The Editors

NICK BROMELL is Professor of English at the University of Massachusetts, Amherst. He is the author of *By the Sweat of the Brow: Labor and Literature in Antebellum America*, *The Powers of Dignity: The Black Political Philosophy of Frederick Douglass*, and *The Time Is Always Now: Black Thought and the Transformation of U.S. Democracy*. His articles and essays on Frederick Douglass and African American political thought have appeared in *American Literary History*, the *American Scholar*, *Critical Philosophy of Race*, *Raritan*, and *Political Theory*.

R. BLAKESLEE GILPIN is Assistant Professor of History at Tulane University. His first book, *John Brown Still Lives!: America's Long Reckoning with Violence, Equality, and Change*, was a finalist for the Gilder Lehrman Center's Frederick Douglass Book Prize. With Rose Styron, Gilpin compiled and edited *The Selected Letters of William Styron*. His next book will be about Nat Turner, William Styron, and the longevity of slavery's hold on America's racial imagination.

For a complete list of Norton Critical Editions, visit
wwnorton.com/nortoncriticals

A NORTON CRITICAL EDITION

Frederick Douglass

MY BONDAGE AND MY FREEDOM

AUTHORITATIVE TEXT

CONTEXTS

CRITICISM

Edited by

NICK BROMELL
UNIVERSITY OF MASSACHUSETTS, AMHERST

and

R. BLAKESLEE GILPIN
TULANE UNIVERSITY

W. W. NORTON & COMPANY
Independent Publishers Since 1923

W. W. Norton & Company has been independent since its founding in 1923, when William Warder Norton and Mary D. Herter Norton first published lectures delivered at the People's Institute, the adult education division of New York City's Cooper Union. The firm soon expanded its program beyond the Institute, publishing books by celebrated academics from America and abroad. By mid-century, the two major pillars of Norton's publishing program—trade books and college texts—were firmly established. In the 1950s, the Norton family transferred control of the company to its employees, and today—with a staff of five hundred and hundreds of trade, college, and professional titles published each year—W. W. Norton & Company stands as the largest and oldest publishing house owned wholly by its employees.

Manufacturing by Maple Press
Book design by Antonina Krass
Production manager: Stephen Sajdak

Library of Congress Cataloging-in-Publication Data

Names: Douglass, Frederick, 1818–1895, author. | Bromell, Nicholas Knowles, editor. | Gilpin, R. Blakeslee, editor.
Title: My bondage and my freedom : authoritative text, contexts, criticism / Frederick Douglass; edited by Nick Bromell, University of Massachusetts, Amherst and R. Blakeslee Gilpin, Tulane University.
Description: First edition. | New York : W. W. Norton & Company, [2020] | Series: Norton Critical Edition | Includes bibliographical references.
Identifiers: LCCN 2019047756 | **ISBN 9780393923636 (paperback)**
Subjects: LCSH: African American abolitionists—Biography. | African American abolitionists—Biography—History and criticism. | Abolitionists—United States—Biography. | Abolitionists—United States—Biography—History and criticism. | Fugitive slaves—Maryland—Biography. | Fugitive slaves—Maryland—Biography—History and criticism. | Antislavery movements—United States—History—19th century. | Slaves—Maryland—Social conditions—19th century. | Plantation life—Maryland—History—19th century. | Douglass, Frederick, 1818–1895. My bondage and my freedom.
Classification: LCC E449 .D738 2020 | DDC 973.8092 [B]—dc23
LC record available at https://lccn.loc.gov/2019047756

W. W. Norton & Company, Inc., 500 Fifth Avenue, New York, N.Y. 10110
www.wwnorton.com
W. W. Norton & Company Ltd., 15 Carlisle Street, London W1D 3BS

1 2 3 4 5 6 7 8 9 0

Contents

Criticism

Introduction

Frederick Douglass was born into slavery in Talbot County, Maryland, on the Eastern Shore of the Chesapeake Bay. Named Frederick Augustus Washington Bailey and likely fathered by his mother's owner, Aaron Anthony, he was intentionally kept from knowing the date of his own birth. Only much later did he surmise that he had been born in 1817; the historian Dickson Preston eventually pinpointed the year of his birth as 1818. After Frederick Bailey escaped from slavery and became known to the world as Frederick Douglass,[1] he often recalled this and other deliberate silences to underscore the peculiar cruelties of American slavery.

As a young boy, Frederick was sent to live with his grandmother, whom he describes with great affection in *My Bondage and My Freedom*. She played a crucial role in providing Douglass with a home that stood in marked contrast to the slave quarters of the plantation. Douglass's grandmother cared for him and nurtured his budding sense of self-worth. His mother, whom he barely knew, also helped foster his belief that, enslaved though he might be, he was nonetheless a person who mattered to others. In *My Bondage and My Freedom*, Douglass recalls his mother rescuing him from the abuse of the plantation cook, instilling in him the knowledge that, as he put it, "I was *somebody's* child" (see p. 48 below).

In his first autobiography, *Narrative of the Life of Frederick Douglass, An American Slave, Written by Himself* (1845), Douglass provided only a brief account of his childhood years. Ten years later, in *My Bondage and My Freedom*, he fleshed out that period with an increasingly complex and compelling description of his youth.[2] One of Douglass's deepest interests in these pages was to recover, understand, and explain exactly how he became aware that he was enslaved, how he realized that his enslavement was unjust, and how he resolved to resist slavery and eventually escape from it. Thus, his

---

1. Douglass changed his name to avoid recapture by his master. For the reason he chose the name Douglass, see note 9 on p. 212.
2. Douglass also wrote a third version of his autobiography: *Life and Times of Frederick Douglass* was published in 1881, then reprinted with some revisions in 1882; another edition, substantially revised and expanded, appeared in December 1892, bearing a copyright date of 1893.

second autobiography sought a clearer articulation of Douglass's multi-faceted political awakening. Some of the most significant moments in his account of this process are relatively famous: his hearing the songs the enslaved sang as they passed through the woods, his learning to read, and his sudden decision to fight back against the "slave breaker" Edward Covey. However, *My Bondage and My Freedom* also calls our attention to many subtler moments in his awakening, from the night he learned he was "*somebody's* child" to the afternoons when he walked alone and listened to the red-winged blackbirds.

After seizing his freedom in 1838, Douglass worked for a time as a laborer in New Bedford, Massachusetts. Within a few years, he had become one of the most outspoken and influential voices of the abolitionist movement. His mere presence overwhelmed William Lloyd Garrison when the two men spoke on the same program at the Nantucket Atheneum in 1841. Garrison followed Douglass by leaping to his feet and asking the audience, much in the manner of a revival preacher, "Have we been listening to a thing, a piece of property, or a man?" Garrison's voice was soon drowned out by the enthusiastic audience answering, "A man! A man!"[3]

Douglass was as compelling and inviting in every dimension as slavery was designed to be impenetrable. He provided a missing source and a living testimonial in a way no other fugitive from slavery did. As Garrison so quickly grasped, Douglass quite literally embodied the core message of the abolitionist gospel: that enslaved persons were human beings who possessed human rights. When Douglass published the *Narrative* in 1845, the book became a best seller, and his fame spread so widely that he was forced to go to Britain to avoid being recaptured by his former master.

Douglass's time in Britain bolstered his book sales and international celebrity. More important, while he was abroad, English supporters purchased his emancipation for $711.66. Douglass returned to America in May 1847 with a plan to found his own newspaper, *The North Star* (see p. 316 below), thereby establishing his independence from the increasingly controlling Garrison. By striking out on his own, Douglass broke with Garrison not only on a personal level but also as a thinker, writer, and activist. *The North Star* was yet another key moment of Douglass's lifelong awakening—in this case to a realization that he was called not just to fight slavery in the South but to foster Black solidarity in the North.

Initially, Douglass had accepted and preached Garrison's view that the framers of the Constitution had compromised with the slave-holding states in order to persuade them to join the Union, giving

3. Philip S. Foner, *The Life and Writings of Frederick Douglass* (New York: International Publishers, 1950), vol. 1, p. 26.

slavery legal legitimacy and making the Constitution "a covenant with death and an agreement with hell." Garrison asserted that abolitionists should forswear morally compromised electoral politics and work to abolish slavery only through "moral suasion," a process he imagined as persuading citizens and individual states to condemn slavery, secede from the United States, and eventually draft a new, morally uncompromised Constitution.[4]

As editor of *The North Star*, Douglass sought out the arguments of a wide range of individuals and organizations opposed to slavery. He was particularly impressed by the American and Foreign Anti-Slavery Society, whose supporters believed that abolitionists were morally obliged to use every tool at their disposal, including politics, to defeat the slavery system. Eventually, their arguments convinced him. After Douglass announced his "change of opinion" in 1851, Garrison's reaction that "there's roguery here!" underlined the personal and political nature of their split. Indeed, the path that Douglass pursued in the 1850s made it impossible for him ever to reconcile fully with his old mentor.

One reason Douglass shifted away from Garrisonian abolition was the increasingly unmistakable success of the "slave power." The Compromise of 1850, with its improved and strengthened Fugitive Slave Act, was clearly a major victory for slaveholders, federally sanctioning the pursuit and recapture of fugitive slaves even in states where slavery was illegal. (It is worth remembering that in the decades before Harriet Beecher Stowe's antislavery novel *Uncle Tom's Cabin* was published in 1852, abolitionists were very much in the wilderness of American life; to voice antislavery sentiments was to risk social disapproval and, in many places, physical harm.) Douglass concluded that Garrisonian abstention from politics was a huge strategic blunder: it exacerbated slaveholders' dominance over American politics, even as it reinforced the view that abolitionists were somehow outside the American mainstream.

On the heels of his *Narrative*, which sold thirty thousand copies before the Civil War, Douglass's *North Star* and his increasingly outspoken and prominent public profile established him as a major Black public intellectual whose audience included anyone concerned about racism, slavery, and freedom in 1850s America. Particularly as he addressed the concerns of free Black citizens, Douglass came to believe that racism was both the effect and the cause of slavery. He insisted that the slave power could not be defeated unless racism too was overthrown. But what produced racism? What purpose did it

---

4. William Lloyd Garrison to Rev. Samuel J. May, July 17, 1845, in Walter M. Merrill, ed., *The Letters of William Lloyd Garrison* (Cambridge, MA: Harvard UP, 1973), 3.303. The phrase "moral suasion" was widely used to describe nonpolitical modes of abolitionism.

serve for nonslaveholders? And what role did racism play in American democracy? Beginning in the 1850s, Douglass's writings and speeches included searching efforts to answer these questions, which remain as urgent and stinging today as they were in his lifetime.

This is the broad context within which Douglass sat down to write *My Bondage and My Freedom*, a much longer, more detailed, more complex, and more ambitious autobiography than the earlier *Narrative*. As indicated below, its readers have found it to be at once a major contribution to U.S. history, a literary masterpiece, a probing critical analysis of racism in American society and politics, and an important intervention in American political philosophy.

After Douglass's death in 1895, as the selections by James Monroe Gregory and Frederic May Holland included in this Norton Critical Edition (see pp. 373 and 378 below) suggest, he was at first remembered mainly as an activist and orator. Arguably, his speeches were better known than his three autobiographies. It was the republication of the *Narrative* in 1960, after a century out of print, that prompted new appreciation for his extraordinary literary accomplishments. Over the next fifteen years, as African American students at universities and colleges across the United States demanded that Black history, art, and culture be included in course curricula, Douglass's *Narrative* became a central text in nineteenth-century American literature and history courses; indeed, it was perhaps the most widely taught and read work of Black literature from any period.

This short, powerful work triggered an outpouring of insightful scholarly criticism and analysis. However, the *Narrative* also set in place a somewhat inaccurate image of Douglass as the self-reliant, self-taught, and individualistic hero of his own story. Although many critics applauded Douglass's powers of resistance to enslavement, some feminist critics expressed misgivings about the highly masculinist story the *Narrative* tells, one in which women figure very little, and mainly as slavery's passive victims.

The rediscovery of *My Bondage and My Freedom* in the late 1980s changed everything. As critics and historians familiarized themselves with this second and much expanded autobiography, they judged it to be Douglass's best book by far, brilliantly combining a more complex narrative with vivid portraits of the people he knew, trenchant analyses of slavery and racism, a wealth of historical detail about the period, and a deeply philosophical meditation on the meaning of freedom, power, and dignity. Together with Harriet Jacob's *Incidents in the Life of a Slave Girl* (excerpted on pp. 351–53 below), *My Bondage and My Freedom* endures as one of the undisputed masterpieces of nineteenth-century American literature.

The transcendent self-creation of *My Bondage and My Freedom* may be the main difference between the Douglass of 1845 and the Douglass of 1855. Ten years after writing his *Narrative*, he combined "personal narrative and advocacy" to create a new mode of auto-biography "that encompasses but is not confined to the speaker's firsthand experience of racial oppression."[5] For Douglass, observes the historian John Stauffer, works of art and writing "could dis-solve social barriers" and link audience and creator in a new shared enterprise.[6]

In addition to recounting his personal story in greater detail, Doug-lass's second book reveals much of the experience of daily life under slavery that he had left out of the *Narrative*, and that even today remains largely unknown as a result of the silences enforced by the "peculiar institution." Another important difference that critics have discerned between Douglass's autobiographies is that in *My Bondage and My Freedom* he no longer portrays himself so emphatically as an individualistic, masculine hero who singlehandedly escapes from slavery. Instead, he devotes many pages to describing the formative influences of his grandmother and mother. He also vividly depicts instances of enslaved women physically resisting their masters, not just (as in the *Narrative*) being whipped by them; and he rewrites the famous scene of his physical combat with Edward Covey to make clear that his victory depended on assistance from other enslaved persons in the Covey household, including the cook Caroline, who "was a powerful woman, and could have mastered me very easily" (p. 154 below) if she had obeyed Covey's command to help him subdue Douglass.[7] But as literary historian Robert S. Levine argues in his contribution to this volume (see p. 410), perhaps the single most important change Douglass made in *My Bondage and My Freedom* was to place himself within a genealogy of Black insurrectionaries who were willing to use violence to overturn slavery. At the same time, as critic Eric J. Sundquist has observed, Douglass also "returned

5. Jeannine Marie DeLombard, *Slavery on Trial: Law, Abolitionism, and Print Culture* (Chapel Hill: U of North Carolina P, 2007), pp. 142, 149.
6. John Stauffer, ed., *Frederick Douglass: My Bondage and My Freedom* (New York: Mod-ern Library, 2003), p. xxvii.
7. There is a rich body of critical work on masculinity and individualism in Douglass's writings. See, for example, Deborah McDowell, "In the First Place: Making Frederick Douglass and the Afro-American Narrative Tradition," in Frederick Douglass, *Narra-tive of the Life of Frederick Douglass, an American Slave, Written by Himself*, ed. Wil-liam L. Andrews and William S. McFeely (New York: Norton, 1997), 172–83; Kimberly Drake, "Rewriting the American Self: Race, Gender, and Identity in the Autobiogra-phies of Frederick Douglass and Harriet Jacobs," *Melus* 22.4 (1997), 91–108; Rafia Zafar, "Franklinian Douglass: The Representative Afro-American Man," in *Frederick Douglass: New Literary and Historical Essays*, ed. Eric J. Sundquist (New York: Cam-bridge UP, 1990), 199–217; Ange-Marie Hancock Alfaro, "Black Masculinity Achieves Nothing without Restorative Care: An Intersectional Rearticulation of Frederick Doug-lass," in *A Political Companion to Frederick Douglass*, ed. Neil Roberts (Lexington: UP of Kentucky, 2018), 236–51.

to the American Revolution for his political principles." Thus, "his revised life story links him alternately with the white founding fathers and those Black men—Toussaint L'Ouverture, Gabriel Prosser, Nat Turner, and Madison Washington, among others[8]—who also belong to the era of revolutionary greatness."[9]

The rediscovery of *My Bondage and My Freedom* has led to a broad range of still-evolving interpretive scholarship, most of it in the fields of history and literary studies. As the editors of this volume, we have aimed to represent the interests of both disciplines. R. Blakeslee Gilpin, a historian, has made most of the selections for the "Contexts" section; Nick Bromell, a literary scholar with an interest in political theory, has selected the pieces in the "Criticism" section. As readers will see, historians have been most interested in what the book tells us about the histories of slavery, the abolition movement, and the free Black community living in the Northern states. Among literary critics, approaches have varied. The most common, perhaps, has been to approach Douglass's second autobiography as his carefully crafted representation of himself as he wished to be seen by his contemporaries in the mid-1850s. Considered in this light, as William L. Andrews argues (p. 392 below), *My Bondage and My Freedom* expresses his new identity as an independent Black activist and intellectual who has broken free of Garrison and other white mentors; at the same time, as Andrews demonstrates, Douglass also tries to place himself in the revolutionary tradition of the founding fathers. Robert S. Levine, again contrasting *My Bondage and My Freedom* with the *Narrative* (p. 410 below), shows that the narrative arc of Douglass's second autobiography is very different from that of the first: "instead of ending with Douglass being enlisted by a white-led abolitionist organization, it concludes with him identifying with the black community and standing in solidarity with black leaders of slave insurrections."

New Historicism is the literary method that most scholars have employed in studying Douglass's works, analyzing them in relation to the historical moment in which each was written and first read.

8. Dominique-François Toussaint L'Ouverture (1743–1803) was the principal leader of the Haitian Revolution (1791–1804). Gabriel Prosser (1776–1800) was an enslaved blacksmith who planned an insurrection near Richmond, Virginia, in 1800. Denmark Vesey (1776–1822) was born into slavery and became a skilled carpenter; he was convicted of planning a slave revolt in Charleston, South Carolina, in 1822, and executed. Nat Turner (1800–1831) led a two-day insurrection of enslaved and free African Americans in Virginia in 1831; he was captured and executed. Madison Washington (dates unknown) led a successful slave rebellion on the ship *Creole* in 1841; all 128 enslaved persons on board gained their liberty. (Frederick Douglass's novella *The Heroic Slave* [1852] is based on Washington's life.)
9. Eric J. Sundquist, *To Wake the Nations: Race in the Making of American Literature* (Cambridge, MA: Harvard UP, 1993), 84.

This Norton Critical Edition includes four New Historicist essays providing a broad range of perspectives on Douglass and *My Bondage and My Freedom*. Nick Bromell (p. 403) places the book in the context of a wider antebellum cultural crisis over the meaning of work and labor, exploring how Douglass represented the labor of the enslaved and thought about it in relation to his own labor as a writer. Jeannine DeLombard (p. 421) focuses on the law as a profession in Douglass's time, and on the difficulties Black lawyers had in gaining acceptance when they tried to present legal arguments to judges and juries in the court system. She shows how Douglass rose to the challenge of making the slave's cause heard by taking his own "lawyerly" arguments directly to the "court of public opinion" in *My Bondage and My Freedom* and in his speeches. Cody Marrs (p. 434) situates the book in the context of the revolutionary upheavals in Europe in 1848 and shows how often Douglass quoted English poetry that voiced the period's revolutionary hopes and sentiments; the Douglass of *My Bondage and My Freedom* is thus remarkably cosmopolitan and transnational in his outlook. Finally, Cristin Ellis (p. 441) looks closely at antebellum Southern worries that plantation cotton agriculture was depleting the land and leading to an economic collapse. She goes on to show that *My Bondage and My Freedom* makes numerous agricultural references, and that the book offers a macroeconomic, environmental case against slavery that operates independently of its more familiar moral argument.

Scholars in the field of African American studies have long been interested in Douglass's contributions to Black American history, literature, and politics, with an early focus on *My Bondage and My Freedom* as a major work in the genre of Black autobiography. Beginning with nineteenth-century slave narratives and extending through W. E. B. DuBois's *The Souls of Black Folk* (1903) and Angela Davis's *An Autobiography* (1974) to Ta-Nehisi Coates's *Between the World and Me* (2015), this rich tradition of autobiography has provided a sustained and penetrating critique of white racism, while at the same time testifying to both the strength of Black resistance and the vitality of Black culture. In his essay in this volume, William L. Andrews argues that *My Bondage and My Freedom* was a foundational work in this tradition, while Henry Louis Gates, Jr. (p. 385) provides a keen analysis of Douglass's use and subversion of cultural binaries.

Scholars working in the fields of Black politics and political theory have found *My Bondage and My Freedom* to be a profound—and for some, controversial—contribution to these traditions. In different ways, the essays by Neil Roberts (p. 453) and Juliet Hooker (p. 460) develop the idea, first suggested by Angela Davis, that Douglass was not just an orator, activist, and writer, but also a radical Black political philosopher. Roberts argues that Douglass proposes a new way of thinking of freedom as "comparative," one actualized by the historical phenomena of "fugitivity" and "marronage," in which fugitives from slavery established their own, quasi-independent communities. Hooker also argues that Douglass can be understood as a philosopher of "fugitive democracy," while she emphasizes that he was also a transnational theorist of multiracial democracy, with a deep interest in Black republics in Latin America.

Douglass makes no mention of philosophy in the *Narrative*, but he repeatedly signals his commitment to it in *My Bondage and My Freedom*. In Chapter 23, he tells us that after joining the Massachusetts Anti-Slavery Society and becoming one of its paid lecturers, he quickly grew tired of giving the same speech night after night. He wanted to do more than bear witness to the horrors of slavery; he also wanted to analyze its workings in order to better condemn it. But his fellow abolitionists discouraged this aspiration: "Give us the facts," counseled his white colleague John Collins; "we will take care of the philosophy" (p. 222). Douglass did not take their advice, of course. Indeed, as he relates in Chapter 25, upon returning from England, he told his fellow abolitionists in Massachusetts that he planned to become an editor and to publish his own Black newspaper. In sentences dripping with irony, he tells us how his "friends" reacted to the idea:

> My American friends looked at me with astonishment! "A wood-sawyer" offering himself to the public as an editor! A slave, brought up in the very depths of ignorance, assuming to instruct the highly civilized people of the north in the principles of liberty, justice, and humanity! The thing looked absurd. (p. 242)

Why did it seem "absurd" to them that a Black man could "instruct" white citizens in the principles of democracy? To those who assumed that philosophy was a matter of reflecting on life from a certain distance, Douglass's claim that a former slave and wood-sawyer could philosophize was deeply unsettling. It exposed the degree to which conventional philosophy was self-limiting and narrow, resting as it did on leisure, privilege, and disengagement from the struggles of everyday life. At the same time, Douglass's plan to philosophize suggested that persons who are caught up in such struggles have a perspective on life that is valuable both to themselves and to other citizens. Finally, as Douglass hints many times throughout *My Bondage and My Freedom*, his friends might have reacted dismissively and defensively to his plan because it threatened to expose something about their own identity that they disavowed: its whiteness. For, as philosopher Charles Mills has observed, "insofar as . . . persons are conceived of as having their personhood uncontested, insofar as their culture and cognition are unhesitatingly respected, insofar as their moral prescriptions take for granted an already achieved citizenship and a history of freedom—insofar, that is, as race is not an issue for them, then they are already tacitly positioned as white persons, culturally and cognitively European, racially privileged members of the West."[1]

"Whiteness studies" is an important and growing academic field: it gives a detailed historical account of when and how different skin colors started to be accorded enormous importance, justifying the enslavement of millions of Africans and making the political domination of whites seem natural and unremarkable. Whiteness studies also has a sociological dimension that analyzes the reasons why some persons invest so deeply in their whiteness, and investigates how the idea of whiteness continues to function as a concept that demeans its "opposite," Blackness. Douglass was a pioneer in this field, often looking back at and gently mocking whites' unconscious attitudes and pretensions. One amusing story (from an 1881 essay) is worth telling here:

> A good but simple-minded Abolitionist said to me that he was not ashamed to walk with me down Broadway arm-in arm, in open daylight, and evidently thought he was saying something that must be very pleasing to my self importance, but it occurred to me, at the moment, that this man does not dream of any reason why I might be ashamed to walk arm-in-arm with him through Broadway in open daylight.[2]

As we hope this overview has shown, the meaning of Frederick Douglass's life and of *My Bondage and My Freedom* has changed over time, and has varied depending on the historical, literary, or political concerns of its readers. As we write this introduction in the spring of 2020, we are keenly aware of our own moment in time, and of the ways *My Bondage and My Freedom* speaks to our situation. Two aspects of its relevance particularly command our attention, although they are somewhat in tension with each other.

On the one hand, it is becoming increasingly possible to read African American literature in a new way: not just for its indispensable *critiques* of racism and oppression, but also for its compelling *visions* of a transformed American society and culture. Over the years, we have heard from many students and teachers that they are weary of approaches to African American literature that focus exclusively on the pain and injustice of the Black experience, and the dynamics of

---

1. Charles W. Mills, *Blackness Visible: Essays on Philosophy and* Race (Ithaca, NY: Cornell UP, 1998), xv.
2. Frederick Douglass, "The Color Line," in *The Life and Writings of Frederick Douglass*, Vol. 4, ed. Philip S. Foner (New York: International Publishers, 1975), 351.

Black resistance and endurance. While these remain as important today as ever, we must also emphasize that Black American culture is much more than just a reaction to racism; it also embodies and expresses its own values, ideas, discoveries, dispositions, and aesthetics that contribute powerfully not just to "American culture" (as if there were such a thing apart from its Black dimension) but to world culture. This contribution is also, potentially, transformative. Frederick Douglass recognized this potential and strove to realize it, above all in his literary masterpiece *My Bondage and My Freedom*.

At the same time, however, we cannot ignore the tenacity of white racism and its effects—or what is now being called "the afterlife of slavery."[3] The unjust imprisonment of hundreds of thousands of African Americans, the unwarranted violence many experience at the hands of law enforcement officials, the continuing damage caused by structural forms of racism, and the countless acts of "microaggression" experienced on a daily basis by most persons of color, all remind us that the need for a critique of racial injustice is greater than ever. [4] Here, too, *My Bondage and My Freedom* has much to offer, as it brilliantly diagnoses the racial underpinnings of the slavery system and its deliberate encouragement of a racist culture in the Northern, "free" states of the United States.

We live in what Frederick Douglass called the "ever-present now." Our own *now*, with respect to racial injustice and the history of race in the United States, is characterized by a paradox: hope for new possibilities is stronger than ever, yet the reasons to despair of progress are also compelling. To help us meet the challenges of this moment, we can have no better guide than Frederick Douglass, and no better book in hand than *My Bondage and My Freedom*.

The text of this Norton Critical Edition follows that of the original 1855 publication, with only minor changes to modernize punctuation and enhance consistency and readability. In the editorial apparatus, the term "Black" has been capitalized when it refers to any person who is part of the African Diaspora. This capitalization recognizes a shared history, culture, and ethnic identity. In contrast, "white" has not been capitalized, because that term does not represent a collective experience.

---

3. Saidya Hartman, *Lose Your Mother: A Journey Along the Atlantic Slave Route* (New York: Farrar, Straus and Giroux, 2007), 6.
4. Michelle Alexander, *The New Jim Crow: Mass Incarceration in the Age of Colorblindness* (New York: New P, 2010); Claudia Rankine, *Citizen: An American Lyric* (Minneapolis: Graywolf P, 2014).

The Text of
MY BONDAGE AND
MY FREEDOM

Frederick Douglass

The frontispiece from the edition this text is based on: *My Bondage and My Freedom* (New York and Auburn, NY: Miller, Orton & Mulligan, 1855).

MY BONDAGE

AND

MY FREEDOM.

Part I.—Life as a Slave.   Part II.—Life as a Freeman.

By FREDERICK DOUGLASS.

WITH

AN INTRODUCTION.

By DR. JAMES M'CUNE SMITH.[1]

By a principle essential to christianity, a PERSON is eternally differenced from a THING; so that the idea of a HUMAN BEING, necessarily excludes the idea of PROPERTY IN THAT BEING.   COLERIDGE.

———•———

NEW YORK AND AUBURN:

MILLER, ORTON & MULLIGAN.

New York: 25 Park Row.—Auburn: 107 Genesee-st.

1855.

1. James McCune Smith (1813–1865) was the first professionally trained Black doctor in the United States. A close friend to Gerrit Smith (no relation; see note 2 on p. 4) and Frederick Douglass, he became a radical abolitionist.

3

TO

HONORABLE GERRIT SMITH,[2]

AS A SLIGHT TOKEN OF

ESTEEM FOR HIS CHARACTER,

ADMIRATION FOR HIS GENIUS AND BENEVOLENCE,

AFFECTION FOR HIS PERSON, AND

GRATITUDE FOR HIS FRIENDSHIP,

AND AS

A Small but most Sincere Acknowledgment of

HIS PRE-EMINENT SERVICES IN BEHALF OF THE RIGHTS AND LIBERTIES

OF AN

AFFLICTED, DESPISED AND DEEPLY OUTRAGED PEOPLE,

BY RANKING SLAVERY WITH PIRACY AND MURDER,

AND BY
DENYING IT EITHER A LEGAL OR CONSTITUTIONAL EXISTENCE,

This Volume is Respectfully Dedicated,

BY HIS FAITHFUL AND FIRMLY ATTACHED FRIEND,

FREDERICK DOUGLASS.

ROCHESTER, N. Y.

---

2. Wealthy abolitionist, philanthropist, and U.S. congressman (1797–1874). Deeply involved in radical abolitionism, Smith was one of Douglass's closest friends and helped fund the antislavery newspaper *Frederick Douglass' Paper*.

Editor's Preface

IF the volume now presented to the public were a mere work of ART, the history of its misfortune might be written in two very simple words—TOO LATE. The nature and character of slavery have been subjects of an almost endless variety of artistic representation; and after the brilliant achievements in that field, and while those achievements are yet fresh in the memory of the million, he who would add another to the legion, must possess the charm of transcendent exellence, or apologize for something worse than rashness. The reader is, therefore, assured, with all due promptitude, that his attention is not invited to a work of ART, but to a work of FACTS—Facts, terrible and almost incredible, it may be—yet FACTS, nevertheless.

I am authorized to say that there is not a fictitious name nor place in the whole volume; but that names and places are literally given, and that every transaction therein described actually transpired.

Perhaps the best Preface to this volume is furnished in the following letter of Mr. Douglass, written in answer to my urgent solicitation for such a work:

ROCHESTER, N. Y. *July* 2, 1855.

DEAR FRIEND: I have long entertained, as you very well know, a somewhat positive repugnance to writing or speaking anything for the public, which could, with any degree of plausibility, make me liable to the imputation of seeking personal notoriety, for its own sake. Entertaining that feeling very sincerely, and permitting its control, perhaps, quite unreasonably, I have often refused to narrate my personal experience in public anti-slavery meetings, and in sympathizing circles, when urged to do so by friends, with whose views and wishes, ordinarily, it were a pleasure to comply. In my letters and speeches, I have generally aimed to discuss the question of Slavery in the light of fundamental principles, and upon facts, notorious and open to all; making, I trust, no more of the fact of my own former enslavement, than circumstances seemed absolutely to require. I have never placed my opposition to slavery on a basis so narrow as my own enslavement, but rather upon the indestructible and unchangeable laws of human nature, every one of which is perpetually and flagrantly violated by the slave system. I have also felt that it was best for those having histories worth the writing—or supposed to be so—to commit such work to hands other than their own. To write of one's self, in such a manner as not to incur the imputation of weakness, vanity, and egotism, is a work within the ability of but few; and I have little reason to believe that I belong to that fortunate few.

These considerations caused me to hesitate, when first you kindly urged me to prepare for publication a full account of my life as a slave, and my life as a freeman.

Nevertheless, I see, with you, many reasons for regarding my autobiography as exceptional in its character, and as being, in some sense, naturally beyond the reach of those reproaches which honorable and sensitive minds dislike to incur. It is not to illustrate any heroic achievements of a man, but to vindicate a just and beneficent principle, in its application to the whole human family, by letting in the light of truth upon a system, esteemed by some as a blessing, and by others as a curse and a crime. I agree with you, that this system is now at the bar of public opinion—not only of this country, but of the whole civilized world—for judgment. Its friends have made for it the usual plea—"not guilty;" the case must, therefore, proceed. Any facts, either from slaves, slaveholders, or by-standers, calculated to enlighten the public mind, by revealing the true nature, character, and tendency of the slave system, are in order, and can scarcely be innocently withheld.

I see, too, that there are special reasons why I should write my own biography, in preference to employing another to do it. Not only is slavery on trial, but unfortunately, the enslaved people are also on trial. It is alleged, that they are, naturally, inferior; that they are *so low* in the scale of humanity, and so utterly stupid, that they are unconscious of their wrongs, and do not apprehend their rights. Looking, then, at your request, from this stand-point, and wishing everything of which you think me capable to go to the benefit of my afflicted people, I part with my doubts and hesitation, and proceed to furnish you the desired manuscript; hoping that you may be able to make such arrangements for its publication as shall be best adapted to accomplish that good which you so enthusiastically anticipate.

FREDERICK DOUGLASS.

There was little necessity for doubt and hesitation on the part of Mr. Douglass, as to the propriety of his giving to the world a full account of himself. A man who was born and brought up in slavery, a living witness of its horrors; who often himself experienced its cruelties; and who, despite the depressing influences surrounding his birth, youth and manhood, has risen, from a dark and almost absolute obscurity, to the distinguished position which he now occupies, might very well assume the existence of a commendable curiosity, on the part of the public, to know the facts of his remarkable history.

EDITOR.[1]

---

1. I.e., the publisher, Miller, Orton & Mulligan. Among the several popular titles the house published in the 1850s was the second edition of Solomon Northup's memoir *Twelve Years a Slave*.

Contents

CHAPTER IV
A GENERAL SURVEY OF THE SLAVE PLANTATION

CHAPTER V
GRADUAL INITIATION INTO THE MYSTERIES OF SLAVERY

CHAPTER VI
TREATMENT OF SLAVES ON LLOYD'S PLANTATION

CHAPTER XI
"A CHANGE CAME O'ER THE SPIRIT OF MY DREAM."

CHAPTER XII
RELIGIOUS NATURE AWAKENED

CHAPTER XIII
THE VICISSITUDES OF SLAVE LIFE

CHAPTER XIV
EXPERIENCE IN ST. MICHAEL'S

CHAPTER XV
COVEY, THE NEGRO-BREAKER

CHAPTER XVI
ANOTHER PRESSURE OF THE TYRANT'S VICE

CHAPTER XVII
THE LAST FLOGGING

CHAPTER XVIII
NEW RELATIONS AND DUTIES

CHAPTER XIX
THE RUNAWAY PLOT

CHAPTER XX
APPRENTICESHIP LIFE

CHAPTER XXI
MY ESCAPE FROM SLAVERY

CHAPTER XXII
LIBERTY ATTAINED

CHAPTER XXIII
INTRODUCED TO THE ABOLITIONISTS

CHAPTER XXIV
TWENTY-ONE MONTHS IN GREAT BRITAIN

CHAPTER XXV
VARIOUS INCIDENTS

APPENDIX
EXTRACTS FROM SPEECHES, ETC.

Introduction

WHEN a man raises himself from the lowest condition in society to the highest, mankind pay him the tribute of their admiration; when he accomplishes this elevation by native energy, guided by prudence and wisdom, their admiration is increased; but when his course, onward and upward, excellent in itself, furthermore proves a possible, what had hitherto been regarded as an impossible, reform, then he becomes a burning and a shining light, on which the aged may look with gladness, the young with hope, and the down-trodden, as a representative of what they may themselves become. To such a man, dear reader, it is my privilege to introduce you.

The life of Frederick Douglass, recorded in the pages which follow, is not merely an example of self-elevation under the most adverse circumstances; it is, moreover, a noble vindication of the highest aims of the American anti-slavery movement. The real object of that movement is not only to disenthrall, it is, also, to bestow upon the negro the exercise of all those rights, from the possession of which he has been so long debarred.

But this full recognition of the colored man to the right, and the entire admission of the same to the full privileges, political, religious and social, of manhood, requires powerful effort on the part of the enthralled, as well as on the part of those who would disenthrall them. The people at large must feel the conviction, as well as admit the abstract logic, of human equality; the negro, for the first time in the world's history, brought in full contact with high civilization, must prove his title to all that is demanded for him; in the teeth of unequal chances, he must prove himself equal to the mass of those who oppress him—therefore, absolutely superior to his apparent fate, and to their relative ability. And it is most cheering to the friends of freedom, to-day, that evidence of this equality is rapidly accumulating, not from the ranks of the half-freed colored people of the free states, but from the very depths of slavery itself; the indestructible equality of man to man is demonstrated by the ease with which black men, scarce one remove from barbarism—if slavery can be honored with such a distinction—vault into the high places of the most advanced and painfully acquired civilization. Ward and Garnett,

Wells Brown and Pennington, Loguen and Douglass,[1] are banners
on the outer wall, under which abolition is fighting its most successful battles, because they are living exemplars of the practicability of the most radical abolitionism; for, they were all of them born
to the doom of slavery, some of them remained slaves until adult
age, yet they all have not only won equality to their white fellow
citizens, in civil, religious, political and social rank, but they have
also illustrated and adorned our common country by their genius,
learning and eloquence.

The characteristies whereby Mr. Douglass has won first rank
among these remarkable men, and is still rising toward highest rank
among living Americans, are abundantly laid bare in the book before
us. Like the autobiography of Hugh Miller,[2] it carries us so far back
into early childhood, as to throw light upon the question, "when positive and persistent memory begins in the human being." And, like
Hugh Miller, he must have been a shy old fashioned child, occasionally oppressed by what he could not well account for, peering and
poking about among the layers of right and wrong, of tyrant and
thrall, and the wonderfulness of that hopeless tide of things which
brought power to one race, and unrequited toil to another, until,
finally, he stumbled upon his "first-found Ammonite," hidden away
down in the depths of his own nature, and which revealed to him
the fact that liberty and right, for all men, were anterior to slavery
and wrong. When his knowledge of the world was bounded by the
visible horizon on Col. Lloyd's plantation,[3] and while every thing
around him bore a fixed, iron stamp, as if it had always been so, this
was, for one so young, a notable discovery.

To his uncommon memory, then, we must add a keen and accurate insight into men and things; an original breadth of common
sense which enabled him to see, and weigh, and compare whatever
passed before him, and which kindled a desire to search out and
define their relations to other things not so patent, but which never
succumbed to the marvelous nor the supernatural; a sacred thirst
for liberty and for learning, first as a means of attaining liberty, then
as an end in itself most desirable; a will; an unfaltering energy and

---

1. Samuel Ringgold Ward (1817–1867), Henry Highland Garnet (1815–1882), William
   Wells Brown (1818–1884), James William Charles Pennington (1807–1870), and Jer-
   main Wesley Loguen (1813–1872), Black abolitionists and writers who were born into
   slavery. Ward's *Autobiography of a Fugitive Slave*, Garnet's "Address to the Slaves,"
   Pennington's *The Fugitive Blacksmith*, Loguen's *The Rev. J. W. Loguen*, and Brown's
   seven books (see his essay in this volume, pp. 368–72) formed the core of the antislavery
   canon with Douglass's autobiographies.
2. Scottish geologist and journalist (1802–1856) who refuted evolution. Miller's widely
   read autobiography, *My Schools and Schoolmasters* (1872), contributed to his reputation
   as a self-made man.
3. Col. Edward Lloyd V (1779–1834) was a prominent and wealthy landowner in Maryland. He served as U.S. congressman 1807–09, thirteenth governor of the state 1809–11,
   and U.S. senator 1819–26.

determination to obtain what his soul pronounced desirable; a majestic self-hood; determined courage; a deep and agonizing sympathy with his embruted, crushed and bleeding fellow slaves, and an extraordinary depth of passion, together with that rare alliance between passion and intellect, which enables the former, when deeply roused, to excite, develop and sustain the latter.

With these original gifts in view, let us look at his schooling; the fearful discipline through which it pleased God to prepare him for the high calling on which he has since entered—the advocacy of emancipation by the people who are not slaves. And for this special mission, his plantation education was better than any he could have acquired in any lettered school. What he needed, was facts and experiences, welded to acutely wrought up sympathies, and these he could not elsewhere have obtained, in a manner so peculiarly adapted to his nature. His physical being was well trained, also, running wild until advanced into boyhood; hard work and light diet, thereafter, and a skill in handicraft in youth.

For his special mission, then, this was, considered in connection with his natural gifts, a good schooling; and, for his special mission, he doubtless "left school" just at the proper moment. Had he remained longer in slavery—had he fretted under bonds until the ripening of manhood and its passions, until the drear agony of slave-wife and slave-children had been piled upon his already bitter experiences—then, not only would his own history have had another termination, but the drama of American slavery would have been essentially varied; for I cannot resist the belief, that the boy who learned to read and write as he did, who taught his fellow slaves these precious acquirements as he did, who plotted for their mutual escape as he did, would, when a man at bay, strike a blow which would make slavery reel and stagger. Furthermore, blows and insults he bore, at the moment, without resentment; deep but suppressed emotion rendered him insensible to their sting; but it was afterward, when the memory of them went seething through his brain, breeding a fiery indignation at his injured self-hood, that the resolve came to resist, and the time fixed when to resist, and the plot laid, how to resist; and he always kept his self-pledged word. In what he undertook, in this line, he looked fate in the face, and had a cool, keen look at the relation of means to ends. Henry Bibb,[4] to avoid chastisement, strewed his master's bed with charmed leaves—and *was whipped*. Frederick Douglass quietly pocketed a like *fetiche*, compared his muscles with those of Covey—and *whipped him*.

---

4. Henry Watson Bibb (1815–1854), Black abolitionist and author of the *Narrative of the Life and Adventures of Henry Bibb*.

In the history of his life in bondage, we find, well developed, that inherent and continuous energy of character which will ever render him distinguished. What his hand found to do, he did with his might; even while conscious that he was wronged out of his daily earnings, he worked, and worked hard. At his daily labor he went with a will; with keen, well set eye, brawny chest, lithe figure, and fair sweep of arm, he would have been king among calkers,[5] had that been his mission.

It must not be overlooked, in this glance at his education, that Mr. Douglass lacked one aid to which so many men of mark have been deeply indebted—he had neither a mother's care, nor a mother's culture, save that which slavery grudgingly meted out to him. Bitter nurse! may not even her features relax with human feeling, when she gazes at such offspring! How susceptible he was to the kindly influences of mother-culture, may be gathered from his own words, on page 57 [p. 48 in this Norton Critical Edition]: "It has been a life-long, standing grief to me, that I know so little of my mother, and that I was so early separated from her. The counsels of her love must have been beneficial to me. The side view of her face is imaged on my memory, and I take few steps in life, without feeling her presence; but the image is mute, and I have no striking words of hers treasured up."

From the depths of chattel slavery in Maryland, our author escaped into the caste-slavery of the north, in New Bedford, Massachusetts. Here he found oppression assuming another, and hardly less bitter, form; of that very handicraft which the greed of slavery had taught him, his half-freedom denied him the exercise for an honest living; he found himself one of a class—free colored men—whose position he has described in the following words:

"Aliens are we in our native land. The fundamental principles of the republic, to which the humblest white man, whether born here or elsewhere, may appeal with confidence, in the hope of awakening a favorable response, are held to be inapplicable to us. The glorious doctrines of your revolutionary fathers, and the more glorious teachings of the Son of God, are construed and applied against us. We are literally scourged beyond the beneficent range of both authorities, human and divine. * * * [6] American humanity hates us, scorns us, disowns and denies, in a thousand ways, our very personality. The outspread wing of American christianity, apparently broad enough to give shelter to a perishing world, refuses to cover us. To us, its bones are brass, and its features iron. In running thither

---

5. "calkers": workers who prepared and repaired the seams of sailing ships by stuffing gaps between planks with a tarred fiber called "oakum."
6. Asterisks in this introduction are the author's, i.e., James McCune Smith's.

for shelter and succor, we have only fled from the hungry blood-hound to the devouring wolf—from a corrupt and selfish world, to a hollow and hypocritical church."—*Speech before American and Foreign Anti-Slavery Society, May*, 1854.

Four years or more, from 1837 to 1841, he struggled on, in New Bedford, sawing wood, rolling casks, or doing what labor he might, to support himself and young family; four years he brooded over the scars which slavery and semi-slavery had inflicted upon his body and soul; and then, with his wounds yet unhealed, he fell among the Garrisonians—a glorious waif to those most ardent reformers.[7] It happened one day, at Nantucket, that he, diffidently and reluctantly, was led to address an anti-slavery meeting. He was about the age when the younger Pitt[8] entered the House of Commons; like Pitt, too, he stood up a born orator.

William Lloyd Garrison, who was happily present, writes thus of Mr. Douglass' maiden effort;[9] "I shall never forget his first speech at the convention—the extraordinary emotion it excited in my own mind—the powerful impression it created upon a crowded auditory, completely taken by surprise. * * * I think I never hated slavery so intensely as at that moment; certainly, my perception of the enormous outrage which is inflicted by it on the godlike nature of its victims, was rendered far more clear than ever. There stood one in physical proportions and stature commanding and exact—in intellect richly endowed—in natural eloquence a prodigy."[1]

It is of interest to compare Mr. Douglass's account of this meeting with Mr. Garrison's. Of the two, I think the latter the most correct. It must have been a grand burst of eloquence! The pent up agony, indignation and pathos of an abused and harrowed boyhood and youth, bursting out in all their freshness and overwhelming earnestness!

This unique introduction to its great leader, led immediately to the employment of Mr. Douglass as an agent by the American Anti-Slavery Society. So far as his self-relying and independent character would permit, he became, after the strictest sect, a Garrisonian. It is not too much to say, that he formed a complement which they needed, and they were a complement equally necessary to his "make-up." With his deep and keen sensitiveness to wrong, and his wonderful memory, he came from the land of bondage full of its woes and its evils, and painting them in characters of living light; and,

---

7. Abolitionists working with William Lloyd Garrison (1805–1879), who established the abolitionist newspaper *The Liberator* on January 1, 1831, and cofounded the American Anti-Slavery Society in December 1833.
8. William Pitt the Younger (1759–1806) was a British political leader who became Britain's youngest prime minister at age twenty-four.
9. See the extract from Douglass's speech on pp. 251–61 below.
1. Letter, Introduction to Life of Frederick Douglass, Boston, 1845 [*Author's note*].

on his part, he found, told out in sound Saxon phrase, all those principles of justice and right and liberty, which had dimly brooded over the dreams of his youth, seeking definite forms and verbal expression. It must have been an electric flashing of thought, and a knitting of soul, granted to but few in this life, and will be a life-long memory to those who participated in it. In the society, more-over, of Wendell Phillips, Edmund Quincy,[2] William Lloyd Garrison, and other men of earnest faith and refined culture, Mr. Douglass enjoyed the high advantage of their assistance and counsel in the labor of self-culture, to which he now addressed himself with wonted energy. Yet, these gentlemen, although proud of Frederick Douglass, failed to fathom, and bring out to the light of day, the highest quali-ties of his mind; the force of their own education stood in their own way: they did not delve into the mind of a colored man for capaci-ties which the pride of race led them to believe to be restricted to their own Saxon blood. Bitter and vindictive sarcasm, irresistible mimicry, and a pathetic narrative of his own experiences of slavery, were the intellectual manifestations which they encouraged him to exhibit on the platform or in the lecture desk.

A visit to England, in 1845, threw Mr. Douglass among men and women of earnest souls and high culture, and who, moreover, had never drank of the bitter waters of American caste. For the first time in his life, he breathed an atmosphere congenial to the longings of his spirit, and felt his manhood free and unrestricted. The cordial and manly greetings of the British and Irish audiences in public, and the refinement and elegance of the social circles in which he min-gled, not only as an equal, but as a recognized man of genius, were, doubtless genial and pleasant resting places in his hitherto thorny and troubled journey through life. There are joys on the earth, and, to the wayfaring fugitive from American slavery or American caste, this is one of them.

But his sojourn in England was more than a joy to Mr. Douglass. Like the platform at Nantucket, it awakened him to the conscious-ness of new powers that lay in him. From the pupilage of Garrison-ism he rose to the dignity of a teacher and a thinker; his opinions on the broader aspects of the great American question were earnestly and incessantly sought, from various points of view, and he must, perforce, bestir himself to give suitable answer. With that prompt and truthful perception which has led their sisters in all ages of the world to gather at the feet and support the hands of reformers, the

2. Wendell Phillips (1811–1884) was a prominent abolitionist, a famous orator, and a close friend of Garrison who wrote a letter in support of Douglass that was printed in Douglass's *Narrative* (1845). Edward Quincy (1808–1877) was a lesser-known but dedi-cated abolitionist in Garrison's inner circle.

gentlewomen of England[3] were foremost to encourage and strengthen him to carve out for himself a path fitted to his powers and energies, in the life-battle against slavery and caste to which he was pledged. And one stirring thought, inseparable from the British idea of the evangel of freedom, must have smote his ear from every side—

> "Hereditary bondmen! know ye not
> Who would be free, themselves must strike the blow?"[4]

The result of this visit was, that on his return to the United States, he established a newspaper. This proceeding was sorely against the wishes and the advice of the leaders of the American Anti-Slavery Society, but our author had fully grown up to the conviction of a truth which they had once promulged,[5] but now forgotten, to wit: that in their own elevation—self-elevation—colored men have a blow to strike "on their own hook," against slavery and caste. Differing from his Boston friends in this matter, diffident in his own abilities, reluctant at their dissuadings, how beautiful is the loyalty with which he still clung to their principles in all things else, and even in this.

Now came the trial hour. Without cordial support from any large body of men or party on this side the Atlantic, and too far distant in space and immediate interest to expect much more, after the much already done, on the other side, he stood up, almost alone, to the arduous labor and heavy expenditure of editor and lecturer. The Garrison party, to which he still adhered, did not want a *colored* newspaper—there was an odor of *caste* about it; the Liberty party[6] could hardly be expected to give warm support to a man who smote their principles as with a hammer; and the wide gulf which separated the free colored people from the Garrisonians, also separated them from their brother, Frederick Douglass.

The arduous nature of his labors, from the date of the establishment of his paper, may be estimated by the fact, that anti-slavery papers in the United States, even while the organs of, and when

3. One of these ladies, impelled by the same noble spirit which carried Miss Nightingale to Scutari, has devoted her time, her untiring energies, to a great extent her means, and her high literary abilities, to the advancement and support of Frederick Douglass' Paper, the only organ of the downtrodden, edited and published by one of themselves, in the United States [*Author's note*].
   "One of the these ladies" refers to Julia Griffiths, a British woman whom Douglass met on a speaking tour in 1846. Florence Nightingale (1820–1910) was a nurse at Scutari Hospital during the Crimean War. After the war she founded her own nursing school for women in London and went on to campaign for social reforms [*Editors' note*].
4. Cf. *Childe Harold's Pilgramage* (1812), 2.76.1–2, by the English poet Lord Byron (1788–1824); often used by abolitionists as an affirmation of the right to strike for freedom.
5. A nineteenth-century variant of "promulgated."
6. The Liberty Party broke with the American Anti-Slavery Society in 1840 to advocate against William Lloyd Garrison's belief that the Constitution was a proslavery document. The founders overlapped a great deal with early members of both the Free Soil Party and the Republican Party.

supported by, anti-slavery parties, have, with a single exception, failed to pay expenses. Mr. Douglass has maintained, and does maintain, his paper without the support of any party, and even in the teeth of the opposition of those from whom he had reason to expect counsel and encouragement. He has been compelled, at one and the same time, and almost constantly, during the past seven years, to contribute matter to its columns as editor, and to raise funds for its support as lecturer. It is within bounds to say, that he has expended twelve thousand dollars of his own hard earned money, in publishing this paper, a larger sum than has been contributed by any one individual for the general advancement of the colored people. There had been many other papers published and edited by colored men, beginning as far back as 1827, when the Rev. Samuel E. Cornish and John B. Russworm (a graduate of Bowdoin college, and afterward Governor of Cape Palmas) published the Freedom's Journal, in New York city; probably not less than one hundred newspaper enterprises have been started in the United States, by free colored men, born free, and some of them of liberal education and fair talents for this work; but, one after another, they have fallen through, although, in several instances, anti-slavery friends contributed to their support.[7] It had almost been given up, as an impracticable thing, to maintain a colored newspaper, when Mr. Douglass, with fewest early advantages of all his competitors, essayed, and has proved, the thing perfectly practicable, and, moreover, of great public benefit. This paper, in addition to its power in holding up the hands of those to whom it is especially devoted, also affords irrefutable evidence of the justice, safety and practicability of Immediate Emancipation; it further proves the immense loss which slavery inflicts on the land while it dooms such energies as his to the hereditary degradation of slavery.

It has been said in this Introduction, that Mr. Douglass had raised himself by his own efforts to the highest position in society. As a successful editor, in our land, he occupies this position. Our editors rule the land, and he is one of them. As an orator and thinker, his position is equally high, in the opinion of his countrymen. If a stranger in the United States would seek its most distinguished men—the movers of public opinion—he will find their names mentioned, and their movements chronicled, under the head of "By Magnetic Telegraph,"[8] in the daily papers. The keen caterers for the public attention, set down, in this column, such men only as have won

---

7. Mr. Stephen Myers, of Albany, deserves mention as one of the most persevering among the colored editorial fraternity. [*Author's note*]. Myers, a Black journalist, founded the newspaper *The Northern Star and Freeman's Advocate*, which preceded Douglass's *Northern Star*. He also planned a Black farming community on land donated by Gerrit Smith [*Editors' note*].
8. Device that sends messages some distance in the form of electric pulses through wires.

high mark in the public esteem. During the past winter—1854–5—
very frequent mention of Frederick Douglass was made under this
head in the daily papers; his name glided as often—this week from
Chicago, next week from Boston—over the lightning wires, as the
name of any other man, of whatever note. To no man did the people
more widely nor more earnestly say, "*Tell me thy thought!*" And,
somehow or other, revolution seemed to follow in his wake. His were
not the mere words of eloquence which Kossuth[9] speaks of, that
delight the ear and then pass away. No! They were *work*-able, *do*-
able words, that brought forth fruits in the revolution in Illinois,[1]
and in the passage of the franchise resolutions[2] by the Assembly of
New York.

And the secret of his power, what is it? He is a Representative
American man—a type of his countrymen. Naturalists tell us that
a full grown man is a resultant or representative of all animated
nature on this globe; beginning with the early embryo state, then
representing the lowest forms of organic life,[3] and passing through
every subordinate grade or type, until he reaches the last and highest—
manhood. In like manner, and to the fullest extent, has Frederick
Douglass passed through every gradation of rank comprised in our
national make-up, and bears upon his person and upon his soul
every thing that is American. And he has not only full sympathy with
every thing American; his proclivity or bent, to active toil and visible
progress, are in the strictly national direction, delighting to outstrip
"all creation."

Nor have the natural gifts, already named as his, lost anything by
his severe training. When unexcited, his mental processes are probably slow, but singularly clear in perception, and wide in vision, the
unfailing memory bringing up all the facts in their every aspect;
incongruities he lays hold of incontinently, and holds up on the edge
of his keen and telling wit. But this wit never descends to frivolity;
it is rigidly in the keeping of his truthful common sense, and always
used in illustration or proof of some point which could not so readily be reached any other way. "Beware of a Yankee when he is feeding," is a shaft that strikes home in a matter never so laid bare by
satire before. "The Garrisonian views of disunion, if carried to a successful issue, would only place the people of the north in the same

---

9. Louis Kossuth (1802–1894), a leader of the Hungarian revolution for independence
   1848–49). Kossuth's tour of the United States in 1851–52 inspired many abolitionists.
1. "revolution in Illinois": In the election of November 7, 1854, candidates opposing
   expansion of slavery captured five of the nine congressional districts that were being
   contested.
2. "franchise resolutions": In 1855, the New York Assembly passed a resolution favoring the
   repeal of the $250 property qualification imposed earlier on the state's African American
   voters but not on whites. However, the Assembly never acted on the resolution.
3. The German physiologists have even discovered vegetable matter—starch—in the
   human body. See Med. Chirurgical Rev., Oct., 1854, p. 889 [*Author's note*].

relation to American slavery which they now bear to the slavery of Cuba or the Brazils," is a statement, in a few words, which contains the result and the evidence of an argument which might cover pages, but could not carry stronger conviction, nor be stated in less pregnable form. In proof of this, I may say, that having been submitted to the attention of the Garrisonians in print, in March, it was repeated before them at their business meeting in May—the platform, *par excellence*, on which they invite free fight, *a l'outrance*,[4] to all comers. It was given out in the clear, ringing tones, wherewith the hall of shields was wont to resound of old, yet neither Garrison, nor Phillips, nor May, nor Remond, nor Foster, nor Burleigh, with his subtle steel of "the ice brook's temper,"[5] ventured to break a lance upon it! The doctrine of the dissolution of the Union, as a means for the abolition of American slavery, was silenced upon the lips that gave it birth, and in the presence of an array of defenders who compose the keenest intellects in the land.

"*The man who is right is a majority*," is an aphorism struck out by Mr. Douglass in that great gathering of the friends of freedom,[6] at Pittsburgh, in 1852, where he towered among the highest, because, with abilities inferior to none, and moved more deeply than any, there was neither policy nor party to trammel the outpourings of his soul. Thus we find, opposed to all the disadvantages which a black man in the United States labors and struggles under, is this one vantage ground—when the chance comes, and the audience where he may have a say, he stands forth the freest, most deeply moved and most earnest of all men.

It has been said of Mr. Douglass, that his descriptive and declamatory powers, admitted to be of the very highest order, take precedence of his logical force. Whilst the schools might have trained him to the exhibition of the formulas of deductive logic, nature and circumstances forced him into the exercise of the higher faculties required by induction. The first ninety pages of this "Life in Bondage," afford specimens of observing, comparing, and careful classifying, of such superior character, that it is difficult to believe them the results of a child's thinking; he questions the earth, and the children and the slaves around him again and again, and finally looks to "*God in the sky*" for the why and the wherefore of the unnatural thing, slavery. "*Yere, if indeed thou art, wherefore dost thou suffer us to be slain?*" is the only prayer and worship of the God-forsaken Dodos in the heart

---

4. "*par excellence*" and "*a l'outrance*": French for "most suitable" and "to the utmost."
5. Cf. Shakespeare, *Othello* 5.2.247. Samuel Joseph May (1797–1871), Charles Lenox Remond (1810–1873), Stephen Symonds Foster (1809–1881), Charles Calistus Burleigh (1810–1878), abolitionists close to Garrison.
6. On August 11–12, 1852, hundreds of antislavery activists attended the national convention of the Free Democratic or Free Soil Party.

of Africa. Almost the same was his prayer. One of his earliest observations was that white children should know their ages, while the colored children were ignorant of theirs; and the songs of the slaves grated on his inmost soul, because a something told him that harmony in sound, and music of the spirit, could not consociate with miserable degradation.

To such a mind, the ordinary processes of logical deduction are like proving that two and two make four. Mastering the intermediate steps by an intuitive glance, or recurring to them as Ferguson[7] resorted to geometry, it goes down to the deeper relation of things, and brings out what may seem, to some, mere statements, but which are new and brilliant generalizations, each resting on a broad and stable basis. Thus, Chief Justice Marshall gave his decisions, and then told Brother Story[8] to look up the authorities—and they never differed from him. Thus, also, in his "Lecture on the Anti-Slavery Movement," delivered before the Rochester Ladies' Anti-Slavery Society, Mr. Douglass presents a mass of thought, which, without any showy display of logic on his part, requires an exercise of the reasoning faculties of the reader to keep pace with him. And his "Claims of the Negro Ethnologically Considered," is full of new and fresh thoughts on the dawning science of race-history.

If, as has been stated, his intellection is slow, when unexcited, it is most prompt and rapid when he is thoroughly aroused. Memory, logic, wit, sarcasm, invective, pathos and bold imagery of rare structural beauty, well up as from a copious fountain, yet each in its proper place, and contributing to form a whole, grand in itself, yet complete in the minutest proportions. It is most difficult to hedge him in a corner, for his positions are taken so deliberately, that it is rare to find a point in them undefended aforethought. Professor Reason[9] tells me the following: "On a recent visit of a public nature, to Philadelphia, and in a meeting composed mostly of his colored brethren, Mr. Douglass proposed a comparison of views in the matters of the relations and duties of 'our people;' he holding that prejudice was the result of condition, and could be conquered by the efforts of the degraded themselves. A gentleman present, distinguished for logical acumen and subtlety, and who had devoted no small portion of the last twenty-five years to the study and elucidation of this very question, held the opposite view, that prejudice is innate and unconquerable. He terminated a series of well

---

7. James Ferguson (1710–1776), self-educated Scottish astronomer.
8. Joseph Story (1779–1845), Supreme Court justice 1812–45; John Marshall (1755–1835), Supreme Court chief justice 1801–35. Story was a central player in the *Amistad* controversy but earned the ire of abolitionists in 1842 when he upheld the constitutionality of the Fugitive Slave Law of 1793 in *Prigg v. Pennsylvania*.
9. Charles Lewis Reason (1818–1893), the first African American professor and a friend of Douglass.

dove-tailed, Socratic questions to Mr. Douglass, with the following:
'If the legislature at Harrisburgh should awaken, to-morrow morning, and find each man's skin turned black and his hair woolly,
what could they do to remove prejudice?' 'Immediately pass laws
entitling black men to all civil, political and social privileges,' was
the instant reply—and the questioning ceased."

The most remarkable mental phenomenon in Mr. Douglass, is his
style in writing and speaking. In March, 1855, he delivered an
address in the assembly chamber before the members of the legislature of the state of New York. An eye witness[1] describes the crowded
and most intelligent audience, and their rapt attention to the speaker,
as the grandest scene he ever witnessed in the capitol. Among those
whose eyes were riveted on the speaker full two hours and a half,
were Thurlow Weed and Lieutenant Governor Raymond;[2] the latter, at the conclusion of the address, exclaimed to a friend, "I
would give twenty thousand dollars, if I could deliver that address
in that manner." Mr. Raymond is a first class graduate of Dart-
mouth, a rising politician, ranking foremost in the legislature; of
course, his ideal of oratory must be of the most polished and finished description.

The style of Mr. Douglass in writing, is to me an intellectual puzzle. The strength, affluence and terseness may easily be accounted
for, because the style of a man is the man; but how are we to account
for that rare polish in his style of writing, which, most critically
examined, seems the result of careful early culture among the best
classics of our language; it equals if it do not surpass the style of
Hugh Miller, which was the wonder of the British literary public,
until he unraveled the mystery in the most interesting of autobiographies. But Frederick Douglass was still calking the seams of Baltimore clippers, and had only written a "pass,"[3] at the age when
Miller's style was already formed.

I asked William Whipper,[4] of Pennsylvania, the gentleman
alluded to above, whether he thought Mr. Douglass's power inherited from the Negroid, or from what is called the Caucasian side of
his make-up? After some reflection, he frankly answered, "I must
admit, although sorry to do so, that the Caucasian predominates."
At that time, I almost agreed with him; but, facts narrated in the

---

1. Mr. Wm. H. Topp, of Albany [*Author's note*]. Topp (1812–1857) was a merchant and
   abolitionist [*Editors' note*].
2. Weed (1797–1882), editor of the *Albany Evening Post*, helped get Henry Jarvis Raymond (1820–1869), cofounder of the *New York Daily Times*, elected as lieutenant
   governor.
3. Enslaved persons were often required to carry papers granting them official permission to travel from their master's home or plantation during slavery.
4. Wealthy African American abolitionist (1804–1876).

first part of this work, throw a different light on this interesting question.

We are left in the dark as to who was the paternal ancestor of our author; a fact which generally holds good of the Romuluses and Remuses[5] who are to inaugurate the new birth of our republic. In the absence of testimony from the Caucasian side, we must see what evidence is given on the other side of the house.

"My grandmother, though advanced in years, * * * was yet a woman of power and spirit. She was marvelously straight in figure, elastic and muscular." (p. 46.) [pp. 42–43]

After describing her skill in constructing nets, her perseverance in using them, and her wide-spread fame in the agricultural way he adds, "It happened to her—as it will happen to any careful and thrifty person residing in an ignorant and improvident neighborhood—to enjoy the reputation of being born to good luck." And his grandmother was a black woman.

"My mother was tall, and finely proportioned; of deep black, glossy complexion; had regular features; and among other slaves was remarkably sedate in her manners." "Being a field hand, she was obliged to walk twelve miles and return, between nightfall and daybreak, to see her children" (p. 54.) [pp. 45–46] "I shall never forget the indescribable expression of her countenance when I told her that I had had no food since morning. * * * There was pity in her glance at me, and a fiery indignation at Aunt Katy at the same time; * * * * she read Aunt Katy a lecture which she never forgot." (p. 56.) [p. 48] "I learned, after my mother's death, that she could read, and that she was the *only* one of all the slaves and colored people in Tuckahoe who enjoyed that advantage. How she acquired this knowledge, I know not, for Tuckahoe is the last place in the world where she would be apt to find facilities for learning." (p. 57.) [pp. 48–49] "There is, in 'Prichard's Natural History of Man,' the head of a figure—on page 157—the features of which so resemble those of my mother, that I often recur to it with something of the feeling which I suppose others experience when looking upon the pictures of dear departed ones." (p. 52.) [p. 46]

The head alluded to is copied from the statue of Ramses the Great, an Egyptian king of the nineteenth dynasty. The authors of the "Types of Mankind"[6] give a side view of the same on page 148, remarking that the profile, "like Napoleon's, is superbly European!" The nearness of its resemblance to Mr. Douglass' mother, rests upon

---

5. "Romuluses and Remuses": Twin brothers adopted by wolves, Romulus and Remus were the legendary founders of the ancient city of Rome.
6. In this influential work of ethnology (1854), Josiah Nott and George Gliddon categorized races as species and even discussed Douglass as an exceptional example of European genealogy.

the evidence of his memory, and judging from his almost marvelous feats of recollection of forms and outlines recorded in this book, this testimony may be admitted.

These facts show that for his energy, perseverance, eloquence, invective, sagacity, and wide sympathy, he is indebted to his negro blood. The very marvel of his style would seem to be a development of that other marvel,—how his mother learned to read. The versatility of talent which he wields, in common with Dumas, Ira Aldridge, and Miss Greenfield,[7] would seem to be the result of the grafting of the Anglo-Saxon on good, original, negro stock. If the friends of "Caucasus" choose to claim, for that region, what remains after this analysis—to wit: combination—they are welcome to it. They will forgive me for reminding them that the term "Caucasian" is dropped by recent writers on Ethnology; for the people about Mount Caucasus, are, and have ever been, Mongols. The great "white race" now seek paternity, according to Dr. Pickering, in Arabia—"Arida Nutrix"[8] of the best breed of horses &c. Keep on, gentlemen; you will find yourselves in Africa, by-and-by. The Egyptians, like the Americans, were a *mixed race*, with some negro blood circling around the throne, as well as in the mud hovels.

This is the proper place to remark of our author, that the same strong self-hood, which led him to measure strength with Mr. Covey, and to wrench himself from the embrace of the Garrisonians, and which has borne him through many resistances to the personal indignities offered him as a colored man, sometimes becomes a hyper-sensitiveness to such assaults as men of his mark will meet with, on paper. Keen and unscrupulous opponents have sought, and not unsuccessfully, to pierce him in this direction; for well they know, that if assailed, he will smite back.

It is not without a feeling of pride, dear reader, that I present you with this book. The son of a self-emancipated bond-woman, I feel joy in introducing to you my brother, who has rent his own bonds, and who, in his every relation—as a public man, as a husband and as a father—is such as does honor to the land which gave him birth. I shall place this book in the hands of the only child spared me, bidding him to strive and emulate its noble example. You may do likewise. It is an American book, for Americans, in the fullest sense of

---

7. Alexandre Dumas (1807–1870) was a famous French author of serials such as *The Count of Monte Cristo* and *The Three Musketeers*; his paternal grandmother was an enslaved African on the French colony of Saint-Domingue (present-day Haiti). Ira F. Aldridge (1807?–1867) was an African American stage actor and playwright who performed in England and the United States. Elizabeth Taylor Greenfield (1809–1876), an African American singer known as the "Black Swan," achieved international fame in the 1850s.
8. A dry nurse, or woman employed to care for an infant but not to breastfeed it (Latin). In *The Races of Man and Their Geographical Distribution*, Charles Pickering (1805–1878) argued that there were eleven races.

the idea. It shows that the worst of our institutions, in its worst aspect, cannot keep down energy, truthfulness, and earnest struggle for the right. It proves the justice and practicability of Immediate Emancipation. It shows that any man in our land, "no matter in what battle his liberty may have been cloven down, * * * * no matter what complexion an Indian or an African sun may have burned upon him," not only may "stand forth redeemed and disenthralled," but may also stand up a candidate for the highest suffrage of a great people—the tribute of their honest, hearty admiration.   Reader, *Vale!*[9]

New York.   JAMES M'CUNE SMITH.

9. Farewell (Latin). The preceding quote is a paraphrased extract from the Irish politican John Philpot Curran's (1750–1817) famous speech on liberty and universal emancipation.

Life as a Slave

CHAPTER I

The Author's Childhood

PLACE OF BIRTH—CHARACTER OF THE DISTRICT—TUCKAHOE—
ORIGIN OF THE NAME—CHOPTANK RIVER—TIME OF BIRTH—
GENEALOGICAL TREES—MODE OF COUNTING TIME—NAMES OF
GRANDPARENTS—THEIR POSITION—GRANDMOTHER ESPECIALLY
ESTEEMED—"BORN TO GOOD LUCK"—SWEET POTATOES—
SUPERSTITION—THE LOG CABIN—ITS CHARMS—SEPARATING
CHILDREN—AUTHOR'S AUNTS—THEIR NAMES—FIRST KNOWLEDGE
OF BEING A SLAVE—"OLD MASTER"—GRIEFS AND JOYS OF
CHILDHOOD—COMPARATIVE HAPPINESS OF THE SLAVE-BOY AND THE
SON OF A SLAVEHOLDER

In Talbot county, Eastern Shore, Maryland, near Easton, the county town of that county, there is a small district of country, thinly populated, and remarkable for nothing that I know of more than for the worn-out, sandy, desert-like appearance of its soil, the general dilapidation of its farms and fences, the indigent and spiritless character of its inhabitants, and the prevalence of ague and fever.

The name of this singularly unpromising and truly famine stricken district is Tuckahoe, a name well known to all Marylanders, black and white. It was given to this section of country probably, at the first, merely in derision; or it may possibly have been applied to it, as I have heard, because some one of its earlier inhabitants had been guilty of the petty meanness of stealing a hoe—or taking a hoe—that did not belong to him. Eastern Shore men usually pronounce the word *took*, as *tuck*; *Took-a-hoe*, therefore, is, in Maryland parlance, *Tuckahoe*. But, whatever may have been its origin—and about this I will not be positive—that name has stuck to the district in question; and it is seldom mentioned but with contempt and derision, on account of the barrenness of its soil, and the ignorance, indolence, and poverty of its people. Decay and ruin are everywhere visible, and the thin population of the place would have quitted it long ago, but for the Choptank river, which runs through it, from which they take abundance of shad and herring, and plenty of ague and fever.

It was in this dull, flat, and unthrifty district, or neighborhood, surrounded by a white population of the lowest order, indolent and drunken to a proverb, and among slaves, who seemed to ask, "*Oh! what's the use?*" every time they lifted a hoe, that I—without any fault of mine—was born, and spent the first years of my childhood.

The reader will pardon so much about the place of my birth, on the score that it is always a fact of some importance to know where a man is born, if, indeed, it be important to know anything about him. In regard to the *time* of my birth, I cannot be as definite as I have been respecting the *place*. Nor, indeed, can I impart much knowledge concerning my parents. Genealogical trees do not flourish among slaves. A person of some consequence here in the north, sometimes designated *father*, is literally abolished in slave law and slave practice. It is only once in a while that an exception is found to this statement. I never met with a slave who could tell me how old he was. Few slave-mothers know anything of the months of the year, nor of the days of the month. They keep no family records, with marriages, births, and deaths. They measure the ages of their children by spring time, winter time, harvest time, planting time, and the like; but these soon become undistinguishable and forgotten. Like other slaves, I cannot tell how old I am. This destitution was among my earliest troubles. I learned when I grew up, that my master—and this is the case with masters generally—allowed no questions to be put to him, by which a slave might learn his age. Such questions are deemed evidence of impatience, and even of impudent curiosity. From certain events, however, the dates of which I have since learned, I suppose myself to have been born about the year 1817.[1]

The first experience of life with me that I now remember—and I remember it but hazily—began in the family of my grandmother and grandfather, Betsey and Isaac Baily.[2] They were quite advanced in life, and had long lived on the spot where they then resided. They were considered old settlers in the neighborhood, and, from certain circumstances, I infer that my grandmother, especially, was held in high esteem, far higher than is the lot of most colored persons in the slave states. She was a good nurse, and a capital hand at

---

1. In *Young Frederick Douglass: The Maryland Years* (Baltimore: Johns Hopkins UP, 1980) Dickson J. Preston established that Douglass was actually born in February 1818.
2. Betsey (also Betsy or Betty; 1774–1849) was the slave of Douglass's first master, Aaron Anthony (1767–1826), schooner captain turned overseer. Her husband, Isaac, was a free Black man.

making nets for catching shad and herring; and these nets were in great demand, not only in Tuckanoe, but at Denton and Hillsboro, neighboring villages. She was not only good at making the nets, but was also somewhat famous for her good fortune in taking the fishes referred to. I have known her to be in the water half the day. Grandmother was likewise more provident than most of her neighbors in the preservation of seedling sweet potatoes, and it happened to her—as it will happen to any careful and thrifty person residing in an ignorant and improvident community—to enjoy the reputation of having been born to "good luck." Her "good luck" was owing to the exceeding care which she took in preventing the succulent root from getting bruised in the digging, and in placing it beyond the reach of frost, by actually burying it under the hearth of her cabin during the winter months. In the time of planting sweet potatoes, "Grandmother Betty," as she was familiarly called, was sent for in all directions, simply to place the seedling potatoes in the hills; for superstition had it, that if "Grandmamma Betty but touches them at planting, they will be sure to grow and flourish." This high reputation was full of advantage to her, and to the children around her. Though Tuckahoe had but few of the good things of life, yet of such as it did possess grandmother got a full share, in the way of presents. If good potato crops came after her planting, she was not forgotten by those for whom she planted; and as she was remembered by others, so she remembered the hungry little ones around her.

The dwelling of my grandmother and grandfather had few pretensions. It was a log hut, or cabin, built of clay, wood, and straw. At a distance it resembled—though it was much smaller, less commodious and less substantial—the cabins erected in the western states by the first settlers. To my child's eye, however, it was a noble structure, admirably adapted to promote the comforts and conveniences of its inmates. A few rough, Virginia fence-rails, flung loosely over the rafters above, answered the triple purpose of floors, ceilings, and bedsteads. To be sure, this upper apartment was reached only by a ladder—but what in the world for climbing could be better than a ladder? To me, this ladder was really a high invention, and possessed a sort of charm as I played with delight upon the rounds of it. In this little hut there was a large family of children: I dare not say how many. My grandmother—whether because too old for field service, or because she had so faithfully discharged the duties of her station in early life, I know not—enjoyed the high privilege of living in a cabin, separate from the quarter, with no other burden than her own support, and the necessary care of the little children, imposed. She evidently esteemed it a great fortune to live so. The children were

not her own, but her grandchildren—the children of her daughters.
She took delight in having them around her, and in attending to their
few wants. The practice of separating children from their mothers,
and hiring the latter out at distances too great to admit of their meeting, except at long intervals, is a marked feature of the cruelty and
barbarity of the slave system. But it is in harmony with the grand
aim of slavery, which, always and everywhere, is to reduce man to a
level with the brute. It is a successful method of obliterating from
the mind and heart of the slave, all just ideas of the sacredness of
the family, as an institution.

Most of the children, however, in this instance, being the children
of my grandmother's daughters, the notions of family, and the reciprocal duties and benefits of the relation, had a better chance of
being understood than where children are placed—as they often
are—in the hands of strangers, who have no care for them, apart
from the wishes of their masters. The daughters of my grandmother
were five in number. Their names were JENNY, ESTHER, MILLY, PRIS-
CILLA, and HARRIET. The daughter last named was my mother, of
whom the reader shall learn more by-and by.

Living here, with my dear old grandmother and grandfather, it
was a long time before I knew myself to be *a slave*. I knew many
other things before I knew that. Grandmother and grandfather
were the greatest people in the world to me; and being with them
so snugly in their own little cabin—I supposed it be their own—
knowing no higher authority over me or the other children than
the authority of grandmamma, for a time there was nothing to dis-
turb me; but, as I grew larger and older, I learned by degrees the
sad fact, that the "little hut," and the lot on which it stood, belonged
not to my dear old grandparents, but to some person who lived a
great distance off, and who was called, by grandmother, "OLD
MASTER." I further learned the sadder fact, that not only the
house and lot, but that grandmother herself, (grandfather was
free,) and all the little children around her, belonged to this mysterious personage, called by grandmother, with every mark of reverence, "Old Master." Thus early did clouds and shadows begin to
fall upon my path. Once on the track—troubles never come singly—I was not long in finding out another fact, still more grievous
to my childish heart. I was told that this "old master," whose name
seemed ever to be mentioned with fear and shuddering, only
allowed the children to live with grandmother for a limited time,
and that in fact as soon as they were big enough, they were
promptly taken away, to live with the said "old master." These were
distressing revelations indeed; and though I was quite too young to
comprehend the full import of the intelligence, and mostly spent

my childhood days in gleesome sports with the other children, a
shade of disquiet rested upon me.

The absolute power of this distant "old master" had touched my
young spirit with but the point of its cold, cruel iron, and left me
something to brood over after the play and in moments of repose.
Grandmammy was, indeed, at that time, all the world to me; and
the thought of being separated from her, in any considerable time,
was more than an unwelcome intruder. It was intolerable.

Children have their sorrows as well as men and women; and it
would be well to remember this in our dealings with them. SLAVE-
children *are* children, and prove no exceptions to the general rule.
The liability to be separated from my grandmother, seldom or never
to see her again, haunted me. I dreaded the thought of going to live
with that mysterious "old master," whose name I never heard mentioned with affection, but always with fear. I look back to this as
among the heaviest of my childhood's sorrows. My grandmother!
my grandmother! and the little hut, and the joyous circle under her
care, but especially *she*, who made us sorry when she left us but for
an hour, and glad on her return,—how could I leave her and the
good old home?

But the sorrows of childhood, like the pleasures of after life, are
transient. It is not even within the power of slavery to write *indeli-
ble* sorrow, at a single dash, over the heart of a child.

> "The tear down childhood's cheek that flows,
> Is like the dew-drop on the rose,—
> When next the summer breeze comes by,
> And waves the bush,—the flower is dry."[3]

There is, after all, but little difference in the measure of contentment felt by the slave-child neglected and the slaveholder's child
cared for and petted. The spirit of the All Just mercifully holds the
balance for the young.

The slaveholder, having nothing to fear from impotent childhood, easily affords to refrain from cruel inflictions; and if cold
and hunger do not pierce the tender frame, the first seven or eight
years of the slave-boy's life are about as full of sweet content as
those of the most favored and petted *white* children of the slaveholder. The slave-boy escapes many troubles which befall and vex
his white brother. He seldom has to listen to lectures on propriety
of behavior, or on anything else. He is never chided for handling
his little knife and fork improperly or awkwardly, for he uses none.
He is never reprimanded for soiling the table-cloth, for he takes

3. Cf. *Rokeby* (1813) 4.11.1–4, by the Scottish poet Sir Walter Scott (1771–1832).

his meals on the clay floor. He never has the misfortune, in his games or sports, of soiling or tearing his clothes, for he has almost none to soil or tear. He is never expected to act like a nice little gentleman, for he is only a rude little slave. Thus, freed from all restraint, the slave-boy can be, in his life and conduct, a genuine boy, doing whatever his boyish nature suggests; enacting, by turns, all the strange anties and freaks of horses, dogs, pigs, and barn-door fowls, without in any manner compromising his dignity, or incurring reproach of any sort. He literally runs wild; has no pretty little verses to learn in the nursery; no nice little speeches to make for aunts, uncles, or cousins, to show how smart he is; and, if he can only manage to keep out of the way of the heavy feet and fists of the older slave boys, he may trot on, in his joyous and roguish tricks, as happy as any little heathen under the palm trees of Africa. To be sure, he is occasionally reminded, when he stumbles in the path of his master—and this he early learns to avoid—that he is eating his "*white bread*," and that he will be made to "*see sights*" by-and-by. The threat is soon forgotten; the shadow soon passes, and our sable boy continues to roll in the dust, or play in the mud, as bests suits him, and in the veriest freedom. If he feels uncomfortable, from mud or from dust, the coast is clear; he can plunge into the river or the pond, without the ceremony of undressing, or the fear of wetting his clothes; his little tow-linen shirt—for that is all he has on—is easily dried; and it needed ablution as much as did his skin. His food is of the coarsest kind, consisting for the most part of cornmeal mush, which often finds it way from the wooden tray to his mouth in an oyster shell. His days, when the weather is warm, are spent in the pure, open air, and in the bright sunshine. He always sleeps in airy apartments; he seldom has to take powders, or to be paid to swallow pretty little sugar-coated pills, to cleanse his blood, or to quicken his appetite. He eats no candies; gets no lumps of loaf sugar; always relishes his food; cries but little, for nobody cares for his crying; learns to esteem his bruises but slight, because others so esteem them. In a word, he is, for the most part of the first eight years of his life, a spirited, joyous, uproarious, and happy boy, upon whom troubles fall only like water on a duck's back. And such a boy, so far as I can now remember, was the boy whose life in slavery I am now narrating.

CHAPTER II

The Author Removed from His First Home

THAT mysterious individual referred to in the first chapter as an object of terror among the inhabitants of our little cabin, under the ominous title of "old master," was really a man of some consequence. He owned several farms in Tuckahoe; was the chief clerk and butler on the home plantation of Col. Edward Lloyd;[1] had overseers on his own farms; and gave directions to overseers on the farms belonging to Col. Lloyd. This plantation is situated on Wye river—the river receiving its name, doubtless, from Wales, where the Lloyds originated. They (the Lloyds) are an old and honored family in Maryland, exceedingly wealthy. The home plantation, where they have resided, perhaps for a century or more, is one of the largest, most fertile, and best appointed, in the state.

About this plantation, and about that queer old master—who must be something more than a man, and something worse than an angel—the reader will easily imagine that I was not only curious, but eager, to know all that could be known. Unhappily for me, however, all the information I could get concerning him but increased my great dread of being carried thither—of being separated from and deprived of the protection of my grandmother and grandfather. It was, evidently, a great thing to go to Col. Lloyd's; and I was not without a little curiosity to see the place; but no amount of coaxing could induce in me the wish to remain there. The fact is, such was my dread of leaving the little cabin, that I wished to remain little forever, for I knew the taller I grew the shorter my stay. The old cabin, with its rail floor and rail bedsteads up stairs, and its clay floor down stairs, and its dirt chimney, and windowless sides, and that most curious piece of workmanship of all the rest, the ladder stairway, and the hole curiously dug in front of the fire-place, beneath which grandmammy placed the sweet potatoes to keep them from the frost, was MY HOME—the only home I ever had; and I loved it, and all connected with it. The old fences around it, and the stumps

1. See note 3 on p. 20.

in the edge of the woods near it, and the squirrels that ran, skipped, and played upon them, were objects of interest and affection. There, too, right at the side of the hut, stood the old well, with its stately and skyward-pointing beam, so aptly placed between the limbs of what had once been a tree, and so nicely balanced that I could move it up and down with only one hand, and could get a drink myself without calling for help. Where else in the world could such a well be found, and where could such another home be met with? Nor were these all the attractions of the place. Down in a little valley, not far from grandmammy's cabin, stood Mr. Lee's mill, where the people came often in large numbers to get their corn ground. It was a water-mill; and I never shall be able to tell the many things thought and felt, while I sat on the bank and watched that mill, and the turning of that ponderous wheel. The mill-pond, too, had its charms; and with my pin-hook, and thread line, I could get *nibbles*, if I could catch no fish. But, in all my sports and plays, and in spite of them, there would, occasionally, come the painful foreboding that I was not long to remain there, and that I must soon be called away to the home of old master.

I was A SLAVE—born a slave—and though the fact was incomprehensible to me, it conveyed to my mind a sense of my entire dependence on the will of *somebody* I had never seen; and, from some cause or other, I had been made to fear this somebody above all else on earth. Born for another's benefit, as the *firstling* of the cabin flock I was soon to be selected as a meet offering to the fearful and inexorable *demigod*, whose huge image on so many occasions haunted my childhood's imagination. When the time of my departure was decided upon, my grandmother, knowing my fears, and in pity for them, kindly kept me ignorant of the dreaded event about to transpire. Up to the morning (a beautiful summer morning) when we were to start, and, indeed, during the whole journey—a journey which, child as I was, I remember as well as if it were yesterday—she kept the sad fact hidden from me. This reserve was necessary; for, could I have known all, I should have given grandmother some trouble in getting me started. As it was, I was helpless, and she—dear woman!—led me along by the hand, resisting, with the reserve and solemnity of a priestess, all my inquiring looks to the last.

The distance from Tuckahoe to Wye river—where my old master lived—was full twelve miles, and the walk was quite a severe test of the endurance of my young legs. The journey would have proved too severe for me, but that my dear old grandmother—blessings on her memory!—afforded occasional relief by "toting" me (as Marylanders have it) on her shoulder. My grandmother, though advanced in years—as was evident from more than one gray hair, which peeped from between the ample and graceful folds of her newly-ironed bandana turban—was yet a woman of power and spirit. She was marvelously straight in figure, elastic, and muscular. I seemed hardly to be a burden to her. She would have "toted" me farther, but that I felt myself too much of a man to allow it, and insisted on walking. Releasing dear grandmamma from carrying me, did not make me altogether independent of her, when we happened to pass through portions of the somber woods which lay between Tuckahoe and Wye river. She often found me increasing the energy of my grip, and holding her clothing, lest something should come out of the woods and eat me up. Several old logs and stumps imposed upon me, and got themselves taken for wild beasts. I could see their legs, eyes, and ears, or I could see something like eyes, legs, and ears, till I got close enough to them to see that the eyes were knots, washed white with rain, and the legs were broken limbs, and the ears, only ears owing to the point from which they were seen. Thus early I learned that the point from which a thing is viewed is of some importance.

As the day advanced the heat increased; and it was not until the afternoon that we reached the much dreaded end of the journey. I found myself in the midst of a group of children of many colors; black, brown, copper colored, and nearly white. I had not seen so many children before. Great houses loomed up in different directions, and a great many men and women were at work in the fields. All this hurry, noise, and singing was very different from the stillness of Tuckahoe. As a new comer, I was an object of special interest; and, after laughing and yelling around me, and playing all sorts of wild tricks, they (the children) asked me to go out and play with them. This I refused to do, preferring to stay with grandmamma. I could not help feeling that our being there boded no good to me. Grandmamma looked sad. She was soon to lose another object of affection, as she had lost many before. I knew she was unhappy, and the shadow fell from her brow on me, though I knew not the cause.

All suspense, however, must have an end; and the end of mine, in this instance, was at hand. Affectionately patting me on the head, and exhorting me to be a good boy, grandmamma told me to go and play with the little children. "They are kin to you," said she; "go and play with them." Among a number of cousins were Phil, Tom, Steve, and Jerry, Nance and Betty.

Grandmother pointed out my brother PERRY, my sister SARAH, and my sister ELIZA,[2] who stood in the group. I had never seen my brother nor my sisters before; and, though I had sometimes heard of them, and felt a curious interest in them, I really did not understand what

2. Perry was born in 1813, Sarah in 1814, and Eliza in 1816.

they were to me, or I to them. We were brothers and sisters, but what of that? Why should they be attached to me, or I to them? Brothers and sisters we were by blood; but *slavery* had made us strangers. I heard the words brother and sisters, and knew they must mean something; but slavery had robbed these terms of their true meaning. The experience through which I was passing, they had passed through before. They had already been initiated into the mysteries of old master's domicile, and they seemed to look upon me with a certain degree of compassion; but my heart clave to my grandmother. Think it not strange, dear reader, that so little sympathy of feeling existed between us. The conditions of brotherly and sisterly feeling were wanting—we had never nestled and played together. My poor mother, like many other slave-women, had *many children*, but no family! The domestic hearth, with its holy lessons and precious endearments, is abolished in the case of a slave-mother and her children. "Little children, love one another,"[3] are words seldom heard in a slave cabin.

I really wanted to play with my brother and sisters, but they were strangers to me, and I was full of fear that grandmother might leave without taking me with her. Entreated to do so, however, and that, too, by my dear grandmother, I went to the back part of the house, to play with them and the other children. *Play*, however, I did not, but stood with my back against the wall, witnessing the playing of the others. At last, while standing there, one of the children, who had been in the kitchen, ran up to me, in a sort of roguish glee, exclaiming, "Fed, Fed! grandmammy gone! grandmammy gone!" I could not believe it; yet, fearing the worst, I ran into the kitchen, to see for myself, and found it even so. Grandmammy had indeed gone, and was now far away, "clean" out of sight. I need not tell all that happened now. Almost heart-broken at the discovery, I fell upon the ground, and wept a boy's bitter tears, refusing to be comforted. My brother and sisters came around me, and said, "Don't cry," and gave me peaches and pears, but I flung them away, and refused all their kindly advances. I had never been deceived before; and I felt not only grieved at parting—as I supposed forever—with my grandmother, but indignant that a trick had been played upon me in a matter so serious.

It was now late in the afternoon. The day had been an exciting and wearisome one, and I knew not how or where, but I suppose I sobbed myself to sleep. There is a healing in the angel wing of sleep, even for the slave-boy; and its balm was never more welcome to any wounded soul than it was to mine, the first night I spent at the domicile of old master. The reader may be surprised that I narrate so minutely an incident apparently so trivial, and which must have

3. In Christian tradition, the apostle John's summary of Jesus's message.

occurred when I was not more than seven years old; but as I wish to give a faithful history of my experience in slavery, I cannot withhold a circumstance which, at the time, affected me so deeply. Besides, this was, in fact, my first introduction to the realities of slavery.

CHAPTER III

The Author's Parentage

AUTHOR'S FATHER SHROUDED IN MYSTERY—AUTHOR'S MOTHER—HER PERSONAL APPEARANCE—INTERFERENCE OF SLAVERY WITH THE NATURAL AFFECTIONS OF MOTHER AND CHILDREN—SITUATION OF AUTHOR'S MOTHER—HER NIGHTLY VISITS TO HER BOY—STRIKING INCIDENT—HER DEATH—HER PLACE OF BURIAL

If the reader will now be kind enough to allow me time to grow bigger, and afford me an opportunity for my experience to become greater, I will tell him something, by-and-by, of slave life, as I saw, felt, and heard it, on Col. Edward Lloyd's plantation, and at the house of old master, where I had now, despite of myself, most suddenly, but not unexpectedly, been dropped. Meanwhile, I will redeem my promise to say something more of my dear mother.

I say nothing of *father*, for he is shrouded in a mystery I have never been able to penetrate. Slavery does away with fathers, as it does away with families. Slavery has no use for either fathers or families, and its laws do not recognize their existence in the social arrangements of the plantation. When they *do* exist, they are not the outgrowths of slavery, but are antagonistic to that system. The order of civilization is reversed here. The name of the child is not expected to be that of its father, and his condition does not necessarily affect that of the child. He may be the slave of Mr. Tilgman; and his child, when born, may be the slave of Mr. Gross. He may be a *freeman*; and yet his child may be a *chattel*. He may be white, glorying in the purity of his Anglo-Saxon blood; and his child may be ranked with the blackest slaves. Indeed, he *may* be, and often *is*, master and father to the same child. He can be father without being a husband, and may sell his child without incurring reproach, if the child be by a woman in whose veins courses one thirty-second part of African blood. My father was a white man, or nearly white. It was sometimes whispered that my master was my father.

But to return, or rather, to begin. My knowledge of my mother is very scanty, but very distinct. Her personal appearance and bearing are ineffaceably stamped upon my memory. She was tall, and finely proportioned; of deep black, glossy complexion; had regular features, and, among the other slaves, was remarkably sedate in her manners. There is in "*Prichard's Natural History of Man,*" the head of a figure—on page 157—the features of which so resemble those of my mother, that I often recur to it with something of the feeling which I suppose others experience when looking upon the pictures of dear departed ones.

Yet I cannot say that I was very deeply attached to my mother; certainly not so deeply as I should have been had our relations in childhood been different. We were separated, according to the common custom, when I was but an infant, and, of course, before I knew my mother from any one else.

The germs of affection with which the Almighty, in his wisdom and mercy, arms the helpless infant against the ills and vicissitudes of his lot, had been directed in their growth toward that loving old grandmother, whose gentle hand and kind deportment it was the first effort of my infantile understanding to comprehend and appreciate. Accordingly, the tenderest affection which a beneficent Father allows, as a partial compensation to the mother for the pains and lacerations of her heart, incident to the maternal relation, was, in my case, diverted from its true and natural object, by the envious, greedy, and treacherous hand of slavery. The slave-mother can be spared long enough from the field to endure all the bitterness of a mother's anguish, when it adds another name to a master's ledger, but *not* long enough to receive the joyous reward afforded by the intelligent smiles of her child. I never think of this terrible interference of slavery with my infantile affections, and its diverting them from their natural course, without feelings to which I can give no adequate expression.

I do not remember to have seen my mother at my grandmother's at any time. I remember her only in her visits to me at Col. Lloyd's plantation, and in the kitchen of my old master. Her visits to me there were few in number, brief in duration, and mostly made in the night. The pains she took, and the toil she endured, to see me, tells me that a true mother's heart was hers, and that slavery had difficulty in paralyzing it with unmotherly indifference.

My mother was hired out to a Mr. Stewart, who lived about twelve miles from old master's, and, being a field hand, she seldom had leisure, by day, for the performance of the journey. The nights and the distance were both obstacles to her visits. She was obliged to walk, unless chance flung into her way an opportunity to ride; and the latter was sometimes her good luck. But she always had to walk one way or the other. It was a greater luxury than slavery could afford, to allow a black slave-mother a horse or a mule, upon which to travel twenty-four miles, when she could walk the distance. Besides, it is deemed a foolish whim for a slave-mother to manifest concern to see her children, and, in one point of view, the case is made out—she can do nothing for them. She has no control over them; the master is even more than the mother, in all matters touching the fate of her child. Why, then, should she give herself any concern? She has no responsibility. Such is the reasoning, and such the practice. The iron rule of the plantation, always passionately and violently enforced in that neighborhood, makes flogging the penalty of failing to be in the field before sunrise in the morning, unless special permission be given to the absenting slave. "I went to see my child," is no excuse to the ear or heart of the overseer.

One of the visits of my mother to me, while at Col. Lloyd's, I remember very vividly, as affording a bright gleam of a mother's love, and the earnestness of a mother's care.

I had on that day offended "Aunt Katy," (called "Aunt" by way of respect,) the cook of old master's establishment. I do not now remember the nature of my offense in this instance, for my offenses were numerous in that quarter, greatly depending, however, upon the mood of Aunt Katy, as to their heinousness; but she had adopted, that day, her favorite mode of punishing me, namely, making me go without food all day—that is, from after breakfast. The first hour or two after dinner, I succeeded pretty well in keeping up my spirits; but though I made an excellent stand against the foe, and fought bravely during the afternoon, I knew I must be conquered at last, unless I got the accustomed reënforcement of a slice of corn bread, at sundown. Sundown came, but *no bread*, and, in its stead, their came the threat, with a scowl well suited to its terrible import, that she "meant to *starve the life out of me!*" Brandishing her knife, she chopped off the heavy slices for the other children, and put the loaf away, muttering, all the while, her savage designs upon myself. Against this disappointment, for I was expecting that her heart would relent at last, I made an extra effort to maintain my dignity; but when I saw all the other children around me with merry and satisfied faces, I could stand it no longer. I went out behind the house, and cried like a fine fellow! When tired of this, I returned to the kitchen, sat by the fire, and brooded over my hard lot. I was too hungry to sleep. While I sat in the corner, I caught sight of an ear of Indian corn on an upper shelf of the kitchen. I watched my chance, and got it, and, shelling off a few grains, I put it back again. The grains in my hand, I quickly put in some ashes, and covered them with embers, to roast them. All this I did at the risk of getting a brutal thumping, for Aunt Katy could beat, as well as starve me. My corn was not long in roasting, and, with my keen appetite, it did not matter even if the grains were not exactly done. I eagerly pulled them out, and placed them on my stool, in a clever little pile. Just as I began to help myself to my very dry meal, in came my dear mother. And now, dear reader, a scene occurred which was altogether worth beholding, and to me it was instructive as well as interesting. The friendless and hungry boy, in his extremest need—and when he did not dare to look for succor—found himself in the strong, protecting arms of a mother; a mother who was, at the moment (being endowed with high powers of manner as well as matter) more than a match for all his enemies. I shall never forget the indescribable expression of her countenance, when I told her that I had had no food since morning; and that Aunt Katy said she "meant to starve the life out of me." There was pity in her glance at me, and a fiery indignation at Aunt Katy at the same time; and, while she took the corn from me, and gave me a large ginger cake, in its stead, she read Aunt Katy a lecture which she never forgot. My mother threatened her with complaining to old master in my behalf; for the latter, though harsh and cruel himself, at times, did not sanction the meanness, injustice, partiality and oppressions enacted by Aunt Katy in the kitchen. That night I learned the fact, that I was not only a child, but *somebody's* child. The "sweet cake" my mother gave me was in the shape of a heart, with a rich, dark ring glazed upon the edge of it. I was victorious, and well off for the moment; prouder, on my mother's knee, than a king upon his throne. But my triumph was short. I dropped off to sleep, and waked in the morning only to find my mother gone, and myself left at the mercy of the sable virago, dominant in my old master's kitchen, whose fiery wrath was my constant dread.

I do not remember to have seen my mother after this occurrence. Death soon ended the little communication that had existed between us; and with it, I believe, a life—judging from her weary, sad, downcast countenance and mute demeanor—full of heartfelt sorrow. I was not allowed to visit her during any part of her long illness; nor did I see her for a long time before she was taken ill and died. The heartless and ghastly form of *slavery* rises between mother and child, even at the bed of death. The mother, at the verge of the grave, may not gather her children, to impart to them her holy admonitions, and invoke for them her dying benediction. The bond-woman lives as a slave, and is left to die as a beast; often with fewer attentions than are paid to a favorite horse. Scenes of sacred tenderness, around the death-bed, never forgotten, and which often arrest the vicious and confirm the virtuous during life, must be looked for among the free, though they sometimes occur among the slaves. It has been a life-long, standing grief to me, that I knew so little of my mother; and that I was so early separated from her. The counsels of her love must have been beneficial to me. The side view of her face is imaged on my memory, and I take few steps in life, without feeling her presence; but the image is mute, and I have no striking words of her's treasured up.

I learned, after my mother's death, that she could read, and that she was the *only* one of all the slaves and colored people in Tuckahoe who enjoyed that advantage. How she acquired this knowledge, I know not, for Tuckahoe is the last place in the world where she would be apt to find facilities for learning. I can, therefore, fondly and proudly ascribe to her an earnest love of knowledge. That a "field hand" should learn to read, in any slave state, is remarkable; but the achievement of my mother, considering the place, was very extraordinary; and, in view of that fact, I am quite willing, and even happy, to attribute any love of letters I possess, and for which I have got—despite of prejudices—only too much credit, *not* to my admitted Anglo-Saxon paternity, but to the native genius of my sable, unprotected, and uncultivated *mother*—a woman, who belonged to a race whose mental endowments it is, at present, fashionable to hold in disparagement and contempt.

Summoned away to her account, with the impassable gulf of slavery between us during her entire illness, my mother died without leaving me a single intimation of *who* my father was. There was a whisper, that my master was my father; yet it was only a whisper, and I cannot say that I ever gave it credence. Indeed, I now have reason to think he was not; nevertheless, the fact remains, in all its glaring odiousness, that, by the laws of slavery, children, in all cases, are reduced to the condition of their mothers. This arrangement admits of the greatest license to brutal slaveholders, and their profligate sons, brothers, relations and friends, and gives to the pleasure of sin, the additional attraction of profit. A whole volume might be written on this single feature of slavery, as I have observed it.

One might imagine, that the children of such connections, would fare better, in the hands of their masters, than other slaves. The rule is quite the other way; and a very little reflection will satisfy the reader that such is the case. A man who will enslave his own blood, may not be safely relied on for magnanimity. Men do not love those who remind them of their sins—unless they have a mind to repent—and the mulatto child's face is a standing accusation against him who is master and father to the child. What is still worse, perhaps, such a child is a constant offense to the wife. She hates its very presence, and when a slaveholding woman hates, she wants not means to give that hate telling effect. Women—white women, I mean—are IDOLS at the south, not WIVES, for the slave women are preferred in many instances; and if these *idols* but nod, or lift a finger, woe to the poor victim: kicks, cuffs and stripes are sure to follow. Masters are frequently compelled to sell this class of their slaves, out of deference to the feelings of their white wives; and shocking and scandalous as it may seem for a man to sell his own blood to the traffickers in human flesh, it is often an act of humanity toward the slave-child to be thus removed from his merciless tormentors.

It is not within the scope of the design of my simple story, to comment upon every phase of slavery not within my experience as a slave.

But, I may remark, that, if the lineal descendants of Ham are only to be enslaved, according to the scriptures, slavery in this country will soon become an unscriptural institution; for thousands are ushered into the world, annually, who—like myself—owe their existence to white fathers, and, most frequently, to their masters, and master's sons. The slave-woman is at the mercy of the fathers, sons or brothers of her master. The thoughtful know the rest.

After what I have now said of the circumstances of my mother, and my relations to her, the reader will not be surprised, nor be disposed to censure me, when I tell but the simple truth, viz: that I received the tidings of her death with no strong emotions of sorrow for her, and with very little regret for myself on account of her loss. I had to learn the value of my mother long after her death, and by witnessing the devotion of other mothers to their children.

There is not, beneath the sky, an enemy to filial affection so destructive as slavery. It had made my brothers and sisters strangers to me; it converted the mother that bore me, into a myth; it shrouded my father in mystery, and left me without an intelligible beginning in the world.

My mother died when I could not have been more than eight or nine years old, on one of old master's farms in Tuckahoe, in the neighborhood of Hillsborough. Her grave is, as the grave of the dead at sea, unmarked, and without stone or stake.

CHAPTER IV

A General Survey of the Slave Plantation

ISOLATION OF LLOYD'S PLANTATION—PUBLIC OPINION THERE NO PROTECTION TO THE SLAVE—ABSOLUTE POWER OF THE OVERSEER—NATURAL AND ARTIFICIAL CHARMS OF THE PLACE—ITS BUSINESS-LIKE APPEARANCE—SUPERSTITION ABOUT THE BURIAL GROUND—GREAT IDEAS OF COL. LLOYD—ETIQUETTE AMONG SLAVES—THE COMIC SLAVE DOCTOR—PRAYING AND FLOGGING—"OLD MASTER" LOSING ITS TERRORS—HIS BUSINESS—CHARACTER OF "AUNT KATY"—SUFFERINGS FROM HUNGER—OLD MASTER'S HOME—JARGON OF THE PLANTATION—GUINEA SLAVES—MASTER DANIEL—FAMILY OF COL. LLOYD—FAMILY OF CAPT. ANTHONY—HIS SOCIAL POSITION—NOTIONS OF RANK AND STATION

IT is generally supposed that slavery, in the state of Maryland, exists in its mildest form, and that it is totally divested of those harsh and terrible peculiarities, which mark and characterize the slave system, in the southern and south-western states of the American union. The argument in favor of this opinion, is the contiguity of the free states, and the exposed condition of slavery in Maryland to the moral, religious and humane sentiment of the free states.

I am not about to refute this argument, so far as it relates to slavery in that State, generally; on the contrary, I am willing to admit that, to this general point, the argument is well grounded. Public opinion is, indeed, an unfailing restraint upon the cruelty and barbarity of masters, overseers, and slave-drivers, whenever and wherever it can reach them; but there are certain secluded and out-of-the way places, even in the state of Maryland, seldom visited by a single ray of healthy public sentiment—where slavery, wrapt in its own congenial, midnight darkness, *can*, and *does*, develop all its malign and shocking characteristics; where it can be indecent without shame, cruel without shuddering, and murderous without apprehension or fear of exposure.

Just such a secluded, dark, and out-of-the-way place, is the "home plantation" of Col. Edward Lloyd, on the Eastern Shore, Maryland. It is far away from all the great thoroughfares, and is proximate to no town or village. There is neither school-house, nor town-house in its neighborhood. The school-house is unnecessary, for there are no children to go to school. The children and grand-children of Col. Lloyd were taught in the house, by a private tutor—a Mr. Page—a tall, gaunt sapling of a man, who did not speak a dozen words to a slave in a whole year. The overseers' children go off somewhere to school; and they, therefore, bring no foreign or dangerous influence from abroad, to embarrass the natural operation of the slave system of the place. Not even the mechanics—through whom there is an occasional out-burst of honest and telling indignation, at cruelty and wrong on other plantations—are white men, on this plantation. Its whole public is made up of, and divided into, three classes— SLAVEHOLERS, SLAVES and OVERSEERS. Its blacksmiths, wheelwrights, shoemakers, weavers, and coopers, are slaves. Not even commerce, selfish and iron-hearted at it is, and ready, as it ever is, to side with the strong against the weak—the rich against the poor—is trusted or permitted within its secluded precincts. Whether with a view of guarding against the escape of its secrets, I know not, but it is a fact, that every leaf and grain of the produce of this plantation, and those of the neighboring farms belonging to Col. Lloyd, are transported to Baltimore in Col. Lloyd's own vessels; every man and boy on board of which—except the captain—are owned by him. In return, everything brought to the plantation, comes through the same channel. Thus, even the glimmering and unsteady light of trade, which sometimes exerts a civilizing influence, is excluded from this "tabooed" spot.

Nearly all the plantations or farms in the vicinity of the "home plantation" of Col. Lloyd, belong to him; and those which do not, are owned by personal friends of his, as deeply interested in maintaining the slave system, in all its rigor, as Col. Lloyd himself. Some of his neighbors are said to be even more stringent than he. The Skinners, the Peakers, the Tilgmans, the Lockermans, and the Gipsons, are in the same boat; being slaveholding neighbors, they may have strengthened each other in their iron rule. They are on intimate terms, and their interests and tastes are identical.

Public opinion in such a quarter, the reader will see, is not likely to be very efficient in protecting the slave from cruelty. On the contrary, it must increase and intensify his wrongs. Public opinion seldom differs very widely from public practice. To be a restraint upon cruelty and vice, public opinion must emanate from a humane and virtuous community. To no such humane and virtuous community, is Col. Lloyd's plantation exposed. That plantation is a little nation of its own, having its own language, its own rules, regulations and customs. The laws and institutions of the state, apparently touch it nowhere. The troubles arising here, are not settled by the civil power of the state. The overseer is generally accuser, judge, jury, advocate and executioner. The criminal is always dumb. The overseer attends to all sides of a case.

There are no conflicting rights of property, for all the people are owned by one man; and they can themselves own no property. Religion and politics are alike excluded. One class of the population is too high to be reached by the preacher; and the other class is too low to be cared for by the preacher. The poor have the gospel preached to them, in this neighborhood, only when they are able to pay for it. The slaves, having no money, get no gospel. The politician keeps away, because the people have no votes, and the preacher keeps away, because the people have no money. The rich planter can afford to learn politics in the parlor, and to dispense with religion altogether.

In its isolation, seclusion, and self-reliant independence, Col. Lloyd's plantation resembles what the baronial domains were, during the middle ages in Europe. Grim, cold, and unapproachable by all genial influences from communities without, *there it stands*; full three hundred years behind the age, in all that relates to humanity and morals.

This, however, is not the only view that the place presents. Civilization is shut out, but nature cannot be. Though separated from the rest of the world; though public opinion, as I have said, seldom gets a chance to penetrate its dark domain; though the whole place is stamped with its own peculiar, ironlike individuality; and though crimes, high-handed and atrocious, may there be committed, with almost as much impunity as upon the deck of a pirate ship,—it is, nevertheless, altogether, to outward seeming, a most strikingly interesting place, full of life, activity, and spirit; and presents a very favorable contrast to the indolent monotony and languor of Tuckahoe. Keen as was my regret and great as was my sorrow at leaving the latter, I was not long in adapting myself to this, my new home. A man's troubles are always half disposed of, when he finds endurance his only remedy. I found myself here; there was no getting away; and what remained for me, but to make the best of it? Here were plenty of children to play with, and plenty of places of pleasant resort for boys of my age, and boys older. The little tendrils of affection, so rudely and treacherously broken from around the darling objects of my grandmother's hut, gradually began to extend, and to entwine about the new objects by which I now found myself surrounded.

There was a windmill (always a commanding object to a child's eye) on Long Point—a tract of land dividing Miles river from the Wye—a mile or more from my old master's house. There was a creek to swim in, at the bottom of an open flat space, of twenty acres or more, called "the Long Green"—a very beautiful play-ground for the children.

In the river, a short distance from the shore, lying quietly at anchor, with her small boat dancing at her stern, was a large sloop— the Sally Lloyd; called by that name in honor of a favorite daughter of the colonel. The sloop and the mill were wondrous things, full of thoughts and ideas. A child cannot well look at such objects without *thinking*.

Then here were a great many houses; human habitations, full of the mysteries of life at every stage of it. There was the little red house, up the road, occupied by Mr. Sevier, the overseer. A little nearer to my old master's, stood a very long, rough, low building, literally alive with slaves, of all ages, conditions and sizes. This was called "the Long Quarter." Perched upon a hill, across the Long Green, was a very tall, dilapidated, old brick building—the architectural dimensions of which proclaimed its erection for a different purpose—now occupied by slaves, in a similar manner to the Long Quarter. Besides these, there were numerous other slave houses and huts, scattered around in the neighborhood, every nook and corner of which was completely occupied. Old master's house, a long, brick building, plain, but substantial, stood in the center of the plantation life, and constituted one independent establishment on the premises of Col. Lloyd.

Besides these dwellings, there were barns, stables, store-houses, and tobacco-houses; blacksmiths' shops, wheelwrights' shops, coopers' shops—all objects of interest; but, above all, there stood the grandest building my eyes had then ever beheld, called, by every one on the plantation, the "Great House." This was occupied by Col. Lloyd and his family. They occupied it; *I* enjoyed it. The great house was surrounded by numerous and variously shaped out-buildings. There were kitchens, wash-houses, dairies, summer-house, green-houses, hen-houses, turkey-houses, pigeon-houses, and arbors, of many sizes and devices, all neatly painted, and altogether interspersed with grand old trees, ornamental and primitive, which afforded delightful shade in summer, and imparted to the scene a high degree of stately beauty. The great house itself was a large, white, wooden building, with wings on three sides of it. In front, a large portico, extending the entire length of the building, and supported by a long range of columns, gave to the whole establishment an air of solemn grandeur. It was a treat to my young and gradually opening mind, to behold this elaborate exhibition of wealth, power, and vanity. The carriage entrance to the house was a large gate, more than a quarter of a mile distant from it; the intermediate space was a beautiful lawn, very neatly trimmed, and watched with the greatest care. It was dotted thickly over with delightful trees, shrubbery, and flowers. The road, or lane, from the gate to the great house, was richly paved with white pebbles from the beach, and, in its course, formed a complete circle around the beautiful lawn. Carriages going in and retiring from the great house, made the circuit of the lawn, and their passengers were permitted to behold a scene of almost Eden-like beauty. Outside this select inclosure, were parks, where—as about the residences of the English nobility—rabbits, deer, and other wild game, might be seen, peering and playing about, with none to molest them or make them afraid. The tops of the stately poplars were often covered with the red-winged blackbirds, making all nature vocal with the joyous life and beauty of their wild, warbling notes. These all belonged to me, as well as to Col. Edward Lloyd, and for a time I greatly enjoyed them.

A short distance from the great house, were the stately mansions of the dead, a place of somber aspect. Vast tombs, embowered beneath the weeping willow and the fir tree, told of the antiquities of the Lloyd family, as well as of their wealth. Superstition was rife among the slaves about this family burying ground. Strange sights had been seen there by some of the older slaves. Shrouded ghosts, riding on great black horses, had been seen to enter; balls of fire had been seen to fly there at midnight, and horrid sounds had been repeatedly heard. Slaves know enough of the rudiments of theology to believe that those go to hell who die slaveholders; and they often fancy such persons wishing themselves back again, to wield the lash. Tales of sights and sounds, strange and terrible, connected with the huge black tombs, were a very great security to the grounds about them, for few of the slaves felt like approaching them even in the day time. It was a dark, gloomy and forbidding place, and it was difficult to feel that the spirits of the sleeping dust there deposited, reigned with the blest in the realms of eternal peace.

The business of twenty or thirty farms was transacted at this, called, by way of eminence, "great house farm." These farms all belonged to Col. Lloyd, as did, also, the slaves upon them. Each farm was under the management of an overseer. As I have said of the overseer of the home plantation, so I may say of the overseers on the smaller ones; they stand between the slave and all civil constitutions— their word is law, and is implicitly obeyed.

The colonel, at this time, was reputed to be, and he apparently was, very rich. His slaves, alone, were an immense fortune. These small and great, could not have been fewer than one thousand in number, and though scarcely a month passed without the sale of one or more lots to the Georgia traders, there was no apparent diminution in the number of his human stock: the home plantation merely groaned at a removal of the young increase, or human crop, then proceeded as lively as ever. Horse-shoeing, cart-mending, plow-repairing, coopering, grinding, and weaving, for all the neighboring farms, were performed here, and slaves were employed in all these branches. "Uncle Tony" was the blacksmith; "Uncle Harry" was the cartwright; "Uncle Abel" was the shoemaker; and all these had hands to assist them in their several departments.

These mechanics were called "uncles" by all the younger slaves, not because they really sustained that relationship to any, but according to plantation *etiquette*, as a mark of respect, due from the younger to the older slaves. Strange, and even ridiculous as it may seem, among a people so uncultivated, and with so many stern trials to look in the face, there is not to be found, among any people, a more rigid enforcement of the law of respect to elders, than they maintain. I set this down as partly constitutional with my race, and partly conventional. There is no better material in the world for making a gentleman, than is furnished in the African. He shows to others, and exacts for himself, all the tokens of respect which he is compelled to manifest toward his master. A young slave must approach the company of the older with hat in hand, and woe betide him, if he fails to acknowledge a favor, of any sort, with the accustomed "*tank'ee*," &c. So uniformly are good manners enforced among slaves, that I can easily detect a "bogus" fugitive by his manners.

Among other slave notabilities of the plantation, was one called by everybody Uncle Isaac Copper. It is seldom that a slave gets a surname from anybody in Maryland; and so completely has the south shaped the manners of the north, in this respect, that even abolitionists make very little of the surname of a negro. The only improvement on the "Bills," "Jacks," "Jims," and "Neds" of the south, observable here is, that "William," "John," "James," "Edward," are substituted. It goes against the grain to treat and address a negro precisely as they would treat and address a white man. But, once in a while, in slavery as in the free states, by some extraordinary circumstance, the negro has a surname fastened to him, and holds it against all conventionalties. This was the case with Uncle Isaac Copper. When the "uncle" was dropped, he generally had the prefix "doctor," in its stead. He was our doctor of medicine, and doctor of divinity as well.[1] Where he took his degree I am unable to say, for he was not very communicative to inferiors, and I was emphatically such, being but a boy seven or eight years old. He was too well established in his profession to permit questions as to his native skill, or his attainments. One qualification he undoubtedly had—he was a confirmed *cripple*; and he could neither work, nor would he bring anything if offered for sale in the market. The old man, though lame, was no sluggard. He was a man that made his crutches do him good service. He was always on the alert, looking up the sick, and all such as were supposed to need his counsel. His remedial prescriptions embraced four articles. For diseases of the body, *Epsom salts* and *castor oil*; for those of the soul, *the Lord's Prayer*, and *hickory switches*!

I was not long at Col. Lloyd's before I was placed under the care of Doctor Isaac Copper. I was sent to him with twenty or thirty other children, to learn the "Lord's Prayer." I found the old gentleman seated on a huge three-legged oaken stool, armed with several large hickory switches; and, from his position, he could reach—lame as he was—any boy in the room. After standing awhile to learn what was expected of us, the old gentleman, in any other than a devotional tone, commanded us to kneel down. This done, he commenced telling us to say everything he said. "Our Father"—this we repeated after him with promptness and uniformity; "Who art in heaven"—was less promptly and uniformly repeated; and the old gentleman paused in the prayer, to give us a short lecture upon the consequences of inattention, both immediate and future, and especially those more immediate. About these he was absolutely certain, for he held in his right hand the means of bringing all his predictions and warnings to pass. On he proceeded with the prayer; and we with our thick tongues and unskilled ears, followed him to the

---

1. Isaac Cooper had been a house servant and breeder of fighting cocks before being put in charge of the spiritual and medical needs of the enslaved on the population.

best of our ability. This, however, was not sufficient to please the old gentleman. Everybody, in the south, wants the privilege of whipping somebody else. Uncle Isaac shared the common passion of his country, and, therefore, seldom found any means of keeping his disciples in order short of flogging. "Say everything I say;" and bang would come the switch on some poor boy's undevotional head. "*What you looking at there*"—"*Stop that pushing*"—and down again would come the lash.

The whip is all in all. It is supposed to secure obedience to the slaveholder, and is held as a sovereign remedy among the slaves themselves, for every form of disobedience, temporal or spiritual. Slaves, as well as slaveholders, use it with an unsparing hand. Our devotions at Uncle Isaac's combined too much of the tragic and comic, to make them very salutary in a spiritual point of view; and it is due to truth to say, I was often a truant when the time for attending the praying and flogging of Doctor Isaac Copper came on.

The windmill under the care of Mr. Kinney, a kind hearted old Englishman, was to me a source of infinite interest and pleasure. The old man always seemed pleased when he saw a troop of darkey little urchins, with their tow-linen shirts fluttering in the breeze, approaching to view and admire the whirling wings of his wondrous machine. From the mill we could see other objects of deep interest. These were, the vessels from St. Michael's, on their way to Baltimore. It was a source of much amusement to view the flowing sails and complicated rigging, as the little crafts dashed by, and to speculate upon Baltimore, as to the kind and quality of the place. With so many sources of interest around me, the reader may be prepared to learn that I began to think very highly of Col. L.'s plantation. It was just a place to my boyish taste. There were fish to be caught in the creek, if one only had a hook and line; and crabs, clams and oysters were to be caught by wading, digging and raking for them. Here was a field for industry and enterprise, strongly inviting; and the reader may be assured that I entered upon it with spirit.

Even the much dreaded old master, whose merciless fiat had brought me from Tuckahoe, gradually, to my mind, parted with his terrors. Strange enough, his reverence seemed to take no particular notice of me, nor of my coming. Instead of leaping out and devouring me, he scarcely seemed conscious of my presence. The fact is, he was occupied with matters more weighty and important than either looking after or vexing me. He probably thought as little of my advent, as he would have thought of the addition of a single pig to his stock!

As the chief butler on Col. Lloyd's plantation, his duties were numerous and perplexing. In almost all important matters he answered in Col. Lloyd's stead. The overseers of all the farms were in some sort under him, and received the law from his mouth. The colonel himself seldom addressed an overseer, or allowed an overseer to address him. Old master carried the keys of all the store houses; measured out the allowance for each slave at the end of every month; superintended the storing of all goods brought to the plantation; dealt out the raw material to all the handicraftsmen; shipped the grain, tobacco, and all saleable produce of the plantation to market, and had the general oversight of the coopers' shop, wheelwrights' shop, blacksmiths' shop, and shoemakers' shop. Besides the care of these, he often had business for the plantation which required him to be absent two and three days.

Thus largely employed, he had little time, and perhaps as little disposition, to interfere with the children individually. What he was to Col. Lloyd, he made Aunt Katy to him. When he had anything to say or do about us, it was said or done in a wholesale manner; disposing of us in classes or sizes, leaving all minor details to Aunt Katy, a person of whom the reader has already received no very favorable impression. Aunt Katy was a woman who never allowed herself to act greatly within the margin of power granted to her, no matter how broad that authority might be. Ambitious, ill-tempered and cruel, she found in her present position an ample field for the exercise of her ill-omened qualities. She had a strong hold on old master—she was considered a first rate cook, and she really was very industrious. She was, therefore, greatly favored by old master, and as one mark of his favor, she was the only mother who was permitted to retain her children around her. Even to these children she was often fiendish in her brutality. She pursued her son Phil, one day, in my presence, with a huge butcher knife, and dealt a blow with its edge which left a shocking gash on his arm, near the wrist. For this, old master did sharply rebuke her, and threatened that if she ever should do the like again, he would take the skin off her back. Cruel, however, as Aunt Katy was to her own children, at times she was not destitute of maternal feeling, as I often had occasion to know, in the bitter pinches of hunger I had to endure. Differing from the practice of Col. Lloyd, old master, instead of allowing so much for each slave, committed the allowance for all to the care of Aunt Katy, to be divided after cooking it, amongst us. The allowance, consisting of coarse corn-meal, was not very abundant—indeed, it was very slender; and in passing through Aunt Katy's hands, it was made more slender still, for some of us. William, Phil and Jerry were her children, and it is not to accuse her too severely, to allege that she was often guilty of starving myself and the other children, while she was literally cramming her own. Want of food was my chief trouble the first summer at my old master's. Oysters and clams would do very well, with an occasional supply of bread, but they soon failed in the absence of bread. I speak but the simple truth, when I say, I have often been so pinched with hunger, that I have fought with the dog—"Old Nep"—for the smallest crumbs that fell from the kitchen table, and have been glad when I won a single crumb in the combat. Many times have I followed, with eager step, the waiting-girl when she went out to shake the table cloth, to get the crumbs and small bones flung out for the cats. The water, in which meat had been boiled, was as eagerly sought for by me. It was a great thing to get the privilege of dipping a piece of bread in such water; and the skin taken from rusty bacon, was a positive luxury. Nevertheless, I sometimes got full meals and kind words from sympathizing old slaves, who knew my sufferings, and received the comforting assurance that I should be a man some day. "Never mind, honey—better day comin'," was even then a solace, a cheering consolation to me in my troubles. Nor were all the kind words I received from slaves. I had a friend in the parlor, as well, and one to whom I shall be glad to do justice, before I have finished this part of my story.

I was not long at old master's, before I learned that his surname was Anthony, and that he was generally called "Captain Anthony"—a title which he probably acquired by sailing a craft in the Chesapeake Bay. Col. Lloyd's slaves never called Capt. Anthony "old master," but always Capt. Anthony; and *me* they called "Captain Anthony Fed." There is not, probably, in the whole south, a plantation where the English language is more imperfectly spoken than on Col. Lloyd's. It is a mixture of Guinea and everything else you please. At the time of which I am now writing, there were slaves there who had been brought from the coast of Africa. They never used the "*s*" in indication of the possessive case. "Cap'n Ant'ney Tom," "Lloyd Bill," "Aunt Rose Harry," means "Captain Anthony's Tom," "Lloyd's Bill," &c. "*Oo you dem long to?*" means, "Whom do you belong to?" "*Oo dem got any peachy?*" means, "Have you got any peaches?" I could scarcely understand them when I first went among them, so broken was their speech; and I am persuaded that I could not have been dropped anywhere on the globe, where I could reap less, in the way of knowledge, from my immediate associates, than on this plantation. Even "Mas' Daniel," by his association with his father's slaves, had measurably adopted their dialect and their ideas, so far as they had ideas to be adopted. The equality of nature is strongly asserted in childhood, and childhood requires children for associates. *Color* makes no difference with a child. Are you a child with wants, tastes and pursuits common to children, not put on, but natural? then, were you black as ebony you would be welcome to the child of alabaster whiteness. The law of compensation holds here, as well as elsewhere. Mas' Daniel could not associate with ignorance without sharing its shade;

and he could not give his black playmates his company, without giving them his intelligence, as well. Without knowing this, or caring about it, at the time, I, for some cause or other, spent much of my time with Mas' Daniel, in preference to spending it with most of the other boys.

Mas' Daniel was the youngest son of Col. Lloyd; his older brothers were Edward and Murray—both grown up, and fine looking men. Edward was especially esteemed by the children, and by me among the rest; not that he ever said anything to us or for us, which could be called especially kind; it was enough for us, that he never looked nor acted scornfully toward us. There were also three sisters, all married; one to Edward Winder; a second to Edward Nicholson; a third to Mr. Lownes.

The family of old master consisted of two sons, Andrew and Richard; his daughter, Lucretia, and her newly married husband, Capt. Auld.[2] This was the house family. The kitchen family consisted of Aunt Katy, Aunt Esther, and ten or a dozen children, most of them older than myself. Capt. Anthony was not considered a rich slave-holder, but was pretty well off in the world. He owned about thirty "*head*" of slaves, and three farms in Tuckahoe. The most valuable part of his property was his slaves, of whom he could afford to sell one every year. This crop, therefore, brought him seven or eight hundred dollars a year, besides his yearly salary, and other revenue from his farms.

The idea of rank and station was rigidly maintained on Col. Lloyd's plantation. Our family never visited the great house, and the Lloyds never came to our home. Equal non-intercourse was observed between Capt. Anthony's family and that of Mr. Sevier, the overseer.

Such, kind reader, was the community, and such the place, in which my earliest and most lasting impressions of slavery, and of slave-life, were received; of which impressions you will learn more in the coming chapters of this book.

2. Thomas Auld (1795–1880) captained the *Sally Lloyd*, Edward Lloyd's sloop.

CHAPTER V

Gradual Initiation into the Mysteries of Slavery

GROWING ACQUAINTANCE WITH OLD MASTER—HIS CHARACTER—
EVILS OF UNRESTRAINED PASSION—APPARENT TENDERNESS—OLD
MASTER A MAN OF TROUBLE—CUSTOM OF MUTTERING TO HIMSELF—
NECESSITY OF BEING AWARE OF HIS WORDS—THE SUPPOSED
OBTUSENESS OF SLAVE-CHILDREN—BRUTAL OUTRAGE—DRUNKEN
OVERSEER—SLAVEHOLDERS' IMPATIENCE—WISDOM OF APPEALING
TO SUPERIORS—THE SLAVEHOLDER'S WRATH BAD AS THAT OF THE
OVERSEER—A BASE AND SELFISH ATTEMPT TO BREAK UP A
COURTSHIP—A HARROWING SCENE

ALTHOUGH my old master—Capt. Anthony—gave me at first, (as the reader will have already seen,) very little attention, and although that little was of a remarkably mild and gentle description, a few months only were sufficient to convince me that mildness and gentleness were not the prevailing or governing traits of his character. These excellent qualities were displayed only occasionally. He could, when it suited him, appear to be literally insensible to the claims of humanity, when appealed to by the helpless against an aggressor, and he could himself commit outrages, deep, dark and nameless. Yet he was not by nature worse than other men. Had he been brought up in a free state, surrounded by the just restraints of free society—restraints which are necessary to the freedom of all its members, alike and equally—Capt. Anthony might have been as humane a man, and every way as respectable, as many who now oppose the slave system; certainly as humane and respectable as are members of society generally. The slaveholder, as well as the slave, is the victim of the slave system. A man's character greatly takes its hue and shape from the form and color of things about him. Under the whole heavens there is no relation more unfavorable to the development of honorable character, than that sustained by the slaveholder to the slave. Reason is imprisoned here, and passions run wild. Like the fires of the prairie, once lighted, they are at the mercy of every wind, and must burn, till they have consumed all that is combustible within their remorseless grasp. Capt. Anthony could be kind, and, at times, he even showed an affectionate disposition. Could the reader have seen him gently leading me by the hand—as he sometimes did—patting me on the head, speaking to me in soft, caressing tones and calling me his "little Indian boy," he would have deemed him a kind old man, and, really, almost fatherly. But the pleasant moods of a slaveholder are remarkably brittle; they are easily snapped; they neither come often, nor remain long. His temper is subjected to perpetual trials; but, since these trials are never borne patiently, they add nothing to his natural stock of patience.

Old master very early impressed me with the idea that he was an unhappy man. Even to my child's eye, he wore a troubled, and at times, a haggard aspect. His strange movements excited my curiosity, and awakened my compassion. He seldom walked alone without muttering to himself; and he occasionally stormed about, as if defying an army of invisible foes. "He would do this, that, and the other; he'd be d—d if he did not,"—was the usual form of his threats. Most of his leisure was spent in walking, cursing and gesticulating, like one possessed by a demon. Most evidently, he was a wretched man, at war with his own soul, and with all the world around him. To be overheard by the children, disturbed him very little. He made no more of *our* presence, than of that of the ducks and geese which he met on the green. He little thought that the little black urchins around him, could see, through those vocal crevices, the very secrets of his heart. Slaveholders ever underrate the intelligence with which they have to grapple. I really understood the old man's mutterings, attitudes and gestures, about as well as he did himself. But slaveholders never encourage that kind of communication, with the slaves, by which they might learn to measure the depths of his knowledge. Ignorance is a high virtue in a human chattel; and as the master studies to keep the slave ignorant, the slave is cunning enough to make the master think he succeeds. The slave fully appreciates the saying, "where ignorance is bliss, 'tis folly to be wise." When old master's gestures were violent, ending with a threatening shake of the head, and a sharp snap of his middle finger and thumb, I deemed it wise to keep at a respectable distance from him; for, at such times, trifling faults stood, in his eyes, as momentous offenses; and, having both the power and the disposition, the victim had only to be near him to catch the punishment, deserved or undeserved.

One of the first circumstances that opened my eyes to the cruelty and wickedness of slavery, and the heartlessness of my old master, was the refusal of the latter to interpose his authority, to protect and shield a young woman, who had been most cruelly abused and beaten by his overseer in Tuckahoe. This overseer—a Mr. Plummer—was a man like most of his class, little better than a human brute; and, in addition to his general profligacy and repulsive coarseness, the creature was a miserable drunkard. He was, probably, employed by my old master, less on account of the excellence of his services, than for the cheap rate at which they could be obtained. He was not fit to have the management of a drove of mules. In a fit of drunken madness, he committed the outrage which brought the young woman in question down to my old master's for protection. This young woman was the daughter of Milly, an own aunt of mine. The poor girl, on arriving at our house, presented a pitiable appearance. She had left in haste, and without preparation; and, probably, without the knowledge of Mr. Plummer. She had traveled twelve miles, bare-footed, bare-necked and bare-headed. Her neck and shoulders were covered with scars, newly made; and, not content with marring her neck and shoulders, with the cowhide, the cowardly brute had dealt her a blow on the head with a hickory club, which cut a horrible gash, and left her face literally covered with blood. In this condition, the poor young woman came down, to implore protection at the hands of my old master. I expected to see him boil over with rage at the revolting deed, and to hear him fill the air with curses upon the brutal Plummer; but I was disappointed. He sternly told her, in an angry tone, he "believed she deserved every bit of it," and, if she did not go home instantly, he would himself take the remaining skin from her neck and back. Thus was the poor girl compelled to return, without redress, and perhaps to receive an additional flogging for daring to appeal to old master against the overseer.

Old master seemed furious at the thought of being troubled by such complaints. I did not, at that time, understand the philosophy of his treatment of my cousin. It was stern, unnatural, violent. Had the man no bowels of compassion? Was he dead to all sense of humanity? No. I think I now understand it. This treatment is a part of the system, rather than a part of the man. Were slaveholders to listen to complaints of this sort against the overseers, the luxury of owning large numbers of slaves, would be impossible. It would do away with the office of overseer, entirely; or, in other words, it would convert the master himself into an overseer. It would occasion great loss of time and labor, leaving the overseer in fetters, and without the necessary power to secure obedience to his orders. A privilege so dangerous as that of appeal, is, therefore, strictly prohibited; and any one exercising it, runs a fearful hazard. Nevertheless, when a slave has nerve enough to exercise it, and boldly approaches his master, with a well-founded complaint against an overseer, though he may be repulsed, and may even have that of which he complains repeated at the time, and, though he may be beaten by his master, as well as by the overseer, for his temerity, in the end the policy of complaining is, generally, vindicated by the relaxed rigor of the overseer's treatment. The latter becomes more careful, and less disposed to use the lash upon such slaves thereafter. It is with this final result in view, rather than with any expectation of immediate good, that the outraged slave is induced to meet his master with a complaint. The overseer very naturally dislikes to have the ear of the master disturbed by complaints; and, either upon this consideration, or upon advice and warning privately given him by his employers, he generally modifies the rigor of his rule, after an outbreak of the kind to which I have been referring.

Howsoever the slaveholder may allow himself to act toward his slave, and, whatever cruelty he may deem it wise, for example's sake, or for the gratification of his humor, to inflict, he cannot, in the absence of all provocation, look with pleasure upon the bleeding wounds of a defenseless slave-woman. When he drives her from his presence without redress, or the hope of redress, he acts, generally, from motives of policy, rather than from a hardened nature, or from innate brutality. Yet, let but his own temper be stirred, his own passions get loose, and the slave-owner will go *far beyond* the overseer in cruelty. He will convince the slave that his wrath is far more terrible and boundless, and vastly more to be dreaded, than that of the underling overseer. What may have been mechanically and heartlessly done by the overseer, is now done with a will. The man who now wields the lash is irresponsible. He may, if he pleases, cripple or kill, without fear of consequences; except in so far as it may concern profit or loss. To a man of violent temper—as my old master was—this was but a very slender and inefficient restraint. I have seen him in a tempest of passion, such as I have just described—a passion into which entered all the bitter ingredients of pride, hatred, envy, jealousy, and the thirst for revenge.

The circumstances which I am about to narrate, and which gave rise to this fearful tempest of passion, are not singular nor isolated in slave life, but are common in every slaveholding community in which I have lived. They are incidental to the relation of master and slave, and exist in all sections of slaveholding countries.

The reader will have noticed that, in enumerating the names of the slaves who lived with my old master, *Esther* is mentioned. This was a young woman who possessed that which is ever a curse to the slave-girl; namely,—personal beauty. She was tall, well formed, and made a fine appearance. The daughters of Col. Lloyd could scarcely surpass her in personal charms. Esther was courted by Ned Roberts, and he was as fine looking a young man, as she was a woman. He was the son of a favorite slave of Col. Lloyd. Some slaveholders would have been glad to promote the marriage of two such persons; but, for some reason or other, my old master took it upon him to break up the growing intimacy between Esther and Edward. He strictly ordered her to quit the company of said Roberts, telling her that he would punish her severely if he ever found her again in Edward's company. This unnatural and heartless order was, of course, broken. A woman's love is not to be annihilated by the peremptory command of any one, whose breath is in his nostrils. It was impossible to keep Edward and Esther apart. Meet they would, and meet they did. Had old master been a man of honor and purity, his motives, in this matter, might have been viewed more favorably. As it was, his motives were as abhorrent, as his methods were foolish and contemptible. It was too evident that he was not concerned for the girl's welfare. It is one of the damning characteristics of the slave system, that it robs its victims of every earthly incentive to a holy life. The fear of God, and the hope of heaven, are found sufficient to sustain many slave-women, amidst the snares and dangers of their strange lot; but, this side of God and heaven, a slave-woman is at the mercy of the power, caprice and passion of her owner. Slavery provides no means for the honorable continuance of the race. Marriage—as imposing obligations on the parties to it—has no existence here, except in such hearts as are purer and higher than the standard morality around them. It is one of the consolations of my life, that I know of many honorable instances of persons who maintained their honor, where all around was corrupt.

Esther was evidently much attached to Edward, and abhorred—as she had reason to do—the tyrannical and base behavior of old master. Edward was young, and fine looking, and he loved and courted her. He might have been her husband, in the high sense just alluded to; but WHO and *what* was this old master? His attentions were plainly brutal and selfish, and it was as natural that Esther should loathe him, as that she should love Edward. Abhorred and circumvented as he was, old master, having the power, very easily took revenge. I happened to see this exhibition of his rage and cruelty toward Esther. The time selected was singular. It was early in the morning, when all besides was still, and before any of the family, in the house or kitchen, had left their beds. I saw but few of the shocking preliminaries, for the cruel work had begun before I awoke. I was probably awakened by the shrieks and piteous cries of poor Esther. My sleeping place was on the floor of a little, rough closet, which opened into the kitchen; and through the cracks of its unplaned boards, I could dictinctly see and hear what was going on, without being seen by old master. Esther's wrists were firmly tied, and the twisted rope was fastened to a strong staple in a heavy wooden joist above, near the fire-place. Here she stood, on a bench, her arms tightly drawn over her breast. Her back and shoulders were bare to the waist. Behind her stood old master, with cowskin in hand, preparing his barbarous work with all manner of harsh, coarse, and tantalizing epithets. The screams of his victim were most piercing. He was cruelly deliberate, and protracted the torture, as one who was delighted with the scene. Again and again he drew the hateful whip through his hand, adjusting it with a view of dealing the most pain-giving blow. Poor Esther had never yet been severely whipped, and her shoulders were plump and tender. Each blow, vigorously laid on, brought screams as well as blood. "*Have mercy; Oh! have mercy*" she cried; "*I won't do so no more;*" but her piercing cries seemed only to increase his fury. His answers to them are too coarse and blasphemous to be produced here. The whole scene, with all its attendants, was revolting and shocking, to the last degree; and when the motives of this brutal castigation are considered, language has no power to convey a just sense of its awful criminality. After laying on some thirty or forty stripes, old master untied his suffering victim, and let her get down. She could scarcely stand, when untied. From my heart I pitied her, and—child though I was—the outrage kindled in me a feeling far from peaceful; but I was hushed, terrified, stunned, and could do nothing, and the fate of Esther might be mine next. The scene here described was often repeated in the case of poor Esther, and her life, as I knew it, was one of wretchedness.

CHAPTER VI

Treatment of Slaves on Lloyd's Plantation

THE AUTHOR'S EARLY REFLECTIONS ON SLAVERY—PRESENTIMENT OF ONE DAY BEING A FREEMAN—COMBAT BETWEEN AN OVERSEER AND A SLAVE-WOMAN—THE ADVANTAGES OF RESISTANCE—ALLOWANCE DAY ON THE HOME PLANTATION—THE SINGING OF SLAVES—AN EXPLANATION—THE SLAVES' FOOD AND CLOTHING—NAKED CHILDREN—LIFE IN THE QUARTER—DEPRIVATION OF SLEEP— NURSING CHILDREN CARRIED TO THE FIELD—DESCRIPTION OF THE COWSKIN—THE ASH-CAKE—MANNER OF MAKING IT—THE DINNER HOUR—THE CONTRAST

THE heart-rending incidents, related in the foregoing chapter, led me, thus early, to inquire into the nature and history of slavery. *Why am I a slave? Why are some people slaves, and others masters? Was there ever a time when this was not so? How did the relation commence?* These were the perplexing questions which began now to claim my thoughts, and to exercise the weak powers of my mind, for I was still but a child, and knew less than children of the same age in the free states. As my questions concerning these things were only put to children a little older, and little better informed than myself, I was not rapid in reaching a solid footing. By some means I learned from these inquiries, that "*God, up in the sky,*" made every body; and that he made *white* people to be masters and mistresses, and *black* people to be slaves. This did not satisfy me, nor lessen my interest in the subject. I was told, too, that God was good, and that He knew what was best for me, and best for everybody. This was less satisfactory than the first statement; because it came, point blank, against all my notions of goodness. It was not good to let old master cut the flesh off Esther, and make her cry so. Besides, how did people know that God made black people to be slaves? Did they go up in the sky and learn it? or, did He come down and tell them so? All was dark here. It was some relief to my hard notions of the goodness of God, that, although he made white men to be slaveholders, he did not make them to be *bad* slaveholders, and that, in due time, he would punish the bad slaveholders; that he would, when they died, send them to the bad place, where they would be "burnt up." Nevertheless, I could not reconcile the relation of slavery with my crude notions of goodness.

Then, too, I found that there were puzzling exceptions to this theory of slavery on both sides, and in the middle. I knew of blacks who were *not* slaves; I knew of whites who were *not* slaveholders; and I knew of persons who were *nearly* white, who were slaves. *Color*, therefore, was a very unsatisfactory basis for slavery.

Once, however, engaged in the inquiry, I was not very long in finding out the true solution of the matter. It was not *color*, but *crime*, not *God*, but *man*, that afforded the true explanation of the existence of slavery; nor was I long in finding out another important truth, viz: what man can make, man can unmake. The appalling darkness faded away, and I was master of the subject. There were slaves here, direct from Guinea; and there were many who could say that their fathers and mothers were stolen from Africa—forced from their homes, and compelled to serve as slaves. This, to me, was knowledge; but it was a kind of knowledge which filled me with a burning hatred of slavery, increased my suffering, and left me without the means of breaking away from my bondage. Yet it was knowledge quite worth possessing. I could not have been more than seven or eight years old, when I began to make this subject my study. It was with me in the woods and fields; along the shore of the river, and wherever my boyish wanderings led me; and though I was, at that time, quite ignorant of the existence of the free states, I distinctly remember being, *even then*, most strongly impressed with the idea of being a freeman some day. This cheering assurance was an inborn dream of my human nature—a constant menace to slavery—and one which all the powers of slavery were unable to silence or extinguish.

Up to the time of the brutal flogging of my Aunt Esther—for she was my own aunt—and the horrid plight in which I had seen my cousin from Tuckahoe, who had been so badly beaten by the cruel Mr. Plummer, my attention had not been called, especially, to the gross features of slavery. I had, of course, heard of whippings, and of savage *rencontres* between overseers and slaves, but I had always been out of the way at the times and places of their occurrence. My plays and sports, most of the time, took me from the corn and tobacco fields, where the great body of the hands were at work, and where scenes of cruelty were enacted and witnessed. But, after the whipping of Aunt Esther, I saw many cases of the same shocking nature, not only in my master's house, but on Col. Lloyd's plantation. One of the first which I saw, and which greatly agitated me, was the whipping of a woman belonging to Col. Lloyd, named Nelly.[1] The offense alleged against Nelly, was one of the commonest and most indefinite in the whole catalogue of offenses usually laid to the charge of slaves, viz: "impudence." This may mean almost anything, or nothing at all, just according to the caprice of the master or overseer, at the moment. But, whatever it is, or is not, if it gets the name of "impudence," the party charged with it is sure of a flogging. This offense may be committed in various ways; in the tone of an answer; in answering at all; in not answering; in the expression of countenance; in the motion of the head; in the gait, manner and bearing of the slave. In the case under consideration, I can easily believe that, according to all slaveholding standards, here was a genuine instance of impudence. In Nelly there were all the necessary conditions for committing the offense. She was a bright mulatto, the recognized wife of a favorite "hand" on board Col. Lloyd's sloop, and the mother of five sprightly children. She was a vigorous and spirited woman, and one of the most likely, on the plantation, to be guilty of impudence. My attention was called to the scene, by the noise, curses and screams that proceeded from it; and, on going a little in that direction, I came upon the parties engaged in the skirmish. Mr. Sevier, the overseer, had hold of Nelly, when I caught sight of them; he was endeavoring to drag her toward a tree, which endeavor Nelly was sternly resisting; but to no purpose, except to retard the progress of the overseer's plans. Nelly—as I have said—was the mother of five children; three of them were present, and though quite small, (from seven to ten years old, I should think,) they gallantly came to their mother's defense, and gave the overseer an excellent pelting with stones. One of the little fellows ran up, seized the overseer by the leg and bit him; but the monster was too busily engaged with Nelly, to pay any attention to the assaults of the children. There were numerous bloody marks on Mr. Sevier's face, when I first saw him, and they increased as the struggle went on. The imprints of Nelly's fingers were visible, and I was glad to see them. Amidst the wild screams of the children—"*Let my mammy go*"—"*let my mammy go*"—there escaped, from between the teeth of the bullet-headed overseer, a few bitter curses, mingled with threats, that "he would teach the d—d b—h how to give a white man

1. Nelly Kellum, then a 37-year-old enslaved person on the Wye Plantation.

impudence." There is no doubt that Nelly felt herself superior, in some respects, to the slaves around her. She was a wife and a mother; her husband was a valued and favorite slave. Besides, he was one of the first hands on board of the sloop, and the sloop hands—since they had to represent the plantation abroad—were generally treated tenderly. The overseer never was allowed to whip Harry; why then should he be allowed to whip Harry's wife? Thoughts of this kind, no doubt, influenced her; but, for whatever reason, she nobly resisted, and, unlike most of the slaves, seemed determined to make her whipping cost Mr. Sevier as much as possible. The blood on his (and her) face, attested her skill, as well as her courage and dexterity in using her nails. Maddened by her resistance, I expected to see Mr. Sevier level her to the ground by a stunning blow; but no; like a savage bull-dog—which he resembled both in temper and appearance—he maintained his grip, and steadily dragged his victim toward the tree, disregarding alike her blows, and the cries of the children for their mother's release. He would, doubtless, have knocked her down with his hickory stick, but that such act might have cost him his place. It is often deemed advisable to knock a *man* slave down, in order to tie him, but it is considered cowardly and inexcusable, in an overseer, thus to deal with a *woman*. He is expected to tie her up, and to give her what is called, in southern parlance, a "genteel flogging," without any very great outlay of strength or skill. I watched, with palpitating interest, the course of the preliminary struggle, and was saddened by every new advantage gained over her by the ruffian. There were times when she seemed likely to get the better of the brute, but he finally overpowered her, and succeeded in getting his rope around her arms, and in firmly tying her to the tree, at which he had been aiming. This done, and Nelly was at the mercy of his merciless lash; and now, what followed, I have no heart to describe. The cowardly creature made good his every threat; and wielded the lash with all the hot zest of furious revenge. The cries of the woman, while undergoing the terrible infliction, were mingled with those of the children, sounds which I hope the reader may never be called upon to hear. When Nelly was untied, her back was covered with blood. The red stripes were all over her shoulders. She was whipped—severely whipped; but she was not subdued, for she continued to denounce the overseer, and to call him every vile name. He had bruised her flesh, but had left her invincible spirit undaunted. Such floggings are seldom repeated by the same overseer. They prefer to whip those who are most easily whipped. The old doctrine that submission is the best cure for outrage and wrong, does not hold good on the slave plantation. He is whipped oftenest, who is whipped easiest; and that slave who has the courage to stand up for himself against the overseer, although he may have many hard stripes at the first, becomes, in the end, a freeman, even though he sustain the formal relation of a slave. "You can shoot me but you can't whip me," said a slave to Rigby Hopkins; and the result was that he was neither whipped nor shot. If the latter had been his fate, it would have been less deplorable than the living and lingering death to which cowardly and slavish souls are subjected. I do not know that Mr. Sevier ever undertook to whip Nelly again. He probably never did, for it was not long after his attempt to subdue her, that he was taken sick, and died. The wretched man died as he had lived, unrepentant; and it was said—with how much truth I know not—that in the very last hours of his life, his ruling passion showed itself, and that when wrestling with death, he was uttering horrid oaths, and flourishing the cowskin, as though he was tearing the flesh off some helpless slave. One thing is certain, that when he was in health, it was enough to chill the blood, and to stiffen the hair of an ordinary man, to hear Mr. Sevier talk. Nature, or his cruel habits, had given to his face an expression of unusual savageness, even for a slave-driver. Tobacco and rage had worn his teeth short, and nearly every sentence that escaped their compressed grating, was commenced or concluded with some outburst of profanity. His presence made the field alike the field of blood, and of blasphemy. Hated for his cruelty, despised for his cowardice, his death was deplored by no one outside his own house—if indeed it was deplored there; it was regarded by the slaves as a merciful interposition of Providence. Never went there a man to the grave loaded with heavier curses. Mr. Sevier's place was promptly taken by a Mr. Hopkins, and the change was quite a relief, he being a very different man. He was, in all respects, a better man than his predecessor; as good as any man can be, and yet be an overseer. His course was characterized by no extraordinary cruelty; and when he whipped a slave, as he sometimes did, he seemed to take no especial pleasure in it, but, on the contrary, acted as though he felt it to be a mean business. Mr. Hopkins stayed but a short time; his place—much to the regret of the slaves generally—was taken by a Mr. Gore,[2] of whom more will be said hereafter. It is enough, for the present, to say, that he was no improvement on Mr. Sevier, except that he was less noisy and less profane.

I have already referred to the business-like aspect of Col. Lloyd's plantation. This business-like appearance was much increased on the two days at the end of each month, when the slaves from the different farms came to get their monthly allowance of meal and

---

2. Gore's first name was Orson. Douglass misspells it as Austin in both the *Narrative* and *My Bondage and My Freedom*. See Preston, *Young Frederick Douglass*, 72–73 (cited in note 1 on p. 36).

meat. These were gala days for the slaves, and there was much rivalry among them as to *who* should be elected to go up to the great house farm for the allowance, and, indeed, to attend to any business at this, (for them,) the capital. The beauty and grandeur of the place, its numerous slave population, and the fact that Harry, Peter and Jake— the sailors of the sloop—almost always kept, privately, little trinkets which they bought at Baltimore, to sell, made it a privilege to come to the great house farm. Being selected, too, for this office, was deemed a high honor. It was taken as a proof of confidence and favor; but, probably, the chief motive of the competitors for the place, was, a desire to break the dull monotony of the field, and to get beyond the overseer's eye and lash. Once on the road with an ox team, and seated on the tongue of his cart, with no overseer to look after him, the slave was comparatively free; and, if thoughtful, he had time to think. Slaves are generally expected to sing as well as to work. A silent slave is not liked by masters or overseers. "*Make a noise*," "*make a noise*," and "*bear a hand*," are the words usually addressed to the slaves when there is silence amongst them. This may account for the almost constant singing heard in the southern states. There was, generally, more or less singing among the teamsters, as it was one means of letting the overseer know where they were, and that they were moving on with the work. But, on allowance day, those who visited the great house farm were peculiarly excited and noisy. While on their way, they would make the dense old woods, for miles around, reverberate with their wild notes. These were not always merry because they were wild. On the contrary, they were mostly of a plaintive cast, and told a tale of grief and sorrow. In the most boisterous outbursts of rapturous sentiment, there was ever a tinge of deep melancholy. I have never heard any songs like those anywhere since I left slavery, except when in Ireland. There I heard the same *wailing notes*, and was much affected by them. It was during the famine of 1845–6. In all the songs of the slaves, there was ever some expression in praise of the great house farm; something which would flatter the pride of the owner, and, possibly, draw a favorable glance from him.

> "I am going away to the great house farm,
>   O yea! O yea! O yea!
> My old master is a good old master,
>   Oh yea! O yea! O yea!"

This they would sing, with other words of their own improvising— jargon to others, but full of meaning to themselves. I have sometimes thought, that the mere hearing of those songs would do more to impress truly spiritual-minded men and women with the soul-crushing and death-dealing character of slavery, than the reading of whole volumes of its mere physical cruelties. They speak to the heart and to the soul of the thoughtful. I cannot better express my sense of them now, than ten years ago, when, in sketching my life, I thus spoke of this feature of my plantation experience:[3]

> "I did not, when a slave, understand the deep meanings of those rude, and apparently incoherent songs. I was myself within the circle, so that I neither saw nor heard as those without might see and hear. They told a tale which was then altogether beyond my feeble comprehension; they were tones, loud, long and deep, breathing the prayer and complaint of souls boiling over with the bitterest anguish. Every tone was a testimony against slavery, and a prayer to God for deliverance from chains. The hearing of those wild notes always depressed my spirits, and filled my heart with ineffable sadness. The mere recurrence, even now, afflicts my spirit, and while I am writing these lines, my tears are falling. To those songs I trace my first glimmering conceptions of the dehumanizing character of slavery. I can never get rid of that conception. Those songs still follow me, to deepen my hatred of slavery, and quicken my sympathies for my brethren in bonds. If any one wishes to be impressed with a sense of the soul-killing power of slavery, let him go to Col. Lloyd's plantation, and, on allowance day, place himself in the deep, pine woods, and there let him, in silence, thoughtfully analyze the sounds that shall pass through the chambers of his soul, and if he is not thus impressed, it will only be because 'there is no flesh in his obdurate heart.'"[4]

The remark is not unfrequently made, that slaves are the most contented and happy laborers in the world. They dance and sing, and make all manner of joyful noises—so they do; but it is a great mistake to suppose them happy because they sing. The songs of the slave represent the sorrows, rather than the joys, of his heart; and he is relieved by them, only as an aching heart is relieved by its tears. Such is the constitution of the human mind, that, when pressed to extremes, it often avails itself of the most opposite methods. Extremes meet in mind as in matter. When the slaves on board of the "Pearl" were overtaken, arrested, and carried to prison—their hopes for freedom blasted—as they marched in chains they sang, and found (as Emily Edmunson tells us) a melancholy relief in singing.[5] The singing of a man cast away on a desolate island, might be as appropriately

---

3. This block quotation is from Chapter 2 of Douglass's *Narrative*.
4. A slightly revised quotation from *The Task* (1785), by the English poet William Cowper (1731–1800).
5. On April 15, 1848, seventy-seven enslaved persons from Washington, D.C., attempted to escape to freedom on the schooner *The Pearl*. Emily Edmonson was one of two enslaved persons whose freedom was purchased by abolitionists. She went on to tell her story to Harriet Beecher Stowe, who included it in *A Key to Uncle Tom's Cabin* (1853).

considered an evidence of his contentment and happiness, as the singing of a slave. Sorrow and desolation have their songs, as well as joy and peace. Slaves sing more to *make* themselves happy, than to express their happiness.

It is the boast of slaveholders, that their slaves enjoy more of the physical comforts of life than the peasantry of any country in the world. My experience contradicts this. The men and the women slaves on Col. Lloyd's farm, received, as their monthly allowance of food, eight pounds of pickled pork, or their equivalent in fish. The pork was often tainted, and the fish was of the poorest quality—herrings, which would bring very little if offered for sale in any northern market. With their pork or fish, they had one bushel of Indian meal—unbolted[6]—of which quite fifteen per cent. was fit only to feed pigs. With this, one pint of salt was given; and this was the entire monthly allowance of a full grown slave, working constantly in the open field, from morning until night, every day in the month except Sunday, and living on a fraction more than a quarter of a pound of meat per day, and less than a peck of corn-meal per week. There is no kind of work that a man can do which requires a better supply of food to prevent physical exhaustion, than the field-work of a slave. So much for the slave's allowance of food; now for his raiment. The yearly allowance of clothing for the slaves on this plantation, consisted of two tow-linen shirts—such linen as the coarsest crash towels are made of; one pair of trowsers of the same material, for summer, and a pair of trowsers and a jacket of woolen, most slazily[7] put together, for winter; one pair of yarn stockings, and one pair of shoes of the coarsest description. The slave's entire apparel could not have cost more than eight dollars per year. The allowance of food and clothing for the little children, was committed to their mothers, or to the older slave-women having the care of them. Children who were unable to work in the field, had neither shoes, stockings, jackets nor trowsers given them. Their clothing consisted of two coarse tow-linen shirts—already described—per year; and when these failed them, as they often did, they went naked until the next allowance day. Flocks of little children from five to ten years old, might be seen on Col. Lloyd's plantation, as destitute of clothing as any little heathen on the west coast of Africa; and this, not merely during the summer months, but during the frosty weather of March. The little girls were no better off than the boys; all were nearly in a state of nudity.

6. "unbolted": unsifted.
7. I.e., sleazily.

As to beds to sleep on, they were known to none of the field hands; nothing but a coarse blanket—not so good as those used in the north to cover horses—was given them, and this only to the men and women. The children stuck themselves in holes and corners, about the quarters; often in the corner of the huge chimneys, with their feet in the ashes to keep them warm. The want of beds, however, was not considered a very great privation. Time to sleep was of far greater importance, for, when the day's work is done, most of the slaves have their washing, mending and cooking to do; and, having few or none of the ordinary facilities for doing such things, very many of their sleeping hours are consumed in necessary preparations for the duties of the coming day.

The sleeping apartments—if they may be called such—have little regard to comfort or decency. Old and young, male and female, married and single, drop down upon the common clay floor, each covering up with his or her blanket,—the only protection they have from cold or exposure. The night, however, is shortened at both ends. The slaves work often as long as they can see, and are late in cooking and mending for the coming day; and, at the first gray streak of morning, they are summoned to the field by the driver's horn.

More slaves are whipped for oversleeping than for any other fault. Neither age nor sex finds any favor. The overseer stands at the quarter door, armed with stick and cowskin, ready to whip any who may be a few minutes behind time. When the horn is blown, there is a rush for the door, and the hindermost one is sure to get a blow from the overseer. Young mothers who worked in the field, were allowed an hour, about ten o'clock in the morning, to go home to nurse their children. Sometimes they were compelled to take their children with them, and to leave them in the corner of the fences, to prevent loss of time in nursing them. The overseer generally rides about the field on horseback. A cowskin and a hickory stick are his constant companions. The cowskin is a kind of whip seldom seen in the northern states. It is made entirely of untanned, but dried, ox hide, and is about as hard as a piece of well-seasoned live oak. It is made of various sizes, but the usual length is about three feet. The part held in the hand is nearly an inch in thickness; and, from the extreme end of the butt or handle, the cowskin tapers its whole length to a point. This makes it quite elastic and springy. A blow with it, on the hardest back, will gash the flesh, and make the blood start. Cowskins are painted red, blue and green, and are the favorite slave whip. I think this whip worse than the "cat-o'-nine-tails." It condenses the whole strength of the arm to a single point, and comes with a spring that makes the air whistle. It is a terrible instrument, and is so handy, that the overseer can always have it on his person, and ready for use. The temptation to use it is ever strong; and an overseer can, if disposed, always have cause for using it. With him, it is literally a word and a blow, and, in most cases, the blow comes first.

As a general rule, slaves do not come to the quarters for either breakfast or dinner, but take their "ash cake"[8] with them, and eat it in the field. This was so on the home plantation; probably, because the distance from the quarter to the field, was sometimes two, and even three miles.

The dinner of the slaves consisted of a huge piece of ash cake, and a small piece of pork, or two salt herrings. Not having ovens, nor any suitable cooking utensils, the slaves mixed their meal with a little water, to such thickness that a spoon would stand erect in it; and, after the wood had burned away to coals and ashes, they would place the dough between oak leaves and lay it carefully in the ashes, completely covering it; hence, the bread is called ash cake. The surface of this peculiar bread is covered with ashes, to the depth of a sixteenth part of an inch, and the ashes, certainly, do not make it very grateful to the teeth, nor render it very palatable. The bran, or coarse part of the meal, is baked with the fine, and bright scales run through the bread. This bread, with its ashes and bran, would disgust and choke a northern man, but it is quite liked by the slaves. They eat it with avidity, and are more concerned about the quantity than about the quality. They are far too scantily provided for, and are worked too steadily, to be much concerned for the quality of their food. The few minutes allowed them at dinner time, after partaking of their coarse repast, are variously spent. Some lie down on the "turning row," and go to sleep; others draw together, and talk; and others are at work with needle and thread, mending their tattered garments. Sometimes you may hear a wild, hoarse laugh arise from a circle, and often a song. Soon, however, the overseer comes dashing through the field. "*Tumble up! Tumble up,* and to *work, work,*" is the cry; and, now, from twelve o'clock (mid-day) till dark, the human cattle are in motion, wielding their clumsy hoes; hurried on by no hope of reward, no sense of gratitude, no love of children, no prospect of bettering their condition; nothing, save the dread and terror of the slave-driver's lash. So goes one day, and so comes and goes another.

But, let us now leave the rough usage of the field, where vulgar coarseness and brutal cruelty spread themselves and flourish, rank as weeds in the tropics; where a vile wretch, in the shape of a man, rides, walks, or struts about, dealing blows, and leaving gashes on broken-spirited men and helpless women, for thirty dollars per month—a business so horrible, hardening, and disgraceful, that, rather than engage in it, a decent man would blow his own brains

8. "ash cake": rough cornmeal bread or cake baked in hot ashes.

out—and let the reader view with me the equally wicked, but less repulsive aspects of slave life; where pride and pomp roll luxuriously at ease; where the toil of a thousand men supports a single family in easy idleness and sin. This is the great house; it is the home of the LLOYDS! Some idea of its splendor has already been given—and, it is here that we shall find that height of luxury which is the opposite of that depth of poverty and physical wretchedness that we have just now been contemplating. But, there is this difference in the two extremes; viz: that in the case of the slave, the miseries and hardships of his lot are imposed by others, and, in the master's case, they are imposed by himself. The slave is a subject, subjected by others; the slaveholder is a subject, but he is the author of his own subjection. There is more truth in the saying, that slavery is a greater evil to the master than to the slave, than many, who utter it, suppose. The self-executing laws of eternal justice follow close on the heels of the evil-doer here, as well as elsewhere; making escape from all its penalties impossible. But, let others philosophize; it is my province here to relate and describe; only allowing myself a word or two, occasionally, to assist the reader in the proper understanding of the facts narrated.

CHAPTER VII

Life in the Great House

COMFORTS AND LUXURIES—ELABORATE EXPENDITURE—HOUSE SERVANTS—MEN SERVANTS AND MAID SERVANTS—APPEARANCES— SLAVE ARISTOCRACY—STABLE AND CARRIAGE HOUSE—BOUNDLESS HOSPITALITY—FRAGRANCE OF RICH DISHES—THE DECEPTIVE CHARACTER OF SLAVERY—SLAVES SEEM HAPPY—SLAVES AND SLAVEHOLDERS ALIKE WRETCHED—FRETFUL DISCONTENT OF SLAVEHOLDERS—FAULT-FINDING—OLD BARNEY—HIS PROFESSION— WHIPPING—HUMILIATING SPECTACLE—CASE EXCEPTIONAL— WILLIAM WILKS—SUPPOSED SON OF COL. LLOYD—CURIOUS INCIDENT—SLAVES PREFER RICH MASTERS TO POOR ONES

THE close-fisted stinginess that fed the poor slave on coarse corn-meal and tainted meat; that clothed him in crashy tow-linen, and hurried him on to toil through the field, in all weathers, with wind and rain beating through his tattered garments; that scarcely gave even the young slave-mother time to nurse her hungry infant in the fence corner; wholly vanishes on approaching the sacred precincts of the great house, the home of the Lloyds. There the scriptural phrase finds an exact illustration; the highly favored inmates of this mansion are literally arrayed "in purple and fine linen,"[1] and fare sumptuously every day! The table groans under the heavy and blood-bought luxuries gathered with pains-taking care, at home and abroad. Fields, forests, rivers and seas, are made tributary here. Immense wealth, and its lavish expenditure, fill the great house with all that can please the eye, or tempt the taste. Here, appetite, not food, is the great *desideratum*. Fish, flesh and fowl, are here in pro-fusion. Chickens, of all breeds; ducks, of all kinds, wild and tame, the common, and the huge Muscovite; Guinea fowls, turkeys, geese, and pea fowls, are in their several pens, fat and fatting for the des-tined vortex. The graceful swan, the mongrels, the black-necked wild goose; partridges, quails, pheasants and pigeons; choice water fowl, with all their strange varieties, are caught in this huge family net. Beef, veal, mutton and venison, of the most select kinds and qual-ity, roll bounteously to this grand consumer. The teeming riches of the Chesapeake bay, its rock, perch, drums, crocus, trout, oysters, crabs, and terrapin, are drawn hither to adorn the glittering table of the great house. The dairy, too, probably the finest on the Eastern Shore of Maryland—supplied by cattle of the best English stock, imported for the purpose, pours its rich donations of fragrant cheese, golden butter, and delicious cream, to heighten the attraction of the gorgeous, unending round of feasting. Nor are the fruits of the earth forgotten or neglected. The fertile garden, many acres in size, constituting a separate establishment, distinct from the common farm—with its scientific gardener, imported from Scotland, (a Mr. McDermott,) with four men under his direction, was not behind, either in the abundance or in the delicacy of its contributions to the same full board. The tender asparagus, the succulent celery, and the delicate cauliflower; egg plants, beets, lettuce, parsnips, peas, and French beans, early and late; radishes, cantelopes, melons of all kinds; the fruits and flowers of all climes and of all descriptions, from the hardy apple of the north, to the lemon and orange of the south, culminated at this point. Baltimore gathered figs, raisins, almonds and juicy grapes from Spain. Wines and brandies from France; teas of various flavor, from China; and rich, aromatic cof-fee from Java, all conspired to swell the tide of high life, where pride and indolence rolled and lounged in magnificence and satiety.

Behind the tall-backed and elaborately wrought chairs, stand the servants, men and maidens—fifteen in number—discriminately selected, not only with a view to their industry and faithfulness, but with special regard to their personal appearance, their graceful agil-ity and captivating address. Some of these are armed with fans, and are fanning reviving breezes toward the over-heated brows of the

1. Cf. Luke 16.19.

alabaster ladies; others watch with eager eye, and with fawn-like step anticipate and supply, wants before they are sufficiently formed to be announced by word or sign.

These servants constituted a sort of black aristocracy on Col. Lloyd's plantation. They resembled the field hands in nothing, except in color, and in this they held the advantage of a velvet-like glossiness, rich and beautiful. The hair, too, showed the same advantage. The delicate colored maid rustled in the scarcely worn silk of her young mistress, while the servant men were equally well attired from the overflowing wardrobe of their young masters; so that, in dress, as well as in form and feature, in manner and speech, in tastes and habits, the distance between these favored few, and the sorrow and hunger-smitten multitudes of the quarter and the field, was immense; and this is seldom passed over.

Let us now glance at the stables and the carriage house, and we shall find the same evidences of pride and luxurious extravagance. Here are three splendid coaches, soft within and lustrous without. Here, too, are gigs, phætons, barouches, sulkeys and sleighs. Here are saddles and harnesses—beautifully wrought and silver mounted—kept with every care. In the stable you will find, kept only for pleasure, full thirty-five horses, of the most approved blood for speed and beauty. There are two men here constantly employed in taking care of these horses. One of these men must be always in the stable, to answer every call from the great house. Over the way from the stable, is a house built expressly for the hounds—a pack of twenty-five or thirty—whose fare would have made glad the heart of a dozen slaves. Horses and hounds are not the only consumers of the slave's toil. There was practiced, at the Lloyd's, a hospitality which would have astonished and charmed any health-seeking northern divine or merchant, who might have chanced to share it. Viewed from his own table, and *not* from the field, the colonel was a model of generous hospitality. His house was, literally, a hotel, for weeks during the summer months. At these times, especially, the air was freighted with the rich fumes of baking, boiling, roasting and broiling. The odors I shared with the winds; but the meats were under a more stringent monopoly—except that, occasionally, I got a cake from Mas' Daniel.[2] In Mas' Daniel I had a friend at court, from whom I learned many things which my eager curiosity was excited to know. I always knew when company was expected, and who they were, although I was an outsider, being the property, not of Col. Lloyd, but of a servant of the wealthy colonel. On these occasions, all that pride, taste and money could do, to dazzle and charm, was done.

2. Daniel Lloyd was Col. Edward Lloyd's youngest son (see note 3 on p. 20).

Who could say that the servants of Col. Lloyd were not well clad and cared for, after witnessing one of his magnificent entertainments? Who could say that they did not seem to glory in being the slaves of such a master? Who, but a fanatic, could get up any sympathy for persons whose every movement was agile, easy and graceful, and who evinced a consciousness of high superiority? And who would ever venture to suspect that Col. Lloyd was subject to the troubles of ordinary mortals? Master and slave seem alike in their glory here? Can it all be seeming? Alas! it may only be a sham at last! This immense wealth; this gilded splendor; this profusion of luxury; this exemption from toil; this life of ease; this sea of plenty; aye, what of it all? Are the pearly gates of happiness and sweet content flung open to such suitors? *far from it!* The poor slave, on his hard, pine plank, but scantily covered with his thin blanket, sleeps more soundly than the feverish voluptuary who reclines upon his feather bed and downy pillow. Food, to the indolent lounger, is poison, not sustenance. Lurking beneath all their dishes, are invisible spirits of evil, ready to feed the self-deluded gormandizers with aches, pains, fierce temper, uncontrolled passions, dyspepsia, rheumatism, lumbago and gout; and of these the Lloyds got their full share. To the pampered love of ease, there is no resting place. What is pleasant to-day, is repulsive to-morrow; what is soft now, is hard at another time; what is sweet in the morning, is bitter in the evening. Neither to the wicked, nor to the idler, is there any solid peace: "*Troubled, like the restless sea.*"[3]

I had excellent opportunities of witnessing the restless discontent and the capricious irritation of the Lloyds. My fondness for horses—not peculiar to me more than to other boys—attracted me, much of the time, to the stables. This establishment was especially under the care of "old" and "young" Barney—father and son. Old Barney was a fine looking old man, of a brownish complexion, who was quite portly, and wore a dignified aspect for a slave. He was, evidently, much devoted to his profession, and held his office an honorable one. He was a farrier as well as an ostler; he could bleed, remove lampers[4] from the mouths of the horses, and was well instructed in horse medicines. No one on the farm knew, so well as Old Barney, what to do with a sick horse. But his gifts and acquirements were of little advantage to him. His office was by no means an enviable one. He often got presents, but he got stripes as well; for in nothing was Col. Lloyd more unreasonable and exacting, than in respect to the management of his pleasure horses. Any supposed inattention to these animals was sure to be visited with degrading punishment. His

3. Jeremiah 49.23.
4. I.e., lampas, swelling of the hard palate during the eruption of incisors.

horses and dogs fared better than his men. Their beds must be softer and cleaner than those of his human cattle. No excuse could shield Old Barney, if the colonel only suspected something wrong about his horses; and, consequently, he was often punished when faultless. It was absolutely painful to listen to the many unreasonable and fretful scoldings, poured out at the stable, by Col. Lloyd, his sons and sons-in-law. Of the latter, he had three—Messrs. Nicholson, Winder and Lownes. These all lived at the great house a portion of the year, and enjoyed the luxury of whipping the servants when they pleased, which was by no means unfrequently. A horse was seldom brought out of the stable to which no objection could be raised. "There was dust in his hair;" "there was a twist in his reins;" "his mane did not lie straight;" "he had not been properly grained;" "his head did not look well;" "his foretop was not combed out;" "his fetlocks had not been properly trimmed;" something was always wrong. Listening to complaints, however groundless, Barney must stand, hat in hand, lips sealed, never answering a word. He must make no reply, no explanation; the judgment of the master must be deemed infallible, for his power is absolute and irresponsible. In a free state, a master, thus complaining without cause, of his ostler, might be told—"Sir, I am sorry I cannot please you, but, since I have done the best I can, your remedy is to dismiss me." Here, however, the ostler must stand, listen and tremble. One of the most heart-saddening and humiliating scenes I ever witnessed, was the whipping of Old Barney, by Col. Lloyd himself. Here were two men, both advanced in years; there were the silvery locks of Col. L., and there was the bald and toil-worn brow of Old Barney; master and slave; superior and inferior here, but *equals* at the bar of God; and, in the common course of events, they must both soon meet in another world, in a world where all distinctions, except those based on obedience and disobedience, are blotted out forever. "Uncover your head!" said the imperious master; he was obeyed. "Take off your jacket, you old rascal!" and off came Barney's jacket. "Down on your knees!" down knelt the old man, his shoulders bare, his bald head glistening in the sun, and his aged knees on the cold, damp ground. In this humble and debasing attitude, the master—that master to whom he had given the best years and the best strength of his life—came forward, and laid on thirty lashes, with his horse whip. The old man bore it patiently, to the last, answering each blow with a slight shrug of the shoulders, and a groan. I cannot think that Col. Lloyd succeeded in marring the flesh of Old Barney very seriously, for the whip was a light, riding whip; but the spectacle of an aged man—a husband and a father—humbly kneeling before a worm of the dust,[5] surprised and

---

5. "Worm of the dust" is a traditional Christian appellation for a human being.

shocked me at the time; and since I have grown old enough to think on the wickedness of slavery, few facts have been of more value to me than this, to which I was a witness. It reveals slavery in its true color, and in its maturity of repulsive hatefulness. I owe it to truth, however, to say, that this was the first and the last time I ever saw Old Barney, or any other slave, compelled to kneel to receive a whipping.

I saw, at the stable, another incident, which I will relate, as it is illustrative of a phase of slavery to which I have already referred in another connection. Besides two other coachmen, Col. Lloyd owned one named William, who, strangely enough, was often called by his surname, Wilks, by white and colored people on the home plantation. Wilks was a very fine looking man. He was about as white as anybody on the plantation; and in manliness of form, and comeliness of features, he bore a very striking resemblance to Mr. Murray Lloyd. It was whispered, and pretty generally admitted as a fact, that William Wilks was a son of Col. Lloyd, by a highly favored slavewoman, who was still on the plantation. There were many reasons for believing this whisper, not only in William's appearance, but in the undeniable freedom which he enjoyed over all others, and his apparent consciousness of being something more than a slave to his master. It was notorious, too, that William had a deadly enemy in Murray Lloyd, whom he so much resembled, and that the latter greatly worried his father with importunities to sell William. Indeed, he gave his father no rest until he did sell him, to Austin Woldfolk, the great slave-trader at that time. Before selling him, however, Mr. L. tried what giving William a whipping would do, toward making things smooth; but this was a failure. It was a compromise, and defeated itself; for, immediately after the infliction, the heartsickened colonel atoned to William for the abuse, by giving him a gold watch and chain. Another fact, somewhat curious, is, that though sold to the remorseless *Woldfolk*, taken in irons to Baltimore and cast into prison, with a view to being driven to the south, William, by *some* means—always a mystery to me—outbid all his purchasers, paid for himself, *and now resides in Baltimore, a* FREEMAN. Is there not room to suspect, that, as the gold watch was presented to atone for the whipping, a purse of gold was given him by the same hand, with which to effect his purchase, as an atonement for the indignity involved in selling his own flesh and blood. All the circumstances of William, on the great house farm, show him to have occupied a different position from the other slaves, and, certainly, there is nothing in the supposed hostility of slaveholders to amalgamation, to forbid the supposition that William Wilks was the son of Edward Lloyd. *Practical* amalgamation is common in every neighborhood where I have been in slavery.

Col. Lloyd was not in the way of knowing much of the real opinions and feelings of his slaves respecting him. The distance between him and them was far too great to admit of such knowledge. His slaves were so numerous, that he did not know them when he saw them. Nor, indeed, did all his slaves know him. In this respect, he was inconveniently rich. It is reported of him, that, while riding along the road one day, he met a colored man, and addressed him in the usual way of speaking to colored people on the public highways of the south: "Well, boy, who do you belong to?" "To Col. Lloyd," replied the slave. "Well, does the colonel treat you well?" "No, sir," was the ready reply. "What! does he work you too hard?" "Yes, sir." "Well, don't he give enough to eat?" "Yes, sir, he gives me enough, such as it is." The colonel, after ascertaining where the slave belonged, rode on; the slave also went on about his business, not dreaming that he had been conversing with his master. He thought, said and heard nothing more of the matter, until two or three weeks afterwards. The poor man was then informed by his overseer, that, for having found fault with his master, he was now to be sold to a Georgia trader. He was immediately chained and handcuffed; and thus, without a moment's warning he was snatched away, and forever sundered from his family and friends, by a hand more unrelenting than that of death. *This* is the penalty of telling the simple truth, in answer to a series of plain questions. It is partly in consequence of such facts, that slaves, when inquired of as to their condition and the character of their masters, almost invariably say they are contented, and that their masters are kind. Slaveholders have been known to send spies among their slaves, to ascertain, if possible, their views and feelings in regard to their condition. The frequency of this has had the effect to establish among the slaves the maxim, that a still tongue makes a wise head. They suppress the truth rather than take the consequence of telling it, and, in so doing, they prove themselves a part of the human family. If they have anything to say of their master, it is, generally, something in his favor, especially when speaking to strangers. I was frequently asked, while a slave, if I had a kind master, and I do not remember ever to have given a negative reply. Nor did I, when pursuing this course, consider myself as uttering what was utterly false; for I always measured the kindness of my master by the standard of kindness set up by slaveholders around us. However, slaves are like other people, and imbibe similar prejudices. They are apt to think *their condition* better than that of others. Many, under the influence of this prejudice, think their own masters are better than the masters of other slaves; and this, too, in some cases, when the very reverse is true. Indeed, it is not uncommon for slaves even to fall out and quarrel among themselves about the relative kindness of their masters, each contending for the superior goodness of his own over that of others. At the very same time, they mutually execrate their masters, when viewed separately. It was so on our plantation. When Col. Lloyd's slaves met those of Jacob Jepson, they seldom parted without a quarrel about their masters; Col. Lloyd's slaves contending that he was the richest, and Mr. Jepson's slaves that he was the smartest, man of the two. Col. Lloyd's slaves would boast his ability to buy and sell Jacob Jepson; Mr. Jepson's slaves would boast his ability to whip Col. Lloyd. These quarrels would almost always end in a fight between the parties; those that beat were supposed to have gained the point at issue. They seemed to think that the greatness of their masters was transferable to themselves. To be a SLAVE, was thought to be bad enough; but to be a *poor man's* slave, was deemed a disgrace, indeed.

CHAPTER VIII

A Chapter of Horrors

AUSTIN GORE—A SKETCH OF HIS CHARACTER—OVERSEERS AS A CLASS—THEIR PECULIAR CHARACTERISTICS—THE MARKED INDIVIDUALITY OF AUSTIN GORE—HIS SENSE OF DUTY—HOW HE WHIPPED—MURDER OF POOR DENBY—HOW IT OCCURRED—SENSATION—HOW GORE MADE PEACE WITH COL. LLOYD—THE MURDER UNPUNISHED—ANOTHER DREADFUL MURDER NARRATED—NO LAWS FOR THE PROTECTION OF SLAVES CAN BE ENFORCED IN THE SOUTHERN STATES

As I have already intimated elsewhere, the slaves on Col. Lloyd's plantation, whose hard lot, under Mr. Sevier, the reader has already noticed and deplored, were not permitted to enjoy the comparatively moderate rule of Mr. Hopkins. The latter was succeeded by a very different man. The name of the new overseer was Austin Gore. Upon this individual I would fix particular attention; for under his rule there was more suffering from violence and bloodshed than had—according to the older slaves—ever been experienced before on this plantation. I confess, I hardly know how to bring this man fitly before the reader. He was, it is true, an overseer, and possessed, to a large extent, the peculiar characteristics of his class; yet, to call him merely an overseer, would not give the reader a fair notion of the man. I speak of overseers as a class.[1] They are such. They are as distinct from the slaveholding gentry of the south, as are the fish-women of Paris, and the coal-heavers of London, distinct from other

1. The overseers who supervised the large plantations were usually looked down upon by the plantation owners themselves.

members of society. They constitute a separate fraternity at the
south, not less marked than is the fraternity of Park lane bullies in
New York.[2] They have been arranged and classified by that great law
of attraction, which determines the spheres and affinities of men;
which ordains, that men, whose malign and brutal propensities pre-
dominate over their moral and intellectual endowments, shall, naturally, fall into those employments which promise the largest
gratification to those predominating instincts or propensities. The
office of overseer takes this raw material of vulgarity and brutality,
and stamps it as a distinct class of southern society. But, in this class,
as in all other classes, there are characters of marked individuality,
even while they bear a general resemblance to the mass. Mr. Gore
was one of those, to whom a general characterization would do no
manner of justice. He was an overseer; but he was something more.
With the malign and tyrannical qualities of an overseer, he combined something of the lawful master. He had the artfulness and
the mean ambition of his class; but he was wholly free from the disgusting swagger and noisy bravado of his fraternity. There was an
easy air of independence about him; a calm self-possession, and a
sternness of glance, which might well daunt hearts less timid than
those of poor slaves, accustomed from childhood and through life
to cower before a driver's lash. The home plantation of Col. Lloyd
afforded an ample field for the exercise of the qualifications for over-
seership, which he possessed in such an eminent degree.

Mr. Gore was one of those overseers, who could torture the slightest word or look into impudence; he had the nerve, not only to
resent, but to punish, promptly and severely. He never allowed himself to be answered back, by a slave. In this, he was as lordly and as
imperious as Col. Edward Lloyd, himself; acting always up to the
maxim, practically maintained by slaveholders, that it is better that
a dozen slaves suffer under the lash, without fault, than that the
master or the overseer should *seem* to have been wrong in the presence of the slave. *Everything must be absolute here.* Guilty or not
guilty, it is enough to be accused, to be sure of a flogging. The very
presence of this man Gore was painful, and I shunned him as I
would have shunned a rattlesnake. His piercing, black eyes, and
sharp, shrill voice, ever awakened sensations of terror among the
slaves. For so young a man, (I describe him as he was, twenty-five
or thirty years ago,) Mr. Gore was singularly reserved and grave in
the presence of slaves. He indulged in no jokes, said no funny things,
and kept his own counsels. Other overseers, how brutal soever they
might be, were, at times, inclined to gain favor with the slaves, by

2. A gang led by Tammany Hall ward boss Isaiah Rynders (1804–1885), known for breaking up abolitionist meetings in Manhattan.

indulging a little pleasantry; but Gore was never known to be guilty of any such weakness. He was always the cold, distant, unapproachable *overseer* of Col. Edward Lloyd's plantation, and needed no higher pleasure than was involved in a faithful discharge of the duties of his office. When he whipped, he seemed to do so from a sense of duty, and feared no consequences. What Hopkins did reluctantly, Gore did with alacrity. There was a stern will, an iron-like reality, about this Gore, which would have easily made him the chief of a band of pirates, had his environments been favorable to such a course of life. All the coolness, savage barbarity and freedom from moral restraint, which are necessary in the character of a pirate-chief, centered, I think, in this man Gore. Among many other deeds of shocking cruelty which he perpetrated, while I was at Mr. Lloyd's, was the murder of a young colored man, named Denby. He was sometimes called Bill Denby, or Demby; (I write from sound, and the sounds on Lloyd's plantation are not very certain.)[3] I knew him well. He was a powerful young man, full of animal spirits, and, so far as I know, he was among the most valuable of Col. Lloyd's slaves. In something—I know not what—he offended this Mr. Austin Gore, and, in accordance with the custom of the latter, he undertook to flog him. He gave Denby but few stripes; the latter broke away from him and plunged into the creek, and, standing there to the depth of his neck in water, he refused to come out at the order of the overseer; whereupon, for this refusal, *Gore shot him dead!* It is said that Gore gave Denby three calls, telling him that if he did not obey the last call, he would shoot him. When the third call was given, Denby stood his ground firmly; and this raised the question, in the minds of the by-standing slaves—"will he dare to shoot?" Mr. Gore, without further parley, and without making any further effort to induce Denby to come out of the water, raised his gun deliberately to his face, took deadly aim at his standing victim, and, in an instant, poor Denby was numbered with the dead. His mangled body sank out of sight, and only his warm, red blood marked the place where he had stood.

This devilish outrage, this fiendish murder, produced, as it was well calculated to do, a tremendous sensation. A thrill of horror flashed through every soul on the plantation, if I may except the guilty wretch who had committed the hell-black deed. While the slaves generally were panic-struck, and howling with alarm, the murderer himself was calm and collected, and appeared as though nothing unusual had happened. The atrocity roused my old master, and

---

3. Douglass had a staggering memory for sounds, names, and language. Remembering names phonetically, he often misspelled them. See, e.g., note 2 on p. 70 and note 4 on p. 86.

he spoke out, in reprobation of it; but the whole thing proved to be less than a nine days' wonder. Both Col. Lloyd and my old master arraigned Gore for his cruelty in the matter, but this amounted to nothing. His reply, or explanation—as I remember to have heard it at the time—was, that the extraordinary expedient was demanded by necessity; that Denby had become unmanageable; that he had set a dangerous example to the other slaves; and that, without some such prompt measure as that to which he had resorted, were adopted, there would be an end to all rule and order on the plantation. That very convenient covert for all manner of cruelty and outrage—that cowardly alarm-cry, that the slaves would *"take the place,"* was pleaded, in extenuation of this revolting crime, just as it had been cited in defense of a thousand similar ones. He argued, that if one slave refused to be corrected, and was allowed to escape with his life, when he had been told that he should lose it if he persisted in his course, the other slaves would soon copy his example; the result of which would be, the freedom of the slaves, and the enslavement of the whites. I have every reason to believe that Mr. Gore's defense, or explanation, was deemed satisfactory—at least to Col. Lloyd. He was continued in his office on the plantation. His fame as an overseer went abroad, and his horrid crime was not even submitted to judicial investigation. The murder was committed in the presence of slaves, and they, of course, could neither institute a suit, nor testify against the murderer. His bare word would go further in a court of law, than the united testimony of ten thousand black witnesses.

All that Mr. Gore had to do, was to make his peace with Col. Lloyd. This done, and the guilty perpetrator of one of the most foul murders goes unwhipped of justice, and uncensured by the community in which he lives. Mr. Gore lived in St. Michael's, Talbot county, when I left Maryland; if he is still alive he probably yet resides there; and I have no reason to doubt that he is now as highly esteemed, and as greatly respected, as though his guilty soul had never been stained with innocent blood. I am well aware that what I have now written will by some be branded as false and malicious. It will be denied, not only that such a thing ever did transpire, as I have now narrated, but that such a thing could happen in *Maryland.* I can only say—believe it or not—that I have said nothing but the literal truth, gainsay it who may.

I speak advisedly when I say this,—that killing a slave, or any colored person, in Talbot county, Maryland, is not treated as a crime, either by the courts or the community. Mr. Thomas Lanman,[4] ship carpenter, of St. Michael's, killed two slaves, one of whom he

---

4. Probably Thomas Lambdin.

butchered with a hatchet, by knocking his brains out. He used to boast of the commission of the awful and bloody deed. I have heard him do so, laughingly, saying, among other things, that he was the only benefactor of his country in the company, and that when "others would do as much as he had done, we should be relieved of the d—d niggers."

As an evidence of the reckless disregard of human life—where the life is that of a slave—I may state the notorious fact, that the wife of Mr. Giles Hicks, who lived but a short distance from Col. Lloyd's, with her own hands murdered my wife's cousin,[5] a young girl between fifteen and sixteen years of age—mutilating her person in a most shocking manner. The atrocious woman, in the paroxysm of her wrath, not content with murdering her victim, literally mangled her face, and broke her breast bone. Wild, however, and infuriated as she was, she took the precaution to cause the slave-girl to be buried; but the facts of the case coming abroad, very speedily led to the disinterment of the remains of the murdered slave-girl. A coroner's jury was assembled, who decided that the girl had come to her death by severe beating. It was ascertained that the offense for which this girl was thus hurried out of the world, was this: she had been set that night, and several preceding nights, to mind Mrs. Hicks's baby, and having fallen into a sound sleep, the baby cried, waking Mrs. Hicks, but not the slave-girl. Mrs. Hicks, becoming infuriated at the girl's tardiness, after calling her several times, jumped from her bed and seized a piece of fire-wood from the fire-place; and then, as she lay fast asleep, she deliberately pounded in her skull and breast-bone, and thus ended her life. I will not say that this most horrid murder produced no sensation in the community. It *did* produce a sensation; but, incredible to tell, the moral sense of the community was blunted too entirely by the ordinary nature of slavery horrors, to bring the murderess to punishment. A warrant was issued for her arrest, but, for some reason or other, that warrant was never served. Thus did Mrs. Hicks not only escape condign punishment, but even the pain and mortification of being arraigned before a court of justice.

Whilst I am detailing the bloody deeds that took place during my stay on Col. Lloyd's plantation, I will briefly narrate another dark transaction, which occurred about the same time as the murder of Denby by Mr. Gore.

On the side of the river Wye, opposite from Col. Lloyd's, there lived a Mr. Beal Bondley,[6] a wealthy slaveholder. In the direction of

---

5. No record of this murder exists. Douglass most likely heard the story from his first wife, Anna Murray (see note 6 on p. 210).
6. Identified as John Beale Bordley, Jr.

his land, and near the shore, there was an excellent oyster fishing ground, and to this, some of the slaves of Col. Lloyd occasionally resorted in their little canoes, at night, with a view to make up the deficiency of their scanty allowance of food, by the oysters that they could easily get there. This, Mr. Bondley took it into his head to regard as a trespass, and while an old man belonging to Col. Lloyd was engaged in catching a few of the many millions of oysters that lined the bottom of that creek, to satisfy his hunger, the villainous Mr. Bondley, lying in ambush, without the slightest ceremony, discharged the contents of his musket into the back and shoulders of the poor old man. As good fortune would have it, the shot did not prove mortal, and Mr. Bondley came over, the next day, to see Col. Lloyd—whether to pay him for his property, or to justify himself for what he had done, I know not; but this I *can* say, the cruel and dastardly transaction was speedily hushed up; there was very little said about it at all, and nothing was publicly done which looked like the application of the principle of justice to the man whom *chance*, only, saved from being an actual murderer. One of the commonest sayings to which my ears early became accustomed, on Col. Lloyd's plantation and elsewhere in Maryland, was, that it was *"worth but half a cent to kill a nigger, and a half a cent to bury him;"* and the facts of my experience go far to justify the practical truth of this strange proverb. Laws for the protection of the lives of the slaves, are, as they must needs be, utterly incapable of being enforced, where the very parties who are nominally protected, are not permitted to give evidence, in courts of law, against the only class of persons from whom abuse, outrage and murder might be reasonably apprehended. While I heard of numerous murders committed by slaveholders on the Eastern Shore of Maryland, I never knew a solitary instance in which a slaveholder was either hung or imprisoned for having murdered a slave. The usual pretext for killing a slave is, that the slave has offered resistance. Should a slave, when assaulted, but raise his hand in self-defense, the white assaulting party is fully justified by southern, or Maryland, public opinion, in shooting the slave down. Sometimes this is done, simply because it is alleged that the slave has been saucy. But here I leave this phase of the society of my early childhood, and will relieve the kind reader of these heart-sickening details.

CHAPTER IX

Personal Treatment of the Author

MISS LUCRETIA—HER KINDNESS—HOW IT WAS MANIFESTED—
"IKE"—A BATTLE WITH HIM—THE CONSEQUENCES THEREOF—MISS
LUCRETIA'S BALSAM—BREAD—HOW I OBTAINED IT—BEAMS OF
SUNLIGHT AMIDST THE GENERAL DARKNESS—SUFFERING FROM
COLD—HOW WE TOOK OUR MEALS—ORDERS TO PREPARE FOR
BALTIMORE—OVERJOYED AT THE THOUGHT OF QUITTING THE
PLANTATION—EXTRAORDINARY CLEANSING—COUSIN TOM'S VERSION
OF BALTIMORE—ARRIVAL THERE—KIND RECEPTION GIVEN ME BY
MRS. SOPHIA AULD—LITTLE TOMMY—MY NEW POSITION—MY NEW
DUTIES—A TURNING POINT IN MY HISTORY

I HAVE nothing cruel or shocking to relate of my own personal experience, while I remained on Col. Lloyd's plantation, at the home of my old master. An occasional cuff from Aunt Katy, and a regular whipping from old master, such as any heedless and mischievous boy might get from his father, is all that I can mention of this sort. I was not old enough to work in the field, and, there being little else than field work to perform, I had much leisure. The most I had to do, was, to drive up the cows in the evening, to keep the front yard clean, and to perform small errands for my young mistress, Lucretia Auld. I have reasons for thinking this lady was very kindly disposed toward me, and, although I was not often the object of her attention, I constantly regarded her as my friend, and was always glad when it was my privilege to do her a service. In a family where there was so much that was harsh, cold and indifferent, the slightest word or look of kindness passed, with me, for its full value. Miss Lucretia—as we all continued to call her long after her marriage—had bestowed upon me such words and looks as taught me that she pitied me, if she did not love me. In addition to words and looks, she sometimes gave me a piece of bread and butter; a thing not set down in the bill of fare, and which must have been an extra ration, planned aside from either Aunt Katy or old master, solely out of the tender regard and friendship she had for me. Then, too, I one day got into the wars with Uncle Abel's son, "Ike," and had got sadly worsted; in fact, the little rascal had struck me directly in the forehead with a sharp piece of cinder, fused with iron, from the old blacksmith's forge, which made a cross in my forehead very plainly to be seen now. The gash bled very freely, and I roared very loudly and betook myself home. The cold-hearted Aunt Katy paid no attention either to my wound or my roaring, except to tell me it served me right; I had no business with Ike; it was good for me; I would now keep away "*from dem Lloyd niggers."* Miss Lucretia, in this state of the case, came forward; and, in quite a different spirit from that manifested by Aunt Katy, she called me into the parlor, (an extra privilege of itself,) and, without using toward me any of the hard-hearted and reproachful epithets of my kitchen tormentor, she quietly acted the good Samaritan. With her own soft hand she washed the blood from my head and face, fetched her own balsam bottle, and with the balsam wetted a nice piece of white linen, and bound up my head. The balsam was not more healing to the wound in my head, than her kindness was heal-ing to the wounds in my spirit, made by the unfeeling words of Aunt Katy. After this, Miss Lucretia was my friend. I felt her to be such; and I have no doubt that the simple act of binding up my head, did much to awaken in her mind an interest in my welfare. It is quite true, that this interest was never very marked, and it seldom showed itself in anything more than in giving me a piece of bread when I was very hungry; but this was a great favor on a slave plantation, and I was the only one of the children to whom such attention was paid. When very hungry, I would go into the back yard and play under Miss Lucretia's window. When pretty severely pinched by hun-ger, I had a habit of singing, which the good lady very soon came to understand as a petition for a piece of bread. When I sung under Miss Lucretia's window, I was very apt to get well paid for my music. The reader will see that I now had two friends, both at important points—Mas' Daniel at the great house, and Miss Lucretia at home. From Mas' Daniel I got protection from the bigger boys; and from Miss Lucretia I got bread, by singing when I was hungry, and sym-pathy when I was abused by that termagant, who had the reins of government in the kitchen. For such friendship I felt deeply grate-ful, and bitter as are my recollections of slavery, I love to recall any instances of kindness, any sunbeams of humane treatment, which found way to my soul through the iron grating of my house of bond-age. Such beams seem all the brighter from the general darkness into which they penetrate, and the impression they make is vividly distinct and beautiful.

As I have before intimated, I was seldom whipped—and never severely—by my old master. I suffered little from the treatment I received, except from hunger and cold. These were my two great physical troubles. I could neither get a sufficiency of food nor of clothing; but I suffered less from hunger than from cold. In hottest summer and coldest winter, I was kept almost in a state of nudity; no shoes, no stockings, no jacket, no trowsers; nothing but coarse sack-cloth or tow-linen, made into a sort of shirt, reaching down to my knees. This I wore night and day, changing it once a week. In the day time I could protect myself pretty well, by keeping on the sunny side of the house; and in bad weather, in the corner of the kitchen chimney. The great difficulty was, to keep warm during the night. I had no bed. The pigs in the pen had leaves, and the horses in the stable had straw, but the children had no beds. They lodged anywhere in the ample kitchen. I slept, generally, in a little closet, without even a blanket to cover me. In very cold weather, I sometimes got down the bag in which corn-meal was usually carried to the mill, and crawled into that. Sleeping there, with my head in and feet out, I was partly protected, though not comfortable. My feet have been so cracked with the frost, that the pen with which I am writing might be laid in the gashes. The manner of taking our meals at old master's, indicated but little refinement. Our corn-meal mush, when sufficiently cooled, was placed in a large wooden tray, or trough, like those used in making maple sugar here in the north. This tray was set down, either on the floor of the kitchen, or out of doors on the ground; and the children were called, like so many pigs; and like so many pigs they would come, and literally devour the mush—some with oyster shells, some with pieces of shingles, and none with spoons. He that eat fastest got most, and he that was strongest got the best place; and few left the trough really satisfied. I was the most unlucky of any, for Aunt Katy had no good feeling for me; and if I pushed any of the other children, or if they told her anything unfavorable of me, she always believed the worst, and was sure to whip me.

As I grew older and more thoughtful, I was more and more filled with a sense of my wretchedness. The cruelty of Aunt Katy, the hunger and cold I suffered, and the terrible reports of wrong and outrage which came to my ear, together with what I almost daily witnessed, led me, when yet but eight or nine years old, to wish I had never been born. I used to contrast my condition with the blackbirds, in whose wild and sweet songs I fancied them so happy! Their apparent joy only deepened the shades of my sorrow. There are thoughtful days in the lives of children—at least there were in mine—when they grapple with all the great, primary subjects of knowledge, and reach, in a moment, conclusions which no subsequent experience can shake. I was just as well aware of the unjust, unnatural and murderous character of slavery, when nine years old, as I am now. Without any appeal to books, to laws, or to authorities of any kind, it was enough to accept God as a father, to regard slavery as a crime.

I was not ten years old when I left Col. Lloyd's plantation for Baltimore. I left that plantation with inexpressible joy. I never shall forget the ecstacy with which I received the intelligence from my friend, Miss Lueretia, that my old master had determined to let me go to Baltimore to live with Mr. Hugh Auld,[1] a brother to Mr. Thomas

---

1. Seaman and shipbuilder (1799–1861) in the Fell's Point region of Baltimore.

Auld, my old master's son-in-law. I received this information about three days before my departure. They were three of the happiest days of my childhood. I spent the largest part of these three days in the creek, washing off the plantation scurf, and preparing for my new home. Mrs. Lucretia took a lively interest in getting me ready. She told me I must get all the dead skin off my feet and knees, before I could go to Baltimore, for the people there were very cleanly, and would laugh at me if I looked dirty; and, besides, she was intending to give me a pair of trowsers, which I should not put on unless I got all the dirt off. This was a warning to which I was bound to take heed; for the thought of owning a pair of trowsers, was great, indeed. It was almost a sufficient motive, not only to induce me to scrub off the *mange*, (as pig drovers would call it,) but the skin as well. So I went at it in good earnest, working for the first time in the hope of reward. I was greatly excited, and could hardly consent to sleep, lest I should be left. The ties that, ordinarily, bind children to their homes, were all severed, or they never had any existence in my case, at least so far as the home plantation of Col. L. was concerned. I therefore found no severe trial at the moment of my departure, such as I had experienced when separated from my home in Tuckahoe. My home at my old master's was charmless to me; it was not home, but a prison to me; on parting from it, I could not feel that I was leaving anything which I could have enjoyed by staying. My mother was now long dead; my grandmother was far away, so that I seldom saw her; Aunt Katy was my unrelenting tormentor; and my two sisters and brothers, owing to our early separation in life, and the family-destroying power of slavery, were, comparatively, strangers to me. The fact of our relationship was almost blotted out. I looked for *home* elsewhere, and was confident of finding none which I should relish less than the one I was leaving. If, however, I found in my new home—to which I was going with such blissful anticipations— hardship, whipping and nakedness, I had the questionable consola- tion that I should not have escaped any one of these evils by remaining under the management of Aunt Katy. Then, too, I thought, since I had endured much in this line on Lloyd's plantation, I could endure as much elsewhere, and especially at Baltimore; for I had some- thing of the feeling about that city which is expressed in the saying, that being "hanged in England, is better than dying a natural death in Ireland." I had the strongest desire to see Baltimore. My cousin Tom—a boy two or three years older than I—had been there, and though not fluent (he stuttered immoderately,) in speech, he had inspired me with that desire, by his eloquent description of the place. Tom was, sometimes, Capt. Auld's cabin boy; and when he came from Baltimore, he was always a sort of hero amongst us, at least till his Baltimore trip was forgotten. I could never tell him of anything, or point out anything that struck me as beautiful or powerful, but that he had seen something in Baltimore far surpassing it. Even the great house itself, with all its pictures within, and pillars without, he had the hardihood to say "was nothing to Baltimore." He bought a trumpet, (worth six pence,) and brought it home; told what he had seen in the windows of stores; that he had heard shooting crackers,[2] and seen soldiers; that he had seen a steamboat; that there were ships in Baltimore that could carry four such sloops as the "Sally Lloyd." He said a great deal about the market-house; he spoke of the bells ringing; and of many other things which roused my curiosity very much; and, indeed, which heightened my hopes of happiness in my new home.

We sailed out of Miles river for Baltimore early on a Saturday morning. I remember only the day of the week; for, at that time, I had no knowledge of the days of the month, nor, indeed, of the months of the year. On setting sail, I walked aft, and gave to Col. Lloyd's plantation what I hoped would be the last look I should ever give to it, or to any place like it. My strong aversion to the great house farm, was not owing to my own personal suffering, but the daily suffering of others, and to the certainty, that I must, sooner or later, be placed under the barbarous rule of an overseer, such as the accomplished Gore, or the brutal and drunken Plummer. After taking this last view, I quitted the quarter deck, made my way to the bow of the sloop, and spent the remainder of the day in looking ahead; interesting myself in what was in the distance, rather than what was near by or behind. The vessels, sweeping along the bay, were very interesting objects. The broad bay opened like a shoreless ocean on my boyish vision, filling me with wonder and admiration.

Late in the afternoon, we reached Annapolis, the capital of the state, stopping there not long enough to admit of my going ashore. It was the first large town I had ever seen; and though it was inferior to many a factory village in New England, my feelings, on seeing it, were excited to a pitch very little below that reached by travelers at the first view of Rome. The dome of the state house was especially imposing, and surpassed in grandeur the appearance of the great house. The great world was opening upon me very rapidly, and I was eagerly acquainting myself with its multifarious lessons.

We arrived in Baltimore on Sunday morning, and landed at Smith's wharf, not far from Bowly's wharf. We had on board the sloop a large flock of sheep, for the Baltimore market; and, after assisting in driving them to the slaughter house of Mr. Curtis, on Loudon Slater's Hill, I was speedily conducted by Rich—one of the hands belonging to the sloop—to my new home in Alliciana street,

2. I.e., firecrackers.

near Gardiner's ship-yard, on Fell's Point. Mr. and Mrs. Hugh Auld, my new mistress and master, were both at home, and met me at the door with their rosy cheeked little son, Thomas, to take care of whom was to constitute my future occupation. In fact, it was to "little Tommy," rather than to his parents, that old master made a present of me; and though there was no *legal* form or arrangement entered into, I have no doubt that Mr. and Mrs. Auld felt that, in due time, I should be the legal property of their bright-eyed and beloved boy, Tommy. I was struck with the appearance, especially, of my new mistress. Her face was lighted with the kindliest emotions; and the reflex influence of her countenance, as well as the tenderness with which she seemed to regard me, while asking me sundry little questions, greatly delighted me, and lit up, to my fancy, the pathway of my future. Miss Lucretia was kind; but my new mistress, "Miss Sophy," surpassed her in kindness of manner. Little Thomas was affectionately told by his mother, that "*there was his Freddy*," and that "Freddy would take care of him;" and I was told to "be kind to little Tommy"—an injunction I scarcely needed, for I had already fallen in love with the dear boy; and with these little ceremonies I was initiated into my new home, and entered upon my peculiar duties, with not a cloud above the horizon.

I may say here, that I regard my removal from Col. Lloyd's plantation as one of the most interesting and fortunate events of my life. Viewing it in the light of human likelihoods, it is quite probable that, but for the mere circumstance of being thus removed before the rigors of slavery had fastened upon me; before my young spirit had been crushed under the iron control of the slave-driver, instead of being, today, a FREEMAN, I might have been wearing the galling chains of slavery. I have sometimes felt, however, that there was something more intelligent than *chance*, and something more certain than *luck*, to be seen in the circumstance. If I have made any progress in knowledge; if I have cherished any honorable aspirations, or have, in any manner, worthily discharged the duties of a member of an oppressed people; this little circumstance must be allowed its due weight in giving my life that direction. I have ever regarded it as the first plain manifestation of that

> "Divinity that shapes our ends,
> Rough hew them as we will."[3]

I was not the only boy on the plantation that might have been sent to live in Baltimore. There was a wide margin from which to select. There were boys younger, boys older, and boys of the same age,

---

3. Cf. Shakespeare, *Hamlet* 5.2.10–11. Lincoln quoted the same lines to describe his good fortune at having turned down an appointment to be the territorial governor of Oregon in 1849, a decision that proved beneficial to his subsequent political career.

belonging to my old master—some at his own house, and some at his farm—but the high privilege fell to my lot.

I may be deemed superstitious and egotistical, in regarding this event as a special interposition of Divine Providence in my favor; but the thought is a part of my history, and I should be false to the earliest and most cherished sentiments of my soul, if I suppressed, or hesitated to avow that opinion, although it may be characterized as irrational by the wise, and ridiculous by the scoffer. From my earliest recollections of serious matters, I date the entertainment of something like an ineffaceable conviction, that slavery would not always be able to hold me within its foul embrace; and this conviction, like a word of living faith, strengthened me through the darkest trials of my lot. This good spirit was from God; and to him I offer thanksgiving and praise.

CHAPTER X

Life in Baltimore

CITY ANNOYANCES—PLANTATION REGRETS—MY MISTRESS, MISS SOPHA—HER HISTORY—HER KINDNESS TO ME—MY MASTER, HUGH AULD—HIS SOURNESS—MY INCREASED SENSITIVENESS—MY COMFORTS—MY OCCUPATION—THE BANEFUL EFFECTS OF SLAVEHOLDING ON MY DEAR AND GOOD MISTRESS—HOW SHE COMMENCED TEACHING ME TO READ—WHY SHE CEASED TEACHING ME—CLOUDS GATHERING OVER MY BRIGHT PROSPECTS—MASTER AULD'S EXPOSITION OF THE TRUE PHILOSOPHY OF SLAVERY—CITY SLAVES—PLANTATION SLAVES—THE CONTRAST— EXCEPTIONS—MR. HAMILTON'S TWO SLAVES, HENRIETTA AND MARY— MRS. HAMILTON'S CRUEL TREATMENT OF THEM—THE PITEOUS ASPECT THEY PRESENTED—NO POWER MUST COME BETWEEN THE SLAVE AND THE SLAVEHOLDER.

ONCE in Baltimore, with hard brick pavements under my feet, which almost raised blisters, by their very heat, for it was in the height of summer; walled in on all sides by towering brick buildings; with troops of hostile boys ready to pounce upon me at every street corner; with new and strange objects glaring upon me at every step, and with startling sounds reaching my ears from all directions, I for a time thought that, after all, the home plantation was a more desirable place of residence than my home on Alliciana street, in Baltimore. My country eyes and ears were confused and bewildered here; but the boys were my chief trouble. They chased me, and called me *"Eastern Shore man,"* till really I almost wished myself back on the

Eastern Shore. I had to undergo a sort of moral acclimation, and when that was over, I did much better. My new mistress happily proved to be all she *seemed* to be, when, with her husband, she met me at the door, with a most beaming, benignant countenance. She was, naturally, of an excellent disposition, kind, gentle and cheerful. The supercilious contempt for the rights and feelings of the slave, and the petulance and bad humor which generally characterize slaveholding ladies, were all quite absent from kind "Miss" Sophia's manner and bearing toward me. She had, in truth, never been a slaveholder, but had—a thing quite unusual in the south—depended almost entirely upon her own industry for a living. To this fact the dear lady, no doubt, owed the excellent preservation of her natural goodness of heart, for slavery can change a saint into a sinner, and an angel into a demon. I hardly knew how to behave toward "Miss Sopha," as I used to call Mrs. Hugh Auld. I had been treated as a *pig* on the plantation; I was treated as a *child* now. I could not even approach her as I had formerly approached Mrs. Thomas Auld. How could I hang down my head, and speak with bated breath, when there was no pride to scorn me, no coldness to repel me, and no hatred to inspire me with fear? I therefore soon learned to regard her as something more akin to a mother, than a slaveholding mistress. The crouching servility of a slave, usually so acceptable a quality to the haughty slaveholder, was not understood nor desired by this gentle woman. So far from deeming it impudent in a slave to look her straight in the face, as some slaveholding ladies do, she seemed ever to say, "look up, child; don't be afraid; see, I am full of kindness and good will toward you." The hands belonging to Col. Lloyd's sloop, esteemed it a great privilege to be the bearers of parcels or messages to my new mistress; for whenever they came, they were sure of a most kind and pleasant reception. If little Thomas was her son, and her most dearly beloved child, she, for a time, at least, made me something like his half-brother in her affections. If dear Tommy was exalted to a place on his mother's knee, "Feddy" was honored by a place at his mother's side. Nor did he lack the caressing strokes of her gentle hand, to convince him that, though *motherless*, he was not *friendless*. Mrs. Auld was not only a kind-hearted woman, but she was remarkably pious; frequent in her attendance of public worship, much given to reading the bible, and to chanting hymns of praise, when alone. Mr. Hugh Auld was altogether a different character. He cared very little about religion, knew more of the world, and was more of the world, than his wife. He set out, doubtless, to be—as the world goes—a respectable man, and to get on by becoming a successful ship builder, in that city of ship building. This was his ambition, and it fully occupied him. I was, of course, of very little consequence to him, compared with what I was to good Mrs. Auld; and, when he smiled upon me, as he sometimes did, the smile was borrowed from his lovely wife, and, like all borrowed light, was transient, and vanished with the source whence it was derived. While I must characterize Master Hugh as being a very sour man, and of forbidding appearance, it is due to him to acknowledge, that he was never very cruel to me, according to the notion of cruelty in Maryland. The first year or two which I spent in his house, he left me almost exclusively to the management of his wife. She was my law-giver. In hands so tender as hers, and in the absence of the cruelties of the plantation, I became, both physically and mentally, much more sensitive to good and ill treatment; and, perhaps, suffered more from a frown from my mistress, than I formerly did from a cuff at the hands of Aunt Katy. Instead of the cold, damp floor of my old master's kitchen, I found myself on carpets; for the corn bag in winter, I now had a good straw bed, well furnished with covers; for the coarse corn-meal in the morning, I now had good bread, and mush occasionally; for my poor tow-linen shirt, reaching to my knees, I had good, clean clothes. I was really well off. My employment was to run of errands, and to take care of Tommy; to prevent his getting in the way of carriages, and to keep him out of harm's way generally. Tommy, and I, and his mother, got on swimmingly together, for a time. I say *for a time*, because the fatal poison of irresponsible power, and the natural influence of slavery customs, were not long in making a suitable impression on the gentle and loving disposition of my excellent mistress. At first, Mrs. Auld evidently regarded me simply as a child, like any other child; she had not come to regard me as *property*. This latter thought was a thing of conventional growth. The first was natural and spontaneous. A noble nature, like hers, could not, instantly, be wholly perverted; and it took several years to change the natural sweetness of her temper into fretful bitterness. In her worst estate, however, there were, during the first seven years I lived with her, occasional returns of her former kindly disposition.

The frequent hearing of my mistress reading the bible—for she often read aloud when her husband was absent—soon awakened my curiosity in respect to this *mystery* of reading, and roused in me the desire to learn. Having no fear of my kind mistress before my eyes, (she had then given me no reason to fear,) I frankly asked her to teach me to read; and, without hesitation, the dear woman began the task, and very soon, by her assistance, I was master of the alphabet, and could spell words of three or four letters. My mistress seemed almost as proud of my progress, as if I had been her own child; and, supposing that her husband would be as well pleased, she made no secret of what she was doing for me. Indeed, she exultingly told him of the aptness of her pupil, of her intention to persevere in teaching me, and of the duty which she felt it to teach me, at least to read *the bible*. Here arose the first cloud over my Baltimore prospects, the precursor of drenching rains and chilling blasts.

Master Hugh was amazed at the simplicity of his spouse, and, probably for the first time, he unfolded to her the true philosophy of slavery, and the peculiar rules necessary to be observed by masters and mistresses, in the management of their human chattels. Mr. Auld promptly forbade the continuance of her instruction; telling her, in the first place, that the thing itself was unlawful;[1] that it was also unsafe, and could only lead to mischief. To use his own words, further, he said, "if you give a nigger an inch, he will take an ell;"[2] "he should know nothing but the will of his master, and learn to obey it." "Learning would spoil the best nigger in the world;" "if you teach that nigger—speaking of myself—how to read the bible, there will be no keeping him;" "it would forever unfit him for the duties of a slave;" and "as to himself, learning would do him no good, but probably, a great deal of harm—making him disconsolate and unhappy." "If you learn him now to read, he'll want to know how to write; and, this accomplished, he'll be running away with himself." Such was the tenor of Master Hugh's oracular exposition of the true philosophy of training a human chattel; and it must be confessed that he very clearly comprehended the nature and the requirements of the relation of master and slave. His discourse was the first decidedly anti-slavery lecture to which it had been my lot to listen. Mrs. Auld evidently felt the force of his remarks; and, like an obedient wife, began to shape her course in the direction indicated by her husband. The effect of his words, *on me*, was neither slight nor transitory. His iron sentences—cold and harsh—sunk deep into my heart, and stirred up not only my feelings into a sort of rebellion, but awakened within me a slumbering train of vital thought. It was a new and special revelation, dispelling a painful mystery, against which my youthful understanding had struggled, and struggled in vain, to wit: the *white* man's power to perpetuate the enslavement of the *black* man. "Very well," thought I; "knowledge unfits a child to be a slave." I instinctively assented to the proposition; and from that moment I understood the direct pathway from slavery to freedom. This was just what I needed; and I got it at a time, and from a source, whence I least expected it. I was saddened at the thought of losing the assistance of my kind mistress; but the information, so instantly derived, to some extent compensated me for the loss I had sustained in this direction. Wise as Mr. Auld was, he evidently underrated my comprehension,

1. Teaching enslaved persons to read was not illegal in Maryland, though it was in much of the South.
2. Measure of length that varied according to country.

and had little idea of the use to which I was capable of putting the impressive lesson he was giving to his wife. *He* wanted me to be *a slave*; I had already voted against that on the home plantation of Col. Lloyd. That which he most loved I most hated; and the very determination which he expressed to keep me in ignorance, only rendered me the more resolute in seeking intelligence. In learning to read, therefore, I am not sure that I do not owe quite as much to the opposition of my master, as to the kindly assistance of my amiable mistress. I acknowledge the benefit rendered me by the one, and by the other; believing, that but for my mistress, I might have grown up in ignorance.

I had resided but a short time in Baltimore, before I observed a marked difference in the manner of treating slaves, generally, from that which I had witnessed in that isolated and out-of-the-way part of the country where I began life. A city slave is almost a free citizen, in Baltimore, compared with a slave on Col. Lloyd's plantation. He is much better fed and clothed, is less dejected in his appearance, and enjoys privileges altogether unknown to the whip-driven slave on the plantation. Slavery dislikes a dense population, in which there is a majority of non-slaveholders. The general sense of decency that must pervade such a population, does much to check and prevent those outbreaks of atrocious cruelty, and those dark crimes without a name, almost openly perpetrated on the plantation. He is a desperate slaveholder who will shock the humanity of his non-slaveholding neighbors, by the cries of the lacerated slaves; and very few in the city are willing to incur the odium of being cruel masters. I found, in Baltimore, that no man was more odious to the white, as well as to the colored people, than he, who had the reputation of starving his slaves. Work them, flog them, if need be, but don't starve them. There are, however, some painful exceptions to this rule. While it is quite true that most of the slaveholders in Baltimore feed and clothe their slaves well, there are others who keep up their country cruelties in the city.

An instance of this sort is furnished in the case of a family who lived directly opposite to our house, and were named Hamilton. Mrs. Hamilton owned two slaves. Their names were Henrietta and Mary. They had always been house slaves. One was aged about twenty-two, and the other about fourteen. They were a fragile couple by nature, and the treatment they received was enough to break down the constitution of a horse. Of all the dejected, emaciated, mangled and excoriated creatures I ever saw, those two girls—in the refined, church going and Christian city of Baltimore—were the most deplorable. Of stone must that heart be made, that could look upon Henrietta and Mary, without being sickened to the core with sadness. Especially was Mary a heart-sickening object. Her head, neck and shoulders, were literally cut to pieces. I have frequently felt her head, and found it nearly covered over with festering sores, caused by the lash of her cruel mistress. I do not know that her master ever whipped her, but I have often been an eye witness of the revolting and brutal inflictions by Mrs. Hamilton; and what lends a deeper shade to this woman's conduct, is the fact, that, almost in the very moments of her shocking outrages of humanity and decency, she would charm you by the sweetness of her voice and her seeming piety. She used to sit in a large rocking chair, near the middle of the room, with a heavy cowskin, such as I have elsewhere described; and I speak within the truth when I say, that those girls seldom passed that chair, during the day, without a blow from that cowskin, either upon their bare arms, or upon their shoulders. As they passed her, she would draw her cowskin and give them a blow, saying, "*move faster, you black jip!*" and, again, "*take that, you black jip!*" continuing, "*if you don't move faster, I will give you more.*" Then the lady would go on, singing her sweet hymns, as though her *righteous* soul were sighing for the holy realms of paradise.

Added to the cruel lashings to which these poor slave-girls were subjected—enough in themselves to crush the spirit of men—they were, really, kept nearly half starved; they seldom knew what it was to eat a full meal, except when they got it in the kitchens of neighbors, less mean and stingy than the psalm-singing Mrs. Hamilton. I have seen poor Mary contending for the offal, with the pigs in the street. So much was the poor girl pinched, kicked, cut and pecked to pieces, that the boys in the street knew her only by the name of "*pecked*," a name derived from the scars and blotches on her neck, head and shoulders.

It is some relief to this picture of slavery in Baltimore, to say— what is but the simple truth—that Mrs. Hamilton's treatment of her slaves was generally condemned, as disgraceful and shocking; but while I say this, it must also be remembered, that the very parties who censured the cruelty of Mrs. Hamilton, would have condemned and promptly punished any attempt to interfere with Mrs. Hamilton's *right* to cut and slash her slaves to pieces. There must be no force between the slave and the slaveholder, to restrain the power of the one, and protect the weakness of the other; and the cruelty of Mrs. Hamilton is as justly chargeable to the upholders of the slave system, as drunkenness is chargeable on those who, by precept and example, or by indifference, uphold the drinking system.

CHAPTER XI

"A Change Came o'er the Spirit of My Dream."[1]

HOW THE AUTHOR LEARNED TO READ—MY MISTRESS—HER
SLAVEHOLDING DUTIES—THEIR DEPLORABLE EFFECTS UPON HER
ORIGINALLY NOBLE NATURE—THE CONFLICT IN HER MIND—HER
FINAL OPPOSITION TO MY LEARNING TO READ—TOO LATE—SHE HAD
GIVEN ME THE "INCH," I WAS RESOLVED TO TAKE THE "ELL"—HOW I
PURSUED MY EDUCATION—MY TUTORS—HOW I COMPENSATED
THEM—WHAT PROGRESS I MADE—SLAVERY—WHAT I HEARD SAID
ABOUT IT—THIRTEEN YEARS OLD—THE "COLUMBIAN ORATOR"—A
RICH SCENE—A DIALOGUE—SPEECHES OF CHATHAM, SHERIDAN,
PITT AND FOX—KNOWLEDGE EVER INCREASING—MY EYES OPENED—
LIBERTY—HOW I PINED FOR IT—MY SADNESS—THE DISSATISFACTION
OF MY POOR MISTRESS—MY HATRED OF SLAVERY—ONE UPAS TREE
OVERSHADOWED US BOTH

I LIVED in the family of Master Hugh, at Baltimore, seven years, during which time—as the almanac makers say of the weather—my condition was variable. The most interesting feature of my history here, was my learning to read and write, under somewhat marked disadvantages. In attaining this knowledge, I was compelled to resort to indirections by no means congenial to my nature, and which were really humiliating to me. My mistress—who, as the reader has already seen, had begun to teach me—was suddenly checked in her benevolent design, by the strong advice of her husband. In faithful compliance with this advice, the good lady had not only ceased to instruct me, herself, but had set her face as a flint against my learning to read by any means. It is due, however, to my mistress to say, that she did not adopt this course in all its stringency at the first. She either thought it unnecessary, or she lacked the depravity indispensable to shutting me up in mental darkness. It was, at least, necessary for her to have some training, and some hardening, in the exercise of the slaveholder's prerogative, to make her equal to forgetting my human nature and character, and to treating me as a thing destitute of a moral or an intellectual nature. Mrs. Auld—my mistress—was, as I have said, a most kind and tender-hearted woman; and, in the humanity of her heart, and the simplicity of her mind, she set out, when I first went to live with her, to treat me as she supposed one human being ought to treat another.

It is easy to see, that, in entering upon the duties of a slaveholder, some little experience is needed. Nature has done almost nothing to

1. A line from Byron's poem "The Dream" (1816).

prepare men and women to be either slaves or slaveholders. Nothing but rigid training, long persisted in, can perfect the character of the one or the other. One cannot easily forget to love freedom; and it is as hard to cease to respect that natural love in our fellow creatures. On entering upon the career of a slaveholding mistress, Mrs. Auld was singularly deficient; nature, which fits nobody for such an office, had done less for her than any lady I had known. It was no easy matter to induce her to think and to feel that the curly-headed boy, who stood by her side, and even leaned on her lap; who was loved by little Tommy, and who loved little Tommy in turn; sustained to her only the relation of a chattel. I was *more* than that, and she felt me to be more than that. I could talk and sing; I could laugh and weep; I could reason and remember; I could love and hate. I was human, and she, dear lady, knew and felt me to be so. How could she, then, treat me as a brute, without a mighty struggle with all the noble powers of her own soul. That struggle came, and the will and power of the husband was victorious. Her noble soul was overthrown; but, he that overthrew it did not, himself, escape the consequences. He, not less than the other parties, was injured in his domestic peace by the fall.

When I went into their family, it was the abode of happiness and contentment. The mistress of the house was a model of affection and tenderness. Her fervent piety and watchful uprightness made it impossible to see her without thinking and feeling—*"that woman is a christian."* There was no sorrow nor suffering for which she had not a tear, and there was no innocent joy for which she had not a smile. She had bread for the hungry, clothes for the naked, and comfort for every mourner that came within her reach. Slavery soon proved its ability to divest her of these excellent qualities, and her home of its early happiness. Conscience cannot stand much violence. Once thoroughly broken down, *who* is he that can repair the damage? It may be broken toward the slave, on Sunday, and toward the master on Monday. It cannot endure such shocks. It must stand entire, or it does not stand at all. If my condition waxed bad, that of the family waxed not better. The first step, in the wrong direction, was the violence done to nature and to conscience, in arresting the benevolence that would have enlightened my young mind. In ceasing to instruct me, she must begin to justify herself *to* herself; and, once consenting to take sides in such a debate, she was riveted to her position. One needs very little knowledge of moral philosophy, to see *where* my mistress now landed. She finally became even more violent in her opposition to my learning to read, than was her husband himself. She was not satisfied with simply doing as *well* as her husband had commanded her, but seemed resolved to better his instruction. Nothing appeared to make my poor mistress—after her turning toward the downward path—more angry, than seeing me, seated in some nook or corner, quietly reading a book or a news-paper. I have had her rush at me, with the utmost fury, and snatch from my hand such newspaper or book, with something of the wrath and consternation which a traitor might be supposed to feel on being dis-covered in a plot by some dangerous spy.

Mrs. Auld was an apt woman, and the advice of her husband, and her own experience, soon demonstrated, to her entire satisfaction, that education and slavery are incompatible with each other. When this conviction was thoroughly established, I was most narrowly watched in all my movements. If I remained in a separate room from the family for any considerable length of time, I was sure to be sus-pected of having a book, and was at once called upon to give an account of myself. All this, however, was entirely *too late*. The first, and never to be retraced, step had been taken. In teaching me the alphabet, in the days of her simplicity and kindness, my mistress had given me the "*inch*," and now, no ordinary precaution could prevent me from taking the "*ell*."

Seized with a determination to learn to read, at any cost, I hit upon many expedients to accomplish the desired end. The plea which I mainly adopted, and the one by which I was most successful, was that of using my young white playmates, with whom I met in the street, as teachers. I used to carry, almost constantly, a copy of Web-ster's spelling book[2] in my pocket; and, when sent of errands, or when play time was allowed me, I would step, with my young friends, aside, and take a lesson in spelling. I generally paid my *tuition fee* to the boys, with bread, which I also carried in my pocket. For a single biscuit, any of my hungry little comrades would give me a lesson more valuable to me than bread. Not every one, however, demanded this consideration, for there were those who took pleasure in teach-ing me, whenever I had a chance to be taught by them. I am strongly tempted to give the names of two or three of those little boys, as a slight testimonial of the gratitude and affection I bear them, but pru-dence forbids; not that it would injure me, but it might, possibly, embarrass them; for it is almost an unpardonable offense to do any thing, directly or indirectly, to promote a slave's freedom, in a slave state. It is enough to say, of my warm-hearted little play fellows, that they lived on Philpot street, very near Durgin & Bailey's shipyard.

Although slavery was a delicate subject, and very cautiously talked about among grown up people in Maryland, I frequently talked about it—and that very freely—with the white boys. I would, sometimes, say to them, while seated on a curb stone or a cellar door, "I wish I could be free, as you will be when you get to be men." "You will be

---

2. *The Elementary Spelling Book*, published in 1829 by the American lexicographer and author Noah Webster (1758–1843), remained a hugely popular textbook for a century.

free, you know, as soon as you are twenty-one, and can go where you like, but I am a slave for life. Have I not as good a right to be free as you have?" Words like these, I observed, always troubled them; and I had no small satisfaction in wringing from the boys, occasionally, that fresh and bitter condemnation of slavery, that springs from nature, unseared and unperverted. Of all consciences, let me have those to deal with which have not been bewildered by the cares of life. I do not remember ever to have met with a *boy*, while I was in slavery, who defended the slave system; but I have often had boys to console me, with the hope that something would yet occur, by which I might be made free. Over and over again, they have told me, that "they believed *I* had as good a right to be free as *they* had;" and that "they did not believe God ever made any one to be a slave." The reader will easily see, that such little conversations with my play fellows, had no tendency to weaken my love of liberty, nor to render me contented with my condition as a slave.

When I was about thirteen years old, and had succeeded in learning to read, every increase of knowledge, especially respecting the FREE STATES, added something to the almost intolerable burden of the thought—"I AM A SLAVE FOR LIFE." To my bondage I saw no end. It was a terrible reality, and I shall never be able to tell how sadly that thought chafed my young spirit. Fortunately, or unfortunately, about this time in my life, I had made enough money to buy what was then a very popular school book, viz: the "Columbian Orator."[3] I bought this addition to my library, of Mr. Knight, on Thames street, Fell's Point, Baltimore, and paid him fifty cents for it. I was first led to buy this book, by hearing some little boys say that they were going to learn some little pieces out of it for the Exhibition. This volume was, indeed, a rich treasure, and every opportunity afforded me, for a time, was spent in diligently perusing it. Among much other interesting matter, that which I had perused and reperused with unflagging satisfaction, was a short dialogue between a master and his slave. The slave is represented as having been recaptured, in a second attempt to run away; and the master opens the dialogue with an upbraiding speech, charging the slave with ingratitude, and demanding to know what he has to say in his own defense. Thus upbraided, and thus called upon to reply, the slave rejoins, that he knows how little anything that he can say will avail, seeing that he is completely in the hands of his owner; and with noble resolution, calmly says, "I submit to my fate."

---

3. *The Columbian Orator: Containing a Variety of Original and Selected Pieces Together with Rules Calculated to Improve Youth and Others in the Ornamental and Useful Art of Eloquence* (1797), by the American educator Caleb Bingham (1757–1817), was a manual that celebrated democracy, courage, and freedom and explicitly denounced slavery. Douglass owned a secondhand copy, which he carried with him during his escape from slavery.

Touched by the slave's answer, the master insists upon his further speaking, and recapitulates the many acts of kindness which he has performed toward the slave, and tells him he is permitted to speak for himself. Thus invited to the debate, the quondam slave made a spirited defense of himself, and thereafter the whole argument, for and against slavery, was brought out. The master was vanquished at every turn in the argument; and seeing himself to be thus vanquished, he generously and meekly emancipates the slave, with his best wishes for his prosperity. It is scarcely necessary to say, that a dialogue, with such an origin, and such an ending—read when the fact of my being a slave was a constant burden of grief—powerfully affected me; and I could not help feeling that the day might come, when the well-directed answers made by the slave to the master, in this instance, would find their counterpart in myself.

This, however, was not all the fanaticism which I found in this Columbian Orator. I met there one of Sheridan's mighty speeches, on the subject of Catholic Emancipation,[4] Lord Chatham's speech on the American war, and speeches by the great William Pitt and by Fox. These were all choice documents to me, and I read them, over and over again, with an interest that was ever increasing, because it was ever gaining in intelligence; for the more I read them, the better I understood them. The reading of these speeches added much to my limited stock of language, and enabled me to give tongue to many interesting thoughts, which had frequently flashed through my soul, and died away for want of utterance. The mighty power and heart-searching directness of truth, penetrating even the heart of a slaveholder, compelling him to yield up his earthly interests to the claims of eternal justice, were finely illustrated in the dialogue, just referred to; and from the speeches of Sheridan, I got a bold and powerful denunciation of oppression, and a most brilliant vindication of the rights of man. Here was, indeed, a noble acquisition. If I ever wavered under the consideration, that the Almighty, in some way, ordained slavery, and willed my enslavement for his own glory, I wavered no longer. I had now penetrated the secret of all slavery and oppression, and had ascertained their true foundation to be in the pride, the power and the avarice of man. The dialogue and the speeches were all redolent of the principles of liberty, and poured floods of light on the nature and character of slavery. With a book of this kind in my hand, my own human nature, and the facts of my experience, to help me, I was equal to a contest with the religious advocates of slavery, whether among the whites or among the colored people, for blindness, in this matter, is not confined to the

4. The speech is actually Daniel O'Connell's "Speech in the Irish House of Commons," 1795.

former. I have met many religious colored people, at the south, who are under the delusion that God requires them to submit to slavery, and to wear their chains with meekness and humility. I could entertain no such nonsense as this; and I almost lost my patience when I found any colored man weak enough to believe such stuff. Nevertheless, the increase of knowledge was attended with bitter, as well as sweet results. The more I read, the more I was led to abhor and detest slavery, and my enslavers. "Slaveholders," thought I, "are only a band of successful robbers, who left their homes and went into Africa for the purpose of stealing and reducing my people to slavery." I loathed them as the meanest and the most wicked of men. As I read, behold! the very discontent so graphically predicted by Master Hugh, had already come upon me. I was no longer the light-hearted, gleesome boy, full of mirth and play, as when I landed first at Baltimore. Knowledge had come; light had penetrated the moral dungeon where I dwelt; and, behold! there lay the bloody whip, for my back, and here was the iron chain; and my good, *kind master*, he was the author of my situation. The revelation haunted me, stung me, and made me gloomy and miserable. As I writhed under the sting and torment of this knowledge, I almost envied my fellow slaves their stupid contentment. This knowledge opened my eyes to the horrible pit, and revealed the teeth of the frightful dragon that was ready to pounce upon me, but it opened no way for my escape. I have often wished myself a beast, or a bird—anything, rather than a slave. I was wretched and gloomy, beyond my ability to describe. I was too thoughtful to be happy. It was this everlasting thinking which distressed and tormented me; and yet there was no getting rid of the subject of my thoughts. All nature was redolent of it. Once awakened by the silver trump of knowledge, my spirit was roused to eternal wakefulness. Liberty! the inestimable birthright of every man, had, for me, converted every object into an asserter of this great right. It was heard in every sound, and beheld in every object. It was ever present, to torment me with a sense of my wretched condition. The more beautiful and charming were the smiles of nature, the more horrible and desolate was my condition. I saw nothing without seeing it, and I heard nothing without hearing it. I do not exaggerate, when I say, that it looked from every star, smiled in every calm, breathed in every wind, and moved in every storm.

I have no doubt that my state of mind had something to do with the change in the treatment adopted, by my once kind mistress toward me. I can easily believe, that my leaden, downcast, and discontented look, was very offensive to her. Poor lady! She did not know my trouble, and I dared not tell her. Could I have freely made her acquainted with the real state of my mind, and given her the reasons therefor, it might have been well for both of us. Her abuse of me fell upon me like the blows of the false prophet upon his ass; she did not know that an *angel* stood in the way;[5] and—such is the relation of master and slave—I could not tell her. Nature had made us *friends*; slavery made us *enemies*. My interests were in a direction opposite to hers, and we both had our private thoughts and plans. She aimed to keep me ignorant; and I resolved to know, although knowledge only increased my discontent. My feelings were not the result of any marked cruelty in the treatment I received; they sprung from the consideration of my being a slave at all. It was *slavery*—not its mere *incidents*—that I hated. I had been cheated. I saw through the attempt to keep me in ignorance; I saw that slaveholders would have gladly made me believe that they were merely acting under the authority of God, in making a slave of me, and in making slaves of others; and I treated them as robbers and deceivers. The feeding and clothing me well, could not atone for taking my liberty from me. The smiles of my mistress could not remove the deep sorrow that dwelt in my young bosom. Indeed, these, in time, came only to deepen my sorrow. She had changed; and the reader will see that I had changed, too. We were both victims to the same overshadowing evil—*she*, as mistress, *I*, as slave. I will not censure her harshly; she cannot censure me, for she knows I speak but the truth, and have acted in my opposition to slavery, just as she herself would have acted, in a reverse of circumstances.

CHAPTER XII

Religious Nature Awakened

ABOLITIONISTS SPOKEN OF—MY EAGERNESS TO KNOW WHAT THIS WORD MEANT—MY CONSULTATION OF THE DICTIONARY—INCENDIARY INFORMATION—HOW AND WHERE DERIVED—THE ENIGMA SOLVED—NATHANIEL TURNER'S INSURRECTION—THE CHOLERA—RELIGION—FIRST AWAKENED BY A METHODIST MINISTER, NAMED HANSON—MY DEAR AND GOOD OLD COLORED FRIEND, LAWSON—HIS CHARACTER AND OCCUPATION—HIS INFLUENCE OVER ME—OUR MUTUAL ATTACHMENT—THE COMFORT I DERIVED FROM HIS TEACHING—NEW HOPES AND ASPIRATIONS—HEAVENLY LIGHT AMIDST EARTHLY DARKNESS—THE TWO IRISHMEN ON THE WHARF—THEIR CONVERSATION—HOW I LEARNED TO WRITE—WHAT WERE MY AIMS.

WHILST in the painful state of mind described in the foregoing chapter, almost regretting my very existence, because doomed to a life of bondage, so goaded and so wretched, at times, that I was even

5. Cf. Numbers 22.21–35.

tempted to destroy my own life, I was yet keenly sensitive and eager
to know any, and every thing that transpired, having any relation to
the subject of slavery. I was all ears, all eyes, whenever the words
slave, slavery, dropped from the lips of any white person, and the
occasions were not unfrequent when these words became leading
ones, in high, social debate, at our house. Every little while, I could
overhear Master Hugh, or some of his company, speaking with much
warmth and excitement about *"abolitionists."* Of *who* or *what* these
were, I was totally ignorant. I found, however, that whatever they
might be, they were most cordially hated and soundly abused by
slaveholders, of every grade. I very soon discovered, too, that slavery
was, in some sort, under consideration, whenever the abolitionists
were alluded to. This made the term a very interesting one to me. If
a slave, for instance, had made good his escape from slavery, it was
generally alleged, that he had been persuaded and assisted by the
abolitionists. If, also, a slave killed his master—as was sometimes
the case—or struck down his overseer, or set fire to his master's
dwelling, or committed any violence or crime, out of the common
way, it was certain to be said, that such a crime was the legitimate
fruits of the abolition movement. Hearing such charges often
repeated, I, naturally enough, received the impression that abolition—
whatever else it might be—could not be unfriendly to the slave, nor
very friendly to the slaveholder. I therefore set about finding out, if
possible, *who* and *what* the abolitionists were, and *why* they were so
obnoxious to the slaveholders. The dictionary afforded me very
little help. It taught me that abolition was the "act of abolishing;"
but it left me in ignorance at the very point where I most wanted
information—and that was, as to the *thing* to be abolished. A city
newspaper, the "Baltimore American," gave me the incendiary
information denied me by the dictionary. In its columns I found,
that, on a certain day, a vast number of petitions and memorials had
been presented to congress, praying for the abolition of slavery in
the District of Columbia, and for the abolition of the slave trade
between the states of the Union.[1] This was enough. The vindictive
bitterness, the marked caution, the studied reserve, and the cum-
brous ambiguity, practiced by our white folks, when allluding to this
subject, was now fully explained. Ever, after that, when I heard
the words "abolition," or "abolition movement," mentioned, I felt the
matter one of a personal concern; and I drew near to listen, when I
could do so, without seeming too solicitous and prying. There was
HOPE in those words. Ever and anon, too, I could see some terrible

1. In December 1831, the *Baltimore American* reported a speech by John Quincy Adams
(1767–1848; U.S. president 1825–29) in which he presented Quaker petitions to abolish slavery and the slave trade in the capital.

denunciation of slavery, in our papers—copied from abolition papers at the north,—and the injustice of such denunciation commented on. These I read with avidity. I had a deep satisfaction in the thought, that the rascality of slaveholders was not concealed from the eyes of the world, and that I was not alone in abhorring the cruelty and brutality of slavery. A still deeper train of thought was stirred. I saw that there was *fear*, as well as *rage*, in the manner of speaking of the abolitionists. The latter, therefore, I was compelled to regard as having some power in the country; and I felt that they might, possibly, succeed in their designs. When I met with a slave to whom I deemed it safe to talk on the subject, I would impart to him so much of the mystery as I had been able to penetrate. Thus, the light of this grand movement broke in upon my mind, by degrees; and I must say, that, ignorant as I then was of the philosophy of that movement, I believed in it from the first—and I believed in it, partly, because I saw that it alarmed the consciences of slaveholders. The insurrection of Nathaniel Turner had been quelled, but the alarm and terror had not subsided. The cholera was on its way,[2] and the thought was present, that God was angry with the white people because of their slaveholding wickedness, and, therefore, his judgments were abroad in the land. It was impossible for me not to hope much from the abolition movement, when I saw it supported by the Almighty, and armed with DEATH!

Previous to my contemplation of the anti-slavery movement, and its probable results, my mind had been seriously awakened to the subject of religion. I was not more than thirteen years old, when I felt the need of God, as a father and protector. My religious nature was awakened by the preaching of a white Methodist minister, named Hanson. He thought that all men, great and small, bond and free, were sinners in the sight of God; that they were, by nature, rebels against His government; and that they must repent of their sins, and be reconciled to God, through Christ. I cannot say that I had a very distinct notion of what was required of me; but one thing I knew very well—I was wretched, and had no means of making myself otherwise. Moreover, I knew that I could pray for light. I consulted a good colored man, named Charles Johnson;[3] and, in tones of holy affection, he told me to pray, and what to pray for. I was, for weeks, a poor, broken-hearted mourner, traveling through the darkness and misery of doubts and fears. I finally found that change of heart which

2. A cholera epidemic hit Baltimore in the summer of 1831. In August of that year, in Southampton County, Virginia, Nat Turner (1800–1831), an enslaved man, began the bloodiest slave revolt in American history.
3. Douglass met Johnson, a Black preacher, at Baltimore's Bethel African Methodist Church.

comes by "casting all one's care"[4] upon God, and by having faith in Jesus Christ, as the Redeemer, Friend, and Savior of those who diligently seek Him.

After this, I saw the world in a new light. I seemed to live in a new world, surrounded by new objects, and to be animated by new hopes and desires. I loved all mankind—slaveholders not excepted; though I abhorred slavery more than ever. My great concern was, now, to have the world converted. The desire for knowledge increased, and especially did I want a thorough acquaintance with the contents of the bible. I have gathered scattered pages from this holy book, from the filthy street gutters of Baltimore, and washed and dried them, that in the moments of my leisure, I might get a word or two of wisdom from them. While thus religiously seeking knowledge, I became acquainted with a good old colored man, named Lawson.[5] A more devout man than he, I never saw. He drove a dray for Mr. James Ramsey, the owner of a rope-walk on Fell's Point, Baltimore. This man not only prayed three times a day, but he prayed as he walked through the streets, at his work—on his dray—everywhere. His life was a life of prayer, and his words, (when he spoke to his friends,) were about a better world. Uncle Lawson lived near Master Hugh's house; and, becoming deeply attached to the old man, I went often with him to prayer-meeting, and spent much of my leisure time with him on Sunday. The old man could read a little, and I was a great help to him, in making out the hard words, for I was a better reader than he. I could teach him "*the letter*," but he could teach me "*the spirit*;" and high, refreshing times we had together, in singing, praying and glorifying God. These meetings with Uncle Lawson went on for a long time, without the knowledge of Master Hugh or my mistress. Both knew, however, that I had become religious, and they seemed to respect my conscientious piety. My mistress was still a professor of religion, and belonged to class. Her leader was no less a person than the Rev. Beverly Waugh, the presiding elder, and now one of the bishops of the Methodist Episcopal church. Mr. Waugh was then stationed over Wilk street church. I am careful to state these facts, that the reader may be able to form an idea of the precise influences which had to do with shaping and directing my mind.

In view of the cares and anxieties incident to the life she was then leading, and, especially, in view of the separation from religious associations to which she was subjected, my mistress had, as I have before stated, become lukewarm, and needed to be looked up by her

4. Cf. 1 Peter 5.7.
5. Charles Lawson, a free Black man, was a member of the Bethel African Methodist Church.

leader. This brought Mr. Waugh to our house, and gave me an opportunity to hear him exhort and pray. But my chief instructor, in
matters of religion, was Uncle Lawson. He was my spiritual father;
and I loved him intensely, and was at his house every chance I got.

This pleasure was not long allowed me. Master Hugh became
averse to my going to Father Lawson's, and threatened to whip me
if I ever went there again. I now felt myself persecuted by a wicked
man; and I *would* go to Father Lawson's, notwithstanding the threat.
The good old man had told me, that the "Lord had a great work for
me to do;" and I must prepare to do it; and that he had been shown
that I must preach the gospel. His words made a deep impression
on my mind, and I verily felt that some such work was before me,
though I could not see *how* I should ever engage in its performance.
"The good Lord," he said, "would bring it to pass in his own good
time," and that I must go on reading and studying the scriptures.
The advice and the suggestions of Uncle Lawson, were not without
their influence upon my character and destiny. He threw my thoughts
into a channel from which they have never entirely diverged. He
fanned my already intense love of knowledge into a flame, by assuring me that I was to be a useful man in the world. When I would say
to him, "How can these things be—and what can *I* do?" his simple
reply was, *"Trust in the Lord."* When I told him that "I was a slave,
and a slave FOR LIFE," he said, "the Lord can make you free, my dear.
All things are possible with him, only *have faith in God."* "Ask, and
it shall be given."[6] "If you want liberty," said the good old man, "ask
the Lord for it, *in faith,* AND HE WILL GIVE IT TO YOU."

Thus assured, and cheered on, under the inspiration of hope, I
worked and prayed with a light heart, believing that my life was
under the guidance of a wisdom higher than my own. With all other
blessings sought at the mercy seat,[7] I always prayed that God would,
of His great mercy, and in His own good time, deliver me from my
bondage.

I went, one day, on the wharf of Mr. Waters; and seeing two Irishmen unloading a large scow of stone, or ballast, I went on board,
unasked, and helped them. When we had finished the work, one of
the men came to me, aside, and asked me a number of questions,
and among them, if I were a slave. I told him "I was a slave, and a
slave for life." The good Irishman gave his shoulders a shrug, and
seemed deeply affected by the statement. He said, "it was a pity so
fine a little fellow as myself should be a slave for life." They both
had much to say about the matter, and expressed the deepest sympathy with me, and the most decided hatred of slavery. They went

6. Cf. Matthew 7.7.
7. Cf. Hebrews 9.5; the symbolic seat of God.

so far as to tell me that I ought to run away, and go to the north; that I should find friends there, and that I would be as free as anybody. I, however, pretended not to be interested in what they said, for I feared they might be treacherous. White men have been known to encourage slaves to escape, and then—to get the reward—they have kidnapped them, and returned them to their masters. And while I mainly inclined to the notion that these men were honest and meant me no ill, I feared it might be otherwise. I nevertheless remembered their words and their advice, and looked forward to an escape to the north, as a possible means of gaining the liberty for which my heart panted. It was not my enslavement, at the then present time, that most affected me; the being a slave *for life*, was the saddest thought. I was too young to think of running away immediately; besides, I wished to learn how to write, before going, as I might have occasion to write my own pass.[8] I now not only had the hope of freedom, but a foreshadowing of the means by which I might, some day, gain that inestimable boon. Meanwhile, I resolved to add to my educational attainments the art of writing.

After this manner I began to learn to write: I was much in the ship yard—Master Hugh's, and that of Durgan & Bailey—and I observed that the carpenters, after hewing and getting a piece of timber ready for use, wrote on it the initials of the name of that part of the ship for which it was intended. When, for instance, a piece of timber was ready for the starboard side, it was marked with a capital "S." A piece for the larboard side was marked "L;" larboard forward, "L. F.;" larboard aft, was marked "L. A.;" starboard aft, "S. A.;" and starboard forward "S. F." I soon learned these letters, and for what they were placed on the timbers.

My work was now, to keep fire under the steam box, and to watch the ship yard while the carpenters had gone to dinner. This interval gave me a fine opportunity for copying the letters named. I soon astonished myself with the ease with which I made the letters; and the thought was soon present, "if I can make four, I can make more." But having made these easily, when I met boys about Bethel church, or any of our play-grounds, I entered the lists with them in the art of writing, and would make the letters which I had been so fortunate as to learn, and ask them to "beat that if they could." With playmates for my teachers, fences and pavements for my copy books, and chalk for my pen and ink, I learned the art of writing. I, however, afterward adopted various methods of improving my hand. The most successful, was copying the *italics* in Webster's spelling book, until I could make them all without looking on the book. By this

8. Free Black persons were required to carry handwritten freedom papers. See note 3 on p. 30.

time, my little "Master Tommy" had grown to be a big boy, and had written over a number of copy books, and brought them home. They had been shown to the neighbors, had elicited due praise, and were now laid carefully away. Spending my time between the ship yard and house, I was as often the lone keeper of the latter as of the former. When my mistress left me in charge of the house, I had a grand time; I got Master Tommy's copy books and a pen and ink, and, in the ample spaces between the lines, I wrote other lines, as nearly like his as possible. The process was a tedious one, and I ran the risk of getting a flogging for marring the highly prized copy books of the oldest son. In addition to these opportunities, sleeping, as I did, in the kitchen loft—a room seldom visited by any of the family,—I got a flour barrel up there, and a chair; and upon the head of that barrel I have written, (or endeavored to write,) copying from the bible and the Methodist hymn book, and other books which had accumulated on my hands, till late at night, and when all the family were in bed and asleep. I was supported in my endeavors by renewed advice, and by holy promises from the good Father Lawson, with whom I continued to meet, and pray, and read the scriptures. Although Master Hugh was aware of my going there, I must say, for his credit, that he never executed his threat to whip me, for having thus, innocently, employed my leisure time.

CHAPTER XIII

The Vicissitudes of Slave Life

DEATH OF OLD MASTER'S SON RICHARD, SPEEDILY FOLLOWED BY THAT OF OLD MASTER—VALUATION AND DIVISION OF ALL THE PROPERTY, INCLUDING THE SLAVES—MY PRESENCE REQUIRED AT HILLSBOROUGH TO BE APPRAISED AND ALLOTTED TO A NEW OWNER—MY SAD PROSPECTS AND GRIEF—PARTING—THE UTTER POWERLESSNESS OF THE SLAVES TO DECIDE THEIR OWN DESTINY—A GENERAL DREAD OF MASTER ANDREW—HIS WICKEDNESS AND CRUELTY—MISS LUCRETIA MY NEW OWNER—MY RETURN TO BALTIMORE—JOY UNDER THE ROOF OF MASTER HUGH—DEATH OF MRS. LUCRETIA—MY POOR OLD GRANDMOTHER—HER SAD FATE—THE LONE COT IN THE WOODS— MASTER THOMAS AULD'S SECOND MARRIAGE—AGAIN REMOVED FROM MASTER HUGH'S—REASONS FOR REGRETTING THE CHANGE—A PLAN OF ESCAPE ENTERTAINED.

I MUST now ask the reader to go with me a little back in point of time, in my humble story, and to notice another circumstance that entered into my slavery experience, and which, doubtless, has had a share in deepening my horror of slavery, and increasing my hostility toward those men and measures that practically uphold the slave system.

It has already been observed, that though I was, after my removal from Col. Lloyd's plantation, in *form* the slave of Master Hugh, I was, in *fact*, and in *law*, the slave of my old master, Capt. Anthony. Very well.

In a very short time after I went to Baltimore, my old master's youngest son, Richard, died; and, in three years and six months after his death, my old master himself died, leaving only his son, Andrew, and his daughter, Lucretia, to share his estate. The old man died while on a visit to his daughter, in Hillsborough, where Capt. Auld and Mrs. Lucretia now lived. The former, having given up the command of Col. Lloyd's sloop, was now keeping a store in that town.

Cut off, thus unexpectedly, Capt. Anthony died intestate; and his property must now be equally divided between his two children, Andrew and Lucretia.

The valuation and the division of slaves, among contending heirs, is an important incident in slave life. The character and tendencies of the heirs, are generally well understood among the slaves who are to be divided, and all have their aversions and preferences. But, neither their aversions nor their preferences avail them anything.

On the death of old master, I was immediately sent for, to be valued and divided with the other property. Personally, my concern was, mainly, about my possible removal from the home of Master Hugh, which, after that of my grandmother, was the most endeared to me. But, the whole thing, as a feature of slavery, shocked me. It furnished me a new insight into the unnatural power to which I was subjected. My detestation of slavery, already great, rose with this new conception of its enormity.

That was a sad day for me, a sad day for little Tommy, and a sad day for my dear Baltimore mistress and teacher, when I left for the Eastern Shore, to be valued and divided. We, all three, wept bitterly that day; for we might be parting, and we feared we were parting, forever. No one could tell among which pile of chattels I should be flung. Thus early, I got a foretaste of that painful uncertainty which slavery brings to the ordinary lot of mortals. Sickness, adversity and death may interfere with the plans and purposes of all; but the slave has the added danger of changing homes, changing hands, and of having separations unknown to other men. Then, too, there was the intensified degradation of the spectacle. What an assemblage! Men and women, young and old, married and single; moral and intellectual beings, in open contempt of their humanity, leveled at a blow with horses, sheep, horned cattle and swine! Horses and men—cattle and women—pigs and children—all holding the same rank

in the scale of social existence; and all subjected to the same narrow inspection, to ascertain their value in gold and silver—the only
standard of worth applied by slaveholders to slaves! How vividly, at
that moment, did the brutalizing power of slavery flash before me!
Personality swallowed up in the sordid idea of property! Manhood
lost in chattelhood!

After the valuation, then came the division. This was an hour of
high excitement and distressing anxiety. Our destiny was now to be
fixed for life, and we had no more voice in the decision of the question, than the oxen and cows that stood chewing at the hay-mow.
One word from the appraisers, against all preferences or prayers, was
enough to sunder all the ties of friendship and affection, and even
to separate husbands and wives, parents and children. We were all
appalled before that power, which, to human seeming, could bless
or blast us in a moment. Added to the dread of separation, most painful to the majority of the slaves, we all had a decided horror of the
thought of falling into the hands of Master Andrew. He was distinguished for cruelty and intemperance.

Slaves generally dread to fall into the hands of drunken owners.
Master Andrew was almost a confirmed sot, and had already, by his
reckless mismanagement and profligate dissipation, wasted a large
portion of old master's property. To fall into his hands, was, therefore, considered merely as the first step toward being sold away to
the far south. He would spend his fortune in a few years, and his
farms and slaves would be sold, we thought, at public out-cry; and
we should be hurried away to the cotton fields, and rice swamps, of
the sunny south. This was the cause of deep consternation.

The people of the north, and free people generally, I think, have
less attachment to the places where they are born and brought up,
than have the slaves. Their freedom to go and come, to be here and
there, as they list, prevents any extravagant attachment to any one
particular place, in their case. On the other hand, the slave is a
fixture; he has no choice, no goal, no destination; but is pegged down
to a single spot, and must take root here, or nowhere. The idea of
removal elsewhere, comes, generally, in the shape of a threat, and
in punishment of crime. It is, therefore, attended with fear and
dread. A slave seldom thinks of bettering his condition by being sold,
and hence he looks upon separation from his native place, with none
of the enthusiasm which animates the bosoms of young freemen,
when they contemplate a life in the far west, or in some distant country where they intend to rise to wealth and distinction. Nor can
those from whom they separate, give them up with that cheerful-
ness with which friends and relations yield each other up, when they
feel that it is for the good of the departing one that he is removed
from his native place. Then, too, there is correspondence, and there

is, at least, the hope of reünion, because reünion is *possible*. But, with the slave, all these mitigating circumstances are wanting. There is no improvement in his condition *probable*,—no correspondence *possible*,—no reünion attainable. His going out into the world, is like a living man going into the tomb, who, with open eyes, sees himself buried out of sight and hearing of wife, children and friends of kindred tie.

In contemplating the likelihoods and possibilities of our circumstances, I probably suffered more than most of my fellow servants. I had known what it was to experience kind, and even tender treatment; they had known nothing of the sort. Life, to them, had been rough and thorny, as well as dark. They had—most of them—lived on my old master's farm in Tuckahoe, and had felt the reign of Mr. Plummer's rule. The overseer had written his character on the living parchment of most of their backs, and left them callous; my back (thanks to my early removal from the plantation to Baltimore,) was yet tender. I had left a kind mistress at Baltimore, who was almost a mother to me. She was in tears when we parted, and the probabilities of ever seeing her again, trembling in the balance as they did, could not be viewed without alarm and agony. The thought of leaving that kind mistress forever, and, worse still, of being the slave of Andrew Anthony—a man who, but a few days before the division of the property, had, in my presence, seized my brother Perry by the throat, dashed him on the ground, and with the heel of his boot stamped him on the head, until the blood gushed from his nose and ears—was terrible! This fiendish proceeding had no better apology than the fact, that Perry had gone to play, when Master Andrew wanted him for some trifling service. This cruelty, too, was of a piece with his general character. After inflicting his heavy blows on my brother, on observing me looking at him with intense astonishment, he said, "*That* is the way I will serve you, one of these days;" meaning, no doubt, when I should come into his possession. This threat, the reader may well suppose, was not very tranquilizing to my feelings. I could see that he really thirsted to get hold of me. But I was there only for a few days. I had not received any orders, and had violated none, and there was, therefore, no excuse for flogging me.

At last, the anxiety and suspense were ended; and they ended, thanks to a kind Providence, in accordance with my wishes. I fell to the portion of Mrs. Lucretia—the dear lady who bound up my head, when the savage Aunt Katy was adding to my sufferings her bitterest maledictions.

Capt. Thomas Auld and Mrs. Lucretia at once decided on my return to Baltimore. They knew how sincerely and warmly Mrs. Hugh Auld was attached to me, and how delighted Mr. Hugh's son would be to have me back; and, withal, having no immediate use for one so young, they willingly let me off to Baltimore.

I need not stop here to narrate my joy on returning to Baltimore, nor that of little Tommy; nor the tearful joy of his mother; nor the evident satisfaction of Master Hugh. I was just one month absent from Baltimore, before the matter was decided; and the time really seemed full six months.

One trouble over, and on comes another. The slave's life is full of uncertainty. I had returned to Baltimore but a short time, when the tidings reached me, that my kind friend, Mrs. Lucretia, who was only second in my regard to Mrs. Hugh Auld, was dead, leaving her husband and only child—a daughter, named Amanda.

Shortly after the death of Mrs. Lucretia, strange to say, Master Andrew died, leaving his wife and one child. Thus, the whole family of Anthonys was swept away; only two children remained. All this happened within five years of my leaving Col. Lloyd's.

No alteration took place in the condition of the slaves, in consequence of these deaths, yet I could not help feeling less secure, after the death of my friend, Mrs. Lucretia, than I had done during her life. While she lived, I felt that I had a strong friend to plead for me in any emergency. Ten years ago, while speaking of the state of things in our family, after the events just named, I used this language:[1]

> "Now all the property of my old master, slaves included, was in the hands of strangers—strangers who had nothing to do in accumulating it. Not a slave was left free. All remained slaves, from the youngest to the oldest. If any one thing in my experience, more than another, served to deepen my conviction of the infernal character of slavery, and to fill me with unutterable loathing of slaveholders, it was their base ingratitude to my poor old grandmother. She had served my old master faithfully from youth to old age. She had been the source of all his wealth; she had peopled his plantation with slaves; she had become a great-grandmother in his service. She had rocked him in infancy, attended him in childhood, served him through life, and at his death wiped from his icy brow the cold death-sweat, and closed his eyes forever. She was nevertheless left a slave—a slave for life—a slave in the hands of strangers; and in their hands she saw her children, her grandchildren, and her great-grandchildren, divided, like so many sheep, without being gratified with the small privilege of a single word, as to their or her own destiny. And, to cap the climax of their base ingratitude and fiendish barbarity, my grandmother, who was now very old, having outlived my old master and all

1. This block quotation is from Chapter 8 of Douglass's *Narrative*.

his children, having seen the beginning and end of all of them, and her present owners finding she was of but little value, her frame already racked with the pains of old age, and complete helplessness fast stealing over her once active limbs, they took her to the woods, built her a little hut, put up a little mud-chimney, and then made her welcome to the privilege of supporting herself there in perfect loneliness; thus virtually turning her out to die! If my poor old grandmother now lives, she lives to suffer in utter loneliness; she lives to remember and mourn over the loss of children, the loss of grandchildren, and the loss of great-grandchildren. They are, in the language of the slave's poet, Whittier.—

> 'Gone, gone, sold and gone,
> To the rice swamp dank and lone,
> Where the slave-whip ceaseless swings,
> Where the noisome insect stings,
> Where the fever-demon strews
> Poison with the falling dews,
> Where the sickly sunbeams glare
> Through the hot and misty air:—
>> Gone, gone, sold and gone
>> To the rice swamp dank and lone,
>> From Virginia hills and waters—
>> Woe is me, my stolen daughters!'[2]

"The hearth is desolate. The children, the unconscious children, who once sang and danced in her presence, are gone. She gropes her way, in the darkness of age, for a drink of water. Instead of the voices of her children, she hears by day the moans of the dove, and by night the screams of the hideous owl. All is gloom. The grave is at the door. And now, when weighed down by the pains and aches of old age, when the head inclines to the feet, when the beginning and ending of human existence meet, and helpless infancy and painful old age combine together— at this time, this most needful time, the time for the exercise of that tenderness and affection which children only can exercise toward a declining parent—my poor old grandmother, the devoted mother of twelve children, is left all alone, in yonder little hut, before a few dim embers."

Two years after the death of Mrs. Lucretia, Master Thomas married his second wife. Her name was Rowena Hamilton, the eldest daughter of Mr. William Hamilton, a rich slaveholder on the Eastern Shore of Maryland, who lived about five miles from St. Michael's, the then place of my master's residence.

---

2. Lines 1–12 of "The Farewell of a Virginia Slave Mother to Her Daughters sold into Southern Bondage" (1849), by the American poet John Greenleaf Whittier (1807–1892).

Not long after his marriage, Master Thomas had a misunderstanding with Master Hugh, and, as a means of punishing his brother, he ordered him to send me home.

As the ground of misunderstanding will serve to illustrate the character of southern chivalry, and humanity, I will relate it.

Among the children of my Aunt Milly, was a daughter, named Henny. When quite a child, Henny had fallen into the fire, and had burnt her hands so bad that they were of very little use to her. Her fingers were drawn almost into the palms of her hands. She could make out to do something, but she was considered hardly worth the having—of little more value than a horse with a broken leg. This unprofitable piece of human property, ill shapen, and disfigured, Capt. Auld sent off to Baltimore, making his brother Hugh welcome to her services.

After giving poor Henny a fair trial, Master Hugh and his wife came to the conclusion, that they had no use for the crippled servant, and they sent her back to Master Thomas. This, the latter took as an act of ingratitude, on the part of his brother; and, as a mark of his displeasure, he required him to send me immediately to St. Michael's, saying, if he cannot keep "*Hen*," he shall not have "*Fred*."

Here was another shock to my nerves, another breaking up of my plans, and another severance of my religious and social alliances. I was now a big boy. I had become quite useful to several young colored men, who had made me their teacher. I had taught some of them to read, and was accustomed to spend many of my leisure hours with them. Our attachment was strong, and I greatly dreaded the separation. But regrets, especially in a slave, are unavailing. I was only a slave; my wishes were nothing, and my happiness was the sport of my masters.

My regrets at now leaving Baltimore, were not for the same reasons as when I before left that city, to be valued and handed over to my proper owner. My home was not now the pleasant place it had formerly been. A change had taken place, both in Master Hugh, and in his once pious and affectionate wife. The influence of brandy and bad company on him, and the influence of slavery and social isolation upon her, had wrought disastrously upon the characters of both. Thomas was no longer "little Tommy," but was a big boy, and had learned to assume the airs of his class toward me. My condition, therefore, in the house of Master Hugh, was not, by any means, so comfortable as in former years. My attachments were now outside of our family. They were felt to those to whom I *imparted* instruction, and to those little white boys from whom I *received* instruction. There, too, was my dear old father, the pious Lawson, who was, in christian graces, the very counterpart of

"Uncle" Tom. The resemblance is so perfect, that he might have been the original of Mrs. Stowe's christian hero.[3] The thought of leaving these dear friends, greatly troubled me, for I was going without the hope of ever returning to Baltimore again; the feud between Master Hugh and his brother being bitter and irreconcilable, or, at least, supposed to be so.

In addition to thoughts of friends from whom I was parting, as I supposed, *forever*, I had the grief of neglected chances of escape to brood over. I had put off running away, until now I was to be placed where the opportunities for escaping were much fewer than in a large city like Baltimore.

On my way from Baltimore to St. Michael's, down the Chesapeake bay, our sloop—the Amanda—was passed by the steamers plying between that city and Philadelphia, and I watched the course of those steamers, and, while going to St. Michael's, I formed a plan to escape from slavery; of which plan, and matters connected therewith the kind reader shall learn more hereafter.

CHAPTER XIV

Experience in St. Michael's

THE VILLAGE—ITS INHABITANTS—THEIR OCCUPATION AND LOW PROPENSITIES—CAPTAIN THOMAS AULD—HIS CHARACTER—HIS SECOND WIFE, ROWENA—WELL MATCHED—SUFFERINGS FROM HUNGER—OBLIGED TO TAKE FOOD—MODE OF ARGUMENT IN VINDICATION THEREOF—NO MORAL CODE OF FREE SOCIETY CAN APPLY TO SLAVE SOCIETY—SOUTHERN CAMP MEETING—WHAT MASTER THOMAS DID THERE—HOPES—SUSPICIONS ABOUT HIS CONVERSION—THE RESULT—FAITH AND WORKS ENTIRELY AT VARIANCE—HIS RISE AND PROGRESS IN THE CHURCH—POOR COUSIN "HENNY"—HIS TREATMENT OF HER—THE METHODIST PREACHERS—THEIR UTTER DISREGARD OF US—ONE EXCELLENT EXCEPTION—REV. GEORGE COOKMAN—SABBATH SCHOOL—HOW BROKEN UP AND BY WHOM—A FUNERAL PALL CAST OVER ALL MY PROSPECTS—COVEY THE NEGRO-BREAKER

St. Michael's, the village in which was now my new home, compared favorably with villages in slave states, generally. There were a few comfortable dwellings in it, but the place, as a whole, wore a dull, slovenly, enterprise-forsaken aspect. The mass of the buildings were

---

3. I.e., served as the model for the long-suffering enslaved man in the novel *Uncle Tom's Cabin* (1852), by the American writer Harriet Beecher Stowe (1811–1896; see pp. 331–32).

of wood; they had never enjoyed the artificial adornment of paint, and time and storms had worn off the bright color of the wood, leaving them almost as black as buildings charred by a conflagration.

St. Michael's had, in former years, (previous to 1833, for that was the year I went to reside there,) enjoyed some reputation as a ship building community, but that business had almost entirely given place to oyster fishing, for the Baltimore and Philadelphia markets—a course of life highly unfavorable to morals, industry, and manners. Miles river was broad, and its oyster fishing grounds were extensive; and the fishermen were out, often, all day, and a part of the night, during autumn, winter and spring. This exposure was an excuse for carrying with them, in considerable quantities, spirituous liquors, the then supposed best antidote for cold. Each canoe was supplied with its jug of rum; and tippling, among this class of the citizens of St. Michael's, became general. This drinking habit, in an ignorant population, fostered coarseness, vulgarity and an indolent disregard for the social improvement of the place, so that it was admitted, by the few sober, thinking people who remained there, that St. Michael's had become a very *unsaintly*, as well as an unsightly place, before I went there to reside.

I left Baltimore, for St. Michael's in the month of March, 1833.[1] I know the year, because it was the one succeeding the first cholera in Baltimore, and was the year, also, of that strange phenomenon, when the heavens seemed about to part with its starry train.[2] I witnessed this gorgeous spectacle, and was awe-struck. The air seemed filled with bright, descending messengers from the sky. It was about daybreak when I saw this sublime scene. I was not without the suggestion, at the moment, that it might be the harbinger of the coming of the Son of Man;[3] and, in my then state of mind, I was prepared to hail Him as my friend and deliverer. I had read, that the "stars shall fall from heaven;"[4] and they were now falling. I was suffering much in my mind. It did seem that every time the young tendrils of my affection became attached, they were rudely broken by some unnatural outside power; and I was beginning to look away to heaven for the rest denied me on earth.

But, to my story. It was now more than seven years since I had lived with Master Thomas Auld, in the family of my old master, on Col. Lloyd's plantation. We were almost entire strangers to each other; for, when I knew him at the house of my old master, it was not as a *master*, but simply as "Captain Auld," who had married old

1. Douglass here revises the year he gives in the *Narrative*, 1832.
2. Douglass is describing the great Leonid meteor shower of November 1833.
3. "Son of Man": a phrase spoken frequently by Jesus in the Christian gospels.
4. "stars shall fall from heaven": cf. Matthew 24.29 and Mark 13.25.

master's daughter. All my lessons concerning his temper and disposition, and the best methods of pleasing him, were yet to be learnt.
Slaveholders, however, are not very ceremonious in approaching a
slave; and my ignorance of the new material in the shape of a master was but transient. Nor was my new mistress long in making
known her animus. She was not a "Miss Lucretia," traces of whom
I yet remembered, and the more especially, as I saw them shining in
the face of little Amanda, her daughter, now living under a step-
mother's government. I had not forgotten the soft hand, guided by a
tender heart, that bound up with healing balsam the gash made in
my head by Ike, the son of Abel. Thomas and Rowena, I found to be
a well-matched pair. *He* was stingy, and *she* was cruel; and—what
was quite natural in such cases—she possessed the ability to make
him as cruel as herself, while she could easily descend to the level
of his meanness. In the house of Master Thomas, I was made—for
the first time in seven years—to feel the pinchings of hunger, and
this was not very easy to bear.

For, in all the changes of Master Hugh's family, there was no
change in the bountifulness with which they supplied me with food.
Not to give a slave enough to eat, is meanness intensified, and it is
so recognized among slaveholders generally, in Maryland. The rule
is, no matter how coarse the food, only let there be enough of it.
This is the theory, and—in the part of Maryland I came from—the
general practice accords with this theory. Lloyd's plantation was an
exception, as was, also, the house of Master Thomas Auld.

All know the lightness of Indian corn-meal, as an article of food,
and can easily judge from the following facts whether the statements
I have made of the stinginess of Master Thomas, are borne out.
There were four slaves of us in the kitchen, and four whites in the
great house—Thomas Auld, Mrs. Auld, Hadaway Auld, (brother of
Thomas Auld,) and little Amanda. The names of the slaves in the
kitchen, were Eliza, my sister; Priscilla, my aunt; Henny, my cousin;
and myself. There were eight persons in the family. There was, each
week, one half bushel of corn-meal brought from the mill; and in
the kitchen, corn-meal was almost our exclusive food, for very little
else was allowed us. Out of this half bushel of corn-meal, the family
in the great house had a small loaf every morning; thus leaving us,
in the kitchen, with not quite a half a peck of meal per week, apiece.
This allowance was less than half the allowance of food on Lloyd's
plantation. It was not enough to subsist upon; and we were, therefore, reduced to the wretched necessity of living at the expense of
our neighbors. We were compelled either to beg, or to steal, and we
did both. I frankly confess, that while I hated everything like stealing, *as such*, I nevertheless did not hesitate to take food, when I was

hungry, wherever I could find it. Nor was this practice the mere result of an unreasoning instinct; it was, in my case, the result of a clear apprehension of the claims of morality. I weighed and considered the matter closely, before I ventured to satisfy my hunger by such means. Considering that my labor and person were the property of Master Thomas, and that I was by him deprived of the necessaries of life—necessaries obtained by my own labor—it was easy to deduce the right to supply myself with what was my own. It was simply appropriating what was my own to the use of my master, since the health and strength derived from such food were exerted in *his* service. To be sure, this was stealing, according to the law and gospel I heard from St. Michael's pulpit; but I had already begun to attach less importance to what dropped from that quarter, on that point, while, as yet, I retained my reverence for religion. It was not always convenient to steal from master, and the same reason why I might, innocently, steal from him, did not seem to justify me in stealing from others. In the case of my master, it was only a question of *removal*—the taking his meat out of one tub, and putting it into another; the ownership of the meat was not affected by the transaction. At first, he owned it in the *tub*, and last, he owned it in *me*. His meat house was not always open. There was a strict watch kept on that point, and the key was on a large bunch in Rowena's pocket. A great many times have we, poor creatures, been severely pinched with hunger, when meat and bread have been moulding under the lock, while the key was in the pocket of our mistress. This had been so when she *knew* we were nearly half starved; and yet, that mistress, with saintly air, would kneel with her husband, and pray each morning that a merciful God would bless them in basket and in store, and save them, at last, in his kingdom. But I proceed with the argument.

It was necessary that the right to steal from *others* should be established; and this could only rest upon a wider range of generalization than that which supposed the right to steal from my master.

It was sometime before I arrived at this clear right. The reader will get some idea of my train of reasoning, by a brief statement of the case. "I am," thought I, "not only the slave of Master Thomas, but I am the slave of society at large. Society at large has bound itself, in form and in fact, to assist Master Thomas in robbing me of my rightful liberty, and of the just reward of my labor; therefore, whatever rights I have against Master Thomas, I have, equally, against those confederated with him in robbing me of liberty. As society has marked me out as privileged plunder, on the principle of self-preservation I am justified in plundering in turn. Since each slave belongs to all; all must, therefore, belong to each."

I shall here make a profession of faith which may shock some, offend others, and be dissented from by all. It is this: Within the bounds of his just earnings, I hold that the slave is fully justified in helping himself to the *gold and silver, and the best apparel of his master, or that of any other slaveholder; and that such taking is not stealing in any just sense of that word.*

The morality of *free* society can have no application to *slave* society. Slaveholders have made it almost impossible for the slave to commit any crime, known either to the laws of God or to the laws of man. If he steals, he takes his own; if he kills his master, he imitates only the heroes of the revolution. Slaveholders I hold to be individually and collectively responsible for all the evils which grow out of the horrid relation, and I believe they will be so held at the judgment, in the sight of a just God. Make a man a slave, and you rob him of moral responsibility. Freedom of choice is the essence of all accountability. But my kind readers are, probably, less concerned about my opinions, than about that which more nearly touches my personal experience; albeit, my opinions have, in some sort, been formed by that experience.

Bad as slaveholders are, I have seldom met with one so entirely destitute of every element of character capable of inspiring respect, as was my present master, Capt. Thomas Auld.

When I lived with him, I thought him incapable of a noble action. The leading trait in his character was intense selfishness. I think he was fully aware of this fact himself, and often tried to conceal it. Capt. Auld was not a *born* slaveholder—not a birthright member of the slaveholding oligarchy. He was only a slaveholder by *marriage-right*; and, of all slaveholders, these latter are, *by far*, the most exacting. There was in him all the love of domination, the pride of mastery, and the swagger of authority, but his rule lacked the vital element of consistency. He could be cruel; but his methods of showing it were cowardly, and evinced his meanness rather than his spirit. His commands were strong, his enforcement weak.

Slaves are not insensible to the whole-souled characteristics of a generous, dashing slaveholder, who is fearless of consequences; and they prefer a master of this bold and daring kind—even with the risk of being shot down for impudence—to the fretful, little soul, who never uses the lash but at the suggestion of a love of gain.

Slaves, too, readily distinguish between the birthright bearing of the original slaveholder and the assumed attitudes of the accidental slaveholder; and while they cannot respect either, they certainly despise the latter more than the former.

The luxury of having slaves wait upon him was something new to Master Thomas; and for it he was wholly unprepared. He was a slaveholder, without the ability to hold or manage his slaves. We seldom called him "master," but generally addressed him by his "bay craft" title—"*Capt. Auld.*" It is easy to see that such conduct might do much to make him appear awkward, and, consequently, fretful. His wife was especially solicitous to have us call her husband "master." "Is your *master* at the store?"—"Where is your *master*?"—"God and tell your *master*"—"I will make your *master* acquainted with your conduct"—she would say; but we were inapt scholars. Especially were I and my sister Eliza inapt in this particular. Aunt Priscilla was less stubborn and defiant in her spirit than Eliza and myself; and, I think, her road was less rough than ours.

In the month of August, 1833, when I had almost become desperate under the treatment of Master Thomas, and when I entertained more strongly than ever the oft-repeated determination to run away, a circumstance occurred which seemed to promise brighter and better days for us all. At a Methodist camp-meeting, held in the Bay Side, (a famous place for camp-meetings,) about eight miles from St. Michael's, Master Thomas came out with a profession of religion. He had long been an object of interest to the church, and to the ministers, as I had seen by the repeated visits and lengthy exhortations of the latter. He was a fish quite worth catching, for he had money and standing. In the community of St. Michael's he was equal to the best citizen. He was strictly temperate; *perhaps*, from principle, but most likely, from interest. There was very little to do for him, to give him the appearance of piety, and to make him a pillar in the church. Well, the camp-meeting continued a week; people gathered from all parts of the county, and two steamboat loads came from Baltimore. The ground was happily chosen; seats were arranged; a stand erected; a rude altar fenced in, fronting the preachers' stand, with straw in it for the accommodation of mourners. This latter would hold at least one hundred persons. In front, and on the sides of the preachers' stand, and outside the long rows of seats, rose the first class of stately tents, each vieing with the other in strength, neatness, and capacity for accommodating its inmates. Behind this first circle of tents was another, less imposing, which reached round the camp-ground to the speakers' stand. Outside this second class of tents were covered wagons, ox carts, and vehicles of every shape and size. These served as tents to their owners. Outside of these, huge fires were burning, in all directions, where roasting, and boiling, and frying, were going on, for the benefit of those who were attending to their own spiritual welfare within the circle. *Behind* the preachers' stand, a narrow space was marked out for the use of the colored people. There were no seats provided for this class of persons; the preachers addressed them, "*over the left*," if they addressed them at all. After the preaching was over, at every service, an invitation was given to mourners to come into the pen; and, in some cases, ministers went out to persuade men and women to come in. By one of these ministers, Master Thomas Auld was persuaded to go inside the pen. I was deeply interested in that matter, and followed; and, though colored people were not allowed either in the pen or in front of the preachers' stand, I ventured to take my stand at a sort of half-way place between the blacks and whites, where I could distinctly see the movements of mourners, and especially the progress of Master Thomas.

"If he has got religion," thought I, "he will emancipate his slaves; and if he should not do so much as this, he will, at any rate, behave toward us more kindly, and feed us more generously than he has heretofore done." Appealing to my own religious experience, and judging my master by what was true in my own case, I could not regard him as soundly converted, unless some such good results followed his profession of religion.

But in my expectations I was doubly disappointed; Master Thomas was *Master Thomas* still. The fruits of his righteousness were to show themselves in no such way as I had anticipated. His conversion was not to change his relation toward men—at any rate not toward BLACK men—but toward God. My faith, I confess, was not great. There was something in his appearance that, in my mind, cast a doubt over his conversion. Standing where I did, I could see his every movement. I watched very narrowly while he remained in the little pen; and although I saw that his face was extremely red, and his hair disheveled, and though I heard him groan, and saw a stray tear halting on his cheek, as if inquiring "which way shall I go?"—I could not wholly confide in the genuineness of his conversion. The hesitating behavior of that tear-drop, and its loneliness, distressed me, and cast a doubt upon the whole transaction, of which it was a part. But people said, *"Capt. Auld had come through,"* and it was for me to hope for the best. I was bound to do this, in charity, for I, too, was religious, and had been in the church full three years, although now I was not more than sixteen years old. Slaveholders may, sometimes, have confidence in the piety of some of their slaves; but the slaves seldom have confidence in the piety of their masters. *"He cant go to heaven with our blood in his skirts,"* is a settled point in the creed of every slave; rising superior to all teaching to the contrary, and standing forever as a fixed fact. The highest evidence the slaveholder can give the slave of his acceptance with God, is the emancipation of his slaves. This is proof that he is willing to give up all to God, and for the sake of God. Not to do this, was, in my estimation, and in the opinion of all the slaves, an evidence of half-heartedness, and wholly inconsistent with the idea of genuine conversion. I had read, also, somewhere in the Methodist Discipline, the following question and answer:[5]

"*Question.* What shall be done for the extirpation of slavery?

"*Answer.* We declare that we are as much as ever convinced of the great evil of slavery; therefore, no slaveholder shall be eligible to any official station in our church."

These words sounded in my ears for a long time, and encouraged me to hope. But, as I have before said, I was doomed to disappointment. Master Thomas seemed to be aware of my hopes and expectations concerning him. I have thought, before now, that he looked at me in answer to my glances, as much as to say, "I will teach you, young man, that, though I have parted with my sins, I have not parted with my sense. I shall hold my slaves, and go to heaven too."

Possibly, to convince us that we must not presume *too much* upon his recent conversion, he became rather more rigid and stringent in his exactions. There always was a scarcity of good nature about the man; but now his whole countenance was *soured* over with the seemings of piety. His religion, therefore, neither made him emancipate his slaves, nor caused him to treat them with greater humanity. If religion had any effect on his character at all, it made him more cruel and hateful in all his ways. The natural wickedness of his heart had not been removed, but only reënforced, by the profession of religion. Do I judge him harshly? God forbid. Facts *are* facts. Capt. Auld made the greatest profession of piety. His house was, literally, a house of prayer. In the morning, and in the evening, loud prayers and hymns were heard there, in which both himself and his wife joined; yet, *no more meal* was brought from the mill, *no more attention* was paid to the moral welfare of the kitchen; and nothing was done to make us feel that the heart of Master Thomas was one whit better than it was before he went into the little pen, opposite to the preachers' stand, on the camp ground.

Our hopes (founded on the discipline) soon vanished; for the authorities let him into the church *at once*, and before he was out of his term of *probation*, I heard of his leading class! He distinguished himself greatly among the brethren, and was soon an exhorter. His progress was almost as rapid as the growth of the fabled vine of Jack's bean.[6] No man was more active than he, in revivals. He would go many miles to assist in carrying them on, and in getting outsiders interested in religion. His house being one of the holiest, if not the happiest in St. Michael's, became the "preachers' home." These preachers evidently liked to share Master Thomas's hospitality; for while he *starved* us, he *stuffed* them. Three or four of

---

5. From *The Doctrines and Discipline of the Methodist Episcopal Church* (1832), 191–92.
6. In the English fairy tale "Jack and the Beanstalk."

these ambassadors of the gospel—according to slavery—have been there at a time; all living on the fat of the land, while we, in the kitchen, were nearly starving. Not often did we get a smile of recognition from these holy men. They seemed almost as unconcerned about our getting to heaven, as they were about our getting out of slavery. To this general charge there was one exception—the Rev. GEORGE COOKMAN. Unlike Rev. Messrs. Storks, Ewry, Hickey, Humphrey and Cooper,[7] (all whom were on the St. Michael's circuit,) he kindly took an interest in our temporal and spiritual welfare. Our souls and our bodies were all alike sacred in his sight; and he really had a good deal of genuine anti-slavery feeling mingled with his colonization ideas.[8] There was not a slave in our neighborhood that did not love, and almost venerate, Mr. Cookman. It was pretty generally believed that he had been chiefly instrumental in bringing one of the largest slaveholders—Mr. Samuel Harrison—in that neighborhood, to emancipate all his slaves,[9] and, indeed, the general impression was, that Mr. Cookman had labored faithfully with slaveholders, whenever he met them, to induce them to emancipate their bondmen, and that he did this as a religious duty. When this good man was at our house, we were all sure to be called in to prayers in the morning; and he was not slow in making inquiries as to the state of our minds, nor in giving us a word of exhortation and of encouragement. Great was the sorrow of all the slaves, when this faithful preacher of the gospel was removed from the Talbot county circuit. He was an eloquent preacher, and possessed what few ministers, south of Mason Dixon's line,[1] possess, or *dare* to show, viz: a warm and philanthropic heart. The Mr. Cookman, of whom I speak, was an Englishman by birth, and perished while on his way to England, on board the ill-fated President. Could the thousands of slaves in Maryland, know the fate of the good man, to whose words of comfort they were so largely indebted, they would thank me for dropping a tear on this page, in memory of their favorite preacher, friend and benefactor.

But, let me return to Master Thomas, and to my experience, after his conversion. In Baltimore, I could, occasionally, get into a Sabbath school, among the free children, and receive lessons, with

---

7. George Cookman, who abandoned his career in business for the ministry, was an anti-slavery preacher who became chaplain to the U.S. Congress. Levi Storks and Joshua Humphries were church elders. William Urey and William Hickey were traveling ministers. Ignatius T. Cooper was a former attorney who became a circuit preacher.
8. Refers to the notion that persons of African descent living in the United States—both enslaved and free—should return to Africa and establish Christian colonies there.
9. In his will, Harrison emancipated his enslaved persons and left a legacy to George Cookman.
1. Mason and Dixon's Line was surveyed 1763–67 by Charles Mason and Jeremiah Dixon to resolve a border dispute among Maryland, Pennsylvania, Delaware, and Virginia (now West Virginia). Before the Missouri Compromise of 1820, the Mason-Dixon Line marked the northern limit of slavery.

the rest; but, having already learned both to read and to write, I was more of a teacher than a pupil, even there. When, however, I went back to the Eastern Shore, and was at the house of Master Thomas, I was neither allowed to teach, nor to be taught. The whole community—with but a single exception, among the whites—frowned upon everything like imparting instruction either to slaves or to free colored persons. That single exception, a pious young man, named Wilson, asked me, one day, if I would like to assist him in teaching a little Sabbath school, at the house of a free colored man in St. Michael's, named James Mitchell. The idea was to me a delightful one, and I told him I would gladly devote as much of my Sabbaths as I could command, to that most laudable work. Mr. Wilson soon mustered up a dozen old spelling books, and a few testaments; and we commenced operations, with some twenty scholars, in our Sunday school. Here, thought I, is something worth living for; here is an excellent chance for usefulness; and I shall soon have a company of young friends, lovers of knowledge, like some of my Baltimore friends, from whom I now felt parted forever.

Our first Sabbath passed delightfully, and I spent the week after very joyously. I could not go to Baltimore, but I could make a little Baltimore here. At our second meeting, I learned that there was some objection to the existence of the Sabbath school; and, sure enough, we had scarcely got at work—*good work*, simply teaching a few colored children how to read the gospel of the Son of God—when in rushed a mob, headed by Mr. Wright Fairbanks and Mr. Garrison West—two class-leaders[2]—and Master Thomas; who, armed with sticks and other missiles, drove us off, and commanded us never to meet for such a purpose again. One of this pious crew told me, that as for my part, I wanted to be another Nat Turner; and if I did not look out, I should get as many balls into me, as Nat did into him.[3] Thus ended the infant Sabbath school, in the town of St. Michael's. The reader will not be surprised when I say, that the breaking up of my Sabbath school, by these class-leaders, and professedly holy men, did not serve to strengthen my religious convictions. The cloud over my St. Michael's home grew heavier and blacker than ever.

It was not merely the agency of Master Thomas, in breaking up and destroying my Sabbath school, that shook my confidence in the power of southern religion to make men wiser or better; but I saw in him all the cruelty and meanness, *after* his conversion, which he had

2. West was an illiterate oysterman and Wrightson Fairbanks was a prominent figure at Sardis Chapel. "Class-leaders": respected members of the Methodist Church who led a "class" consisting of twelve church members.
3. See note 2 on p. 109. "Balls" refer to musket balls fired from a shotgun. In fact, Nat Turner died by hanging (though the rebel leader was flayed and beheaded afterwards).

exhibited before he made a profession of religion. His cruelty and meanness were especially displayed in his treatment of my unfortunate cousin, Henny, whose lameness made her a burden to him. I have no extraordinary personal hard usage toward myself to complain of, against him, but I have seen him tie up the lame and maimed woman, and whip her in a manner most brutal, and shocking; and then, with blood-chilling blasphemy, he would quote the passage of scripture, "That servant which knew his lord's will, and prepared not himself, neither did according to his will, shall be beaten with many stripes."[4] Master would keep this lacerated woman tied up by her wrists, to a bolt in the joist, three, four and five hours at a time. He would tie her up early in the morning, whip her with a cowskin before breakfast; leave her tied up; go to his store, and, returning to his dinner, repeat the castigation; laying on the rugged lash, on flesh already made raw by repeated blows. He seemed desirous to get the poor girl out of existence, or, at any rate, off his hands. In proof of this, he afterwards gave her away to his sister Sarah, (Mrs. Cline;) but, as in the case of Master Hugh, Henny was soon returned on his hands. Finally, upon a pretense that he could do nothing with her, (I use his own words,) he "set her adrift, to take care of herself." Here was a recently converted man, holding, with tight grasp, the well-framed, and able bodied slaves left him by old master—the persons, who, in freedom, could have taken care of themselves; yet, turning loose the only cripple among them, virtually to starve and die.

No doubt, had Master Thomas been asked, by some pious northern brother, *why* he continued to sustain the relation of a slaveholder, to those whom he retained, his answer would have been precisely the same as many other religious slaveholders have returned to that inquiry, viz: "I hold my slaves for their own good."

Bad as my condition was when I lived with Master Thomas, I was soon to experience a life far more goading and bitter. The many differences springing up between myself and Master Thomas, owing to the clear perception I had of his character, and the boldness with which I defended myself against his capricious complaints, led him to declare that I was unsuited to his wants; that my city life had affected me perniciously; that, in fact, it had almost ruined me for every good purpose, and had fitted me for everything that was bad. One of my greatest faults, or offenses, was that of letting his horse get away, and go down to the farm belonging to his father-in-law. The animal had a liking for that farm, with which I fully sympathized. Whenever I let it out, it would go dashing down the road to Mr. Hamilton's, as if going on a grand frolic. My horse gone, of

4. Cf. Luke 12.47.

course I must go after it. The explanation of our mutual attachment to the place is the same; the horse found there good pasturage, and I found there plenty of bread. Mr. Hamilton had his faults, but starving his slaves was not among them. He gave food, in abundance, and that, too, of an excellent quality. In Mr. Hamilton's cook—Aunt Mary—I found a most generous and considerate friend. She never allowed me to go there without giving me bread enough to make good the deficiencies of a day or two. Master Thomas at last resolved to endure my behavior no longer; he could neither keep me, nor his horse, we liked so well to be at his father-in-law's farm. I had now lived with him nearly nine months, and he had given me a number of severe whippings, without any visible improvement in my character, or my conduct; and now he was resolved to put me out—as he said—"*to be broken.*"

There was, in the Bay Side, very near the camp ground, where my master got his religious impressions, a man named Edward Covey, who enjoyed the execrated reputation, of being a first rate hand at breaking young negroes.[5] This Covey was a poor man, a farm renter; and this reputation, (hateful as it was to the slaves and to all good men,) was, at the same time, of immense advantage to him. It enabled him to get his farm tilled with very little expense, compared with what it would have cost him without this most extraordinary reputation. Some slaveholders thought it an advantage to let Mr. Covey have the government of their slaves a year or two, almost free of charge, for the sake of the excellent training such slaves got under his happy management! Like some horse breakers, noted for their skill, who ride the best horses in the country without expense, Mr. Covey could have under him, the most fiery bloods of the neighborhood, for the simple reward of returning them to their owners, *well broken.* Added to the natural fitness of Mr. Covey for the duties of his profession, he was said to "enjoy religion," and was as strict in the cultivation of piety, as he was in the cultivation of his farm. I was made aware of his character by some who had been under his hand; and while I could not look forward to going to him with any pleasure, I was glad to get away from St. Michael's. I was sure of getting enough to eat at Covey's, even if I suffered in other respects. *This*, to a hungry man, is not a prospect to be regarded with indifference.

5. Douglass's vivid description of Covey (1806–1875) transformed the slave breaker into one of the most notorious villains in American literature.

CHAPTER XV

Covey, the Negro Breaker

JOURNEY TO MY NEW MASTER'S—MEDITATIONS BY THE WAY—VIEW OF
COVEY'S RESIDENCE—THE FAMILY—THE AUTHOR'S AWKWARDNESS AS
A FIELD HAND—A CRUEL BEATING—WHY IT WAS GIVEN—
DESCRIPTION OF COVEY—FIRST ADVENTURE AT OX DRIVING—HAIR
BREADTH ESCAPES—OX AND MAN ALIKE PROPERTY—COVEY'S
MANNER OF PROCEEDING TO WHIP—HARD LABOR BETTER THAN THE
WHIP FOR BREAKING DOWN THE SPIRIT—CUNNING AND TRICKERY OF
COVEY—FAMILY WORSHIP—SHOCKING CONTEMPT FOR CHASTITY—
THE AUTHOR BROKEN DOWN—GREAT MENTAL AGITATION IN
CONTRASTING THE FREEDOM OF THE SHIPS WITH HIS OWN
SLAVERY—ANGUISH BEYOND DESCRIPTION

THE morning of the first of January, 1834, with its chilling wind and
pinching frost, quite in harmony with the winter in my own mind,
found me, with my little bundle of clothing on the end of a stick,
swung across my shoulder, on the main road, bending my way toward
Covey's, whither I had been imperiously ordered by Master Thomas.
The latter had been as good as his word, and had committed me,
without reserve, to the mastery of Mr. Edward Covey. Eight or ten
years had now passed since I had been taken from my grandmother's
cabin, in Tuckahoe; and these years, for the most part, I had spent
in Baltimore, where—as the reader has already seen—I was treated
with comparative tenderness. I was now about to sound profounder
depths in slave life. The rigors of a field, less tolerable than the field
of battle, awaited me. My new master was notorious for his fierce
and savage disposition, and my only consolation in going to live with
him was, the certainty of finding him precisely as represented by
common fame. There was neither joy in my heart, nor elasticity in
my step, as I started in search of the tyrant's home. Starvation made
me glad to leave Thomas Auld's, and the cruel lash made me dread
to go to Covey's. Escape was impossible; so, heavy and sad, I paced
the seven miles, which separated Covey's house from St. Michael's—
thinking much by the solitary way—averse to my condition; but
thinking was all I could do. Like a fish in a net, allowed to play for a
time, I was now drawn rapidly to the shore, secured at all points.
"I am," thought I, "but the sport of a power which makes no
account, either of my welfare or of my happiness. By a law which I
can clearly comprehend, but cannot evade nor resist, I am ruthlessly snatched from the hearth of a fond grandmother, and hurried away to the home of a mysterious 'old master;' again I am
removed from there, to a master in Baltimore; thence am I snatched

away to the Eastern Shore, to be valued with the beasts of the field, and, with them, divided and set apart for a possessor; then I am sent back to Baltimore; and by the time I have formed new attachments, and have begun to hope that no more rude shocks shall touch me, a difference arises between brothers, and I am again broken up, and sent to St. Michael's; and now, from the latter place, I am footing my way to the home of a new master, where, I am given to understand, that, like a wild young working animal, I am to be broken to the yoke of a bitter and life-long bondage."

With thoughts and reflections like these, I came in sight of a small wood-colored building, about a mile from the main road, which, from the description I had received, at starting, I easily recognized as my new home. The Chesapeake bay—upon the jutting banks of which the little wood-colored house was standing—white with foam, raised by the heavy north-west wind; Poplar Island, covered with a thick, black pine forest, standing out amid this half ocean; and Kent Point, stretching its sandy, desert-like shores out into the foam-crested bay,—were all in sight, and deepened the wild and desolate aspect of my new home.

The good clothes I had brought with me from Baltimore were now worn thin, and had not been replaced; for Master Thomas was as little careful to provide us against cold, as against hunger. Met here by a north wind, sweeping through an open space of forty miles, I was glad to make any port; and, therefore, I speedily pressed on to the little wood-colored house. The family consisted of Mr. and Mrs. Covey; Miss Kemp, (a broken-backed woman,) a sister of Mrs. Covey; William Hughes, cousin to Edward Covey; Caroline, the cook; Bill Smith, a hired man; and myself. Bill Smith, Bill Hughes, and myself, were the working force of the farm, which consisted of three or four hundred acres. I was now, for the first time in my life, to be a field hand; and in my new employment I found myself even more awkward than a green country boy may be supposed to be, upon his first entrance into the bewildering scenes of city life; and my awkwardness gave me much trouble. Strange and unnatural as it may seem, I had been at my new home but three days, before Mr. Covey, (my brother in the Methodist church,) gave me a bitter foretaste of what was in reserve for me. I presume he thought, that since he had but a single year in which to complete his work, the sooner he began, the better. Perhaps he thought that, by coming to blows at once, we should mutually better understand our relations. But to whatever motive, direct or indirect, the cause may be referred, I had not been in his possession three whole days, before he subjected me to a most brutal chastisement. Under his heavy blows, blood flowed freely, and wales were left on my back as large as my little finger. The sores on my back, from this flogging, continued for weeks, for they were kept open by the rough and coarse cloth which I wore for shirting. The occasion and details of this first chapter of my experience as a field hand, must be told, that the reader may see how unreasonable, as well as how cruel, my new master, Covey, was. The whole thing I found to be characteristic of the man; and I was probably treated no worse by him than scores of lads who had previously been committed to him, for reasons similar to those which induced my master to place me with him. But, here are the facts connected with the affair, precisely as they occurred.

On one of the coldest days of the whole month of January, 1834, I was ordered, at day break, to get a load of wood, from a forest about two miles from the house. In order to perform this work, Mr. Covey gave me a pair of unbroken oxen, for, it seems, his breaking abilities had not been turned in this direction; and I may remark, in passing, that working animals in the south, are seldom so well trained as in the north. In due form, and with all proper ceremony, I was introduced to this huge yoke of unbroken oxen, and was carefully told which was "Buck," and which was "Darby"—which was the "in hand," and which was the "off hand" ox. The master of this important ceremony was no less a person than Mr. Covey, himself; and the introduction, was the first of the kind I had ever had. My life, hitherto, had led me away from horned cattle, and I had no knowledge of the art of managing them. What was meant by the "in ox," as against the "off ox," when both were equally fastened to one cart, and under one yoke, I could not very easily divine; and the difference, implied by the names, and the peculiar duties of each, were alike *Greek* to me. Why was not the "off ox" called the "in ox?" Where and what is the reason for this distinction in names, when there is none in the things themselves? After initiating me into the "*woa*," "*back*" "*gee*," "*hither*"—the entire spoken language between oxen and driver—Mr. Covey took a rope, about ten feet long and one inch thick, and placed one end of it around the horns of the "in hand ox," and gave the other end to me, telling me that if the oxen started to run away, as the scamp knew they would, I must hold on to the rope and stop them. I need not tell any one who is acquainted with either the strength or the disposition of an untamed ox, that this order was about as unreasonable, as a command to shoulder a mad bull! I had never driven oxen before, and I was as awkward, as a driver, as it is possible to conceive. It did not answer for me to plead ignorance, to Mr. Covey; there was something in his manner that quite forbade that. He was a man to whom a slave seldom felt any disposition to speak. Cold, distant, morose, with a face wearing all the marks of captions pride and malicious sternness, he repelled all advances. Covey was not a large man; he was only about five feet ten inches in height, I should think; short necked, round shoulders; of quick and wiry motion, of thin and wolfish visage; with a pair of small, greenish-gray eyes, set well back under a forehead without dignity, and constantly in motion, and floating his passions, rather than his thoughts, in sight, but denying them utterance in words. The creature presented an appearance altogether ferocious and sinister, disagreeable and forbidding, in the extreme. When he spoke, it was from the corner of his mouth, and in a sort of light growl, like a dog, when an attempt is made to take a bone from him. The fellow had already made me believe him even *worse* than he had been represented. With his directions, and without stopping to question, I started for the woods, quite anxious to perform my first exploit in driving, in a creditable manner. The distance from the house to the woods gate—a full mile, I should think—was passed over with very little difficulty; for although the animals ran, I was fleet enough, in the open field, to keep pace with them; especially as they pulled me along at the end of the rope; but, on reaching the woods, I was speedily thrown into a distressing plight. The animals took fright, and started off ferociously into the woods, carrying the cart, full tilt, against trees, over stumps, and dashing from side to side, in a manner altogether frightful. As I held the rope, I expected every moment to be crushed between the cart and the huge trees, among which they were so furiously dashing. After running thus for several minutes, my oxen were, finally, brought to a stand, by a tree, against which they dashed themselves with great violence, upsetting the cart, and entangling themselves among sundry young saplings. By the shock, the body of the cart was flung in one direction, and the wheels and tongue in another, and all in the greatest confusion. There I was, all alone, in a thick wood, to which I was a stranger; my cart upset and shattered; my oxen entangled, wild, and enraged; and I, poor soul! but a green hand, to set all this disorder right. I knew no more of oxen, than the ox driver is supposed to know of wisdom. After standing a few moments surveying the damage and disorder, and not without a presentiment that this trouble would draw after it others, even more distressing, I took one end of the cart body, and, by an extra outlay of strength, I lifted it toward the axletree, from which it had been violently flung; and after much pulling and straining, I succeeded in getting the body of the cart in its place. This was an important step out of the difficulty, and its performance increased my courage for the work which remained to be done. The cart was provided with an ax, a tool with which I had become pretty well acquainted in the ship yard at Baltimore. With this, I cut down the saplings by which my oxen were entangled, and again pursued my journey, with my heart in my mouth, lest the oxen should again take it into their senseless heads to cut up a caper. My fears were groundless. Their spree was over for the present, and the rascals now moved off as soberly as though their behavior had been natural and exemplary. On reaching the part of the forest where I had been, the day before, chopping wood, I filled the cart with a heavy load, as a security against another running away. But, the neck of an ox is equal in strength to iron. It defies all ordinary burdens, when excited. Tame and docile to a proverb, when *well* trained, the ox is the most sullen and and intractable of animals when but half broken to the yoke.

I now saw, in my situation, several points of similarity with that of the oxen. They were property, so was I; they were to be broken, so was I. Covey was to break me, I was to break them; break and be broken—such is life.

Half the day already gone, and my face not yet homeward! It required only two day's experience and observation to teach me, that such apparent waste of time would not be lightly overlooked by Covey. I therefore hurried toward home; but, on reaching the lane gate, I met with the crowning disaster for the day. This gate was a fair specimen of southern handicraft. There were two huge posts, eighteen inches in diameter, rough hewed and square, and the heavy gate was so hung on one of these, that it opened only about half the proper distance. On arriving here, it was necessary for me to let go the end of the rope on the horns of the "in hand ox;" and now as soon as the gate was open, and I let go of it to get the rope, again, off went my oxen—making nothing of their load—full tilt; and in doing so they caught the huge gate between the wheel and the cart body, literally crushing it to splinters, and coming only within a few inches of subjecting me to a similar crushing, for I was just in advance of the wheel when it struck the left gate post. With these two hair-breadth escapes, I thought I could successfully explain to Mr. Covey the delay, and avert apprehended punishment. I was not without a faint hope of being commended for the stern resolution which I had displayed in accomplishing the difficult task—a task which, I afterwards learned, even Covey himself would not have undertaken, without first driving the oxen for some time in the open field, preparatory to their going into the woods. But, in this I was disappointed. On coming to him, his countenance assumed an aspect of rigid displeasure, and, as I gave him a history of the casualties of my trip, his wolfish face, with his greenish eyes, became intensely ferocious. "Go back to the woods again," he said, muttering something else about wasting time. I hastily obeyed; but I had not gone far on my way, when I saw him coming after me. My oxen now behaved themselves with singular propriety, opposing their present conduct to my representation of their former antics. I almost wished, now that Covey was coming, they would do something in keeping with the character I had given them; but no, they had already had their spree, and they could afford now to be extra good, readily obeying my orders, and seeming to understand them quite as well as I did myself. On reaching the woods, my tormentor—who seemed all the way to be remarking upon the good behavior of his oxen—came up to me, and ordered me to stop the cart, accompanying the same with the threat that he would now teach me how to break gates, and idle away my time, when he sent me to the woods. Suiting the action to the word, Covey paced off, in his own wiry fashion, to a large, black-gum tree, the young shoots of which are generally used for *ox goads*, they being exceedingly tough. Three of these *goads*, from four to six feet long, he cut off, and trimmed up, with his large jack-knife. This done, he ordered me to take off my clothes. To this unreasonable order I made no reply, but sternly refused to take off my clothing. "If you will beat me," thought I, "you shall do so over my clothes." After many threats, which made no impression on me, he rushed at me with something of the savage fierceness of a wolf, tore off the few and thinly worn clothes I had on, and proceeded to wear out, on my back, the heavy goads which he had cut from the gum tree. This flogging was the first of a series of floggings; and though very severe, it was less so than many which came after it, and these, for offenses far lighter than the gate breaking.

I remained with Mr. Covey one year, (I cannot say I *lived* with him,) and during the first six months that I was there, I was whipped, either with sticks or cowskins, every week. Aching bones and a sore back were my constant companions. Frequent as the lash was used, Mr. Covey thought less of it, as a means of breaking down my spirit, than that of hard and long continued labor. He worked me steadily, up to the point of my powers of endurance. From the dawn of day in the morning, till the darkness was complete in the evening, I was kept at hard work, in the field or the woods. At certain seasons of the year, we were all kept in the field till eleven and twelve o'clock at night. At these times, Covey would attend us in the field, and urge us on with words or blows, as it seemed best to him. He had, in his life, been an overseer, and he well understood the business of slave driving. There was no deceiving him. He knew just what a man or boy could do, and he held both to strict account. When he pleased, he would work himself, like a very Turk,[1] making everything fly before him. It was, however, scarcely necessary for Mr. Covey to be really present in the field, to have his work go on industriously. He

---

1. "like a very Turk": idiomatic 19th-century American proverb often attached to slave-owners. Here it conveys the meaning of working with great intensity.

had the faculty of making us feel that he was always present. By a series of adroitly managed surprises, which he practiced, I was prepared to expect him at any moment. His plan was, never to approach the spot where his hands were at work, in an open, manly and direct manner. No thief was ever more artful in his devices than this man Covey. He would creep and crawl, in ditches and gullies; hide behind stumps and bushes, and practice so much of the cunning of the serpent, that Bill Smith and I—between ourselves—never called him by any other name than "*the snake.*" We fancied that in his eyes and his gait we could see a snakish resemblance. One half of his proficiency in the art of negro breaking, consisted, I should think, in this species of cunning. We were never secure. He could see or hear us nearly all the time. He was, to us, behind every stump, tree, bush and fence on the plantation. He carried this kind of trickery so far, that he would sometimes mount his horse, and make believe he was going to St. Michael's; and, in thirty minutes afterward, you might find his horse tied in the woods, and the snake-like Covey lying flat in the ditch, with his head lifted above its edge, or in a fence corner, watching every movement of the slaves! I have known him walk up to us and give us special orders, as to our work, in advance, as if he were leaving home with a view to being absent several days; and before he got half way to the house, he would avail himself of our inattention to his movements, to turn short on his heels, conceal himself behind a fence corner or a tree, and watch us until the going down of the sun. Mean and contemptible as is all this, it is in keeping with the character which the life of a slaveholder is calculated to produce. There is no earthly inducement, in the slave's condition, to incite him to labor faithfully. The fear of punishment is the sole motive for any sort of industry, with him. Knowing this fact, as the slaveholder does, and judging the slave by himself, he naturally concludes the slave will be idle whenever the cause for this fear is absent. Hence, all sorts of petty deceptions are practiced, to inspire this fear.

But, with Mr. Covey, trickery was natural. Everything in the shape of learning or religion, which he possessed, was made to conform to this semi-lying propensity. He did not seem conscious that the practice had anything unmanly, base or contemptible about it. It was a part of an important system, with him, essential to the relation of master and slave. I thought I saw, in his very religious devotions, this controlling element of his character. A long prayer at night made up for the short prayer in the morning; and few men could seem more devotional than he, when he had nothing else to do.

Mr. Covey was not content with the cold style of family worship, adopted in these cold latitudes, which begin and end with a simple prayer. No! the voice of praise, as well as of prayer, must be heard in his house, night and morning. At first, I was called upon to bear some part in these exercises; but the repeated flogging given me by Covey, turned the whole thing into mockery. He was a poor singer, and mainly relied on me for raising the hymn for the family, and when I failed to do so, he was thrown into much confusion. I do not think that he ever abused me on account of these vexations. His religion was a thing altogether apart from his worldly concerns. He knew nothing of it as a holy principle, directing and controlling his daily life, making the latter conform to the requirements of the gospel. One or two facts will illustrate his character better than a volume of generalities.

I have already said, or implied, that Mr. Edward Covey was a poor man. He was, in fact, just commencing to lay the foundation of his fortune, as fortune is regarded in a slave state. The first condition of wealth and respectability there, being the ownership of human property, every nerve is strained, by the poor man, to obtain it, and very little regard is had to the manner of obtaining it. In pursuit of this object, pious as Mr. Covey was, he proved himself to be as unscrupulous and base as the worst of his neighbors. In the beginning, he was only able—as he said—"to buy one slave;" and, scandalous and shocking as is the fact, he boasted that he bought her simply "*as a breeder.*" But the worst is not told in this naked statement. This young woman (Caroline was her name) was virtually compelled by Mr. Covey to abandon herself to the object for which he had purchased her; and the result was, the birth of twins at the end of the year. At this addition to his human stock, both Edward Covey and his wife, Susan, were extatic with joy. No one dreamed of reproaching the woman, or of finding fault with the hired man—Bill Smith—the father of the children, for Mr. Covey himself had locked the two up together every night, thus inviting the result.

But I will pursue this revolting subject no further. No better illustration of the unchaste and demoralizing character of slavery can be found, than is furnished in the fact that this professedly christian slaveholder, amidst all his prayers and hymns, was shamelessly and boastfully encouraging, and actually compelling, in his own house, undisguised and unmitigated fornication, as a means of increasing his human stock. I may remark here, that, while this fact will be read with disgust and shame at the north, it will be *laughed at*, as smart and praiseworthy in Mr. Covey, at the south; for a man is no more condemned there for buying a woman and devoting her to this life of dishonor, than for buying a cow, and raising stock from her. The same rules are observed, with a view to increasing the number and quality of the former, as of the latter.

I will here reproduce what I said of my own experience in this wretched place, more than ten years ago:[2]

"If at any one time of my life, more than another, I was made to drink the bitterest dregs of slavery, that time was during the first six months of my stay with Mr. Covey. We were worked all weathers. It was never too hot or too cold; it could never rain, blow, snow, or hail too hard for us to work in the field. Work, work, work, was scarcely more the order of the day than of the night. The longest days were too short for him, and the shortest nights were too long for him. I was somewhat unmanageable when I first went there; but a few months of this discipline tamed me. Mr. Covey succeeded in breaking me. I was broken in body, soul and spirit. My natural elasticity was crushed; my intellect languished; the disposition to read departed; the cheerful spark that lingered about my eye died; the dark night of slavery closed in upon me; and behold a man transformed into a brute!

"Sunday was my only leisure time. I spent this in a sort of beast-like stupor, between sleep and wake, under some large tree. At times, I would rise up, a flash of energetic freedom would dart through my soul, accompanied with a faint beam of hope, that flickered for a moment, and then vanished. I sank down again, mourning over my wretched condition. I was sometimes prompted to take my life, and that of Covey, but was prevented by a combination of hope and fear. My sufferings on this plantation seem now like a dream rather than a stern reality.

"Our house stood within a few rods of the Chesapeake bay, whose broad bosom was ever white with sails from every quarter of the habitable globe. Those beautiful vessels, robed in purest white, so delightful to the eye of freemen, were to me so many shrouded ghosts, to terrify and torment me with thoughts of my wretched condition. I have often, in the deep stillness of a summer's Sabbath, stood all alone upon the banks of that noble bay, and traced, with saddened heart and tearful eye, the countless number of sails moving off to the mighty ocean. The sight of these always affected me powerfully. My thoughts would compel utterance; and there, with no audience but the Almighty, I would pour out my soul's complaint in my rude way, with an apostrophe to the moving multitude of ships:

"'You are loosed from your moorings, and free; I am fast in my chains, and am a slave! You move merrily before the gentle gale, and I sadly before the bloody whip! You are freedom's

---

2. This block quotation is from Chapter 10 of Douglass's *Narrative*.

swift-winged angels, that fly around the world; I am confined in bands of iron! O, that I were free! O, that I were on one of your gallant decks, and under your protecting wing! Alas! betwixt me and you the turbid waters roll. Go on, go on. O that I could also go! Could I but swim! If I could fly! O, why was I born a man, of whom to make a brute! The glad ship is gone; she hides in the dim distance. I am left in the hottest hell of unending slavery. O God, save me! God, deliver me! Let me be free! Is there any God? Why am I a slave? I will run away. I will not stand it. Get caught, or get clear, I'll try it. I had as well die with ague as with fever. I have only one life to lose. I had as well be killed running as die standing. Only think of it; one hundred miles straight north, and I am free! Try it? Yes! God helping me, I will. It cannot be that I shall live and die a slave. I will take to the water. This very bay shall yet bear me into freedom. The steamboats steered in a north-east coast from North Point. I will do the same; and when I get to the head of the bay, I will turn my canoe adrift, and walk straight through Delaware into Pennsylvania. When I get there, I shall not be required to have a pass;[3] I will travel without being disturbed. Let but the first opportunity offer, and, come what will, I am off. Meanwhile, I will try to bear up under the yoke. I am not the only slave in the world. Why should I fret? I can bear as much as any of them. Besides, I am but a boy, and all boys are bound to some one. It may be that my misery in slavery will only increase my happiness when I get free. There is a better day coming.'"

I shall never be able to narrate the mental experience through which it was my lot to pass during my stay at Covey's. I was completely wrecked, changed and bewildered; goaded almost to madness at one time, and at another reconciling myself to my wretched condition. Everything in the way of kindness, which I had experienced at Baltimore; all my former hopes and aspirations for usefulness in the world, and the happy moments spent in the exercises of religion, contrasted with my then present lot, but increased my anguish.

I suffered bodily as well as mentally. I had neither sufficient time in which to eat or to sleep, except on Sundays. The over work, and the brutal chastisements of which I was the victim, combined with that ever-gnawing and soul-devouring thought—"*I am a slave—a slave for life—a slave with no rational ground to hope for freedom*"—rendered me a living embodiment of mental and physical wretchedness.

3. See note 8 on p. 112.

CHAPTER XVI

Another Pressure of the Tyrant's Vice

EXPERIENCE AT COVEY'S SUMMED UP—FIRST SIX MONTHS SEVERER
THAN THE SECOND—PRELIMINARIES TO THE CHANGE—REASONS FOR
NARRATING THE CIRCUMSTANCES—SCENE IN THE TREADING YARD—
AUTHOR TAKEN ILL—UNUSUAL BRUTALITY OF COVEY—AUTHOR
ESCAPES TO ST. MICHAEL'S—THE PURSUIT—SUFFERING IN THE
WOODS—DRIVEN BACK AGAIN TO COVEY'S—BEARING OF "MASTER
THOMAS"—THE SLAVE IS NEVER SICK—NATURAL TO EXPECT SLAVES
TO FEIGN SICKNESS—LAZINESS OF SLAVEHOLDERS.

THE foregoing chapter, with all its horrid incidents and shocking features, may be taken as a fair representation of the first six months of my life at Covey's. The reader has but to repeat, in his own mind, once a week, the scene in the woods, where Covey subjected me to his merciless lash, to have a true idea of my bitter experience there, during the first period of the breaking process through which Mr. Covey carried me. I have no heart to repeat each separate transaction, in which I was a victim of his violence and brutality. Such a narration would fill a volume much larger than the present one. I aim only to give the reader a truthful impression of my slave life, without unnecessarily affecting him with harrowing details.

As I have elsewhere intimated that my hardships were much greater during the first six months of my stay at Covey's, than during the remainder of the year, and as the change in my condition was owing to causes which may help the reader to a better understanding of human nature, when subjected to the terrible extremities of slavery, I will narrate the circumstances of this change, although I may seem thereby to applaud my own courage.

You have, dear reader, seen me humbled, degraded, broken down, enslaved, and brutalized, and you understand how it was done; now let us see the converse of all this, and how it was brought about; and this will take us through the year 1834.

On one of the hottest days of the month of August, of the year just mentioned, had the reader been passing through Covey's farm, he might have seen me at work, in what is there called the "treading yard"—a yard upon which wheat is trodden out from the straw, by the horses' feet. I was there, at work, feeding the "fan," or rather bringing wheat to the fan, while Bill Smith was feeding. Our force consisted of Bill Hughes, Bill Smith, and a slave by the name of Eli; the latter having been hired for this occasion. The work was simple, and required strength and activity, rather than any skill or intelligence, and yet, to one entirely unused to such work, it came very hard. The heat was intense and overpowering, and there was much hurry to get the wheat, trodden out that day, through the fan; since, if that work was done an hour before sundown, the hands would have, according to a promise of Covey, that hour added to their night's rest. I was not behind any of them in the wish to complete the day's work before sundown, and, hence, I struggled with all my might to get the work forward. The promise of one hour's repose on a week day, was sufficient to quicken my pace, and to spur me on to extra endeavor. Besides, we had all planned to go fishing, and I certainly wished to have a hand in that. But I was disappointed, and the day turned out to be one of the bitterest I ever experienced. About three o'clock, while the sun was pouring down his burning rays, and not a breeze was stirring, I broke down; my strength failed me; I was seized with a violent aching of the head, attended with extreme dizziness, and trembling in every limb. Finding what was coming, and feeling it would never do to stop work, I nerved myself up, and staggered on until I fell by the side of the wheat fan, feeling that the earth had fallen upon me. This brought the entire work to a dead stand. There was work for four; each one had his part to perform, and each part depended on the other, so that when one stopped, all were compelled to stop. Covey, who had now become my dread, as well as my tormentor, was at the house, about a hundred yards from where I was fanning, and instantly, upon hearing the fan stop, he came down to the treading yard, to inquire into the cause of our stopping. Bill Smith told him I was sick, and that I was unable longer to bring wheat to the fan.

I had, by this time, crawled away, under the side of a post-and-rail fence, in the shade, and was exceedingly ill. The intense heat of the sun, the heavy dust rising from the fan, the stooping, to take up the wheat from the yard, together with the hurrying, to get through, had caused a rush of blood to my head. In this condition, Covey finding out where I was, came to me; and, after standing over me a while, he asked me what the matter was. I told him as well as I could, for it was with difficulty that I could speak. He then gave me a savage kick in the side, which jarred my whole frame, and commanded me to get up. The man had obtained complete control over me; and if he had commanded me to do any possible thing, I should, in my then state of mind, have endeavored to comply. I made an effort to rise, but fell back in the attempt, before gaining my feet. The brute now gave me another heavy kick, and again told me to rise. I again tried to rise, and succeeded in gaining my feet; but, upon stooping to get the tub with which I was feeding the fan, I again staggered and fell to the ground; and I must have so fallen, had I been sure that a hundred bullets would have pierced me, as the consequence. While down, in this sad condition, and perfectly helpless, the merciless negro breaker took up the hickory slab, with which Hughes had been striking off the wheat to a level with the sides of the half bushel measure, (a very hard weapon,) and with the sharp edge of it, he dealt me a heavy blow on my head which made a large gash, and caused the blood to run freely, saying, at the same time, "If *you have got the headache, I'll cure you.*" This done, he ordered me again to rise, but I made no effort to do so; for I had made up my mind that it was useless, and that the heartless monster might *now* do his worst; he could but kill me, and that might put me out of my misery. Finding me unable to rise, or rather despairing of my doing so, Covey left me, with a view to getting on with the work without me. I was bleeding very freely, and my face was soon covered with my warm blood. Cruel and merciless as was the motive that dealt that blow, dear reader, the wound was fortunate for me. Bleeding was never more efficacious. The pain in my head speedily abated, and I was soon able to rise. Covey had, as I have said, now left me to my fate; and the question was, shall I return to my work, or shall I find my way to St. Michael's, and make Capt. Auld acquainted with the atrocious cruelty of his brother Covey, and beseech him to get me another master? Remembering the object he had in view, in placing me under the management of Covey, and further, his cruel treatment of my poor crippled cousin, Henny, and his meanness in the matter of feeding and clothing his slaves, there was little ground to hope for a favorable reception at the hands of Capt. Thomas Auld. Nevertheless, I resolved to go straight to Capt. Auld, thinking that, if not animated by motives of humanity, he might be induced to interfere on my behalf from selfish considerations. "He cannot," thought I, "allow his property to be thus bruised and battered, marred and defaced; and I will go to him, and tell him the simple truth about the matter." In order to get to St. Michael's, by the most favorable and direct road, I must walk seven miles; and this, in my sad condition, was no easy performance. I had already lost much blood; I was exhausted by over exertion; my sides were sore from the heavy blows planted there by the stout boots of Mr. Covey; and I was, in every way, in an unfavorable plight for the journey. I however watched my chance, while the cruel and cunning Covey was looking in an opposite direction, and started off, across the field, for St. Michael's. This was a daring step; if it failed, it would only exasperate Covey, and increase the rigors of my bondage, during the remainder of my term of service under him; but the step was taken, and I must go forward. I succeeded in getting nearly half way across the broad field, toward the woods, before Mr. Covey observed me. I was still bleeding, and the exertion of running had started the blood afresh. *"Come back! Come back!"* vociferated Covey, with threats of what he would do if I did not return instantly. But, disregarding his calls and his threats, I pressed on toward the woods as fast as my feeble state would allow. Seeing no signs of my stopping, Covey caused his horse to be brought out and saddled, as if he intended to pursue me. The race was now to be an unequal one; and, thinking I might be overhauled by him, if I kept the main road, I walked nearly the whole distance in the woods, keeping far enough from the road to avoid detection and pursuit. But, I had not gone far, before my little strength again failed me, and I laid down. The blood was still oozing from the wound in my head; and, for a time, I suffered more than I can describe. There I was, in the deep woods, sick and emaciated, pursued by a wretch whose character for revolting cruelty beggars all opprobrious speech—bleeding, and almost bloodless. I was not without the fear of bleeding to death. The thought of dying in the woods, all alone, and of being torn to pieces by the buzzards, had not yet been rendered tolerable by my many troubles and hardships, and I was glad when the shade of the trees, and the cool evening breeze, combined with my matted hair to stop the flow of blood. After lying there about three quarters of an hour, brooding over the singular and mournful lot to which I was doomed, my mind passing over the whole scale or circle of belief and unbelief, from faith in the overruling providence of God, to the blackest atheism,[1] I again took up my journey toward St. Michael's, more weary and sad than in the morning when I left Thomas Auld's for the home of Mr. Covey. I was bare-footed and bare-headed, and in my shirt sleeves. The way was through bogs and briers, and I tore my feet often during the journey. I was full five hours in going the seven or eight miles; partly, because of the difficulties of the way, and partly, because of the feebleness induced by my illness, bruises and loss of blood. On gaining my master's store, I presented an appearance of wretchedness and woe, fitted to move any but a heart of stone. From the crown of my head to the sole of my feet, there were marks of blood. My hair was all clotted with dust and blood, and the back of my shirt was literally stiff with the same. Briers and thorns had scarred and torn my feet and legs, leaving blood marks there. Had I escaped from a den of tigers, I could not have looked worse than I did on reaching St. Michael's. In this unhappy plight, I

1. Douglass's reading of *Representative Men* (1850), by the American writer Ralph Waldo Emerson (1803–1882), may have influenced this passage. Emerson's collection of seven lectures explored the notion of "great men" in society, a concept particularly relevant to Douglass since it was applied to him during his lifetime, and even more so after his death.

appeared before my professedly *christian* master, humbly to invoke the interposition of his power and authority, to protect me from further abuse and violence. I had begun to hope, during the latter part of my tedious journey toward St. Michael's, that Capt. Auld would now show himself in a nobler light than I had ever before seen him. I was disappointed. I had jumped from a sinking ship into the sea; I had fled from the tiger to something worse. I told him all the circumstances, as well as I could; how I was endeavoring to please Covey; how hard I was at work in the present instance; how unwillingly I sunk down under the heat, toil and pain; the brutal manner in which Covey had kicked me in the side; the gash cut in my head; my hesitation about troubling him (Capt. Auld) with complaints; but, that now I felt it would not be best longer to conceal from him the outrages committed on me from time to time by Covey. At first, master Thomas seemed somewhat affected by the story of my wrongs, but he soon repressed his feelings and became cold as iron. It was impossible—as I stood before him at the first—for him to seem indifferent. I distinctly saw his human nature asserting its conviction against the slave system, which made cases like mine *possible*; but, as I have said, humanity fell before the systematic tyranny of slavery. He first walked the floor, apparently much agitated by my story, and the sad spectacle I presented; but, presently, it was *his* turn to talk. He began moderately, by finding excuses for Covey, and ending with a full justification of him, and a passionate condemnation of me. "He had no doubt I deserved the flogging. He did not believe I was sick; I was only endeavoring to get rid of work. My dizziness was laziness, and Covey did right to flog me, as he had done." After thus fairly annihilating me, and rousing himself by his own eloquence, he fiercely demanded what I wished *him* to do in the case!

With such a complete knock-down to all my hopes, as he had given me, and feeling, as I did, my entire subjection to his power, I had very little heart to reply. I must not affirm my innocence of the allegations which he had piled up against me; for that would be impudence, and would probably call down fresh violence as well as wrath upon me. The guilt of a slave is always, and everywhere, presumed; and the innocence of the slaveholder or the slave employer, is always asserted. The word of the slave, against this presumption, is generally treated as impudence, worthy of punishment. "Do you contradict me, you rascal?" is a final silencer of counter statements from the lips of a slave.

Calming down a little in view of my silence and hesitation, and, perhaps, from a rapid glance at the picture of misery I presented, he inquired again, "what I would have him do?" Thus invited a second time, I told Master Thomas I wished him to allow me to get a new home and to find a new master; that, as sure as I went back to live with Mr. Covey again, I should be killed by him; that he would never forgive my coming to him (Capt Auld) with a complaint against him (Covey;) that, since I had lived with him, he had almost crushed my spirit, and I believed that he would ruin me for future service; that my life was not safe in his hands. This, Master Thomas (*my brother in the church*) regarded as "nonsense." "There was no danger of Mr. Covey's killing me; he was a good man, industrious and religious, and he would not think of removing me from that home; "besides," said he,—and this I found was the most distressing thought of all to him—"if you should leave Covey now, that your year has but half expired, I should lose your wages for the entire year. You belong to Mr. Covey for one year, and you *must go back* to him, come what will. You must not trouble me with any more stories about Mr. Covey; and if you do not go immediately home, I will get hold of you myself." This was just what I expected, when I found he had *prejudged* the case against me. "But, Sir," I said, "I am sick and tired, and I cannot get home to-night." At this, he again relented, and finally he allowed me to remain all night at St. Michael's; but said I must be off early in the morning, and concluded his directions by making me swallow a huge dose of *epsom salts*—about the only medicine ever administered to slaves.

It was quite natural for Master Thomas to presume I was feigning sickness to escape work, for he probably thought that were *he* in the place of a slave—with no wages for his work, no praise for well doing, no motive for toil but the lash—he would try every possible scheme by which to escape labor. I say I have no doubt of this; the reason is, that there are not, under the whole heavens, a set of men who cultivate such an intense dread of labor as do the slaveholders. The charge of laziness against the slaves is ever on their lips, and is the standing apology for every species of cruelty and brutality. These men literally "bind heavy burdens, grievous to be borne, and lay them on men's shoulders; but they, themselves, will not move them with one of their fingers."[2]

My kind readers shall have, in the next chapter—what they were led, perhaps, to expect to find in this—namely: an account of my partial disenthrallment from the tyranny of Covey, and the marked change which it brought about.

2. Cf. Matthew 23.4.

CHAPTER XVII

The Last Flogging

A SLEEPLESS NIGHT—RETURN TO COVEY'S—PURSUED BY COVEY—THE
CHASE DEFEATED—VENGEANCE POSTPONED—MUSINGS IN THE
WOODS—THE ALTERNATIVE—DEPLORABLE SPECTACLE—NIGHT IN
THE WOODS—EXPECTED ATTACK—ACCOSTED BY SANDY, A FRIEND,
NOT A HUNTER—SANDY'S HOSPITALITY—THE "ASH CAKE" SUPPER—
THE INTERVIEW WITH SANDY—HIS ADVICE—SANDY A CONJURER AS
WELL AS A CHRISTIAN—THE MAGIC ROOT—STRANGE MEETING WITH
COVEY—HIS MANNER—COVEY'S SUNDAY FACE—AUTHOR'S DEFENSIVE
RESOLVE—THE FIGHT—THE VICTORY, AND ITS RESULTS

SLEEP itself does not always come to the relief of the weary in
body, and the broken in spirit; especially when past troubles only
foreshadow coming disasters. The last hope had been extin-
guished. My master, who I did not venture to hope would protect
me as *a man*, had even now refused to protect me as *his property*;
and had cast me back, covered with reproaches and bruises, into
the hands of a stranger to that mercy which was the soul of the
religion he professed. May the reader never spend such a night as
that allotted to me, previous to the morning which was to herald
my return to the den of horrors from which I had made a temporary escape.

I remained all night—sleep I did not—at St. Michael's; and in the
morning (Saturday) I started off, according to the order of Master
Thomas, feeling that I had no friend on earth, and doubting if I had
one in heaven. I reached Covey's about nine o'clock; and just as I
stepped into the field, before I had reached the house, Covey, true
to his snakish habits, darted out at me from a fence corner, in which
he had secreted himself, for the purpose of securing me. He was
amply provided with a cowskin and a rope; and he evidently intended
to *tie me up*, and to wreak his vengeance on me to the fullest extent.
I should have been an easy prey, had he succeeded in getting his
hands upon me, for I had taken no refreshment since noon on Friday; and this, together with the pelting, excitement, and the loss of
blood, had reduced my strength. I, however, darted back into the
woods, before the ferocious hound could get hold of me, and buried
myself in a thicket, where he lost sight of me. The corn-field afforded
me cover, in getting to the woods. But for the tall corn, Covey would
have overtaken me, and made me his captive. He seemed very much
chagrined that he did not catch me, and gave up the chase, very
reluctantly; for I could see his angry movements, toward the house
from which he had sallied, on his foray.

Well, now I am clear of Covey, and of his wrathful lash, for the present. I am in the wood, buried in its somber gloom, and hushed in its solemn silence; hid from all human eyes; shut in with nature and nature's God, and absent from all human contrivances. Here was a good place to pray; to pray for help for deliverance—a prayer I had often made before. But how could I pray? Covey could pray— Capt. Auld could pray—I would fain pray; but doubts (arising partly from my own neglect of the means of grace, and partly from the sham religion which everywhere prevailed, cast in my mind a doubt upon all religion, and led me to the conviction that prayers were unavailing and delusive) prevented my embracing the opportunity, as a religious one. Life, in itself, had almost become burdensome to me. All my outward relations were against me; I must stay here and starve, (I was already hungry,) or go home to Covey's, and have my flesh torn to pieces, and my spirit humbled under the cruel lash of Covey. This was the painful alternative presented to me. The day was long and irksome. My physical condition was deplorable. I was weak, from the toils of the previous day, and from the want of food and rest; and had been so little concerned about my appearance, that I had not yet washed the blood from my garments. I was an object of horror, even to myself. Life, in Baltimore, when most oppressive, was a paradise to this. What had I done, what had my parents done, that such a life as this should be mine? That day, in the woods, I would have exchanged my manhood for the brutehood of an ox.

Night came. I was still in the woods, unresolved what to do. Hunger had not yet pinched me to the point of going home, and I laid myself down in the leaves to rest; for I had been watching for hunters all day, but not being molested during the day, I expected no disturbance during the night. I had come to the conclusion that Covey relied upon hunger to drive me home; and in this I was quite correct—the facts showed that he had made no effort to catch me, since morning.

During the night, I heard the step of a man in the woods. He was coming toward the place where I lay. A person lying still has the advantage over one walking in the woods, in the day time, and this advantage is much greater at night. I was not able to engage in a physical struggle, and I had recourse to the common resort of the weak. I hid myself in the leaves to prevent discovery. But, as the night rambler in the woods drew nearer, I found him to be a *friend*, not an enemy; it was a slave of Mr. William Groomes, of Easton, a kind hearted fellow, named "Sandy." Sandy lived with Mr. Kemp that year, about four miles from St. Michael's. He, like myself, had been hired out by the year; but, unlike myself, had not been hired out to be broken. Sandy was the husband of a free woman, who lived in the lower part of "*Potpie Neck*," and he was now on his way through the woods, to see her, and to spend the Sabbath with her.

As soon as I had ascertained that the disturber of my solitude was not an enemy, but the good-hearted Sandy—a man as famous among the slaves of the neighborhood for his good nature, as for his good sense—I came out from my hiding place, and made myself known to him. I explained the circumstances of the past two days, which had driven me to the woods, and he deeply compassionated my distress. It was a bold thing for him to shelter me, and I could not ask him to do so; for, had I been found in his hut, he would have suffered the penalty of thirty-nine lashes on his bare back, if not something worse. But, Sandy was too generous to permit the fear of punishment to prevent his relieving a brother bondman from hunger and exposure; and, therefore, on his own motion, I accompanied him to his home, or rather to the home of his wife—for the house and lot were hers. His wife was called up—for it was now about midnight—a fire was made, some Indian meal was soon mixed with salt and water, and an ash cake[1] was baked in a hurry to relieve my hunger. Sandy's wife was not behind him in kindness—both seemed to esteem it a privilege to succor me; for, although I was hated by Covey and by my master, I was loved by the colored people, because *they* thought I was hated for my knowledge, and persecuted because I was feared. I was the *only* slave *now* in that region who could read and write. There had been one other man, belonging to Mr. Hugh Hamilton, who could read, (his name was "Jim,") but he, poor fellow, had, shortly after my coming into the neighborhood, been sold off to the far south. I saw Jim ironed, in the cart, to be carried to Easton for sale,—pinioned like a yearling for the slaughter. My knowledge was now the pride of my brother slaves; and, no doubt, Sandy felt something of the general interest in me on that account. The supper was soon ready, and though I have feasted since, with honorables, lord mayors and aldermen, over the sea, my supper on ash cake and cold water, with Sandy, was the meal, of all my life, most sweet to my taste, and now most vivid in my memory.

Supper over, Sandy and I went into a discussion of what was *possible* for me, under the perils and hardships which now overshadowed my path. The question was, must I go back to Covey, or must I now attempt to run away? Upon a careful survey, the latter was found to be impossible; for I was on a narrow neck of land, every avenue from which would bring me in sight of pursuers. There was the Chesapeake bay to the right, and "Pot-pie" river to the left, and St. Michael's and its neighborhood occupying the only space through which there was any retreat.

1. See note 8 on p. 75.

I found Sandy an old adviser. He was not only a religious man, but he professed to believe in a system for which I have no name. He was a genuine African, and had inherited some of the so called magical powers, said to be possessed by African and eastern nations. He told me that he could help me; that, in those very woods, there was an herb, which in the morning might be found, possessing all the powers required for my protection, (I put his thoughts in my own language;) and that, if I would take his advice, he would procure me the root of the herb of which he spoke. He told me further, that if I would take that root and wear it on my right side, it would be impossible for Covey to strike me a blow; that with this root about my person, no white man could whip me. He said he had carried it for years, and that he had fully tested its virtues. He had never received a blow from a slaveholder since he carried it; and he never expected to receive one, for he always meant to carry that root as a protection. He knew Covey well, for Mrs. Covey was the daughter of Mr. Kemp; and he (Sandy) had heard of the barbarous treatment to which I was subjected, and he wanted to do something for me.

Now all this talk about the root, was, to me, very absurd and ridiculous, if not positively sinful. I at first rejected the idea that the simple carrying a root on my right side, (a root, by the way, over which I walked every time I went into the woods,) could possess any such magic power as he ascribed to it, and I was, therefore, not disposed to cumber my pocket with it. I had a positive aversion to all pretenders to "*divination.*" It was beneath one of my intelligence to countenance such dealings with the devil, as this power implied. But, with all my learning—it was really precious little—Sandy was more than a match for me. "My book learning," he said, "had not kept Covey off me," (a powerful argument just then,) and he entreated me, with flashing eyes, to try this. If it did me no good, it could do me no harm, and it would cost me nothing, any way. Sandy was so earnest, and so confident of the good qualities of this weed, that, to please him, rather than from any conviction of its excellence, I was induced to take it. He had been to me the good Samaritan, and had, almost providentially, found me, and helped me when I could not help myself; how did I know but that the hand of the Lord was in it? With thoughts of this sort, I took the roots from Sandy, and put them in my right hand pocket.

This was, of course, Sunday morning. Sandy now urged me to go home, with all speed, and to walk up bravely to the house, as though nothing had happened. I saw in Sandy too deep an insight into human nature, with all his superstition, not to have some respect for his advice; and perhaps, too, a slight gleam or shadow of his superstition had fallen upon me. At any rate, I started off toward Covey's, as directed by Sandy. Having, the previous night, poured my griefs into Sandy's ears, and got him enlisted in my behalf, having made his wife a sharer in my sorrows, and having, also, become well refreshed by sleep and food, I moved off, quite courageously, toward the much dreaded Covey's. Singularly enough, just as I entered his yard gate, I met him and his wife, dressed in their Sunday best—looking as smiling as angels—on their way to church. The manner of Covey astonished me. There was something really benignant in his countenance. He spoke to me as never before; told me that the pigs had got into the lot, and he wished me to drive them out; inquired how I was, and seemed an altered man. This extraordinary conduct of Covey, really made me begin to think that Sandy's herb had more virtue in it than I, in my pride, had been willing to allow; and, had the day been other than Sunday, I should have attributed Covey's altered manner solely to the magic power of the root. I suspected, however, that the *Sabbath*, and not the *root*, was the real explanation of Covey's manner. His religion hindered him from breaking the Sabbath, but not from breaking my skin. He had more respect for the *day* than for the *man*, for whom the day was mercifully given; for while he would cut and slash my body during the week, he would not hesitate, on Sunday, to teach me the value of my soul, or the way of life and salvation by Jesus Christ.

All went well with me till Monday morning; and then, whether the root had lost its virtue, or whether my tormentor had gone deeper into the black art than myself, (as was sometimes said of him,) or whether he had obtained a special indulgence, for his faithful Sabbath day's worship, it is not necessary for me to know, or to inform the reader; but, this much I *may* say,—the pious and benignant smile which graced Covey's face on *Sunday*, wholly disappeared on *Monday*. Long before daylight, I was called up to go and feed, rub, and curry the horses. I obeyed the call, and I would have so obeyed it, had it been made at an earlier hour, for I had brought my mind to a firm resolve, during that Sunday's reflection, viz: to obey every order, however unreasonable, if it were possible, and, if Mr. Covey should then undertake to beat me, to defend and protect myself to the best of my ability. My religious views on the subject of resisting my master, had suffered a serious shock, by the savage persecution to which I had been subjected, and my hands were no longer tied by my religion. Master Thomas's indifference had severed the last link. I had now to this extent "backslidden" from this point in the slave's religious creed; and I soon had occasion to make my fallen state known to my Sunday-pious brother, Covey.

Whilst I was obeying his order to feed and get the horses ready for the field, and when in the act of going up the stable loft for the purpose of throwing down some blades, Covey sneaked into the stable, in his peculiar snake-like way, and seizing me suddenly by the leg, he brought me to the stable floor, giving my newly mended body a fearful jar. I now forgot my *roots*, and remembered my pledge to *stand up in my own defense*. The brute was endeavoring skillfully to get a slip-knot on my legs, before I could draw up my feet. As soon as I found what he was up to, I gave a sudden spring, (my two day's rest had been of much service to me,) and by that means, no doubt, he was able to bring me to the floor so heavily. He was defeated in his plan of tying me. While down, he seemed to think he had me very securely in his power. He little thought he was—as the rowdies say—"in" for a "rough and tumble" fight; but such was the fact. Whence came the daring spirit necessary to grapple with a man who, eight-and-forty hours before, could, with his slightest word have made me tremble like a leaf in a storm, I do not know; at any rate, *I was resolved to fight*, and, what was better still, I was actually hard at it. The fighting madness had come upon me, and I found my strong fingers firmly attached to the throat of my cowardly tormentor; as heedless of consequences, at the moment, as though we stood as equals before the law. The very color of the man was forgotten. I felt as supple as a cat, and was ready for the snakish creature at every turn. Every blow of his was parried, though I dealt no blows in turn. I was strictly on the *defensive*, preventing him from injuring me, rather than trying to injure him. I flung him on the ground several times, when he meant to have hurled me there. I held him so firmly by the throat, that his blood followed my nails. He held me, and I held him.

All was fair, thus far, and the contest was about equal. My resistance was entirely unexpected, and Covey was taken all aback by it, for he trembled in every limb. *"Are you going to resist*, you scoundrel?" said he. To which, I returned a polite *"yes sir;"* steadily gazing my interrogator in the eye, to meet the first approach or dawning of the blow, which I expected my answer would call forth. But, the conflict did not long remain thus equal. Covey soon cried out lustily for help; not that I was obtaining any marked advantage over him, or was injuring him, but because he was gaining none over me, and was not able, single handed, to conquer me. He called for his cousin Hughes, to come to his assistance, and now the scene was changed. I was compelled to give blows, as well as to parry them; and, since I was, in any case, to suffer for resistance, I felt (as the musty proverb goes) that "I might as well be hanged for an old sheep as a lamb." I was still *defensive* toward Covey, but *aggressive* toward Hughes; and, at the first approach of the latter, I dealt a blow, in my desperation, which fairly sickened my youthful assailant. He went off, bending over with pain, and manifesting no disposition to come within my reach again. The poor fellow was in the act of trying to catch and tie my right hand, and while flattering himself with success, I gave him the kick which sent him staggering away in pain, at the same time that I held Covey with a firm hand.

Taken completely by surprise, Covey seemed to have lost his usual strength and coolness. He was frightened, and stood puffing and blowing, seemingly unable to command words or blows. When he saw that poor Hughes was standing half bent with pain—his courage quite gone—the cowardly tyrant asked if I "meant to persist in my resistance." I told him "I *did mean to resist, come what might;*" that I had been by him treated like a *brute*, during the last six months; and that I should stand it *no longer*. With that, he gave me a shake, and attempted to drag me toward a stick of wood, that was lying just outside the stable door. He meant to knock me down with it; but, just as he leaned over to get the stick, I seized him with both hands by the collar, and, with a vigorous and sudden snatch, I brought my assailant harmlessly, his full length, on the *not over* clean ground—for we were now in the cow yard. He had selected the place for the fight, and it was but right that he should have all the advantages of his own selection.

By this time, Bill, the hired man, came home. He had been to Mr. Hemsley's, to spend the Sunday with his nominal wife, and was coming home on Monday morning, to go to work. Covey and I had been skirmishing from before daybreak, till now, that the sun was almost shooting his beams over the eastern woods, and we were still at it. I could not see where the matter was to terminate. He evidently was afraid to let me go, lest I should again make off to the woods; otherwise, he would probably have obtained arms from the house, to frighten me. Holding me, Covey called upon Bill for assistance. The scene here, had something comic about it. "Bill," who knew *precisely* what Covey wished him to do, affected ignorance, and pretended he did not know what to do. "What shall I do, Mr. Covey," said Bill. "Take hold of him—take hold of him!" said Covey. With a toss of his head, peculiar to Bill, he said, "indeed, Mr. Covey, I want to go to work." "*This is* your work," said Covey; "take hold of him." Bill replied, with spirit, "My master hired me here, to work, and *not* to help you whip Frederick." It was now my turn to speak. "Bill," said I, "don't put your hands on me." To which he replied, "My God! Frederick, I aint goin' to tech ye," and Bill walked off, leaving Covey and myself to settle our matters as best we might.

But, my present advantage was threatened when I saw Caroline (the slave-woman of Covey) coming to the cow yard to milk, for she was a powerful woman, and could have mastered me very easily, exhausted as I now was. As soon as she came into the yard, Covey attempted to rally her to his aid. Strangely—and, I may add, fortunately—Caroline was in no humor to take a hand in any such sport. We were all in open rebellion, that morning. Caroline answered the command of her master to "*take hold of me*," precisely as Bill had answered, but in *her*, it was at greater peril so to answer; she was the slave of Covey, and he could do what he pleased with her. It was *not* so with Bill, and Bill knew it. Samuel Harris, to whom Bill belonged, did not allow his slaves to be beaten, unless they were guilty of some crime which the law would punish. But, poor Caroline, like myself, was at the mercy of the merciless Covey; nor did she escape the dire effects of her refusal. He gave her several sharp blows.

Covey at length (two hours had elapsed) gave up the contest. Letting me go, he said,—puffing and blowing at a great rate—"now, you scoundrel, go to your work; I would not have whipped you half so much as I have had you not resisted." The fact was, *he had not whipped me at all*. He had not, in all the scuffle, drawn a single drop of blood from me. I had drawn blood from him; and, even without this satisfaction, I should have been victorious, because my aim had not been to injure him, but to prevent his injuring me.

During the whole six months that I lived with Covey, after this transaction, he never laid on me the weight of his finger in anger. He would, occasionally, say he did not want to have to get hold of me again—a declaration which I had no difficulty in believing; and I had a secret feeling, which answered, "you need not wish to get hold of me again, for you will be likely to come off worse in a second fight than you did in the first."

Well, my dear reader, this battle with Mr. Covey,—undignified as it was, and as I fear my narration of it is—was the turning point in my "*life as a slave*." It rekindled in my breast the smouldering embers of liberty; it brought up my Baltimore dreams, and revived a sense of my own manhood. I was a changed being after that fight. I was *nothing* before; I WAS A MAN NOW. It recalled to life my crushed self-respect and my self-confidence, and inspired me with a renewed determination to be A FREEMAN. A man, without force, is without the essential dignity of humanity. Human nature is so constituted, that it cannot *honor* a helpless man, although it can *pity* him; and even this it cannot do long, if the signs of power do not arise.

He only can understand the effect of this combat on my spirit, who has himself incurred something, hazarded something, in repelling the unjust and cruel aggressions of a tyrant. Covey was a tyrant, and a cowardly one, withal. After resisting him, I felt as I had never felt before. It was a resurrection from the dark and pestiferous tomb of slavery, to the heaven of comparative freedom. I was no longer a servile coward, trembling under the frown of a brother worm of the dust,[2] but, my long-cowed spirit was roused to an attitude of manly independence. I had reached the point, at which I was

2. See note 5 on p. 80.

not afraid to die. This spirit made me a freeman in *fact*, while I remained a slave in *form*. When a slave cannot be flogged he is more than half free. He has a domain as broad as his own manly heart to defend, and he is really "*a power on earth.*"[3] While slaves prefer their lives, with flogging, to instant death, they will always find christians enough, like unto Covey, to accommodate that preference. From this time, until that of my escape from slavery, I was never fairly whipped. Several attempts were made to whip me, but they were always unsuccessful. Bruises I did get, as I shall hereafter inform the reader; but the case I have been describing, was the end of the brutification to which slavery had subjected me.

The reader will be glad to know why, after I had so grievously offended Mr. Covey, he did not have me taken in hand by the authorities; indeed, why the law of Maryland, which assigns hanging to the slave who resists his master, was not put in force against me; at any rate, why I was not taken up, as is usual in such cases, and publicly whipped, for an example to other slaves, and as a means of deterring me from committing the same offense again. I confess, that the easy manner in which I got off, was, for a long time, a surprise to me, and I cannot, even now, fully explain the cause.

The only explanation I can venture to suggest, is the fact, that Covey was, probably, ashamed to have it known and confessed that he had been mastered by a boy of sixteen. Mr. Covey enjoyed the unbounded and very valuable reputation, of being a first rate overseer and *negro breaker.* By means of this reputation, he was able to procure his hands for *very trifling* compensation, and with very great ease. His interest and his pride mutually suggested the wisdom of passing the matter by, in silence. The story that he had undertaken to whip a lad, and had been resisted, was, of itself, sufficient to damage him; for his bearing should, in the estimation of slaveholders, be of that imperial order that should make such an occurrence *impossible.* I judge from these circumstances, that Covey deemed it best to give me the go-by. It is, perhaps, not altogether creditable to my natural temper, that, after this conflict with Mr. Covey, I did, at times, purposely aim to provoke him to an attack, by refusing to keep with the other hands in the field, but I could never bully him to another battle. I had made up my mind to do him serious damage, if he ever again attempted to lay violent hands on me.

> "Hereditary bondmen, know ye not
> Who would be free, themselves must strike the blow?"[4]

---

3. Cf. Matthew 28.18 and Mark 2.10.
4. See note 4 on p. 25.

CHAPTER XVIII

New Relations and Duties

My term of actual service to Mr. Edward Covey ended on Christmas day, 1834. I gladly left the snakish Covey, although he was now as gentle as a lamb. My home for the year 1835 was already secured—my next master was already selected. There is always more or less excitement about the matter of changing hands, but I had become somewhat reckless. I cared very little into whose hands I fell—I meant to fight my way. Despite of Covey, too, the report got abroad, that I was hard to whip; that I was guilty of kicking back; that though generally a good tempered negro, I sometimes *"got the devil in me."* These sayings were rife in Talbot county, and they distinguished me among my servile brethren. Slaves, generally, will fight each other, and die at each other's hands; but there are few who are not held in awe by a white man. Trained from the cradle up, to think and feel that their masters are superior, and invested with a sort of sacredness, there are few who can outgrow or rise above the control which that sentiment exercises. I had now got free from it, and the thing was known. One bad sheep will spoil a whole flock. Among the slaves, I was a bad sheep. I hated slavery, slaveholders, and all pertaining to them; and I did not fail to inspire others with the same feeling, wherever and whenever opportunity was presented. This made me a marked lad among the slaves, and a suspected one among the slaveholders. A knowledge of my ability to read and write, got pretty widely spread, which was very much against me.

The days between Christmas day and New Year's, are allowed the slaves as holidays. During these, all regular work was suspended, and there was nothing to do but to keep fires, and look after the stock. This time we regarded as our own, by the grace of our masters, and we, therefore used it, or abused it, as we pleased. Those who had families at a distance, were now expected to visit them, and to spend with them the entire week. The younger slaves, or the unmarried ones, were expected to see to the cattle, and attend to incidental duties at home. The holidays were variously spent. The sober, thinking and industrious ones of our number, would employ themselves in manufacturing corn brooms, mats, horse collars and baskets, and some of these were very well made. Another class spent their time in hunting opossums, coons, rabbits, and other game. But the majority spent the holidays in sports, ball playing, wrestling, boxing, running foot races, dancing, and drinking whisky; and this latter mode of spending the time was generally most agreeable to their masters. A slave who would work during the holidays, was thought, by his master, undeserving of holidays. Such an one had rejected the favor of his master. There was, in this simple act of continued work, an accusation against slaves; and a slave could not help thinking, that if he made three dollars during the holidays, he might make three hundred during the year. Not to be drunk during the holidays, was disgraceful; and he was esteemed a lazy and improvident man, who could not afford to drink whisky during Christmas.

The fiddling, dancing and "*jubilee beating,*" was going on in all directions. This latter performance is strickly southern. It supplies the place of a violin, or of other musical instruments, and is played so easily, that almost every farm has its "Juba" beater. The performer improvises as he beats, and sings his merry songs, so ordering the words as to have them fall pat with the movement of his hands. Among a mass of nonsense and wild frolic, once in a while a sharp hit is given to the meanness of slaveholders. Take the following, for an example:

> "We raise de wheat,
> Dey gib us de corn;
> We bake de bread,
> Dey gib us de cruss;
> We sif de meal,
> Dey gib us de huss;
> We peal de meat,
> Dey gib us de skin,
> And dat's de way
> Dey takes us in.
> We skim de pot,
> Dey gib us the liquor,
> And say dat's good enough for nigger.
>   Walk over! walk over!

Tom butter and de fat;
Poor nigger you can't get over dat;
Walk over!"

This is not a bad summary of the palpable injustice and fraud of slavery, giving—as it does—to the lazy and idle, the comforts which God designed should be given solely to the honest laborer. But to the holiday's.

Judging from my own observation and experience, I believe these holidays to be among the most effective means, in the hands of slaveholders, of keeping down the spirit of insurrection among the slaves.

To enslave men, successfully and safely, it is necessary to have their minds occupied with thoughts and aspirations short of the liberty of which they are deprived. A certain degree of attainable good must be kept before them. These holidays serve the purpose of keeping the minds of the slaves occupied with prospective pleasure, within the limits of slavery. The young man can go wooing; the married man can visit his wife; the father and mother can see their children; the industrious and money loving can make a few dollars; the great wrestler can win laurels; the young people can meet, and enjoy each other's society; the drunken man can get plenty of whisky; and the religious man can hold prayer meetings, preach, pray and exhort during the holidays. Before the holidays, these are pleasures in prospect; after the holidays, they become pleasures of memory, and they serve to keep out thoughts and wishes of a more dangerous character. Were slaveholders at once to abandon the practice of allowing their slaves these liberties, periodically, and to keep them, the year round, closely confined to the narrow circle of their homes, I doubt not that the south would blaze with insurrections. These holidays are conductors or safety valves to carry off the explosive elements inseparable from the human mind, when reduced to the condition of slavery. But for these, the rigors of bondage would become too severe for endurance, and the slave would be forced up to dangerous desperation. Woe to the slaveholder when he undertakes to hinder or to prevent the operation of these electric conductors. A succession of earthquakes would be less destructive, than the insurrectionary fires which would be sure to burst forth in different parts of the south, from such interference.

Thus, the holidays, become part and parcel of the gross fraud, wrongs and inhumanity of slavery. Ostensibly, they are institutions of benevolence, designed to mitigate the rigors of slave life, but, practically, they are a fraud, instituted by human selfishness, the better to secure the ends of injustice and oppression. The slave's happiness is not the end sought, but, rather, the master's safety. It is not from a generous unconcern for the slave's labor that this cessation from labor is allowed, but from a prudent regard to the safety of the slave system. I am strengthened in this opinion, by the fact, that most slaveholders like to have their slaves spend the holidays in such a manner as to be of no real benefit to the slaves. It is plain, that every-thing like rational enjoyment among the slaves, is frowned upon; and only those wild and low sports, peculiar to semi-civilized people, are encouraged. All the license allowed, appears to have no other object than to disgust the slaves with their temporary freedom, and to make them as glad to return to their work, as they were to leave it. By plunging them into exhausting depths of drunkenness and dissipa-tion, this effect is almost certain to follow. I have known slaveholders resort to cunning tricks, with a view of getting their slaves deplorably drunk. A usual plan is, to make bets on a slave, that he can drink more whisky than any other; and so to induce a rivalry among them, for the mastery in this degradation. The scenes, brought about in this way, were often scandalous and loathsome in the extreme. Whole multitudes might be found stretched out in brutal drunkenness, at once helpless and disgusting. Thus, when the slave asks for a few hours of virtuous freedom, his cunning master takes advantage of his ignorance, and cheers him with a dose of vicious and revolting dis-sipation, artfully labeled with the name of LIBERTY. We were induced to drink, I among the rest, and when the holidays were over, we all staggered up from our filth and wallowing, took a long breath, and went away to our various fields of work; feeling, upon the whole, rather glad to go from that which our masters artfully deceived us into the belief was freedom, back again to the arms of slavery. It was not what we had taken it to be, nor what it might have been, had it not been abused by us. It was about as well to be a slave to *master*, as to be a slave to *rum* and *whisky*.[1]

I am the more induced to take this view of the holiday system, adopted by slaveholders, from what I know of their treatment of slaves, in regard to other things. It is the commonest thing for them to try to disgust their slaves with what they do not want them to have, or to enjoy. A slave, for instance, likes molasses; he steals some; to cure him of the taste for it, his master, in many cases, will go away to town, and buy a large quantity of the *poorest* quality, and set it before his slave, and, with whip in hand, compel him to eat it, until the poor fellow is made to sicken at the very thought of molasses. The same course is often adopted to cure slaves of the disagreeable and inconvenient practice of asking for more food, when their allow-ance has failed them. The same disgusting process works well, too, in other things, but I need not cite them. When a slave is drunk,

---

1. Douglass, like many abolitionists, did not drink.

the slaveholder has no fear that he will plan an insurrection; no fear that he will escape to the north. It is the sober, thinking slave who is dangerous, and needs the vigilance of his master, to keep him a slave. But, to proceed with my narrative.

On the first of January, 1835, I proceeded from St. Michael's to Mr. William Freeland's, my new home.[2] Mr. Freeland lived only three miles from St. Michael's, on an old worn out farm, which required much labor to restore it to anything like a self-supporting establishment.

I was not long in finding Mr Freeland to be a very different man from Mr. Covey. Though not rich, Mr. Freeland was what may be called a well-bred southern gentleman, as different from Covey, as a well-trained and hardened negro breaker is from the best specimen of the first families of the south. Though Freeland was a slaveholder, and shared many of the vices of his class, he seemed alive to the sentiment of honor. He had some sense of justice, and some feelings of humanity. He was fretful, impulsive and passionate, but I must do him the justice to say, he was free from the mean and selfish characteristics which distinguished the creature from which I had now, happily, escaped. He was open, frank, imperative, and practiced no concealments, disdaining to play the spy. In all this, he was the opposite of the crafty Covey.

Among the many advantages gained in my change from Covey's to Freeland's—startling as the statement may be—was the fact that the latter gentleman made no profession of religion. I assert *most unhesitatingly*, that the religion of the south—as I have observed it and proved it—is a mere covering for the most horrid crimes; the justifier of the most appalling barbarity; a sanctifier of the most hateful frauds; and a secure shelter, under which the darkest, foulest, grossest, and most infernal abominations fester and flourish. Were I again to be reduced to the condition of a slave, *next* to that calamity, I should regard the fact of being the slave of a religious slaveholder, the greatest that could befall me. For of all slaveholders with whom I have ever met, religious slaveholders are the worst. I have found them, almost invariably, the vilest, meanest and basest of their class. Exceptions there may be, but this is true of religious slaveholders, *as a class*. It is not for me to explain the fact. Others may do that; I simply state it as a fact, and leave the theological, and psychological inquiry, which it raises, to be decided by others more competent than myself. Religious slaveholders, like religious persecutors, are ever extreme in their malice and violence. Very near my new home, on an adjoining farm, there lived the Rev. Daniel Weeden, who was both pious and cruel after the real Covey pattern. Mr. Weeden

2. Thomas Auld hired Douglass out to Freeland.

was a local preacher of the Protestant Methodist persuasion, and a most zealous supporter of the ordinances of religion, generally. This Weeden owned a woman called "Ceal," who was a standing proof of his mercilessness. Poor Ceal's back, always scantily clothed, was kept literally raw, by the lash of this religious man and gospel minister. The most notoriously wicked man—so called in distinction from church members—could hire hands more easily than this brute. When sent out to find a home, a slave would never enter the gates of the preacher Weeden, while a sinful sinner needed a hand. Behave ill, or behave well, it was the known maxim of Weeden, that it is the duty of a master to use the lash. If, for no other reason, he contended that this was essential to remind a slave of his condition, and of his master's authority. The good slave must be whipped, to be *kept* good, and the bad slave must be whipped, to be *made* good. Such was Weeden's theory, and such was his practice. The back of his slave-woman will, in the judgment, be the swiftest witness against him.

While I am stating particular cases, I might as well immortalize another of my neighbors, by calling him by name, and putting him in print. He did not think that a "chiel"[3] was near, "taking notes," and will, doubtless, feel quite angry at having his character touched off in the ragged style of a slave's pen. I beg to introduce the reader to Rev. Rigby Hopkins.[4] Mr. Hopkins resides between Easton and St. Michael's, in Talbot county, Maryland. The severity of this man made him a perfect terror to the slaves of his neighborhood. The peculiar feature of his government, was, his system of whipping slaves, as he said, *in advance* of deserving it. He always managed to have one or two slaves to whip on Monday morning, so as to start his hands to their work, under the inspiration of a new assurance on Monday, that his preaching about kindness, mercy, brotherly love, and the like, on Sunday, did not interfere with, or prevent him from establishing his authority, by the cowskin. He seemed to wish to assure them, that his tears over poor, lost and ruined sinners, and his pity for them, did not reach to the blacks who tilled his fields. This saintly Hopkins used to boast, that he was the best hand to manage a negro in the county. He whipped for the smallest offenses, by way of preventing the commission of large ones.

The reader might imagine a difficulty in finding faults enough for such frequent whipping. But this is because you have no idea how easy a matter it is to offend a man who is on the look-out for offenses. The man, unaccustomed to slaveholding, would be astonished to observe how many *floggable* offenses there are in the slaveholder's

---

3. "Child," pronounced "chile," in Southern dialect.
4. Methodist Evangelical minister.

catalogue of crimes; and how easy it is to commit any one of them, even when the slave least intends it. A slaveholder, bent on finding fault, will hatch up a dozen a day, if he chooses to do so, and each one of these shall be of a punishable description. A mere look, word, or motion, a mistake, accident, or want of power, are all matters for which a slave may be whipped at any time. Does a slave look dissatisfied with his condition? It is said, that he has the devil in him, and it must be whipped out. Does he answer *loudly*, when spoken to by his master, with an air of self-consciousness? Then, must he be taken down a button-hole lower, by the lash, well laid on. Does he forget, and omit to pull off his hat, when approaching a white person? Then, he must, or may be, whipped for his bad manners. Does he ever venture to vindicate his conduct, when harshly and unjustly accused? Then, he is guilty of impudence, one of the greatest crimes in the social catalogue of southern society. To allow a slave to escape punishment, who has impudently attempted to exculpate himself from unjust charges, preferred against him by some white person, is to be guilty of great dereliction of duty. Does a slave ever venture to suggest a better way of doing a thing, no matter what? he is, altogether, too officious—wise above what is written—and he deserves, even if he does not get, a flogging for his presumption. Does he, while plowing, break a plow, or while hoeing, break a hoe, or while chopping, break an ax? no matter what were the imperfections of the implement broken, or the natural liabilities for breaking, the slave can be whipped for carelessness. The *reverend* slaveholder could always find something of this sort, to justify him in using the lash several times during the week. Hopkins—like Covey and Weeden—were shunned by slaves who had the privilege (as many had) of finding their own masters at the end of each year; and yet, there was not a man in all that section of country, who made a louder profession of religion, than did Mr. RIGBY HOPKINS.

But, to continue the thread of my story, through my experience when at Mr. William Freeland's.

My poor, weather-beaten bark now reached smoother water, and gentler breezes. My stormy life at Covey's had been of service to me. The things that would have seemed very hard, had I gone direct to Mr. Freeland's, from the home of Master Thomas, were now (after the hardships at Covey's) "trifles light as air."[5] I was still a field hand, and had come to prefer the severe labor of the field, to the enervating duties of a house servant. I had become large and strong; and had begun to take pride in the fact, that I could do as much hard work as some of the older men. There is much rivalry among slaves, at times, as to which can do the most work, and masters generally

5. Cf. Shakespeare, *Othello* 3.3.323.

seek to promote such rivalry. But some of us were too wise to race with each other very long. Such racing, we had the sagacity to see, was not likely to pay. We had our times for measuring each other's strength, but we knew too much to keep up the competition so long as to produce an extraordinary day's work. We knew that if, by extraordinary exertion, a large quantity of work was done in one day, the fact, becoming known to the master, might lead him to require the same amount every day. This thought was enough to bring us to a dead halt when ever so much excited for the race.

At Mr. Freeland's, my condition was every way improved. I was no longer the poor scape-goat that I was when at Covey's, where every wrong thing done was saddled upon me, and where other slaves were whipped over my shoulders. Mr. Freeland was too just a man thus to impose upon me, or upon any one else.

It is quite usual to make one slave the object of especial abuse, and to beat him often, with a view to its effect upon others, rather than with any expectation that the slave whipped will be improved by it, but the man with whom I now was, could descend to no such meanness and wickedness. Every man here was held individually responsible for his own conduct.

This was a vast improvement on the rule at Covey's. There, I was the general pack horse. Bill Smith was protected, by a positive pro-hibition made by his rich master, and the command of the rich slave-holder is LAW to the poor one; Hughes was favored, because of his relationship to Covey; and the hands hired temporarily, escaped flog-ging, except as they got it over my poor shoulders. Of course, this comparison refers to the time when Covey *could* whip me.

Mr. Freeland, like Mr. Covey, gave his hands enough to eat, but, unlike Mr. Covey, he gave them time to take their meals; he worked us hard during the day, but gave us the night for rest—another advan-tage to be set to the credit of the sinner, as against that of the saint. We were seldom in the field after dark in the evening, or before sun-rise in the morning. Our implements of husbandry were of the most improved pattern, and much superior to those used at Covey's.

Notwithstanding the improved condition which was now mine, and the many advantages I had gained by my new home, and my new master, I was still restless and discontented. I was about as hard to please by a master, as a master is by a slave. The freedom from bodily torture and unceasing labor, had given my mind an increased sensibility, and imparted to it greater activity. I was not yet exactly in right relations. "How be it, that was not first which is spiritual, but that which is natural, and afterward that which is spiritual."[6] When entombed at Covey's, shrouded in darkness and physical

6. Cf. 1 Corinthians 15.46.

wretchedness, temporal well-being was the grand *desideratum*; but, temporal wants supplied, the spirit puts in its claims. Beat and cuff your slave, keep him hungry and spiritless, and he will follow the chain of his master like a dog; but, feed and clothe him well,— work him moderately—surround him with physical comfort,—and dreams of freedom intrude. Give him a *bad* master, and he aspires to a *good* master; give him a good master, and he wishes to become his *own* master. Such is human nature. You may hurl a man so low, beneath the level of his kind, that he loses all just ideas of his natural position; but elevate him a little, and the clear conception of rights rises to life and power, and leads him onward. Thus elevated, a little, at Freeland's, the dreams called into being by that good man, Father Lawson, when in Baltimore, began to visit me; and shoots from the tree of liberty began to put forth tender buds, and dim hopes of the future began to dawn.

I found myself in congenial society, at Mr. Freeland's. There were Henry Harris, John Harris, Handy Caldwell, and Sandy Jenkins.[7]

Henry and John were brothers, and belonged to Mr. Freeland. They were both remarkably bright and intelligent, though neither of them could read. Now for mischief! I had not been long at Freeland's before I was up to my old tricks. I early began to address my companions on the subject of education, and the advantages of intelligence over ignorance, and, as far as I dared, I tried to show the agency of ignorance in keeping men in slavery. Webster's spelling book and the Columbian Orator were looked into again.[8] As summer came on, and the long Sabbath days stretched themselves over our idleness, I became uneasy, and wanted a Sabbath school, in which to exercise my gifts, and to impart the little knowledge of letters which I possessed, to my brother slaves. A house was hardly necessary in the summer time; I could hold my school under the shade of an old oak tree, as well as any where else. The thing was, to get the scholars, and to have them thoroughly imbued with the desire to learn. Two such boys were quickly secured, in Henry and John, and from them the contagion spread. I was not long in bringing around me twenty or thirty young men, who enrolled themselves, gladly, in my Sabbath school, and were willing to meet me regularly, under the trees or elsewhere, for the purpose of learning to read. It was surprising with what ease they provided themselves with spelling books. These were mostly the cast off books of their young

---

7. This is the same man who gave me the roots to prevent my being whipped by Mr. Covey [see pp. 149–51]. He was "a clever soul." We used frequently to talk about the fight with Covey, and as often as we did so, he would claim my success as the result of the roots which he gave me. This superstition is very common among the more ignorant slaves. A slave seldom dies, but that his death is attributed to trickery [*Author's note*].
8. See note 2 on p. 103 and note 3 on p. 104.

masters or mistresses. I taught, at first, on our own farm. All were impressed with the necessity of keeping the matter as private as possible, for the fate of the St. Michael's attempt was notorious, and fresh in the minds of all. Our pious masters, at St. Michael's, must not know that a few of their dusky brothers were learning to read the word of God, lest they should come down upon us with the lash and chain. We might have met to drink whisky, to wrestle, fight, and to do other unseemly things, with no fear of interruption from the saints or the sinners of St. Michael's.

But, to meet for the purpose of improving the mind and heart, by learning to read the sacred scriptures, was esteemed a most dangerous nuisance, to be instantly stopped. The slaveholders of St. Michael's, like slaveholders elsewhere, would always prefer to see the slaves engaged in degrading sports, rather than to see them acting like moral and accountable beings.

Had any one asked a religious white man, in St. Michael's, twenty years ago, the names of three men in that town, whose lives were most after the pattern of our Lord and Master, Jesus Christ, the first three would have been as follows:

GARRISON WEST, *Class Leader.*
WRIGHT FAIRBANKS, *Class Leader*
THOMAS AULD, *Class Leader.*

And yet, these were the men who ferociously rushed in upon my Sabbath school, at St. Michael's, armed with mob-like missiles, and forbade our meeting again, on pain of having our backs made bloody by the lash. This same Garrison West was my class leader, and I must say, I thought him a christian, until he took part in breaking up my school. He led me no more after that. The plea for this outrage was then, as it is now and at all times,—the danger to good order. If the slaves learnt to read, they would learn something else, and something worse. The peace of slavery would be disturbed; slave rule would be endangered. I leave the reader to characterize a system which is endangered by such causes. I do not dispute the soundness of the reasoning. It is perfectly sound; and, if slavery be *right*, Sabbath schools for teaching slaves to read the bible are *wrong*, and ought to be put down. These christian class leaders were, to this extent, consistent. They had settled the question, that slavery is *right*, and, by that standard, they determined that Sabbath schools are wrong. To be sure, they were Protestant, and held to the great Protestant right of every man to "*search the scriptures*" for himself; but, then, to all general rules, there are *exceptions*. How convenient! what crimes, may not be committed under the doctrine of the last remark. But, my dear, class leading Methodist brethren, did not condescend to give give me a reason for breaking up the Sabbath school at St. Michael's; it was enough that they had determined upon its destruction. I am, however, digressing.

After getting the school cleverly into operation, the second time— holding it in the woods, behind the barn, and in the shade of trees—I succeeded in inducing a free colored man, who lived several miles from our house, to permit me to hold my school in a room at his house. He, very kindly, gave me this liberty; but he incurred much peril in doing so, for the assemblage was an unlawful one. I shall not mention, here, the name of this man; for it might, even now, subject him to persecution, although the offenses were committed more than twenty years ago. I had, at one time, more than forty scholars, all of the right sort; and many of them succeeded in learning to read. I have met several slaves from Maryland, who were once my scholars; and who obtained their freedom, I doubt not, partly in consequence of the ideas imparted to them in that school. I have had various employments during my short life; but I look back to *none* with more satisfaction, than to that afforded by my Sunday school. An attachment, deep and lasting, sprung up between me and my persecuted pupils, which made my parting from them intensely grievous; and, when I think that most of these dear souls are yet shut up in this abject thralldom, I am overwhelmed with grief.

Besides my Sunday school, I devoted three evenings a week to my fellow slaves, during the winter. Let the reader reflect upon the fact, that, in this christian country, men and women are hiding from professors of religion, in barns, in the woods and fields, in order to learn to read the *holy bible*. Those dear souls, who came to my Sabbath school, came *not* because it was popular or reputable to attend such a place, for they came under the liability of having forty stripes laid on their naked backs. Every moment they spent in my school, they were under this terrible liability; and, in this respect, I was a sharer with them. Their minds had been cramped and starved by their cruel masters; the light of education had been completely excluded; and their hard earnings had been taken to educate their master's children. I felt a delight in circumventing the tyrants, and in blessing the victims of their curses.

The year at Mr. Freeland's passed off very smoothly, to outward seeming. Not a blow was given me during the whole year. To the credit of Mr. Freeland,—irreligious though he was—it must be stated, that he was the best master I ever had, until I became my own master, and assumed for myself, as I had a right to do, the responsibility of my own existence and the exercise of my own powers. For much of the happiness—or absence of misery—with which I passed this year with Mr. Freeland, I am indebted to the genial temper and ardent friendship of my brother slaves. They were, every one of them, manly, generous and brave, yes; I say they were brave, and I will add, fine looking. It is seldom the lot of mortals to have truer and better friends than were the slaves on this farm. It is not uncommon to charge slaves with great treachery toward each other, and to believe them incapable of confiding in each other; but I must say, that I never loved, esteemed, or confided in men, more than I did in these. They were as true as steel, and no band of brothers could have been more loving. There were no mean advantages taken of each other, as is sometimes the case where slaves are situated as we were; no tattling; no giving each other bad names to Mr. Freeland; and no elevating one at the expense of the other. We never undertook to do any thing, of any importance, which was likely to affect each other, without mutual consultation. We were generally a unit, and moved together. Thoughts and sentiments were exchanged between us, which might well be called very incendiary, by oppressors and tyrants; and perhaps the time has not even now come, when it is safe to unfold all the flying suggestions which arise in the minds of intelligent slaves. Several of my friends and brothers, if yet alive, are still in some part of the house of bondage; and though twenty years have passed away, the suspicious malice of slavery might punish them for even listening to my thoughts.

The slaveholder, kind or cruel, is a slaveholder still—the every hour violator of the just and inalienable rights of man; and he is, therefore, every hour silently whetting the knife of vengeance for his own throat. He never lisps a syllable in commendation of the fathers of this republic, nor denounces any attempted oppression of himself, without inviting the knife to his own throat, and asserting the rights of rebellion for his own slaves.

The year is ended, and we are now in the midst of the Christmas holidays, which are kept this year as last, according to the general description previously given.

CHAPTER XIX

The Run-Away Plot

I AM now at the beginning of the year 1836, a time favorable for serious thoughts. The mind naturally occupies itself with the mysteries of life in all its phases—the ideal, the real and the actual. Sober people look both ways at the beginning of the year, surveying the errors of the past, and providing against possible errors of the future. I, too, was thus exercised. I had little pleasure in retrospect, and the prospect was not very brilliant. "Notwithstanding," thought I, "the many resolutions and prayers I have made, in behalf of freedom, I am, this first day of the year 1836, still a slave, still wandering in the depths of spirit-devouring thralldom. My faculties and powers of body and soul are not my own, but are the property of a fellow mortal, in no sense superior to me, except that he had the physical power to compel me to be owned and controlled by him. By the combined physical force of the community, I am his slave,—a slave for life." With thoughts like these, I was perplexed and chafed; they rendered me gloomy and disconsolate. The anguish of my mind may not be written.

At the close of the year 1835, Mr. Freeland, my temporary master, had bought me of Capt. Thomas Auld, for the year 1836. His promptness in securing my services, would have been flattering to my vanity, had I been ambitious to win the reputation of being a valuable slave. Even as it was, I felt a slight degree of complacency at the circumstance. It showed he was as well pleased with me as a slave, as I was with him as a master. I have already intimated my regard for Mr. Freeland, and I may say here, in addressing northern readers—where there is no selfish motive for speaking in praise of a slaveholder—that Mr. Freeland was a man of many excellent qualities, and to me quite preferable to any master I ever had.

But the kindness of the slavemaster only gilds the chain of slavery, and detracts nothing from its weight or power. The thought that men are made for other and better uses than slavery, thrives best under the gentle treatment of a kind master. But the grim visage of slavery can assume no smiles which can fascinate the partially enlightened slave, into a forgetfulness of his bondage, nor of the desirableness of liberty.

I was not through the first month of this, my second year with the kind and gentlemanly Mr. Freeland, before I was earnestly considering and devising plans for gaining that freedom, which, when I was but a mere child, I had ascertained to be the natural and inborn right of every member of the human family. The desire for this freedom had been benumbed, while I was under the brutalizing dominion of Covey; and it had been postponed, and rendered inoperative, by my truly pleasant Sunday school engagements with my friends, during the year 1835, at Mr. Freeland's. It had, however, never entirely subsided. I hated slavery, always, and the desire for freedom only needed a favorable breeze, to fan it into a blaze, at any moment. The thought of only being a creature of the *present* and the *past,* troubled me, and I longed to have a *future*—a future with hope in it. To be shut up entirely to the past and present, is abhorrent to the human mind; it is to the soul—whose life and happiness is unceasing progress—what the prison is to the body; a blight and mildew, a hell of horrors. The dawning of this, another year, awakened me from my temporary slumber, and roused into life my latent, but long cherished aspirations for freedom. I was now not only ashamed to be contented in slavery, but ashamed to *seem* to be contented, and in my present favorable condition, under the mild rule of Mr. F., I am not sure that some kind reader will not condemn me for being over ambitious, and greatly wanting in proper humility, when I say the truth, that I now drove from me all thoughts of making the best of my lot, and welcomed only such thoughts as led me away from the house of bondage. The intense desire, now felt, *to be free*, quickened by my present favorable circumstances, brought me to the determination to *act*, as well as to think and speak. Accordingly, at the beginning of this year 1836, I took upon me a solemn vow, that the year which had now dawned upon me should not close, without witnessing an earnest attempt, on my part, to gain my liberty. This vow only bound me to make my escape individually; but the year spent with Mr. Freeland had attached me, as with "hooks of steel,"[1] to my brother slaves. The most affectionate and confiding friendship existed between us; and I felt it my duty to give them an opportunity to share in my virtuous determination, by frankly disclosing to them my plans and purposes. Toward Henry and John Harris, I felt a friendship as strong as one man can feel for another; for I could have died with and for them. To them, therefore, with a suitable degree of caution, I began to disclose my sentiments and plans; sounding them, the while, on the subject of running away, provided a good chance should offer. I scarcely need tell the reader, that I did my *very best* to imbue the minds of my dear friends with my own views and feelings. Thoroughly awakened, now, and with a definite vow upon me, all my little reading, which had any bearing on the subject of human rights, was rendered available in my communications with my friends. That (to me) gem of a book, the Columbian Orator,[2] with its eloquent orations and spicy dialogues, denouncing oppression and slavery—telling of what had been dared, done and suffered by men, to obtain the inestimable boon of liberty—was still fresh in my memory, and whirled into the ranks of my speech with the aptitude of well trained soldiers, going through the drill. The fact is, I here began my public speaking. I canvassed, with Henry and John, the subject of slavery, and dashed against it the condemning brand of God's eternal justice, which it every hour violates. My fellow servants were neither indifferent, dull, nor inapt. Our feelings were more alike than our opinions. All, however, were ready to act, when a feasible plan should be proposed. "Show us *how* the thing is to be done," said they, "and all else is clear."

We were all, except Sandy, quite free from slaveholding priestcraft. It was in vain that we had been taught from the pulpit at St. Michael's, the duty of obedience to our masters; to recognize God as the author of our enslavement; to regard running away an offense, alike against God and man; to deem our enslavement a merciful and beneficial arrangement; to esteem our condition, in this country, a paradise to that from which we had been snatched in Africa; to consider our hard hands and dark color as God's mark of displeasure,

1. Cf. Shakespeare, *Hamlet* 1.3.62.
2. See note 3 on p. 104.

and as pointing us out as the proper subjects of slavery; that the relation of master and slave was one of reciprocal benefits; that our work was not more serviceable to our masters, than our master's thinking was serviceable to us. I say, it was in vain that the pulpit of St. Michael's had constantly inculcated these plausible doctrines. Nature laughed them to scorn. For my own part, I had now become altogether too big for my chains. Father Lawson's solemn words, of what I ought to be, and might be, in the providence of God, had not fallen dead on my soul. I was fast verging toward manhood, and the prophecies of my childhood were still unfulfilled. The thought, that year after year had passed away, and my best resolutions to run away had failed and faded—that I was *still a slave*, and a slave, too, with chances for gaining my freedom diminished and still diminishing—was not a matter to be slept over easily; nor did I easily sleep over it.

But here came a new trouble. Thoughts and purposes so incendiary as those I now cherished, could not agitate the mind long, without danger of making themselves manifest to scrutinizing and unfriendly beholders. I had reason to fear that my sable face might prove altogether too transparent for the safe concealment of my hazardous enterprise. Plans of greater moment have leaked through stone walls, and revealed their projectors. But, here was no stone wall to hide my purpose. I would have given my poor, tell tale face for the immovable countenance of an Indian, for it was far from being proof against the daily, searching glances of those with whom I met.

It is the interest and business of slaveholders to study human nature, with a view to practical results, and many of them attain astonishing proficiency in discerning the thoughts and emotions of slaves. They have to deal not with earth, wood, or stone, but with *men*; and, by every regard they have for their safety and prosperity, they must study to know the material on which they are at work. So much intellect as the slaveholder has around him, requires watching. Their safety depends upon their vigilance. Conscious of the injustice and wrong they are every hour perpetrating, and knowing what they themselves would do if made the victims of such wrongs, they are looking out for the first signs of the dread retribution of justice. They watch, therefore, with skilled and practiced eyes, and have learned to read, with great accuracy, the state of mind and heart of the slave, through his sable face. These uneasy sinners are quick to inquire into the matter, where the slave is concerned. Unusual sobriety, apparent abstraction, sullenness and indifference—indeed, any mood out of the common way—afford ground for suspicion and inquiry. Often relying on their superior position and wisdom, they hector and torture the slave into a confession, by affecting to know the truth of their accusations. "You have got the devil in you," say they, "and we will whip him out of you." I have often been

put thus to the torture, on bare suspicion. This system has its disadvantages as well as their opposite. The slave is sometimes whipped
into the confession of offenses which he never committed. The
reader will see that the good old rule—"a man is to be held innocent
until proved to be guilty"—does not hold good on the slave plantation. Suspicion and torture are the approved methods of getting at
the truth, here. It was necessary for me, therefore, to keep a watch
over my deportment, lest the enemy should get the better of me.

But with all our caution and studied reserve, I am not sure that
Mr. Freeland did not suspect that all was not right with us. It *did*
seem that he watched us more narrowly, after the plan of escape
had been conceived and discussed amongst us. Men seldom see
themselves as others see them; and while, to ourselves, everything
connected with our contemplated escape appeared concealed,
Mr. Freeland may have, with the peculiar prescience of a slaveholder, mastered the huge thought which was disturbing our peace
in slavery.

I am the more inclined to think that he suspected us, because,
prudent as we were, as I now look back, I can see that we did many
silly things, very well calculated to awaken suspicion. We were, at
times, remarkably buoyant, singing hymns and making joyous excla-
mations, almost as triumphant in their tone as if we had reached a
land of freedom and safety. A keen observer might have detected in
our repeated singing of

> "O Canaan, sweet Canaan,
> I am bound for the land of Canaan,"[3]

something more than a hope of reaching heaven. We meant to reach
the *north*—and the north was our Canaan

> "I thought I heard them say,
> There were lions in the way,
> I don't expect to stay
>   Much longer here.
> Run to Jesus—shun the danger—
> I don't expect to stay
>   Much longer here,"[4]

was a favorite air, and had a double meaning. In the lips of some, it
meant the expectation of a speedy summons to a world of spirits;
but, in the lips of *our* company, it simply meant, a speedy pilgrim-
age toward a free state, and deliverance from all the evils and dangers of slavery.

---

3. Lines from the chorus of the spiritual "Sweet Canaan."
4. Verse from the spiritual "Run to Jesus."

I had succeeded in winning to my (what slaveholders would call wicked) scheme, a company of five young men, the very flower of the neighborhood, each of whom would have commanded one thousand dollars in the home market. At New Orleans, they would have brought fifteen hundred dollars a piece, and, perhaps, more. The names of our party were as follows: Henry Harris; John Harris, brother to Henry; Sandy Jenkins, of root memory;[5] Charles Roberts, and Henry Bailey. I was the youngest, but one, of the party. I had, however, the advantage of them all, in experience, and in a knowledge of letters. This gave me great influence over them. Perhaps not one of them, left to himself, would have dreamed of escape as a possible thing. Not one of them was self-moved in the matter. They all wanted to be free; but the serious thought of running away, had not entered into their minds, until I won them to the undertaking. They all were tolerably well off—for slaves—and had dim hopes of being set free, some day, by their masters. If any one is to blame for disturbing the quiet of the slaves and slave-masters of the neighborhood of St. Michael's, *I am the man*. I claim to be the instigator of the high crime, (as the slaveholders regard it,) and I kept life in it, until life could be kept in it no longer.

Pending the time of our contemplated departure out of our Egypt,[6] we met often by night, and on every Sunday. At these meetings we talked the matter over; told our hopes and fears, and the difficulties discovered or imagined; and, like men of sense, we counted the cost of the enterprise to which we were committing ourselves.

These meetings must have resembled, on a small scale, the meetings of revolutionary conspirators, in their primary condition. We were plotting against our (so called) lawful rulers; with this difference—that we sought our own good, and not the harm of our enemies. We did not seek to overthrow them, but to escape from them. As for Mr. Freeland, we all liked him, and would have gladly remained with him, *as freemen*. LIBERTY was our aim; and we had now come to think that we had a right to liberty, against every obstacle—even against the lives of our enslavers.

We had several words, expressive of things, important to us, which we understood, but which, even if distinctly heard by an outsider, would convey no certain meaning. I have reasons for suppressing these *pass-words*, which the reader will easily divine. I hated the secrecy; but where slavery is powerful, and liberty is weak, the latter is driven to concealment or to destruction.

---

5. See note 7 on p. 165.
6. Refers to the story in the Book of Exodus about the deliverance of the Jews from Egypt. See also note 3 on p. 173.

The prospect was not always a bright one. At times, we were almost tempted to abandon the enterprise, and to get back to that comparative peace of mind, which even a man under the gallows might feel, when all hope of escape had vanished. Quiet bondage was felt to be better than the doubts, fears and uncertainties, which now so sadly perplexed and disturbed us.

The infirmities of humanity, generally, were represented in our little band. We were confident, bold and determined, at times; and, again, doubting, timid and wavering; whistling, like the boy in the graveyard, to keep away the spirits.

To look at the map, and observe the proximity of Eastern Shore, Maryland, to Delaware and Pennsylvania, it may seem to the reader quite absurd, to regard the proposed escape as a formidable undertaking. But to *understand*, some one has said a man must *stand under*. The real distance was great enough, but the imagined distance was, to our ignorance, even greater. Every slaveholder seeks to impress his slave with a belief in the boundlessness of slave territory, and of his own almost illimitable power. We all had vague and indistinct notions of the geography of the country.

The distance, however, is not the chief trouble. The nearer are the lines of a slave state and the borders of a free one, the greater the peril. Hired kidnappers infest these borders. Then, too, we knew that merely reaching a free state did not free us; that, wherever caught, we could be returned to slavery. We could see no spot on this side the ocean, where we could be free. We had heard of Canada, the real Canaan of the American bondmen, simply as a country to which the wild goose and the swan repaired at the end of winter, to escape the heat of summer, but not as the home of man. I knew something of theology, but nothing of geography. I really did not, at that time, know that there was a state of New York, or a state of Massachusetts. I had heard of Pennsylvania, Delaware and New Jersey, and all the southern states, but was ignorant of the free states, generally. New York city was our northern limit, and to go there, and to be forever harassed with the liability of being hunted down and returned to slavery—with the certainty of being treated ten times worse than we had ever been treated before—was a prospect far from delightful, and it might well cause some hesitation about engaging in the enterprise. The case, sometimes, to our excited visions, stood thus: At every gate through which we had to pass, we saw a watchman; at every ferry, a guard; on every bridge, a sentinel; and in every wood, a patrol or slave-hunter. We were hemmed in on every side. The good to be sought, and the evil to be shunned, were flung in the balance, and weighed against each other. On the one hand, there stood slavery; a stern reality, glaring frightfully upon us, with the blood of millions in his polluted skirts—terrible to behold—greedily devouring our hard earnings and feeding himself upon our flesh. Here was the evil from which to escape. On the other hand, far away, back in the hazy distance, where all forms seemed but shadows, under the flickering light of the north star—behind some craggy hill or snow-covered mountain—stood a doubtful freedom, half frozen, beckoning us to her icy domain. This was, the good to be sought. The inequality was as great as that between certainty and uncertainty. This, in itself, was enough to stagger us; but when we came to survey the untrodden road, and conjecture the many possible difficulties, we were appalled, and at times, as I have said, were upon the point of giving over the struggle altogether.

The reader can have little idea of the phantoms of trouble which flit, in such circumstances, before the uneducated mind of the slave. Upon either side, we saw grim death assuming a variety of horrid shapes. Now, it was starvation, causing us, in a strange and friendless land, to eat our own flesh. Now, we were contending with the waves, (for our journey was in part by water,) and were drowned. Now, we were hunted by dogs, and overtaken and torn to pieces by their merciless fangs. We were stung by scorpions—chased by wild beasts—bitten by snakes; and, worst of all, after having succeeded in swimming rivers—encountering wild beasts—sleeping in the woods—suffering hunger, cold, heat and nakedness—we supposed ourselves to be overtaken by hired kidnappers, who, in the name of the law, and for their thrice accursed reward, would, perchance, fire upon us—kill some, wound others, and capture all. This dark picture, drawn by ignorance and fear, at times greatly shook our determination, and not unfrequently caused us to

> "Rather bear those ills we had
> Than fly to others which we knew not of."[7]

I am not disposed to magnify this circumstance in my experience, and yet I think I shall seem to be so disposed, to the reader. No man can tell the intense agony which is felt by the slave, when wavering on the point of making his escape. All that he has is at stake; and even that which he has not, is at stake, also. The life which he has, may be lost, and the liberty which he seeks, may not be gained.

Patrick Henry, to a listening senate, thrilled by his magic eloquence, and ready to stand by him in his boldest flights, could say, "Give me Liberty or give me Death,"[8] and this saying was a sublime one, even for a freeman; but, incomparably more sublime, is

---

7. Cf. Shakespeare, *Hamlet* 3.1.82–83.
8. On March 23, 1775, the American Statesman Patrick Henry (1736–1799) delivered this famous line as part of a speech to the Second Virginia Convention of Delegates: "I know not what course others may take; but as for me, give me liberty, or give me death!"

the same sentiment, when *practically* asserted by men accustomed to the lash and chain—men whose sensibilities must have become more or less deadened by their bondage. With us it was a *doubtful* liberty, at best, that we sought; and a certain, lingering death in the rice swamps and sugar fields, if we failed. Life is not lightly regarded by men of sane minds. It is precious, alike to the pauper and to the prince—to the slave, and to his master; and yet, I believe there was not one among us, who would not rather have been shot down, than pass away life in hopeless bondage.

In the progress of our preparations, Sandy, the root man, became troubled. He began to have dreams, and some of them were very distressing. One of these, which happened on a Friday night, was, to him, of great significance; and I am quite ready to confess, that I felt somewhat damped by it myself. He said, "I dreamed, last night, that I was roused from sleep, by strange noises, like the voices of a swarm of angry birds, that caused a roar as they passed, which fell upon my ear like a coming gale over the tops of the trees. Looking up to see what it could mean," said Sandy, "I saw you, Frederick, in the claws of a huge bird, surrounded by a large number of birds, of all colors and sizes. These were all picking at you, while you, with your arms, seemed to be trying to protect your eyes. Passing over me, the birds flew in a south-westerly direction, and I watched them until they were clean out of sight. Now, I saw this as plainly as I now see you; and furder, honey, watch de Friday night dream; dare is sumpon in it, shoes you born; dare is, indeed, honey."

I confess I did not like this dream; but I threw off concern about it, by attributing it to the general excitement and perturbation consequent upon our contemplated plan of escape. I could not, however, shake off its effect at once. I felt that it boded me no good. Sandy was unusually emphatic and oracular, and his manner had much to do with the impression made upon me.

The plan of escape which I recommended, and to which my comrades assented, was to take a large canoe, owned by Mr. Hamilton, and, on the Saturday night previous to the Easter holidays, launch out into the Chesapeake bay, and paddle for its head,—a distance of seventy miles—with all our might. Our course, on reaching this point, was, to turn the canoe adrift, and bend our steps toward the north star, till we reached a free state.

There were several objections to this plan. One was, the danger from gales on the bay. In rough weather, the waters of the Chesapeake are much agitated, and there is danger, in a canoe, of being swamped by the waves. Another objection was, that the canoe would soon be missed; the absent persons would, at once, be suspected of having taken it; and we should be pursued by some of the fast sailing bay craft out of St. Michael's. Then, again, if we reached the head of the bay, and turned the canoe adrift, she might prove a guide to our track, and bring the land hunters after us.

These and other objections were set aside, by the stronger ones which could be urged against every other plan that could then be suggested. On the water, we had a chance of being regarded as fishermen, in the service of a master. On the other hand, by taking the land route, through the counties adjoining Delaware, we should be subjected to all manner of interruptions, and many very disagreeable questions, which might give us serious trouble. Any white man is authorized to stop a man of color, on any road, and examine him, and arrest him, if he so desires.

By this arrangement, many abuses (considered such even by slaveholders) occur. Cases have been known, where freemen have been called upon to show their free papers, by a pack of ruffians—and, on the presentation of the papers, the ruffians have torn them up, and seized their victim, and sold him to a life of endless bondage.

The week before our intended start, I wrote a pass for each of our party, giving them permission to visit Baltimore, during the Easter holidays. The pass ran after this manner:

> "This is to certify, that I, the undersigned, have given the bearer, my servant, John, full liberty to go to Baltimore, to spend the Easter holidays.
>
> > "W. H.
> >
> > "Near St. Michael's, Talbot county, Maryland."

Although we were not going to Baltimore, and were intending to land east of North Point, in the direction where I had seen the Philadelphia steamers go, these passes might be made useful to us in the lower part of the bay, while steering toward Baltimore. These were not, however, to be shown by us, until all other answers failed to satisfy the inquirer. We were all fully alive to the importance of being calm and self-possessed, when accosted, if accosted we should be; and we more times than one rehearsed to each other how we should behave in the hour of trial.

Those were long, tedious days and nights. The suspense was painful, in the extreme. To balance probabilities, where life and liberty hang on the result, requires steady nerves. I panted for action, and was glad when the day, at the close of which we were to start, dawned upon us. Sleeping, the night before, was out of the question. I probably felt more deeply than any of my companions, because I was the instigator of the movement. The responsibility of the whole enterprise rested on my shoulders. The glory of success, and the shame and confusion of failure, could not be matters of indifference to me. Our food was prepared; our clothes were packed up; we were all ready to go, and impatient for Saturday morning—considering that the last morning of our bondage.

I cannot describe the tempest and tumult of my brain, that morning. The reader will please to bear in mind, that, in a slave state, an unsuccessful run-away is not only subjected to cruel torture, and sold away to the far south, but he is frequently execrated by the other slaves. He is charged with making the condition of the other slaves intolerable, by laying them all under the suspicion of their masters— subjecting them to greater vigilance, and imposing greater limitations on their privileges. I dreaded murmurs from this quarter. It is difficult, too, for a slave-master to believe that slaves escaping have not been aided in their flight by some one of their fellow slaves. When, therefore, a slave is missing, every slave on the place is closely examined as to his knowledge of the undertaking; and they are sometimes even tortured, to make them disclose what they are suspected of knowing of such escape.

Our anxiety grew more and more intense, as the time of our intended departure for the north drew nigh. It was truly felt to be a matter of life and death with us; and we fully intended to *fight* as well as *run*, if necessity should occur for that extremity. But the trial hour was not yet come. It was easy to resolve, but not so easy to act. I expected there might be some drawing back, at the last. It was natural that there should be; therefore, during the intervening time, I lost no opportunity to explain away difficulties, to remove doubts, to dispel fears, and to inspire all with firmness. It was too late to look back; and *now* was the time to go forward. Like most other men, we had done the talking part of our work, long and well; and the time had come to *act* as if we were in earnest, and meant to be as true in action as in words. I did not forget to appeal to the pride of my comrades, by telling them that, if after having solemnly promised to go, as they had done, they now failed to make the attempt, they would, in effect, brand themselves with cowardice, and might as well sit down, fold their arms, and acknowledge themselves as fit only to be *slaves*. This detestable character, all were unwilling to assume. Every man except Sandy (he, much to our regret, withdrew) stood firm; and at our last meeting we pledged ourselves afresh, and in the most solemn manner, that, at the time appointed, we *would* certainly start on our long journey for a free country. This meeting was in the middle of the week, at the end of which we were to start.

Early that morning we went, as usual, to the field, but with hearts that beat quickly and anxiously. Any one intimately acquainted with us, might have seen that all was not well with us, and that some monster lingered in our thoughts. Our work that morning was the same as it had been for several days past—drawing out and spreading manure. While thus engaged, I had a sudden presentiment, which flashed upon me like lightning in a dark night, revealing to the lonely traveler the gulf before, and the enemy behind. I instantly turned to Sandy Jenkins, who was near me, and said to him, "*Sandy, we are betrayed*; something has just told me so." I felt as sure of it, as if the officers were there in sight. Sandy said, "Man, dat is strange; but I feel just as you do." If my mother—then long in her grave— had appeared before me, and told me that we were betrayed, I could not, at that moment, have felt more certain of the fact.

In a few minutes after this, the long, low and distant notes of the horn summoned us from the field to breakfast. I felt as one may be supposed to feel before being led forth to be executed for some great offense. I wanted no breakfast; but I went with the other slaves toward the house, for form's sake. My feelings were not disturbed as to the right of running away; on that point I had no trouble, whatever. My anxiety arose from a sense of the consequences of failure.

In thirty minutes after that vivid presentiment, came the apprehended crash. On reaching the house, for breakfast, and glancing my eye toward the lane gate, the worst was at once made known. The lane gate of Mr. Freeland's house, is nearly a half a mile from the door, and much shaded by the heavy wood which bordered the main road. I was, however, able to descry four white men, and two colored men, approaching. The white men were on horseback, and the colored men were walking behind, and seemed to be tied. "*It is all over with us*," thought I, "*we are surely betrayed.*" I now became composed, or at least comparatively so, and calmly awaited the result. I watched the ill-omened company, till I saw them enter the gate. Successful flight was impossible, and I made up my mind to stand, and meet the evil, whatever it might be; for I was now not without a slight hope that things might turn differently from what I at first expected. In a few moments, in came Mr. William Hamilton, riding very rapidly, and evidently much excited. He was in the habit of riding very slowly, and was seldom known to gallop his horse. This time, his horse was nearly at full speed, causing the dust to roll thick behind him. Mr. Hamilton, though one of the most resolute men in the whole neighborhood, was, nevertheless, a remarkably mild spoken man; and, even when greatly excited, his language was cool and circumspect. He came to the door, and inquired if Mr. Freeland was in. I told him that Mr. Freeland was at the barn. Off the old gentleman rode, toward the barn, with unwonted speed. Mary, the cook, was at a loss to know what was the matter, and I did not profess any skill in making her understand. I knew she would have united, as readily as any one, in cursing me for bringing trouble into the family; so I held my peace, leaving matters to develop themselves, without my assistance. In a few moments, Mr. Hamilton and Mr. Freeland came down from the barn to the house; and, just as they made their appearance in the front yard, three men (who proved to be constables) came dashing into the lane, on horseback, as if summoned by a sign requiring quick work. A few seconds brought them into the front yard, where they hastily dismounted, and tied their horses. This done, they joined Mr. Freeland and Mr. Hamilton, who were standing a short distance from the kitchen. A few moments were spent, as if in consulting how to proceed, and then the whole party walked up to the kitchen door. There was now no one in the kitchen but myself and John Harris. Henry and Sandy were yet at the barn. Mr. Freeland came inside the kitchen door, and with an agitated voice, called me by name, and told me to come forward; that there were some gentlemen who wished to see me. I stepped toward them, at the door, and asked what they wanted, when the constables grabbed me, and told me that I had better not resist; that I had been in a scrape, or was said to have been in one; that they were merely going to take me where I could be examined; that they were going to carry me to St. Michael's, to have me brought before my master. They further said, that, in case the evidence against me was not true, I should be acquitted. I was now firmly tied, and completely at the mercy of my captors. Resistance was idle. They were five in number, armed to the very teeth. When they had secured me, they next turned to John Harris, and, in a few moments, succeeded in tying him as firmly as they had already tied me. They next turned toward Henry Harris, who had now returned from the barn. "Cross your hands," said the constables, to Henry. "I won't" said Henry, in a voice so firm and clear, and in a manner so determined, as for a moment to arrest all proceedings. "Won't you cross your hands?" said Tom Graham, the constable. "*No I won't*," said Henry, with increasing emphasis. Mr. Hamilton, Mr. Freeland, and the officers, now came near to Henry. Two of the constables drew out their shining pistols, and swore by the name of God, that he should cross his hands, or they would shoot him down. Each of these hired ruffians now cocked their pistols, and, with fingers apparently on the triggers, presented their deadly weapons to the breast of the unarmed slave, saying, at the same time, if he did not cross his hands, they would "blow his d—d heart out of him."

"*Shoot! shoot me!*" said Henry. "*You can't kill me but once.* Shoot!—shoot! and be d—d. *I won't be tied.*" This, the brave fellow said in a voice as defiant and heroic in its tone, as was the language itself; and, at the moment of saying this, with the pistols at his very breast, he quickly raised his arms, and dashed them from the puny hands of his assassins, the weapons flying in opposite directions.

Now came the struggle. All hands now rushed upon the brave fellow, and, after beating him for some time, they succeeded in overpowering and tying him. Henry put me to shame; he fought, and fought bravely. John and I had made no resistance. The fact is, I never see much use in fighting, unless there is a reasonable probability of whipping somebody. Yet there was something almost providential in the resistance made by the gallant Henry. But for that resistance, every soul of us would have been hurried off to the far south. Just a moment previous to the trouble with Henry, Mr. Hamilton *mildly* said—and this gave me the unmistakable clue to the cause of our arrest—"Perhaps we had now better make a search for those protections, which we understand Frederick has written for himself and the rest." Had these passes been found, they would have been point blank proof against us, and would have confirmed all the statements of our betrayer. Thanks to the resistance of Henry, the excitement produced by the scuffle drew all attention in that direction, and I succeeded in flinging my pass, unobserved, into the fire. The confusion attendant upon the scuffle, and the apprehension of further trouble, perhaps, led our captors to forego, for the present, any search for *"those protections" which Frederick was said to have written for his companions*; so we were not yet convicted of the purpose to run away; and it was evident that there was some doubt, on the part of all, whether we had been guilty of such a purpose.

Just as we were all completely tied, and about ready to start toward St. Michael's, and thence to jail, Mrs. Betsey Freeland (mother to William, who was very much attached—after the southern fashion—to Henry and John, they having been reared from childhood in her house) came to the kitchen door, with her hands full of biscuits,—for we had not had time to take our breakfast that morning—and divided them between Henry and John. This done, the lady made the following parting address to me, looking and pointing her bony finger at me. "You devil! You yellow devil! It was you that put it into the heads of Henry and John to run away. But for *you*, you *long legged yellow devil*, Henry and John would never have thought of running away." I gave the lady a look, which called forth a scream of mingled wrath and terror, as she slammed the kitchen door, and went in, leaving me, with the rest, in hands as harsh as her own broken voice.

Could the kind reader have been quietly riding along the main road to or from Easton, that morning, his eye would have met a painful sight. He would have seen five young men, guilty of no crime, save that of preferring *liberty* to a life of *bondage*, drawn along the public highway—firmly bound together—tramping through dust and heat, bare-footed and bare-headed—fastened to three strong horses, whose riders were armed to the teeth, with pistols and daggers—on their way to prison, like felons, and suffering every possible insult from the crowds of idle, vulgar people, who clustered around, and heartlessly made their failure the occasion for all manner of ribaldry and sport. As I looked upon this crowd of vile persons, and saw myself and friends thus assailed and persecuted, I could not help seeing the fulfillment of Sandy's dream. I was in the hands of moral vultures, and firmly held in their sharp talons, and was being hurried away toward Easton, in a southeasterly direction, amid the jeers of new birds of the same feather, through every neighborhood we passed. It seemed to me, (and this shows the good understanding between the slaveholders and their allies,) that every body we met knew the cause of our arrest, and were out, awaiting our passing by, to feast their vindictive eyes on our misery and to gloat over our ruin. Some said, *I ought to be hanged*, and others, *I ought to be burnt*; others, I ought to have the "*hide*" taken from my back; while no one gave us a kind word or sympathizing look, except the poor slaves, who were lifting their heavy hoes, and who cautiously glanced at us through the post-and-rail fences, behind which they were at work. Our sufferings, that morning, can be more easily imagined than described. Our hopes were all blasted, at a blow. The cruel injustice, the victorious crime, and the helplessness of innocence, led me to ask, in my ignorance and weakness—"Where now is the God of justice and mercy? and why have these wicked men the power thus to trample upon our rights, and to insult our feelings?" And yet, in the next moment, came the consoling thought, "*the day of the oppressor will come at last.*" Of one thing I could be glad—not one of my dear friends, upon whom I had brought this great calamity, either by word or look, reproached me for having led them into it. We were a band of brothers, and never dearer to each other than now. The thought which gave us the most pain, was the probable separation which would now take place, in case we were sold off to the far south, as we were likely to be. While the constables were looking forward, Henry and I, being fastened together, could occasionally exchange a word, without being observed by the kidnappers who had us in charge. "What shall I do with my pass?" said Henry. "Eat it with your biscuit," said I; "it won't do to tear it up." We were now near St. Michael's. The direction concerning the passes was passed around, and executed. "*Own nothing!*" said I. "*Own nothing!*" was passed around and enjoined, and assented to. Our confidence in each other was unshaken; and we were quite resolved to succeed or fail together—as much after the calamity which had befallen us, as before.

On reaching St. Michael's, we underwent a sort of examination at my master's store, and it was evident to my mind, that Master Thomas suspected the truthfulness of the evidence upon which they had acted in arresting us; and that he only affected, to some extent, the positiveness with which he asserted our guilt. There was nothing said by any of our company, which could, in any manner, prejudice our cause; and there was hope, yet, that we should be able to return to our homes—if for nothing else, at least to find out the guilty man or woman who had betrayed us.

To this end, we all denied that we had been guilty of intended flight. Master Thomas said that the evidence he had of our intention to run away, was strong enough to hang us, in a case of murder. "But," said I, "the cases are not equal. If murder were committed, some one must have committed it—the thing is done! In our case, nothing has been done! We have not run away. Where is the evidence against us? We were quietly at our work." I talked thus, with unusual freedom, to bring out the evidence against us, for we all wanted, above all things, to know the guilty wretch who had betrayed us, that we might have something tangible upon which to pour our execrations. From something which dropped, in the course of the talk, it appeared that there was but one witness against us—and that that witness could not be produced. Master Thomas would not tell us *who* his informant was; but we suspected, and suspected *one* person *only*. Several circumstances seemed to point SANDY out, as our betrayer. His entire knowledge of our plans—his participation in them—his withdrawal from us—his dream, and his simultaneous presentiment that we were betrayed—the taking us, and the leaving him—were calculated to turn suspicion toward him; and yet, we could not suspect him. We all loved him too well to think it *possible* that he could have betrayed us. So we rolled the guilt on other shoulders.

We were literally dragged, that morning, behind horses, a distance of fifteen miles, and placed in the Easton jail. We were glad to reach the end of our journey, for our pathway had been the scene of insult and mortification. Such is the power of public opinion, that it is hard, even for the innocent, to feel the happy consolations of innocence, when they fall under the maledictions of this power. How could we regard ourselves as in the right, when all about us denounced us as criminals, and had the power and the disposition to treat us as such.

In jail, we were placed under the care of Mr. Joseph Graham, the sheriff of the county. Henry, and John, and myself, were placed in one room, and Henry Baily and Charles Roberts, in another, by themselves. This separation was intended to deprive us of the advantage of concert, and to prevent trouble in jail.

Once shut up, a new set of tormentors came upon us. A swarm of imps, in human shape—the slave-traders, deputy slave-traders, and agents of slave-traders—that gather in every country town of the state, watching for chances to buy human flesh, (as buzzards to eat carrion,) flocked in upon us, to ascertain if our masters had placed us in jail to be sold. Such a set of debased and villainous creatures, I never saw before, and hope never to see again. I felt myself surrounded as by a pack of *fiends*, fresh from *perdition*. They laughed, leered, and grinned at us; saying, "Ah! boys, we've got you, havn't we? So you were about to make your escape? Where were you going to?" After taunting us, and jeering at us, as long as they liked, they one by one subjected us to an examination, with a view to ascertain our value; feeling our arms and legs, and shaking us by the shoulders to see if we were sound and healthy; impudently asking us, "how we would like to have them for masters?" To such questions, we were, very much to their annoyance, quite dumb, disdaining to answer them. For one, I detested the whisky-bloated gamblers in human flesh; and I believe I was as much detested by them in turn. One fellow told me, "if he had me, he would cut the devil out of me pretty quick."

These negro buyers are very offensive to the genteel southron christian public. They are looked upon, in respectable Maryland society, as necessary, but detestable characters. As a class, they are hardened ruffians, made such by nature and by occupation. Their ears are made quite familiar with the agonizing cry of outraged and woe-smitten humanity. Their eyes are forever open to human misery. They walk amid desecrated affections, insulted virtue, and blasted hopes. They have grown intimate with vice and blood; they gloat over the wildest illustrations of their soul-damning and earth-polluting business, and are moral pests. Yes; they are a legitimate fruit of slavery; and it is a puzzle to make out a case of greater villainy for them, than for the slaveholders, who make such a class *possible*. They are mere hucksters of the surplus slave produce of Maryland and Virginia—coarse, cruel, and swaggering bullies, whose very breathing is of blasphemy and blood.

Aside from these slave-buyers, who infested the prison, from time to time, our quarters were much more comfortable than we had any right to expect they would be. Our allowance of food was small and coarse, but our room was the best in the jail—neat and spacious, and with nothing about it necessarily reminding us of being in prison, but its heavy locks and bolts and the black, iron lattice-work at the windows. We were prisoners of state, compared with most slaves who are put into that Easton jail. But the place was not one of contentment. Bolts, bars and grated windows are not acceptable to freedom-loving people of any color. The suspense, too, was painful. Every step on the stairway was listened to, in the hope that the comer would cast a ray of light on our fate. We would have given the hair off our heads for half a dozen words with one of the waiters in Sol. Lowe's hotel. Such waiters were in the way of hearing, at the table, the probable course of things. We could see them flitting about in their white jackets, in front of this hotel, but could speak to none of them.

Soon after the holidays were over, contrary to all our expectations, Messrs. Hamilton and Freeland came up to Easton; not to make a bargain with the "Georgia traders," nor to send us up to Austin Woldfolk, as is usual in the case of run-away slaves, but to release Charles, Henry Harris, Henry Baily and John Harris, from prison, and this, too, without the infliction of a single blow. I was now left entirely alone in prison. The innocent had been taken, and the guilty left. My friends were separated from me, and apparently forever. This circumstance caused me more pain than any other incident connected with our capture and imprisonment. Thirty-nine lashes on my naked and bleeding back, would have been joyfully borne, in preference to this separation from these, the friends of my youth. And yet, I could not but feel that I was the victim of something like justice. Why should these young men, who were led into this scheme by me, suffer as much as the instigator? I felt glad that they were released from prison, and from the dread prospect of a life (or death I should rather say) in the rice swamps. It is due to the noble Henry, to say, that he seemed almost as reluctant to leave the prison with me in it, as he was to be tied and dragged to prison. But he and the rest knew that we should, in all the likelihoods of the case, be separated, in the event of being sold; and since we were now completely in the hands of our owners, we all concluded it would be best to go peaceably home.

Not until this last separation, dear reader, had I touched those profounder depths of desolation, which it is the lot of slaves often to reach. I was solitary in the world, and alone within the walls of a stone prison, left to a fate of life-long misery. I had hoped and expected much, for months before, but my hopes and expectations were now withered and blasted. The ever dreaded slave life in Georgia, Louisiana and Alabama—from which escape is next to impossible—now, in my loneliness, stared me in the face. The possibility of ever becoming anything but an abject slave, a mere machine in the hands of an owner, had now fled, and it seemed to me it had fled forever. A life of living death, beset with the innumerable horrors of the cotton field, and the sugar plantation, seemed to be my doom. The fiends, who rushed into the prison when we were first put there, continued to visit me, and to ply me with questions and with their tantalizing remarks. I was insulted, but helpless; keenly alive to the demands of justice and liberty, but with no means of asserting them. To talk to those imps about justice and mercy, would have been as absurd as to reason with bears and tigers. Lead and steel are the only arguments that they understand.

After remaining in this life of misery and despair about a week, which, by the way, seemed a month, Master Thomas, very much to my surprise, and greatly to my relief, came to the prison, and took me out, for the purpose, as he said, of sending me to Alabama, with a friend of his, who would emancipate me at the end of eight years. I was glad enough to get out of prison; but I had no faith in the story that this friend of Capt. Auld would emancipate me, at the end of the time indicated. Besides, I never had heard of his having a friend in Alabama, and I took the announcement, simply as an easy and comfortable method of shipping me off to the far south. There was a little scandal, too, connected with the idea of one christian selling another to the Georgia traders, while it was deemed every way proper for them to sell to others. I thought this friend in Alabama was an invention, to meet this difficulty, for Master Thomas was quite jealous of his christian reputation, however unconcerned he might be about his real christian character. In these remarks, however, it is possible that I do Master Thomas Auld injustice. He certainly did not exhaust his power upon me, in the case, but acted, upon the whole, very generously, considering the nature of my offense. He had the power and the provocation to send me, without reserve, into the very everglades of Florida, beyond the remotest hope of emancipation; and his refusal to exercise that power, must be set down to his credit.

After lingering about St. Michael's a few days, and no friend from Alabama making his appearance, to take me there, Master Thomas decided to send me back again to Baltimore, to live with his brother Hugh, with whom he was now at peace; possibly he became so by his profession of religion, at the camp-meeting in the Bay Side. Master Thomas told me that he wished me to go to Baltimore, and learn a trade; and that, if I behaved myself properly, he would *emancipate me at twenty-five!* Thanks for this one beam of hope in the future. The promise had but one fault; it seemed too good to be true.

CHAPTER XX

Apprenticeship Life

NOTHING LOST BY THE ATTEMPT TO RUN AWAY—COMRADES IN THEIR
OLD HOMES—REASONS FOR SENDING AUTHOR AWAY—RETURN TO
BALTIMORE—CONTRAST BETWEEN "TOMMY" AND THAT OF HIS
COLORED COMPANION—TRIALS IN GARDINER'S SHIP YARD—
DESPERATE FIGHT—ITS CAUSES—CONFLICT BETWEEN WHITE AND
BLACK LABOR—DESCRIPTION OF THE OUTRAGE—COLORED
TESTIMONY NOTHING—CONDUCT OF MASTER HUGH—SPIRIT OF
SLAVERY IN BALTIMORE—AUTHOR'S CONDITION IMPROVES—NEW
ASSOCIATIONS—SLAVEHOLDERS' RIGHT TO TAKE HIS WAGES—HOW
TO MAKE A CONTENTED SLAVE.

WELL! dear reader, I am not, as you may have already inferred, a
loser by the general upstir, described in the foregoing chapter. The
little domestic revolution, notwithstanding the sudden snub it got
by the treachery of somebody—I dare not say or think *who*—did not,
after all, end so disastrously, as, when in the iron cage at Easton, I
conceived it would. The prospect, from that point, did look about as
dark as any that ever cast its gloom over the vision of the anxious,
out-looking, human spirit. "All is well that ends well."[1] My affectionate comrades, Henry and John Harris, are still with Mr. William
Freeland. Charles Roberts and Henry Baily are safe at their homes.
I have not, therefore, any thing to regret on their account. Their masters have mercifully forgiven them, probably on the ground suggested in the spirited little speech of Mrs. Freeland, made to me just
before leaving for the jail—namely: that they had been allured into
the wicked scheme of making their escape, by me; and that, but for
me, they would never have dreamed of a thing so shocking! My
friends had nothing to regret, either; for while they were watched
more closely on account of what had happened, they were, doubtless, treated more kindly than before, and got new assurances that
they would be legally emancipated, some day, provided their behavior should make them deserving, from that time forward. Not a blow,
as I learned, was struck any one of them. As for Master William
Freeland, good, unsuspecting soul, he did not believe that we were
intending to run away at all. Having given—as he thought—no occasion to his boys to leave him, he could not think it probable that
they had entertained a design so grievous. This, however, was not
the view taken of the matter by "Mas' Billy," as we used to call the
soft spoken, but crafty and resolute Mr. William Hamilton. He had

1. Cf. Shakespeare, *All's Well That Ends Well* 4.4.35 and 5.1.25.

no doubt that the crime had been meditated; and regarding me as the instigator of it, he frankly told Master Thomas that he must remove me from that neighborhood, or he would shoot me down. He would not have one so dangerous as "Frederick" tampering with his slaves. William Hamilton was not a man whose threat might be safely disregarded. I have no doubt that he would have proved as good as his word, had the warning given not been promptly taken. He was furious at the thought of such a piece of high-handed *theft*, as we were about to perpetrate—the stealing of our own bodies and souls! The feasibility of the plan, too, could the first steps have been taken, was marvelously plain. Besides, this was a *new* idea, this use of the bay. Slaves escaping, until now, had taken to the woods; they had never dreamed of profaning and abusing the waters of the noble Chesapeake, by making them the highway from slavery to freedom. Here was a broad road of destruction to slavery, which, before, had been looked upon as a wall of security by slaveholders. But Master Billy could not get Mr. Freeland to see matters precisely as he did; nor could he get Master Thomas so excited as he was himself. The latter—I must say it to his credit—showed much humane feeling in his part of the transaction, and atoned for much that had been harsh, cruel and unreasonable in his former treatment of me and others. His clemency was quite unusual and unlooked for. "Cousin Tom" told me that while I was in jail, Master Thomas was very unhappy; and that the night before his going up to release me, he had walked the floor nearly all night, evincing great distress; that very tempting offers had been made to him, by the negro-traders, but he had rejected them all, saying that *money could not tempt him to sell me to the far south.* All this I can easily believe, for he seemed quite reluctant to send me away, at all. He told me that he only consented to do so, because of the very strong prejudice against me in the neighborhood, and that he feared for my safety if I remained there.

Thus, after three years spent in the country, roughing it in the field, and experiencing all sorts of hardships, I was again permitted to return to Baltimore, the very place, of all others, short of a free state, where I most desired to live. The three years spent in the country, had made some difference in me, and in the household of Master Hugh. "Little Tommy" was no longer *little* Tommy; and I was not the slender lad who had left for the Eastern Shore just three years before. The loving relations between me and Mas' Tommy were broken up. He was no longer dependent on me for protection, but felt himself a *man*, with other and more suitable associates. In childhood, he scarcely considered me inferior to himself—certainly, as good as any other boy with whom he played; but the time had come when his *friend* must become his *slave*. So we were cold, and we parted. It was a sad thing to me, that, loving each other as we had done, we must now take different roads. To him, a thousand avenues were open. Education had made him acquainted with all the treasures of the world, and liberty had flung open the gates thereunto; but I, who had attended him seven years, and had watched over him with the care of a big brother, fighting his battles in the street, and shielding him from harm, to an extent which had induced his mother to say, "Oh! Tommy is always safe, when he is with Freddy," must be confined to a single condition. He could grow, and become a MAN; I could grow, though I could *not* become a man, but must remain, all my life, a minor—a mere boy. Thomas Auld, junior, obtained a situation on board the brig Tweed, and went to sea. I know not what has become of him; he certainly has my good wishes for his welfare and prosperity. There were few persons to whom I was more sincerely attached than to him, and there are few in the world I would be more pleased to meet.

Very soon after I went to Baltimore to live, Master Hugh succeeded in getting me hired to Mr. William Gardiner, an extensive ship builder on Fell's Point. I was placed here to learn to calk, a trade of which I already had some knowledge, gained while in Mr. Hugh Auld's ship-yard, when he was a master builder. Gardiner's, however, proved a very unfavorable place for the accomplishment of that object. Mr. Gardiner was, that season, engaged in building two large man-of-war vessels, professedly for the Mexican government. These vessels were to be launched in the month of July, of that year, and, in failure thereof, Mr. G. would forfeit a very considerable sum of money. So, when I entered the ship-yard, all was hurry and driving. There were in the yard about one hundred men; of these about seventy or eighty were regular carpenters—privileged men. Speaking of my condition here, I wrote, years ago—and I have now no reason to vary the picture—as follows:[2]

> "There was no time to learn any thing. Every man had to do that which he knew how to do. In entering the ship-yard, my orders from Mr. Gardiner were, to do whatever the carpenters commanded me to do. This was placing me at the beck and call of about seventy-five men. I was to regard all these as masters. Their word was to be my law. My situation was a most trying one. At times I needed a dozen pair of hands. I was called a dozen ways in the space of a single minute. Three or four voices would strike my ear at the same moment. It was—'Fred., come help me to cant this timber here."—'Fred., come carry this timber yonder.'—'Fred., bring that roller here.'—'Fred., go get a fresh can of water.'—'Fred., come help saw off the end of this timber.'—'Fred., go quick and get the crowbar.'—'Fred., hold on

2. This block quotation is from Chapter 10 of Douglass's *Narrative*.

the end of this fall.'—'Fred., go the blacksmith's shop, and get a new punch.'—'Hurra, Fred.! run and bring me a cold chisel.'—'I say, Fred., bear a hand, and get up a fire as quick as lightning under that steam-box.'—'Halloo, nigger! come, turn this grindstone.'—'Come, come! move, move! and *bowse* this timber forward.'—'I say, darkey, blast your eyes, why don't you heat up some pitch?'—'Halloo! halloo! halloo!' (Three voices at the same time.) 'Come here!—Go there!—Hold on where you are! D—n you, if you move, I'll knock your brains out!'"

Such, dear reader, is a glance at the school which was mine, during the first eight months of my stay at Baltimore. At the end of eight months, Master Hugh refused longer to allow me to remain with Mr. Gardiner. The circumstance which led to his taking me away, was a brutal outrage, committed upon me by the white apprentices of the ship-yard. The fight was a desperate one, and I came out of it most shockingly mangled. I was cut and bruised in sundry places, and my left eye was nearly knocked out of its socket. The facts, leading to this barbarous outrage upon me, illustrate a phase of slavery destined to become an important element in the overthrow of the slave system, and I may, therefore state them with some minuteness. That phase is this: *the conflict of slavery with the interests of the white mechanics and laborers of the south.* In the country, this conflict is not so apparent; but, in cities, such as Baltimore, Richmond, New Orleans, Mobile, &c., it is seen pretty clearly. The slaveholders, with a craftiness peculiar to themselves, by encouraging the enmity of the poor, laboring white man against the blacks, succeeds in making the said white man almost as much a slave as the black slave himself. The difference between the white slave, and the black slave, is this: the latter belongs to *one* slaveholder, and the former belongs to *all* the slaveholders, collectively. The white slave has taken from him, by indirection, what the black slave has taken from him, directly, and without ceremony. Both are plundered, and by the same plunderers. The slave is robbed, by his master, of all his earnings, above what is required for his bare physical necessities; and the white man is robbed by the slave system, of the just results of his labor, because he is flung into competition with a class of laborers who work without wages. The competition, and its injurious consequences, will, one day, array the non-slaveholding white people of the slave states, against the slave system, and make them the most effective workers against the great evil. At present, the slaveholders blind them to this competition, by keeping alive their prejudice against the slaves, *as men*—not against them *as slaves.* They appeal to their pride, often denouncing emancipation, as tending to place the white working man, on an equality with negroes, and, by this means, they succeed in drawing off the minds of the poor whites from the real fact, that, by the rich slave-master, they are already regarded as but a single remove from equality with the slave. The impression is cunningly made, that slavery is the only power that can prevent the laboring white man from falling to the level of the slave's poverty and degradation. To make this enmity deep and broad, between the slave and the poor white man, the latter is allowed to abuse and whip the former, without hinderance. But—as I have suggested—this state of facts prevails *mostly* in the country. In the city of Baltimore, there are not unfrequent murmurs, that educating the slaves to be mechanics may, in the end, give slave-masters power to dispense with the services of the poor white man altogether. But, with characteristic dread of offending the slaveholders, these poor, white mechanics in Mr. Gardiner's ship-yard—instead of applying the natural, honest remedy for the apprehended evil, and objecting at once to work there by the side of slaves—made a cowardly attack upon the free colored mechanics, saying *they* were eating the bread which should be eaten by American freemen, and swearing that they would not work with them. The feeling was, *really*, against having their labor brought into competition with that of the colored people at all; but it was too much to strike directly at the interest of the slaveholders; and, therefore—proving their servility and cowardice—they dealt their blows on the poor, colored freeman, and aimed to prevent *him* from serving himself, in the evening of life, with the trade with which he had served his master, during the more vigorous portion of his days. Had they succeeded in driving the black freemen out of the ship yard, they would have determined also upon the removal of the black slaves. The feeling was very bitter toward all colored people in Baltimore, about this time, (1836,) and they—free and slave—suffered all manner of insult and wrong.

Until a very little while before I went there, white and black ship carpenters worked side by side, in the ship yards of Mr. Gardiner, Mr. Duncan, Mr. Walter Price, and Mr. Robb.[3] Nobody seemed to see any impropriety in it. To outward seeming, all hands were well satisfied. Some of the blacks were first rate workmen, and were given jobs requiring the highest skill. All at once, however, the white carpenters knocked off, and swore that they would no longer work on the same stage with free negroes. Taking advantage of the heavy contract resting upon Mr. Gardiner, to have the war vessels for Mexico ready to launch in July, and of the difficulty of getting other hands at that season of the year, they swore they would not strike another blow for him, unless he would discharge his free colored workmen.

3. Levin Dunkin, Walter Price, and John Robb all owned shipyards in Fell's Point.

Now, although this movement did not extend to me, *in form*, it did reach me, *in fact*. The spirit which it awakened was one of malice and bitterness, toward colored people *generally*, and I suffered with the rest, and suffered severely. My fellow apprentices very soon began to feel it to be degrading to work with me. They began to put on high looks, and to talk contemptuously and maliciously of "*the niggers;*" saying, that "they would take the country," that "they ought to be killed." Encouraged by the cowardly workmen, who, knowing me to be a slave, made no issue with Mr. Gardiner about my being there, these young men did their utmost to make it impossible for me to stay. They seldom called me to do anything, without coupling the call with a curse, and, Edward North, the biggest in every thing, rascality included, ventured to strike me, whereupon I picked him up, and threw him into the dock. Whenever any of them struck me, I struck back again, regardless of consequences. I could manage any of them *singly*; and, while I could keep them from combining, I succeeded very well. In the conflict which ended my stay at Mr. Gardiner's, I was beset by four of them at once—Ned North, Ned Hays, Bill Stewart, and Tom Humphreys. Two of them were as large as myself, and they came near killing me, in broad day light. The attack was made suddenly, and simultaneously. One came in front, armed with a brick; there was one at each side, and one behind, and they closed up around me. I was struck on all sides; and, while I was attending to those in front, I received a blow on my head, from behind, dealt with a heavy hand-spike. I was completely stunned by the blow, and fell, heavily, on the ground, among the timbers. Taking advantage of my fall, they rushed upon me, and began to pound me with their fists. I let them lay on, for a while, after I came to myself, with a view of gaining strength. They did me little damage, so far; but, finally, getting tired of that sport, I gave a sudden surge, and, despite their weight, I rose to my hands and knees. Just as I did this, one of their number (I know not which) planted a blow with his boot in my left eye, which, for a time, seemed to have burst my eyeball. When they saw my eye completely closed, my face covered with blood, and I staggering under the stunning blows they had given me, they left me. As soon as I gathered sufficient strength, I picked up the hand-spike, and, madly enough, attempted to pursue them; but here the carpenters interfered, and compelled me to give up my frenzied pursuit. It was impossible to stand against so many.

Dear reader, you can hardly believe the statement, but it is true, and, therefore, I write it down: not fewer than fifty white men stood by, and saw this brutal and shameless outrage committed, and not a man of them all interposed a single word of mercy. There were four against one, and that one's face was beaten and battered most horribly, and no one said, "that is enough;" but some cried out, "kill him—kill him—kill the d—d nigger! knock his brains out—he struck a white person." I mention this inhuman outcry, to show the character of the men, and the spirit of the times, at Gardiner's ship yard, and, indeed, in Baltimore generally, in 1836. As I look back to this period, I am almost amazed that I was not murdered outright, in that ship yard, so murderous was the spirit which prevailed there. On two occasions, while there, I came near losing my life. I was driving bolts in the hold, through the keelson, with Hays. In its course, the bolt bent. Hays cursed me, and said that it was my blow which bent the bolt. I denied this, and charged it upon him. In a fit of rage he seized an adze, and darted toward me. I met him with a maul, and parried his blow, or I should have then lost my life. A son of old Tom Lamman,[4] (the latter's double murder I have elsewhere charged upon him,) in the spirit of his miserable father, made an assault upon me, but the blow with his maul missed me. After the united assault of North, Stewart, Hays and Humphreys, finding that the carpenters were as bitter toward me as the apprentices, and that the latter were probably set on by the former, I found my only chance for life was in flight. I succeeded in getting away, without an additional blow. To strike a white man, was death, by Lynch law,[5] in Gardiner's ship yard; nor was there much of any other law toward colored people, at that time, in any other part of Maryland. The whole sentiment of Baltimore was murderous.

After making my escape from the ship yard, I went straight home, and related the story of the outrage to Master Hugh Auld; and it is due to him to say, that his conduct—though he was not a religious man—was every way more humane than that of his brother, Thomas, when I went to the latter in a somewhat similar plight, from the hands of "*Brother Edward Covey*."[6] He listened attentively to my narration of the circumstances leading to the ruffianly outrage, and gave many proofs of his strong indignation at what was done. Hugh was a rough, but manly-hearted fellow, and, at this time, his best nature showed itself.

The heart of my once almost over-kind mistress, Sophia, was again melted in pity toward me. My puffed-out eye, and my scarred and blood-covered face, moved the dear lady to tears. She kindly drew a chair by me, and with friendly, consoling words, she took water, and washed the blood from my face. No mother's hand could have been more tender than hers. She bound up my head, and covered my wounded eye with a lean piece of fresh beef. It was almost compensation for the murderous assault, and my suffering,

---

4. See note 4 on p. 86.
5. "Lynch law": term coined in 1782 to describe the extralegal actions of Virginian Charles Lynch against suspected Loyalists during the American Revolution.
6. See note 5 on p. 131.

that it furnished an occasion for the manifestation, once more, of the originally characteristic kindness of my mistress. Her affectionate heart was not yet dead, though much hardened by time and by circumstances.

As for Master Hugh's part, as I have said, he was furious about it; and he gave expression to his fury in the usual forms of speech in that locality. He poured curses on the heads of the whole ship yard company, and swore that he would have satisfaction for the outrage. His indignation was really strong and healthy; but, unfortunately, it resulted from the thought that his rights of property, in my person, had not been respected, more than from any sense of the outrage committed on me *as a man*. I inferred as much as this, from the fact that he could, himself, beat and mangle when it suited him to do so. Bent on having satisfaction, as he said, just as soon as I got a little the better of my bruises, Master Hugh took me to Esquire Watson's office,[7] on Bond street, Fell's Point, with a view to procuring the arrest of those who had assaulted me. He related the outrage to the magistrate, as I had related it to him, and seemed to expect that a warrant would, at once, be issued for the arrest of the lawless ruffians.

Mr. Watson heard it all, and instead of drawing up his warrant, he inquired.—

"Mr. Auld, who saw this assault of which you speak?"

"It was done, sir, in the presence of a ship yard full of hands."

"Sir," said Watson, "I am sorry, but I cannot move in this matter except upon the oath of white witnesses."

"But here's the boy; look at his head and face," said the excited Master Hugh; "*they* show *what* has been done."

But Watson insisted that he was not authorized to do anything, unless *white* witnesses of the transaction would come forward, and testify to what had taken place. He could issue no warrant on my word, against white persons; and, if I had been killed in the presence of a *thousand blacks*, their testimony, combined, would have been insufficient to arrest a single murderer. Master Hugh, for once, was compelled to say, that this state of things was *too bad*; and he left the office of the magistrate, disgusted.

Of course, it was impossible to get any white man to testify against my assailants. The carpenters saw what was done; but the actors were but the agents of their malice, and did only what the carpenters sanctioned. They had cried, with one accord, "*kill the nigger! kill the nigger!*" Even those who may have pitied me, if any such were among them, lacked the moral courage to come and volunteer their evidence. The slightest manifestation of sympathy or justice toward

7. The office of William H. Watson, justice of the peace.

a person of color, was denounced as abolitionism; and the name of abolitionist, subjected its bearer to frightful liabilities. "D——n *abolitionists*," and "*Kill the niggers*," were the watch-words of the foul-mouthed ruffians of those days. Nothing was done, and probably there would not have been any thing done, had I been killed in the affray. The laws and the morals of the christian city of Baltimore, afforded no protection to the sable denizens of that city.

Master Hugh, on finding he could get no redress for the cruel wrong, withdrew me from the employment of Mr. Gardiner, and took me into his own family, Mrs. Auld kindly taking care of me, and dressing my wounds, until they were healed, and I was ready to go again to work.

While I was on the Eastern Shore, Master Hugh had met with reverses, which overthrew his business; and he had given up ship building in his own yard, on the City Block, and was now acting as foreman of Mr. Walter Price. The best he could now do for me, was to take me into Mr. Price's yard, and afford me the facilities there, for completing the trade which I had began to learn at Gardiner's.[8] Here I rapidly became expert in the use of my calking tools; and, in the course of a single year, I was able to command the highest wages paid to journeymen calkers in Baltimore.

The reader will observe that I was now of some pecuniary value to my master. During the busy season, I was bringing six and seven dollars per week. I have, sometimes, brought him as much as nine dollars a week, for the wages were a dollar and a half per day.

After learning to calk, I sought my own employment, made my own contracts, and collected my own earnings; giving Master Hugh no trouble in any part of the transactions to which I was a party.

Here, then, were better days for the Eastern Shore *slave*. I was now free from the vexatious assaults of the apprentices at Mr. Gardiner's; and free from the perils of plantation life, and once more in a favorable condition to increase my little stock of education, which had been at a dead stand since my removal from Baltimore. I had, on the Eastern Shore, been only a teacher, when in company with other slaves, but now there were colored persons who could instruct me. Many of the young calkers could read, write and cipher. Some of them had high notions about mental improvement; and the free ones, on Fell's Point, organized what they called the "*East Baltimore*

---

8. In 1836–37, Walter Price's shipyard built three illegal slave-trading ships: the *Delorez*, the *Teayer*, and the *Eagle*. Douglass would not have known their eventual use, but he almost certainly helped build them. (American participation in the international slave trade had been made illegal in 1807.)

Mental Improvement Society." To this society, notwithstanding it was intended that only free persons should attach themselves, I was admitted, and was, several times, assigned a prominent part in its debates. I owe much to the society of these young men.

The reader already knows enough of the *ill* effects of good treatment on a slave, to anticipate what was now the case in my improved condition. It was not long before I began to show signs of disquiet with slavery, and to look around for means to get out of that condition by the shortest route. I was living among *freemen*; and was, in all respects, equal to them by nature and by attainments. *Why should I be a slave?* There was *no* reason why I should be the thrall of any man.

Besides, I was now getting—as I have said—a dollar and fifty cents per day. I contracted for it, worked for it, earned it, collected it; it was paid to me, and it was *rightfully* my own; and yet, upon every returning Saturday night, this money—my own hard earnings, every cent of it—was demanded of me, and taken from me by Master Hugh. He did not earn it; he had no hand in earning it; why, then, should he have it? I owed him nothing. He had given me no schooling, and I had received from him only my food and raiment; and for these, my services were supposed to pay, from the first. The right to take my earnings, was the right of the robber. He had the power to compel me to give him the fruits of my labor, and this power was his only right in the case. I became more and more dissatisfied with this state of things; and, in so becoming, I only gave proof of the same human nature which every reader of this chapter in my life—slaveholder, or non-slaveholder—is conscious of possessing.

To make a contented slave, you must make a thoughtless one. It is necessary to darken his moral and mental vision, and, as far as possible, to annihilate his power of reason. He must be able to detect no inconsistencies in slavery. The man that takes his earnings, must be able to convince him that he has a perfect right to do so. It must not depend upon mere force; the slave must know no Higher Law than his master's will. The whole relationship must not only demonstrate, to his mind, its necessity, but its absolute rightfulness. If there be one crevice through which a single drop can fall, it will certainly rust off the slave's chain.

CHAPTER XXI

My Escape from Slavery

CLOSING INCIDENTS OF MY "LIFE AS A SLAVE"—REASONS WHY FULL
PARTICULARS OF THE MANNER OF MY ESCAPE WILL NOT BE GIVEN—
CRAFTINESS AND MALICE OF SLAVEHOLDERS—SUSPICION OF AIDING A
SLAVE'S ESCAPE ABOUT AS DANGEROUS AS POSITIVE EVIDENCE—WANT
OF WISDOM SHOWN IN PUBLISHING DETAILS OF THE ESCAPE OF
FUGITIVES—PUBLISHED ACCOUNTS REACH THE MASTERS, NOT THE
SLAVES—SLAVEHOLDERS STIMULATED TO GREATER WATCHFULNESS—
AUTHOR'S CONDITION—DISCONTENT—SUSPICIONS IMPLIED BY
MASTER HUGH'S MANNER, WHEN RECEIVING MY WAGES—HIS
OCCASIONAL GENEROSITY!—DIFFICULTIES IN THE WAY OF ESCAPE—
EVERY AVENUE GUARDED—PLAN TO OBTAIN MONEY—AUTHOR
ALLOWED TO HIRE HIS TIME—A GLEAM OF HOPE—ATTENDS CAMP-
MEETING, WITHOUT PERMISSION—ANGER OF MASTER HUGH
THEREAT—THE RESULT—MY PLANS OF ESCAPE ACCELERATED
THEREBY—THE DAY FOR MY DEPARTURE FIXED—HARASSED BY
DOUBTS AND FEARS—PAINFUL THOUGHTS OF SEPARATION FROM
FRIENDS—THE ATTEMPT MADE—ITS SUCCESS

I WILL now make the kind reader acquainted with the closing incidents of my "Life as a Slave," having already trenched upon the limit
allotted to my "Life as a Freeman." Before, however, proceeding with
this narration, it is, perhaps, proper that I should frankly state, in
advance, my intention to withhold a part of the facts connected with
my escape from slavery. There are reasons for this suppression,
which I trust the reader will deem altogether valid. It may be easily
conceived, that a full and complete statement of all the facts pertaining to the flight of a bondman, might implicate and embarrass
some who may have, wittingly or unwittingly, assisted him; and no
one can wish me to involve any man or woman who has befriended
me, even in the liability of embarrassment or trouble.

Keen is the scent of the slaveholder; like the fangs of the rattlesnake, his malice retains its poison long; and, although it is now
nearly seventeen years since I made my escape, it is well to be careful, in dealing with the circumstances relating to it. Were I to give
but a shadowy outline of the process adopted, with characteristic
aptitude, the crafty and malicious among the slaveholders might,
possibly, hit upon the track I pursued, and involve some one in suspicion, which, in a slave state, is about as bad as positive evidence.
The colored man, there, must not only shun evil, but shun the very
appearance of evil, or be condemned as a criminal. A slaveholding
community has a peculiar taste for ferreting out offenses against the

slave system, justice there being more sensitive in its regard for the peculiar rights of this system, than for any other interest or institution. By stringing together a train of events and circumstances, even if I were not very explicit, the means of escape might be ascertained, and, possibly, those means be rendered, thereafter, no longer available to the liberty-seeking children of bondage I have left behind me. No anti-slavery man can wish me to do anything favoring such results, and no slaveholding reader has any right to expect the impartment of such information.

While, therefore, it would afford me pleasure, and perhaps would materially add to the interest of my story, were I at liberty to gratify a curiosity which I know to exist in the minds of many, as to the manner of my escape, I must deprive myself of this pleasure, and the curious of the gratification, which such a statement of facts would afford. I would allow myself to suffer under the greatest imputations that evil minded men might suggest, rather than exculpate myself by an explanation, and thereby run the hazard of closing the slightest avenue by which a brother in suffering might clear himself of the chains and fetters of slavery.

The practice of publishing every new invention by which a slave is known to have escaped from slavery, has neither wisdom nor necessity to sustain it. Had not Henry Box Brown[1] and his friends attracted slaveholding attention to the manner of his escape, we might have had a thousand *Box Browns* per annum. The singularly original plan adopted by William and Ellen Crafts,[2] perished with the first using, because every slaveholder in the land was apprised of it. The *salt water slave* who hung in the guards of a steamer, being washed three days and three nights—like another Jonah[3]—by the waves of the sea, has, by the publicity given to the circumstance, set a spy on the guards of every steamer departing from southern ports.

I have never approved of the very public manner, in which some of our western friends have conducted what *they* call the "*Under-ground Railroad*,"[4] but which, I think, by their open declarations, has been made, most emphatically, the "*Upper*-ground Railroad." Its stations are far better known to the slaveholders than to the slaves. I honor those good men and women for their noble daring, in willingly subjecting themselves to persecution, by openly avowing

1. Brown escaped from slavery in 1849 by shipping himself in a wooden crate to Philadelphia. His own *Narrative* (1849) made him a prominent lecturer on the abolitionist circuit.
2. This couple fled Macon, Georgia, in 1848 by train, disguised as an elderly white man and his valet.
3. The central character in the biblical book of Jonah. He is cast overboard during a storm and is saved by being swallowed by a whale, in whose belly he spends three days.
4. The Underground Railroad was a network of safe houses and secret routes used by enslaved persons to escape into free states.

their participation in the escape of slaves; nevertheless, the good resulting from such avowals, is of a very questionable character. It may kindle an enthusiasm, very pleasant to inhale; but that is of no practical benefit to themselves, nor to the slaves escaping. Nothing is more evident, than that such disclosures are a positive evil to the slaves remaining, and seeking to escape. In publishing such accounts, the anti-slavery man addresses the slaveholder, *not the slave*; he stimulates the former to greater watchfulness, and adds to his facilities for capturing his slave. We owe something to the slaves, south of Mason and Dixon's line,[5] as well as to those north of it; and, in discharging the duty of aiding the latter, on their way to freedom, we should be careful to do nothing which would be likely to hinder the former, in making their escape from slavery. Such is my detestation of slavery, that I would keep the merciless slaveholder profoundly ignorant of the means of flight adopted by the slave. He should be left to imagine himself surrounded by myriads of invisible tormentors, ever ready to snatch, from his infernal grasp, his trembling prey. In pursuing his victim, let him be left to feel his way in the dark; let shades of darkness, commensurate with his crime, shut every ray of light from his pathway; and let him be made to feel, that, at every step he takes, with the hellish purpose of reducing a brother man to slavery, he is running the frightful risk of having his hot brains dashed out by an invisible hand.

But, enough of this. I will now proceed to the statement of those facts, connected with my escape, for which I am alone responsible, and for which no one can be made to suffer but myself.

My condition in the year (1838) of my escape, was, comparatively, a free and easy one, so far, at least, as the wants of the physical man were concerned; but the reader will bear in mind, that my troubles from the beginning, have been less physical than mental, and he will thus be prepared to find, after what is narrated in the previous chapters, that slave life was adding nothing to its charms for me, as I grew older, and became better acquainted with it. The practice, from week to week, of openly robbing me of all my earnings, kept the nature and character of slavery constantly before me. I could be robbed by *indirection*, but this was *too* open and barefaced to be endured. I could see no reason why I should, at the end of each week, pour the reward of my honest toil into the purse of any man. The thought itself vexed me, and the manner in which Master Hugh received my wages, vexed me more than the original wrong. Carefully counting the money and rolling it out, dollar by dollar, he would look me in the face, as if he would search my heart as well as my pocket, and reproachfully ask me, "*Is that all?*"—implying that I had,

5. See note 1 on p. 128.

perhaps, kept back part of my wages; or, if not so, the demand was made, possibly, to make me feel, that, after all, I was an "unprofit-able servant."[6] Draining me of the last cent of my hard earnings, he would, however, occasionally—when I brought home an extra large sum—dole out to me a sixpence or a shilling, with a view, perhaps, of kindling up my gratitude; but this practice had the opposite effect—it was an admission of *my right to the whole sum.* The fact, that he gave me any part of my wages, was proof that he suspected that I had a right *to the whole of them.* I always felt uncomfortable, after having received anything in this way, for I feared that the giv-ing me a few cents, might, possibly, ease his conscience, and make him feel himself a pretty honorable robber, after all!

Held to a strict account, and kept under a close watch—the old suspicion of my running away not having been entirely removed—escape from slavery, even in Baltimore, was very difficult. The rail-road from Baltimore to Philadelphia was under regulations so stringent, that even *free* colored travelers were almost excluded. They must have *free* papers; they must be measured and carefully exam-ined, before they were allowed to enter the cars; they only went in the day time, even when so examined. The steamboats were under regulations equally stringent. All the great turnpikes, leading north-ward, were beset with kidnappers, a class of men who watched the newspapers for advertisements for runaway slaves, making their liv-ing by the accursed reward of slave hunting.

My discontent grew upon me, and I was on the look-out for means of escape. With money, I could easily have managed the matter, and, therefore, I hit upon the plan of soliciting the privilege of hiring my time. It is quite common, in Baltimore, to allow slaves this privilege, and it is the practice, also, in New Orleans. A slave who is considered trust-worthy, can, by paying his master a definite sum regularly, at the end of each week, dispose of his time as he likes. It so happened that I was not in very good odor,[7] and I was far from being a trust-worthy slave. Nevertheless, I watched my opportunity when Master Thomas came to Baltimore, (for I was still his property, Hugh only acted as his agent,) in the spring of 1838, to purchase his spring supply of goods, and applied to him, directly, for the much-coveted privilege of hiring my time. This request Master Thomas unhesitatingly refused to grant; and he charged me, with some sternness, with inventing this stratagem to make my escape. He told me, "I could go *nowhere* but he could catch me; and, in the event of my running away, I might be assured he should spare no pains in his efforts to recapture me. He recounted, with a good deal of eloquence, the many kind offices

6. Cf. Luke 17.10.
7. Displeasing, out of favor.

he had done me, and exhorted me to be contented and obedient. "Lay out no plans for the future," said he. "If you behave yourself properly, I will take care of you." Now, kind and considerate as this offer was, it failed to soothe me into repose. In spite of Master Thomas, and, I may say, in spite of myself, also, I continued to think, and worse still, to think almost exclusively about the injustice and wickedness of slavery. No effort of mine or of his could silence this trouble-giving thought, or change my purpose to run away.

About two months after applying to Master Thomas for the privilege of hiring my time, I applied to Master Hugh for the same liberty, supposing him to be unacquainted with the fact that I had made a similar application to Master Thomas, and had been refused. My boldness in making this request, fairly astounded him at the first. He gazed at me in amazement. But I had many good reasons for pressing the matter; and, after listening to them awhile, he did not absolutely refuse, but told me he would think of it. Here, then, was a gleam of hope. Once master of my own time, I felt sure that I could make, over and above my obligation to him, a dollar or two every week. Some slaves have made enough, in this way, to purchase their freedom. It is a sharp spur to industry; and some of the most enterprising colored men in Baltimore hire themselves in this way. After mature reflection—as I must suppose it was—Master Hugh granted me the privilege in question, on the following terms: I was to be allowed all my time; to make all bargains for work; to find my own employment, and to collect my own wages; and, in return for this liberty, I was required, or obliged, to pay him three dollars at the end of each week, and to board and clothe myself, and buy my own calking tools. A failure in any of these particulars would put an end to my privilege. This was a hard bargain. The wear and tear of clothing, the losing and breaking of tools, and the expense of board, made it necessary for me to earn at least six dollars per week, to keep even with the world. All who are acquainted with calking, know how uncertain and irregular that employment is. It can be done to advantage only in dry weather, for it is useless to put wet oakum into a seam. Rain or shine, however, work or no work, at the end of each week the money must be forthcoming.

Master Hugh seemed to be very much pleased, for a time, with this arrangement; and well he might be, for it was decidedly in his favor. It relieved him of all anxiety concerning me. His money was sure. He had armed my love of liberty with a lash and a driver, far more efficient than any I had before known; and, while he derived all the benefits of slaveholding by the arrangement, without its evils, I endured all the evils of being a slave, and yet suffered all the care and anxiety of a responsible freeman. "Nevertheless," thought I, "it is a valuable privilege—another step in my career toward freedom."

It was something even to be permitted to stagger under the disadvantages of liberty, and I was determined to hold on to the newly gained footing, by all proper industry. I was ready to work by night as well as by day; and being in the enjoyment of excellent health, I was able not only to meet my current expenses, but also to lay by a small sum at the end of each week. All went on thus, from the month of May till August; then—for reasons which will become apparent as I proceed—my much valued liberty was wrested from me.

During the week previous to this (to me) calamitous event, I had made arrangements with a few young friends, to accompany them, on Saturday night, to a camp-meeting, held about twelve miles from Baltimore. On the evening of our intended start for the camp-ground, something occurred in the ship yard where I was at work, which detained me unusually late, and compelled me either to disappoint my young friends, or to neglect carrying my weekly dues to Master Hugh. Knowing that I had the money, and could hand it to him on another day, I decided to go to camp-meeting, and to pay him the three dollars, for the past week, on my return. Once on the camp-ground, I was induced to remain one day longer than I had intended, when I left home. But, as soon as I returned, I went straight to his house on Fell street, to hand him his (my) money. Unhappily, the fatal mistake had been committed. I found him exceedingly angry. He exhibited all the signs of apprehension and wrath, which a slaveholder may be surmised to exhibit on the supposed escape of a favorite slave. "You rascal! I have a great mind to give you a severe whipping. How dare you go out of the city without first asking and obtaining my permission?" "Sir," said I, "I hired my time and paid you the price you asked for it. I did not know that it was any part of the bargain that I should ask you when or where I should go."

"You did not know, you rascal! You are bound to show yourself here every Saturday night." After reflecting, a few moments, he became somewhat cooled down; but, evidently greatly troubled, he said, "Now, you scoundrel! you have done for yourself; you shall hire your time no longer. The next thing I shall hear of, will be your running away. Bring home your tools and your clothes, at once. I'll teach you how to go off in this way."

Thus ended my partial freedom. I could hire my time no longer; and I obeyed my master's orders at once. The little taste of liberty which I had had—although as the reader will have seen, it was far from being unalloyed—by no means enhanced my contentment with slavery. Punished thus by Master Hugh, it was now my turn to punish him. "Since," thought I, "you *will* make a slave of me, I will await your orders in all things;" and, instead of going to look for work on Monday morning, as I had formerly done, I remained at home during the entire week, without the performance of a single stroke of work.

Saturday night came, and he called upon me, as usual, for my wages. I, of course, told him I had done no work, and had no wages. Here we were at the point of coming to blows. His wrath had been accumulating during the whole week; for he evidently saw that I was making no effort to get work, but was most aggravatingly awaiting his orders, in all things. As I look back to this behavior of mine, I scarcely know what possessed me, thus to trifle with those who had such unlimited power to bless or to blast me. Master Hugh raved and swore his determination to "*get hold of me*;" but, wisely for *him*, and happily for *me*, his wrath only employed those very harmless, impalpable missiles, which roll from a limber tongue. In my desperation, I had fully made up my mind to measure strength with Master Hugh, in case he should undertake to execute his threats. I am glad there was no necessity for this; for resistance to him could not have ended so happily for me, as it did in the case of Covey. He was not a man to be safely resisted by a slave; and I freely own, that in my conduct toward him, in this instance, there was more folly than wisdom. Master Hugh closed his reproofs, by telling me that, hereafter, I need give myself no uneasiness about getting work; that he "would, himself, see to getting work for me, and enough of it, at that." This threat I confess had some terror in it; and, on thinking the matter over, during the Sunday, I resolved, not only to save him the trouble of getting me work, but that, upon the third day of September, I would attempt to make my escape from slavery. The refusal to allow me to hire my time, therefore, hastened the period of my flight. I had three weeks, now, in which to prepare for my journey.

Once resolved, I felt a certain degree of repose, and on Monday, instead of waiting for Master Hugh to seek employment for me, I was up by break of day, and off to the ship yard of Mr. Butler, on the City Block, near the draw-bridge. I was a favorite with Mr. B., and, young as I was, I had served as his foreman on the float stage, at calking. Of course, I easily obtained work, and, at the end of the week—which by the way was exceedingly fine—I brought Master Hugh nearly nine dollars. The effect of this mark of returning good sense, on my part, was excellent. He was very much pleased; he took the money, commended me, and told me I might have done the same thing the week before. It is a blessed thing that the tyrant may not always know the thoughts and purposes of his victim. Master Hugh little knew what my plans were. The going to camp-meeting without asking his permission—the insolent answers made to his reproaches—the sulky deportment the week after being deprived of the privilege of hiring my time—had awakened in him the suspicion that I might be cherishing disloyal purposes. My object, therefore, in working steadily, was to remove suspicion, and in this I succeeded admirably. He probably thought I was never better satisfied with my condition, than at the very time I was planning my escape. The second week passed, and again I carried him my full week's wages—*nine dollars*; and so well pleased was he, that he gave me TWENTY-FIVE CENTS! and "bade me make good use of it!" I told him I would, for one of the uses to which I meant to put it, was to pay my fare on the underground railroad.

Things without went on as usual; but I was passing through the same internal excitement and anxiety which I had experienced two years and a half before. The failure, in that instance, was not calculated to increase my confidence in the success of this, my second attempt; and I knew that a second failure could not leave me where my first did—I must either get to the *far north*, or be sent to the *far south*. Besides the exercise of mind from this state of facts, I had the painful sensation of being about to separate from a circle of honest and warm hearted friends, in Baltimore. The thought of such a separation, where the hope of ever meeting again is excluded, and where there can be no correspondence, is very painful. It is my opinion, that thousands would escape from slavery who now remain there, but for the strong cords of affection that bind them to their families, relatives and friends. The daughter is hindered from escaping, by the love she bears her mother, and the father, by the love he bears his children; and so, to the end of the chapter. I had no relations in Baltimore, and I saw no probability of ever living in the neighborhood of sisters and brothers; but the thought of leaving my friends, was among the strongest obstacles to my running away. The last two days of the week—Friday and Saturday—were spent mostly in collecting my things together, for my journey. Having worked four days that week, for my master, I handed him six dollars, on Saturday night. I seldom spent my Sundays at home; and, for fear that something might be discovered in my conduct, I kept up my custom, and absented myself all day. On Monday, the third day of September, 1838, in accordance with my resolution, I bade farewell to the city of Baltimore, and to that slavery which had been my abhorrence from childhood.

How I got away—in what direction I traveled—whether by land or by water; whether with or without assistance—must, for reasons already mentioned, remain unexplained.

Life as a Freeman

CHAPTER XXII

Liberty Attained

TRANSITION FROM SLAVERY TO FREEDOM—A WANDERER IN NEW YORK—FEELINGS ON REACHING THAT CITY—AN OLD ACQUAINTANCE MET—UNFAVORABLE IMPRESSIONS—LONELINESS AND INSECURITY—APOLOGY FOR SLAVES WHO RETURN TO THEIR MASTERS—COMPELLED TO TELL MY CONDITION—SUCCORED BY A SAILOR—DAVID RUGGLES—THE UNDERGROUND RAILROAD—MARRIAGE—BAGGAGE TAKEN FROM ME—KINDNESS OF NATHAN JOHNSON—THE AUTHOR'S CHANGE OF NAME—DARK NOTIONS OF NORTHERN CIVILIZATION—THE CONTRAST—COLORED PEOPLE IN NEW BEDFORD—AN INCIDENT ILLUSTRATING THEIR SPIRIT—THE AUTHOR AS A COMMON LABORER—DENIED WORK AT HIS TRADE—THE FIRST WINTER AT THE NORTH—REPULSE AT THE DOORS OF THE CHURCH—SANCTIFIED HATE—THE LIBERATOR AND ITS EDITOR

THERE is no necessity for any extended notice of the incidents of this part of my life. There is nothing very striking or peculiar about my career as a freeman, when viewed apart from my life as a slave. The relation subsisting between my early experience and that which I am now about to narrate, is, perhaps, my best apology for adding another chapter to this book.

Disappearing from the kind reader, in a flying cloud or balloon, (pardon the figure,) driven by the wind, and knowing not where I should land—whether in slavery or in freedom—it is proper that I should remove, at once, all anxiety, by frankly making known where I alighted. The flight was a bold and perilous one; but here I am, in the great city of New York, safe and sound, without loss of blood or bone. In less than a week after leaving Baltimore, I was walking amid the hurrying throng, and gazing upon the dazzling wonders of Broadway. The dreams of my childhood and the purposes of my manhood were now fulfilled. A free state around me, and a free earth under my feet! What a moment was this to me! A whole year was pressed into a single day. A new world burst upon my agitated vision. I have often been asked, by kind friends to whom I have told my story, how I felt when first I found myself beyond the limits of slavery; and I must say here, as I have often said to them, there is scarcely anything about which I could not give a more satisfactory answer. It was a moment of joyous excitement, which no words can describe. In a letter to a friend, written soon after reaching New York, I said I felt as one might be supposed to feel, on escaping from a den of hungry lions. But, in a moment like that, sensations are too intense and too rapid for words. Anguish and grief, like darkness and rain, may be described, but joy and gladness, like the rainbow of promise, defy alike the pen and pencil.

For ten or fifteen years I had been dragging a heavy chain, with a huge block attached to it, cumbering my every motion. I had felt myself doomed to drag this chain and this block through life. All efforts, before, to separate myself from the hateful encumbrance, had only seemed to rivet me the more firmly to it. Baffled and discouraged at times, I had asked myself the question, May not this, after all, be God's work? May He not, for wise ends, have doomed me to this lot? A contest had been going on in my mind for years, between the clear consciousness of right and the plausible errors of superstition; between the wisdom of manly courage, and the foolish weakness of timidity. The contest was now ended; the chain was severed; God and right stood vindicated. I WAS A FREEMAN, and the voice of peace and joy thrilled my heart.

Free and joyous, however, as I was, joy was not the only sensation I experienced. It was like the quick blaze, beautiful at the first, but which subsiding, leaves the building charred and desolate. I was soon taught that I was still in an enemy's land. A sense of loneliness and insecurity oppressed me sadly. I had been but a few hours in New York, before I was met in the streets by a fugitive slave, well known to me, and the information I got from him respecting New York, did nothing to lessen my apprehension of danger. The fugitive in question was "Allender's Jake," in Baltimore; but, said he, I am "WILLIAM DIXON," in New York![1] I knew Jake well, and knew when Tolly Allender and Mr. Price (for the latter employed Master Hugh as his foreman, in his shipyard on Fell's Point) made an attempt to recapture Jake, and failed. Jake told me all about his circumstances, and how narrowly he escaped being taken back to slavery; that the city was now full of southerners, returning from the springs; that

---

1. William Dixon had escaped from Baltimore and fled to New York, where he was arrested and imprisoned in 1837. He met Douglas soon after being freed from prison for lack of evidence. Runaway slaves, by the terms of the Constitution, should be arrested anywhere as property. States where slavery had ended tended to be more hostile to these laws, especially after 1850.

the black people in New York were not to be trusted; that there were
hired men on the lookout for fugitives from slavery, and who, for a
few dollars, would betray me into the hands of the slave-catchers;
that I must trust no man with my secret; that I must not think of
going either on the wharves to work, or to a boarding-house to board;
and, worse still, this same Jake told me it was not in his power to
help me. He seemed, even while cautioning me, to be fearing lest,
after all, I might be a party to a second attempt to recapture him.
Under the inspiration of this thought, I must suppose it was, he gave
signs of a wish to get rid of me, and soon left me—his whitewash
brush in hand—as he said, for his work. He was soon lost to sight
among the throng, and I was alone again, an easy prey to the kidnappers, if any should happen to be on my track.

New York, seventeen years ago, was less a place of safety for a runaway slave than now, and all know how unsafe it now is, under the
new fugitive slave bill.[2] I was much troubled. I had very little
money—enough to buy me a few loaves of bread, but not enough to
pay board, outside a lumber yard.[3] I saw the wisdom of keeping away
from the ship yards, for if Master Hugh pursued me, he would naturally expect to find me looking for work among the calkers. For a
time, every door seemed closed against me. A sense of my loneliness
and helplessness crept over me, and covered me with something bor-
dering on despair. In the midst of thousands of my fellow-men, and
yet a perfect stranger! In the midst of human brothers, and yet more
fearful of them than of hungry wolves! I was without home, without friends, without work, without money, and without any definite
knowledge of which way to go, or where to look for succor.

Some apology can easily be made for the few slaves who have,
after making good their escape, turned back to slavery, preferring
the actual rule of their masters, to the life of loneliness, apprehension, hunger, and anxiety, which meets them on their first arrival in
a free state. It is difficult for a freeman to enter into the feelings of
such fugitives. He cannot see things in the same light with the slave,
because he does not, and cannot, look from the same point from
which the slave does. "Why do you tremble," he says to the slave—
"you are in a free state;" but the difficulty is, in realizing that he is
in a free state, the slave might reply. A freeman cannot understand
why the slave-master's shadow is bigger, to the slave, than the might

2. The Fugitive Slave Act, or Fugitive Slave Law, was the central feature of the Compromise of 1850, a series of resolutions intended to bridge over the intensifying differences
between the slaveholding South and the free states of the North. In effect, the Act made
escaping from slavery a federal offense. It required states and state officials to cooperate
in the hunting, capture, and extradition of escaped enslaved persons. It infuriated not
just abolitionists but many Northerners who hitherto had been critics of abolitionism.
3. Douglass humorously implies that at night he secretly could take shelter in a lumber-
yard free of charge.

and majesty of a free state; but when he reflects that the slave knows more about the slavery of his master than he does of the might and majesty of the free state, he has the explanation. The slave has been all his life learning the power of his master—being trained to dread his approach—and only a few hours learning the power of the state. The master is to him a stern and flinty reality, but the state is little more than a dream. He has been accustomed to regard every white man as the friend of his master, and every colored man as more or less under the control of his master's friends—the white people. It takes stout nerves to stand up, in such circumstances. A man, home-less, shelterless, breadless, friendless, and moneyless, is not in a condition to assume a very proud or joyous tone; and in just this condition was I, while wandering about the streets of New York city and lodging, at least one night, among the barrels on one of its wharves. I was not only free from slavery, but I was free from home, as well. The reader will easily see that I had something more than the simple fact of being free to think of, in this extremity.

I kept my secret as long as I could, and at last was forced to go in search of an honest man[4]—a man sufficiently *human* not to betray me into the hands of slave-catchers. I was not a bad reader of the human face, nor long in selecting the right man, when once com-pelled to disclose the facts of my condition to some one.

I found my man in the person of one who said his name was Stew-art. He was a sailor, warm-hearted and generous, and he listened to my story with a brother's interest. I told him I was running for my freedom—knew not where to go—money almost gone—was hungry—thought it unsafe to go the shipyards for work, and needed a friend. Stewart promptly put me in the way of getting out of my trouble. He took me to his house, and went in search of the late David Ruggles,[5] who was then the secretary of the New York Vigi-lance Committee, and a very active man in all anti-slavery works. Once in the hands of Mr. Ruggles, I was comparatively safe. I was hidden with Mr. Ruggles several days. In the meantime, my intended wife, Anna,[6] came on from Baltimore—to whom I had written, informing her of my safe arrival at New York—and, in the presence of Mrs. Mitchell and Mr. Ruggles, we were married, by Rev. James W. C. Pennington.

---

4. Reference to Diogenes, an ancient Greek wise man who traveled widely and unsuc-cessfully in search of an honest man.
5. Prominent black leader in New York (1810–1849) who helped found the New York Committee of Vigilance to both shield fugitive slaves and protect free Blacks.
6. Anna Murray Douglass (1813–1882) was a free Black woman and domestic servant in Baltimore. She had encouraged Douglass's escape from slavery, but the two did not have a happy marriage, and he rarely mentioned her.

Mr. Ruggles[7] was the first officer on the underground railroad with whom I met after reaching the north, and, indeed, the first of whom I ever heard anything. Learning that I was a calker by trade, he promptly decided that New Bedford was the proper place to send me. "Many ships," said he, "are there fitted out for the whaling business, and you may there find work at your trade, and make a good living." Thus, in one fortnight after my flight from Maryland, I was safe in New Bedford, regularly entered upon the exercise of the rights, responsibilities, and duties of a freeman.

I may mention a little circumstance which annoyed me on reaching New Bedford. I had not a cent of money, and lacked two dollars toward paying our fare from Newport, and our baggage—not very costly—was taken by the stage driver,[8] and held until I could raise the money to redeem it. This difficulty was soon surmounted. Mr. Nathan Johnson, to whom we had a line from Mr. Ruggles, not only received us kindly and hospitably, but, on being informed about our baggage, promptly loaned me two dollars with which to redeem my little property. I shall ever be deeply grateful, both to Mr. and Mrs. Nathan Johnson, for the lively interest they were pleased to take in me, in this the hour of my extremest need. They not only gave myself and wife bread and shelter, but taught us how to begin to secure those benefits for ourselves. Long may they live, and may blessings attend them in this life and in that which is to come!

Once initiated into the new life of freedom, and assured by Mr. Johnson that New Bedford was a safe place, the comparatively unimportant matter, as to what should be my name, came up for consideration. It was necessary to have a name in my new relations. The name given me by my beloved mother was no less pretentious than "Frederick Augustus Washington Bailey." I had, however, before leaving Maryland, dispensed with the *Augustus Washington*, and retained the name *Frederick Bailey*. Between Baltimore and New Bedford, however, I had several different names, the better to avoid being overhauled by the hunters, which I had good reason to believe would be put on my track. Among honest men an honest man may well be content with one name, and to acknowledge it at all times .

---

7. He was a whole-souled man, fully imbued with a love of his afflicted and hunted people, and took pleasure in being to me, as was his wont, "Eyes to the blind, and legs to the lame" [Cf. Job 29.15] This brave and devoted man suffered much from the persecutions common to all who have been prominent benefactors. He at last became blind, and needed a friend to guide him, even as he had been a guide to others. Even in his blindness, he exhibited his manly character. In search of health, he became a physician. When hope of gaining his own was gone, he had hope for others. Believing in hydropathy, he established, at Northampton, Massachusetts, a large "*Water Cure*," and became one of the most successful of all engaged in that mode of treatment [*Author's note*].
8. "stage driver": the person controlling the horses pulling a stagecoach.

and in all places; but toward fugitives, Americans are not honest. When I arrived at New Bedford, my name was Johnson; and finding that the Johnson family in New Bedford were already quite numerous—sufficiently so to produce some confusion in attempts to distinguish one from another—there was the more reason for making another change in my name. In fact, "Johnson" had been assumed by nearly every slave who had arrived in New Bedford from Maryland, and this, much to the annoyance of the original "Johnsons" (of whom there were many) in that place. Mine host, unwilling to have another of his own name added to the community in this unauthorized way, after I spent a night and a day at his house, gave me my present name. He had been reading the "Lady of the Lake," and was pleased to regard me as a suitable person to wear this, one of Scotland's many famous names.[9] Considering the noble hospitality and manly character of Nathan Johnson, I have felt that he, better than I, illustrated the virtues of the great Scottish chief. Sure I am, that had any slave-catcher entered his domicile, with a view to molest any one of his household, he would have shown himself like him of the "stalwart hand."

The reader will be amused at my ignorance, when I tell the notions I had of the state of northern wealth, enterprise, and civilization. Of wealth and refinement, I supposed the north had none. My Columbian Orator,[1] which was almost my only book, had not done much to enlighten me concerning northern society. The impressions I had received were all wide of the truth. New Bedford, especially, took me by surprise, in the solid wealth and grandeur there exhibited. I had formed my notions respecting the social condition of the free states, by what I had seen and known of free, white, non-slaveholding people in the slave states. Regarding slavery as the basis of wealth, I fancied that no people could become very wealthy without slavery. A free white man, holding no slaves, in the country, I had known to be the most ignorant and poverty-stricken of men, and the laughing stock even of slaves themselves—called generally by them, in derision, *"poor white trash."* Like the non-slaveholders at the south, in holding no slaves, I supposed the northern people like them, also, in poverty and degradation. Judge, then, of my amazement and joy, when I found—as I did find—the very laboring population of New Bedford living in better houses, more elegantly furnished—surrounded by more comfort and refinement—than a majority of the slaveholders on the Eastern Shore of Maryland. There was my friend, Mr. Johnson, himself a

9. Douglass named himself after Lord James of Douglas, a Scottish chieftain celebrated—in part for his "stalwart hand"—in the narrative poem *The Lady of the Lake* (1810), by Sir Walter Scott (see note 3 on p. 39).
1. See note 3 on p. 104.

colored man, (who at the south would have been regarded as a proper marketable commodity,) who lived in a better house—dined at a richer board—was the owner of more books—the reader of more newspapers—was more conversant with the political and social condition of this nation and the world—than nine-tenths of all the slaveholders of Talbot county, Maryland. Yet Mr. Johnson was a working man, and his hands were hardened by honest toil. Here, then, was something for observation and study. Whence the difference? The explanation was soon furnished, in the superiority of mind over simple brute force. Many pages might be given to the contrast, and in explanation of its causes. But an incident or two will suffice to show the reader as to how the mystery gradually vanished before me.

My first afternoon, on reaching New Bedford, was spent in visiting the wharves and viewing the shipping. The sight of the broad brim and the plain, Quaker dress, which met me at every turn, greatly increased my sense of freedom and security. "I am among the Quakers," thought I, "and am safe." Lying at the wharves and riding in the stream, were full-rigged ships of finest model, ready to start on whaling voyages. Upon the right and the left, I was walled in by large granite-fronted warehouses, crowded with the good things of this world. On the wharves, I saw industry without bustle, labor without noise, and heavy toil without the whip. There was no loud singing, as in southern ports, where ships are loading or unloading—no loud cursing or swearing—but everything went on as smoothly as the works of a well adjusted machine. How different was all this from the noisily fierce and clumsily absurd manner of labor-life in Baltimore and St. Michael's! One of the first incidents which illustrated the superior mental character of northern labor over that of the south, was the manner of unloading a ship's cargo of oil. In a southern port, twenty or thirty hands would have been employed to do what five or six did here, with the aid of a single ox attached to the end of a fall. Main strength, unassisted by skill, is slavery's method of labor. An old ox, worth eighty dollars, was doing, in New Bedford, what would have required fifteen thousand dollars worth of human bones and muscles to have performed in a southern port. I found that everything was done here with a scrupulous regard to economy, both in regard to men and things, time and strength. The maid servant, instead of spending at least a tenth part of her time in bringing and carrying water, as in Baltimore, had the pump at her elbow. The wood was dry, and snugly piled away for winter. Wood-houses, in-door pumps, sinks, drains, self-shutting gates, washing machines, pounding barrels, were all new things, and told me that I was among a thoughtful and sensible people. To the ship-repairing dock I went, and saw the same wise prudence. The carpenters struck where they aimed, and the calkers wasted no blows in idle flourishes of the mallet. I learned that men went from New Bedford to Baltimore, and bought old ships, and brought them here to repair, and made them better and more valuable than they ever were before. Men talked here of going whaling on a four *years'* voyage with more coolness than sailors where I came from talked of going [on] a four *months'* voyage.

I now find that I could have landed in no part of the United States, where I should have found a more striking and gratifying contrast to the condition of the free people of color in Baltimore, than I found here in New Bedford. No colored man is really free in a slaveholding state. He wears the badge of bondage while nominally free, and is often subjected to hardships to which the slave is a stranger; but here in New Bedford, it was my good fortune to see a pretty near approach to freedom on the part of the colored people. I was taken all aback when Mr. Johnson—who lost no time in making me acquainted with the fact—told me that there was nothing in the constitution of Massachusetts to prevent a colored man from holding any office in the state. There, in New Bedford, the black man's children—although anti-slavery was then far from popular—went to school side by side with the white children, and apparently without objection from any quarter. To make me at home, Mr. Johnson assured me that no slaveholder could take a slave from New Bedford; that there were men there who would lay down their lives, before such an outrage could be perpetrated. The colored people themselves were of the best metal, and would fight for liberty to the death.

Soon after my arrival in New Bedford, I was told the following story, which was said to illustrate the spirit of the colored people in that goodly town: A colored man and a fugitive slave happened to have a little quarrel, and the former was heard to threaten the latter with informing his master of his whereabouts. As soon as this threat became known, a notice was read from the desk of what was then the only colored church in the place, stating that business of importance was to be then and there transacted. Special measures had been taken to secure the attendance of the would-be Judas, and had proved successful. Accordingly, at the hour appointed, the people came, and the betrayer also. All the usual formalities of public meetings were scrupulously gone through, even to the offering prayer for Divine direction in the duties of the occasion. The president himself performed this part of the ceremony, and I was told that he was unusually fervent. Yet, at the close of his prayer, the old man (one of the numerous family of Johnsons) rose from his knees, deliberately surveyed his audience, and then said, in a tone of solemn resolution, "*Well, friends, we have got him here, and I would now recommend*

*that you young men should just take him outside the door and kill
him."* With this, a large body of the congregation, who well understood the business they had come there to transact, made a rush at
the villain, and doubtless would have killed him, had he not availed
himself of an open sash, and made good his escape. He has never
shown his head in New Bedford since that time. This little incident
is perfectly characteristic of the spirit of the colored people in New
Bedford. A slave could not be taken from that town seventeen years
ago, any more than he could be so taken away now. The reason is, that
the colored people in that city are educated up to the point of fighting
for their freedom, as well as speaking for it.

Once assured of my safety in New Bedford, I put on the habiliments of a common laborer, and went on the wharf in search of
work. I had no notion of living on the honest and generous sympathy of my colored brother, Johnson, or that of the abolitionists.
My cry was like that of Hood's laborer, "Oh! only give me work."[2]
Happily for me, I was not long in searching. I found employment,
the third day after my arrival in New Bedford, in stowing a sloop
with a load of oil for the New York market. It was new, hard, and
dirty work, even for a calker, but I went at it with a glad heart and
a willing hand. I was now my own master—a tremendous fact—
and the rapturous excitement with which I seized the job, may
not easily be understood, except by some one with an experience
something like mine. The thoughts—"I can work! I can work for a
living; I am not afraid of work; I have no Master Hugh to rob me
of my earnings"—placed me in a state of independence, beyond
seeking friendship or support of any man. That day's work I considered the real starting point of something like a new existence.
Having finished this job and got my pay for the same, I went next in
pursuit of a job at calking. It so happened that Mr. Rodney French,
late mayor of the city of New Bedford, had a ship fitting out for sea,
and to which there was a large job of calking and coppering to be
done. I applied to that noble-hearted man for employment, and he
promptly told me to go to work; but going on the float-stage for the
purpose, I was informed that every white man would leave the ship if
I struck a blow upon her. "Well, well," thought I, "this is a hardship,
but yet not a very serious one for me." The difference between the
wages of a calker and that of a common day laborer, was an hundred per cent. in favor of the former; but then I was free, and free
to work, though not at my trade. I now prepared myself to do anything which came to hand in the way of turning an honest penny;
sawed wood—dug cellars—shoveled coal—swept chimneys with

2. Cf. line 43 of "The Lay of the Laborer," by the English poet Thomas Flood (1799–
1845).

Uncle Lucas Debuty—rolled oil casks on the wharves—helped to load and unload vessels—worked in Ricketson's candle works—in Richmond's brass foundery, and elsewhere; and thus supported myself and family for three years.

The first winter was unusually severe, in consequence of the high prices of food; but even during that winter we probably suffered less than many who had been free all their lives. During the hardest of the winter, I hired out for nine dollars a month; and out of this rented two rooms for nine dollars per quarter, and supplied my wife—who was unable to work—with food and some necessary articles of furniture. We were closely pinched to bring our wants within our means; but the jail stood over the way, and I had a wholesome dread of the consequences of running in debt. This winter past, and I was up with the times—got plenty of work—got well paid for it—and felt that I had not done a foolish thing to leave Master Hugh and Master Thomas. I was now living in a new world, and was wide awake to its advantages. I early began to attend the meetings of the colored people of New Bedford, and to take part in them. I was somewhat amazed to see colored men drawing up resolutions and offering them for consideration. Several colored young men of New Bedford, at that period, gave promise of great usefulness. They were educated, and possessed what seemed to me, at that time, very superior talents. Some of them have been cut down by death, and others have removed to different parts of the world, and some remain there now, and justify, in their present activities, my early impressions of them.

Among my first concerns on reaching New Bedford, was to become united with the church, for I had never given up, in reality, my religious faith. I had become lukewarm and in a backslidden state, but I was still convinced that it was my duty to join the Methodist church. I was not then aware of the powerful influence of that religious body in favor of the enslavement of my race, nor did I see how the northern churches could be responsible for the conduct of southern churches; neither did I fully understand how it could be my duty to remain separate from the church, because bad men were connected with it. The slaveholding church, with its Coveys, Weedens, Aulds, and Hopkins, I could see through at once, but I could not see how Elm Street church, in New Bedford, could be regarded as sanctioning the christianity of these characters in the church at St. Michael's. I therefore resolved to join the Methodist church in New Bedford, and to enjoy the spiritual advantage of public worship. The minister of the Elm Street Methodist church, was the Rev. Mr. Bonney; and although I was not allowed a seat in the body of the house, and was proscribed on account of my color, regarding this proscription simply as an accommodation of the unconverted congregation who had not yet been won to Christ and his brotherhood,

I was willing thus to be proscribed, lest sinners should be driven away from the saving power of the gospel. Once converted, I thought they would be sure to treat me as a man and a brother. "Surely," thought I, "these christian people have none of this feeling against color. They, at least, have renounced this unholy feeling." Judge, then, dear reader, of my astonishment and mortification, when I found, as soon I did find, all my charitable assumptions at fault.

An opportunity was soon afforded me for ascertaining the exact position of Elm Street church on that subject. I had a chance of seeing the religious part of the congregation by themselves; and although they disowned, in effect, their black brothers and sisters, before the world, I did think that where none but the saints were assembled, and no offense could be given to the wicked, and the gospel could not be "blamed," they would certainly recognize us as children of the same Father, and heirs of the same salvation, on equal terms with themselves.

The occasion to which I refer, was the sacrament of the Lord's Supper, that most sacred and most solemn of all the ordinances of the christian church. Mr. Bonney had preached a very solemn and searching discourse, which really proved him to be acquainted with the inmost secrets of the human heart. At the close of his discourse, the congregation was dismissed, and the church remained to partake of the sacrament. I remained to see, as I thought, this holy sacrament celebrated in the spirit of its great Founder.

There were only about a half dozen colored members attached to the Elm Street church, at this time. After the congregation was dismissed, these descended from the gallery, and took a seat against the wall most distant from the altar. Brother Bonney was very animated, and sung very sweetly, "Salvation 'tis a joyful sound," and soon began to administer the sacrament. I was anxious to observe the bearing of the colored members, and the result was most humiliating. During the whole ceremony, they looked like sheep without a shepherd. The white members went forward to the altar by the bench full; and when it was evident that all the whites had been served with the bread and wine, Brother Bonney—pious Brother Bonney—after a long pause, as if inquiring whether all the white members had been served, and fully assuring himself on that important point, then raised his voice to an unnatural pitch, and looking to the corner where his black sheep seemed penned, beckoned with his hand, exclaiming, "Come forward, colored friends!—come forward! You, too, have an interest in the blood of Christ. God is no respecter of persons. Come forward, and take this holy sacrament to your comfort." The colored members—poor, slavish souls—went forward, as invited. I went *out*, and have never been in that church since, although I honestly went there with a view to joining that body. I found it impossible to respect the religious profession of any who were under the dominion of this wicked prejudice, and I could not, therefore, feel that in joining them, I was joining a christian church, at all. I tried other churches in New Bedford, with the same result, and, finally, I attached myself to a small body of colored Methodists, known as the Zion Methodists.[3] Favored with the affection and confidence of the members of this humble communion, I was soon made a class-leader and a local preacher among them. Many seasons of peace and joy I experienced among them, the remembrance of which is still precious, although I could not see it to be my duty to remain with that body, when I found that it consented to the same spirit which held my brethren in chains.

In four or five months after reaching New Bedford, there came a young man to me, with a copy of the "Liberator," the paper edited by William Lloyd Garrison, and published by Isaac Knapp,[4] and asked me to subscribe for it. I told him I had but just escaped from slavery, and was of course very poor, and remarked further, that I was unable to pay for it then; the agent, however, very willingly took me as a subscriber, and appeared to be much pleased with securing my name to his list. From this time I was brought in contact with the mind of William Lloyd Garrison. His paper took its place with me next to the bible.

The Liberator was a paper after my own heart. It detested slavery— exposed hypocrisy and wickedness in high places—made no truce with the traffickers in the bodies and souls of men; it preached human brotherhood, denounced oppression, and, with all the solemnity of God's word, demanded the complete emancipation of my race. I not only liked—I *loved* this paper, and its editor. He seemed a match for all the opponents of emancipation, whether they spoke in the name of the law, or the gospel. His words were few, full of holy fire, and straight to the point. Learning to love him, through his paper, I was prepared to be pleased with his presence. Something of a hero worshiper, by nature, here was one, on first sight, to excite my love and reverence.

Seventeen years ago, few men possessed a more heavenly countenance than William Lloyd Garrison, and few men evinced a more genuine or a more exalted piety. The bible was his text book—held sacred, as the word of the Eternal Father—sinless perfection—complete submission to insults and injuries—literal

---

3. New Bedford Zion Methodists were part of the African Methodist Episcopal Church.
4. Printer and abolitionist (1804–1843) and one of William Lloyd Garrison's earliest collaborators. On Garrison, see note 7 on p. 23.

obedience to the injunction, if smitten on one side to turn the other also.[5] Not only was Sunday a Sabbath, but all days were Sabbaths, and to be kept holy. All sectarism false and mischievous—the regenerated, throughout the world, members of one body, and the HEAD Christ Jesus. Prejudice against color was rebellion against God. Of all men beneath the sky, the slaves, because most neglected and despised, were nearest and dearest to his great heart. Those ministers who defended slavery from the bible, were of their "father the devil;"[6] and those churches which fellowshiped slaveholders as christians, were synagogues of Satan, and our nation was a nation of liars. Never loud or noisy—calm and serene as a summer sky, and as pure. "You are the man, the Moses, raised up by God, to deliver his modern Israel from bondage,"[7] was the spontaneous feeling of my heart, as I sat away back in the hall and listened to his mighty words; mighty in truth—mighty in their simple earnestness.

I had not long been a reader of the Liberator, and listener to its editor, before I got a clear apprehension of the principles of the anti-slavery movement. I had already the spirit of the movement, and only needed to understand its principles and measures. These I got from the Liberator, and from those who believed in that paper. My acquaintance with the movement increased my hope for the ultimate freedom of my race, and I united with it from a sense of delight, as well as duty.

Every week the Liberator came, and every week I made myself master of its contents. All the anti-slavery meetings held in New Bedford I promptly attended, my heart burning at every true utterance against the slave system, and every rebuke of its friends and supporters. Thus passed the first three years of my residence in New Bedford. I had not then dreamed of the possibility of my becoming a public advocate of the cause so deeply imbedded in my heart. It was enough for me to listen—to receive and applaud the great words of others, and only whisper in private, among the white laborers on the wharves, and elsewhere, the truths which burned in my breast.

5. Cf. Matthew 5.39.
6. Cf. John 8.44.
7. Douglass is comparing Garrison to Moses, who, in the Bible's Book of Exodus, led his people out of slavery to freedom.

CHAPTER XXIII

Introduced to the Abolitionists

FIRST SPEECH AT NANTUCKET—MUCH SENSATION—EXTRAORDINARY
SPEECH OF MR. GARRISON—AUTHOR BECOMES A PUBLIC
LECTURER—FOURTEEN YEARS' EXPERIENCE—YOUTHFUL
ENTHUSIASM—A BRAND NEW FACT—MATTER OF THE AUTHOR'S
SPEECH—HE COULD NOT FOLLOW THE PROGRAMME—HIS FUGITIVE
SLAVESHIP DOUBTED—TO SETTLE ALL DOUBT HE WRITES HIS
EXPERIENCE OF SLAVERY—DANGER OF RECAPTURE INCREASED

IN the summer of 1841, a grand anti-slavery convention was held in
Nantucket, under the auspices of Mr. Garrison and his friends.[1]
Until now, I had taken no holiday since my escape from slavery. Having worked very hard that spring and summer, in Richmond's brass
foundery—sometimes working all night as well as all day—and
needing a day or two of rest, I attended this convention, never supposing that I should take part in the proceedings. Indeed, I was not
aware that any one connected with the convention even so much as
knew my name. I was, however, quite mistaken. Mr. William C.
Coffin,[2] a prominent abolitionist in those days of trial, had heard
me speaking to my colored friends, in the little school house on
Second street, New Bedford, where we worshiped. He sought me
out in the crowd, and invited me to say a few words to the convention. Thus sought out, and thus invited, I was induced to speak out
the feelings inspired by the occasion, and the fresh recollection of
the scenes through which I had passed as a slave. My speech on this
occasion is about the only one I ever made, of which I do not remember a single connected sentence. It was with the utmost difficulty
that I could stand erect, or that I could command and articulate two
words without hesitation and stammering. I trembled in every limb.
I am not sure that my embarrassment was not the most effective
part of my speech, if speech it could be called. At any rate, this is
about the only part of my performance that I now distinctly remember. But excited and convulsed as I was, the audience, though
remarkably quiet before, became as much excited as myself.
Mr. Garrison followed me, taking me as his text; and now, whether
I had made an eloquent speech in behalf of freedom or not, his was
one never to be forgotten by those who heard it. Those who had
heard Mr. Garrison oftenest, and had known him longest, were

1. See note 7 on p. 23.
2. A passionate abolitionist, best known for encouraging Douglass to speak at the Nantucket Atheneum, where he first encountered William Lloyd Garrison (see p. viii).

astonished. It was an effort of unequaled power, sweeping down, like a very tornado, every opposing barrier, whether of sentiment or opinion. For a moment, he possessed that almost fabulous inspiration, often referred to but seldom attained, in which a public meeting is transformed, as it were, into a single individuality—the orator wielding a thousand heads and hearts at once, and by the simple majesty of his all controlling thought, converting his hearers into the express image of his own soul. That night there were at least one thousand Garrisonians in Nantucket! At the close of this great meeting, I was duly waited on by Mr. John A. Collins—then the general agent of the Massachusetts anti-slavery society[3]—and urgently solicited by him to become an agent of that society, and to publicly advocate its anti-slavery principles. I was reluctant to take the proffered position. I had not been quite three years from slavery—was honestly distrustful of my ability—wished to be excused; publicity exposed me to discovery and arrest by my master; and other objections came up, but Mr. Collins was not to be put off, and I finally consented to go out for three months, for I supposed that I should have got to the end of my story and my usefulness, in that length of time.

Here opened upon me a new life—a life for which I had had no preparation. I was a "graduate from the peculiar institution," Mr. Collins used to say, when introducing me, "*with my diploma written on my back!*" The three years of my freedom had been spent in the hard school of adversity. My hands had been furnished by nature with something like a solid leather coating, and I had bravely marked out for myself a life of rough labor, suited to the hardness of my hands, as a means of supporting myself and rearing my children.

Now what shall I say of this fourteen years' experience as a public advocate of the cause of my enslaved brothers and sisters? The time is but as a speck, yet large enough to justify a pause for retrospection—and a pause it must only be.

Young, ardent, and hopeful, I entered upon this new life in the full gush of unsuspecting enthusiasm. The cause was good; the men engaged in it were good; the means to attain its triumph, good; Heaven's blessing must attend all, and freedom must soon be given to the pining millions under a ruthless bondage. My whole heart went with the holy cause, and my most fervent prayer to the Almighty Disposer of the hearts of men, were continually offered for its early triumph. "Who or what," thought I, "can withstand a cause so good, so holy, so indescribably glorious. The God of Israel is with us. The might of the Eternal is on our side. Now let but the truth be

---

3. Collins (1810–c. 1879) remained with the Society until 1843.

spoken, and a nation will start forth at the sound!" In this enthusiastic spirit, I dropped into the ranks of freedom's friends, and went forth to the battle. For a time I was made to forget that my skin was dark and my hair crisped. For a time I regretted that I could not have shared the hardships and dangers endured by the earlier workers for the slave's release. I soon, however, found that my enthusiasm had been extravagant; that hardships and dangers were not yet passed; and that the life now before me, had shadows as well as sunbeams.

Among the first duties assigned me, on entering the ranks, was to travel, in company with Mr. George Foster, to secure subscribers to the "Anti-slavery Standard"[4] and the "Liberator." With him I traveled and lectured through the eastern counties of Massachusetts. Much interest was awakened—large meetings assembled. Many came, no doubt, from curiosity to hear what a negro could say in his own cause. I was generally introduced as a "*chattel*"—a "*thing*"— a piece of southern "*property*"—the chairman assuring the audience that *it* could speak. Fugitive slaves, at that time, were not so plentiful as now; and as a fugitive slave lecturer, I had the advantage of being a "*brand new fact*"—the first one out. Up to that time, a colored man was deemed a fool who confessed himself a runaway slave, not only because of the danger to which he exposed himself of being retaken, but because it was a confession of a very *low* origin! Some of my colored friends in New Bedford thought very badly of my wisdom for thus exposing and degrading myself. The only precaution I took, at the beginning, to prevent Master Thomas from knowing where I was, and what I was about, was the withholding my former name, my master's name, and the name of the state and county from which I came. During the first three or four months, my speeches were almost exclusively made up of narrations of my own personal experience as a slave. "Let us have the facts," said the people. So also said Friend George Foster, who always wished to pin me down to my simple narrative. "Give us the facts," said Collins, "we will take care of the philosophy." Just here arose some embarrassment. It was impossible for me to repeat the same old story month after month, and to keep up my interest in it. It was new to the people, it is true, but it was an old story to me; and to go through with it night after night, was a task altogether too mechanical for my nature. "Tell your story, Frederick," would whisper my then revered friend, William Lloyd Garrison, as I stepped upon the platform. I could not always obey, for I was now reading and thinking. New views of the subject

4. The *National Anti-Slavery Standard*, a newspaper published in New York City 1840–72, represented the views of the American Anti-Slavery Society. George Foster, a member of the Society, traveled with Douglass in the early 1840s, giving abolitionist lectures.

were presented to my mind. It did not entirely satisfy me to *narrate* wrongs; I felt like *denouncing* them. I could not always curb my moral indignation for the perpetrators of slaveholding villainy, long enough for a circumstantial statement of the facts which I felt almost everybody must know. Besides, I was growing, and needed room. "People won't believe you ever was a slave, Frederick, if you keep on this way," said Friend Foster. "Be yourself," said Collins, "and tell your story." It was said to me, "Better have a *little* of the plantation manner of speech than not; 'tis not best that you seem too learned." These excellent friends were actuated by the best of motives, and were not altogether wrong in their advice; and still I must speak just the word that seemed to *me* the word to be spoken *by* me.

At last the apprehended trouble came. People doubted if I had ever been a slave. They said I did not talk like a slave, look like a slave, nor act like a slave, and that they believed I had never been south of Mason and Dixon's line.[5] "He don't tell us where he came from— what his master's name was—how he got away—nor the story of his experience. Besides, he is educated, and is, in this, a contradiction of all the facts we have concerning the ignorance of the slaves." Thus, I was in a pretty fair way to be denounced as an impostor. The committee of the Massachusetts anti-slavery society knew all the facts in my case, and agreed with me in the prudence of keeping them private. They, therefore, never doubted my being a genuine fugitive; but going down the aisles of the churches in which I spoke, and hearing the free spoken Yankees saying, repeatedly, *"He's never been a slave, I'll warrant ye,"* I resolved to dispel all doubt, at no distant day, by such a revelation of facts as could not be made by any other than a genuine fugitive.

In a little less than four years, therefore, after becoming a public lecturer, I was induced to write out the leading facts connected with my experience in slavery, giving names of persons, places, and dates—thus putting it in the power of any who doubted, to ascertain the truth or falsehood of my story of being a fugitive slave. This statement soon became known in Maryland, and I had reason to believe that an effort would be made to recapture me.

It is not probable that any open attempt to secure me as a slave could have succeeded, further than the obtainment, by my master, of the money value of my bones and sinews. Fortunately for me, in the four years of my labors in the abolition cause, I had gained many friends, who would have suffered themselves to be taxed to almost any extent to save me from slavery. It was felt that I had committed the double offense of running away, and exposing the secrets and crimes of slavery and slaveholders. There was a double motive for

5. See note 1 on p. 128.

seeking my reënslavement—avarice and vengeance; and while, as I have said, there was little probability of successful recapture, if attempted openly, I was constantly in danger of being spirited away, at a moment when my friends could render me no assistance. In traveling about from place to place—often alone—I was much exposed to this sort of attack. Any one cherishing the design to betray me, could easily do so, by simply tracing my whereabouts through the anti-slavery journals, for my meetings and movements were promptly made known in advance. My true friends, Mr. Garrison and Mr. Phillips,[6] had no faith in the power of Massachusetts to protect me in my right to liberty. Public sentiment and the law, in their opinion, would hand me over to the tormentors. Mr. Phillips, especially, considered me in danger, and said, when I showed him the manuscript of my story, if in my place, he would throw it into the fire. Thus, the reader will observe, the settling of one difficulty only opened the way for another; and that though I had reached a free state, and had attained a position for public usefulness, I was still tormented with the liability of losing my liberty. How this liability was dispelled, will be related, with other incidents, in the next chapter.

CHAPTER XXIV

Twenty-One Months in Great Britain

GOOD ARISING OUT OF UNPROPITIOUS EVENTS—DENIED CABIN PASSAGE—PROSCRIPTION TURNED TO GOOD ACCOUNT—THE HUTCHINSON FAMILY—THE MOB ON BOARD THE CAMBRIA—HAPPY INTRODUCTION TO THE BRITISH PUBLIC—LETTER ADDRESSED TO WILLIAM LLOYD GARRISON—TIME AND LABORS WHILE ABROAD— FREEDOM PURCHASED—MRS. HENRY RICHARDSON—FREE PAPERS— ABOLITIONISTS DISPLEASED WITH THE RANSOM—HOW THE AUTHOR'S ENERGIES WERE DIRECTED—RECEPTION SPEECH IN LONDON— CHARACTER OF THE SPEECH DEFENDED—CIRCUMSTANCES EXPLAINED—CAUSES CONTRIBUTING TO THE SUCCESS OF HIS MISSION—FREE CHURCH OF SCOTLAND—TESTIMONIAL

THE allotments of Providence, when coupled with trouble and anxiety, often conceal from finite vision the wisdom and goodness in which they are sent; and, frequently, what seemed a harsh and invidious dispensation, is converted by after experience into a happy and beneficial arrangement. Thus, the painful liability to be returned

6. See note 2 on p. 24.

again to slavery, which haunted me by day, and troubled my dreams by night, proved to be a necessary step in the path of knowledge and usefulness. The writing of my pamphlet, in the spring of 1845, endangered my liberty, and led me to seek a refuge from republican slavery in monarchical England. A rude, uncultivated fugitive slave was driven, by stern necessity, to that country to which young American gentlemen go to increase their stock of knowledge, to seek pleasure, to have their rough, democratic manners softened by contact with English aristocratic refinement. On applying for a passage to England, on board the Cambria, of the Cunard line, my friend, James N. Buffum,[1] of Lynn, Massachusetts, was informed that I could not be received on board as a cabin passenger. American prejudice against color triumphed over British liberality and civilization, and erected a color test and condition for crossing the sea in the cabin of a British vessel. The insult was keenly felt by my white friends, but to me, it was common, expected, and therefore, a thing of no great consequence, whether I went in the cabin or in the steerage. Moreover, I felt that if I could not go into the first cabin, first-cabin passengers could come into the second cabin, and the result justified my anticipations to the fullest extent. Indeed, I soon found myself an object of more general interest than I wished to be; and so far from being degraded by being placed in the second cabin, that part of the ship became the scene of as much pleasure and refinement, during the voyage, as the cabin itself. The Hutchinson Family,[2] celebrated vocalists—fellow-passengers—often came to my rude forecastle deck, and sung their sweetest songs, enlivening the place with eloquent music, as well as spirited conversation, during the voyage. In two days after leaving Boston, one part of the ship was about as free to me as another. My fellow-passengers not only visited me, but invited me to visit them, on the saloon deck. My visits there, however, were but seldom. I preferred to live within my privileges, and keep upon my own premises. I found this quite as much in accordance with good policy, as with my own feelings. The effect was, that with the majority of the passengers, all color distinctions were flung to the winds, and I found myself treated with every mark of respect, from the beginning to the end of the voyage, except in a single instance; and in that, I came near being mobbed, for complying with an invitation given me by the passengers, and the captain of the "Cambria," to deliver a lecture on slavery. Our New Orleans and Georgia passengers were pleased to regard my lecture as an insult offered to them, and swore I should not speak. They went so

---

1. Garrisonian abolitionist (1807–1888) who accompanied Douglass on his first trip to Great Britain, 1845–47 (see p. viii).
2. Musical quartet who supported abolitionism and performed frequently at abolitionist meetings.

far as to threaten to throw me overboard, and but for the firmness of Captain Judkins, probably would have (under the inspiration of *slavery* and *brandy*) attempted to put their threats into execution. I have no space to describe this scene, although its tragic and comic peculiarities are well worth describing. An end was put to the *melee*, by the captain's calling the ship's company to put the salt water mobocrats in irons. At this determined order, the gentlemen of the lash scampered, and for the rest of the voyage conducted themselves very decorously.

This incident of the voyage, in two days after landing at Liverpool, brought me at once before the British public, and that by no act of my own. The gentlemen so promptly snubbed in their meditated violence, flew to the press to justify their conduct, and to denounce me as a worthless and insolent negro. This course was even less wise than the conduct it was intended to sustain; for, besides awakening something like a national interest in me, and securing me an audience, it brought out counter statements, and threw the blame upon themselves, which they had sought to fasten upon me and the gallant captain of the ship.

Some notion may be formed of the difference in my feelings and circumstances, while abroad, from the following extract from one of a series of letters addressed by me to Mr. Garrison, and published in the Liberator. It was written on the first day of January, 1846:

> "MY DEAR FRIEND GARRISON: Up to this time, I have given no direct expression of the views, feelings, and opinions which I have formed, respecting the character and condition of the people of this land. I have refrained thus, purposely. I wish to speak advisedly, and in order to do this, I have waited till, I trust, experience has brought my opinions to an intelligent maturity. I have been thus careful, not because I think what I say will have much effect in shaping the opinions of the world, but because whatever of influence I may possess, whether little or much, I wish it to go in the right direction, and according to truth. I hardly need say that, in speaking of Ireland, I shall be influenced by no prejudices in favor of America. I think my circumstances all forbid that. I have no end to serve, no creed to uphold, no government to defend; and as to nation, I belong to none. I have no protection at home, or resting-place abroad. The land of my birth welcomes me to her shores only as a slave, and spurns with contempt the idea of treating me differently; so that I am an outcast from the society of my childhood, and an outlaw in the land of my birth. 'I am a stranger with thee, and a sojourner, as all my fathers were.'[3] That men should be

---

3. Cf. Psalm 39.12.

patriotic, is to me perfectly natural; and as a philosophical fact, I am able to give it an *intellectual* recognition. But no further can I go. If ever I had any patriotism, or any capacity for the feeling, it was whipped out of me long since, by the lash of the American soul-drivers.

In thinking of America, I sometimes find myself admiring her bright blue sky, her grand old woods, her fertile fields, her beautiful rivers, her mighty lakes, and star-crowned mountains. But my rapture is soon checked, my joy is soon turned to mourning. When I remember that all is cursed with the infernal spirit of slaveholding, robbery, and wrong; when I remember that with the waters of her noblest rivers, the tears of my brethren are borne to the ocean, disregarded and forgotten, and that her most fertile fields drink daily of the warm blood of my outraged sisters; I am filled with unutterable loathing, and led to reproach myself that anything could fall from my lips in praise of such a land. America will not allow her children to love her. She seems bent on compelling those who would be her warmest friends, to be her worst enemies. May God give her repentance, before it is too late, is the ardent prayer of my heart. I will continue to pray, labor, and wait, believing that she cannot always be insensible to the dictates of justice, or deaf to the voice of humanity.

"My opportunities for learning the character and condition of the people of this land have been very great. I have traveled almost from the Hill of Howth to the Giant's Causeway, and from the Giant's Causeway to Cape Clear.[4] During these travels, I have met with much in the character and condition of the people to approve, and much to condemn; much that has thrilled me with pleasure, and very much that has filled me with pain. I will not, in this letter, attempt to give any description of those scenes which have given me pain. This I will do hereafter. I have enough, and more than your subscribers will be disposed to read at one time, of the bright side of the picture. I can truly say, I have spent some of the happiest moments of my life since landing in this country. I seem to have undergone a transformation. I live a new life. The warm and generous coöperation extended to me by the friends of my despised race; the prompt and liberal manner with which the press has rendered me its aid; the glorious enthusiasm with which thousands have flocked to hear the cruel wrongs of my down-trodden and long-enslaved fellow-countrymen portrayed; the deep sympathy for the slave, and the strong abhorrence of the slaveholder, everywhere evinced; the cordiality with which members and

---

4. I.e., from the eastern coast of Ireland to the north coast, and from the north coast to the south coast.

ministers of various religious bodies, and of various shades of religious opinion, have embraced me, and lent me their aid; the kind hospitality constantly proffered to me by persons of the highest rank in society; the spirit of freedom that seems to animate all with whom I come in contact, and the entire absence of everything that looked like prejudice against me, on account of the color of my skin—contrasted so strongly with my long and bitter experience in the United States, that I look with wonder and amazement on the transition. In the southern part of the United States, I was a slave, thought of and spoken of as property; in the language of the LAW, '*held, taken, reputed, and adjudged to be a chattel in the hands of my owners and possessors, and their executors, administrators, and assigns, to all intents, constructions, and purposes whatsoever.*' (Brev. Digest,[5] 224.) In the northern states, a fugitive slave, liable to be hunted at any moment, like a felon, and to be hurled into the terrible jaws of slavery—doomed by an inveterate prejudice against color to insult and outrage on every hand, (Massachusetts out of the question)[6]—denied the privileges and courtesies common to others in the use of the most humble means of conveyance— shut out from the cabins on steamboats—refused admission to respectable hotels—caricatured, scorned, scoffed, mocked, and maltreated with impunity by any one, (no matter how black his heart,) so [long as] he has a white skin. But now behold the change! Eleven days and a half gone, and I have crossed three thousand miles of the perilous deep. Instead of a democratic government, I am under a monarchical government. Instead of the bright, blue sky of America, I am covered with the soft, grey fog of the Emerald Isle. I breathe, and lo! the chattel becomes a man. I gaze around in vain for one who will question my equal humanity, claim me as his slave, or offer me an insult. I employ a cab—I am seated beside white people—I reach the hotel—I enter the same door—I am shown into the same parlor—I dine at the same table—and no one is offended. No delicate nose grows deformed in my presence. I find no difficulty here in obtaining admission into any place of worship, instruction, or amusement, on equal terms with people as white as any I ever saw in the United States. I meet nothing to remind me of my complexion. I find myself regarded and treated at every turn with the kindness and deference paid to white people. When I go to church, I am met by no upturned nose and scornful lip to tell me, '*We don't allow niggers in here!*'

---

5. *Brevard's Digest*, shorthand name for a compendium of South Carolina laws pertaining to slavery, compiled by the judge and legal scholar Joseph Brevard (1766–1821).
6. Douglass makes an exception of Massachusetts, which in 1843 passed a law prohibiting racial discrimination on the state's railroads. (Douglass refers to this legislation on p. 246 of this volume.)

"I remember, about two years ago, there was in Boston, near the south-west corner of Boston Common, a menagerie. I had long desired to see such a collection as I understood was being exhibited there. Never having had an opportunity while a slave, I resolved to seize this, my first, since my escape. I went, and as I approached the entrance to gain admission, I was met and told by the door-keeper, in a harsh and contemptuous tone, 'We don't allow niggers in here.' I also remember attending a revival meeting in the Rev. Henry Jackson's meeting-house, at New Bedford, and going up the broad aisle to find a seat, I was met by a good deacon, who told me, in a pious tone, 'We don't allow niggers in here!' Soon after my arrival in New Bedford, from the south, I had a strong desire to attend the Lyceum, but was told, 'They don't allow niggers in here!' While passing from New York to Boston, on the steamer Massachusetts, on the night of the 9th of December, 1843, when chilled almost through with the cold, I went into the cabin to get a little warm. I was soon touched upon the shoulder, and told, 'We don't allow niggers in here!' On arriving in Boston, from an anti-slavery tour, hungry and tired, I went into an eating-house, near my friend, Mr. Campbell's, to get some refreshments. I was met by a lad in a white apron, 'We don't allow niggers in here!' A week or two before leaving the United States, I had a meeting appointed at Weymouth, the home of that glorious band of true abolitionists, the Weston family, and others. On attempting to take a seat in the omnibus to that place, I was told by the driver, (and I never shall forget his fiendish hate,) 'I don't allow niggers in here!' Thank heaven for the respite I now enjoy! I had been in Dublin but a few days, when a gentleman of great respectability kindly offered to conduct me through all the public buildings of that beautiful city; and a little afterward, I found myself dining with the lord mayor of Dublin. What a pity there was not some American democratic christian at the door of his splendid mansion, to bark out at my approach, 'They don't allow niggers in here!' The truth is, the people here know nothing of the republican negro hate prevalent in our glorious land. They measure and esteem men according to their moral and intellectual worth, and not according to the color of their skin. Whatever may be said of the aristocracies here, there is none based on the color of a man's skin. This species of aristocracy belongs preëminently to 'the land of the free, and the home of the brave.' I have never found it abroad, in any but Americans. It sticks to them wherever they go. They find it almost as hard to get rid of, as to get rid of their skins.

"The second day after my arrival at Liverpool, in company with my friend, Buffum, and several other friends, I went to Eaton Hall, the residence of the Marquis of Westminster, one of the most splendid buildings in England. On approaching the door, I found several of our American passengers, who came out with us in the Cambria, waiting for admission, as but one party was allowed in the house at a time. We all had to wait till the company within came out. And of all the faces, expressive of chagrin, those of the Americans were preeminent. They looked as sour as vinegar, and as bitter as gall, when they found I was to be admitted on equal terms with themselves. When the door was opened, I walked in, on an equal footing with my white fellow-citizens, and from all I could see, I had as much attention paid me by the servants that showed us through the house, as any with a paler skin. As I walked through the building, the statuary did not fall down, the pictures did not leap from their places, the doors did not refuse to open, and the servants did not say, *'We don't allow niggers in here!'*

"A happy new-year to you, and all the friends of freedom."

My time and labors, while abroad, were divided between England, Ireland, Scotland, and Wales. Upon this experience alone, I might write a book twice the size of this, *"My Bondage and my Freedom."* I visited and lectured in nearly all the large towns and cities in the United Kingdom, and enjoyed many favorable opportunities for observation and information. But books on England are abundant, and the public may, therefore, dismiss any fear that I am meditating another infliction in that line; though, in truth, I should like much to write a book on those countries, if for nothing else, to make grateful mention of the many dear friends, whose benevolent actions toward me are ineffaceably stamped upon my memory, and warmly treasured in my heart. To these friends I owe my freedom in the United States. On their own motion, without any solicitation from me, (Mrs. Henry Richardson, a clever lady, remarkable for her devotion to every good work, taking the lead,) they raised a fund sufficient to purchase my freedom, and actually paid it over, and placed the papers[7] of my manumission in my hands, before they would

---

7. The following is a copy of these curious papers, both of my transfer from Thomas to Hugh Auld, and from Hugh to myself:

"Know all men by these Presents, That I, Thomas Auld, of Talbot county, and state of Maryland, for and in consideration of the sum of one hundred dollars, current money, to me paid by Hugh Auld, of the city of Baltimore, in the said state, at and before the sealing and delivery of these presents, the receipt whereof, I, the said Thomas Auld, do hereby acknowledge, have granted, bargained, and sold, and by these presents do grant, bargain, and sell unto the said Hugh Auld, his executors, administrators, and assigns, ONE NEGRO MAN, by the name of FREDERICK BAILY, or DOUGLASS, as he calls himself—he is now about twenty-eight years of age—to have and to hold the said negro man for life. And I, the said Thomas Auld, for myself, my heirs, executors, and administrators, all and singular, the said FREDERICK BAILY, *alias* DOUGLASS, unto the said Hugh Auld, his executors, administrators, and assigns, against me, the said Thomas Auld, my executors, and administrators, and against all and every other person or persons whatsoever, shall and will warrant and forever defend

tolerate the idea of my returning to this, my native country. To this commercial transaction I owe my exemption from the democratic operation of the fugitive slave bill of 1850.[8] But for this, I might at any time become a victim of this most cruel and scandalous enactment, and be doomed to end my life, as I began it, a slave. The sum paid for my freedom was one hundred and fifty pounds sterling.[9]

Some of my uncompromising anti-slavery friends in this country failed to see the wisdom of this arrangement, and were not pleased that I consented to it, even by my silence. They thought it a violation of anti-slavery principles—conceding a right of property in man—and a wasteful expenditure of money. On the other hand, viewing it simply in the light of a ransom, or as money extorted by a robber, and my liberty of more value than one hundred and fifty pounds sterling, I could not see either a violation of the laws of morality, or those of economy, in the transaction.

It is true, I was not in the possession of my claimants, and could have easily remained in England, for the same friends who had so generously purchased my freedom, would have assisted me in establishing myself in that country. To this, however, I could not consent. I felt that I had a duty to perform—and that was, to labor and suffer with the oppressed in my native land. Considering, therefore, all the circumstances—the fugitive slave bill included—I think the very best thing was done in letting Master Hugh have the hundred and fifty pounds sterling, and leaving me free to return to my appropriate field of labor. Had I been a private person, having no other relations or duties than those of a personal and family nature, I

---

by these presents. In witness whereof, I set my hand and seal, this thirteenth day of November, eighteen hundred and forty-six.   THOMAS AULD.
   "Signed, sealed, and delivered in presence of Wrightson Jones.
"JOHN C. LEAS."

The authenticity of this bill of sale is attested by N. Harrington, a justice of the peace of the state of Maryland, and for the county of Talbot, dated same day as above.

"To all whom it may concern: Be it known, that I, Hugh Auld, of the city of Baltimore, in Baltimore county, in the state of Maryland, for divers good causes and considerations, me thereunto moving, have released from slavery, liberated, manumitted, and set free, and by these presents do hereby release from slavery, liberate, manumit, and set free, MY NEGRO MAN, named FREDERICK BAILY, otherwise called DOUGLASS, being of the age of twenty-eight years, or thereabouts, and able to work and gain a sufficient livelihood and maintenance; and him the said negro man, named FREDERICK BAILY, otherwise called FREDERICK DOUGLASS, I do declare to be henceforth free, manumitted, and discharged from all manner of servitude to me, my executors, and administrators forever.
   "In witness whereof, I, the said Hugh Auld, have hereunto set my hand and seal, the fifth of December, in the year one thousand eight hundred and forty-six.   HUGH AULD.
   "Sealed and delivered in presence of T. Hanson Belt.
"JAMES N. S. T. WRIGHT." [Author's note]

8. See note 2 on p. 209.
9. While in Great Britain, Douglass was persuaded by a group of English friends to let them purchase his freedom from his master.

should never have consented to the payment of so large a sum for the privilege of living securely under our glorious republican form of government. I could have remained in England, or have gone to some other country; and perhaps I could even have lived unobserved in this. But to this I could not consent. I had already become somewhat notorious, and withal quite as unpopular as notorious; and I was, therefore, much exposed to arrest and recapture.

The main object to which my labors in Great Britain were directed, was the concentration of the moral and religious sentiment of its people against American slavery. England is often charged with having established slavery in the United States, and if there were no other justification than this, for appealing to her people to lend their moral aid for the abolition of slavery, I should be justified. My speeches in Great Britain were wholly extemporaneous, and I may not always have been so guarded in my expressions, as I otherwise should have been. I was ten years younger then than now, and only seven years from slavery. I cannot give the reader a better idea of the nature of my discourses, than by republishing one of them, delivered in Finsbury chapel, London, to an audience of about two thousand persons, and which was published in the "London Universe," at the time.[1]

Those in the United States who may regard this speech as being harsh in its spirit and unjust in its statements, because delivered before an audience supposed to be anti-republican in their principles and feelings, may view the matter differently, when they learn that the case supposed did not exist. It so happened that the great mass of the people in England who attended and patronized my antislavery meetings, were, in truth, about as good republicans as the mass of Americans, and with this decided advantage over the latter—they are lovers of republicanism for all men, for black men as well as for white men. They are the people who sympathize with Louis Kossuth and Mazzini,[2] and with the oppressed and enslaved, of every color and nation, the world over. They constitute the democratic element in British politics, and are as much opposed to the union of church and state as we, in America, are to such an union. At the meeting where this speech was delivered, Joseph Sturge[3]—a world-wide philanthropist, and a member of the society of Friends— presided, and addressed the meeting. George William Alexander,[4] another Friend, who has spent more than an American fortune in promoting the anti-slavery cause in different sections of the world,

---

1. See Appendix to this volume, page 407 [*Author's note*; see p. 251].
2. Giuseppe Mazzini (1805–1872), leader of the Italian movement for independence from France. On Kossuth, see note 9 on p. 27.
3. English reformer and antislavery advocate (1793–1859).
4. Wealthy English reformer and antislavery activist (1802–1890).

was on the platform; and also Dr. Campbell, (now of the "British Banner,") who combines all the humane tenderness of Melancthon, with the directness and boldness of Luther.[5] He is in the very front ranks of non-conformists, and looks with no unfriendly eye upon America. George Thompson, too, was there; and America will yet own that he did a true man's work in relighting the rapidly dying-out fire of true republicanism in the American heart, and be ashamed of the treatment he met at her hands.[6] Coming generations in this country will applaud the spirit of this much abused republican friend of freedom. There were others of note seated on the platform, who would gladly ingraft upon English institutions all that is purely republican in the institutions of America. Nothing, therefore, must be set down against this speech on the score that it was delivered in the presence of those who cannot appreciate the many excellent things belonging to our system of government, and with a view to stir up prejudice against republican institutions.

Again, let it also be remembered—for it is the simple truth—that neither in this speech, nor in any other which I delivered in England, did I ever allow myself to address Englishmen as against Americans. I took my stand on the high ground of human brotherhood, and spoke to Englishmen as men, in behalf of men. Slavery is a crime, not against Englishmen, but against God, and all the members of the human family; and it belongs to the whole human family to seek its suppression. In a letter to Mr. Greeley,[7] of the New York Tribune, written while abroad, I said:

> "I am, nevertheless, aware that the wisdom of exposing the sins of one nation in the ear of another, has been seriously questioned by good and clear-sighted people, both on this and on your side of the Atlantic. And the thought is not without weight on my own mind. I am satisfied that there are many evils which can be best removed by confining our efforts to the immediate locality where such evils exist. This, however, is by no means the case with the system of slavery. It is such a giant sin—such a monstrous aggregation of iniquity—so hardening to the human heart—so destructive to the moral sense, and so well

5. John Campbell (1795–1867), English clergyman and editor, exhibits qualities of the German scholar and religious reformer Philipp Melanchthon (1497–1560) and German Reformation leader Martin Luther (1483–1546). The *British Banner* newspaper was published 1848–58.
6. George Donisthorpe Thompson (1804–1878) was a self-educated English reformer best known for his staunch opposition to slavery. After the British Emancipation Act of 1833, he focused on abolishing slavery in the United States. He became a friend of William Lloyd Garrison and Wendell Phillips and traveled twice to the United States to give antislavery lectures.
7. Horace Greeley (1811–1872), American newspaper editor, orator, and politician. A founder of the then-liberal Republican Party (1854), he was a strong ally of the abolitionist movement.

calculated to beget a character, in every one around it, favorable to its own continuance,—that I feel not only at liberty, but
abundantly justified, in appealing to the whole world to aid in
its removal."

But, even if I had—as has been often charged—labored to bring
American institutions generally into disrepute, and had not confined
my labors strictly within the limits of humanity and morality, I
should not have been without illustrious examples to support me.
Driven into semi-exile by civil and barbarous laws, and by a system
which cannot be thought of without a shudder, I was fully justified
in turning, if possible, the tide of the moral universe against the
heaven-daring outrage.

Four circumstances greatly assisted me in getting the question of
American slavery before the British public. First, the mob on board
the Cambria, already referred to, which was a sort of national
announcement of my arrival in England. Secondly, the highly rep-
rehensible course pursued by the Free Church of Scotland,[8] in soliciting, receiving, and retaining money in its sustentation fund for
supporting the gospel in Scotland, which was evidently the ill-
gotten gain of slaveholders and slave-traders. Third, the great Evangelical Alliance[9]—or rather the attempt to form such an alliance,
which should include slaveholders of a certain description—added
immensely to the interest felt in the slavery question. About the same
time, there was the World's Temperance Convention, where I had
the misfortune to come in collision with sundry American doctors
of divinity—Dr. Cox among the number—with whom I had a small
controversy.[1]

It has happened to me—as it has happened to most other men
engaged in a good cause—often to be more indebted to my enemies
than to my own skill or to the assistance of my friends, for whatever
success has attended my labors. Great surprise was expressed by
American newspapers, north and south, during my stay in Great
Britain, that a person so illiterate and insignificant as myself could
awaken an interest so marked in England. These papers were not
the only parties surprised. I was myself not far behind them in surprise. But the very contempt and scorn, the systematic and extravagant disparagement of which I was the object, served, perhaps, to
magnify my few merits, and to render me of some account, whether

8. Denomination of the Church of Scotland, founded in 1843.
9. Association of Evangelical churches in Britain, founded in 1846.
1. A World's Temperance Convention to promote sobriety was held in London August 4–8,
   1846. In attendance, Douglass was repeatedly called on to speak. When he did so, he
   introduced the topic of the abolition of slavery, much to the displeasure of many participants. Dr. Samuel L. Cox (1793–1880), another attendee, afterward wrote critically
   about Douglass's remarks in the *Evangelist*, a Presbyterian newspaper published in
   New York City 1830–1902.

deserving or not. A man is sometimes made great, by the greatness of the abuse a portion of mankind may think proper to heap upon him. Whether I was of as much consequence as the English papers made me out to be, or not, it was easily seen, in England, that I could not be the ignorant and worthless creature, some of the American papers would have them believe I was. Men, in their senses, do not take bowie-knives to kill mosquitoes, nor pistols to shoot flies; and the American passengers who thought proper to get up a mob to silence me, on board the Cambria, took the most effective method of telling the British public that I had something to say.

But to the second circumstance, namely, the position of the Free Church of Scotland, with the great Doctors Chalmers, Cunningham, and Candlish[2] at its head. That church, with its leaders, put it out of the power of the Scotch people to ask the old question, which we in the north have often most wickedly asked—*What have we to do with slavery?*" That church had taken the price of blood into its treasury, with which to build *free* churches, and to pay *free* church ministers for preaching the gospel; and, worse still, when honest John Murray, of Bowlien Bay—now gone to his reward in heaven—with William Smeal, Andrew Paton, Frederick Card, and other sterling anti-slavery men in Glasgow, denounced the transaction as disgraceful and shocking to the religious sentiment of Scotland, this church, through its leading divines, instead of repenting and seeking to mend the mistake into which it had fallen, made it a flagrant sin, by undertaking to defend, in the name of God and the bible, the principle not only of taking the money of slave-dealers to build churches, but of holding fellowship with the holders and traffickers in human flesh. This, the reader will see, brought up the whole question of slavery, and opened the way to its full discussion, without any agency of mine. I have never seen a people more deeply moved than were the people of Scotland, on this very question. Public meeting succeeded public meeting. Speech after speech, pamphlet after pamphlet, editorial after editorial, sermon after sermon, soon lashed the conscientious Scotch people into a perfect *furore*. "Send back the money!" was indignantly cried out, from Greenock to Edinburgh, and from Edinburgh to Aberdeen. George Thompson, of London, Henry C. Wright,[3] of the United States, James N. Buffum, of Lynn, Massachusetts, and myself were on the anti-slavery side; and Doctors Chalmers, Cunningham, and Candlish on the other. In a conflict where the latter could have had even the show of right,

---

2. Thomas Chalmers (1780–1847), Dr. William Cunningham (1805–1861), and the Rev. Robert Smith Candlish (1806–1873), leaders in the Free Church of Scotland who defended the church's right to accept contributions from American slaveholders.
3. Associate of William Lloyd Garrison and member of the American Anti-Slavery Society (1797–1870).

the truth, in our hands as against them, must have been driven to the wall; and while I believe we were able to carry the conscience of the country against the action of the Free Church, the battle, it must be confessed, was a hard-fought one. Abler defenders of the doctrine of fellowshiping slaveholders as christians, have not been met with. In defending this doctrine, it was necessary to deny that slavery is a sin. If driven from this position, they were compelled to deny that slaveholders were responsible for the sin; and if driven from both these positions, they must deny that it is a sin in such a sense, and that slaveholders are sinners in such a sense, as to make it wrong, in the circumstances in which they were placed, to recognize them as christians. Dr. Cunningham was the most powerful debater on the slavery side of the question; Mr. Thompson was the ablest on the anti-slavery side. A scene occurred between these two men, a parallel to which I think I never witnessed before, and I know I never have since. The scene was caused by a single exclamation on the part of Mr. Thompson.

The general assembly of the Free Church was in progress at Cannon Mills, Edinburgh. The building would hold about twenty-five hundred persons; and on this occasion it was densely packed, notice having been given that Doctors Cunningham and Candlish would speak, that day, in defense of the relations of the Free Church of Scotland to slavery in America. Messrs. Thompson, Buffum, myself, and a few anti-slavery friends, attended, but sat at such a distance, and in such a position, that, perhaps, we were not observed from the platform. The excitement was intense, having been greatly increased by a series of meetings held by Messrs. Thompson, Wright, Buffum, and myself, in the most splendid hall in that most beautiful city, just previous to the meetings of the general assembly. "Send back the money!" stared at us from every street corner; "Send back the money!" in large capitals, adorned the broad flags of the pavement; "Send back the money!" was the chorus of the popular street songs; "Send back the money!" was the heading of leading editorials in the daily newspapers. This day, at Cannon Mills, the great doctors of the church were to give an answer to this loud and stern demand. Men of all parties and all sects were most eager to hear. Something great was expected. The occasion was great, the men great, and great speeches were expected from them.

In addition to the outside pressure upon Doctors Cunningham and Candlish, there was wavering in their own ranks. The conscience of the church itself was not at ease. A dissatisfaction with the position of the church touching slavery, was sensibly manifest among the members, and something must be done to counteract this untoward influence. The great Dr. Chalmers was in feeble health, at the time. His most potent eloquence could not now be summoned to Cannon Mills, as formerly. He whose voice was able to rend asunder and dash down the granite walls of the established church of Scotland, and to lead a host in solemn procession from it, as from a doomed city, was now old and enfeebled. Besides, he had said his word on this very question; and his word had not silenced the clamor without, nor stilled the anxious heavings within. The occasion was momentous, and felt to be so. The church was in a perilous condition. A change of some sort must take place in her condition, or she must go to pieces. To stand where she did, was impossible. The whole weight of the matter fell on Cunningham and Candlish. No shoulders in the church were broader than theirs; and I must say, badly as I detest the principles laid down and defended by them, I was compelled to acknowledge the vast mental endowments of the men. Conningham rose; and his rising was the signal for almost tumultuous applause. You will say this was scarcely in keeping with the solemnity of the occasion, but to me it served to increase its grandeur and gravity. The applause, though tumultuous, was not joyous. It seemed to me, as it thundered up from the vast audience, like the fall of an immense shaft, flung from shoulders already galled by its crushing weight. It was like saying, "Doctor, we have borne this burden long enough, and willingly fling it upon you. Since it was you who brought it upon us, take it now, and do what you will with it, for we are too weary to bear it."

Doctor Cunningham proceeded with his speech, abounding in logic, learning, and eloquence, and apparently bearing down all opposition; but at the moment—the fatal moment—when he was just bringing all his arguments to a point, and that point being, that neither Jesus Christ nor his holy apostles regarded slaveholding as a sin, George Thompson, in a clear, sonorous, but rebuking voice, broke the deep stillness of the audience, exclaiming, "Hear! hear! hear!" The effect of this simple and common exclamation is almost incredible. It was as if a granite wall had been suddenly flung up against the advancing current of a mighty river. For a moment, speaker and audience were brought to a dead silence. Both the doctor and his hearers seemed appalled by the audacity, as well as the fitness of the rebuke. At length a shout went up to the cry of "*Put him out!*" Happily, no one attempted to execute this cowardly order, and the doctor proceeded with his discourse. Not, however, as before, did the learned doctor proceed. The exclamation of Thompson must have reëchoed itself a thousand times in his memory, during the remainder of his speech, for the doctor never recovered from the blow.

The deed was done, however; the pillars of the church—*the proud, Free Church of Scotland*—were committed, and the humility of repentance was absent. The Free Church held on to the blood-stained money, and continued to justify itself in its position—and of course to apologize for slavery—and does so till this day. She lost a glorious opportunity for giving her voice, her vote, and her example to the cause of humanity; and to-day she is staggering under the curse of the enslaved, whose blood is in her skirts. The people of Scotland are, to this day, deeply grieved at the course pursued by the Free Church, and would hail, as a relief from a deep and blighting shame, the "sending back the money" to the slaveholders from whom it was gathered.

One good result followed the conduct of the Free Church; it furnished an occasion for making the people of Scotland thoroughly acquainted with the character of slavery, and for arraying against the system the moral and religious sentiment of that country. Therefore, while we did not succeed in accomplishing the specific object of our mission, namely—procure the sending back of the money—we were amply justified by the good which really did result from our labors.

Next comes the Evangelical Alliance. This was an attempt to form a union of all evangelical christians throughout the world. Sixty or seventy American divines attended, and some of them went there merely to weave a world-wide garment with which to clothe evangelical slaveholders. Foremost among these divines, was the Rev. Samuel Hanson Cox, moderator of the New School Presbyterian General Assembly. He and his friends spared no pains to secure a platform broad enough to hold American slaveholders, and in this they partly succeeded. But the question of slavery is too large a question to be finally disposed of, even by the Evangelical Alliance. We appealed from the judgment of the Alliance, to the judgment of the people of Great Britain, and with the happiest effect. This controversy with the Alliance might be made the subject of extended remark, but I must forbear, except to say, that this effort to shield the christian character of slaveholders greatly served to open a way to the British ear for anti-slavery discussion, and that it was well improved.

The fourth and last circumstance that assisted me in getting before the British public, was an attempt on the part of certain doctors of divinity to silence me on the platform of the World's Temperance Convention. Here I was brought into point blank collision with Rev. Dr. Cox, who made me the subject not only of bitter remark in the convention, but also of a long denunciatory letter published in the New York Evangelist and other American papers. I replied to the doctor as well as I could, and was successful in getting a respectful hearing before the British public, who are by nature and practice ardent lovers of fair play, especially in a conflict between the weak and the strong.

Thus did circumstances favor me, and favor the cause of which I strove to be the advocate. After such distinguished notice, the public in both countries was compelled to attach some importance to my labors. By the very ill usage I received at the hands of Dr. Cox and his party, by the mob on board the Cambria, by the attacks made upon me in the American newspapers, and by the aspersions cast upon me through the organs of the Free Church of Scotland, I became one of that class of men, who, for the moment, at least, "have greatness forced upon them."[4] People became the more anxious to hear for themselves, and to judge for themselves, of the truth which I had to unfold. While, therefore, it is by no means easy for a stranger to get fairly before the British public, it was my lot to accomplish it in the easiest manner possible.

Having continued in Great Britain and Ireland nearly two years, and being about to return to America—not as I left it, a slave, but a freeman—leading friends of the cause of emancipation in that country intimated their intention to make me a testimonial, not only on grounds of personal regard to myself, but also to the cause to which they were so ardently devoted. How far any such thing could have succeeded, I do not know; but many reasons led me to prefer that my friends should simply give me the means of obtaining a printing press and printing materials, to enable me to start a paper, devoted to the interests of my enslaved and oppressed people. I told them that perhaps the greatest hinderance to the adoption of abolition principles by the people of the United States, was the low estimate, everywhere in that country, placed upon the negro, as a man; that because of his assumed natural inferiority, people reconciled themselves to his enslavement and oppression, as things inevitable, if not desirable. The grand thing to be done, therefore, was to change the estimation in which the colored people of the United States were held; to remove the prejudice which depreciated and depressed them; to prove them worthy of a higher consideration; to disprove their alleged inferiority, and demonstrate their capacity for a more exalted civilization than slavery and prejudice had assigned to them. I further stated, that, in my judgment, a tolerably well conducted press, in the hands of persons of the despised race, by calling out the mental energies of the race itself; by making them acquainted with their own latent powers; by enkindling among them the hope that for them there is a future; by developing their moral power; by combining and reflecting their talents—would prove a most powerful means of removing prejudice, and of awakening an interest in them. I further informed them—and at that time the statement was

4. Cf. Shakespeare, *Twelfth Night* 2.5.127–28.

true—that there was not, in the United States, a single newspaper regularly published by the colored people; that many attempts had been made to establish such papers; but that, up to that time, they had all failed. These views I laid before my friends. The result was, nearly two thousand five hundred dollars were speedily raised toward starting my paper. For this prompt and generous assistance, rendered upon my bare suggestion, without any personal efforts on my part, I shall never cease to feel deeply grateful; and the thought of fulfilling the noble expectations of the dear friends who gave me this evidence of their confidence, will never cease to be a motive for persevering exertion.

Proposing to leave England, and turning my face toward America, in the spring of 1847, I was met, on the threshold, with something which painfully reminded me of the kind of life which awaited me in my native land. For the first time in the many months spent abroad, I was met with proscription on account of my color. A few weeks before departing from England, while in London, I was careful to purchase a ticket, and secure a berth for returning home, in the Cambria—the steamer in which I left the United States— paying therefor the round sum of forty pounds and nineteen shillings sterling. This was first cabin fare. But on going aboard the Cambria, I found that the Liverpool agent had ordered my berth to be given to another, and had forbidden my entering the saloon! This contemptible conduct met with stern rebuke from the British press. For, upon the point of leaving England, I took occasion to expose the disgusting tyranny, in the columns of the London Times.[5] That journal, and other leading journals throughout the United Kingdom, held up the outrage to unmitigated condemnation. So good an opportunity for calling out a full expression of British sentiment on the subject, had not before occurred, and it was most fully embraced. The result was, that Mr. Cunard came out in a letter to the public journals, assuring them of his regret at the outrage, and promising that the like should never occur again on board his steamers; and the like, we believe, has never since occurred on board the steamships of the Cunard line.

It is not very pleasant to be made the subject of such insults; but if all such necessarily resulted as this one did, I should be very happy to bear, patiently, many more than I have borne, of the same sort. Albeit, the lash of proscription, to a man accustomed to equal social position, even for a time, as I was, has a sting for the soul hardly less severe than that which bites the flesh and draws the blood from the back of the plantation slave. It was rather hard, after having enjoyed nearly two years of equal social privileges in England, often

5. A major British newspaper, founded in 1785.

dining with gentlemen of great literary, social, political, and religious eminence—never, during the whole time, having met with a single word, look, or gesture, which gave me the slightest reason to think my color was an offense to anybody—now to be cooped up in the stern of the Cambria, and denied the right to enter the saloon, lest my dark presence should be deemed an offense to some of my democratic fellow-passengers. The reader will easily imagine what must have been my feelings.

CHAPTER XXV

Various Incidents

NEWSPAPER ENTERPRISE—UNEXPECTED OPPOSITION—THE OBJECTIONS TO IT—THEIR PLAUSIBILITY ADMITTED—MOTIVES FOR COMING TO ROCHESTER—DISCIPLE OF MR. GARRISON—CHANGE OF OPINION—CAUSES LEADING TO IT—THE CONSEQUENCES OF THE CHANGE—PREJUDICE AGAINST COLOR—AMUSING CONDESCENSION— "JIM CROW CARS"—COLLISIONS WITH CONDUCTORS AND BRAKEMEN— TRAINS ORDERED NOT TO STOP AT LYNN—AMUSING DOMESTIC SCENE—SEPARATE TABLES FOR MASTER AND MAN—PREJUDICE UNNATURAL—ILLUSTRATIONS—THE AUTHOR IN HIGH COMPANY— ELEVATION OF THE FREE PEOPLE OF COLOR—PLEDGE FOR THE FUTURE

I HAVE now given the reader an imperfect sketch of nine years' experience in freedom—three years as a common laborer on the wharves of New Bedford, four years as a lecturer in New England, and two years of semi-exile in Great Britain and Ireland. A single ray of light remains to be flung upon my life during the last eight years, and my story will be done.

A trial awaited me on my return from England to the United States, for which I was but very imperfectly prepared. My plans for my then future usefulness as an anti-slavery advocate were all settled. My friends in England had resolved to raise a given sum to purchase for me a press and printing materials; and I already saw myself wielding my pen, as well as my voice, in the great work of renovating the public mind, and building up a public sentiment which should, at least, send slavery and oppression to the grave, and restore to "liberty and the pursuit of happiness" the people with whom I had suffered, both as a slave and as a freeman. Intimation had reached my friends in Boston[1] of what I intended to do, before

1. William Lloyd Garrison (see note 7 on p. 23), Wendell Phillips (see note 2 on p. 24), Maria Chapman, and other friends and associates in the Massachusetts Anti-Slavery Society. Maria Weston Chapman (1806–1885), a member of the Society, disbursed

my arrival, and I was prepared to find them favorably disposed toward my much cherished enterprise. In this I was mistaken. I found them very earnestly opposed to the idea of my starting a paper, and for several reasons. First, the paper was not needed; secondly, it would interfere with my usefulness as a lecturer; thirdly, I was better fitted to speak than to write; fourthly, the paper could not succeed. This opposition, from a quarter so highly esteemed, and to which I had been accustomed to look for advice and direction, caused me not only to hesitate, but inclined me to abandon the enterprise. All previous attempts to establish such a journal having failed, I felt that probably I should but add another to the list of failures, and thus contribute another proof of the mental and moral deficiencies of my race. Very much that was said to me in respect to my imperfect literary acquirements, I felt to be most painfully true. The unsuccessful projectors of all the previous colored newspapers were my superiors in point of education, and if they failed, how could I hope for success? Yet I did hope for success, and persisted in the undertaking. Some of my English friends greatly encouraged me to go forward, and I shall never cease to be grateful for their words of cheer and generous deeds.

I can easily pardon those who have denounced me as ambitions and presumptuous, in view of my persistence in this enterprise. I was but nine years from slavery. In point of mental experience, I was but nine years old. That one, in such circumstances, should aspire to establish a printing press, among an educated people, might well be considered, if not ambitious, quite silly. My American friends looked at me with astonishment! "A wood-sawyer" offering himself to the public as an editor! A slave, brought up in the very depths of ignorance, assuming to instruct the highly civilized people of the north in the principles of liberty, justice, and humanity! The thing looked absurd. Nevertheless, I persevered. I felt that the want of education, great as it was, could be overcome by study, and that knowledge would come by experience; and further, (which was perhaps the most controlling consideration,) I thought that an intelligent public, knowing my early history, would easily pardon a large share of the deficiencies which I was sure that my paper[2] would exhibit. The most distressing thing, however, was the offense which I was about to give my Boston friends, by what seemed to them a reckless disregard of their sage advice. I am not sure that I was not under the influence of something like a slavish adoration of my Boston friends, and I labored hard to convince them of the wisdom of my

---

payments to Douglass and monitored his activities in Britain during his service to the organization as a lecturer.

2. Douglass refers to the antislavery newspaper he would soon found and edit, *The North Star* (1847–51), later titled *Frederick Douglass' Paper* (1851–60).

undertaking, but without success. Indeed, I never expect to succeed, although time has answered all their original objections. The paper has been successful. It is a large sheet, costing eighty dollars per week—has three thousand subscribers—has been published regularly nearly eight years—and bids fair to stand eight years longer. At any rate, the eight years to come are as full of promise as were the eight that are past.

It is not to be concealed, however, that the maintenance of such a journal, under the circumstances, has been a work of much difficulty; and could all the perplexity, anxiety, and trouble attending it, have been clearly foreseen, I might have shrunk from the undertaking. As it is, I rejoice in having engaged in the enterprise, and count it joy to have been able to suffer, in many ways, for its success, and for the success of the cause to which it has been faithfully devoted. I look upon the time, money, and labor bestowed upon it, as being amply rewarded, in the development of my own mental and moral energies, and in the corresponding development of my deeply injured and oppressed people.

From motives of peace, instead of issuing my paper in Boston, among my New England friends, I came to Rochester, Western New York, among strangers, where the circulation of my paper could not interfere with the local circulation of the Liberator and the Standard;[3] for at that time I was, on the anti-slavery question, a faithful disciple of William Lloyd Garrison, and fully committed to his doctrine touching the pro-slavery character of the constitution of the United States, and the *non-voting principle*,[4] of which he is the known and distinguished advocate. With Mr. Garrison, I held it to be the first duty of the non-slaveholding states to dissolve the union with the slaveholding states; and hence my cry, like his, was, "No union with slaveholders." With these views, I came into Western New York; and during the first four years of my labor here, I advocated them with pen and tongue, according to the best of my ability.

About four years ago, upon a reconsideration of the whole subject, I became convinced that there was no necessity for dissolving the "union between the northern and southern states;" that to seek this dissolution was no part of my duty as an abolitionist; that to abstain from voting, was to refuse to exercise a legitimate and powerful means for abolishing slavery; and that the constitution of the United States not only contained no guarantees in favor of slavery,

3. See note 4 on p. 222.
4. Douglass refers to the position taken by William Lloyd Garrison and other members of the Massachusetts Anti-Slavery Society that the Constitution gave legal sanction to slavery. Garrison argued that for this reason resistance to slavery must steer clear of formal politics, including voting, and should pursue instead a strategy of persuading individual states to secede from the Union and the slaveholding South.

but, on the contrary, it is, in its letter and spirit, an anti-slavery instrument, demanding the abolition of slavery as a condition of its own existence, as the supreme law of the land.

Here was a radical change in my opinions, and in the action logically resulting from that change. To those with whom I had been in agreement and in sympathy, I was now in opposition. What they held to be a great and important truth, I now looked upon as a dangerous error. A very painful, and yet a very natural, thing now happened. Those who could not see any honest reasons for changing their views, as I had done, could not easily see any such reasons for my change, and the common punishment of apostates was mine.

The opinions first entertained were naturally derived and honestly entertained, and I trust that my present opinions have the same claims to respect. Brought directly, when I escaped from slavery, into contact with a class of abolitionists regarding the constitution as a slaveholding instrument, and finding their views supported by the united and entire history of every department of the government, it is not strange that I assumed the constitution to be just what their interpretation made it. I was bound, not only by their superior knowledge, to take their opinions as the true ones, in respect to the subject, but also because I had no means of showing their unsoundness. But for the responsibility of conducting a public journal, and the necessity imposed upon me of meeting opposite views from abolitionists in this state, I should in all probability have remained as firm in my disunion views as any other disciple of William Lloyd Garrison.

My new circumstances compelled me to re-think the whole subject, and to study, with some care, not only the just and proper rules of legal interpretation, but the origin, design, nature, rights, powers, and duties of civil government, and also the relations which human beings sustain to it. By such a course of thought and reading, I was conducted to the conclusion that the constitution of the United States—inaugurated "to form a more perfect union, establish justice, insure domestic tranquillity, provide for the common defense, promote the general welfare, and secure the blessings of liberty"[5]—could not well have been designed at the same time to maintain and perpetuate a system of rapine and murder like slavery; especially, as not one word can be found in the constitution to authorize such a belief. Then, again, if the declared purposes of an instrument are to govern the meaning of all its parts and details, as they clearly should, the constitution of our country is our warrant for the abolition of slavery in every state in the American Union. I mean, however, not to argue, but simply to state my views. It would

5. From the first sentence of the Preamble to the United States Constitution.

require very many pages of a volume like this, to set forth the arguments demonstrating the unconstitutionality and the complete illegality of slavery in our land; and as my experience, and not my arguments, is within the scope and contemplation of this volume, I omit the latter and proceed with the former.

I will now ask the kind reader to go back a little in my story, while I bring up a thread left behind for convenience sake, but which, small as it is, cannot be properly omitted altogether; and that thread is American prejudice against color, and its varied illustrations in my own experience.

When I first went among the abolitionists of New England, and began to travel, I found this prejudice very strong and very annoying. The abolitionists themselves were not entirely free from it, and I could see that they were nobly struggling against it. In their eagerness, sometimes, to show their contempt for the feeling, they proved that they had not entirely recovered from it; often illustrating the saying, in their conduct, that a man may "stand up so straight as to lean backward." When it was said to me, "Mr. Douglass, I will walk to meeting with you; I am not afraid of a black man," I could not help thinking—seeing nothing very frightful in my appearance— "And why should you be?" The children at the north had all been educated to believe that if they were bad, the old *black* man—not the old *devil*—would get them; and it was evidence of some courage, for any so educated to get the better of their fears.

The custom of providing separate cars for the accommodation of colored travelers, was established on nearly all the railroads of New England, a dozen years ago. Regarding this custom as fostering the spirit of caste, I made it a rule to seat myself in the cars for the accommodation of passengers generally. Thus seated, I was sure to be called upon to betake myself to the "*Jim Crow car*." Refusing to obey, I was often dragged out of my seat, beaten, and severely bruised, by conductors and brakemen. Attempting to start from Lynn, one day, for Newburyport, on the Eastern railroad, I went, as my custom was, into one of the best railroad carriages on the road. The seats were very luxuriant and beautiful. I was soon waited upon by the conductor, and ordered out; whereupon I demanded the reason for my invidious removal. After a good deal of parleying, I was told that it was because I was black. This I denied, and appealed to the company to sustain my denial; but they were evidently unwilling to commit themselves, on a point so delicate, and requiring such nice powers of discrimination, for they remained as dumb as death. I was soon waited on by half a dozen fellows of the baser sort, (just such as would volunteer to take a bull-dog out of a meeting-house in time of public worship,) and told that I must move out of that seat, and if I did not, they would drag me out. I refused to move, and they clutched me, head, neck, and shoulders. But, in anticipation of the stretching to which I was about to be subjected, I had interwoven myself among the seats. In dragging me out, on this occasion, it must have cost the company twenty-five or thirty dollars, for I tore up seats and all. So great was the excitement in Lynn, on the subject, that the superintendent, Mr. Stephen A. Chase, ordered the trains to run through Lynn without stopping, while I remained in that town; and this ridiculous farce was enacted. For several days the trains went dashing through Lynn without stopping. At the same time that they excluded a free colored man from their cars, this same company allowed slaves, in company with their masters and mistresses, to ride unmolested.

After many battles with the railroad conductors, and being roughly handled in not a few instances, proscription was at last abandoned; and the "Jim Crow car"—set up for the degradation of colored people—is nowhere found in New England. This result was not brought about without the intervention of the people, and the threatened enactment of a law compelling railroad companies to respect the rights of travelers. Hon. Charles Francis Adams performed signal service in the Massachusetts legislature,[6] in bringing about this reformation; and to him the colored citizens of that state are deeply indebted.

Although often annoyed, and sometimes outraged, by this prejudice against color, I am indebted to it for many passages of quiet amusement. A half-cured subject of it is sometimes driven into awkward straits, especially if he happens to get a genuine specimen of the race into his house.

In the summer of 1843, I was traveling and lecturing, in company with William A. White,[7] Esq., through the state of Indiana. Antislavery friends were not very abundant in Indiana, at that time, and beds were not more plentiful than friends. We often slept out, in preference to sleeping in the houses, at some points. At the close of one of our meetings, we were invited home with a kindly-disposed old farmer, who, in the generous enthusiasm of the moment, seemed to have forgotten that he had but one spare bed, and that his guests were an ill-matched pair. All went on pretty well, till near bed time, when signs of uneasiness began to show themselves, among the unsophisticated sons and daughters. White is remarkably fine looking, and very evidently a born gentleman; the idea of putting us in the same bed was hardly to be tolerated; and yet, there we were, and but the one bed for us, and that, by the way, was in the same room occupied by the other members of the family. White, as well as I,

6. Adams (1807–1886) served in the Massachusetts state legislature 1841–45.
7. William Abijah White (1818–1856), abolitionist and friend of a friend of Douglass's.

perceived the difficulty, for yonder slept the old folks, there the sons, and a little farther along slept the daughters; and but one other bed remained. Who should have this bed, was the puzzling question. There was some whispering between the old folks, some confused looks among the young, as the time for going to bed approached. After witnessing the confusion as long as I liked, I relieved the kindly-disposed family by playfully saying, "Friend White, having got entirely rid of my prejudice against color, I think, as a proof of it, I must allow you to sleep with me to-night." White kept up the joke, by seeming to esteem himself the favored party, and thus the difficulty was removed. If we went to a hotel, and called for dinner, the landlord was sure to set one table for White and another for me, always taking him to be master, and me the servant. Large eyes were generally made when the order was given to remove the dishes from my table to that of White's. In those days, it was thought strange that a white man and a colored man could dine peaceably at the same table, and in some parts the strangeness of such a sight has not entirely subsided.

Some people will have it that there is a natural, an inherent, and an invincible repugnance in the breast of the white race toward dark-colored people; and some very intelligent colored men think that their proscription is owing solely to the color which nature has given them. They hold that they are rated according to their color, and that it is impossible for white people ever to look upon dark races of men, or men belonging to the African race, with other than feelings of aversion. My experience, both serious and mirthful, combats this conclusion. Leaving out of sight, for a moment, grave facts, to this point, I will state one or two, which illustrate a very interesting feature of American character as well as American prejudice. Riding from Boston to Albany, a few years ago, I found myself in a large car, well filled with passengers. The seat next to me was about the only vacant one. At every stopping place we took in new passengers, all of whom, on reaching the seat next to me, cast a disdainful glance upon it, and passed to another car, leaving me in the full enjoyment of a whole form. For a time, I did not know but that my riding there was prejudicial to the interest of the railroad company. A circumstance occurred, however, which gave me an elevated position at once. Among the passengers on this train was Gov. George N. Briggs.[8] I was not acquainted with him, and had no idea that I was known to him. Known to him, however, I was, for upon observing me, the governor left his place, and making his way toward me, respectfully asked the privilege of a seat by my side; and upon introducing himself, we entered into a conversation very pleasant and

8. Briggs (1796–1861) was governor of Massachusetts 1851–55.

instructive to me. The despised seat now became honored. His excellency had removed all the prejudice against sitting by the side of a negro; and upon his leaving it, as he did, on reaching Pittsfield, there were at least one dozen applicants for the place. The governor had, without changing my skin a single shade, made the place respectable which before was despicable.

A similar incident happened to me once on the Boston and New Bedford railroad, and the leading party to it has since been governor of the state of Massachusetts. I allude to Col. John Henry Clifford.[9] Lest the reader may fancy I am aiming to elevate myself, by claiming too much intimacy with great men, I must state that my only acquaintance with Col. Clifford was formed while I was *his hired servant*, during the first winter of my escape from slavery. I owe it him to say, that in that relation I found him always kind and gentlemanly. But to the incident. I entered a car at Boston, for New Bedford, which, with the exception of a single seat, was full, and found I must occupy this, or stand up, during the journey. Having no mind to do this, I stepped up to the man having the next seat, and who had a few parcels on the seat, and gently asked leave to take a seat by his side. My fellow-passenger gave me a look made up of reproach and indignation, and asked me why I should come to that particular seat. I assured him, in the gentlest manner, that of all others this was the seat for me. Finding that I was actually about to sit down, he sang out, "O! stop, stop! and let me get out!" Suiting the action to the word, up the agitated man got, and sauntered to the other end of the car, and was compelled to stand for most of the way thereafter. Half-way to New Bedford, or more, Col. Clifford, recognizing me, left his seat, and not having seen me before since I had ceased to wait on him, (in everything except hard arguments against his pro-slavery position,) apparently forgetful of his rank, manifested, in greeting me, something of the feeling of an old friend. This demonstration was not lost on the gentleman whose dignity I had, an hour before, most seriously offended. Col. Clifford was known to be about the most aristocratic gentleman in Bristol county; and it was evidently thought that I must be somebody, else I should not have been thus noticed, by a person so distinguished. Sure enough, after Col. Clifford left me, I found myself surrounded with friends; and among the number, my offended friend stood nearest, and with an apology for his rudeness, which I could not resist, although it was one of the lamest ever offered. With such facts as these before me—and I have many of them—I am inclined to think that pride and fashion have much to do with the treatment

9. Lawyer, Massachusetts state legislator, and district attorney for southern Massachusetts (1809–1876).

commonly extended to colored people in the United States. I once heard a very plain man say, (and he was cross-eyed, and awkwardly flung together in other respects,) that he should be a handsome man when public opinion shall be changed.

Since I have been editing and publishing a journal devoted to the cause of liberty and progress, I have had my mind more directed to the condition and circumstances of the free colored people than when I was the agent of an abolition society. The result has been a corresponding change in the disposition of my time and labors. I have felt it to be a part of my mission—under a gracious Providence—to impress my sable brothers in this country with the conviction that, notwithstanding the ten thousand discouragements and the powerful hinderances, which beset their existence in this country—notwithstanding the blood-written history of Africa, and her children, from whom we have descended, or the clouds and darkness, (whose stillness and gloom are made only more awful by wrathful thunder and lightning,) now overshadowing them—progress is yet possible, and bright skies shall yet shine upon their pathway; and that "Ethiopia shall yet reach forth her hand unto God."[1]

Believing that one of the best means of emancipating the slaves of the south is to improve and elevate the character of the free colored people of the north I shall labor in the future, as I have labored in the past, to promote the moral, social, religious, and intellectual elevation of the free colored people; never forgetting my own humble origin, nor refusing, while Heaven lends me ability, to use my voice, my pen, or my vote, to advocate the great and primary work of the universal and unconditional emancipation of my entire race.

---

1. Cf. Psalm 68.31.

Appendix,

CONTAINING EXTRACTS FROM

SPEECHES, ETC[1]

[FREDERICK DOUGLASS]

Reception Speech

AT FINSBURY CHAPEL,[2] MOORFIELDS, ENGLAND, MAY 12, 1846

MR. DOUGLASS rose amid loud cheers, and said: I feel exceedingly glad of the opportunity now afforded me of presenting the claims of my brethren in bonds in the United States, to so many in London and from various parts of Britain, who have assembled here on the present occasion. I have nothing to commend me to your consideration in the way of learning, nothing in the way of education, to entitle me to your attention; and you are aware that slavery is a very bad school for rearing teachers of morality and religion. Twenty-one years of my life have been spent in slavery—personal slavery—surrounded by degrading influences, such as can exist nowhere beyond the pale of slavery; and it will not be strange, if under such circumstances, I should betray, in what I have to say to you, a deficiency of that refinement which is seldom or ever found, except among persons that have experienced superior advantages to those which I have enjoyed. But I will take it for granted that you know something about the degrading influences of slavery, and that you will not expect great things from me this evening, but simply such facts as I may be able to advance immediately in connection with my own experience of slavery.

Now, what is this system of slavery? This is the subject of my lecture this evening—what is the character of this institution? I am

---

1. Mr. Douglass' published speeches alone, would fill two volumes of the size of this. Our space will only permit the insertion of the extracts which follow; and which, for originality of thought, beauty and force of expression, and for impassioned, indignatory eloquence, have seldom been equaled [*Original editor's note*; see note 1 on p. 7].
2. Congregational chapel in London.

about to answer the inquiry, what is American slavery? I do this the more readily, since I have found persons in this country who have identified the term slavery with that which I think it is not, and in some instances, I have feared, in so doing, have rather (unwittingly, I know,) detracted much from the horror with which the term slavery is contemplated. It is common in this country to distinguish every bad thing by the name of slavery. Intemperance is slavery; to be deprived of the right to vote is slavery, says one; to have to work hard is slavery, says another; and I do not know but that if we should let them go on, they would say that to eat when we are hungry, to walk when we desire to have exercise, or to minister to our necessities, or have necessities at all, is slavery. I do not wish for a moment to detract from the horror with which the evil of intemperance is contemplated—not at all; nor do I wish to throw the slightest obstruction in the way of any political freedom that any class of persons in this country may desire to obtain. But I am here to say that I think the term slavery is sometimes abused by identifying it with that which it is not. Slavery in the United States is the granting of that power by which one man exercises and enforces a right of property in the body and soul of another. The condition of a slave is simply that of the brute beast. He is a piece of property—a marketable commodity, in the language of the law, to be bought or sold at the will and caprice of the master who claims him to be his property; he is spoken of, thought of, and treated as property. His own good, his conscience, his intellect, his affections, are all set aside by the master. The will and the wishes of the master are the law of the slave. He is as much a piece of property as a horse. If he is fed, he is fed because he is property. If he is clothed, it is with a view to the increase of his value as property. Whatever of comfort is necessary to him for his body or soul that is inconsistent with his being property, is carefully wrested from him, not only by public opinion, but by the law of the country. He is carefully deprived of everything that tends in the slightest degree to detract from his value as property. He is deprived of education. God has given him an intellect; the slaveholder declares it shall not be cultivated. If his moral perception leads him in a course contrary to his value as property, the slaveholder declares he shall not exercise it. The marriage institution cannot exist among slaves, and one-sixth of the population of democratic America is denied its privileges by the law of the land. What is to be thought of a nation boasting of its liberty, boasting of its humanity, boasting of its Christianity, boasting of its love of justice and purity, and yet having within its own borders three millions of persons denied by law the right of marriage?—what must be the condition of that people? I need not lift up the veil by giving you any experience of my own. Every one that can put two ideas together, must see the most fearful results from such a state of things as I have just mentioned. If any of these three millions find for themselves companions, and prove themselves honest, upright, virtuous persons to each other, yet in these cases—few as I am bound to confess they are—the virtuous live in constant apprehension of being torn asunder by the merciless men-stealers that claim them as their property. This is American slavery; no marriage—no education—the light of the gospel shut out from the dark mind of the bondman—and he forbidden by law to learn to read. If a mother shall teach her children to read, the law in Louisiana proclaims that she may be hanged by the neck. If the father attempt to give his son a knowledge of letters, he may be punished by the whip in one instance, and in another be killed, at the discretion of the court. Three millions of people shut out from the light of knowledge! It is easy for you to conceive the evil that must result from such a state of things.

I now come to the physical evils of slavery. I do not wish to dwell at length upon these, but it seems right to speak of them, not so much to influence your minds on this question, as to let the slaveholders of America know that the curtain which conceals their crimes is being lifted abroad; that we are opening the dark cell, and leading the people into the horrible recesses of what they are pleased to call their domestic institution. We want them to know that a knowledge of their whippings, their scourgings, their brandings, their chainings, is not confined to their plantations, but that some negro of their has broken loose from his chains—has burst through the dark incrustation of slavery, and is now exposing their deeds of deep damnation to the gaze of the christian people of England.

The slaveholders resort to all kinds of cruelty. If I were disposed, I have matter enough to interest you on this question for five or six evenings, but I will not dwell at length upon these cruelties. Suffice it to say, that all the peculiar modes of torture that were resorted to in the West India islands, are resorted to, I believe, even more frequently, in the United States of America. Starvation, the bloody whip, the chain, the gag, the thumb-screw, cat-hauling, the cat-o'-nine-tails, the dungeon, the blood-hound, are all in requisition to keep the slave in his condition as a slave in the United States. If any one has a doubt upon this point, I would ask him to read the chapter on slavery in Dickens's *Notes on America*.[3] If any man has a doubt upon it, I have here the "testimony of a thousand witnesses,"[4] which

---

3. In October 1842, the English novelist Charles Dickens (1812–1870) published *American Notes for General Circulation*, an account of his travels in the United States from January to June of that year. The book includes a scathing attack on slavery.
4. A reference to the influential book *Slavery As It Is: Testimony of a Thousand Witnesses* (1839), by the abolitionist Theodore Weld (1803–1895).

I can give at any length, all going to prove the truth of my statement.
The blood-hound is regularly trained in the United States, and advertisements are to be found in the southern papers of the Union,
from persons advertising themselves as blood-hound trainers, and
offering to hunt down slaves at fifteen dollars a piece, recommend-
ing their hounds as the fleetest in the neighborhood, never known
to fail. Advertisements are from time to time inserted, stating that
slaves have escaped with iron collars about their necks, with bands
of iron about their feet, marked with the lash, branded with red-hot
irons, the initials of their master's name burned into their flesh; and
the masters advertise the fact of their being thus branded with their
own signature, thereby proving to the world, that, however damning it may appear to non-slaveholders, such practices are not regarded
discreditable among the slaveholders themselves. Why, I believe if a
man should brand his horse in this country—burn the initials of his
name into any of his cattle, and publish the ferocious deed here—
that the united execrations of christians in Britain would descend
upon him. Yet, in the United States, human beings are thus branded.
As Whittier says—

> ". . . . Our countrymen in chains,
>   The whip on woman's shrinking flesh,
> Our soil yet reddening with the stains
>   Caught from her scourgings warm and fresh."[5]

The slave-dealer boldly publishes his infamous acts to the world.
Of all things that have been said of slavery to which exception has
been taken by slaveholders, this, the charge of cruelty, stands foremost, and yet there is no charge capable of clearer demonstration,
than that of the most barbarous inhumanity on the part of the slaveholders toward their slaves. And all this is necessary; it is necessary
to resort to these cruelties, in order to *make the slave a slave*, and to
keep him a slave. Why, my experience all goes to prove the truth of
what you will call a marvelous proposition, that the better you treat
a slave, the more you destroy his value *as a slave*, and enhance the
probability of his eluding the grasp of the slaveholder; the more
kindly you treat him, the more wretched you make him, while you
keep him in the condition of a slave. My experience, I say, confirms
the truth of this proposition. When I was treated exceedingly ill;
when my back was being scourged daily; when I was whipped within
an inch of my life—*life* was all I cared for. "Spare my life," was my
continual prayer. When I was looking for the blow about to be
inflicted upon my head, I was not thinking of my liberty; it was my

---

5. Cf. lines 17–20 of "Our Countrymen in Chains" (1842), by John Greenleaf Whittier
(see note 2 on p. 118). This work circulated widely in an 1837 broadside edition.

life. But, as soon as the blow was not to be feared, then came the longing for liberty. If a slave has a bad master, his ambition is to get a better; when he gets a better, he aspires to have the best; and when he gets the best, he aspires to be his own master. But the slave must be brutalized to keep him as a slave. The slaveholder feels this necessity. I admit this necessity. If it be right to hold slaves at all, it is right to hold them in the only way in which they can be held; and this can be done only by shutting out the light of education from their minds, and brutalizing their persons. The whip, the chain, the gag, the thumb-screw, the blood-hound, the stocks, and all the other bloody paraphernalia of the slave system, are indispensably necessary to the relation of master and slave. The slave must be subjected to these, or he ceases to be a slave. Let him know that the whip is burned; that the fetters have been turned to some useful and profitable employment; that the chain is no longer for his limbs; that the bloodhound is no longer to be put upon his track; that his master's authority over him is no longer to be enforced by taking his life— and immediately he walks out from the house of bondage and asserts his freedom as a man. The slaveholder finds it necessary to have these implements to keep the slave in bondage; finds it necessary to be able to say, "Unless you do so and so; unless you do as I bid you—I will take away your life!"

Some of the most awful scenes of cruelty are constantly taking place in the middle states of the Union. We have in those states what are called the slave-breeding states. Allow me to speak plainly. Although it is harrowing to your feelings, it is necessary that the facts of the case should be stated. We have in the United States slave-breeding states. The very state from which the minister from our court to yours comes, is one of these states—Maryland, where men, women, and children are reared for the market, just as horses, sheep, and swine are raised for the market. Slave-rearing is there looked upon as a legitimate trade; the law sanctions it, public opinion upholds it, the church does not condemn it. It goes on in all its bloody horrors, sustained by the auctioneer's block. If you would see the cruelties of this system, hear the following narrative. Not long since the following scene occurred. A slave-woman and a slave-man had united themselves as man and wife in the absence of any law to protect them as man and wife. They had lived together by the permission, not by right, of their master, and they had reared a family. The master found it expedient, and for his interest, to sell them. He did not ask them their wishes in regard to the matter at all; they were not consulted. The man and woman were brought to the auctioneer's block, under the sound of the hammer. The cry was raised, "Here goes; who bids cash?" Think of it—a man and wife to be sold! The woman was placed on the auctioneer's block; her limbs, as is customary, were brutally exposed to the purchasers, who examined her with all the freedom with which they would examine a horse. There stood the husband, powerless; no right to his wife; the master's right preëminent. She was sold. He was next brought to the auctioneer's block. His eyes followed his wife in the distance; and he looked beseechingly, imploringly, to the man that had bought his wife, to buy him also. But he was at length bid off to another person. He was about to be separated forever from her he loved. No word of his, no work of his, could save him from this separation. He asked permission of his new master to go and take the hand of his wife at parting. It was denied him. In the agony of his soul he rushed from the man who had just bought him, that he might take a farewell of his wife; but his way was obstructed, he was struck over the head with a loaded whip, and was held for a moment; but his agony was too great. When he was let go, he fell a corpse at the feet of his master. His heart was broken. Such scenes are the every-day fruits of American slavery. Some two years sinee, the Hon. Seth M. Gates, an anti-slavery gentleman of the state of New York, a representative in the congress of the United States, told me he saw with his own eyes the following circumstance. In the national District of Columbia, over which the star-spangled emblem is constantly waving, where orators are ever holding forth on the subject of American liberty, American democracy, American republicanism, there are two slave prisons. When going across a bridge, leading to one of these prisons, he saw a young woman run out, bare-footed and bare-headed, and with very little clothing on. She was running with all speed to the bridge he was approaching. His eye was fixed upon her, and he stopped to see what was the matter. He had not paused long before he saw three men run out after her. He now knew what the nature of the case was; a slave escaping from her chains—a young woman, a sister—escaping from the bondage in which she had been held. She made her way to the bridge, but had not reached it, ere from the Virginia side there came two slaveholders. As soon as they saw them, her pursuers called out, "Stop her!" True to their Virginian instincts, they came to the rescue of their brother kidnappers, across the bridge. The poor girl now saw that there was no chance for her. It was a trying time. She knew if she went back, she must be a slave forever—she must be dragged down to the scenes of pollution which the slaveholders continually provide for most of the poor, sinking, wretched young women, whom they call their property. She formed her resolution; and just as those who were about to take her, were going to put hands upon her, to drag her back, she leaped over the balustrades of the bridge, and down she went to rise no more. She chose death, rather than to go back into the hands of those christian slaveholders from whom she had escaped.

Can it be possible that such things as these exist in the United States? Are not these the exceptions? Are any such scenes as this general? Are not such deeds condemned by the law and denounced by public opinion? Let me read to you a few of the laws of the slave-holding states of America. I think no better exposure of slavery can be made than is made by the laws of the states in which slavery exists. I prefer reading the laws to making any statement in confirmation of what I have said myself; for the slaveholders cannot object to this testimony, since it is the calm, the cool, the deliberate enactment of their wisest heads, of their most clear-sighted, their own constituted representatives. "If more than seven slaves together are found in any road without a white person, twenty lashes a piece; for visiting a plantation without a written pass, ten lashes; for letting loose a boat from where it is made fast, thirty-nine lashes for the first offense; and for the second, shall have cut off from his head one ear; for keeping or carrying a club, thirty-nine lashes; for having any article for sale, without a ticket from his master, ten lashes; for traveling in any other than the most usual and accustomed road, when going alone to any place, forty lashes; for traveling in the night without a pass, forty lashes." I am afraid you do not understand the awful character of these lashes. You must bring it before your mind. A human being in a perfect state of nudity, tied hand and foot to a stake, and a strong man standing behind with a heavy whip, knotted at the end, each blow cutting into the flesh, and leaving the warm blood dripping to the feet; and for these trifles. "For being found in another person's negro-quarters, forty lashes; for hunting with dogs in the the woods, thirty lashes; for being on horseback without the written permission of his master, twenty-five lashes; for riding or going abroad in the night, or riding horses in the day time, without leave, a slave may be whipped, cropped, or branded in the cheek with the letter R, or otherwise punished, such punishment not extending to life, or so as to render him unfit for labor." The laws referred to, may be found by consulting Brevard's Digest; Haywood's Manual; Virginia Revised Code; Prince's Digest; Missouri Laws; Mississippi Revised Code.[6] A man, for going to visit his brethren, without the permission of his master—and in many instances he may not have that permission; his master, from caprice or other reasons, may not be willing to allow it—may be caught on his way, dragged to a post, the branding-iron heated, and the name of his master or the letter R branded into his cheek or on his forehead. They treat slaves

6. These were all compendia of laws pertaining to slavery. See, e.g., note 5 on p. 228.

thus, on the principle that they must punish for light offenses, in order to prevent the commission of larger ones. I wish you to mark that in the single state of Virginia there are seventy-one crimes for which a colored man may be executed; while there are only three of these crimes, which, when committed by a white man, will subject him to that punishment. There are many of these crimes which if the white man did not commit, he would be regarded as a scoundrel and a coward. In the state of Maryland, there is a law to this effect: that if a slave shall strike his master, he may be hanged, his head severed from his body, his body quartered, and his head and quarters set up in the most prominent places in the neighborhood. If a colored woman, in the defense of her own virtue, in defense of her own person, should shield herself from the brutal attacks of her tyrannical master, or make the slightest resistance, she may be killed on the spot. No law whatever will bring the guilty man to justice for the crime.

But you will ask me, can these things be possible in a land professing christianity? Yes, they are so; and this is not the worst. No; a darker feature is yet to be presented than the mere existence of these facts. I have to inform you that the religion of the southern states, at this time, is the great supporter, the great sanctioner of the bloody atrocities to which I have referred. While America is printing tracts and bibles; sending missionaries abroad to convert the heathen; expending her money in various ways for the promotion of the gospel in foreign lands—the slave not only lies forgotten, uncared for, but is trampled under foot by the very churches of the land. What have we in America? Why, we have slavery made part of the religion of the land. Yes, the pulpit there stands up as the great defender of this cursed *institution*, as it is called. Ministers of religion come forward and torture the hallowed pages of inspired wisdom to sanction the bloody deed. They stand forth as the foremost, the strongest defenders of this "institution." As a proof of this, I need not do more than state the general fact, that slavery has existed under the droppings of the sanctuary of the south for the last two hundred years, and there has not been any war between the *religion* and the *slavery* of the south. Whips, chains, gags, and thumb-screws have all lain under the droppings of the sanctuary, and instead of rusting from off the limbs of the bondman, those droppings have served to preserve them in all their strength. Instead of preaching the gospel against this tyranny, rebuke, and wrong, ministers of religion have sought, by all and every means, to throw in the background whatever in the bible could be construed into opposition to slavery, and to bring forward that which they could torture into its support. This I conceive to be the darkest feature of slavery, and the most difficult to attack, because it is identified with religion, and exposes those who denounce it to the charge of infidelity. Yes, those with whom I have been laboring, namely, the old organization anti-slavery society of America, have been again and again stigmatized as infidels, and for what reason? Why, solely in consequence of the faithfulness of their attacks upon the slaveholding religion of the southern states, and the northern religion that sympathizes with it. I have found it difficult to speak on this matter without persons coming forward and saying, "Douglass, are you not afraid of injuring the cause of Christ? You do not desire to do so, we know; but are you not undermining religion?" This has been said to me again and again, even since I came to this country, but I cannot be induced to leave off these exposures. I love the religion of our blessed Savior. I love that religion that comes from above, in the "wisdom of God, which is first pure, then peaceable, gentle, and easy to be entreated, full of mercy and good fruits, without partiality and without hypocrisy." I love that religion that sends its votaries to bind up the wounds of him that has fallen among thieves. I love that religion that makes it the duty of its disciples to visit the fatherless and the widow in their affliction. I love that religion that is based upon the glorious principle, of love to God and love to man; which makes its followers do unto others as they themselves would be done by. If you demand liberty to yourself, it says, grant it to your neighbors. If you claim a right to think for yourself, it says, allow your neighbors the same right. If you claim to act for yourself, it says, allow your neighbors the same right. It is because I love this religion that I hate the slaveholding, the woman-whipping, the mind-darkening, the soul-destroying religion that exists in the southern states of America. It is because I regard the one as good, and pure, and holy, that I cannot but regard the other as bad, corrupt, and wicked. Loving the one I must hate the other; holding to the one I must reject the other.

I may be asked, why I am so anxious to bring this subject before the British public—why I do not confine my efforts to the United States? My answer is, first, that slavery is the common enemy of mankind, and all mankind should be made acquainted with its abominable character. My next answer is, that the slave is a man, and, as such, is entitled to your sympathy as a brother. All the feelings, all the susceptibilities, all the capacities, which you have, he has. He is a part of the human family. He has been the prey—the common prey—of christendom for the last three hundred years, and it is but right, it is but just, it is but proper, that his wrongs should be known throughout the world. I have another reason for bringing this matter before the British public, and it is this: slavery is a system of wrong, so blinding to all around, so hardening to the heart, so corrupting to the morals, so deleterious to religion, so sapping to all the principles of justice in its immediate vicinity, that the community surrounding it lack the moral stamina necessary to its removal. It is a system of such gigantic evil, so strong, so overwhelming in its power, that no one nation is equal to its removal. It requires the humanity of Christianity, the morality of the world to remove it. Hence, I call upon the people of Britain to look at this matter, and to exert the influence I am about to show they possess, for the removal of slavery from America. I can appeal to them, as strongly by their regard for the slaveholder as for the slave, to labor in this cause. I am here, because you have an influence on America that no other nation can have. You have been drawn together by the power of steam to a marvelous extent; the distance between London and Boston is now reduced to some twelve or fourteen days, so that the denunciations against slavery, uttered in London this week, may be heard in a fortnight in the streets of Boston, and reverberating amidst the hills of Massachusetts. There is nothing said here against slavery that will not be recorded in the United States. I am here, also, because the slaveholders do not want me to be here; they would rather that I were not here. I have adopted a maxim laid down by Napoleon,[7] never to occupy ground which the enemy would like me to occupy. The slaveholders would much rather have me, if I will denounce slavery, denounce it in the northern states, where their friends and supporters are, who will stand by and mob me for denouncing it. They feel something as the man felt, when he uttered his prayer, in which he made out a most horrible case for himself, and one of his neighbors touched him and said, "My friend, I always had the opinion of you that you have now expressed for yourself— that you are a very great sinner." Coming from himself, it was all very well, but coming from a stranger it was rather cutting. The slaveholders felt that when slavery was denounced among themselves, it was not so bad; but let one of the slaves get loose, let him summon the people of Britain, and make known to them the conduct of the slaveholders toward their slaves, and it cuts them to the quick, and produces a sensation such as would be produced by nothing else. The power I exert now is something like the power that is exerted by the man at the end of the lever; my influence now is just in proportion to the distance that I am from the United States. My exposure of slavery abroad will tell more upon the hearts and consciences of slaveholders, than if I was attacking them in America; for almost every paper that I now receive from the United States, comes teeming with statements about this fugitive negro, calling him a "glib-tongued scoundrel," and saying that he is running out against the institutions and people of America. I deny the charge

7. Napoléon Bonaparte (1769–1821), French emperor 1804–15.

that I am saying a word against the institutions of America, or the people, as such. What I have to say is against slavery and slaveholders. I feel at liberty to speak on this subject. I have on my back the marks of the lash; I have four sisters and one brother now under the galling chain. I feel it my duty to cry aloud and spare not. I am not averse to having the good opinion of my fellow-creatures. I am not averse to being kindly regarded by all men; but I am bound, even at the hazard of making a large class of religionists in this country hate me, oppose me, and malign me as they have done—I am bound by the prayers, and tears, and entreaties of three millions of kneeling bondsmen, to have no compromise with men who are in any shape or form connected with the slaveholders of America. I expose slavery in this country, because to expose it is to kill it. Slavery is one of those monsters of darkness to whom the light of truth is death. Expose slavery, and it dies. Light is to slavery what the heat of the sun is to the root of a tree; it must die under it. All the slaveholder asks of me is silence. He does not ask me to go abroad and preach *in favor* of slavery; he does not ask any one to do that. He would not say that slavery is a good thing, but the best under the circumstances. The slaveholders want total darkness on the subject. They want the hatchway shut down, that the monster may crawl in his den of darkness, crushing human hopes and happiness, destroying the bondman at will, and having no one to reprove or rebuke him. Slavery shrinks from the light; it hateth the light, neither cometh to the light, lest its deeds should be reproved. To tear off the mask from this abominable system, to expose it to the light of heaven, aye, to the heat of the sun, that it may burn and wither it out of existence, is my object in coming to this country. I want the slaveholder surrounded, as by a wall of anti-slavery fire, so that he may see the condemnation of himself and his system glaring down in letters of light. I want him to feel that he has no sympathy in England, Scotland, or Ireland; that he has none in Canada, none in Mexico, none among the poor wild Indians; that the voice of the civilized, aye, and savage world is against him. I would have condemnation blaze down upon him in every direction, till, stunned and overwhelmed with shame and confusion, he is compelled to let go the grasp he holds upon the persons of his victims, and restore them to their long-lost rights.

[REVEREND DR. CAMPBELL][1]

Dr. Campbell's Reply

From Rev. Dr. Campbell's brilliant reply we extract the following:

FREDERICK DOUGLASS, the "beast of burden," the portion of "goods and chattels," the representative of three millions of men, has been raised up! Shall I say the *man?* If there is a man on earth, he is a man. My blood boiled within me when I heard his address tonight, and thought that he had left behind him three millions of such men.

We must see more of this man; we must have more of this man. One would have taken a voyage round the globe some forty years back—especially since the introduction of steam—to have heard such an exposure of slavery from the lips of a slave. It will be an era in the individual history of the present assembly. Our children—our boys and girls—I have to-night seen the delightful sympathy of their hearts evinced by their heaving breasts, while their eyes sparkled with wonder and admiration, that this black man—this slave—had so much logic, so much wit, so much fancy, so much eloquence. He was something more than a man, according to their little notions. Then, I say, we must hear him again. We have got a purpose to accomplish. He has appealed to the pulpit of England. The English pulpit is with him. He has appealed to the press of England; the press of England is conducted by English hearts, and that press will do him justice. About ten days hence, and his second master, who may well prize "such a piece of goods," will have the pleasure of reading his burning words, and his first master will bless himself that he has got quit of him. We have to create public opinion, or rather, not to create it, for it is created already; but we have to foster it; and when to-night I heard those magnificent words—the words of Curran,[2] by which my heart, from boyhood, has ofttimes been deeply moved—I rejoice to think that they embody an instinct of an Englishman's nature. I heard, with inexpressible delight, how they told on this mighty mass of the citizens of the metropolis.

Britain has now no slaves; we can therefore talk to the other nations now, as we could not have talked a dozen years ago. I want the whole of the London ministry to meet Douglass. For as his appeal is to England, and throughout England, I should rejoice in the idea of churchmen and dissenters merging all

1. See note 5 on p. 233.
2. John Philpot Curran (1750–1817), Irish politician, lawyer, and orator.

sectional distinctions in this cause. Let us have a public breakfast. Let the ministers meet him; let them hear him; let them
grasp his hand; and let him enlist their sympathies on behalf
of the slave. Let him inspire them with abhorrence of the man-
stealer—the slaveholder. No slaveholding American shall ever
cross my door. No slaveholding or slavery-supporting minister
shall ever pollute my pulpit. While I have a tongue to speak, or a
hand to write, I will, to the utmost of my power, oppose these
slaveholding men. We must have Douglass amongst us to aid
in fostering public opinion.

The great conflict with slavery must now take place in America; and while they are adding other slave states to the Union,
our business is to step forward and help the abolitionists
there. It is a pleasing circumstance that such a body of men
has risen in America, and whilst we hurl our thunders against
her slavers, let us make a distinction between those who advocate slavery and those who oppose it. George Thompson has
been there.[3] This man, Frederick Douglass, has been there,
and has been compelled to flee. I wish, when he first set foot
on our shores, he had made a solemn vow, and said, "Now that
I am free, and in the sanctuary of freedom, I will never return
till I have seen the emancipation of my country completed."
He wants to surround these men, the slaveholders, as by a
wall of fire; and he himself may do much toward kindling it.
Let him travel over the island—east, west, north, and
south—everywhere diffusing knowledge and awakening principle, till the whole nation become a body of petitioners to
America. He will, he must, do it. He must for a season make
England his home. He must send for his wife. He must send
for his children. I want to see the sons and daughters of such a
sire. We, too, must do something for him and them worthy of
the English name. I do not like the idea of a man of such
mental dimensions, such moral courage, and all but incompa-
rable talent, having his own small wants, and the wants of a
distant wife and children, supplied by the poor profits of his
publication, the sketch of his life. Let the pamphlet be bought
by tens of thousands.[4] But we will do something more for him,
shall we not?

It only remains that we pass a resolution of thanks to Frederick Douglass, the slave that was, the man that is! He that was
covered with chains, and that is now being covered with glory,
and whom we will send back a gentleman.

---

3. See note 6 on p. 233.
4. Refers to Douglass's 1845 *Narrative*, which was republished in Dublin, Ireland, in 1845
and 1846; the book sold very well in Great Britain, and the proceeds were a major
source of Douglass's income while he resided there.

[FREDERICK DOUGLASS]

Letter to His Old Master[1]

To My Old Master, Thomas Auld

SIR—The long and intimate, though by no means friendly, relation which unhappily subsisted between you and myself, leads me to hope that you will easily account for the great liberty which I now take in addressing you in this open and public manner. The same fact may possibly remove any disagreeable surprise which you may experience on again finding your name coupled with mine, in any other way than in an advertisement, accurately describing my person, and offering a large sum for my arrest. In thus dragging you again before the public, I am aware that I shall subject myself to no inconsiderable amount of censure. I shall probably be charged with an unwarrantable, if not a wanton and reckless disregard of the rights and proprieties of private life. There are those north as well as south who entertain a much higher respect for rights which are merely conventional, than they do for rights which are personal and essential. Not a few there are in our country, who, while they have no scruples against robbing the laborer of the hard-earned results of his patient industry, will be shocked by the extremely indelicate manner of bringing your name before the public. Believing this to be the case, and wishing to meet every reasonable or plausible objection to my conduct, I will frankly state the ground upon which I justify myself in this instance, as well as on former occasions when I have thought proper to mention your name in public. All will agree that a man guilty of theft, robbery, or murder, has forfeited the right to concealment and private life; that the community have a right to subject such persons to the most complete exposure. However much they may desire retirement, and aim to conceal themselves and their movements from the popular gaze, the public have a right to ferret them out, and bring their conduct before the proper tribunals of the country for investigation. Sir, you will undoubtedly make the proper application of these generally admitted principles, and will easily see the light in which you are regarded by me; I will not therefore manifest ill temper, by calling you hard names. I know you to be a man of some intelligence, and can readily determine the precise estimate which I entertain of your character. I may therefore indulge in

---

1. It is not often that chattels address their owners. The following letter is unique; and probably the only specimen of the kind extant. It was written while in England [*Original editor's note*; see note 1 on p. 7].

language which may seem to others indirect and ambiguous, and yet be quite well understood by yourself.

I have selected this day on which to address you, because it is the anniversary of my emancipation;[2] and knowing no better way, I am led to this as the best mode of celebrating that truly important event. Just ten years ago this beautiful September morning, yon bright sun beheld me a slave—a poor degraded chattel—trembling at the sound of your voice, lamenting that I was a man, and wishing myself a brute. The hopes which I had treasured up for weeks of a safe and successful escape from your grasp, were powerfully confronted at this last hour by dark clouds of doubt and fear, making my person shake and my bosom to heave with the heavy contest between hope and fear. I have no words to describe to you the deep agony of soul which I experienced on that never-to-be-forgotten morning—for I left by daylight. I was making a leap in the dark. The probabilities, so far as I could by reason determine them, were stoutly against the undertaking. The preliminaries and precautions I had adopted previously, all worked badly. I was like one going to war without weapons—ten chances of defeat to one of victory. One in whom I had confided, and one who had promised me assistance, appalled by fear at the trial hour, deserted me, thus leaving the responsibility of success or failure solely with myself. You, sir, can never know my feelings. As I look back to them, I can scarcely realize that I have passed through a scene so trying. Trying, however, as they were, and gloomy as was the prospect, thanks be to the Most High, who is ever the God of the oppressed, at the moment which was to determine my whole earthly career, His grace was sufficient; my mind was made up. I embraced the golden opportunity, took the morning tide at the flood, and a free man, young, active, and strong, is the result.

I have often thought I should like to explain to you the grounds upon which I have justified myself in running away from you. I am almost ashamed to do so now, for by this time you may have discovered them yourself. I will, however, glance at them. When yet but a child about six years old, I imbibed the determination to run away. The very first mental effort that I now remember on my part, was an attempt to solve the mystery—why am I a slave? and with this question my youthful mind was troubled for many days, pressing upon me more heavily at times than others. When I saw the slave-driver whip a slave-woman, cut the blood out of her neck, and heard her piteous cries, I went away into the corner of the fence, wept and pondered over the mystery. I had, through some medium, I know not what, got some idea of God, the Creator of all mankind, the black and the white, and that he had made the blacks to serve the

2. Douglass refers to the day he escaped from slavery, September 3, 1838.

whites as slaves. How he could do this and be *good*, I could not tell. I was not satisfied with this theory, which made God responsible for slavery, for it pained me greatly, and I have wept over it long and often. At one time, your first wife, Mrs. Lucretia, heard me sighing and saw me shedding tears, and asked of me the matter, but I was afraid to tell her. I was puzzled with this question, till one night while sitting in the kitchen, I heard some of the old slaves talking of their parents having been stolen from Africa by white men, and were sold here as slaves. The whole mystery was solved at once. Very soon after this, my Aunt Jinny and Uncle Noah ran away, and the great noise made about it by your father-in-law, made me for the first time acquainted with the fact, that there were free states as well as slave states. From that time, I resolved that I would some day run away. The morality of the act I dispose of as follows: I am myself; you are yourself; we are two distinct persons, equal persons. What you are, I am. You are a man, and so am I. God created both, and made us separate beings. I am not by nature bond to you, or you to me. Nature does not make your existence depend upon me, or mine to depend upon yours. I cannot walk upon your legs, or you upon mine. I cannot breathe for you, or you for me; I must breathe for myself, and you for yourself. We are distinct persons, and are each equally provided with faculties necessary to our individual existence. In leaving you, I took nothing but what belonged to me, and in no way lessened your means for obtaining an *honest* living. Your faculties remained yours, and mine became useful to their rightful owner. I therefore see no wrong in any part of the transaction. It is true, I went off secretly; but that was more your fault than mine. Had I let you into the secret, you would have defeated the enterprise entirely; but for this, I should have been really glad to have made you acquainted with my intentions to leave.

You may perhaps want to know how I like my present condition. I am free to say, I greatly prefer it to that which I occupied in Maryland. I am, however, by no means prejudiced against the state as such. Its geography, climate, fertility, and products, are such as to make it a very desirable abode for any man; and but for the existence of slavery there, it is not impossible that I might again take up my abode in that state. It is not that I love Maryland less, but freedom more. You will be surprised to learn that people at the north labor under the strange delusion that if the slaves were emancipated at the south, they would flock to the north. So far from this being the case, in that event, you would see many old and familiar faces back again to the south. The fact is, there are few here who would not return to the south in the event of emancipation. We want to live in the land of our birth, and to lay our bones by the side of our fathers; and nothing short of an intense love of personal freedom keeps us from the south. For the sake of this, most of us would live on a crust of bread and a cup of cold water.

Since I left you, I have had a rich experience. I have occupied stations which I never dreamed of when a slave. Three out of the ten years since I left you, I spent as a common laborer on the wharves of New Bedford, Massachusetts. It was there I earned my first free dollar. It was mine. I could spend it as I pleased. I could buy hams or herring with it, without asking any odds of anybody. That was a precious dollar to me. You remember when I used to make seven, or eight, or even nine dollars a week in Baltimore, you would take every cent of it from me every Saturday night, saying that I belonged to you, and my earnings also. I never liked this conduct on your part—to say the best, I thought it a little mean. I would not have served you so. But let that pass. I was a little awkward about counting money in New England fashion when I first landed in New Bedford. I came near betraying myself several times. I caught myself saying phip, for fourpence; and at one time a man actually charged me with being a runaway, whereupon I was silly enough to become one by running away from him, for I was greatly afraid he might adopt measures to get me again into slavery, a condition I then dreaded more than death.

I soon learned, however, to count money, as well as to make it, and got on swimmingly. I married soon after leaving you; in fact, I was engaged to be married before I left you; and instead of finding my companion a burden, she was truly a helpmate. She went to live at service, and I to work on the wharf, and though we toiled hard the first winter, we never lived more happily. After remaining in New Bedford for three years, I met with William Lloyd Garrison, a person of whom you have *possibly* heard, as he is pretty generally known among slaveholders. He put it into my head that I might make myself serviceable to the cause of the slave, by devoting a portion of my time to telling my own sorrows, and those of other slaves, which had come under my observation. This was the commencement of a higher state of existence than any to which I had ever aspired. I was thrown into society the most pure, enlightened, and benevolent, that the country affords. Among these I have never forgotten you, but have invariably made you the topic of conversation—thus giving you all the notoriety I could do. I need not tell you that the opinion formed of you in these circles is far from being favorable. They have little respect for your honesty, and less for your religion.

But I was going on to relate to you something of my interesting experience. I had not long enjoyed the excellent society to which I have referred, before the light of its excellence exerted a beneficial influence on my mind and heart. Much of my early dislike of white persons was removed, and their manners, habits, and customs, so entirely unlike what I had been used to in the kitchen-quarters on the plantations of the south, fairly charmed me, and gave me a strong disrelish for the coarse and degrading customs of my former condition. I therefore made an effort so to improve my mind and deportment, as to be somewhat fitted to the station to which I seemed almost providentially called. The transition from degradation to respectability was indeed great, and to get from one to the other without carrying some marks of one's former condition, is truly a difficult matter. I would not have you think that I am now entirely clear of all plantation peculiarities, but my friends here, while they entertain the strongest dislike to them, regard me with that charity to which my past life somewhat entitles me, so that my condition in this respect is exceedingly pleasant. So far as my domestic affairs are concerned, I can boast of as comfortable a dwelling as your own. I have an industrious and neat companion, and four dear children— the oldest a girl of nine years, and three fine boys, the oldest eight, the next six, and the youngest four years old. The three oldest are now going regularly to school—two can read and write, and the other can spell, with tolerable correctness, words of two syllables. Dear fellows! they are all in comfortable beds, and are sound asleep, perfectly secure under my own roof. There are no slaveholders here to rend my heart by snatching them from my arms, or blast a mother's dearest hopes by tearing them from her bosom. These dear children are ours—not to work up into rice, sugar, and tobacco, but to watch over, regard, and protect, and to rear them up in the nurture and admonition of the gospel—to train them up in the paths of wisdom and virtue, and, as far as we can, to make them useful to the world and to themselves. Oh! sir, a slaveholder never appears to me so completely an agent of hell, as when I think of and look upon my dear children. It is then that my feelings rise above my control. I meant to have said more with respect to my own prosperity and happiness, but thoughts and feelings which this recital has quickened, unfits me to proceed further in that direction. The grim horrors of slavery rise in all their ghastly terror before me; the wails of millions pierce my heart and chill my blood. I remember the chain, the gag, the bloody whip; the death-like gloom overshadowing the broken spirit of the fettered bondman; the appalling liability of his being torn away from wife and children, and sold like a beast in the market. Say not that this is a picture of fancy. You well know that I wear stripes on my back, inflicted by your direction; and that you, while we were brothers in the same church, caused this right hand, with which I am now penning this letter, to be closely tied to my left, and my person dragged, at the pistol's mouth, fifteen miles, from the Bay Side to Easton, to be sold like a beast in the market, for the alleged crime of intending to escape from your possession.

All this, and more, you remember, and know to be perfectly true, not only of yourself, but of nearly all of the slaveholders around you.

At this moment, you are probably the guilty holder of at least three of my own dear sisters, and my only brother, in bondage. These you regard as your property. They are recorded on your ledger, or perhaps have been sold to human flesh-mongers, with a view to filling your own ever-hungry purse. Sir, I desire to know how and where these dear sisters are. Have you sold them? or are they still in your possession? What has become of them? are they living or dead? And my dear old grandmother, whom you turned out like an old horse to die in the woods—is she still alive?[3] Write and let me know all about them. If my grandmother be still alive, she is of no service to you, for by this time she must be nearly eighty years old—too old to be cared for by one to whom she has ceased to be of service; send her to me at Rochester, or bring her to Philadelphia, and it shall be the crowning happiness of my life to take care of her in her old age. Oh! She was to me a mother and a father, so far as hard toil for my comfort could make her such. Send me my grandmother! that I may watch over and take care of her in her old age. And my sisters—let me know all about them. I would write to them, and learn all I want to know of them, without disturbing you in any way, but that, through your unrighteous conduct, they have been entirely deprived of the power to read and write. You have kept them in utter ignorance, and have therefore robbed them of the sweet enjoyments of writing or receiving letters from absent friends and relatives. Your wickedness and cruelty, committed in this respect on your fellow-creatures, are greater than all the stripes you have laid upon my back or theirs. It is an outrage upon the soul, a war upon the immortal spirit, and one for which you must give account at the bar of our common Father and Creator.

The responsibility which you have assumed in this regard is truly awful, and how you could stagger under it these many years is marvelous. Your mind must have become darkened, your heart hardened, your conscience seared and petrified, or you would have long since thrown off the accursed load, and sought relief at the hands of a sin-forgiving God. How, let me ask, would you look upon me, were I, some dark night, in company with a band of hardened villains, to enter the precincts of your elegant dwelling, and seize the person of your own lovely daughter, Amanda, and carry her off from your family, friends, and all the loved ones of her youth—make her my slave—compel her to work, and I take her wages—place her name

---

3. Douglass subsequently learned that his grandmother, who figures importantly in the early chapters of this book, had not been ill-treated by Auld, and in a second letter to him apologized for these accusations.

on my ledger as property—disregard her personal rights—fetter the powers of her immortal soul by denying her the right and privilege of learning to read and write—feed her coarsely—clothe her scantily, and whip her on the naked back occasionally; more, and still more horrible, leave her unprotected—a degraded victim to the brutal lust of fiendish overseers, who would pollute, blight, and blast her fair soul—rob her of all dignity—destroy her virtue, and annihilate in her person all the graces that adorn the character of virtuous womanhood? I ask, how would you regard me, if such were my conduct? Oh! The vocabulary of the damned would not afford a word sufficiently infernal to express your idea of my God-provoking wickedness. Yet, sir, your treatment of my beloved sisters is in all essential points precisely like the case I have now supposed. Damning as would be such a deed on my part, it would be no more so than that which you have committed against me and my sisters.

I will now bring this letter to a close; you shall hear from me again unless you let me hear from you. I intend to make use of you as a weapon with which to assail the system of slavery—as a means of concentrating public attention on the system, and deepening the horror of trafficking in the souls and bodies of men. I shall make use of you as a means of exposing the character of the American church and clergy—and as a means of bringing this guilty nation, with yourself, to repentance. In doing this, I entertain no malice toward you personally. There is no roof under which you would be more safe than mine, and there is nothing in my house which you might need for your comfort, which I would not readily grant. Indeed, I should esteem it a privilege to set you an example as to how mankind ought to treat each other.

I am your fellow-man, but not your slave.

From The Nature of Slavery

EXTRACT FROM A LECTURE ON SLAVERY, AT ROCHESTER, DECEMBER 1, 1850[1]

More than twenty years of my life were consumed in a state of slavery. My childhood was environed by the baneful peculiarities of the slave system. I grew up to manhood in the presence of this hydra-headed monster[2]—not as a master—not as an idle spectator—not as the guest of the slaveholder—but as a slave, eating the bread and

1. Douglass selected this and the other excerpts from his speeches that appear in *My Bondage and My Freedom.*
2. In ancient Greek mythology, the Hydra, a many-headed and highly lethal monster, was slain by the hero Hercules.

drinking the cup of slavery with the most degraded of my brother-bondmen, and sharing with them all the painful conditions of their wretched lot. In consideration of these facts, I feel that I have a right to speak, and to speak *strongly*. Yet, my friends, I feel bound to speak truly.

Goading as have been the cruelties to which I have been subjected—bitter as have been the trials through which I have passed—exasperating as have been, and still are, the indignities offered to my manhood—I find in them no excuse for the slightest departure from truth in dealing with any branch of this subject.

First of all, I will state, as well as I can, the legal and social relation of master and slave. A master is one—to speak in the vocabulary of the southern states—who claims and exercises a right of property in the person of a fellow-man. This he does with the force of the law and the sanction of southern religion. The law gives the master absolute power over the slave. He may work him, flog him, hire him out, sell him, and, in certain contingencies, *kill* him, with perfect impunity. The slave is a human being, divested of all rights—reduced to the level of a brute—a mere "chattel" in the eye of the law—placed beyond the circle of human brotherhood—cut off from his kind—his name, which the "recording angel" may have enrolled in heaven,[3] among the blest, is impiously inserted in a *master's ledger,* with horses, sheep, and swine. In law, the slave has no wife, no children, no country, and no home. He can own nothing, possess nothing, acquire nothing, but what must belong to another. To eat the fruit of his own toil, to clothe his person with the work of his own hands, is considered stealing. He toils that another may reap the fruit; he is industrious that another may live in idleness; he eats unbolted meal that another may eat the bread of fine flour; he labors in chains at home, under a burning sun and biting lash, that another may ride in ease and splendor abroad; he lives in ignorance that another may be educated; he is abused that another may be exalted; he rests his toil-worn limbs on the cold, damp ground that another may repose on the softest pillow; he is clad in coarse and tattered raiment that another may be arrayed in purple and fine linen; he is sheltered only by the wretched hovel that a master may dwell in a magnificent mansion; and to this condition he is bound down as by an arm of iron.

From this monstrous relation there springs an unceasing stream of most revolting cruelties. The very accompaniments of the slave system stamp it as the offspring of hell itself. To ensure good behavior, the slaveholder relies on the whip; to induce proper humility, he

3. In Judeo-Christian mythology, one or more angels record all human events, actions, and prayers.

relies on the whip; to rebuke what he is pleased to term insolence, he relies on the whip; to supply the place of wages as an incentive to toil, he relies on the whip; to bind down the spirit of the slave, to imbrute and destroy his manhood, he relies on the whip, the chain, the gag, the thumb-screw, the pillory, the bowie-knife, the pistol, and the blood-hound. These are the necessary and unvarying accompaniments of the system. Wherever slavery is found, these horrid instruments are also found. Whether on the coast of Africa, among the savage tribes, or in South Carolina, among the refined and civilized, slavery is the same, and its accompaniments one and the same. It makes no difference whether the slaveholder worships the God of the christians, or is a follower of Mahomet,[4] he is the minister of the same cruelty, and the author of the same misery. *Slavery* is always *slavery*; always the same foul, haggard, and damning scourge, whether found in the eastern or in the western hemisphere.

There is a still deeper shade to be given to this picture. The physical cruelties are indeed sufficiently harassing and revolting; but they are as a few grains of sand on the sea shore, or a few drops of water in the great ocean, compared with the stupendous wrongs which it inflicts upon the mental, moral, and religious nature of its hapless victims. It is only when we contemplate the slave as a moral and intellectual being, that we can adequately comprehend the unparalleled enormity of slavery, and the intense criminality of the slaveholder. I have said that the slave was a man. "What a piece of work is man! How noble in reason! How infinite in faculties! In form and moving how express and admirable! In action how like an angel! In apprehension how like a God! the beauty of the world! the paragon of animals!"[5]

The slave is a man, "the image of God," but "a little lower than the angels;"[6] possessing a soul, eternal and indestructible; capable of endless happiness, or immeasurable woe; a creature of hopes and fears, of affections and passions, of joys and sorrows, and he is endowed with those mysterious powers by which man soars above the things of time and sense, and grasps, with undying tenacity, the elevating and sublimely glorious idea of a God. It is *such* a being that is smitten and blasted. The first work of slavery is to mar and deface those characteristics of its victims which distinguish *men* from *things*, and *persons* from *property*. Its first aim is to destroy all sense of high moral and religious responsibility. It reduces man to a mere machine. It cuts him off from his Maker, it hides from him the laws of God, and leaves him to grope his way from time to eternity in the

4. Muhammad (c. 570–632), the prophet who founded the religion of Islam.
5. Cf. Shakespeare, *Hamlet* 2.2.265–68.
6. Cf. Genesis 1.27 and Psalm 8.5.

dark, under the arbitrary and despotic control of a frail, depraved, and sinful fellow-man. As the serpent-charmer of India is compelled to extract the deadly teeth of his venomous prey before he is able to handle him with impunity, so the slaveholder must strike down the conscience of the slave before he can obtain the entire mastery over his victim.

It is, then, the first business of the enslaver of men to blunt, deaden, and destroy the central principle of human responsibility. Conscience is, to the individual soul, and to society, what the law of gravitation is to the universe. It holds society together; it is the basis of all trust and confidence; it is the pillar of all moral rectitude. Without it, suspicion would take the place of trust; vice would be more than a match for virtue; men would prey upon each other, like the wild beasts of the desert; and earth would become a *hell*.

Nor is slavery more adverse to the conscience than it is to the mind. This is shown by the fact, that in every state of the American Union, where slavery exists, except the state of Kentucky, there are laws absolutely prohibitory of education among the slaves. The crime of teaching a slave to read is punishable with severe fines and impris-onment, and, in some instances, with *death itself*.

Nor are the laws respecting this matter a dead letter. Cases may occur in which they are disregarded, and a few instances may be found where slaves may have learned to read; but such are isolated cases, and only prove the rule. The great mass of slaveholders look upon education among the slaves as utterly subversive of the slave system. I well remember when my mistress first announced to my master that she had discovered that I could read. His face colored at once with surprise and chagrin. He said that "I was ruined, and my value as a slave destroyed; that a slave should know nothing but to obey his master; that to give a negro an inch would lead him to take an ell; that having learned how to read, I would soon want to know how to write; and that by-and-by I would be running away." I think my audience will bear witness to the correctness of this phi-losophy, and to the literal fulfillment of this prophecy.

It is perfectly well understood at the south, that to educate a slave is to make him discontented with slavery, and to invest him with a power which shall open to him the treasures of freedom; and since the object of the slaveholder is to maintain complete authority over his slave, his constant vigilance is exercised to prevent everything which militates against, or endangers, the stability of his authority. Education being among the menacing influences, and, perhaps, the most dangerous, is, therefore, the most cautiously guarded against.

It is true that we do not often hear of the enforcement of the law, punishing as a crime the teaching of slaves to read, but this is not because of a want of disposition to enforce it. The true reason or explanation of the matter is this: there is the greatest unanimity of opinion among the white population in the south in favor of the policy of keeping the slave in ignorance. There is, perhaps, another reason why the law against education is so seldom violated. The slave is too poor to be able to offer a temptation sufficiently strong to induce a white man to violate it; and it is not to be supposed that in a community where the moral and religious sentiment is in favor of slavery, many martyrs will be found sacrificing their liberty and lives by violating those prohibitory enactments.

As a general rule, then, darkness reigns over the abodes of the enslaved, and "how great is that darkness!"[7]

We are sometimes told of the contentment of the slaves, and are entertained with vivid pictures of their happiness. We are told that they often dance and sing; that their masters frequently give them wherewith to make merry; in fine, that they have little of which to complain. I admit that the slave does sometimes sing, dance, and appear to be merry. But what does this prove? It only proves to my mind, that though slavery is armed with a thousand stings, it is not able entirely to kill the elastic spirit of the bondman. That spirit will rise and walk abroad, despite of whips and chains, and extract from the cup of nature occasional drops of joy and gladness. No thanks to the slaveholder, nor to slavery, that the vivacious captive may sometimes dance in his chains; his very mirth in such circumstances stands before God as an accusing angel against his enslaver.

It is often said, by the opponents of the anti-slavery cause, that the condition of the people of Ireland is more deplorable than that of the American slaves. Far be it from me to underrate the sufferings of the Irish people. They have been long oppressed; and the same heart that prompts me to plead the cause of the American bondman, makes it impossible for me not to sympathize with the oppressed of all lands. Yet I must say that there is no analogy between the two cases. The Irishman is poor, but he is not a slave. He may be in rags, but he is not a slave. He is still the master of his own body, and can say with the poet, "The hand of Douglass is his own."[8] "The world is all before him, where to choose;"[9] and poor as may be my opinion of the British parliament, I cannot believe that it will ever sink to such a depth of infamy as to pass a law for the recapture of fugitive Irishmen! The shame and scandal of kidnapping will long remain wholly monopolized by the American congress. The Irishman has not only the liberty to emigrate from his country, but

7. Cf. Matthew 6.23.
8. Cf. *Marmion* (1808) 6.13.406, by Sir Walter Scott (see note 3 on p. 39).
9. Cf. *Paradise Lost* (1674) 12.646, by the English poet John Milton (1608–1674).

he has liberty at home. He can write, and speak, and coöperate for the attainment of his rights and the redress of his wrongs.

The multitude can assemble upon all the green hills and fertile plains of the Emerald Isle; they can pour out their grievances, and proclaim their wants without molestation; and the press, that "swift-winged messenger,"[1] can bear the tidings of their doings to the extreme bounds of the civilized world. They have their "Conciliation Hall," on the banks of the Liffey,[2] their reform clubs, and their newspapers; they pass resolutions, send forth addresses, and enjoy the right of petition. But how is it with the American slave? Where may he assemble? Where is his Conciliation Hall? Where are his newspapers? Where is his right of petition? Where is his freedom of speech? his liberty of the press? and his right of locomotion? He is said to be happy; happy men can speak. But ask the slave what is his condition—what his state of mind—what he thinks of enslavement? and you had as well address your inquiries to the *silent dead.* There comes no *voice* from the enslaved. We are left to gather his feelings by imagining what ours would be, were our souls in his soul's stead.

If there were no other fact descriptive of slavery, than that the slave is dumb, this alone would be sufficient to mark the slave system as a grand aggregation of human horrors.

Most who are present, will have observed that leading men in this country have been putting forth their skill to secure quiet to the nation. A system of measures to promote this object was adopted a few months ago in congress.[3] The result of those measures is known. Instead of quiet, they have produced alarm; instead of peace, they have brought us war; and so it must ever be.

While this nation is guilty of the enslavement of three millions of innocent men and women, it is as idle to think of having a sound and lasting peace, as it is to think there is no God to take cognizance of the affairs of men. There can be no peace to the wicked while slavery continues in the land. It will be condemned; and while it is condemned there will be agitation. Nature must cease to be nature; men must become monsters; humanity must be transformed; christianity must be exterminated; all ideas of justice and the laws of eternal goodness must be utterly blotted out from the human soul,—ere a system so foul and infernal can escape condemnation, or this guilty republic can have a sound, enduring peace.

1. Epithet for the Greek mythological character Hermes, who delivered messages for the gods.
2. River that flows through Dublin; built in 1841, the hall served as a meeting place for activists working to repeal the union of Great Britain and Ireland.
3. Referring to the Compromise of 1850. See note 2 on p. 209.

From Inhumanity of Slavery

EXTRACT FROM A LECTURE ON SLAVERY, AT ROCHESTER,
DECEMBER 8, 1850

THE relation of master and slave has been called patriarchal, and only second in benignity and tenderness to that of the parent and child. This representation is doubtless believed by many northern people; and this may account, in part, for the lack of interest which we find among persons whom we are bound to believe to be honest and humane. What, then, are the facts? Here I will not quote my own experience in slavery; for this you might call one-sided testimony. I will not cite the declarations of abolitionists; for these you might pronounce exaggerations. I will not rely upon advertisements cut from newspapers; for these you might call isolated cases. But I will refer you to the laws adopted by the legislatures of the slave states. I give you such evidence, because it cannot be invalidated nor denied. I hold in my hand sundry extracts from the slave codes of our country, from which I will quote. * * *[1]

Now, if the foregoing be an indication of kindness, *what is cruelty?* If this be parental affection, *what is bitter malignity?* A more atrocious and blood-thirsty string of laws could not well be conceived of. And yet I am bound to say that they fall short of indicating the horrible cruelties constantly practiced in the slave states.

I admit that there are individual slaveholders less cruel and barbarous than is allowed by law; but these form the exception. The majority of slaveholders find it necessary, to insure obedience, at times, to avail themselves of the utmost extent of the law, and many go beyond it. If kindness were the rule, we should not see advertisements filling the columns of almost every southern newspaper, offering large rewards for fugitive slaves, and describing them as being branded with irons, loaded with chains, and scarred by the whip. One of the most telling testimonies against the pretended kindness of slaveholders, is the fact that uncounted numbers of fugitives are now inhabiting the Dismal Swamp,[2] preferring the untamed wilderness to their cultivated homes—choosing rather to encounter hunger and thirst, and to roam with the wild beasts of the forest, running the hazard of being hunted and shot down, than to submit to the authority of *kind* masters.

---

1. Asterisks in this selection are Douglass's.
2. The Great Dismal Swamp, covering nearly a million acres in southeastern Virginia and northeastern North Carolina.

I tell you, my friends, humanity is never driven to such an unnatural course of life, without great wrong. The slave finds more of the milk of human kindness in the bosom of the savage Indian, than in the heart of his *christian* master. He leaves the man of the *bible*, and takes refuge with the man of the *tomahawk*. He rushes from the praying slaveholder into the paws of the bear. He quits the homes of men for the haunts of wolves. He prefers to encounter a life of trial, however bitter, or death, however terrible, to dragging out his existence under the dominion of these *kind* masters.

The apologists for slavery often speak of the abuses of slavery; and they tell us that they are as much opposed to those abuses as we are; and that they would go as far to correct those abuses and to ameliorate the condition of the slave as anybody. The answer to that view is, that slavery is *itself* an abuse; that it lives by abuse; and dies by the absence of abuse. Grant that slavery is right; grant that the relation of master and slave may innocently exist; and there is not a single outrage which was ever committed against the slave but what finds an apology in the very necessity of the case. As was said by a slaveholder, (the Rev. A. G. Few,) to the Methodist conference, "If the relation be right, the means to maintain it are also right;" for without those means slavery could not exist. Remove the dreadful scourge—the plaited thong—the galling fetter—the accursed chain—and let the slaveholder rely solely upon moral and religious power, by which to secure obedience to his orders, and how long do you suppose a slave would remain on his plantation? The case only needs to be stated; it carries its own refutation with it.

Absolute and arbitrary power can never be maintained by one man over the body and soul of another man, without brutal chastisment and enormous cruelty.

To talk of *kindness* entering into a relation in which one party is robbed of wife, of children, of his hard earnings, of home, of friends, of society, of knowledge, and of all that makes this life desirable, is most absurd, wicked, and preposterous.

I have shown that slavery is wicked—wicked, in that it violates the great law of liberty, written on every human heart—wicked, in that it violates the first command of the decalogue[3]—wicked, in that it fosters the most disgusting licentiousness—wicked, in that it mars and defaces the image of God by cruel and barbarous inflictions—wicked, in that it contravenes the laws of eternal justice, and tramples in the dust all the humane and heavenly precepts of the New Testament.

---

3. The first of the Ten Commandments: "You shall have no other gods before me."

The evils resulting from this huge system of iniquity are not confined to the states south of Mason and Dixon's line.[4] Its noxious
influence can easily be traced throughout our northern borders. It
comes even as far north as the state of New York. Traces of it may
be seen even in Rochester; and travelers have told me it casts its
gloomy shadows across the lake, approaching the very shores of
Queen Victoria's dominions.[5]

The presence of slavery may be explained by—as it is the explanation of—the mobocratic violence which lately disgraced New York,
and which still more recently disgraced the city of Boston.[6] These
violent demonstrations, these outrageous invasions of human rights,
faintly indicate the presence and power of slavery here. It is a significant fact, that while meetings for almost any purpose under
heaven may be held unmolested in the city of Boston, that in the
same city, a meeting cannot be peaceably held for the purpose of
preaching the doctrine of the American Declaration of Independence, "that all men are created equal." The pestiferous breath of
slavery taints the whole moral atmosphere of the north, and ener-
vates the moral energies of the whole people.

The moment a foreigner ventures upon our soil, and utters a natural repugnance to oppression, that moment he is made to feel that
there is little sympathy in this land for him. If he were greeted with
smiles before, he meets with frowns now; and it shall go well with
him if he be not subjected to that peculiarly fitting method of showing fealty to slavery, the assaults of a mob.

Now, will any man tell me that such a state of things is natural,
and that such conduct on the part of the people of the north, springs
from a consciousness of rectitude? No! every fibre of the human
heart unites in detestation of tyranny, and it is only when the human
mind has become familiarized with slavery, is accustomed to its
injustice, and corrupted by its selfishness, that it fails to record its
abhorrence of slavery, and does not exult in the triumphs of liberty.

The northern people have been long connected with slavery; they
have been linked to a decaying corpse, which has destroyed the
moral health. The union of the government; the union of the north
and south, in the political parties; the union in the religious organizations of the land, have all served to deaden the moral sense of the

---

4. See note 1 on p. 128.
5. "dominions": British constitutional term signifying independent Commonwealth realms.
   The Canadian Confederation, established in 1867, was the first of these realms.
6. Abolitionist speakers and meetings were frequently mobbed by Northern supporters of
   slavery. Douglass refers here to mob violence in May 1850 against a meeting of the
   American Anti-Slavery Society in New York, and similar violence in November of that
   year against a meeting at Faneuil Hall, Boston, that welcomed the British reformer
   George Thompson (see note 6 on p. 233).

northern people, and to impregnate them with sentiments and ideas forever in conflict with what as a nation we call *genius of American institutions*. Rightly viewed, this is an alarming fact, and ought to rally all that is pure, just, and holy in one determined effort to crush the monster of corruption, and to scatter "its guilty profits" to the winds.[7] In a high moral sense, as well as in a national sense, the whole American people are responsible for slavery, and must share, in its guilt and shame, with the most obdurate men-stealers of the south.

While slavery exists, and the union of these states endures, every American citizen must bear the chagrin of hearing his country branded before the world as a nation of liars and hypocrites; and behold his cherished national flag pointed at with the utmost scorn and derision. Even now an American *abroad* is pointed out in the crowd, as coming from a land where men gain their fortunes by "the blood of souls,"[8] from a land of slave markets, of blood-hounds, and slave-hunters; and, in some circles, such a man is shunned altogether, as a moral pest. Is it not time, then, for every American to awake, and inquire into his duty with respect to this subject?

Wendell Phillips[9]—the eloquent New England orator—on his return from Europe, in 1842, said, "As I stood upon the shores of Genoa, and saw floating on the placid waters of the Mediterranean, the beautiful American war ship Ohio, with her masts tapering proportionately aloft, and an eastern sun reflecting her noble form upon the sparkling waters, attracting the gaze of the multitude, my first impulse was of pride, to think myself an American; but when I thought that the first time that gallant ship would gird on her gorgeous apparel, and wake from beneath her sides her dormant thunders, it would be in defense of the African slave trade, I blushed in utter *shame* for my country."

Let me say again, *slavery is alike the sin and the shame of the American people*; it is a blot upon the American name, and the only national reproach which need make an American hang his head in shame, in the presence of monarchical governments.

With this gigantic evil in the land, we are constantly told to look *at home*; if we say ought against crowned heads, we are pointed to our enslaved millions; if we talk of sending missionaries and bibles abroad, we are pointed to three millions now lying in worse than heathen darkness; if we express a word of sympathy for Kossuth[1] and

---

7. Douglass refers here to a famous line by the prominent antislavery politician Lord Chancellor Henry Brougham (1778–1868).
8. Cf. Jeremiah 2.34.
9. See note 2 on p. 24.
1. See note 9 on p. 27.

his Hungarian fugitive brethren, we are pointed to that horrible and hell-black enactment, "the fugitive slave bill."[2]

Slavery blunts the edge of all our rebukes of tyranny abroad—the criticisms that we make upon other nations, only call forth ridicule, contempt, and scorn. In a word, we are made a reproach and a by-word to a mocking earth, and we must continue to be so made, so long as slavery continues to pollute our soil.

We have heard much of late of the virtue of patriotism, the love of country, &c., and this sentiment, so natural and so strong, has been impiously appealed to, by all the powers of human selfishness, to cherish the viper which is stinging our national life away. In its name, we have been called upon to deepen our infamy before the world, to rivet the fetter more firmly on the limbs of the enslaved, and to become utterly insensible to the voice of human woe that is wafted to us on every southern gale. We have been called upon, in its name, to desecrate our whole land by the footprints of slave-hunters, and even to engage ourselves in the horrible business of kidnapping.

I, too, would invoke the spirit of patriotism; not in a narrow and restricted sense, but, I trust, with a broad and manly signification; not to cover up our national sins, but to inspire us with sincere repentance; not to hide our shame from the world's gaze, but utterly to abolish the cause of that shame; not to explain away our gross inconsistencies as a nation, but to remove the hateful, jarring, and incongruous elements from the land; not to sustain an egregious wrong, but to unite all our energies in the grand effort to remedy that wrong.

I would invoke the spirit of patriotism, in the name of the law of the living God, natural and revealed, and in the full belief that "righteousness exalteth a nation, while sin is a reproach to any people."[3] "He that walketh righteously, and speaketh uprightly; he that despiseth the gain of oppressions, that shaketh his hands from the holding of bribes, he shall dwell on high, his place of defense shall be the munitions of rocks, bread shall be given him, his water shall be sure."[4]

We have not only heard much lately of patriotism, and of its aid being invoked on the side of slavery and injustice, but the very prosperity of this people has been called in to deafen them to the voice of duty, and to lead them onward in the pathway of sin. Thus has the blessing of God been converted into a curse. In the spirit of genuine patriotism, I warn the American people, by all that is just and honorable, to BEWARE!

2. See note 2 on p. 209.
3. Cf. Proverbs 14.34.
4. Cf. Isaiah 33.15–16.

I warn them that, strong, proud, and prosperous though we be, there is a power above us that can "bring down high looks;[5] at the breath of whose mouth our wealth may take wings; and before whom every knee shall bow;" and who can tell how soon the avenging angel may pass over our land, and the sable bondmen now in chains, may become the instruments of our nation's chastisement! Without appealing to any higher feeling, I would warn the American people, and the American government, to be wise in their day and generation. I exhort them to remember the history of other nations; and I remind them that America cannot always sit "as a queen,"[6] in peace and repose; that prouder and stronger governments than this have been shattered by the bolts of a just God; that the time *may* come when those they now despise and hate, may be needed; when those whom they now compel by oppression to be enemies, may be wanted as friends. What has been, may be again. There is a point beyond which human endurance cannot go. The crushed worm may yet turn under the heel of the oppressor. I warn them, then, with all solemnity, and in the name of retributive justice, *to look to their ways*; for in an evil hour, those sable arms that have, for the last two centuries, been engaged in cultivating and adorning the fair fields of our country, may yet become the instruments of terror, desolation, and death, throughout our borders.

It was the sage of the Old Dominion that said—while speaking of the possibility of a conflict between the slaves and the slaveholders— "God has no attribute that could take sides with the oppressor in such a contest. I tremble for my country when I reflect that God *is just*, and that his justice cannot sleep forever." Such is the warning voice of Thomas Jefferson;[7] and every day's experience since its utterance until now, confirms its wisdom, and commends its truth.

From What to the Slave Is the Fourth of July?

EXTRACT FROM AN ORATION, AT ROCHESTER, JULY 5, 1852

FELLOW-CITIZENS—Pardon me, and allow me to ask, why am I called upon to speak here to-day? What have I, or those I represent, to do with your national independence? Are the great principles of political freedom and of natural justice, embodied in that Declaration of Independence, extended to us? and am I, therefore, called upon to bring our humble offering to the national altar, and to confess the

5. Cf. Psalm 18.27.
6. Source unknown.
7. Jefferson (1743–1826), U.S. president 1801–09, is here quoted from his *Notes on the State of Virginia* (1785), Query XVIII. "Old Dominion" is a nickname for Virginia.

benefits, and express devout gratitude for the blessings, resulting from your independence to us?

Would to God, both for your sakes and ours, that an affirmative answer could be truthfully returned to these questions! Then would my task be light, and my burden easy and delightful. For who is there so cold that a nation's sympathy could not warm him? Who so obdurate and dead to the claims of gratitude, that would not thankfully acknowledge such priceless benefits? Who so stolid and selfish, that would not give his voice to swell the hallelujahs of a nation's jubilee, when the chains of servitude had been torn from his limbs? I am not that man. In a case like that, the dumb might eloquently speak, and the "lame man leap as an hart."[1]

But, such is not the state of the case. I say it with a sad sense of the disparity between us. I am not included within the pale of this glorious anniversary! Your high independence only reveals the immeasurable distance between us. The blessings in which you this day rejoice, are not enjoyed in common. The rich inheritance of justice, liberty, prosperity, and independence, bequeathed by your fathers, is shared by you, not by me. The sunlight that brought life and healing to you, has brought stripes and death to me. This Fourth of July is *yours*, not *mine*. *You* may rejoice, *I* must mourn. To drag a man in fetters into the grand illuminated temple of liberty, and call upon him to join you in joyous anthems, were inhuman mockery and sacrilegious irony. Do you mean, citizens, to mock me, by asking me to speak to-day? If so, there is a parallel to your conduct. And let me warn you that it is dangerous to copy the example of a nation whose crimes, towering up to heaven, were thrown down by the breath of the Almighty, burying that nation in irrecoverable ruin! I can to-day take up the plaintive lament of a peeled and woe-smitten people.

"By the rivers of Babylon, there we sat down. Yea! we wept when we remembered Zion. We hanged our harps upon the willows in the midst thereof. For there, they that carried us away captive, required of us a song; and they who wasted us required of us mirth, saying, Sing us one of the songs of Zion. How can we sing the Lord's song in a strange land? If I forget thee, O Jerusalem, let my right hand forget her cunning. If I do not remember thee, let my tongue cleave to the roof of my mouth."[2]

Fellow-citizens, above your national, tumultuous joy, I hear the mournful wail of millions, whose chains, heavy and grievous yesterday, are to-day rendered more intolerable by the jubilant shouts that reach them. If I do forget, if I do not faithfully remember those

1. Cf. Isaiah 35.6.
2. Cf. Psalm 137:1–6.

bleeding children of sorrow this day, "may my right hand forget her cunning, and may my tongue cleave to the roof of my mouth!" To forget them, to pass lightly over their wrongs, and to chime in with the popular theme, would be treason most scandalous and shocking, and would make me a reproach before God and the world. My subject, then, fellow-citizens, is AMERICAN SLAVERY. I shall see this day and its popular characteristics from the slave's point of view. Standing there, identified with the American bondman, making his wrongs mine, I do not hesitate to declare, with all my soul, that the character and conduct of this nation never looked blacker to me than on this Fourth of July. Whether we turn to the declarations of the past, or to the professions of the present, the conduct of the nation seems equally hideous and revolting. America is false to the past, false to the present, and solemnly binds herself to be false to the future. Standing with God and the crushed and bleeding slave on this occasion, I will, in the name of humanity which is outraged, in the name of liberty which is fettered, in the name of the constitution and the bible, which are disregarded and trampled upon, dare to call in question and to denounce, with all the emphasis I can command, everything that serves to perpetuate slavery—the great sin and shame of America! "I will not equivocate; I will not excuse;"[3] I will use the severest language I can command; and yet not one word shall escape me that any man, whose judgment is not blinded by prejudice, or who is not at heart a slaveholder, shall not confess to be right and just.

But I fancy I hear some one of my audience say, it is just in this circumstance that you and your brother abolitionists fail to make a favorable impression on the public mind. Would you argue more, and denounce less, would you persuade more and rebuke less, your cause would be much more likely to succeed. But, I submit, where all is plain there is nothing to be argued. What point in the anti-slavery creed would you have me argue? On what branch of the subject do the people of this country need light? Must I undertake to prove that the slave is a man? That point is conceded already. Nobody doubts it. The slaveholders themselves acknowledge it in the enactment of laws for their government. They acknowledge it when they punish disobedience on the part of the slave. There are seventy-two crimes in the state of Virginia, which, if committed by a black man, (no matter how ignorant he be,) subject him to the punishment of death; while only two of these same crimes will subject a white man to the like punishment. What is this but the acknowledgment that the slave is a moral, intellectual, and responsible being. The manhood of the

---

3. These famous words of William Lloyd Garrison appeared in the first issue of *The Liberator* (see note 7 on p. 23).

slave is conceded. It is admitted in the fact that southern statute books are covered with enactments forbidding, under severe fines and penalties, the teaching of the slave to read or write. When you can point to any such laws, in reference to the beasts of the field, then I may consent to argue the manhood of the slave. When the dogs in your streets, when the fowls of the air, when the cattle on your hills, when the fish of the sea, and the reptiles that crawl, shall be unable to distinguish the slave from a brute, then will I argue with you that the slave is a man!

For the present, it is enough to affirm the equal manhood of the negro race. Is it not astonishing that, while we are plowing, planting, and reaping, using all kinds of mechanical tools, erecting houses, constructing bridges, building ships, working in metals of brass, iron, copper, silver, and gold; that, while we are reading, writing, and cyphering, acting as clerks, merchants, and secretaries, having among us lawyers, doctors, ministers, poets, authors, editors, orators, and teachers; that, while we are engaged in all manner of enterprises common to other men—digging gold in California, capturing the whale in the Pacific, feeding sheep and cattle on the hillside, living, moving, acting, thinking, planning, living in families as husbands, wives, and children, and, above all, confessing and worshiping the christian's God, and looking hopefully for life and immortality beyond the grave,—we are called upon to prove that we are men!

Would you have me argue that man is entitled to liberty? that he is the rightful owner of his own body? You have already declared it. Must I argue the wrongfulness of slavery? Is that a question for republicans? Is it to be settled by the rules of logic and argumentation, as a matter beset with great difficulty, involving a doubtful application of the principle of justice, hard to be understood? How should I look to-day in the presence of Americans, dividing and subdividing a discourse, to show that men have a natural right to freedom, speaking of it relatively and positively, negatively and affirmatively? To do so, would be to make myself ridiculous, and to offer an insult to your understanding. There is not a man beneath the canopy of heaven that does not know that slavery is wrong *for him*.

What! am I to argue that it is wrong to make men brutes, to rob them of their liberty, to work them without wages, to keep them ignorant of their relations to their fellow-men, to beat them with sticks, to flay their flesh with the lash, to load their limbs with irons, to hunt them with dogs, to sell them at auction, to sunder their families, to knock out their teeth, to burn their flesh, to starve them into obedience and submission to their masters? Must I argue that a system, thus marked with blood and stained with pollution, is wrong? No; I will not. I have better employment for my time and strength than such arguments would imply.

What, then, remains to be argued? Is it that slavery is not divine; that God did not establish it; that our doctors of divinity are mistaken? There is blasphemy in the thought. That which is inhuman cannot be divine. Who can reason on such a proposition! They that can, may; I cannot. The time for such argument is past.

At a time like this, scorching irony, not convincing argument, is needed. Oh! had I the ability, and could I reach the nation's ear, I would to-day pour out a fiery stream of biting ridicule, blasting reproach, withering sarcasm, and stern rebuke. For it is not light that is needed, but fire; it is not the gentle shower, but thunder. We need the storm, the whirlwind, and the earthquake. The feeling of the nation must be quickened; the conscience of the nation must be roused; the propriety of the nation must be startled; the hypocrisy of the nation must be exposed; and its crimes against God and man must be proclaimed and denounced.

What to the American slave is your Fourth of July? I answer, a day that reveals to him, more than all other days in the year, the gross injustice and cruelty to which he is the constant victim. To him, your celebration is a sham; your boasted liberty, an unholy license; your national greatness, swelling vanity; your sounds of rejoicing are empty and heartless; your denunciations of tyrants, brass-fronted impudence; your shouts of liberty and equality, hollow mockery; your prayers and hymns, your sermons and thanks givings, with all your religious parade and solemnity, are to him mere bombast, fraud, deception, impiety, and hypocrisy—a thin veil to cover up crimes which would disgrace a nation of savages. There is not a nation on the earth guilty of practices more shocking and bloody, than are the people of these United States, at this very hour.

Go where you may, search where you will, roam through all the monarchies and despotisms of the old world, travel through South America, search out every abuse, and when you have found the last, lay your facts by the side of the every-day practices of this nation, and you will say with me, that, for revolting barbarity and shameless hypocrisy, America reigns without a rival.

From The Internal Slave Trade

EXTRACT FROM AN ORATION, AT ROCHESTER, JULY 5, 1852

TAKE the American slave trade, which, we are told by the papers, is especially prosperous just now. Ex-senator Benton[1] tells us that the price of men was never higher than now. He mentions the fact to

---

1. Thomas Hart Benton (1782–1852), U.S. senator from Missouri 1821–51.

show that slavery is in no danger. This trade is one of the peculiarities of American institutions. It is carried on in all the large towns
and cities in one-half of this confederacy; and millions are pocketed
every year by dealers in this horrid traffic. In several states this trade
is a chief source of wealth. It is called (in contradistinction to the
foreign slave trade) "*the internal slave trade.*" It is, probably, called
so, too, in order to divert from it the horror with which the foreign
slave trade is contemplated. That trade has long since been denounced
by this government as piracy. It has been denounced with burning
words, from the high places of the nation, as an execrable traffic.
To arrest it, to put an end to it, this nation keeps a squadron, at
immense cost, on the coast of Africa. Everywhere in this country, it
is safe to speak of this foreign slave trade as a most inhuman traffic, opposed alike to the laws of God and of man. The duty to extir-
pate and destroy it is admitted even by our *doctors of divinity.* In order
to put an end to it, some of these last have consented that their
colored brethren (nominally free) should leave this country, and
establish themselves on the western coast of Africa. It is, however,
a notable fact, that, while so much execration is poured out by Americans, upon those engaged in the foreign slave trade, the men
engaged in the slave trade between the states pass without condemnation, and their business is deemed honorable.

Behold the practical operation of this internal slave trade—the
American slave trade sustained by American politics and American
religion! Here you will see men and women reared like swine for the
market. You know what is a swine-drover? I will show you a man-
drover. They inhabit all our southern states. They perambulate the
country, and crowd the highways of the nation with droves of human
stock. You will see one of these human-flesh-jobbers, armed with pistol, whip, and bowie-knife, driving a company of a hundred men,
women, and children, from the Potomac[2] to the slave market at New
Orleans. These wretched people are to be sold singly, or in lots, to
suit purchasers. They are food for the cotton-field and the deadly
sugar-mill. Mark the sad procession as it moves wearily along, and
the inhuman wretch who drives them. Hear his savage yells and his
blood-chilling oaths, as he hurries on his affrighted captives. There,
see the old man, with locks thinned and gray. Cast one glance, if
you please, upon that young mother, whose shoulders are bare to
the scorching sun, her briny tears falling on the brow of the babe in
her arms. See, too, that girl of thirteen, weeping, yes, weeping, as
she thinks of the mother from whom she has been torn. The drove
moves tardily. Heat and sorrow have nearly consumed their strength.

---

2. The Potomac River flows from the Potomac Highlands of West Virginia into Chesapeake Bay, an estuary forming the eastern border of Maryland and Virginia.

Suddenly you hear a quick snap, like the discharge of a rifle; the fetters clank, and the chain rattles simultaneously; your ears are saluted with a scream that seems to have torn its way to the center of your soul. The crack you heard was the sound of the slave whip; the scream you heard was from the woman you saw with the babe. Her speed had faltered under the weight of her child and her chains; that gash on her shoulder tells her to move on. Follow this drove to New Orleans. Attend the auction; see men examined like horses; see the forms of women rudely and brutally exposed to the shocking gaze of American slave-buyers. See this drove sold and separated forever; and never forget the deep, sad sobs that arose from that scattered multitude. Tell me, citizens, where, under the sun, can you witness a spectacle more fiendish and shocking. Yet this is but a glance at the American slave trade, as it exists at this moment, in the ruling part of the United States.

I was born amid such sights and scenes. To me the American slave trade is a terrible reality. When a child, my soul was often pierced with a sense of its horrors. I lived on Philpot street, Fell's Point, Baltimore, and have watched from the wharves the slave ships in the basin, anchored from the shore, with their cargoes of human flesh, waiting for favorable winds to waft them down the Chesapeake. There was, at that time, a grand slave mart kept at the head of Pratt street, by Austin Woldfolk.[3] His agents were sent into every town and county in Maryland, announcing their arrival through the papers, and on flaming hand-bills, headed, "cash for negroes." These men were generally well dressed, and very captivating in their manners; ever ready to drink, to treat, and to gamble. The fate of many a slave has depended upon the turn of a single card; and many a child has been snatched from the arms of its mother by bargains arranged in a state of brutal drunkenness.

The flesh-mongers gather up their victims by dozens, and drive them, chained, to the general depot at Baltimore. When a sufficient number have been collected here, a ship is chartered, for the purpose of conveying the forlorn crew to Mobile or to New Orleans. From the slave-prison to the ship, they are usually driven in the darkness of night; for since the anti-slavery agitation a certain caution is observed.

In the deep, still darkness of midnight, I have been often aroused by the dead, heavy footsteps and the piteous cries of the chained gangs that passed our door. The anguish of my boyish heart was intense; and I was often consoled, when speaking to my mistress in the morning, to hear her say that the custom was very wicked; that

---

3. See the reference to Woldfolk on p. 81.

she hated to hear the rattle of the chains, and the heart-rending cries. I was glad to find one who sympathized with me in my horror.

Fellow-citizens, this murderous traffic is to-day in active operation in this boasted republic. In the solitude of my spirit, I see clouds of dust raised on the highways of the south; I see the bleeding footsteps; I hear the doleful wail of fettered humanity, on the way to the slave markets, where the victims are to be sold like horses, sheep, and swine, knocked off to the highest bidder. There I see the tenderest ties ruthlessly broken, to gratify the lust, caprice, and rapacity of the buyers and sellers of men. My soul sickens at the sight.

> "Is this the land your fathers loved?
> The freedom which they toiled to win?
> Is this the earth whereon they moved?
> Are these the graves they slumber in?"[4]

But a still more inhuman, disgraceful, and scandalous state of things remains to be presented. By an act of the American congress, not yet two years old,[5] slavery has been nationalized in its most horrible and revolting form. By that act, Mason and Dixon's line[6] has been obliterated; New York has become as Virginia; and the power to hold, hunt, and sell men, women, and children as slaves, remains no longer a mere state institution, but is now an institution of the whole United States. The power is co-extensive with the star-spangled banner and American christianity. Where these go, may also go the merciless slave-hunter. Where these are, man is not sacred. He is a bird for the sportsman's gun. By that most foul and fiendish of all human decrees, the liberty and person of every man are put in peril. Your broad republican domain is a hunting-ground for *men*. Not for thieves and robbers, enemies of society, merely, but for men guilty of no crime. Your law-makers have commanded all good citizens to engage in this hellish sport. Your president, your secretary of state, your lords, nobles, and ecclesiastics, enforce as a duty you owe to your free and glorious country and to your God, that you do this accursed thing. Not fewer than forty Americans have within the past two years been hunted down, and without a moment's warning, hurried away in chains, and consigned to slavery and excruciating torture. Some of these have had wives and children dependent on them for bread; but of this no account was made. The right of the hunter to his prey, stands superior to the right of marriage, and to *all* rights in this republic, the rights of God included! For black men there are neither law, justice,

---

4. Cf. lines 1–4 of "Stanzas for the Times" (1835), by John Greenleaf Whittier (see note 2 on p. 118).
5. See note 2 on p. 209.
6. See note 1 on p. 128.

humanity, nor religion. The fugitive slave law makes MERCY TO THEM A CRIME; and bribes the judge who tries them. An American judge GETS TEN DOLLARS FOR EVERY VICTIM HE CONSIGNS to slavery, and five, when he fails to do so. The oath of and two villains is sufficient, under this hell-black enactment, to send the most pious and exemplary black man into the remorseless jaws of slavery! His own testimony is nothing. He can bring no witnesses for himself. The minister of American justice is bound by the law to hear but *one side*; and that side is the side of the oppressor. Let this damning fact be perpetually told. Let it be thundered around the world, that, in tyrant-killing, king-hating, people-loving, democratic, christian America, the seats of justice are filled with judges, who hold their office under an open and palpable *bribe*, and are bound, in deciding in the case of a man's liberty, *to hear only his accusers!*

In glaring violation of justice, in shamelesss disregard of the forms of administering law, in cunning arrangement to entrap the defenseless, and in diabolical intent, this fugitive slave law stands alone in the annals of tyrannical legislation. I doubt if there be another nation on the globe having the brass and the baseness to put such a law on the statute-book. If any man in this assembly thinks differently from me in this matter, and feels able to disprove my statements, I will gladly confront him at any suitable time and place he may select.

From The Slavery Party

EXTRACT FROM A SPEECH DELIVERED BEFORE THE
A. A. S. SOCIETY,[1] IN NEW YORK, MAY, 1853

SIR, it is evident that there is in this country a purely slavery party— a party which exists for no other earthly purpose but to promote the interests of slavery. The presence of this party is felt everywhere in the republic. It is known by no particular name, and has assumed no definite shape; but its branches reach far and wide in the church and in the state. This shapeless and nameless party is not intangible in other and more important respects. That party, sir, has determined upon a fixed, definite, and comprehensive policy toward the whole colored population of the United States. What that policy is, it becomes us as abolitionists, and especially does it become the colored people themselves, to consider and to understand fully. We ought to know who our enemies are, where they are, and what are

---

1. The American Anti-Slavery Society (1833–70), an abolitionist society based in New York City, was cofounded by William Lloyd Garrison (see note 7 on p. 23) and Arthur Tappan.

their objects and measures. Well, sir, here is my version of it—not original with me—but mine because I hold it to be true.

I understand this policy to comprehend five cardinal objects. They are these: 1st. The complete suppression of all anti-slavery discussion. 2d. The expatriation of the entire free people of color from the United States. 3d. The unending perpetuation of slavery in this republic. 4th. The nationalization of slavery to the extent of making slavery respected in every state of the Union. 5th. The extension of slavery over Mexico and the entire South American states.

Sir, these objects are forcibly presented to us in the stern logic of passing events; in the facts which are and have been passing around us during the last three years. The country has been and is now dividing on these grand issues. In their magnitude, these issues cast all others into the shade, depriving them of all life and vitality. Old party ties are broken. Like is finding its like on either side of these great issues, and the great battle is at hand. For the present, the best representative of the slavery party in politics is the democratic party. Its great head for the present is President Pierce,[2] whose boast it was, before his election, that his whole life had been consistent with the interests of slavery, that he is above reproach on that score. In his inaugural address, he reassures the south on this point. Well, the head of the slave power[3] being in power, it is natural that the pro-slavery elements should cluster around the administration, and this is rapidly being done. A fraternization is going on. The stringent protectionists and the free-traders strike hands. The supporters of Fillmore[4] are becoming the supporters of Pierce. The silver-gray whig[5] shakes hands with the hunker democrat;[6] the former only differing from the latter in name. They are of one heart, one mind, and the union is natural and perhaps inevitable. Both hate negroes; both hate progress; both hate the "higher law;"

2. Franklin Pierce (1804–1869), U.S. president 1853–57. He opposed the abolitionist movement and signed into law the Kansas-Nebraska Act (1854), a proslavery measure that provoked widespread outrage in the North.
3. This phrase expresses the view—first articulated by Ohio politician Salmon P. Chase (1808–1873), U.S. Supreme Court chief justice 1864–73—that the slaveholders of the South had organized themselves into a unitary force that conspired to control the U.S. government and the national electoral system.
4. Millard Fillmore (1800–1874), member of the Whig Party (see next note), U.S. president 1850–53. He signed the Fugitive Slave Act of 1850 into law, thereby angering the abolitionist movement (see note 2 on p. 209).
5. The Whig Party came into being in opposition to the Democrat Andrew Jackson (1767–1845), U.S. president 1829–37. In general, Whigs were suspicious of democratic rule by a majority, favoring instead a more limited democratic system dominated by enlightened and educated elites, including businessmen and clergymen. The party split over the expansion of slavery into new territories following the 1860 election. One Whig faction supported Fillmore and became known as the Silver Gray Whigs, so-called for Francis Granger, a New York congressman.
6. There were two factions of the Democratic Party in New York in the mid-19th century. The Barnburners were explicitly antislavery, while the Hunkers were reluctant to antagonize the South.

both hate William H. Seward;[7] both hate the free democratic party; and upon this hateful basis they are forming a union of hatred. "Pilate and Herod are thus made friends."[8] Even the central organ of the whig party is extending its beggar hand for a morsel from the table of slavery democracy, and when spurned from the feast by the more deserving, it pockets the insult; when kicked on one side it turns the other, and perseveres in its importunities. The fact is, that paper comprehends the demands of the times; it understands the age and its issues; it wisely sees that slavery and freedom are the great antagonistic forces in the country, and it goes to its own side. Silver grays and hunkers all understand this. They are, therefore, rapidly sinking all other questions to nothing, compared with the increasing demands of slavery. They are collecting, arranging, and consolidating their forces for the accomplishment of their appointed work.

The keystone to the arch of this grand union of the slavery party of the United States, is the compromise of 1850. In that compromise we have all the objects of our slaveholding policy specified. It is, sir, favorable to this view of the designs of the slave power, that both the whig and the democratic party bent lower, sunk deeper, and strained harder, in their conventions, preparatory to the late presidential election, to meet the demands of the slavery party than at any previous time in their history. Never did parties come before the northern people with propositions of such undisguised contempt for the moral sentiment and the religious ideas of that people. They virtually asked them to unite in a war upon free speech, and upon conscience, and to drive the Almighty presence from the councils of the nation. Resting their platforms upon the fugitive slave bill, they boldly asked the people for political power to execute the horrible and hell-black provisions of that bill. The history of that election reveals, with great clearness, the extent to which slavery has shot its leprous distillment through the life-blood of the nation. The party most thoroughly opposed to the cause of justice and humanity, triumphed; while the party suspected of a leaning toward liberty, was overwhelmingly defeated, some say annihilated.

But here is a still more important fact, illustrating the designs of the slave power. It is a fact full of meaning, that no sooner did the democratic slavery party come into power, than a system of

7. Politician (1801–1872), originally a Whig, who served as governor of New York 1839–42 and U.S. senator from New York 1849–61. In 1850, Seward, a supporter of the abolitionist movement, delivered a speech to the New York Senate in which he advanced "higher law," the idea that constitutional law is not the final arbiter of political disputes such as that over slavery because a higher moral law is more authoritative. In the mid-1850s, he joined the newly formed Republican Party.
8. Cf. Luke 23.12.

legislation was presented to the legislatures of the northern states, designed to put the states in harmony with the fugitive slave law, and the malignant bearing of the national government toward the colored inhabitants of the country. This whole movement on the part of the states, bears the evidence of having one origin, emanating from one head, and urged forward by one power. It was simultaneous, uniform, and general, and looked to one end. It was intended to put thorns under feet already bleeding; to crush a people already bowed down; to enslave a people already but half free; in a word, it was intended to discourage, dishearten, and drive the free colored people out of the country. In looking at the recent black law of Illinois,[9] one is struck dumb with its enormity. It would seem that the men who enacted that law, had not only banished from their minds all sense of justice, but all sense of shame. It coolly proposes to sell the bodies and souls of the black to increase the intelligence and refinement of the whites; to rob every black stranger who ventures among them, to increase their literary fund.

While this is going on in the states, a pro-slavery, political board of health is established at Washington. Senators Hale, Chase, and Sumner[1] are robbed of a part of their senatorial dignity and consequence as representing sovereign states, because they have refused to be inoculated with the slavery virus. Among the services which a senator is expected by his state to perform, are many that can only be done efficiently on committees; and, in saying to these honorable senators, you shall not serve on the committees of this body, the slavery party took the responsibility of robbing and insulting the states that sent them. It is an attempt at Washington to decide for the states who shall be sent to the senate. Sir, it strikes me that this aggression on the part of the slave power did not meet at the hands of the proscribed senators the rebuke which we had a right to expect would be administered. It seems to me that an opportunity was lost, that the great principle of senatorial equality was left undefended, at a time when its vindication was sternly demanded. But it is not to the purpose of my present statement to criticise the conduct of our friends. I am persuaded that much ought to be left to the discretion of anti-slavery men in congress, and charges of recreancy should never be made but on the most sufficient grounds. For, of all the places in the world where an anti-slavery man needs

9. Enacted in 1853, the law was designed to prevent African American immigration into the state. It stipulated that any "negro or mulatto" seeking residence in Illinois could be fined fifty dollars and that those unable to pay the fine would be sold at auction for a period of servitude.
1. John P. Hale (1806–1873), U.S. senator for New Hampshire 1847–53 and 1855–65; Salmon P. Chase (see note 3 on p. 290); and Charles Sumner (1811–1874), U.S. Senator from Massachusetts 1851–74, ardently supported abolitionism.

the confidence and encouragement of friends, I take Washington to be that place.

Let me now call attention to the social influences which are operating and coöperating with the slavery party of the country, designed to contribute to one or all of the grand objects aimed at by that party. We see here the black man attacked in his vital interests; prejudice and hate are excited against him; enmity is stirred up between him and other laborers. The Irish people, warm-hearted, generous, and sympathizing with the oppressed everywhere, when they stand upon their own green island, are instantly taught, on arriving in this christian country, to hate and despise the colored people. They are taught to believe that we eat the bread which of right belongs to them. The cruel lie is told the Irish, that our adversity is essential to their prosperity. Sir, the Irish-American will find out his mistake one day. He will find that in assuming our avocation he also has assumed our degradation. But for the present we are sufferers. The old employments by which we have heretofore gained our livelihood, are gradually, and it may be inevitably, passing into other hands. Every hour sees us elbowed out of some employment to make room perhaps for some newly-arrived emigrants, whose hunger and color are thought to give them a title to especial favor. White men are becoming house-servants, cooks, and stewards, common laborers, and flunkeys to our gentry, and, for aught I see, they adjust themselves to their stations with all becoming obsequiousness. This fact proves that if we cannot rise to the whites, the whites can fall to us. Now, sir, look once more. While the colored people are thus elbowed out of employment; while the enmity of emigrants is being excited against us; while state after state enacts laws against us; while we are hunted down, like wild game, and oppressed with a general feeling of insecurity,—the American colonization society[2]—that old offender against the best interests and slanderer of the colored people—awakens to new life, and vigorously presses its scheme upon the consideration of the people and the government. New papers are started—some for the north and some for the south—and each in its tone adapting itself to its latitude. Government, state and national, is called upon for appropriations to enable the society to send us out of the country by steam! They want steamers to carry letters and negroes to Africa. Evidently, this society looks upon our "extremity as its opportunity,"[3] and we may expect that it will use the occasion well. They do not deplore, but glory, in our misfortunes.

---

2. Officially named the Society for the Colonization of Free People of Color, established in 1816 to promote the emigration of free African Americans to Africa.
3. Cf. the Christian saying "Man's extremity is God's opportunity."

But, sir, I must hasten. I have thus briefly given my view of one aspect of the present condition and future prospects of the colored people of the United States. And what I have said is far from encouraging to my afflicted people. I have seen the cloud gather upon the sable brows of some who hear me. I confess the case looks black enough. Sir, I am not a hopeful man. I think I am apt even to undercalculate the benefits of the future. Yet, sir, in this seemingly desperate case, I do not despair for my people. There is a bright side to almost every picture of this kind; and ours is no exception to the general rule. If the influences against us are strong, those for us are also strong. To the inquiry, will our enemies prevail in the execution of their designs. In my God and in my soul, I believe they *will not*. Let us look at the first object sought for by the slavery party of the country, viz: the suppression of anti-slavery discussion. They desire to suppress discussion on this subject, with a view to the peace of the slaveholder and the security of slavery. Now, sir, neither the principle nor the subordinate objects here declared, can be at all gained by the slave power, and for this reason: It involves the proposition to padlock the lips of the whites, in order to secure the fetters on the limbs of the blacks. The right of speech, precious and priceless, *cannot, will not*, be surrendered to slavery. Its suppression is asked for, as I have said, to give peace and security to slaveholders. Sir, that thing cannot be done. God has interposed an insuperable obstacle to any such result. "There can be *no peace*, saith my God, to the wicked."[4] Suppose it were possible to put down this discussion, what would it avail the guilty slaveholder, pillowed as he is upon the heaving bosoms of ruined souls? He could not have a peaceful spirit. If every anti-slavery tongue in the nation were silent—every anti-slavery organization dissolved—every anti-slavery press demolished—every anti-slavery periodical, paper, book, pamphlet, or what not, were searched out, gathered together, deliberately burned to ashes, and their ashes given to the four winds of heaven, still, still the slaveholder could have "*no peace*." In every pulsation of his heart, in every throb of his life, in every glance of his eye, in the breeze that soothes, and in the thunder that startles, would be waked up an accuser, whose cause is, "Thou art, verily, guilty concerning thy brother."[5]

---

4. Cf. Isaiah 48.22, 57.21.
5. Cf. Genesis 42.21.

From The Anti-Slavery Movement

EXTRACTS FROM A LECTURE BEFORE VARIOUS ANTI-SLAVERY
BODIES, IN THE WINTER OF 1855[1]

A GRAND movement on the part of mankind, in any direction, or for any purpose, moral or political, is an interesting fact, fit and proper to be studied. It is such, not only for those who eagerly participate in it, but also for those who stand aloof from it—even for those by whom it is opposed. I take the anti-slavery movement to be such an one, and a movement as sublime and glorious in its character, as it is holy and beneficent in the ends it aims to accomplish. At this moment, I deem it safe to say, it is properly engrossing more minds in this country than any other subject now before the American people. The late John C. Calhoun[2]—one of the mightiest men that ever stood up in the American senate—did not deem it beneath him; and he probably studied it as deeply, though not as honestly, as Gerrit Smith, or William Lloyd Garrison.[3] He evinced the greatest familiarity with the subject; and the greatest efforts of his last years in the senate had direct reference to this movement. His eagle eye watched every new development connected with it; and he was ever prompt to inform the south of every important step in its progress. He never allowed himself to make light of it; but always spoke of it and treated it as a matter of grave import; and in this he showed himself a master of the mental, moral, and religious constitution of human society. Daniel Webster,[4] too, in the better days of his life, before he gave his assent to the fugitive slave bill, and trampled upon all his earlier and better convictions—when his eye was yet single— he clearly comprehended the nature of the elements involved in this movement; and in his own majestic eloquence, warned the south, and the country, to have a care how they attempted to put it down. He is an illustration that it is easier to give, than to take, good advice. To these two men—the greatest men to whom the nation has yet given birth—may be traced the two great facts of the present—the south triumphant, and the north humbled. Their names may stand thus,—Calhoun and domination—Webster and degradation. Yet again. If to the enemies of liberty this subject is one of engrossing

---

1. Material in brackets in this selection are the original editor's notes.
2. Politician (1782–1850) who served as U.S. representative from South Carolina 1811–17, U.S. vice president 1825–32, and U.S. senator from South Carolina 1845–50. He vigorously defended states' rights and slavery.
3. See note 2 on p. 4 and note 7 on p. 23.
4. Politician (1782–1852) who served as U.S. senator from Massachusetts 1845–50 and U.S. secretary of state 1841–43 and 1850–52. He outraged abolitionists when he supported the Compromise of 1850 (see note 2 on p. 209).

interest, vastly more so should it be such to freedom's friends. The latter, it leads to the gates of all valuable knowledge—philanthropic, ethical, and religious; for it brings them to the study of man, wonderfully and fearfully made—the proper study of man through all time—the open book, in which are the records of time and eternity.

Of the existence and power of the anti-slavery movement, as a fact, you need no evidence. The nation has seen its face, and felt the controlling pressure of its hand. You have seen it moving in all directions, and in all weathers, and in all places, appearing most where desired least, and pressing hardest where most resisted. No place is exempt. The quiet prayer meeting, and the stormy halls of national debate, share its presence alike. It is a common intruder, and of course has the name of being ungentlemanly. Brethren who had long sung, in the most affectionate fervor, and with the greatest sense of security,

"Together let us sweetly live—together let us die,"[5]

have been suddenly and violently separated by it, and ranged in hostile attitude toward each other. The Methodist, one of the most powerful religious organizations of this country, has been rent asunder, and its strongest bolts of denominational brotherhood started at a single surge.[6] It has changed the tone of the northern pulpit, and modified that of the press. A celebrated divine,[7] who, four years ago, was for flinging his own mother, or brother, into the remorseless jaws of the monster slavery, lest he should swallow up the Union, now recognizes anti-slavery as a characteristic of future civilization. Signs and wonders follow this movement; and the fact just stated is one of them. Party ties are loosened by it; and men are compelled to take sides for or against it, whether they will or not. Come from where he may, or come for what he may, he is compelled to show his hand. What is this mighty force? What is its history? and what is its destiny? Is it ancient or modern, transient or permanent? Has it turned aside, like a stranger and a sojourner, to tarry for a night? or has it come to rest with us forever? Excellent chances are here for speculation; and some of them are quite profound. We might, for instance, proceed to inquire not only into the philosophy of the anti-slavery movement, but into the philosophy of the law, in obedience to which that movement started into existence. We might demand to know what is that law or power which, at different times, disposes the minds of men to this or that particular object—now for peace, and now for war—now for freedom, and now for slavery; but this

---

5. The first line of a hymn of that title.
6. In 1844, the Methodist Church split into two factions: antislavery in the North and proslavery in the South.
7. Unitarian minister Orville Dewey (1794–1882).

profound question I leave to the abolitionists of the superior class
to answer. The speculations which must precede such answer, would
afford, perhaps, about the same satisfaction as the learned theories
which have rained down upon the world, from time to time, as to
the origin of evil. I shall, therefore, avoid water in which I cannot
swim, and deal with anti-slavery as a fact, like any other fact in
the history of mankind, capable of being described and understood, both as to its internal forces, and its external phases and
relations.

> [After an eloquent, a full, and highly interesting exposition of
> the nature, character, and history of the anti-slavery movement,
> from the insertion of which want of space precludes us, he con-
> cluded in the following happy manner.]

Present organizations may perish, but the cause will go on. That
cause has a life, distinct and independent of the organizations
patched up from time to time to carry it forward. Looked at, apart
from the bones and sinews and body, it is a thing immortal. It is the
very essence of justice, liberty, and love. The moral life of human
society, it cannot die while conscience, honor, and humanity remain.
If but one be filled with it, the cause lives. Its incarnation in any
one individual man, leaves the whole world a priesthood, occupying
the highest moral eminence—even that of disinterested benevolence. Whoso has ascended this height, and has the grace to stand
there, has the world at his feet, and is the world's teacher, as of divine
right. He may set in judgment on the age, upon the civilization of
the age, and upon the religion of the age; for he has a test, a sure
and certain test, by which to try all institutions, and to measure all
men. I say, he may do this, but this is not the chief business for which
he is qualified. The great work to which he is called is not that of
judgment. Like the Prince of Peace, he may say, if I judge, I judge
righteous judgment;[8] still mainly, like him, he may say, this is not
his work. The man who has thoroughly embraced the principles of
justice, love, and liberty, like the true preacher of christianity, is less
anxious to reproach the world of its sins, than to win it to repentance. His great work on earth is to exemplify, and to illustrate, and
to ingraft those principles upon the living and practical understandings of all men within the reach of his influence. This is his work;
long or short his years, many or few his adherents, powerful or weak
his instrumentalities, through good report, or through bad report,
this is his work. It is to snatch from the bosom of nature the latent
facts of each individual man's experience, and with steady hand to

---

8. Douglass also used this passage in his lecture to the Rochester Ladies' Anti-Slavery
Society in 1855.

hold them up fresh and glowing, enforcing, with all his power, their acknowledgment and practical adoption. If there be but *one* such man in the land, no matter what becomes of abolition societies and parties, there will be an anti-slavery cause, and an anti-slavery movement. Fortunately for that cause, and fortunately for him by whom it is espoused, it requires no extraordinary amount of talent to preach it or to receive it when preached. The grand secret of its power is, that each of its principles is easily rendered appreciable to the faculty of reason in man, and that the most unenlightened conscience has no difficulty in deciding on which side to register its testimony. It can call its preachers from among the fishermen, and raise them to power. In every human breast, it has an advocate which can be silent only when the heart is dead. It comes home to every man's understanding, and appeals directly to every man's conscience. A man that does not recognize and approve for himself the rights and privileges contended for, in behalf of the American slave, has not yet been found. In whatever else men may differ, they are alike in the apprehension of their natural and personal rights. The difference between abolitionists and those by whom they are opposed, is not as to principles. All are agreed in respect to these. The manner of applying them is the point of difference.

The slaveholder himself, the daily robber of his equal brother, discourses eloquently as to the excellency of justice, and the man who employs a brutal driver to flay the flesh of his negroes, is not offended when kindness and humanity are commended. Every time the abolitionist speaks of justice, the anti-abolitionist assents—says, yes, I wish the world were filled with a disposition to render to every man what is rightfully due him; I should then get what is due me. That's right; let us have justice. By all means, let us have justice. Every time the abolitionist speaks in honor of human liberty, he touches a chord in the heart of the anti-abolitionist, which responds in harmonious vibrations. Liberty—yes, that is very evidently my right, and let him beware who attempts to invade or abridge that right. Every time he speaks of love, of human brotherhood, and the reciprocal duties of man and man, the anti-abolitionist assents—says, yes, all right—all true—we cannot have such ideas too often, or too fully expressed. So he says, and so he feels, and only shows thereby that he is a man as well as an anti-abolitionist. You have only to keep out of sight the manner of applying your principles, to get them endorsed every time. Contemplating himself, he sees truth with absolute clearness and distinctness. He only blunders when asked to lose sight of himself. In his own cause he can beat a Boston lawyer, but he is dumb when asked to plead the cause of others. He knows very well whatsoever he would have done unto himself, but is quite in doubt as to having the same thing done unto others. It is just here, that lions spring up in the path of duty, and the battle once fought in heaven is refought on the earth. So it is, so hath it ever been, and so must it ever be, when the claims of justice and mercy make their demand at the door of human selfishness. Nevertheless, there is that within which ever pleads for the right and the just.

In conclusion, I have taken a sober view of the present anti-slavery movement. I am sober, but not hopeless. There is no denying, for it is everywhere admitted, that the anti-slavery question is the great moral and social question now before the American people. A state of things has gradually been developed, by which that question has become the first thing in order. It must be met. Herein is my hope. The great idea of impartial liberty is now fairly before the American people. Anti-slavery is no longer a thing to be prevented. The time for prevention is past. This is great gain. When the movement was younger and weaker—when it [was] wrought in a Boston garret to human apprehension, it might have been silently put out of the way. Things are different now. It has grown too large—its friends are too numerous—its facilities too abundant—its ramifications too extended—its power too omnipotent, to be snuffed out by the contingencies of infancy. A thousand strong men might be struck down, and its ranks still be invincible. One flash from the heart-supplied intellect of Harriet Beecher Stowe[9] could light a million camp fires in front of the embattled host of slavery, which not all the waters of the Mississippi, mingled as they are with blood, could extinguish. The present will be looked to by after coming genera-tions, as the age of anti-slavery literature—when supply on the gal-lop could not keep pace with the ever-growing demand—when a picture of a negro on the cover was a help to the sale of a book—when conservative lyceums and other American literary associations began first to select their orators for distinguished occasions from the ranks of the previously despised abolitionists. If the anti-slavery movement shall fail now, it will not be from outward opposition, but from inward decay. Its auxiliaries are everywhere. Scholars, authors, orators, poets, and statesmen give it their aid. The most brilliant of American poets volunteer in its service. Whittier speaks in burning verse to more than thirty thousand, in the National Era.[1] Your own Longfellow whispers, in every hour of trial and disappointment, "labor and wait."[2] James Russell Lowell is reminding us that "men

9. See note 3 on p. 120.
1. Washington, D.C., abolitionist newspaper, 1847–60; it published Stowe's *Uncle Tom's Cabin* serially and many poems by Whittier (see note 2 on p. 118).
2. Cf. line 36 of "A Psalm of Life" (1838), by the American poet Henry Wadsworth Long-fellow (1807–1882).

are more than institutions."[3] Pierpont cheers the heart of the pilgrim in search of liberty, by singing the praises of "the north star."[4] Bryant, too, is with us; and though chained to the car of party,[5] and dragged on amidst a whirl of political excitement, he snatches a moment for letting drop a smiling verse of sympathy for the man in chains. The poets are with us. It would seem almost absurd to say it, considering the use that has been made of them, that we have allies in the Ethiopian songs; those songs that constitute our national music, and without which we have no national music. They are heart songs, and the finest feelings of human nature are expressed in them. "Lucy Neal," "Old Kentucky Home," and "Uncle Ned,"[6] can make the heart sad as well as merry, and can call forth a tear as well as a smile. They awaken the sympathies for the slave, in which antislavery principles take root, grow, and flourish. In addition to authors, poets, and scholars at home, the moral sense of the civilized world is with us. England, France, and Germany, the three great lights of modern civilization, are with us, and every American traveler learns to regret the existence of slavery in his country. The growth of intelligence, the influence of commerce, steam, wind, and lightning are our allies. It would be easy to amplify this summary, and to swell the vast conglomeration of our material forces; but there is a deeper and truer method of measuring the power of our cause, and of comprehending its vitality. This is to be found in its accordance with the best elements of human nature. It is beyond the power of slavery to annihilate affinities recognized and established by the Almighty. The slave is bound to mankind by the powerful and inextricable net-work of human brotherhood. His voice is the voice of a man, and his cry is the cry of a man in distress, and man must cease to be man before he can become insensible to that cry. It is the righteousness of the cause—the humanity of the cause—which constitutes its potency. As one genuine bank-bill is worth more than a thousand counterfeits, so is one man, with right on his side, worth more than a thousand in the wrong. "One may chase a thousand, and put ten thousand to flight."[7] It is, therefore, upon the goodness of our cause, more than upon all other auxiliaries, that we depend for its final triumph.

3. Unidentified quotation or paraphrase from the American poet, essayist, and dramatist James Russell Lowell (1819–1891).
4. In "The Fugitive Slave's Apostrophe to the North Star" (1840), by the American poet John Pierpont (1785–1866).
5. The American poet and editor William Cullen Bryant (1794–1878) was a prominent member of the Free Soil Party, which opposed the expansion of slavery into the Western territories. Around the time Douglass wrote this essay, the Free Soil Party was absorbed into the Republican Party.
6. Minstrel songs by the American songwriter Stephen Foster (1826–1864).
7. Cf. Deuteronomy 32.30.

Another source of congratulation is the fact that, amid all the efforts made by the church, the government, and the people at large, to stay the onward progress of this movement, its course has been onward, steady, straight, unshaken, and unchecked from the beginning. Slavery has gained victories large and numerous; but never as against this movement—against a temporizing policy, and against northern timidity, the slave power has been victorious; but against the spread and prevalence in the country, of a spirit of resistance to its aggression, and of sentiments favorable to its entire overthrow, it has yet accomplished nothing. Every measure, yet devised and executed, having for its object the suppression of anti-slavery, has been as idle and fruitless as pouring oil to extinguish fire. A general rejoicing took place on the passage of "the compromise measures" of 1850.[8] Those measures were called peace measures, and were afterward termed by both the great parties of the country, as well as by leading statesmen, a final settlement of the whole question of slavery; but experience has laughed to scorn the wisdom of proslavery statesmen; and their final settlement of agitation seems to be the final revival, on a broader and grander scale than ever before, of the question which they vainly attempted to suppress forever. The fugitive slave bill has especially been of positive service to the anti-slavery movement. It has illustrated before all the people the horrible character of slavery toward the slave, in hunting him down in a free state, and tearing him away from wife and children, thus setting its claims higher than marriage or parental claims. It has revealed the arrogant and overbearing spirit of the slave states toward the free states; despising their principles—shocking their feelings of humanity, not only by bringing before them the abominations of slavery, but by attempting to make them parties to the crime. It has called into exercise among the colored people, the hunted ones, a spirit of manly resistance well calculated to surround them with a bulwark of sympathy and respect hitherto unknown. For men are always disposed to respect and defend rights, when the victims of oppression stand up manfully for themselves.

There is another element of power added to the anti-slavery movement, of great importance; it is the conviction, becoming every day more general and universal, that slavery must be abolished at the south, or it will demoralize and destroy liberty at the north. It is the nature of slavery to beget a state of things all around it favorable to its own continuance. This fact, connected with the system of bondage, is beginning to be more fully realized. The slave-holder is not satisfied to associate with men in the church or in the state, unless he can thereby stain them with the blood of his slaves. To be a

8. See note 2 on p. 209.

slave-holder is to be a propagandist from necessity; for slavery can only live by keeping down the under-growth morality which nature supplies. Every new-born white babe comes armed from the Eternal presence, to make war on slavery. The heart of pity, which would melt in due time over the brutal chastisements it sees inflicted on the helpless, must be hardened. And this work goes on every day in the year, and every hour in the day.

What is done at home is being done also abroad here in the north. And even now the question may be asked, have we at this moment a single free state in the Union? The alarm at this point will become more general. The slave power must go on in its career of exactions. Give, give, will be its cry, till the timidity which concedes shall give place to courage, which shall resist. Such is the voice of experience, such has been the past, such is the present, and such will be that future, which, so sure as man is man, will come. Here I leave the subject; and I leave off where I began, consoling myself and congratulating the friends of freedom upon the fact that the anti-slavery cause is not a new thing under the sun; not some moral delusion which a few years' experience may dispel. It has appeared among men in all ages, and summoned its advocates from all ranks. Its foundations are laid in the deepest and holiest convictions, and from whatever soul the demon, selfishness, is expelled, there will this cause take up its abode. Old as the everlasting hills; immovable as the throne of God; and certain as the purposes of eternal power, against all hinderances, and against all delays, and despite all the mutations of human instrumentalities, it is the faith of my soul, that this anti-slavery cause will triumph.

CONTEXTS

BENJAMIN FRANKLIN

From The Autobiography of Benjamin Franklin[†]

* * *

Josiah, my father, married young, and carried his wife with three children into New England, about 1682. The conventicles having been forbidden by law, and frequently disturbed, induced some considerable men of his acquaintance to remove to that country, and he was prevailed with to accompany them thither, where they expected to enjoy their mode of religion with freedom. By the same wife he had four children more born there, and by a second wife ten more, in all seventeen; of which I remember thirteen sitting at one time at his table, who all grew up to be men and women, and married; I was the youngest son, and the youngest child but two, and was born in Boston, New England. My mother, the second wife, was Abiah Folger, daughter of Peter Folger, one of the first settlers of New England, of whom honorable mention is made by Cotton Mather, in his church history of that country, entitled Magnalia Christi Americana, as *"a godly, learned Englishman,"* if I remember the words rightly. I have heard that he wrote sundry small occasional pieces, but only one of them was printed, which I saw now many years since. It was written in 1675, in the home-spun verse of that time and people, and addressed to those then concerned in the government there. It was in favor of liberty of conscience, and in behalf of the Baptists, Quakers, and other sectaries that had been under persecution, ascribing the Indian wars, and other distresses that had befallen the country, to that persecution, as so many judgments of God to punish so heinous an offense, and exhorting a repeal of those uncharitable laws. The whole appeared to me as written with a good deal of decent plainness and manly freedom. The six concluding lines I remember, though I have forgotten the two first of the stanza; but the purport of them was, that his censures proceeded from good-will, and, therefore he would be known to be the author.

> "Because to be a libeller (says he)
> I hate it with my heart;
> From Sherburne town, where now I dwell
> My name I do put here;
> Without offense your real friend,
> It is Peter Folgier."

† From *The Autobiography of Benjamin Franklin*, ed. John Bigelow (Philadelphia: J. B. Lippincott & Co., 1868), pp. 82–88. The original editors' notes have been omitted. Franklin's memoirs provide the blueprint of American autobiographical writing. This brief selection foregrounds themes and transformative moments that clearly echo throughout Douglass's writing.

My elder brothers were all put apprentices to different trades. I was put to the grammar-school at eight years of age, my father intending to devote me, as the tithe of his sons, to the service of the Church. My early readiness in learning to read (which must have been very early, as I do not remember when I could not read), and the opinion of all his friends, that I should certainly make a good scholar, encouraged him in this purpose of his. My uncle Benjamin, too, approved of it, and proposed to give me all his short-hand volumes of sermons, I suppose as a stock to set up with, if I would learn his character. I continued, however, at the grammar-school not quite one year, though in that time I had risen gradually from the middle of the class of that year to be the head of it, and farther was removed into the next class above it, in order to go with that into the third at the end of the year. But my father, in the mean time, from a view of the expense of a college education, which having so large a family he could not well afford, and the mean living many so educated were afterwards able to obtain—reasons that he gave to his friends in my hearing—altered his first intention, took me from the grammar-school, and sent me to a school for writing and arithmetic, kept by a then famous man, Mr. George Brownell, very successful in his profession generally, and that by mild, encouraging methods. Under him I acquired fair writing pretty soon, but I failed in the arithmetic, and made no progress in it. At ten years old I was taken home to assist my father in his business, which was that of a tallow-chandler and sope-boiler; a business he was not bred to, but had assumed on his arrival in New England, and on finding his dying trade would not maintain his family, being in little request. Accordingly, I was employed in cutting wick for the candles, filling the dipping mold and the molds for cast candles, attending the shop, going of errands, etc.

I disliked the trade, and had a strong inclination for the sea, but my father declared against it; however, living near the water, I was much in and about it, learnt early to swim well, and to manage boats; and when in a boat or canoe with other boys, I was commonly allowed to govern, especially in any case of difficulty; and upon other occasions I was generally a leader among the boys, and sometimes led them into scrapes, of which I will mention one instance, as it shows an early projecting public spirit, tho' not then justly conducted.

There was a salt-marsh that bounded part of the mill-pond, on the edge of which, at high water, we used to stand to fish for minnows. By much trampling, we had made it a mere quagmire. My proposal was to build a wharff there fit for us to stand upon, and I showed my comrades a large heap of stones, which were intended for a new house near the marsh, and which would very well suit our purpose. Accordingly, in the evening, when the workmen were gone, I assembled a number of my play-fellows, and working with them diligently like so many emmets, sometimes two or three to a stone, we brought them all away and built our little wharff. The next morning the workmen were surprised at missing the stones, which were found in our wharff. Inquiry was made after the removers; we were discovered and complained of; several of us were corrected by our fathers; and, though I pleaded the usefulness of the work, mine convinced me that nothing was useful which was not honest.

I think you may like to know something of his person and character. He had an excellent constitution of body, was of middle stature, but well set, and very strong; he was ingenious, could draw prettily, was skilled a little in music, and had a clear pleasing voice, so that when he played psalm tunes on his violin and sung withal, as he sometimes did in an evening after the business of the day was over, it was extremely agreeable to hear. He had a mechanical genius too, and, on occasion, was very handy in the use of other tradesmen's tools; but his great excellence lay in a sound understanding and solid judgment in prudential matters, both in private and publick affairs. In the latter, indeed, he was never employed, the numerous family he had to educate and the straitness of his circumstances keeping him close to his trade; but I remember well his being frequently visited by leading people, who consulted him for his opinion in affairs of the town or of the church he belonged to, and showed a good deal of respect for his judgment and advice: he was also much consulted by private persons about their affairs when any difficulty occurred, and frequently chosen an arbitrator between contending parties. At his table he liked to have, as often as he could, some sensible friend or neighbor to converse with, and always took care to start some ingenious or useful topic for discourse, which might tend to improve the minds of his children. By this means he turned our attention to what was good, just, and prudent in the conduct of life; and little or no notice was ever taken of what related to the victuals on the table, whether it was well or ill dressed, in or out of season, of good or bad flavor, preferable or inferior to this or that other thing of the kind, so that I was bro't up in such a perfect inattention to those matters as to be quite indifferent what kind of food was set before me, and so unobservant of it, that to this day if I am asked I can scarce tell a few hours after dinner what I dined upon. This has been a convenience to me in travelling, where my companions have been sometimes very unhappy for want of a suitable gratification of their more delicate, because better instructed, tastes and appetites.

* * *

WILLIAM LLOYD GARRISON

From The Liberator

The importance of the relationship between Douglass and William Lloyd Garrison[1] has generated many pages of commentary and controversy. In his third and final autobiography, *Life and Times of Frederick Douglass* (1882, revised 1892), Douglass describes *The Liberator* as

> my meat and my drink. My soul was set all on fire. Its sympathy for my brethren in bonds—its scathing denunciations of slaveholders—its faithful exposures of slavery—and its powerful attacks upon the upholders of the institution—sent a thrill of joy through my soul, such as I had never felt before!
>
> I had not long been a reader of the "Liberator," before I got a pretty correct idea of the principles, measures, and spirit of the anti-slavery reform. I took right hold of the cause. I could do but little; but what I could, I did with a joyful heart, and never felt happier than when in an anti-slavery meeting." (p. 118)

However, Douglass's relationship with Garrison was much more fraught than this recollection would suggest. By the time Douglass published *Narrative of the Life of an American Slave*, in 1845, he had begun to chafe under Garrison's efforts to control the scope of his denunciations of the slavery system. Matters grew worse when Douglass traveled to England later in 1845 and discovered there that Garrison's colleagues were in effect spying on him. The definitive break between the two men came in 1851, when Douglass announced that he had changed his mind on the constitutionality of slavery and now rejected the views espoused by Garrison.

The first selection below, from 1831, reflects Garrison's interest in "elevating" the free Black community so as to persuade white Americans that enslaved Black persons were capable and worthy of citizenship; Douglass adopted a modified version of this view. The second excerpt, from 1843, expresses Garrison's high regard for Douglass when their relationship was at its warmest. The third excerpt is representative of the "battle" the two men engaged in after Douglass changed his mind about slavery's constitutionality.

["*To Our Free Colored Brethren*"][†]

Your moral and intellectual elevation, the advancement of your rights, and the defence of your character, will be a leading object of our paper. We know that you are now struggling against wind and

1. See note 7 on p. 23.
† From *The Liberator* 1.1 (January 1, 1831): 3.

tide, and that adversity 'has marked you for his own;' yet among three hundred thousand of your number, some patronage may be given. We ask, and expect, but little: that little may save the life of 'The Liberator.' Our enemies are numerous, active and inveterate; and a great effort will undoubtedly be made to put us down.

["*I Spoke of Frederick Douglass*"][†]

I spoke of Frederick Douglass as a noble representative and advocate of the colored race. In point of moral worth, or intellectual ability, or native energy of character, I have never met his equal among those who are so ready to despise those of a darker hue than themselves. But if he were not all this, still would he not be my brother? * * *

["*A Battle Has Commenced*"][‡]

A battle has commenced in the Free States of America, between Lloyd Garrison & Co. and Frederick Douglass and party. But what has set them in battle array? Christianity and Infidelity, is the avowed and ostensible reason assigned. But can they be sincere or in earnest, when the one party would drive the ploughshare through Christianity, with all her benevolent, humane and literary institutions, whilst the leader of the other counselled us in Chicago not to be led away with the doctrine of 'Christ and him crucified,' the main pillar of Christianity—the foundation of all hope—and the grand motive to all obedience. The thing is altogether a farce! It is what military men call a 'sham fight.' We had hoped that Douglass, *on breaking away from his old friends*, called the Garrisonian party, had embraced the enlightened principles of Christianity, and resigned his whole being to their influences; but in this we are disappointed. We wish it were so, on behalf of the cause of human freedom, as he would become a more potent instrument for good, both to the bond and free . . . * * *

---

† From *The Liberator* 13.52 (December 29, 1843): 4.
‡ From *The Liberator* 24.1 (January 6, 1854): 1.

FREDERICK DOUGLASS

The Constitution and Slavery[†]

This editorial by Douglass was the culmination of a months-long debate in his newspaper about the character of the U.S. Constitution. Douglass conceded in a letter to the abolitionist C. H. Chase that the document might be read as neutral in wording, but he emphasized that "the original intent and meaning of the Constitution (the one given to it by the men who framed it, those who adopted, and the one given to it by the Supreme Court of the United States) makes it a pro-slavery instrument—such an one as I cannot bring myself to vote under, or swear to support." While Douglass remained supportive of this central tenet of Garrisonian abolitionism—that the Constitution was poisoned by slavery—in analyzing the issue, he showed his curiosity and desire to explore the historical and theoretical foundations of the American polity.[1] As Douglass's ruminations below on "the truly consistent man" suggest, in this editorial we see him beginning to exercise his remarkable powers as a moral and political philosopher.

The assertion which we made five weeks ago, that "the Constitution, *if strictly construed according to its reading*," is not a pro-slavery instrument, has excited some interest amongst our Anti-Slavery brethren. Letters have reached us from different quarters on the subject. Some of these express agreement and pleasure with our views, and others, surprise and dissatisfaction. Each class of opinion and feeling is represented in the letters which we have placed in another part of this week's paper. The one from our friend Gerrit Smith, represents the view which the Liberty party take of this subject, and that of Mr. Robert Forten is consistent with the ground occupied by a majority of the American Anti-Slavery Society.[2]

Whether we shall be able to set ourselves right in the minds of those on the one side of this question or the other, and at the same time vindicate the correctness of our former assertion, remains to be seen. Of one thing, however, we can assure our readers, and this is, that we bring to the consideration of this subject no partisan feelings, nor the slightest wish to make ourselves consistent with the creed of either Anti-Slavery party,[3] and that our only aim is to know what is truth and what is duty in respect to the matter in dispute,

† From *The North Star* (March 16, 1849): 1.

1. It took Douglass nearly a decade to reject the Garrisonian position. On March 26, 1860, he reevaluated nearly each of these arguments in his speech before the Scottish Anti-Slavery Society in Glasgow, Scotland.
2. See note 7 on p. 23. On Smith, see note 2 on p. 4. Robert Bridges Forten (1813–1864) was an African American scholar, activist, and inventor.
3. At this time, abolitionist organizations in the United States were generally split and hostile to each other. Some believed, like Garrison, that the U.S. Constitution

holding ourselves perfectly free to change our opinion in any direction, and at any time which may be indicated by our immediate
apprehension of truth, unbiased by the smiles or frowns of any class
or party of abolitionists. The only truly consistent man is he who will,
for the sake of being right today, contradict what he said wrong yesterday. "Sufficient unto the day is the evil thereof."[4] True stability consists not in being of the same opinion now as formerly, but in a fixed
principle of honesty, even urging us to the adoption or rejection of
that which may seem to us true or false at the ever-present now.

Before entering upon a discussion of the main question, it may
be proper to remove a misapprehension into which Gerrit Smith and
Robert Forten seem to have fallen, in respect to what we mean by
the term, "strictly construed according to its reading," as used by us
in regard to the Constitution. Upon a second reading of these words,
we can readily see how easily they can be made to mean more than
we intended. What we mean then, and what we would be understood
to mean now, is simply this—that the Constitution of the United
States, standing alone, and construed only in the light of its letter,
without reference to the opinions of the men who framed and
adopted it, or to the uniform, universal and undeviating practice of
the nation under it, from the time of its adoption until now, is not a
pro-slavery instrument. Of this admission we are perfectly willing
to give our esteemed friend Gerrit Smith, and all who think with
him on this subject, the fullest benefit; accompanied, however, with
this explanation, that it was made with no view to give the public to
understand that we held this construction to be the proper one of
that instrument, and that it was drawn out merely because we were
unwilling to go before the public on so narrow an issue, and one
about which there could be so little said on either side. How a document would appear under one construction, is one thing; but whether
the construction be the right one, is quite another and a very different thing. Confounding these two things, has led Gerrit Smith to
think too favorably of us, and Robert Forten too unfavorably. We may
agree with the Roman Catholic, that the language of Christ, with
respect to the sacrament, if construed according to reading, teaches
the doctrine of transubstantiation.[5] But the admission is not final,
neither are we understood by doing so, to sanction that irrational
though literal doctrine. Neither Roman Catholic nor Protestant
could attach any importance to such an admission. It would neither

---

legitimated and supported the slavery system; others, like Gerrit Smith, asserted that
it did not, but rather could be used as a powerful weapon to defeat the slavery system.
4. Cf. Matthew 6.34.
5. Transubstantiation is the doctrinal belief that in the ritual of the Eucharist, the bread
and wine offered to participating worshipers are converted into the body and blood of
Christ.

afford pleasure to the Catholic, nor pain to the Protestant. Hoping that we have now made ourselves understood on this point, we proceed to the general question.

The Constitutionality of Slavery

The Constitution of the United States.—What is it? Who made it? For whom and for what was it made? Is it from heaven or from men? How, and in what light are we to understand it? If it be divine, divine light must be our means of understanding it; if human, humanity, with all its vice and crimes, as well as its virtues, must help us to a proper understanding of it. All attempts to explain it in the light of heaven must fail. It is human, and must be explained in the light of those maxims and principles which human beings have laid down as guides to the understanding of all written instruments, covenants, contracts and agreements, emanating from human beings, and to which human beings are parties, both on the first and the second part. It is in such a light that we propose to examine the Constitution; and in this light we hold it to be a most cunningly-devised and wicked compact, demanding the most constant and earnest efforts of the friends of righteous freedom for its complete overthrow. It was "conceived in sin, and shapen in iniquity."[6] But this will be called mere declamation, and assertion—mere "heat without light"—sound and fury signify nothing.[7]—Have it so. Let us then argue the question with all the coolness and clearness of which any learned fugitive slave, smarting under the wrongs inflicted by this unholy Union, is capable. We cannot talk "lawyer like" about law—about its emanating from the bosom of God!—about government, and of its seat in the great heart of the Almighty!—nor can we, in connection with such an ugly matter-of-fact looking thing as the United States Constitution, bring ourselves to split hairs about the alleged legal rule of interpretation, which declares that an "act of the Legislature may be set aside when it contravenes natural justice." We have to do with facts, rather than theory. The Constitution is not an abstraction. It is a living breathing fact, exerting a mighty power over the nation of which it is the bond of the Union.

Had the Constitution dropped down from the blue overhanging sky, upon a land uncursed by slavery, and without an interpreter, although some difficulty might have occurred in applying its manifold provisions, yet so cunningly is it framed, that no one would have imagined that it recognized or sanctioned slavery. But having a terrestrial, and not a celestial origin, we find no difficulty in

6. Cf. Psalm 51.5.
7. Cf. Shakespeare, *Macbeth* 5.5.27–28.

ascertaining its meaning in all the parts which we allege to relate to slavery. Slavery existed before the Constitution, in the very States by whom it was made and adopted.—Slaveholders took a large share in making it. It was made in view of the existence of slavery, and in a manner well calculated to aid and strengthen that heaven-daring crime.

Take, for instance, article 1st, section 2d, to wit: "Representatives and direct taxes shall be apportioned among several States which may be included within this Union, according to their respective numbers, which shall be determined by adding to the whole number of free persons, including those bound to service for a term of years, and including Indians not taxed, three-fifths of all other persons."

A diversity of persons are here described—persons bound to service for a term of years, Indians not taxed, and three-fifths of all other persons. Now, we ask, in the name of common sense, can there be an honest doubt that, in States where there are slaves, that they are included in this basis of representation? To us, it is as plain as the sun in the heavens that this clause does, and was intended to mean, that the slave States should enjoy a representation of their human chattels under this Constitution. Beside, the term free, which is generally, though not always, used as the correlative of slave, "all other persons," settles the question forever that slaves are here included.

It is contended on this point by Lysander Spooner[8] and others, that the words, "all other persons," used in this article of the Constitution, relates only to aliens. We deny that the words bear any such construction. Are we to presume that the Constitution, which so carefully points out a class of persons for exclusion, such as "Indians not taxed," would be silent with respect to another class which it was meant equally to exclude? We have never studied logic, but it does seem to us that such a presumption would be very much like an absurdity. And the absurdity is all the more glaring, when it is remembered and the language used immediately after the words "excluding Indians are not taxed," (having done with exclusions) it includes "all other persons." It is as easy to suppose that the Constitution contemplates including Indians, (against its express declaration to the contrary,) as it is to suppose that it should be construed to mean the exclusion of slaves from the basis of representation, against the express language, "including all other persons." Where all are included, none remain to be excluded. The reasonings of those who are likely to take the opposite view of the clause, appears very much like quibbling, to use no harsher word. One thing is

8. American abolitionist (1808–1887). His book *The Unconstitutionality of Slavery* (1845), which argued that the Constitution did not legitimate the slavery system, influenced Douglass's change of mind on this subject.

certain about this clause of the Constitution. It is this—that under it, the slave system has enjoyed a large and domineering representation in Congress, which has given laws to the whole Union in regard to slavery, ever since the formation of the government.

Satisfied that the view we have given of this clause of the Constitution is the only sound interpretation of it, we throw at once all those parts and particulars of the instrument which refer to slavery, and constitute what we conceive to be the slaveholding compromises of the Constitution, before the reader, and beg that he will look with candor upon the comments which we propose to make upon them.

"Art. 5th, Sect. 8th.—Congress shall have power to suppress insurrections."

"Art. 1st, Sect. 9th.—The migration or importation of any such persons as any of the States now existing shall think proper to admit, shall not be prohibited by Congress prior to the year one thousand eight hundred and eight; but a tax or duty may be imposed, not exceeding ten dollars each person."

"Art. 4th, Sec. 2nd.—No person held to service or labor in one State, escaping into another, shall in consequence of any law or regulation therein, be discharged from such service or labor, but shall be delivered up on claim of the party to whom such service or labor may be due."

"Art. 4th, Sec. 4th—The United States shall guarantee to every State in this Union a Republican form of Government; and shall protect each of them against invasion; and on application of the Legislature, or of the Executive, (when the Legislature cannot be convened,) against Domestic violence."

The first article and ninth section is a full, complete and broad sanction of the slavetrade for twenty years. In this compromise of the Constitution, the parties to it pledged the national arm to protect that infernal trade for twenty years. While all other subjects of commerce were left under the control of Congress, this species of commerce alone was Constitutionally exempted. And why was this the case? Simply because South Carolina and Georgia declared, through their delegates that framed the Constitution, that they would not come into the Union if this traffic in human flesh should be prohibited. Mr. Rutledge, of South Carolina, (a distinguished member of the Convention that framed the Constitution,) said, "if the Convention thinks that North Carolina, South Carolina, and Georgia, will ever agree to the plan, unless their right to import slaves be untouched, the expectation is vain." Mr. Pinckney said, South Carolina could never receive the plan, "if it prohibits the slavetrade." In consequence of the determination of these States to stand out of the Union in case of the traffic in human flesh should be prohibited, and from one was adopted, as a compromise; and shameful as it is, it is by no means more shameful than others which preceded and succeeded it. The slaveholding South, by that unyielding tenacity and consistency which they usually contend for their measures, triumphed, and the doughface North was brought to the disgraceful terms in question, just as they have been ever since on all questions touching the subject of slavery.

As a compensation for their base treachery to human freedom and justice, the North were permitted to impose a tax of ten dollars for each person imported, with which to swell the coffers of the national treasury, thus baptizing the infant Republic with the blood-stained gold.

Art. 4, Sec. 2.—This article was adopted with a view to restoring fugitive slaves to their masters—ambiguous, to be sure, but sufficiently explicit to answer the end sought to be attained. Under it, and in accordance with it, the Congress enacted the atrocious "law of '93," making it penal in a high degree to harbor or shelter the flying fugitive. The whole nation that adopted it, consented to become kidnappers, and the whole land converted into slave-hunting ground.

Art. 4, Sec. 4.—Pledges the national arm to protect the slaveholder from domestic violence, and is the safeguard of the Southern tyrant against the vengeance of the outraged and plundered slave. Under it, the nation is bound to do the bidding of the slaveholder, to bring out the whole naval and military power of the country, to crush the refractory slaves into obedience to their cruel masters. Thus has the North, under the Constitution, not only consented to form bulwarks around the system of slavery, with all its bloody enormities, to prevent the slave from escape, but has planted its uncounted feet and tremendous weight on the heaving hearts of American bondmen, to prevent them from rising to gain their freedom. Could Pandemonium devise a Union more inhuman, unjust, and affronting to God and man, than this? Yet such is the Union consummated under the Constitution of the United States. It is truly a compact demanding immediate disannulment, and one which, with our view of its wicked requirements, we can never enter.

We might just here drop the pen and the subject, and assume the Constitution to be what we have briefly attempted to prove it to be, radically and essentially pro-slavery, in fact as well as in its tendency; and regard our position to be correct beyond the possibility of an honest doubt, and treat those who differ from us as mere cavilers, bent upon making the worse appear the better reason; or we might anticipate the objections which are supposed to be valid against that position. We are, however, disposed to do neither.—We have too much respect for the men opposed to us to do the former, and have too strong a desire to have those objections put in their most favorable light, to do the latter.—We are prepared to hear all sides, and to give the arguments of our opponents a candid consideration. Where an honest expression of views is allowed, Truth has nothing to fear.

And now if our friend Gerrit Smith desires to be heard on the other side, the columns of the *North Star* are at his service. We can assure him that he cannot have a stronger wish to turn every rightful instrumentality against slavery, than we have; and if the Constitution can be so turned, and he can satisfy us of the fact, we shall readily, gladly and zealously, turn our feeble energies in that direction. The case which our friend Gerrit Smith put to us in his letter is a good one, but fails in a most important particular, and that is, analogy. The only likeness which we can see in the supposed case of a bargain with Brown, to that of the bargain entered into by the North and the South, is that there is gross dishonesty in both. So far, there is a striking similarity, but no further. The parties that made the Constitution, aimed to cheat and defraud the slave, who was not himself a party to the compact or agreement. It was entered into understandingly on both sides. They both designed to purchase their freedom and safety at the expense of the imbruted slave. The North are willing to become the body guards of slavery—suppressing insurrection—returning fugitive slaves to bondage—importing slaves for twenty years, and as much longer as the Congress should see fit to leave it unprohibited, and virtually to give slaveholders three votes for every five slaves they could plunder from Africa, and all this to form a Union by which to repel invasion, and otherwise promoted their interest. No, friend Smith, we are not asked to act the honorable part of "Judge Douglass" with respect to this "contract," but to become a guilty party to it, and in reply we say—No!

["The Change in Our Opinion"]†

The debate on the resolution relative to anti-slavery newspapers[1] assumed such a character as to make it our duty to define the position of the *North Star* in respect to the Constitution of the United States. The ground having been directly taken, that no paper ought to receive the recommendation of the American Anti-Slavery Society that did not assume the Constitution to be a pro-slavery document,

---

† From *The North Star* (May 23, 1851): 1. Douglass's editorial touches on the ongoing disagreements and conflicts between various supporters of abolition.
1. At the annual meeting of the American Anti-Slavery Society (see note 7 on p. 23).

we felt in honor bound to announce at once to our old anti-slavery companions that we no longer possessed the requisite qualification for their official approval and commendation; and to assure them that we had arrived at the firm conviction that the Constitution; construed in the light of well established rules of legal interpretation, might be made consistent with its details with the noble purposes avowed in its preamble; and that hereafter we should insist upon the application of such rules to that instrument, and demand that it be wielded in behalf of emancipation. The change in our opinion on this subject has not been hastily arrived at. A careful study of the writings of Lysander Spooner, of Gerrit Smith, and of William Goodell,[2] has brought us to our present conclusion. We found, in our former position, that, when debating the question, we were compelled to go behind the letter of the Constitution, and to seek its meaning in the history and practice of the nation under it—a process always attended with disadvantages; and certainly we feel little inclination to shoulder disadvantages of any kind, in order to give slavery the slightest protection. In short, we hold it to be a system of lawless violence; that it *never was lawful, and never can be made so*; and that it is the first duty of every American citizen, whose conscience permits so to do, to use his *political* as well as his *moral* power for its overthrow. Of course, this avowal did not pass without animadversion, and it would have been strange if it had passed without some crimination; for it is hard for any combination or party to attribute good motives to any one who differs from them in what they deem a vital point. Brother Garrison at once exclaimed, "There is roguery somewhere!" but we can easily forgive this hastily expressed imputation, falling, as it did, from the lips of one to whom we shall never cease to be grateful, and for whom we have cherished (and do now cherish) a veneration only inferior in degree to that which we own to our conscience and our God.

HENRY DAVID THOREAU

From Walden[†]

The high points of antebellum American writing include the works of Frederick Douglass, Harriet Beecher Stowe (see p. 331), and Henry David Thoreau (1817–1862). Acquaintance with their work is essential to understanding the United States' limping progress toward

2. William Goodell (1792–1878) was a prominent abolitionist and cofounder of the American Anti-Slavery Society. On Spooner and Smith, see note 8 on p. 313 and note 2 on p. 4, respectively.
† From *Walden; or, Life in the Woods* (Boston: Ticknor & Fields, 1854), pp. 353–56.

self-understanding and equality for all. Thoreau's most famous work, *Walden* (1854)—a memoir and a meditation on his life in a cabin at Walden Pond, near Concord, Massachusetts—provides an intriguing counterpoint to Douglass's ideas on what the country should be.

* * *

Rather than love, than money, than fame, give me truth. I sat at a table where were rich food and wine in abundance, and obsequious attendance, but sincerity and truth were not; and I went away hungry from the inhospitable board. The hospitality was as cold as the ices. I thought that there was no need of ice to freeze them. They talked to me of the age of the wine and the fame of the vintage; but I thought of an older, a newer, and purer wine, of a more glorious vintage, which they had not got, and could not buy. The style, the house and grounds and "entertainment" pass for nothing with me. I called on the king, but he made me wait in his hall, and conducted like a man incapacitated for hospitality. There was a man in my neighborhood who lived in a hollow tree. His manners were truly regal. I should have done better had I called on him.

How long shall we sit in our porticoes practising idle and musty virtues, which any work would make impertinent? As if one were to begin the day with long-suffering, and hire a man to hoe his potatoes; and in the afternoon go forth to practise Christian meekness and charity with goodness aforethought! Consider the China pride and stagnant self-complacency of mankind. This generation reclines a little to congratulate itself on being the last of an illustrious line; and in Boston and London and Paris and Rome, thinking of its long descent, it speaks of its progress in art and science and literature with satisfaction. There are the Records of the Philosophical Societies, and the public Eulogies of *Great Men!* It is the good Adam contemplating his own virtue. "Yes, we have done great deeds, and sung divine songs, which shall never die,"—that is, as long as *we* can remember them. The learned societies and great men of Assyria,— where are they? What youthful philosophers and experimentalists we are! There is not one of my readers who has yet lived a whole human life. These may be but the spring months in the life of the race. If we have had the seven-years' itch, we have not seen the seventeen-year locust yet in Concord. We are acquainted with a mere pellicle of the globe on which we live. Most have not delved six feet beneath the surface, nor leaped as many above it. We know not where we are. Beside, we are sound asleep nearly half our time. Yet we esteem ourselves wise, and have an established order on the surface. Truly, we are deep thinkers, we are ambitious spirits! As I stand over the insect crawling amid the pine needles on the forest floor, and endeavoring to conceal itself from my sight, and ask myself why it will cherish those humble thoughts, and hide its head from me who might, perhaps, be its benefactor, and impart to its race some cheering information, I am reminded of the greater Benefactor and Intelligence that stands over me the human insect.

There is an incessant influx of novelty into the world, and yet we tolerate incredible dulness. I need only suggest what kind of sermons are still listened to in the most enlightened countries. There are such words as joy and sorrow, but they are only the burden of a psalm, sung with a nasal twang, while we believe in the ordinary and mean. We think that we can change our clothes only. It is said that the British Empire is very large and respectable, and that the United States are a first-rate power. We do not believe that a tide rises and falls behind every man which can float the British Empire like a chip, if he should ever harbor it in his mind. Who knows what sort of seventeen-year locust will next come out of the ground? The government of the world I live in was not framed, like that of Britain, in after-dinner conversations over the wine.

The life in us is like the water in the river. It may rise this year higher than man has ever known it, and flood the parched uplands; even this may be the eventful year, which will drown out all our muskrats. It was not always dry land where we dwell. I see far inland the banks which the stream anciently washed, before science began to record its freshets. Every one has heard the story which has gone the rounds of New England, of a strong and beautiful bug which came out of the dry leaf of an old table of apple-tree wood, which had stood in a farmer's kitchen for sixty years, first in Connecticut, and afterward in Massachusetts,—from an egg deposited in the living tree many years earlier still, as appeared by counting the annual layers beyond it; which was heard gnawing out for several weeks, hatched perchance by the heat of an urn. Who does not feel his faith in a resurrection and immortality strengthened by hearing of this? Who knows what beautiful and winged life, whose egg has been buried for ages under many concentric layers of woodenness in the dead dry life of society, deposited at first in the alburnum of the green and living tree, which has been gradually converted into the semblance of its well-seasoned tomb,—heard perchance gnawing out now for years by the astonished family of man, as they sat round the festive board,—may unexpectedly come forth from amidst society's most trivial and handselled furniture, to enjoy its perfect summer life at last!

FREDERICK DOUGLASS

What to the Slave Is the Fourth of July?[†]

This speech, Douglass's most famous, was delivered at the invitation of the Ladies' Anti-Slavery Society in Douglass's home city of Rochester, New York. The speech celebrated Independence Day on July 5 because July 4, 1852, occurred on a Sunday. Douglass brilliantly used the holiday as a metaphor for the various hypocrisies, shortcomings, and possibilities of the American project. This speech appeared in heavily edited form in the first edition of *My Bondage and My Freedom* (see p. 281). The following text restores the opening thirty paragraphs.

Mr. President, Friends and Fellow Citizens:

He who could address this audience without a quailing sensation, has stronger nerves than I have. I do not remember ever to have appeared as a speaker before any assembly more shrinkingly, nor with greater distrust of my ability, than I do this day. A feeling has crept over me, quite unfavorable to the exercise of my limited powers of speech. The task before me is one which requires much previous thought and study for its proper performance. I know that apologies of this sort are generally considered flat and unmeaning. I trust, however, that mine will not be so considered. Should I seem at ease, my appearance would much misrepresent me. The little experience I have had in addressing public meetings, in country school houses, avails me nothing on the present occasion.

The papers and placards say, that I am to deliver a 4th July oration. This certainly, sounds large, and out of the common way, for me. It is true that I have often had the privilege to speak in this beautiful Hall, and to address many who now honor me with their presence. But neither their familiar faces, nor the perfect gage I think I have of Corinthian Hall, seems to free me from embarrassment.

The fact is, ladies and gentlemen, the distance between this platform and the slave plantation, from which I escaped, is considerable—and the difficulties to be overcome in getting from the latter to the former, are by no means slight. That I am here to-day, is, to me, a matter of astonishment as well as of gratitude. You will not, therefore, be surprised, if in what I have to say, I evince no elaborate preparation, nor grace my speech with any high sounding exordium. With little experience and with less learning, I have been able to throw my thoughts hastily and imperfectly together; and trusting to your patient and generous indulgence, I will proceed to lay them before you.

[†] From *Oration, Delivered in Corinthian Hall, Rochester* (Rochester, NY: Lee, Man, & Co., 1852), pp. 4–20.

This, for the purpose of this celebration, is the 4th of July. It is the birthday of your National Independence, and of your political freedom. This, to you, is what the Passover was to the emancipated people of God. It carries your minds back to the day, and to the act of your great deliverance; and to the signs, and to the wonders, associated with that act, and that day. This celebration also marks the beginning of another year of your national life; and reminds you that the Republic of America is now 76 years old. I am glad, fellow-citizens, that your nation is so young. Seventy-six years, though a good old age for a man, is but a mere speck in the life of a nation. Three score years and ten is the allotted time for individual men; but nations number their years by thousands. According to this fact, you are, even now only in the beginning of your national career, still lingering in the period of childhood. I repeat, I am glad this is so. There is hope in the thought, and hope is much needed, under the dark clouds which lower above the horizon. The eye of the reformer is met with angry flashes, portending disastrous times; but his heart may well beat lighter at the thought that America is young, and that she is still in the impressible stage of her existence. May he not hope that high lessons of wisdom, of justice and of truth, will yet give direction to her destiny? Were the nation older, the patriot's heart might be sadder, and the reformer's brow heavier. Its future might be shrouded in gloom, and the hope of its prophets go out in sorrow. There is consolation in the thought, that America is young.—Great streams are not easily turned from channels, worn deep in the course of ages. They may sometimes rise in quiet and stately majesty, and inundate the land, refreshing and fertilizing the earth with their mysterious properties. They may also rise in wrath and fury, and bear away, on their angry waves, the accumulated wealth of years of toil and hardship. They, however, gradually flow back to the same old channel, and flow on as serenely as ever. But, while the river may not be turned aside, it may dry up, and leave nothing behind but the withered branch, and the unsightly rock, to howl in the abyss-sweeping wind, the sad tale of departed glory. As with rivers so with nations.

Fellow-citizens, I shall not presume to dwell at length on the associations that cluster about this day. The simple story of it is, that, 76 years ago, the people of this country were British subjects. The style and title of your "sovereign people" (in which you now glory) was not then born. You were under the British Crown. Your fathers esteemed the English Government as the home government; and England as the fatherland. This home government, you know, although a considerable distance from your home, did, in the exercise of its parental prerogatives, impose upon its colonial children, such restraints, burdens and limitations, as, in its mature judgment, it deemed wise, right and proper.

But, your fathers, who had not adopted the fashionable idea of this day, of the infallibility of government, and the absolute character of its acts, presumed to differ from the home government in respect to the wisdom and the justice of some of those burdens and restraints. They went so far in their excitement as to pronounce the measures of government unjust, unreasonable, and oppressive, and altogether such as ought not to be quietly submitted to. I scarcely need say, fellow-citizens, that my opinion of those measures fully accords with that of your fathers. Such a declaration of agreement on my part, would not be worth much to anybody. It would, certainly, prove nothing, as to what part I might have taken, had I lived during the great controversy of 1776. To say *now* that America was right, and England wrong, is exceedingly easy. Everybody can say it; the dastard, not less than the noble brave, can flippantly discant on the tyranny of England towards the American Colonies. It is fashionable to do so; but there was a time when, to pronounce against England, and in favor of the cause of the colonies, tried men's souls.[1] They who did so were accounted in their day, plotters of mischief, agitators and rebels, dangerous men. To side with the right, against the wrong, with the weak against the strong, and with the oppressed against the oppressor! *here* lies the merit, and the one which, of all others, seems unfashionable in our day. The cause of liberty may be stabbed by the men who glory in the deeds of your fathers. But, to proceed.

Feeling themselves harshly and unjustly treated, by the home government, your fathers, like men of honesty, and men of spirit, earnestly sought redress. They petitioned and remonstrated; they did so in a decorous, respectful, and loyal manner. Their conduct was wholly unexceptionable. This, however, did not answer the purpose. They saw themselves treated with sovereign indifference, coldness and scorn. Yet they persevered. They were not the men to look back.

As the sheet anchor takes a firmer hold, when the ship is tossed by the storm, so did the cause of your fathers grow stronger, as it breasted the chilling blasts of kingly displeasure. The greatest and best of British statesmen admitted its justice, and the loftiest eloquence of the British Senate came to its support. But, with that blindness which seems to be the unvarying characteristic of tyrants, since Pharoah and his hosts were drowned in the Red sea,[2] the British Government persisted in the exactions complained of.

The madness of this course, we believe, is admitted now, even by England; but we fear the lesson is wholly lost on our present rulers.

---

1. Cf. the first sentence of "Crisis No. 1" (1776), a pamphlet by the English-born American revolutionary Thomas Paine (1737–1809).
2. Cf. Exodus 14.

Oppression makes a wise man mad.[3] Your fathers were wise men, and if they did not go mad, they became restive under this treatment. They felt themselves the victims of grievous wrongs, wholly incurable in their colonial capacity. With brave men there is always a remedy for oppression. Just here, the idea of a total separation of the colonies from the crown was born! It was a startling idea, much more so, than we, at this distance of time, regard it. The timid and the prudent (as has been intimated) of that day, were, of course, shocked and alarmed by it.

Such people lived then, had lived before, and will, probably, ever have a place on this planet; and their course, in respect to any great change, (no matter how great the good to be attained, or the wrong to be redressed by it,) may be calculated with as much precision as can be the course of the stars. They hate all changes, but silver, gold and copper change! Of this sort of change they are always strongly in favor.

These people were called tories[4] in the days of your fathers; and the appellation, probably, conveyed the same idea that is meant by a more modern, though a somewhat less euphonious term, which we often find in our papers, applied to some of our old politicians.

Their opposition to the then dangerous thought was earnest and powerful; but, amid all their terror and affrighted vociferations against it, the alarming and revolutionary idea moved on, and the country with it.

On the 2d of July, 1776, the old Continental Congress, to the dismay of the lovers of ease, and the worshippers of property, clothed that dreadful idea with all the authority of national sanction. They did so in the form of a resolution; and as we seldom hit upon resolutions, drawn up in our day, whose transparency is at all equal to this, it may refresh your minds and help my story if I read it.

> Resolved, That these united colonies are, and of right, ought to be free and Independent States; that they are absolved from all allegiance to the British Crown; and that all political connection between them and the State of Great Britain is, and ought to be, dissolved.

Citizens, your fathers made good that resolution. They succeeded; and to-day you reap the fruits of their success. The freedom gained is yours; and you, therefore, may properly celebrate this anniversary. The 4th of July is the first great fact in your nation's history—the very ring-bolt in the chain of your yet undeveloped destiny.

---

3. Cf. Ecclesiastes 7.7.
4. A term referring to political conservatives in England generally, and used in the United States to mean colonists who remained loyal to England and opposed the American Revolution.

Pride and patriotism, not less than gratitude, prompt you to celebrate and to hold it in perpetual remembrance. I have said that the Declaration of Independence is the RINGBOLT to the chain of your nation's destiny; so, indeed, I regard it. The principles contained in that instrument are saving principles. Stand by those principles, be true to them on all occasions, in all places, against all foes, and at whatever cost.

From the round top of your ship of state, dark and threatening clouds may be seen. Heavy billows, like mountains in the distance, disclose to the leeward huge forms of flinty rocks! That *bolt* drawn, that *chain* broken, and all is lost. *Cling to this day—cling to it*, and to its principles, with the grasp of a storm-tossed mariner to a spar at midnight.

The coming into being of a nation, in any circumstances, is an interesting event. But, besides general considerations, there were peculiar circumstances which make the advent of this republic an event of special attractiveness.

The whole scene, as I look back to it, was simple, dignified and sublime.

The population of the country, at the time, stood at the insignificant number of three millions. The country was poor in the munitions of war. The population was weak and scattered, and the country a wilderness unsubdued. There were then no means of concert and combination, such as exist now. Neither steam nor lightning had then been reduced to order and discipline. From the Potomac to the Delaware[5] was a journey of many days. Under these, and innumerable other disadvantages, your fathers declared for liberty and independence and triumphed.

Fellow Citizens, I am not wanting in respect for the fathers of this republic. The signers of the Declaration of Independence were brave men. They were great men too—great enough to give fame to a great age. It does not often happen to a nation to raise, at one time, such a number of truly great men. The point from which I am compelled to view them is not, certainly the most favorable; and yet I cannot contemplate their great deeds with less than admiration. They were statesmen, patriots and heroes, and for the good they did, and the principles they contended for, I will unite with you to honor their memory.

They loved their country better than their own private interests; and, though this is not the highest form of human excellence, all will concede that it is a rare virtue, and that when it is exhibited, it

5. The Delaware River has two branches that flow from the Catskill Mountains in New York State through New Jersey, Pennsylvania, Maryland, and the river mouth in Delaware Bay. For the Potomac River, see note 2 on p. 286.

ought to command respect. He who will, intelligently, lay down his life for his country, is a man whom it is not in human nature to despise. Your fathers staked their lives, their fortunes, and their sacred honor, on the cause of their country. In their admiration of liberty, they lost sight of all other interests.

They were peace men; but they preferred revolution to peaceful submission to bondage. They were quiet men; but they did not shrink from agitating against oppression. They showed forbearance; but that they knew its limits. They believed in order; but not in the order of tyranny. With them, nothing was "*settled*" that was not right. With them, justice, liberty and humanity were "*final;*" not slavery and oppression. You may well cherish the memory of such men. They were great in their day and generation. Their solid manhood stands out the more as we contrast it with these degenerate times.

How circumspect, exact and proportionate were all their movements! How unlike the politicians of an hour! Their statesmanship looked beyond the passing moment, and stretched away in strength into the distant future. They seized upon eternal principles, and set a glorious example in their defence. Mark them!

Fully appreciating the hardships to be encountered, firmly believing in the right of their cause, honorably inviting the scrutiny of an on-looking world, reverently appealing to heaven to attest their sincerity, soundly comprehending the solemn responsibility they were about to assume, wisely measuring the terrible odds against them, your fathers, the fathers of this republic, did, most deliberately, under the inspiration of a glorious patriotism, and with a sublime faith in the great principles of justice and freedom, lay deep, the corner-stone of the national super-structure, which has risen and still rises in grandeur around you.

Of this fundamental work, this day is the anniversary. Our eyes are met with demonstrations of joyous enthusiasm. Banners and penants wave exultingly on the breeze. The din of business, too, is hushed. Even mammon seems to have quitted his grasp on this day. The ear-piercing fife and the stirring drum unite their accents with the ascending peal of a thousand church bells. Prayers are made, hymns are sung, and sermons are preached in honor of this day; while the quick martial tramp of a great and multitudinous nation, echoed back by all the hills, valleys and mountains of a vast continent, bespeak the occasion one of thrilling and universal interest—a nation's jubilee.

Friends and citizens, I need not enter further into the causes which led to this anniversary. Many of you understand them better than I do. You could instruct me in regard to them. That is a branch of knowledge in which you feel, perhaps, a much deeper interest than your speaker. The causes which led to the separation of the colonies from the British crown have never lacked for a tongue. They

have all been taught in your common schools, narrated at your fire-
sides, unfolded from your pulpits, and thundered from your legisla-
tive halls, and are as familiar to you as household words. They form
the staple of your national poetry and eloquence.

I remember, also, that, as a people, Americans are remarkably
familiar with all facts which make in their own favor. This is
esteemed by some as a national trait—perhaps a national weakness.
It is a fact, that whatever makes for the wealth or for the reputation
of Americans, and can be had *cheap!* will be found by Americans. I
shall not be charged with slandering Americans, if I say I think the
American side of any question may be safely left in American hands.

I leave, therefore, the great deeds of your fathers to other gentlemen whose claim to have been regularly descended will be less likely
to be disputed than mine!

The Present

My business, if I have any here to-day, is with the present. The
accepted time with God and his cause is the ever-living now.

> "Trust no future, however pleasant,
>   Let the dead past bury its dead;
> Act, act in the living present,
>   Heart within, and God overhead."[6]

We have to do with the past only as we can make it useful to the
present and to the future. To all inspiring motives, to noble deeds
which can be gained from the past, we are welcome. But now is the
time, the important time. Your fathers have lived, died, and have
done their work, and have done much of it well. You live and must
die, and you must do your work. You have no right to enjoy a child's
share in the labor of your fathers, unless your children are to be blest
by your labors. You have no right to wear out and waste the hard-
earned fame of your fathers to cover your indolence. Sydney Smith[7]
tells us that men seldom eulogize the wisdom and virtues of their
fathers, but to excuse some folly or wickedness of their own. This
truth is not a doubtful one. There are illustrations of it near and
remote, ancient and modern. It was fashionable, hundreds of years
ago, for the children of Jacob to boast, we have "Abraham to our
father,"[8] when they had long lost Abraham's faith and spirit. That people contented themselves under the shadow of Abraham's great name,
while they repudiated the deeds which made his name great. Need I
remind you that a similar thing is being done all over this country

---

6. Cf. lines 21–24 of Longfellow's "A Psalm of Life" (see note 2 on p. 299).
7. Anglican minister and essayist (1771–1845).
8. Cf. Matthew 3.9.

to-day? Need I tell you that the Jews are not the only people who built the tombs of the prophets, and garnished the sepulchres of the righteous? Washington could not die till he had broken the chains of his slaves.[9] Yet his monument is built up by the price of human blood, and the traders in the bodies and souls of men, shout—"We have Washington to *our father*."—Alas! that it should be so; yet so it is.

> "The evil that men do, lives after them,
> The good is oft' interred with their bones."[1]

Fellow-citizens, pardon me, allow me to ask, why am I called upon to speak here to-day? What have I, or those I represent, to do with your national independence? Are the great principles of political freedom and of natural justice, embodied in that Declaration of Independence, extended to us? and am I, therefore, called upon to bring our humble offering to the national altar, and to confess the benefits and express devout gratitude for the blessings resulting from your independence to us?

Would to God, both for your sakes and ours, that an affirmative answer could be truthfully returned to these questions! Then would my task be light, and my burden easy and delightful. For *who* is there so cold, that a nation's sympathy could not warm him? Who so obdurate and dead to the claims of gratitude, that would not thankfully acknowledge such priceless benefits? Who so stolid and selfish, that would not give his voice to swell the hallelujahs of a nation's jubilee, when the chains of servitude had been torn from his limbs? I am not that man. In a case like that, the dumb might eloquently speak, and the "lame man leap as an hart."[2]

But, such is not the state of the case. I say it with a sad sense of the disparity between us. I am not included within the pale of this glorious anniversary! Your high independence only reveals the immeasurable distance between us. The blessings in which you, this day, rejoice, are not enjoyed in common.—The rich inheritance of justice, liberty, prosperity and independence, bequeathed by your fathers is shared by you, not by me. The sunlight that brought life and healing to you, has brought stripes and death to me. This Fourth July is *yours*, not *mine*. *You* may rejoice, *I* must mourn. To drag a man in fetters into the grand illuminated temple of liberty, and call upon him to join you in joyous anthems, were inhuman mockery and sacrilegious irony. Do you mean, citizens, to mock me, by asking me to speak to-day? If so, there is a parallel to your conduct. And let me warn you that it is dangerous to copy the example of a nation whose

9. In his will, George Washington (1732–1799) stipulated that his plantation's enslaved persons be freed upon his wife's death.
1. Cf. Shakespeare, *Julius Caesar* 3.2.73–74.
2. Cf. Isaiah 35.6.

crimes, towering up to heaven, were thrown down by the breath of the Almighty, burying that nation in irrecoverable ruin! I can today take up the plaintive lament of a peeled and woe-smitten people!

"By the rivers of Babylon, there we sat down. Yea! we wept when we remembered Zion. We hanged our harps upon the willows in the midst thereof. For there, they that carried us away captive, required of us a song; and they who wasted us required of us mirth, saying, Sing us one of the songs of Zion. How can we sing the Lord's song in a strange land? If I forget thee, O Jerusalem, let my right hand forget her cunning. If I do not remember thee, let my tongue cleave to the roof of my mouth."[3]

Fellow citizens; above your national, tumultous joy, I hear the mournful wail of millions! whose chains, heavy and grievous yesterday, are, to-day, rendered more intolerable by the jubilee shouts that reach them. If I do forget, if I do not faithfully remember those bleeding children of sorrow this day, "may my right hand forget her cunning, and may my tongue cleave to the roof of my mouth!" To forget them, to pass lightly over their wrongs, and to chime in with the popular theme, would be treason most scandalous and shocking, and would make me a reproach before God and the world. My subject, then, fellow-citizens, is AMERICAN SLAVERY. I shall see, this day, and its popular characteristics, from the slave's point of view. Standing, there, identified with the American bondman, making his wrongs mine, I do not hesitate to declare, with all my soul, that the character and conduct of this nation never looked blacker to me than on this 4th of July! Whether we turn to the declarations of the past, or to the professions of the present, the conduct of the nation seems equally hideous and revolting. America is false to the past, false to the present, and solemnly binds herself to be false to the future. Standing with God and the crushed and bleeding slave on this occasion, I will, in the name of humanity which is outraged, in the name of liberty which is fettered, in the name of the constitution and the Bible, which are disregarded and trampled upon, dare to call in question and to denounce, with all the emphasis I can command, everything that serves to perpetuate slavery—the great sin and shame of America! "I will not equivocate; I will not excuse;"[4] I will use the severest language I can command; and yet not one word shall escape me that any man, whose judgment is not blinded by prejudice, or who is not at heart a slaveholder, shall not confess to be right and just.

But I fancy I hear some one of my audience say, it is just in this circumstance that you and your brother abolitionists fail to make a

---

3. Cf. Psalm 137.1–6.
4. These famous words of William Lloyd Garrison appeared in the first issue of *The Liberator* (see note 7 on p. 23 and excerpts on pp. 308–09).

favorable impression on the public mind. Would you argue more, and denounce less, would you persuade more, and rebuke less, your cause would be much more likely to succeed. But, I submit, where all is plain there is nothing to be argued. What point in the anti-slavery creed would you have me argue? On what branch of the subject do the people of this country need light? Must I undertake to prove that the slave is a man? That point is conceded already. Nobody doubts it. The slaveholders themselves acknowledge it in the enactment of laws for their government. They acknowledge it when they punish disobedience on the part of the slave. There are seventy-two crimes in the State of Virginia, which, if committed by a black man, (no matter how ignorant he be,) subject him to the punishment of death; while only two of the same crimes will subject a white man to the like punishment.— What is this but the acknowledgement that the slave is a moral, intellectual and responsible being. The manhood of the slave is conceded. It is admitted in the fact that Southern statute books are covered with enactments forbidding, under severe fines and penalties, the teaching of the slave to read or to write.—When you can point to any such laws, in reference to the beasts of the field, then I may consent to argue the manhood of the slave. When the dogs in your streets, when the fowls of the air, when the cattle on your hills, when the fish of the sea, and the reptiles that crawl, shall be unable to distinguish the slave from a brute, *then* will I argue with you that the slave is a man!

For the present, it is enough to affirm the equal manhood of the negro race. Is it not astonishing that, while we are ploughing, planting and reaping, using all kinds of mechanical tools, erecting houses, constructing bridges, building ships, working in metals of brass, iron, copper, silver and gold; that, while we are reading, writing and cyphering, acting as clerks, merchants and secretaries, having among us lawyers, doctors, ministers, poets, authors, editors, orators and teachers; that, while we are engaged in all manner of enterprises common to other men, digging gold in California, capturing the whale in the Pacific, feeding sheep and cattle on the hill-side, living, moving, acting, thinking, planning, living in families as husbands, wives and children, and, above all, confessing and worshipping the Christian's God, and looking hopefully for life and immortality beyond the grave, we are called upon to prove that we are men!

Would you have me argue that man is entitled to liberty? that he is the rightful owner of his own body? You have already declared it. Must I argue the wrongfulness of slavery? Is that a question for Republicans? Is it to be settled by the rules of logic and argumentation, as a matter beset with great difficulty, involving a doubtful application of the principle of justice, hard to be understood? How should I look to-day, in the presence of Americans, dividing, and subdividing a discourse, to show that men have a natural right to freedom?

speaking of it relatively, and positively, negatively, and affirmatively. To do so, would be to make myself ridiculous, and to offer an insult to your understanding.—There is not a man beneath the canopy of heaven, that does not know that slavery is wrong *for him.*

What, am I to argue that it is wrong to make men brutes, to rob them of their liberty, to work them without wages, to keep them ignorant of their relations to their fellow men, to beat them with sticks, to flay their flesh with the lash, to load their limbs with irons, to hunt them with dogs, to sell them at auction, to sunder their families, to knock out their teeth, to burn their flesh, to starve them into obedience and submission to their masters? Must I argue that a system thus marked with blood, and stained with pollution, is *wrong?* No I will not. I have better employment for my time and strength, than such arguments would imply.

What, then, remains to be argued? Is it that slavery is not divine; that God did not establish it; that our doctors of divinity are mistaken? There is blasphemy in the thought. That which is inhuman, cannot be divine! *Who* can reason on such a proposition? They that can, may; I cannot. The time for such argument is past.

At a time like this, scorching irony, not convincing argument, is needed. O! had I the ability, and could I reach the nation's ear, I would, to-day, pour out a fiery stream of biting ridicule, blasting reproach, withering sarcasm, and stern rebuke. For it is not light that is needed, but fire; it is not the gentle shower, but thunder. We need the storm, the whirlwind, and the earthquake. The feeling of the nation must be quickened; the conscience of the nation must be roused; the propriety of the nation must be startled; the hypocrisy of the nation must be exposed; and its crimes against God and man must be proclaimed and denounced.

What, to the American slave, is your 4th of July? I answer; a day that reveals to him, more than all other days in the year, the gross injustice and cruelty to which he is the constant victim. To him, your celebration is a sham; your boasted liberty, an unholy license; your national greatness, swelling vanity; your sounds of rejoicing are empty and heartless; your denunciations of tyrants, brass fronted impudence; your shouts of liberty and equality, hollow mockery; your prayers and hymns, your sermons and thanksgivings, with all your religious parade, and solemnity, are, to him, mere bombast, fraud, deception, impiety, and hypocrisy—a thin veil to cover up crimes which would disgrace a nation of savages. There is not a nation on the earth guilty of practices, more shocking and bloody, than are the people of these United States, at this very hour.

* * *

HARRIET BEECHER STOWE

From Uncle Tom's Cabin[†]

Harriet Beecher Stowe (1811–1896) was the sister of the famed abolitionist minister Henry Ward Beecher (1813–1887) and of Catharine
Esther Beecher (1800–1878), a well-known writer of domestic advice
manuals for women. Stowe became a writer to support her own family,
and she published her best-selling novel *Uncle Tom's Cabin* in 1852.
Douglass admired the work very much and published several excerpts
from it in his newspaper. He and Stowe developed a friendly and mutually respectful relationship. Douglass even defended Stowe from the
criticism of a number of Black readers who objected that her representation of the book's main character, Uncle Tom, inaccurately depicted
enslaved persons as passive, meek, and obedient because they were
happy with their lot. The following excerpt is typical of Stowe's portrayal of Uncle Tom; it indicates how deeply most white abolitionists
like Stowe had absorbed negative stereotypes of enslaved persons, stereotypes that were promulgated by slavery's defenders.

Chapter XXXI

THE MIDDLE PASSAGE

"Thou art of purer eyes than to behold evil, and canst not look
upon iniquity: wherefore lookest thou upon them that deal
treacherously, and holdest thy tongue when the wicked devoureth
the man that is more righteous than he?"   —Hab 1 : 13.

On the lower of part of a small, mean boat, on the Red river, Tom
sat,—chains on his wrists, chains on his feet, and a weight heavier
than chains lay on his heart. All had faded from his sky,—moon and
star; all had passed by him, as the trees and banks were now passing, to return no more. Kentucky home, with wife and children, and
indulgent owners; St. Clare home, with all its refinements and splen-
dors; the golden head of Eva, with its saint-like eyes; the proud, gay,
handsome, seemingly careless, yet ever-kind St. Clare; hours of ease
and indulgent leisure,—all gone! and in place thereof, *what* remains?
   It is one of the bitterest apportionments of a lot of slavery, that
the negro, sympathetic and assimilative, after acquiring, in a refined
family, the tastes and feelings which form the atmosphere of such a
place, is not the less liable to become the bond-slave of the coarsest
and most brutal,—just as a chair or table, which once decorated the
superb saloon, comes, at last, battered and defaced, to the bar-room

† From *Uncle Tom's Cabin*, Vol. 2 (Boston: John P. Jewett & Company, 1852), pp. 168–
69, 170, 176.

of some filthy tavern, or some low haunt of vulgar debauchery. The great difference is, that the table and chair cannot feel, and the *man* can; for even a legal enactment that he shall be "taken, reputed, adjudged in law, to be a chattel personal,"[1] cannot blot out his soul, with its own private little world of memories, hopes, loves, fears, and desires.

Mr. Simon Legree, Tom's master, had purchased slaves at one place and another, in New Orleans, to the number of eight, and driven them, handcuffed, in couples of two and two, down to the good steamer Pirate, which lay at the levee, ready for a trip up the Red river.

* * *

"Well, I'll soon have *that* out of you. I have none o' yer bawling, praying, singing niggers on my place; so remember. Now, mind yourself," he said, with a stamp and a fierce glance of his gray eye, directed at Tom, "*I'm* your church now! You understand,—you've got to be as *I* say."

Something within the silent black man answered *No!* and, as if repeated by an invisible voice, came the words of an old prophetic scroll, as Eva had often read them to him,—"Fear not! for I have redeemed thee. I have called thee by my name. Thou art MINE!"[2]

But Simon Legree heard no voice. That voice is one he never shall hear. He only glared for a moment on the downcast face of Tom, and walked off. He took Tom's trunk, which contained a very neat and abundant wardrobe, to the forecastle, where it was soon surrounded by various hands of the boat. With much laughing, at the expense of niggers who tried to be gentlemen, the articles very readily were sold to one and another, and the empty trunk finally put up at auction. * * *

* * *

The boat moved on,—freighted with its weight of sorrow,—up the red, muddy, turbid current, through the abrupt, tortuous windings of the Red river; and sad eyes gazed wearily on the steep red-clay banks, as they glided by in dreary sameness. At last the boat stopped at a small town, and Legree, with his party, disembarked.

---

1. 2 Brev. Dig. 229 Prince's Digest, 446.
2. Cf. Isaiah 43.1. Little Eva (Evangeline St. Claire) is the kind, frail daughter of a slaveowner who befriends Uncle Tom.

FREDERICK DOUGLASS

Letter to Harriet Beecher Stowe[†]

In his editorials and speeches, Douglass frequently criticized whites' anti-Black racism in the North, excoriating in particular the whites who refused to employ Blacks or to work with them. Nonetheless, convinced that skilled labor employment was crucial for free Blacks' upward mobility, he began trying to persuade free Black people in the North to establish a manual labor school at which free Black men could learn skilled trades. In hopes of raising money to fund such an effort, Douglass wrote to Harriet Beecher Stowe, who had become wealthy following the publication of *Uncle Tom's Cabin*. He also used this appeal as an opportunity to dissuade Stowe from supporting schemes—which she had endorsed in the novel—for Black emigration to Africa. An excerpt from that letter follows.

ROCHESTER, March 8, 1853.

MY DEAR MRS. STOWE:

You kindly informed me, when at your house a fortnight ago, that you designed to do something which should permanently contribute to the improvement and elevation of the free colored people in the United States. You especially expressed an interest in such of this class as had become free by their own exertions, and desired most of all to be of service to them. In what manner and by what means you can assist this class most successfully, is the subject upon which you have done me the honor to ask my opinion. . . . I assert, then, that *poverty, ignorance*, and *degradation* are the combined evils; or in other words, these constitute the social disease of the free colored people of the United States.

To deliver them from this triple malady is to improve and elevate them, by which I mean simply to put them on an equal footing with their white fellow-countrymen in the sacred right to "*Life, Liberty*, and the pursuit of happiness."[1] I am for no fancied or artificial elevation, but only ask fair play. How shall this be obtained? I answer, first, not by establishing for our use high schools and colleges. Such institutions are, in my judgment, beyond our immediate occasions and are not adapted to our present most pressing wants. High schools and colleges are excellent institutions, and will in due season be greatly subservient to our progress; but they are the result, as well as they are the demand, of a point of progress which we as a people have

---

† From *The Life and Times of Frederick Douglass* (Hartford, CT: Park Publishing, 1881), pp. 353–57.
1. Famous phrase in the U.S. Declaration of Independence.

not yet attained. Accustomed as we have been to the rougher and harder modes of living, and of gaining a livelihood, we cannot and we ought not to hope that in a single leap from our low condition, we can reach that of *Ministers, Lawyers, Doctors, Editors, Merchants*, etc. These will doubtless be attained by us; but this will only be when we have patiently and laboriously, and I may add successfully, mastered and passed through the intermediate gradations of agriculture and the mechanic arts. * * *

There must be a certain amount of cultivation among the people, to sustain such a ministry. At present we have not that cultivation amongst us; and, therefore, we value in the preacher strong lungs rather than high learning. I do not say that educated ministers are not needed amongst us, far from it! I wish there were more of them! but to increase their number is *not* the largest benefit you can bestow upon us.

* * *

There is little reason to hope that any considerable number of the free colored people will ever be induced to leave this country, even if such a thing were desirable. The black man (*un*like the Indian) loves civilization. He does not make very great progress in civilization himself, but he likes to be in the midst of it, and prefers to share its most galling evils, to encountering barbarism. Then the love of country, the dread of isolation, the lack of adventurous spirit, and the thought of seeming to desert their "brethren in bonds," are a powerful check upon all schemes of colonization,[2] which look to the removal of the colored people, without the slaves. The truth is, dear madam, we are *here*, and here we are likely to remain. Individuals emigrate—nations never. We have grown up with this republic, and I see nothing in her character, or even in the character of the American people, as yet, which compels the belief that we must leave the United States. If, then, we are to remain here, the question for the wise and good is precisely that you have submitted to me—namely: What can be done to improve the condition of the free people of color in the United States? The plan which I humbly submit in answer to this inquiry (and in the hope that it may find favor with you, and with the many friends of humanity who honor, love, and coöperate with you) is the establishment in Rochester, N. Y.,[3] or in some other part of the United States equally favorable to such an enterprise, of an INDUSTRIAL COLLEGE in which shall be taught several important branches of the mechanic arts. This college to be open to colored youth. I will pass over the details of such an institution

---

2. See note 2 on p. 293.
3. Then Douglass's home city.

as I propose. . . . Never having had a day's schooling in all my life, I may not be expected to map out the details of a plan so comprehensive as that involved in the idea of a college. I repeat, then, I leave the organization and administration to the superior wisdom of yourself and the friends who second your noble efforts. The argument in favor of an Industrial College (a college to be conducted by the best men, and the best workmen which the mechanic arts can afford; a college where colored youth can be instructed to use their hands, as well as their heads; where they can be put in possession of the means of getting a living whether their lot in after life may be cast among civilized or uncivilized men; whether they choose to stay here, or prefer to return to the land of their fathers) is briefly this: Prejudice against the free colored people in the United States has shown itself nowhere so invincible as among mechanics. The farmer and the professional man cherish no feeling so bitter as that cherished by these. The latter would starve us out of the country entirely. At this moment I can more easily get my son into a lawyer's office to study law than I can into a blacksmith's shop to blow the bellows and to wield the sledge-hammer. Denied the means of learning useful trades, we are pressed into the narrowest limits to obtain a livelihood. In times past we have been the hewers of wood and drawers of water for American society, and we once enjoyed a monopoly in menial employments, but this is so no longer. Even these employments are rapidly passing away out of our hands. The fact is (every day begins with the lesson, and ends with the lesson) that colored men must learn trades; must find new employments; new modes of usefulness to society, or that they must decay under the pressing wants to which their condition is rapidly bringing them.

We must become mechanics; we must build as well as live in houses; we must make as well as use furniture; we must construct bridges as well as pass over them, before we can properly live or be respected by our fellow men. We need mechanics as well as ministers. We need workers in iron, clay, and leather. We have orators, authors, and other professional men, but these reach only a certain class, and get respect for our race in certain select circles. To live here as we ought we must fasten ourselves to our countrymen through their every-day, cardinal wants. We must not only be able to *black* boots, but to *make* them. At present we are unknown in the northern States as mechanics. We give no proof of genius or skill at the county, State, or national fairs. We are unknown at any of the great exhibitions of the industry of our fellow-citizens, and being unknown, we are unconsidered.

The fact that we make no show of our ability is held conclusive of our inability to make any, hence all the indifference and contempt with which incapacity is regarded fall upon us, and that too when we have had no means of disproving the infamous opinion of our natural inferiority. I have, during the last dozen years, denied before the Americans that we are an inferior race; but this has been done by arguments based upon admitted principles rather than by the presentation of facts. Now, firmly believing, as I do, that there are skill, invention, power, industry, and real mechanical genius among the colored people, which will bear favorable testimony for them, and which only need the means to develop them, I am decidedly in favor of the establishment of such a college as I have mentioned. The benefits of such an institution would not be confined to the Northern States, nor to the free colored people. They would extend over the whole Union. The slave not less than the freeman would be benefited by such an institution. It must be confessed that the most powerful argument now used by the southern slaveholder, and the one most soothing to his conscience, is that derived from the low condition of the free colored people of the North. I have long felt that too little attention has been given by our truest friends in this country to removing this stumbling-block out of the way of the slave's liberation.

The most telling, the most killing refutation of slavery is the presentation of an industrious, enterprising, thrifty, and intelligent free black population. Such a population I believe would rise in the Northern States under the fostering care of such a college as that supposed.

* * * Allow me to say in conclusion that I believe every intelligent colored man in America will approve and rejoice at the establishment of some such institution as that now suggested. There are many respectable colored men, fathers of large families, having boys nearly grown up, whose minds are tossed by day and by night with the anxious inquiry, What shall I do with my boys? Such an institution would meet the wants of such persons. Then, too, the establishment of such an institution would be in character with the eminently practical philanthropy of your transatlantic friends. America could scarcely object to it as an attempt to agitate the public mind on the subject of slavery, or to *dissolve the Union.* It could not be tortured into a cause for hard words by the American people, but the noble and good of all classes would see in the effort an excellent motive, a benevolent object, temperately, wisely, and practically manifested.

Wishing you, dear madam, renewed health, a pleasant passage, and safe return to your native land,

I am, most truly, your grateful friend,

FREDERICK DOUGLASS.

HARRIET BEECHER STOWE

Letter to William Lloyd Garrison[†]

Following Douglass's change of opinion on the constitutionality of slavery, Harriet Beecher Stowe looked on in alarm as the hostilities been Douglass and Garrison escalated. Eventually, she felt compelled to write a letter of reproof to Garrison, urging him to acknowledge that Douglass's views did not merely emulate those of his white mentors, but originated in "the soil of his own mind."

Cabin - December 19 [1853]
Mr. Garrison
Dear Sir

After seeing you, I enjoyed the pleasure of a personal interview with Mr. Douglas & I feel bound in justice to say that the impression was far more satisfactory, than I had anticipated.

There did not appear to be any underlying stratum of bitterness—he did not seem to me malignant or revengeful. I think that it was only a temporary excitement & one which he will outgrow.

I was much gratified with the growth and development both of his mind and heart. I am satisfied that his change of sentiment was not a mere political one but a genuine growth of his own conviction.

A vigorous reflective mind like his cast among those holding new sentiments is naturally led to modified views.

At all events, he holds no opinion which he cannot defend, with a variety & richness of thought & expression & an aptness of illustration which shows it to be a growth from the soil of his own mind with a living root & not a twig broken off other mens thoughts & stuck down to subserve a temporary purpose.

His plans for the elevation of his own race, are manly, sensible, comprehensive, he has evidently observed closely & thought deeply and will I trust act efficiently.

You speak of him as an apostate—I cannot but regard this language as unjustly severe—why is he to be any more called an apostate for having spoken ill tempered things of former friends than they for having spoken severely and cruelly as they have of him?—where is this work of excommunication to end—Is there but one true anti-slavery church and all others infidels? & who shall declare which it is?

[†] Transcribed by the editors of this Norton Critical Edition from the Boston Public Library Anti-Slavery Collection MS A.1.2 v.23, p.115.

I feel bound to remonstrate with this—for the same reason that I do with slavery—because I think it, an injustice. I must say still further, that if the first allusion to his family concerns was unfortunate this last one is more unjustifiable still—I am utterly surprised at it—as a friend to you, and to him I do view it with the deepest concern and regret.

What Mr. Douglas *is* really, time will show—I trust that he will make no further additions to the already unfortunate controversial literature of the cause. *Silence* in this case will be eminently—*golden.*

I must indulge the hope you will see reason at some future time to alter your opinion & that what you now cast aside as worthless shall yet appear to be a treasure.

There is abundant room in the anti-slavery field for him to perform a work without crossing the track or impeding the movements of his old friends & perhaps in some future time meeting each other from opposite quarters of a victorious field you may yet shake hands together.

I write this note because in the conversation I had with you, and also with Miss Weston I admitted so much that was not favorable to Mr. Douglas that I felt bound in justice to state the more favorable views which had arisen in my mind.

Very sincerely your friend,

H. B. Stowe

FREDERICK DOUGLASS

The Doom of the Black Power[†]

The days of the Black Power are numbered. Its course, indeed, is onward, but with the swiftness of an arrow, it rushes to the tomb. While crushing its millions, it is also crushing itself.—The sword of Retribution, suspended by a single hair, hangs over it.[1] That sword must fall. Liberty must triumph. It possesses an inherent vitality, a recuperative energy, to which its opposite is a stranger. It may to human appearances be dead, the enemy may rejoice at its grave, and

---

[†] From *Frederick Douglass' Paper* (July 27, 1855): 2.

1. Douglass is referring to the sword of Damocles, a moral parable popularized by the Roman philosopher Cicero. In the story, Damocles flatters King Dionysius II, who lets him experience his opulent life but dangles a sword over Damocles' head. Those in power always labor in anxiety and under the threat of death. For Douglass that sword was retribution from enslaved persons principally, but also from those who were fighting the slaveocracy.

sing its funeral requiem, but in the midst of the triumphal shout, it leaps from its well guarded sepulchre, asserts the divinity of its origin, flashes its indignant eye upon the affrighted enemy, and bids him prepare for *the last battle, and the grave.*

We were never more hopeful, than at the present time, of the final triumph of the great Principles which underlie the Abolition movement. We rest our hopes upon a consciousness of their inherent Righteousness. Truth is mighty, and will prevail. This is a maxim, which we do not regard as a mere rhetorical flourish. We are conscious that there is a black side to our picture. The developments of the Slave Power, are anything but pleasant to contemplate. The Present, with its inflexible realities, seems to be but an echo of the terribleness of the Past. We have lived through the one, we are now grappling with the other. We should not, as an oppressed People, grow despondent. Fear and despondency prevent us from working for the overthrow of our common enemy, with that hopeful spirit which causes us to keep our head above the waters, despite the raging of the elements. If we can at the present crisis, catch but one soft, low whisper of peace to our troubled souls, let us cling to it. Let us rejoice in Hope. The arm of the enemy will yet be paralyzed, and *with our withered arm made whole*, we'll rise in all the majesty and might of *Freemen*, and crush the crushers of the dangerous element of Abolitionism.

Whoever will contemplate the diversified phases of the Abolition Movement, from its inception to the present, will readily discern, that at no period of its history, has it presented so favorable an aspect as at the present. Truth is progressive. It ever has been; it always will be. Retrogression cannot be written on its brow. To the gaze of the world, error may appear, robed in the habiliments of gladness, and riding upon the wings of the wind. Truth may seemingly lag behind, and stop to rest upon the weeping willow. But the progress of the latter is sure and steady. The race is not to the swift;[2] Error will soon lie down and die, but Truth will live forever. Let these reflections continually inspire us while battling with the oppressor.

Again: we should rejoice that the People are beginning to read, mark, and inwardly digest the truth. The attention of the masses is being directed to the enormity, the crushing cruelty, the ever-grasping cupidity of Slavery.—They begin to feel and know that Slavery is as relentless as the greedy grave, that its thirst for human blood can only be satiated for the time being; even a gift of nearly a half a million square miles only cools, *pro tempore*, the ardor of its ferocity. They have found out to their hearts' content, the utter inutility of attempting to compromise, or enter into any kind of contract with it, that so soon as compromises and contracts cease to conduce to its

2. Cf. Ecclesiastes 9.11.

own aggrandizement, it spurns the compromise, and those who were gulled by it, and tramples on the contract. They have also found out that the Slavery question is one in which white men, as well as black men, are immediately interested, that Slavery invades the rights of man, irrespective of color and condition. They now begin to realize as Truth, that which a short time ago, they were wont to regard as the freak of disordered imaginations. Hence, the wolfish cry of *"fanaticism,"* has lost its potency; indeed the *"fanatics"* are looked upon as a pretty respectable body of People. Some consolation can be deduced from this reflection.

Another thought: we regard the present developments of the Slave Power as precipitating the era of its disastrous doom. It has over-reached itself, in its efforts to abolish Freedom in the United States, and erect its black standard upon every hill-top and valley in the land. It never wore an aspect so repulsive, as it does to-day. It has made such a frightful noise of late, that the attention of the world is directed toward it. The passage of the Fugitive Slave Act, and the Nebraska Bill; the recent marauding movements of the oligarchy in Kansas,[3] all the ebullitions of its pent-up wrath, are fatal stabs in the monster side. The Anti-Slavery sentiment of the North[4] has been strengthened and increased by these developments; indeed, the Abolitionists have now a most potent ally in the Slave Power. Slaveholders are unconsciously performing good service in the cause of Liberty, by demonstrating in their conduct, the truthfulness of the sentiments advanced and advocated by Abolitionists. The Anti-Slavery men of the land have faithfully admonished the whole country, and held up the Slave Power, as an Oligarchy determined on swaying the sceptre of universal dominion. But they have been regarded fanatics, and enthusiasts, crying wolf, when there was no wolf, inciting peaceful citizens to Rebellion, turning the country upside down, striving to destroy the Union. These and a host of similar allegations have been brought against them.

But now the great masses of the People find out by experience, that the wolf is indeed among them. They see his red, glaring eyes, and they cry out, *"kill the wolf;* he must not be permitted to go any farther in his depredations; our eyes have been opened." Thanks to the Fugitive Slave and Nebraska Bills. They have sealed the doom of the Black Power.

Lastly, we behold that doom written in unmistakable characters, by the great Republican Movement, which is sweeping like a whirlwind over the Free States.[5] We rejoice in this demonstration. It

---

3. See note 2 on p. 209 and note 2 on p. 290.
4. See note 7 on p. 23.
5. The "great Republican Movement" refers to the birth of the modern Republican Party. The party was really a grass-roots political reaction to the Kansas-Nebraska Act of 1854, which rewrote previous compromises in allowing slavery in places where it did

evinces the fact of a growing determination on the part of the North, to redeem *itself* from bondage, to bury party affinities, and predilections, and also the political leaders who have hitherto controlled them; to unite in one grand phalanx, and go forth, and whip the enemy. We cannot join this party, because we think it lacks vitality; it does not go far enough in the right direction; it gives aid and comfort to the Slaveholder, by its concessions, and its willingness to "let Slavery alone where it is"—This is the very place where it should be attacked. We cannot attack it very well where it is not. But we have in former articles commented at length on the inconsistency and absurdity of that phase of Anti-Slavery sentiment and action, denominated Free-Soilism.[6] We are, however, hopeful that this Republican Party as it grows in numbers, will also grow "*in the knowledge of the Truth.*" A few more pro-Slavery demonstrations, a few more presses thrown into the river, a few more northern ministers driven from the South and West, a few more recaptures of Fugitives, near Bunker Hill, and Plymouth Rock, causing the People to see the system in all its native ugliness, and hate it with indescribable intenseness, and all will be well. We have no fears of ultimate success. Let each man do his duty. Let him continue to *agitate* in the circle in which he moves. Let him not lose sight of his individual responsibility, for this gives tone and vigor to associated action. The Slave's complaint must be heard at the fireside, in the street, in the counting house, in the prayer meeting, in the conference room, from the pulpit, in synods, and associations, and conferences, and especially *at the Polls*. We must follow the oppressor whithersoever he goeth, irrespective of the form in which he may develop himself, or the habiliments he may assume. Use the proper means, fight with the right weapons, let there be no cessation of the warfare, no diversion from the *real cause of the battle*, and we shall yet witness the *end of the Black Power in America*.

The Trials and Triumphs of Self-Made Men[†]

The LECTURER on rising was received with immense cheering. He said: I appear before you this evening in an unaccustomed position. I usually speak in public on the subject of American slavery, and it is supposed by some in my country that a coloured man has not thoughts

---

not previously exist. The Republican Party was founded as a single-issue party, dedicated to allowing slavery only where it already existed.

6. See note 5 on p. 300.

† From the *Halifax Courier* (January 7, 1860). Douglass debuted his "Self-Made Men" speech in February 1859, then gave many variations of it throughout his extensive speaking career. The earliest surviving published text is the following version, which recounts Douglass's appearance in Halifax, England, on January 4, 1860.

worth listening to on any other subject. Partly with a view to show the fallacy of this notion, and partly to give expression to what I think sound and important views of life, I have prepared this lecture.

The various uses to which men put the brief space of human existence, and the proportion which their success in the world bears to their several opportunities, are subjects worthy of the attention and study of all men, and especially of those who have something of life still in prospect. It may not be of very serious consequence, what views of life are presented and urged upon the attention of those who have grown old and hardened in the violent and long continued abuse of life's best privileges. Under the whole heavens there is not a sadder sight—a more affecting and melancholy spectacle— than such men present to the eye of a thoughtful man. Standing upon the very verge of misspent time, and looking back only upon wasted opportunities, a whole life wantonly flung away, such men stud the field of human existence only as warnings. And sad warnings they are. The chance to redeem the time for themselves has come and gone, never to return. The past is covered with regrets, the present is without the life and inspirations of hope, and the future is mantled in gloom.

But to the young, with all the bright world before them where to choose, the case is widely and cheeringly different. By wisdom, by firmness, and by a manly and heroic self-denial, these may wholly escape the sharp and flinty rocks, the false lights, and the treacherous shores, the tempest, and the whirlwinds of passion and sin which have sent other voyagers to the bottom wrecked and ruined. Life is the world's greatest and most significant fact. It is the grand reality that realizes all other realities. All that man can know of the dim and shadowy past, and of the solemn and mysterious future have their explanation mainly in this one great fact. It is the now that makes the then, and the here that makes the hereafter to us all. Death itself is only predicated of life, and itself can only comprehend death.

Without trenching upon the forbidden domains of theology, I may venture to say, that if this life shall only be regarded as an individual fact, standing alone, having no relations or bearings, full and complete in itself, wholly independent of, and disconnected with, any other state or place, we still find it a most glorious fact, and crowded with arguments the most convincing, and with motives the most powerful, in favour of the construction and cultivation of a true and manly character. Such are the transcendent rewards of virtue, knowledge, wisdom, and power, even in this life, and the certain misery which a life of inaction, vice, and ignorance entails, that man is ever under the pressure of the highest motives in favour of self-culture and self-improvement.

How to make the best of this life, as a thing of and for itself,—viewed apart from those other considerations to which I have alluded,—must ever be an important and useful enquiry. For he who has best fitted himself to live and serve his fellow men on earth has best fitted himself to live and serve his God in Heaven. While in the world, a man's work is with the world and for the world. It is something to be a man among shady trees and stately halls—but much more to be a man among men, full of the cares, labours, and joys of this life. It is good to think that in Heaven, all injustice, all wrong, all wars, all ignorance, and all vice, will be at an end; but how incomparably better is it, to wage a vigorous war upon these blighting evils and drive them from the present, so that the will of God may be done on earth as in heaven—(cheers).[1]

There have been many daguerrotypes taken of life. They are as various as they are numerous. Each picture is coloured according to the lights and shades surrounding the artist. To the sailor, life is a ship, richly freighted, and with all sail spread to the breeze. To the farmer, life is a fertile field waving with its golden harvests. To the architect, it stands out as a gorgeous palace or temple, with its pillars, domes, towers, and turrets. To the great dramatic poet, all the world is a stage, and men but players;[2] but to all mankind, the world is a vast school. From the cradle to the grave, the oldest and the wisest, not less than the youngest and the simplest, are but learners; and those who learn most, seem to have most to learn—(hear, hear).

The lecturer then spoke at some length on the anomalies of society; the rich and the poor, the lofty and the lowly, the happy and the miserable. But, he observed, even taking this aspect of society, humanity was a great worker, and it sometimes worked wonders. It was a master of all situations, and a match for all adversities. Notwithstanding the vast disparity between the hut and the hall, these two extremes, as well as others, did sometimes meet in life's eventful journey, and shake hands upon a common platform of knowledge, wisdom, usefulness, virtue, honour, and fame—(cheers).

Nevertheless, life presented many puzzles. It was a puzzle that men could resemble each other so closely, yet differ so widely. Possessed of the same faculties, vitalized by the same life-blood, sustained by the same elements, yet how endless were the dissimilarities and contradictions. While some were Miltons, Bacons, and Shakespeares,[3] illuminating and filling a wondering world with the resplendent glories of their achievements, others were as dull as lead, and rose no higher in life than a mere physical existence. The

1. Cf. the Lord's Prayer (Matthew 6.10, Luke 11.2).
2. Cf. Shakespeare, *As You Like It* 2.7.139–40.
3. The English poet John Milton (1608–1674), the English philosopher Francis Bacon (1561–1626), and William Shakespeare (1564–1616).

natural laws for the preservation and development of human faculties were equal, uniform, harmonious, permanent, wise, and perfect; but the subjects of them abounded in oddities, confusions, opposites, and discords—(hear, hear).

A thousand arrows might be shot at the same object, but, though united in aim, they might be divided in flight. And such was life—equal in quiver, but unequal in aim; matched when dormant, but unmatched, mismatched, and countermatched in action. The boundless realms of the past were covered with these fallen arrows. They were to be met with in history, biography, and the other walks of life. Nothing was more natural or instructive than to walk among those fallen arrows and estimate the probable amount of skill and force requisite to bring each to its place. "The proper study of mankind is man"[4] was a saying of which men never tired. It expressed a sublime truth, it came fresh to the ear every time repeated, and vibrated the soul like the lightning the wire; it was felt as well as thought; it was felt before it was thought. A single human being was of more interest than all else on earth. The solitary form of the great navigator, Franklin,[5] wedged in between walls of eternal ice, cast all the gloomy wonders of the Arctic Seas into the shade. He was greater to us than the polar night or the north-west passage[6]—there was a charm about him in the simple quality of manhood—(hear, hear).

The voyage of discovery that evening was over the broad ocean of humanity. They might not find that for which they were searching, but they would find that which would make the search worth undertaking. Men were noble and generous when they found a man who came up to their idea of a hero. The lecturer at this point stated that he once saw a swarm of little boys following the great O'Connell,[7] from square to square in the city of Dublin, forgetful of their poverty and wretchedness, despising cold and rain and mud, swept on by a joyous enthusiasm, making the welkin ring with praises of the great Irish liberator. Why did they follow him? The answer was plain—they could not help it; they obeyed the tide of their nature.

The lecturer having enlarged on this view of human nature, he remarked that the title of his lecture that evening involved something like a solecism. He freely admitted that there could not be self-made men in the world; all had begged, borrowed, or stolen from somebody or somewhere—(cheers). Nevertheless, it was a fit and convenient title to the subject matter of his discourse.

---

4. Line 1 of *An Essay on Man*, Epistle 2 (1733), by the English poet Alexander Pope (1688–1744).
5. John Franklin (1786–1847), Britain's most famous Arctic explorer.
6. Fabled sea route to the Pacific through the Arctic Ocean, much sought by European explorers in earlier centuries.
7. Daniel O'Connell (1775–1847), Irish nationalist.

Four points were suggested as the natural divisions of his subject. First, the class designated as self-made men. Second, the true theory of their success. Third, the advantages which they derived from the ideas and institutions of the country in which they lived. And the fourth, the criticism and disadvantages to which they were exposed.

In a certain sense, most if not all the great characters whose names shone in history, and whose deeds commanded homage and admiration might be regarded as self-made men; but he meant that evening just what the name imported: those men who had without the ordinary helps of favouring circumstances, raised themselves against great odds from the most humble and cheerless positions in life to usefulness, greatness, honour, influence, and fame. These were the men who had built the ladder on which they climbed and built as they climbed—(hear, hear). Such men, whether they were found in the factory or the college, whether at the handles of the plough or in the professor's chair, whether at the bar or in the pulpit, whether of Anglo-Saxon or of Anglo-African origin, ought to have awarded to them the honour of being self-made men—(cheers).

There were three special explanations given as to the cause of success in self-made men. The first attributed to such men superior mental endowments, and assigned this as the true explanation of success. The second made the most of circumstances, favouring opportunities, accidents, chances, &c. The third made industry and application the great secret of success. All had truth in them, and all were capable of being pressed into untruth.

Mr. Douglass entered into a discussion of each point, but the substance of his own views on them was, that industry and application, together with a regard to favourable circumstances and opportunities were the means of success. The lecturer continued:—Such is my theory of self-made men, and, indeed, of all made men. The credit belongs and must be ascribed to brave, honest, earnest, ceaseless heart and soul industry. By this simple means—open and free to all men—whatever may be said of chances, circumstances, and natural endowments—the simple man may become wise, and the wise man become wiser. Striking examples of the truth of this position are abundant.

Hugh Miller,[8] whose lamented death a few years ago cast a dark shadow, not only over this land, but across the broad Atlantic, is, perhaps, among the most striking and brilliant examples of industrious application at self-culture. In a country famous for its colleges and other institutions of learning, this brave son of toil mastered

8. See note 2 on p. 20.

geology while wielding the heavy hammer of the mechanic. As was said of Burns,[9] Miller was himself a college. One is really astonished, on reading this man's works, at what he accomplished by simple, patient application, guided by a steady purpose.

The case of Elihu Burritt[1]—a man whose very goodness overshadows his real mental greatness—may be cited. He had to support his bodily wants by his own hands, while maintaining the struggle for an education. But this did not discourage him. Over the glowing forge, the red-hot steel, the polished anvil, amid the noise and dust of the blacksmith's shop, this brave son of toil mastered, I dare not say how many languages, and is now admitted to be among our best American scholars.

That not many books, or very favourable circumstances are essential to successful education. is amply demonstrated in the life of Louis Kossuth.[2] That eminent man came here from the extreme east of Europe, loaded down with Anglo-Saxon ideas, and clothed with an English eloquence which is absolutely overwhelming. When asked where and when he got his knowledge, he tells us that his school-house was an Austrian prison, that his books were the Bible and Shakespeare, and the English Dictionary, and that his schoolmaster was Louis Kossuth—(cheers and laughter).

The United States has produced no self-made man more worthy of mention than Benjamin Bannecker, the black astronomer of the State of Maryland.[3] With honest pride I turn to this black sage as in part blotting out the charge of natural inferiority so often brought against the negro race. You may know his history. He was black—for slavery had not in his day robbed the negro in America of his colour, as well as of his liberty. Bannecker was distinguished as a mathematician, and was among the surveyors who laid out the present capital of the United States—where freedom has been "laid out" ever since. In the corn field, and by the roadside, this sable son of toil picked up an education which brought him to the favourable notice of eminent men on both sides of the Atlantic. He held a creditable correspondence with a man no less distinguished than Thomas Jefferson, one of the early presidents of the United States. At that time presidents were men, and not as now mere platforms. Bannecker was an astronomer as well as a surveyor, and calculated almanacs. One of his almanacs he sent to Mr. Jefferson, which brought him the following letter in return:—[4]

---

9. Robert Burns (1759–1796), Scottish poet.
1. American writer, lecturer, and social activist (1810–1879).
2. See note 9 on p. 27. Douglass paraphrases the Hungarian exile's speech at Boston's Faneuil Hall.
3. Banneker (1731–1806), a free Black man in Washington, D.C., taught himself mathematics and astronomy and became a prominent writer and scientist.
4. Douglass slightly misquotes Jefferson's letter.

Philadelphia, August 30, 1790.

Sir,—I thank you sincerely for your letter and the almanac it contains. Nobody wishes more than I do to see such proofs as you exhibit that nature has given our black brethren talents equal to those of other colours of men, and that the appearance of a want of them is owing merely to the degraded condition of their existence both in Africa and in America. I have taken the liberty of sending your almanac to Monsieur Condorcet, secretary of the Academy of Science at Paris, and member of the Philanthropic Society, because I considered it as a document to which your whole colour had a right for their justification against the doubts which have been entertained of them.

I am, with great esteem, Sir,
Your most obedient,

THOMAS JEFFERSON.

William Dietz, of Albany, another black man, now living, has risen from the humble condition of a servant in a private family, to be the manager of an estate worth three million dollars.[5] This black man (for he too is black) who would be read out of the human family by the Notts, Gliddens, Mortons,[6] and other American ethnological writers, is admitted to be one of the best designers and draftsmen in the state of New York. He is not only a draftsman but an inventor, and a very ingenious one. He has recently invented a bridge for spanning the Hudson at Albany, which is calculated to overcome all the objections scientific men have raised in behalf of navigation against the erection of a draw-bridge at that point. This is not all: he has invented and planned a railroad for Broadway, New York city, equally obviating the presence of dust, smoke, noise, and horses, in that grand thorough-fare, and should any railway be allowed there, it will be on the plan suggested and modelled by William Dietz, of Albany. An engraving of this railway has been published and commended by the *Scientific American*. Men read of the inventions of Mr. Dietz, but do not know what I know, and what the American people ought to know, that the inventor is a black man. His achievement if known, would do more to elevate the popular estimate of the coloured race than any number of learned dissertations on the natural equality of races. Nothing in logic is so stubborn, and here is a strong one certainly.

5. Dietz was a servant of the businessman and politician Charles E. Dudley, in Albany, N.Y. Dudley's widow turned over the management of her estate to Dietz, who eventually went into business for himself and became one of Albany's wealthiest Black citizens.
6. Josiah Clark Nott (1804–1873), George Robins Gliddon (1809–1857), and Samuel George Morton (1799–1851). See note 6 on p. 31.

There too, stands the bright example of Toussaint l'Ouverture.[7] He is confessed to have been a brave and generous soldier, a clear-headed, calm and sagacious statesman, and the noble liberator and law giver of his brave and dauntless people. A slave during fifty of the best years of his life. A poor scholar, yet rising up in troublous times, and in an age of great men he towered among the tallest of his times. I will not extol his merits. He is already a hero of history, poetry, and eloquence. Wordsworth has encircled his memory with a halo of fadeless glory, while Wendell Phillips has borne his name heavenward in a chariot of matchless eloquence.[8]

I might if time permitted, point to a long list of self-made men, and could I ask these by what means they obtained their high positions among their fellowmen, their answer would come with the startling effect of a blast from a quarry—industry and application.

I now come to the relation which ideas and institutions bear to this class of men, and shall have special reference to America. I seldom find anything either in the ideas or institutions of that country, whereof to glory. The one deep dark veil of human bondage, covering as it does every department of the government, and every class of its people, poisoning the very life blood, the morals, religion, manners, and civilization of that great nation, hides from my dim vision much that might otherwise be seen, noble and beautiful and worthy of admiration and of imitation. But pushing aside this black and clotted covering which mantles all our land, as with the shadow of death, I recognize one feature at least of special and peculiar excellence, and that is the relation of America to self-made men. America is, most unquestionably and pre-eminently, the home and special patron of self-made men. In no country in the world are the conditions more favourable to the production and sustentation of such men than in America. They are found in all the high places, exercising all the powers, and enjoying all the immunities of office and honour. The press flames with the living and quenchless fires of their genius, and the senate listens with respect and admiration to their eloquence. They are foremost men everywhere. They are found among our authors, editors, lawyers, preachers, inventors, poets, philosophers, and statesmen, and the fact that they are self-made is often dwelt upon by the crowd as their highest honour.

Let me give you one or two of the causes of this ample growth of self-made men. One cause, undoubtedly, is to be found in the general respectability of labour, especially in the northern states of the American Union. Work has not yet come to be looked upon as a

---

7. Haitian general and liberator (c. 1743–1803).
8. The English poet William Wordsworth (1770–1850) published the elegy "To Toussaint L'Ouverture" in 1803. Wendell Phillips (see note 2 on p. 24) gave a series of popular lectures on Toussaint-Louverture in the 1850s–60s.

degradation or disgrace. A man may labour there with his hands, or
with his head, or with both hands and head, and yet move in respectable society—that is if he has a white skin. Every stranger landing
upon American shores is struck by the easy, independent, and even
haughty bearing of the labouring classes. This general respectability of labour is an important element in the production of self-made
men. But a second, and perhaps the most powerful, cause is this:
the principle of measuring men by their own individual merits is better observed and enforced there than anywhere else. In Europe

> A king can mak' a belted knight,
> A marquis, duke, and a' that.[9]

But there, a man who wants to be a nobleman, must prove his nobility to his neighbours and the public. The sons of Henry Clay, Daniel Webster, and John C. Calhoun, are put upon trial, and have to
make their way in the world like the rest of us, and they must prove
themselves real Clays, Websters, and Calhouns, if they attract to
themselves any of the respect and generous admiration commanded
by their brilliant fathers.[1] Our departed great men drop down from
their various circles of greatness, like bright stars from the blue overhanging sky, bearing away with them their own silvery light, leaving
the places they have illumined robed in darkness, until the heavens
are re-lighted by the glory of other rising stars—(hear, hear, and
cheers). On the strength of a great name, and upon the accident of
being just what any other man might be, the nephew of his uncle,
Mr. Louis Napoleon,[2] has been able to banish from France many of
the wisest, best, and bravest patriots and statesmen. On the ruins of
broken faith and outraged liberty, he has firmly seated himself on
the throne of a despot. But such an experiment on such a capital of
name and nephewship could never succeed in America. Nobody there
now cares for George Washington, jun., nor for Andrew Jackson,
jun.,[3] and they stand no better chance of being made presidents of
the United States than William or John, or other common men,
whose fathers were never heard of twenty miles from home.

But self-made men are by no means invulnerable men. I do not at
all subscribe to the maxim that self-made men are the best made
men. With many excellent qualities and acquirements, they are apt

---

9. Cf. lines 25–26 of "Is There for Honest Poverty" (1795), by Robert Burns (see note 9 on
   p. 346).
1. Clay (1777–1852), Webster (1782–1852), and Calhoun (1782–1850), distinguished
   statesmen and orators, each had numerous sons, of various accomplishments.
2. Napoléon III (1808–1873), emperor of the French 1852–71.
3. U.S. presidents Washington (1732–1799) and Jackson (1767–1845) did not father any
   children, but each adopted heirs. However, Douglass means that in the United States,
   with its democratic culture, the sons, while noteworthy citizens, do not automatically
   inherit their fathers' prestige.

to possess some which are not so excellent and desirable. It is hard to shake off all the effects of early surroundings. There is, however, one very common defect to be found among such men, to which even I may allude, who may share it; this it is: such men are generally very egotistical. The very nature of the path they have pursued, and the energies they have employed in reaching their position, have served to render them so. A man who is indebted to himself for himself, is apt to think no small pumpkins of himself—(laughter). He has altogether too much to say about being a self-made man. Whatever else shall be forgotten, this is always remembered. "I am a self-made man" is the thread-bare preface to all his words and actions—(cheers).

I have still another criticism to pass upon self-made men; and that is, they too often display a want of respect for the means by which other men have risen above the level of the race. They are too free in disparagement of schools they never attended, and colleges, of which they are ignorant. In this they assume a place that does not become them; for whatever may be their merits they are generally but relative merits—they are out-siders. They may pass judgment upon the best means of self-education, but they may not lay down the law as to the best means of educating others. There never was yet a man who had educated himself who could not, by the same exertion and application and determined perseverance, have been better educated by the helps of the ordinary institutions of learning—(hear, hear). Thus I have given you a peep at both sides of the class of men taken as my subject, having nothing set down in malice, whatever I may have set down in partiality. The lessons which such men teach are valuable in many respects, chief among them is the dignity of humanity. They teach us, too, the value of work, self-reliance, and manly independence. Let us appreciate such men and award to them the mead of praise due to their heroism—give them equal elbow room—no matter from what land they come or from what race they descend—(cheers).

After all, my friends, let it be remembered—let it be rivetted upon our understandings and anchored in our hearts for ever—that neither self-culture, nor any other kind of culture, can amount to much in this world, unless joined to some truly unselfish and noble purpose. Patriotism, religion, philanthropy—some grand motive power other than the simple hope of personal reward must be present, or the candle is under the bushel[4] and will certainly remain there. We all need some grand, some soul-enlarging, some soul-sustaining object to draw out the best energies of our natures and to lift us to the plains of true nobleness and manly life—(cheers).

4. Cf. Matthew 5.15, Mark 4.2, or Luke 11.33.

And is it not a consoling thought that, rich as this great world may be, and poor and small as the individual man may be, there [is] none so small, none so destitute, but that he is rich enough to make this great world a debtor to him for something in the way of example, word, or deed more precious than all the gems of the east?—(loud applause).

HARRIET JACOBS

From Incidents in the Life of a Slave Girl[†]

Harriet Jacobs (1813–1897), an African American, began life as an enslaved person. After escaping and later being freed, she became an abolitionist and a public speaker. Under the pseudonym Linda Brent, she published her autobiography, *Incidents in the Life of a Slave Girl*, as a newspaper serial and then a self-financed book (1861). *Incidents* provides a compelling account of a *woman's* experience of enslavement, one that included constant threat of sexual violation. Precisely to protect herself from her master, Dr. James Norcross (whom Jacobs calls "Dr. Flint" in her book), she sought the protection of another wealthy white man, Samuel Tredwell Sawyer (whom she calls "Mr. Sands"). In the following excerpt, Jacobs struggles to explain this liaison to her readers, who, she worried, would condemn her for it.

X

A PERILOUS PASSAGE IN THE SLAVE GIRL'S LIFE

And now, reader, I come to a period in my unhappy life, which I would gladly forget if I could. The remembrance fills me with sorrow and shame. It pains me to tell you of it; but I have promised to tell you the truth, and I will do it honestly, let it cost me what it may. I will not try to screen myself behind the plea of compulsion from a master; for it was not so. Neither can I plead ignorance or thoughtlessness. For years, my master had done his utmost to pollute my mind with foul images, and to destroy the pure principles inculcated by my grandmother, and the good mistress of my childhood. The influences of slavery had had the same effect on me that they had on other young girls; they had made me prematurely knowing, concerning the evil ways of the world. I know what I did, and I did it with deliberate calculation.

But, O, ye happy women, whose purity has been sheltered from childhood, who have been free to choose the objects of your

---

† From *Incidents in the Life of a Slave Girl*, ed. Lydia Maria Child (Boston: Published for the Author, 1861), pp. 83–86.

affection, whose homes are protected by law, do not judge the poor
desolate slave girl too severely! If slavery had been abolished, I,
also, could have married the man of my choice; I could have had a
home shielded by the laws; and I should have been spared the painful task of confessing what I am now about to relate; but all my
prospects had been blighted by slavery. I wanted to keep myself
pure; and, under the most adverse circumstances, I tried hard to
preserve my self-respect; but I was struggling alone in the powerful
grasp of the demon Slavery; and the monster proved too strong for
me. I felt as if I was forsaken by God and man; as if all my efforts
must be frustrated; and I became reckless in my despair.

I have told you that Dr. Flint's persecutions and his wife's jealousy had given rise to some gossip in the neighborhood. Among
others, it chanced that a white unmarried gentleman had obtained
some knowledge of the circumstances in which I was placed. He
knew my grandmother, and often spoke to me in the street. He
became interested for me, and asked questions about my master,
which I answered in part. He expressed a great deal of sympathy,
and a wish to aid me. He constantly sought opportunities to see me,
and wrote to me frequently. I was a poor slave girl, only fifteen years
old.

So much attention from a superior person was, of course, flattering; for human nature is the same in all. I also felt grateful for his
sympathy, and encouraged by his kind words. It seemed to me a
great thing to have such a friend. By degrees, a more tender feeling
crept into my heart. He was an educated and eloquent gentleman;
too eloquent, alas, for the poor slave girl who trusted in him. Of
course I saw whither all this was tending. I knew the impassable
gulf between us; but to be an object of interest to a man who is not
married, and who is not her master, is agreeable to the pride and
feelings of a slave, if her miserable situation has left her any pride
or sentiment. It seems less degrading to give one's self, than to submit to compulsion. There is something akin to freedom in having a
lover who has no control over you, except that which he gains by
kindness and attachment. A master may treat you as rudely as he
pleases, and you dare not speak; moreover, the wrong does not
seem so great with an unmarried man, as with one who has a wife
to be made unhappy. There may be sophistry in all this; but the
condition of a slave confuses all principles of morality, and, in fact,
renders the practice of them impossible.

When I found that my master had actually begun to build the
lonely cottage, other feelings mixed with those I have described.
Revenge, and calculations of interest, were added to flattered vanity and sincere gratitude for kindness. I knew nothing would enrage
Dr. Flint so much as to know that I favored another; and it was

something to triumph over my tyrant even in that small way. I thought he would revenge himself by selling me, and I was sure my friend, Mr. Sands, would buy me. He was a man of more generosity and feeling than my master, and I thought my freedom could be easily obtained from him. The crisis of my fate now came so near that I was desperate. I shuddered to think of being the mother of children that should be owned by my old tyrant. I knew that as soon as a new fancy took him, his victims were sold far off to get rid of them; especially if they had children. I had seen several women sold, with his babies at the breast. He never allowed his offspring by slaves to remain long in sight of himself and his wife. Of a man who was not my master I could ask to have my children well supported; and in this case, I felt confident I should obtain the boon. I also felt quite sure that they would be made free. With all these thoughts revolving in my mind, and seeing no other way of escaping the doom I so much dreaded, I made a headlong plunge. Pity me, and pardon me, O virtuous reader! You never knew what it is to be a slave; to be entirely unprotected by law or custom; to have the laws reduce you to the condition of a chattel, entirely subject to the will of another. You never exhausted your ingenuity in avoiding the snares, and eluding the power of a hated tyrant; you never shuddered at the sound of his footsteps, and trembled within hearing of his voice. I know I did wrong. No one can feel it more sensibly than I do. The painful and humiliating memory will haunt me to my dying day. Still, in looking back, calmly, on the events of my life, I feel that the slave woman ought not to be judged by the same standard as others.

CRITICISM

Contemporary Criticism

ANONYMOUS

["A Style at Once Terse, Vigorous, Frank, and Ingenuous"]†

Many works within the last few years have been written and published in the United States to illustrate the evils, enormities, dangers, and guilt of Slavery. No other works have been as widely read as some of these. *Uncle Tom's Cabin*, by Harriet Beecher Stowe, and *The White Slave*, by Richard Hildreth,[1] may be cited as examples. The reason is obvious; the subject is an all-engrossing one, and deeply, though variously, affects the interests, the politics, and the feelings of every American, Slavery is the great question which occupies the thoughts of the universal people. The problem to be solved is—whether the largest liberty is compatible with the rankest despotism—or, rather, whether Slavery shall spread itself over the entire extent of the American soil, or Liberty shall triumph, and Republican Institutions be purged from their deformity and disgrace.

A valuable addition has just been made to the Anti-Slavery literature of the United States, by the publication of the self-written life of Frederick Douglass—his life in slavery, and his life as a free man. * * *

The majority of our readers do not require to be told that Frederick Douglass is among the most eloquent of living men—that his descriptive and declamatory powers are of the highest order—and that his talents as a writer are not inferior to those which he has displayed as a speaker. His present work is written in a style at once terse, vigorous, frank, and ingenuous. It sustains his high reputation as a close observer, an original thinker, and a nervous,[2]

---

† From the London *Empire* (September 1, 1855).
1. Hildreth (1807–1865), journalist and historian, published his novel *The White Slave: Or, Memoirs of a Fugitive* in 1852, the same year that Stowe published hers (see p. 331).
2. In the mid-nineteenth century, "nervous" could also mean "energetic."

and, at the same time, elegant composer. That it will be widely read on both sides of the Atlantic we have no doubt; we are also confident that its facts, arguments, and impassioned appeals, will increase the depth of that detestation with which the slavery of America is already regarded, and will hasten its overthrow.

* * *

We conclude with a few words from the pen of
AN AMERICAN CRITIC

My Bondage and My Freedom exhibits the fine genius, and the rapidly developing powers of its author. If he is original and peculiar as a speaker, he is equally so as a writer. We have the fullest confidence, therefore, that this work, the result of his riper experience and of his more mature judgment, will challenge not only the admiration of all the Friends of Freedom, for its spirited and irresistible Anti-Slavery facts and arguments, but of scholars, for the directness, condensation, and affluence of its style, and of the general reader, also, for the graphic interest of the story of his checkered and eventful life.

ANONYMOUS

Books and Negrophilism†

* * * We are forced to bear the leaden dullness of our own day, and cannot but believe that the next generation will have as great an army of Dunciad heroes[1] as our own, if it be not more plenteously favored. The last of these impositions on a forbearing public is a work denominated Bondage and Freedom, the author of which is no less a person than the bosom friend of Philosopher Greeley and Abby Kelly Foster,[2] *Frederick Douglass*. Fred. is a fugitive from labor whom the sagacious negrophilists of Faneuil Hall and the Tribune office,[3] with a few other candidates for State aid as lunatics, have been endeavoring to civilize a good many years for the purpose of proving that God knew not what he was about when he stamped inferiority on every line and lineament of the African. This

---

† From the *Daily Southside Democrat* (September 5, 1855).

† From the *Daily Southside Democrat* (September 5, 1855).
1. As in the mock-heroic poem *The Dunciad* (1728–43), by the English poet Alexander Pope (1688–1744).
2. Notable abolitionist. Horace Greeley (1811–1872), antislavery editor and politician.
3. The *New-York Tribune* was a popular daily newspaper founded and edited by Horace Greeley (see preceding note). Faneuil Hall was a meeting hall in Boston sometimes used by abolitionists.

christian-like task has been undertaken and prosecuted with the usual zeal of monomaniacs, and we may add with about *their* usual success. Fred. has been *feted* and toasted and glorified and dressed up for worship like the shapeless post that receives the homage of a Feejee islander, and the faithful have vowed with many protestations that their idol was a prodigy of intellect and virtue, with the hope that their protestations would induce the censorious world to believe their divinity at least, respectable.

* * *

Can a more significant commentary on abolition fanaticism be imagined than the testimony of this slave (the best treated African in the Northern States) that he is an out cast and a Pariah in the land where he was promised freedom and equality? How powerful is this unwilling evidence, extorted by the bitter consciousness of degradation, and a disgust more bitter, at the falsehood and treachery of his pretended friends!

If it were reasonable to hope for any exhibition of sanity from men so hopelessly crazed as the freesoilers of the North,[4] we might look for some mitigation of a fanaticism so sternly rebuked by the cherished object of its zeal. May we not at least hope that upon the calm, reflecting mind of the North this bitter rebuke may operate some wholesome result? May we not expect that it will bring to the absorbing question of Slavery more rational and deliberative consideration, and that men may learn the short-sighted weakness of their attempts to mend the workmanship of the Omniscient Eternal?

ANONYMOUS

["This Plain Biography of a Living Man"][†]

Compared with the actual and startling revelations of this plain biography of a living man, the melodramatic imaginings of *Uncle Tom's Cabin*[1] are of small value. It may be said, as it has been, that taking a number of isolated circumstances and weaving them together on a wool of fiction, Mrs. STOWE produced a romance of no ordinary power. But here is a man, not yet forty years of age, who was a born thrall; who has himself suffered as a slave; who

4. See note 5 on p. 300.
† From the *New York Daily Times* (September 17, 1855).
1. See p. 331.

felt the iron eat into his soul; who records only what he personally experienced; who gives dates and places; who names circumstances and persons; whose body yet bears the marks of the cruel lash; who remained twenty-one years in bondage; who escaped from that bitter slavery; who, a self-taught man, has exhibited true eloquence of speech and pen, at home and in Europe, in advocacy of his race's claim to freedom; who has conducted a newspaper in this State for several years with success; whose exemption from being claimed as a fugitive is owing solely to the fact that, long after his escape, his friends purchased his freedom from his quondam "master;" and who, living, acting, speaking among us, possesses more vital interest for men who think than would the heroes of twenty negro romances, even though each of them was as highly wrought as that written by Mrs. STOWE. *My Bondage*, so forcible in its evident truth, is one of the most interesting, exciting and thought-awakening books in our language. In every way is it remarkable—not only in what it relates, but in the manner of the relation.

In truth, the literary merit of the book is very great. Suppose that it had been written by some college trained man, the lucidity of its style and the thoroughly Saxon character of its language would have attracted attention. But here is a man of color, instructed merely how to spell words of three letters, while yet a child—subsequently forbidden to acquire any further knowledge of this sort,—gleaning the elements of learning literally on "the highways and by-ways,"—teaching himself to write by copying printed letters—and producing a work which, as a mere literary production, would be creditable to the first English writer of the day. (Actually, the only vulgarity we have found in it is, where passing a eulogy on a friend, he called him a "whole-souled man"—a phrase which, bad enough in colloquial usage, is almost offensive when deliberately *written*). We trust that *My Bondage* will meet with great success, for it stands far above all rivals, at the head of the peculiar class to which it belongs.

ANONYMOUS

["It Is No Fiction"]†

—A third biography before us furnishes a still further contrast—the
Life and Bondage of FREDERICK DOUGLASS, the well-known fugitive
slave, who has come to occupy so conspicuous a position, both as a
writer and speaker. It details the incidents of his experience on the
slave plantation of Maryland, where he was born, of his subsequent
escape, and of his public career in England and the northern States.
We need hardly say that it abounds in interest. The mere fact that
the member of an outcast and enslaved race should accomplish his
freedom, and educate himself up to an equality of intellectual and
moral vigor with the leaders of the race by which he was held in
bondage, is, in itself, so remarkable, that the story of the change cannot be otherwise than exciting. For ourselves, we confess to have
read it with the unbroken attention with which we absorbed Uncle
Tom's Cabin.[1] It has the advantage of the latter book in that it is no
fiction. Of course, it is impossible to say how far the author's prejudices, and remembrances of wrong, may have deepened the color of
his pictures, but the general tone of them is truthful. He writes bitterly, as we might expect of one who writes under a personal provocation, taking incidents of individual experience for essential
characteristics, but not more bitterly than the circumstances seem
to justify. His denunciations of slavery and slaveholders are not indis-
criminate, while he wars upon the system rather than upon the
persons whom that system has made. In the details of his early life
upon the plantation, of his youthful thoughts on life and destiny,
and of the means by which he gradually worked his way to freedom,
there is much that is profoundly touching. Our English literature
has recorded many an example of genius struggling against adversity,—of the poor Ferguson, for instance, making himself an
astronomer, of Burns becoming a poet, of Hugh Miller finding his
geology in a stone quarry,[2] and a thousand similar cases—yet none
of these are so impressive as the case of the solitary slave, in a remote
district, surrounded by none but enemies, conceiving the project
of his escape, teaching himself to read and write to facilitate it,
accomplishing it at last, and subsequently raising himself to a leadership in a great movement in behalf of his brethren. Whatever may

† From *Putnam's Monthly* 6.547 (November 1855).
1. See p. 331.
2. All three of these Scotsmen had humble origins. James Ferguson (1710–1776) was an
   astronomer and globe maker. On Burns, see note 9 on p. 346. On Miller, see note 2 on
   p. 20.

be our opinions of slavery, or of the best means of acting upon it, we cannot but admire the force and integrity of character which has enabled Frederick Douglass to attain his present unique position.

ANONYMOUS

["His Mind Is Essentially Original"][†]

This is in every respect a remarkable production. The author is too well-known in this country to render an introductory notice of him necessary in this place, and we hope that a copy of the volume now before us—which is a valuable addition to anti-slavery literature— will ere long be as well known amongst us as he was himself, and will figure in the library or on the table of every friend of the negro. Frederick Douglass is no common man, and could not write a work of only ordinary merit. His mind is essentially original; therefore he takes novel views of things, even most familiar. Hence his reflexions on them have a freshness and an interest altogether peculiar. Although his experiences of slave life were severe, and extended over a period of twenty-one years, we have been less struck with his recital of them than with his delineation of the mental struggles that made him restless by day and sleepless by night, and which, commencing with the inquiries, "What is a slave? and why am I a slave?" led him by degrees to the irresistible conclusion that he was a slave only because all moral principle had been set aside to make him one, and that, therefore, he had a right to possess himself, and to take advantage of the first opportunity to make that self-possession sure. His narrative, however, presents a graphic picture of the inner life of the system of which he was a victim, and is penned in an admirable style: terse yet flowing, and frequently even elegant. Passages, too, of great humour abound in it; and when he gives the rein to his wit and satire, pointing his shafts against the system, he does so with evident relish. But an undercurrent of profound thought also runs through the whole work, which sometimes—nay often—partakes of the character of the highest philosophy. His arguments and his conclusions strike with irresistible force at the foundation of "the peculiar institution,"[1] and are never more cogent than when levelled at the sophisms of pro-slavery divines. His descriptions of places and portraits of individuals are, we should judge, touched off to the life.

---

† From the *Anti-Slavery Reporter* 4.22–23 (January 1, 1856). Bracketed page references are to this Norton Critical Edition.

1. Nineteenth-century Southern expression for slavery, with "peculiar" meaning "special."

That of Tuckahoe, Maryland, with its not less queer named river Choptank, "from which they take abundance of shad and herring, and plenty of ague and fever" [p. 36], opens the book, for the simple reason that Douglass was born in this district. It is quite a gem. Here, too, we are introduced to a spectral personage known as "Old Master, whose name seemed ever to be mentioned with fear and shuddering" [p. 38], and whose mysterious existence and absolute power first touched the young spirit of Douglass with "the point of its cold cruel iron" [p. 39], and left him something to brood over after play and in moments of repose. As the narrative proceeds, the reader is introduced to other scenes and new personages, all sketched with singular felicity of expression, and probably with equal fidelity to nature. Those of the Reverend Rigby Hopkins, the principal feature of whose government was "his system of whipping slaves *in advance* of deserving it, as he said" [p. 162]; and Edward Covey, "the negro breaker," are equal to any thing in the way of portrait painting ever done by Dickens or Thackeray.[2] * * *

The manner in which the slave-boy picked up learning by the wayside is singularly illustrative of his intelligence, industry, and force of character. It was indeed "the pursuit of knowledge under difficulties;"[3] and the success which attended his efforts deserves to be specially recorded as another proof of the power of self-advancement which has been denied to the negro and the coloured man. An interesting episode in this phase of the writer's career is that which relates to his Baltimore mistress, Sophia Auld, who, in the simplicity and kindness of her heart, began by encouraging the lad's desire to acquire knowledge, but under the influence of the system, gradually awakening to the "danger" of having "larned niggers about the place," not only "set herself at last hard as a flint" against Douglass' learning to read by any means, but would herself fly into a terrible rage, and tear newspaper, book, or scrap of paper out of his hands, whenever she saw him with such in his possession. Still, he bears her in affectionate remembrance on account of her many acts of kindness to him, and of what she would have been if the system had allowed her to follow the natural impulses of her warm heart.

We cannot, within the limits we can allot to a review, do anything like justice to *My Bondage and Freedom*, either as a literary composition or as a simple narrative of slave experience. We would gladly have minutely detailed the incidents of Douglass' life, from the period of his first troubles at Tuckahoe till he found himself a free

2. William Makepeace Thackeray (1811–1863), English writer. On Dickens, see note 3 on p. 253.
3. Referring to the 1830 book of that title, a collection of brief biographies of eminent men, by the Scottish writer George Lillie Craik (1798–1866).

man in New York, and we would in like manner have dwelt upon the subsequent phases of his history to the present time. This, however, our limited space precludes us from doing. We have been particularly interested in those portions of the narrative which embrace his labours in the anti-slavery field, both in the United States and in this country. In them are set forth the circumstances under which he became an agent of the *American Anti-Slavery Society*,[4] and the reasons which influenced him, on his return from England, to make an attempt to establish a newspaper that should be the organ of the coloured people; an enterprise that appears to have led to his severing himself from his former colleagues. He also gives, in a few pithy sentences, an account of the radical change which, about four years ago, took place in his opinions on the subject of the Constitution and non-voting under it, and which now placed him in opposition to those with whom he had been theretofore in agreement. This change, he informs the reader, was brought about by the responsibilities of his new position as an Editor, which imposed upon him the necessity of giving reasons for his views. Hence he was "compelled to re-think the whole subject, and to study, with some care, not only the just and proper rules of legal interpretation, but the origin, design, nature, rights, powers, and duties of civil government, and also the relations which human beings sustain to it" [p. 244]. * * *

Whether right or wrong in the conclusion to which he came, namely; that the Constitution is not a pro-slavery instrument, no one can doubt that his convictions were likely, under such circumstances, to be sincere. From this time he is found urging them with the same zeal, energy, and ability, which distinguished his advocacy of the opposite views whilst he was attached to the *American Anti-Slavery Society.*

F. Douglass' idea of establishing a paper devoted to the interests of the enslaved and oppressed, did not find favour in the eyes of his Boston friends and former colleagues; but he felt so strongly the necessity of disproving the inferiority of his "people," and of demonstrating their capacity for a more exalted civilization than slavery and prejudice had assigned to them, that he resolved to persevere in his new project, notwithstanding the offence he knew he should give to his old friends in Boston, "by what seemed to them a reckless disregard of their sage advice" [p. 242]. * * *

* * *

We have marked for extract several passages in this interesting book, which we shall give in our columns, from time to time, under

4. See note 7 on p. 23.

appropriate heads. Meanwhile we recommend *My Bondage and Freedom* as a work that will repay an attentive perusal, not only on account of its revelations of the inner life of slavery, but as a reflex of the mind of the extraordinary man who has attained his present eminence by the force of his genius and the vigour and energy of his character.

We cannot close our notice of this book without a passing reference to the manly letter from F. Douglass to Dr. J. McCune Smith, in which he states his reasons for yielding to the earnest solicitations of his friend, and writing his own biography. The introductory chapter by Dr. McCune Smith is also extremely able as an exposition of Douglass' peculiar mental qualities, and as a history of their development under circumstances of extraordinary difficulties and dangers.

OTTILIE ASSING

Preface to the German Translation of *My Bondage and My Freedom*†

Ottilie Davida Assing (1819–1884) was a German American feminist, freethinker, and journalist. She first met Douglass in 1856, when she traveled from her home in New York City to his office, in Rochester, New York. There, Douglass wrote for and edited his newspaper, *Frederick Douglass' Paper*. At this meeting, Douglass gave his approval for Assing's planned translation of *My Bondage and My Freedom*, which she completed in 1858 and published in 1860.

Were this life story fiction, artistic invention, one would have to deplore that it was not published a few years earlier, before the interest in such narratives had been exhausted by the almost countless representations of slave life that now, since the publication of the famous *Uncle Tom*,[1] have developed into a whole new branch of literature. Yet the present work is not an invention but a true history, a series of naked, unadorned, terrible facts that are far more effective, moving, and convincing for those who can stand the truth than any work of fiction, because they represent reality and all of its consequences. Instead of an imagined hero, it is the author himself who is at the center of this narrative: he actually lived these

---

† From *Radical Passion: Ottilie Assing's Reports from America and Letters to Frederick Douglass*, ed. and trans. Christoph Lohmann (New York: Peter Lang, 1999), pp. 68–70. Reprinted by permission of the Estate of Christoph Lohmann. Notes are by the editors of this Norton Critical Edition; Lohmann's notes have been omitted.
1. See p. 331.

experiences, and he is now living among us, one of America's famous men. He belongs to that oppressed race—the pariahs of American society—who, because of a decision by the United States Supreme Court last year,[2] are forever barred from becoming citizens of their own country and have no rights that any white person is bound to respect. It is the whole human being—the noble self, the passionate, spirited, gifted, and dynamic man, with his burning love of freedom and the virtuosity of his implacable hatred of slavery and slave masters—who steps from these pages in his irresistible attractiveness and distinction to meet the reader. In the northern United States his autobiography was an overwhelming success, far beyond all expectations. Since 1855, the year when it first appeared, no fewer than 20,000 copies have been issued, even though slavery is the subject of countless daily discussions and controversies in all the papers, causing the reading public to pay attention only to the most outstanding and significant writings on this subject.

The story of the author's life is the most faithful expression of his individuality and therefore needs no further explanation. The reader will get to know all his qualities in the course of this book, except for his brilliance as an orator, which is the basis of his current renown. In this country of great orators Frederick Douglass is one of the greatest. Perfect mastery of the subject, incisive and brilliant logic, and controlled moderation despite all passion are his hallmark. He often soars to tragic heights but then illuminates his subject with brilliant flashes of wit, speaks to the listener's heart, or provides comic relief with a joke. Everything is fresh, original, and compelling, and all these attributes are underscored by a perfect mastery of language and by so mellifluous, sonorous, flexible a voice speaking to the heart as I have ever heard. His abundant intellect and originality are evident in the fact that, even while all the great speakers of this country have also been exploiting the subject, he has been treating it for seventeen years without becoming repetitious or stale. The circumstances that served him well at his first appearance—a time when a fugitive slave was rarely seen on the platform and he had the advantage of novelty—no longer obtain; nevertheless, his success and his influence are still rising. In every town and village of the northern United States the mere announcement of his name is enough to fill the halls to the last remaining seat. Although he addresses it every year, I have even seen the demanding public of New York thrilled and swept away by him as if a new apostle had

---

2. In *Dred Scott v. Sanborn* (1857), the Supreme Court ruled that African Americans were not and could not become citizens of the United States, and that the Missouri Compromise of 1820, which had greatly limited the expansion of slavery, was unconstitutional.

revealed to them for the first time a truth that had lain unspoken in everyone's heart.

Two years ago, I first became acquainted with Frederick Douglass on a visit to Rochester,[3] and I present the following excerpt from the sketch I wrote after that first meeting. All I have to add is that that first positive impression has only been confirmed and strengthened upon further acquaintance.

"At first I went to meet Frederick Douglass in his newspaper office, which is marked by a sign in large letters above the entrance: THE NORTH STAR OFFICE. It refers to the familiar symbol among fugitive slaves, who often have the north star as their only guide as they flee and are transported by the hundreds on the so-called underground railroad[4] from Rochester to Canada. As I did not find him there, I went to his home, about a half hour outside the city. The handsome villa, surrounded by a large garden, is situated on a hill overlooking a charming landscape. Douglass is a rather light mulatto of unusually tall, slender, and powerful stature. His features are striking: the prominently domed forehead with a peculiarly deep cleft at the base of the nose, an aquiline nose, and the narrow, beautifully carved lips betray more of his white than his black origin. The thick hair, here and there with touches of gray, is frizzy and unruly but not woolly. His whole appearance, stamped by past storms and struggles, bespeaks great energy and will power that shuns no obstacle and has been the sole source of his success in reaching his present prominence in the face of all odds. One can easily see how, when little more than a boy, he stood up to his master (who wanted to beat him) and actually cowed him—as he relates in his autobiography; or, when working in the shipyard at Baltimore and finding that the white workers refused to tolerate him, he lifted up his most ardent opponent and tossed him into the water. Despite all the vicissitudes, his whole being expresses a richly endowed, original, happily mature nature. Everything about him is fresh, genuine, true, and good. Endowed with an exceptional talent for conversation, he knows how to inspire and elevate others, and in conversation proves to be cheerful, animated, witty, and knowledgeable. Glowing with passion for the cause to which he has dedicated his life, he is far too wide-ranging in his interests as not to engage other worthy causes with energy. We touched upon a wide variety of things—large and small, general and personal—in the course of our conversation, and everywhere I encountered understanding and sympathy.— Douglass's wife is completely black, and his five children, therefore, have more of the traits of the Negro than he."

3. See note 3 on p. 334.
4. See note 4 on p. 199.

If Frederick Douglass were white, with his talent, endurance, and energy he would have had a brilliant career and achieved some distinguished position despite his humble origins. But as a mulatto— even though he is a famous man whose speeches attract large and eager crowds, whose importance and influence no one can gainsay, a man who belongs to the true elite of society, a man of intellect, personal amiability, and the purest character—he is excluded from any public office and from what is generally called good society. All the greater is the respect and love he enjoys among the friends of the emancipation of the slaves. It is no exaggeration of his accomplishments and the influence of his personality to attribute to him much of the change in public opinion in favor of the colored population that has occurred in the North for a number of years and is making slow but noticeable progress.

May this biography contribute to heighten the interest in the representatives and the cause of a race that, under a so-called republican form of government, has been subjected to a system of oppression whose cruelty has hardly been paralleled in the history of all peoples and countries.

WILLIAM WELLS BROWN
["Eloquent Fugitive"]†

THE career of the distinguished individual whose name heads this page is more widely known than that of any other living colored man, except, perhaps, Alexandre Dumas.[1] The narrative of his life, published in 1845, gave a new impetus to the black man's literature. All other stories of fugitive slaves faded away before the beautifully written, highly descriptive, and thrilling memoir of Frederick Douglass. Other narratives had only brought before the public a few heart-rending scenes connected with the person described. But Mr. Douglass, in his book, brought not only his old master's farm and its occupants before the reader, but the entire country around him, including Baltimore and its ship yard. The manner in which he obtained his education, and especially his learning to write, has been read and re-read by thousands in both hemispheres. His escape from slavery is too well understood to need a recapitulation here. He took up his residence in New Bedford, where he still continued the

---

† From *The Black Man: His Antecedents, His Genius, and His Achievements* (New York: Thomas Hamilton, 1863), pp. 180–87. Notes are by the editors of this Norton Critical Edition.
1. See note 7 on p. 32.

assiduous student—mastering the different branches of education which the accursed institution had deprived him of in early life.

His advent as a lecturer was a remarkable one. White men and black men had talked against slavery, but none had ever spoken like Frederick Douglass. Throughout the north the newspapers were filled with the sayings of the "eloquent fugitive." He often travelled with others, but they were all lost sight of in the eagerness to hear Douglass. His travelling companions would sometimes get angry, and would speak first at the meetings; then they would take the last turn; but it was all the same—the fugitive's impression was the one left upon the mind. He made more persons angry, and pleased more, than any other man. He was praised, and he was censured. He made them laugh, he made them weep, and he made them swear. His "Slaveholder's Sermon" was always a trump card. He awakened an interest in the hearts of thousands who before were dead to the slave and his condition. Many kept away from his lectures, fearing lest they should be converted against their will. Young men and women, in those days of pro-slavery hatred, would return to their fathers' roofs filled with admiration for the "runaway slave," and would be rebuked by hearing the old ones grumble out, "You'd better stay at home and study your lessons, and not be running after the nigger meetings."

In 1841, he was induced to accept an agency as a lecturer for the Anti-slavery Society,[2] and at once became one of the most valuable of its advocates. He visited England in 1845. There he was kindly received, and heartily welcomed; and after going through the length and breadth of the land, and addressing public meetings out of number on behalf of his countrymen in chains, with a power of eloquence which captivated his auditors, and brought the cause which he pleaded home to their hearts, he returned home and commenced the publication of the *North Star*, a weekly newspaper devoted to the advocacy of the cause of freedom.

Mr. Douglass is tall and well made. His vast and fully-developed forehead shows at once that he is a superior man intellectually. He is polished in his language, and gentlemanly in his manners. His voice is full and sonorous. His attitude is dignified, and his gesticulation is full of noble simplicity. He is a man of lofty reason; natural, and without pretension; always master of himself; brilliant in the art of exposing and abstracting. Few persons can handle a subject, with which they are familiar, better than he. There is a kind of eloquence issuing from the depth of the soul as from a spring, rolling along its copious floods, sweeping all before it, overwhelming by its very force, carrying, upsetting, ingulfing its adversaries, and more

2. See note 7 on p. 23.

dazzling and more thundering than the bolt which leaps from crag to crag. This is the eloquence of Frederick Douglass. One of the best mimics of the age, and possessing great dramatic powers, had he taken up the sock and buskin, instead of becoming a lecturer, he would have made as fine a Coriolanus[3] as ever trod the stage.

In his splendidly conceived comparison of Mr. Douglass to S. R. Ward, written for the "Autographs for Freedom," Professor William J. Wilson[4] says of the former, "In his very look, his gesture, his whole manner, there is so much of genuine, earnest eloquence, that they leave no time for reflection. Now you are reminded of one rushing down some fearful steep, bidding you follow; now on some delightful stream, still beckoning you onward. In either case, no matter what your prepossessions or oppositions, you, for the moment at least, forget the justness or unjustness of his cause, and obey the summons, and loath, if at all, you return to your former post. Not always, however, is he successful in retaining you. Giddy as you may be with the descent you have made, delighted as you are with the pleasure afforded, with the Elysium to which he has wafted you, you return too often dissatisfied with his and your own impetuosity and want of firmness. You feel that you had only a dream, a pastime,—not a reality.

"This great power of momentary captivation consists in his eloquence of manners, his just appreciation of words. In listening to him, your whole soul is fired, every nerve strung, every passion inflated, and every faculty you possess ready to perform at a moment's bidding. You stop not to ask why or wherefore. 'Tis a unison of mighty yet harmonious sounds that play upon your imagination; and you give yourself up, for a time, to their irresistible charm. At last, the *cataract* which roared around you is hushed, the *tornado* is passed, and you find yourself sitting upon a bank, (at whose base roll but tranquil waters,) quietly asking yourself why, amid such a display of power, no greater effect had really been produced. After all, it must be admitted there is a power in Mr. Douglass rarely to be found in any other man."

As a speaker, Frederick Douglass has had more imitators than almost any other American, save, perhaps, Wendell Phillips.[5] Unlike most great speakers, he is a superior writer also. Some of his articles, in point of ability, will rank with any thing ever written for the American press. He has taken lessons from the best of teachers,

3. Title character in Shakespeare's tragedy. "Taken up . . . buskin": become an actor, the sock and buskin being ancient symbols of comedy and tragedy, respectively.
4. Black activist and educator (1818–?) who, in the 1853 anthology of antislavery literature *Autographs for Freedom*, compared Douglass to Samuel Ringgold Ward (1817–c. 1866), a noted Black abolitionist who had escaped enslavement in Maryland.
5. See note 2 on p. 24.

amid the homeliest realities of life; hence the perpetual freshness of his delineations, which are never over-colored, never strained, never aiming at difficult or impossible effects, but which always read like living transcripts of experience. The following from his pen, on "What shall be done with the slaves, if emancipated?" is characteristic of his style.

"What shall be done with the four million slaves, if they are emancipated? This question has been answered, and can be answered in many ways. Primarily, it is a question less for man than for God—less for human intellect than for the laws of nature to solve. It assumes that nature has erred; that the law of liberty is a mistake; that freedom, though a natural want of the human soul, can only be enjoyed at the expense of human welfare, and that men are better off in slavery than they would or could be in freedom; that slavery is the natural order of human relations, and that liberty is an experiment. What shall be done with them?

"Our answer is, Do nothing with them; mind your business, and let them mind theirs. Your *doing* with them is their greatest misfortune. They have been undone by your doings, and all they now ask, and really have need of at your hands, is just to let them alone. They suffer by every interference, and succeed best by being let alone. The negro should have been let alone in Africa—let alone when the pirates and robbers offered him for sale in our Christian slave markets (more cruel and inhuman than the Mohammedan slave markets)—let alone by courts, judges, politicians, legislators, and slave-drivers—let alone altogether, and assured that they were thus to be let alone forever, and that they must now make their own way in the world, just the same as any and every other variety of the human family. As colored men, we only ask to be allowed to *do* with ourselves, subject only to the same great laws for the welfare of human society which apply to other men—Jews, Gentiles, Barbarian, Scythian. Let us stand upon our own legs, work with our own hands, and eat bread in the sweat of our own brows. When you, our white fellow-countrymen, have attempted to do any thing for us, it has generally been to deprive us of some right, power, or privilege, which you yourselves would die before you would submit to have taken from you. When the planters of the West Indies used to attempt to puzzle the pure-minded Wilberforce[6] with the question, 'How shall we get rid of slavery?' his simple answer was, 'Quit stealing.' In like manner we answer those who are perpetually puzzling their brains with questions as to what shall be done with the negro, 'Let him alone, and mind your own business.' If you see him

6. William Wilberforce (1759–1833), Englishman who became a leader of the English abolitionist movement.

ploughing in the open field, levelling the forest, at work with a spade, a rake, a hoe, a pickaxe, or a bill—let him alone; he has a right to work. If you see him on his way to school, with spelling-book, geography, and arithmetic in his hands—let him alone. Don't shut the door in his face, nor bolt your gates against him; he has a right to learn—let him alone. Don't pass laws to degrade him. If he has a ballot in his hand, and is on his way to the ballot-box to deposit his vote for the man who, he thinks, will most justly and wisely administer the government which has the power of life and death over him, as well as others—let him ALONE; his right of choice as much deserves respect and protection as your own. If you see him on his way to church, exercising religious liberty in accordance with this or that religious persuasion—let him alone. Don't meddle with him, nor trouble yourselves with any questions as to what shall be done with him.

"What shall be done with the negro, if emancipated? Deal justly with him. He is a human being, capable of judging between good and evil, right and wrong, liberty and slavery, and is as much a subject of law as any other man; therefore, deal justly with him. He is, like other men, sensible of the motives of reward and punishment. Give him wages for his work, and let hunger pinch him if he don't work. He knows the difference between fulness and famine, plenty and scarcity. 'But will he work?' Why should he not? He is used to it, and is not afraid of it. His hands are already hardened by toil, and he has no dreams of ever getting a living by any other means than by hard work. 'But would you turn them all loose?' Certainly! We are no better than our Creator. He has turned them loose, and why should not we? 'But would you let them all stay here?' Why not? What better is *here* than *there*? Will they occupy more room as freemen than as slaves? Is the presence of a black freeman less agreeable than that of a black slave? Is an object of your injustice and cruelty a more ungrateful sight than one of your justice and benevolence? You have borne the one more than two hundred years—can't you bear the other long enough to try the experiment?"

JAMES MONROE GREGORY

["His Style Is Peculiarly His Own"][†]

Chapter VIII

AS ORATOR AND WRITER

By whatever standard judged Mr. Douglass will take high rank as orator and writer. It may be truly said of him that he was born an orator; and, though he is a man of superior intellectual faculties, he has not relied on his natural powers alone for success in this his chosen vocation. He is called a self-made man, but few college bred men have been more diligent students of logic, of rhetoric, of politics, of history, and general literature than he. He belongs to that class of orators of which Fox of England and Henry and Clay[1] in our own country are the most illustrious representatives. His style, however, is peculiarly his own.

Cicero[2] says, "The best orator is he that so speaks as to instruct, to delight, and to move the mind of his hearers." Mr. Douglass is a striking example of this definition. Few men equal him in his power over an audience. He possesses wit and pathos, two qualities which characterized Cicero and which, in the opinion of the rhetorician Quintilian, gave the Roman orator great advantage over Demosthenes.[3] Judge Ruffin of Boston, in his introduction to Mr. Douglass' autobiography,[4] says: "Douglass is brimful of humor,—at times of the driest kind; it is of a quaint kind; you can see it coming a long way off in a peculiar twitch of his mouth; it increases and broadens gradually until it becomes irresistible and all-pervading with his audience." The humor of Mr. Douglass is much like that of Mr. Joseph Jefferson,[5] the great actor, who never makes an effort to be funny, but his humor is of the quiet, suppressed type. Like Mr. Jefferson, now he excites those emotions which cause tears, and now he stirs up those which produce laughter. Grief and mirth may be said to reside in adjoining apartments in the same edifice, and the passing from one apartment to the other is not a difficult thing to do.

[†] From *Frederick Douglass the Orator* (Springfield, MA: Willey Company, 1893; rpt. 1969), pp. 89–96, 99–101. Notes are by the editors of this Norton Critical Edition.

1. George Fox (1624–1691), English preacher and founder of the Religious Society of Friends (Quakers). On Patrick Henry, see note 8 on p. 176. On Henry Clay, see note 1 on p. 349.

2. Marcus Tullius Cicero (106–43 BCE), Roman statesman, author, and orator.

3. The most famous orator of ancient Greece (384–322 BCE). Quintilian: Marcus Fabius Quintilianus (c. 35–100 CE), influential Roman rhetorician.

4. George Lewis Ruffin (1834–1886), an African American attorney, judge, and politician, provided the introduction to *The Life and Times of Frederick Douglass* (1881).

5. Well-known American actor and comedian (1829–1905).

The biographer of Webster[6] gives the following amusing anecdote to show the simplicity of expressing thought for which that Colossus of American intellect is distinguished in his speeches: "On the arrival of that singular genius, David Crockett,[7] at Washington, he had an opportunity of hearing Mr. Webster. A short time afterwards he met him and abruptly accosted him as follows: 'Is this Mr. Webster?' 'Yes, sir.' 'The great Mr. Webster of Massachusetts?' continued he, with a significant tone. 'I am Mr. Webster of Massachusetts,' was the calm reply. 'Well, sir,' continued the eccentric Crockett, 'I had heard that you were a great man, but I don't think so; I heard your speech and *understood every word you said.*'"

President Lincoln gave this reply to the question asked, to what secret he owed his success in public debate: "I always assume that my audiences are in many things wiser than I am, and I say the most sensible things I can to them. I never found that they did not understand me."

The power of simple statement is one of the chief characteristics of Mr. Douglass' style of speaking, and in this respect he resembles Fox,[8] the great British statesman, who, above all his countrymen, was distinguished on account of plainness, and, as I may express it, homeliness of thought which gave him great power in persuading and moving his audience.

Mr. Douglass' influence in public speaking is due largely to the fact that he touches the hearts of his hearers—that he impresses them with the belief of his sincerity and earnestness. His heart is in what he says. "Clearness, force, and earnestness," says Webster, "are the qualities which produce conviction. True eloquence, indeed, does not consist in speech; it cannot be brought from far; labor and learning may toil for it, but they will toil for it in vain. Words and phrases may be marshaled in every way, but they cannot compass it; it must exist in the man, in the subject, and in the occasion."

There have been those of brilliant minds who have gained some reputation as speakers; they have been successful in pleasing and amusing those they addressed, but their success stopped here. They could not reach the depths of the heart, because their own hearts were not touched. The poet Horace[9] admirably enforces this thought when he says: "If you wish me to weep, you must first yourself be deeply grieved."

But to be fully appreciated, Mr. Douglass must be seen and heard. This was also true of Henry Clay. One could form but a faint conception of his eloquence and grandeur by reading his speeches, and

6. See note 4 on p. 295.
7. American frontiersman and politician, better known as Davy Crockett (1786–1836).
8. Charles James Fox (1749–1806).
9. Quintus Horatius Flaccus (65–8 BCE), Roman poet.

yet, as reported, they were both logical and argumentative. The fire and action of the man could not be transferred to paper. Mr. Douglass in speaking does not make many gestures, but those he uses are natural and spontaneous. His manner is simple and graceful, and there is nothing about his style artificial or declamatory. Much of an orator's success depends upon his delivery. The younger Pitt[1] said that he could not discover where lay his father's eloquence by simply reading his speeches. It is related of Garrick[2] that he was asked by a clergyman why it was that he could produce greater effect by a recital of fiction than the clergy by the presentation of the most important truths. Garrick replied: "Because you speak truths as if they were fictions; we speak fictions as if they were truths."

Mr. Douglass, as an extemporaneous speaker, was much more impressive than he has been since he began to write out his speeches and deliver them from manuscript. He remarked to the writer one day that he thought he had made a mistake in thus writing out his lectures; he imbibed the idea that his extemporaneous speeches would be defective and subject him to criticism. He had by so doing lost much power in delivery. "For," said he, "I never was a good reader." The first address he wrote out in full was the paper before the Western Reserve College[3] in 1854. Ever since his return from England in 1860 he has steadily followed the habit of writing what he has to say and reading from manuscript. His former style is what we call extemporaneous, but we do not wish to convey the idea that he spoke without preparation. On the contrary, he gave much thought to the topics which he intended to discuss, and then prepared notes under the different divisions of his subject. By not being confined to his manuscript, he caught the inspiration of his audience. This inspiration, so essential to true eloquence in the orator, can never be secured by the essayist, however finished and perfect he may be.

While Mr. Douglass may have lost much of his eloquence in using manuscript, yet some important advantages have resulted from this practice. He was led to investigate more extensively the subjects on which he wrote, and to take more time for preparation; and thus made his speeches more complete. Formerly, many of his best extemporaneous efforts were never fully reported, and consequently much that he said has been lost. His later lectures and speeches have been preserved in manuscript form, and when published together,

---

1. William Pitt (1759–1806), English statesman, two-time prime minister, and son of the statesman William Pitt the Elder (1708–1778).
2. David Garrick (1717–1779), famous English actor and playwright.
3. Established in Hudson, Ohio, in 1826, and one of the first colleges in the state to admit African Americans.

as they will be one day, will prove a valuable contribution to literature.

Some of his best lectures are The Mission of the War, The Sources of Danger to the Republic, Self-made Men, Recollections of the Anti-slavery Contest, William the Silent, Santo Domingo, The National Capital, Abraham Lincoln, John Brown.

The discourses of Mr. Douglass when reviewed, will bear the test of criticism, and will be found to contain the requisites of a correct and finished style. His language is pure, his words are choice, and in accordance with the best usage. His sentences are constructed in the English idiom, and have the elements of strength because preference is given in their formation to short Anglo-Saxon words, rather than to those derived from Latin and Greek. So carefully is the rule of propriety observed by him that one would think he had thoroughly mastered the principles of grammar and rhetoric under the most competent instructors. From the discrimination he uses in the selection of words to express the idea he wishes to convey, we conclude he must have been for many years a diligent student of the dictionary. His writings are remarkably free from obscurity and affectation, which Macaulay[4] regards as "the two greatest faults in style," and they may, therefore, be taken as models of perspicuity, so essential to one who would become eminent as an essayist. This excellence to which we allude, is due, no doubt, to the fact that he first forms clear and distinct conceptions of the truth he wishes to illustrate, and then making use of simple language to express the ideas arranged in his mind in logical order, writes freely as if under inspiration. Since he has followed the practice of writing his speeches his style has become more argumentative and massive, similar to that of Webster and Burke.[5] In all he says, like these great masters, whom none have surpassed, there is so much beauty of expression, elegance of diction, dignity of thought, and elevation of moral feeling that the most happy and lasting effect is produced upon the mind of the reader.

In the preparation of his speeches and addresses, Mr. Douglass at times requires greater privacy than his library affords, where he is liable to interruption by members of his household and visitors. In order that he may wholly give his attention to the literary work which he has in hand, he retires to his "den," as he calls it, a small, one-room building, situated in the rear of his dwelling, and used by former owners as a storehouse, but now with certain interior

4. Thomas Babington Macaulay (1800–1859), English historian and statesman.
5. Edmund Burke (1729–1797), Irish-born British statesman, writer, philosopher, and orator.

alterations made into a cozy study. It is a pleasant retreat in summer, for it is protected from the heat of the sun by trees and vines, and in winter is made comfortable by a glowing fire in the old-fashioned fireplace found within. The study is furnished simply with a lounge, a high desk, and a stool. It is the practice of Mr. Douglass to write standing, when in this room, where he will remain for hours at a time, denying himself to all visitors. While composing, he thinks accurately and correctly, and on this account his composition requires but little correction. His manuscript is always neat, not marred by erasures and alterations. We mention this fact because it proves that correct writing is the result of care exercised by the writer in the beginning, which in time becomes a fixed habit.

* * *

Mr. Douglass in December, 1841, made an anti-slavery speech in Providence, Rhode Island. This speech * * * was never written out or fully reported. We give the account of it as furnished by that elegant writer, N. P. Rogers.[6]

"Friday evening was chiefly occupied by colored speakers. The fugitive Douglass was up when we entered. This is an extraordinary man. He was cut out for a hero. In a rising for liberty he would have been a Toussaint or a Hamilton.[7] He has the 'heart to conceive, the head to contrive, and the hand to execute!' A commanding person— over six feet, we should say, in height, and of most manly proportions. His head would strike a phrenologist amid a sea of them in Exeter Hall, and his voice would ring like a trumpet in the field. Let the South congratulate herself that he is a fugitive. It would not have been safe for her if he had remained about the plantations a year or two longer. Douglass is his fugitive name. He did not wear it in slavery. We do not know why he assumed it, or who bestowed it on him, but there is some fitness in it, to his commanding figure and heroic part. As a speaker he has few equals. It is not declamation, but oratory, power of debate. He watches the tide of discussion with the eye of the veteran, and dashes into it at once with all the tact of the forum or the bar. He has wit, argument, sarcasm, pathos—all that first-rate men show in their master efforts. His voice is highly melodious and rich, and his enunciation quite elegant, and yet he has been but two or three years out of the house of bondage. We noticed that he had strikingly improved, since we heard him at Dover in September. We say this much of him, for he is esteemed by our

6. Nathaniel Peabody Rogers (1797–1846), abolitionist and editor of the antislavery newspaper *Herald of Freedom*.
7. Alexander Hamilton (1755 or 1757–1804), American revolutionary and statesman. On Toussaint, see note 7 on p. 348.

multitude as of an inferior race. We should like to see him before any New England legislature or bar, and let him feel the freedom of the anti-slavery meeting, and see what would become of his inferiority. Yet he is a thing, in American estimate. He is the chattel of some pale-faced tyrant. How his owner would cower and shiver to hear him thunder in an anti-slavery hall! How he would shrink away, with his infernal whip, from his flaming eye when kindled with anti-slavery emotion! And the brotherhood of thieves, the *posse comitatus* of divines, we wish a hecatomb or two of the proudest and flintiest of them were obliged to hear him thunder for human liberty and lay the enslavement of his people at their doors. They would tremble like Belshazzar."

* * *

FREDERIC MAY HOLLAND

["Rather a Rare Book"]†

* * *

His most important publication previous to 1882 was the enlarged edition of the "Narrative," which appeared in 1855, under the title "My Bondage and My Freedom," with an Introduction by Dr. James M'Cune Smith. There is a portrait, taken from a daguerreotype, and showing much sterner features than those which usher in the volumes of 1845 and 1882. The signature below indicates that his handwriting had become less delicate and feminine than it was ten years before, and had acquired its present manly vigor. The dedication is to Gerrit Smith. The preface by Garrison, which had appeared in 1845, is omitted, with the letter from Phillips[1] and the appendix about religion. The publishers were Miller, Orton, and Mulligan, in New York and Auburn; the volume contains nearly five hundred pages, including the Introduction and appendix; and the latter gives extracts from seven speeches, and also a letter to Thomas Auld. The account in the "Narrative," of the author's life up to 1841, was rewritten, with frequent additions of graphic details, so as to be enlarged to a size almost three times as great as before, and to occupy about fifty per cent. more space in this version of 1855 than in that of 1882,

---

† From *Frederick Douglass: The Colored Orator* (New York: Funk & Wagnalls, 1895; rpt. 1970), pp. 241–50, 400. Notes are by the editors of this Norton Critical Edition. Bracketed page references are to this edition.

1. On Wendell Phillips, see note 2 on p. 24. On William Lloyd Garrison, see note 7 on p. 23.

which did not, I think, gain by abridgment. The period from 1841 to 1855 is given at much greater length in the version of 1882, however, than any part of it had ever been before; and described on the whole with greater vigor, although many characteristic passages have been omitted. This much has been said about "My Bondage and My Freedom," because it seems to have become rather a rare book, and its disappearance would be a great loss.

The most curious thing about this book is an opinion which was passed upon it by Garrison, and which is here quoted as an act of justice to those philanthropic people who differed from him. George Thompson[2] gave "My Bondage and My Freedom" a friendly notice in his own organ, but this led Garrison to write him a letter, part of which soon found its way into the "Liberator," for January 18, 1856. It is a protest against this "panegyric upon Frederick Douglass's new volume, 'My Bondage and My Freedom,' a volume remarkable, it is true, for its thrilling sketches of a slave's life and experience, and for the ability displayed in its pages, but which, in its second portion, is reeking with the virus of personal malignity towards Wendell Phillips, myself, and the old organizationists generally, and full of ingratitude and baseness towards as true and disinterested friends as any man ever yet had upon earth." The only pages which could possibly be referred to, acknowledge that he went to Rochester[3] "from motives of peace" [p. 243], say nothing about Phillips, speak of Garrison as "the known and distinguished advocate" [p. 243] of the non-voting principle, mention that "To abstain from voting was to refuse to exercise a legitimate and powerful means for abolishing slavery" [p. 243], and say, finally, "To those with whom I had been in agreement and sympathy, I was now in opposition. What they held to be a great and important truth, I now looked upon as a dangerous error. A very painful, and yet a very natural thing now happened. Those who could not see any honest reasons for changing their views, as I had done, could not easily see any such reasons for my change; and the common punishment of apostates was mine. The opinions first entertained were naturally derived, and honestly entertained; and I trust that my present opinions have the same title to respect" [p. 244]. If there is any "virus" in these words it is only such as has always been greatly needed for the inoculation of reformers.

I am not aware that Douglass ever spoke more severely of Garrison than in 1879, when he said this:[4]

2. See note 6 on p. 233.
3. City in New York State where Douglass lived 1843–72.
4. This block quote is from Douglass's "Speech on the Death of William Lloyd Garrison," delivered in Washington, D.C., on June 2, 1879. The president presiding was Robert Purvis (1810–1898), a wealthy mixed-race abolitionist.

"Massachusetts is a great State; she has done many great things; she has given to our country many scholars and statesmen, many poets and philosophers, many discoverers and inventors; but no son of hers has won for her a more enduring honor, or for himself a more enduring fame, than William Lloyd Garrison. No one of her sons has stamped his convictions in lines so clear, deep, and ineffaceable into the very life and future of the Republic. Of no man is it more true than of him—that being dead he yet speaketh. The lessons he taught fifty years ago from his garret in Boston are only yet half learned by the nation. His work will not stop at his grave. Our general has fallen; but his army will march on. His words of wisdom, justice, and truth will be echoed by the voices of the millions, till every jot and tittle of all his prophecies shall be fulfilled. Mr. President, this is not the time and place for a critical and accurate measurement of William Lloyd Garrison; but when it comes, no friend of his has need to fear the application to him of the severest test of honest and truthful criticism. He never refused to see, nor allow his readers to see, in the 'Liberator,' the worst that was thought, felt, and said of him. A candid examination of his character and his work in the world may disclose some things we would have had otherwise. Speaking for myself, I must frankly say I have sometimes thought him uncharitable to those who differed from him. Honest himself, he could not always see how men could differ from him and still be honest. To say this of him is simply to say that he was human; and it may be added that when he erred here, he erred in the interest of truth. He revolted at halfness, abhorred compromise, and demanded that men should be either hot or cold. This great quality of the man, though sometimes in excess, is one explanation of his wonderful and successful leadership. What it cost him in breadth and numbers, it gained him in condensation and intensity. He held his little band well in hand all the time, and close to his person; no leader was ever more loved by the circle about him. Absolute in his faith, no sect could proselyte him; inflexible in his principles, no party could use him; content with the little circle about him, he did not mingle directly and largely with the great masses of men. By one simple principle he tried all men, all parties, and all sects. They that were not for him, were against him. What his name stood for in the beginning, it stands for now, and will so stand forever. It is said that the wicked shall not live out half their days. This is true in more senses than one; for 'The coward and the small in soul scarce do live.'[5] Mr. Garrison lived out his whole existence. For to live is to battle; and he battled from first to last. Although he had reached a good

---

5. *Festus* (1839) 7.15, by the English poet Philip James Bailey (1816–1902).

old age, time had not dimmed his intellect, nor darkened his moral vision, nor quenched the ardor of his genius. His letter, published three weeks before his death, on the exodus from Mississippi and Louisiana,[6] had in it all the energy and fire of his youth. Men of three score and ten are apt to live in the past. It was not so with Mr. Garrison. He was during his latest years fully abreast with his times. No event or circumstance bearing upon the cause of justice and humanity escaped his intelligent observation. His letter written a few months ago upon the Chinese question[7] was a crowning utterance. It was in harmony with the guiding sentiment of his life, 'My country is the world; and all mankind are my countrymen.' With him it was not race or color, but humanity."[8]

One result of the publication of "My Bondage and My Freedom," was that a bookseller in Mobile,[9] who had been a slave-holder, bought not only a copy which had been ordered but two others to supply possible customers. A clergyman in the city heard of this, sent his son to buy the books, and stirred up such an excitement against the bookseller that he was glad to steal away in a little sail-boat.

While still busy with the composition of this work, its author was invited by the members of the Legislature to address them, in March, 1855, in the Assembly Chamber at Albany. There he denounced not only the Nebraska and Fugitive Slave Bills,[1] but also the indifference of the North to his people's wrongs. An eye-witness describes the rapt attention of the crowded audience for two hours and a half as the grandest scene he ever saw in the capital; and the Lieutenant-Governor said he would give twenty thousand dollars to be able to speak as powerfully. The May meeting of the A. A. S. S.[2] in New York gave the orator an opportunity to defend a proposition which he had already submitted to them in writing, namely that, "The Garrisonian views of disunion, if carried to a successful issue, would only place the people of the North in the same relation to American slavery which they now bear to the slavery of Cuba or Brazil." He defended this proposition on May 10, in reply to the assertion of another fugitive from slavery, that the Union was of no value to

6. The Exodus of 1879, or Exoduster Movement, refers to the mass migration of freedmen (emancipated slaves) from Southern states along the Mississippi River into Kansas, Oklahoma, and Colorado. Douglass publicly opposed it.
7. The late-nineteenth-century debate as to whether Chinese laborers should be permitted to immigrate to the United States culminated in the passage of the Chinese Exclusion Act of 1882, banning all immigration of Chinese laborers.
8. A quote from a letter by Garrison dated February 27, 1879.
9. City in Alabama.
1. See note 2 on p. 209. The Kansas-Nebraska Act (1854) allowed people residing in the Kansas and Nebraska Territories to decide whether to permit slavery within their borders. Albany is the capital of New York State.
2. The American Anti-Slavery Society.

colored people. Then, according to the "New York Daily News," "A grand and terrific set-to came off between Abby Kelley Foster,[3] Garrison, and Frederick Douglass, who defended the Union while claiming rights for his people. He was insulted, interrupted, and denounced by the Garrison Cabinet, but stood amid them and overtopped them like a giant among pigmies." One thing said against him was, that he had no more right to call himself anti-slavery, than a moderate drinker has to try to pass himself off for a friend of temperance.

Soon after this debate, he told the colored men, with whom he was holding a council to prepare for a national convention in October, that he knew that his plan of an industrial college[4] was opposed by some of the Abolitionist organs:

> "But if the colored people would ever arrive at a respectable place in society, they must do their own thinking. The colored people are now the 'sick man' of America; those who pretend to be their friends measure their places and pat them on the back; but when they step beyond that narrow place, their friends become villifiers and enemies."

On June 26, 27, 28, there was a convention in Syracuse[5] of men who had agreed, a year or two before, to call themselves Radical Political Abolitionists. The editor of "My Bondage and My Freedom," Dr. Smith, presided; and among other speakers were Douglass, Gerrit Smith, Lewis Tappan, and Rev. S. J. May.[6] Ten States were represented, besides New York and Canada. It was unanimously resolved that the members should do what they could to prevent the return of fugitives; but there was some difference of opinion in consequence of a proposal to raise money to enable John Brown, who was going out that fall to join his sons in Kansas, to take out a good supply of weapons. Douglass, who had known him well for eight years, spoke earnestly in his behalf; Tappan and others were unwilling to encourage violence; but as a letter recently received from Hayti says: "The collection was taken up with much spirit, nevertheless; for Captain Brown was present and spoke for himself; and when he spoke, men believed in the man."

The national colored convention came off, as proposed, in Philadelphia, and on the first day, October 16, there was an evident repugnance to the admission of the only delegate from Canada, Miss

---

3. Abby Foster Kelly (1811–1887) was an American abolitionist and women's rights activist.
4. See pp. 333–36 of this volume.
5. City in New York State.
6. On May, see note 5 on p. 28. Lewis Tappan (1788–1873) and his brother Arthur (1786–1865) were wealthy supporters of abolitionism.

Shadd. Her sex was so much against her that Remond[7] thought it best to make a compromise, which would give her a seat as a corresponding member. Douglass insisted on having this vote reconsidered; and his speech caused her to be recognized, by a majority vote, as a member in full standing. The "New York Tribune" had endorsed his plan for an industrial college as "the greatest and most comprehensive for elevating the colored race in this country yet proposed." Some members of the convention saw little need of such an institution, at a time when more than thirty per cent. of those of their brethren in the North who were trained in trades and professions were prevented, as Douglass himself had been, by the color prejudice from carrying them on. It was also urged that a college in one place would do little good at a distance; and much was said in favor of a mechanical bureau, which should employ teachers of special trades wherever such instruction might be demanded. There was also quite a controversy as to whether slavery could be abolished constitutionally; but here Douglass triumphed, with the aid of his friend, Dr. Smith, and his paper was formally acknowledged to be "our organ."

A long quotation has already been made from his pamphlet on "the Anti-Slavery Movement;" it also contains an expression of dissatisfaction with the newly organized Republican party, of which he says:

> "It aims to limit and denationalize slavery, and to relieve the Federal Government from all responsibility for slavery. Its motto is, 'Slavery, Local; Liberty, National.' The objection to this movement is the same as that against the American Anti-Slavery Society. It leaves the slave in his fetters, in the undisturbed possession of his master, and does not grapple with the question of emancipation in the States."

His own preference, in 1855, was for the Liberty party, which was "pledged to continue the struggle while a bondman in his chains remains to weep. Upon its platform must the great battle of freedom be fought out, if upon any short of the bloody field. It must be under no partial cry of 'No union with slave-holders,' nor selfish cry of 'No more slavery extension,' but it must be, 'No slavery for man under the whole heavens.'"

His opinion of the Republican party was fully justified in 1856, when its convention, at Philadelphia, adopted a platform which had nothing to say against the Fugitive Slave Bill, or in favor of

---

7. Charles Lenox Remond (1810–1873) was a Massachusetts-born orator and abolitionist. Mary Ann Shad (1823–1893), an African American educator, abolitionist, editor, and journalist, moved to Canada after the passage of the Fugitive Slave Act.

emancipation in the States; while its candidate, Fremont,[8] was selected with no more reference to his record as an Abolitionist than to his experience as a statesman. So far at least as the conventions of 1852 and 1856 could be compared, there was perfect truth in the statement of our editor in 1860: "The national conventions, held successively in Pittsburgh, Philadelphia, and Chicago, have formed a regular descent from the better utterances of 1848 at Buffalo." No colored man spoke at Philadelphia, and but little was said by Abolitionists. The candidates of the other parties, however, for President were Fillmore, who had signed the Fugitive Slave Bill, and Buchanan,[9] who was pledged to sustain it as well as to hinder Kansas from entering the Union as a Free State. Garrison acknowledged that if he could vote for any one, it would be for Fremont; and Douglass did all he could to elect him.

*   *   *

His whole life from first to last is heroic, in his steady determination to think for himself, and to speak what he thinks at any risk. His mistakes have been only errors in judgment; he has never been false to principle; and his mighty eloquence has poured forth freely in defense, not only of his own oppressed race, but of the disfranchised sex, of downtrodden Ireland, of the maltreated Chinese, and of dumb animals. Never has he called out tears, except for those who deserve pity, nor tried to make the poor and suffering appear ridiculous. His ability to recognize real reforms may not be as keen now as formerly; but he has never been deluded by visionary ones. After more than seventy years of trial and responsibility he is still hopeful and happy as a boy, and almost as active. Quickness of brain, kindness of heart, and richness of imagination characterize his familiar talk, as well as his speeches and books; and there are very few men whose conversation is so free from vulgarity or irritability, and so perfectly refined without any stiffness, dulness, or constraint. He is a gentleman in the fullest sense of the word; and it is very seldom that it can be applied so justly. The man is greater than the speeches and books.

*   *   *

8. John Charles Frémont (1813–1890), American explorer, general, and statesman; first Republican U.S. presidential candidate.
9. James Buchanan (1791–1868), a member of the Democratic Party, served as U.S. president 1857–61. Millard Fillmore (see note 4 on p. 290) was the 1856 candidate for the Know Nothing Party.

Recent Criticism

HENRY LOUIS GATES, Jr.

From Binary Oppositions in Chapter One of *Narrative of the Life of Frederick Douglass an American Slave Written by Himself* †

* * *

In the act of interpretation, we establish a sign relationship between the description and a meaning. The relations most crucial to structural analysis are functional binary oppositions. Roman Jakobson and Morris Halle argue in *Fundamentals of Language* that binary oppositions are inherent in all languages, that they are, indeed, a fundamental principle of language formation itself.[1] Many structuralists, seizing on Jakobson's formulation, hold the binary opposition to be a fundamental operation of the human mind, basic to the production of meaning. Levi-Strauss, who turned topsy-turvy the way we examine mythological discourse, describes the binary opposition as "this elementary logic which is the smallest common denominator of all thought."[2] Levi-Strauss' model of opposition and mediation, which sees the binary opposition as an underlying structural pattern as well as a method for revealing that pattern, has in its many variants become a most satisfying mechanism for retrieving almost primal social contradictions, long ago "resolved" in the

---

† From *Afro-American Literature: The Reconstruction of Instruction*, ed. Dexter Fisher and Robert B. Stepto (New York: Modern Language Association of America, 1979), pp. 212–32. Rpt. in *Critical Essays on Frederick Douglass*, ed. William L. Andrews (Boston: G. K. Hall & Co., 1991), pp. 85–87, 89–93. Reprinted by permission of the Modern Language Association.

    This groundbreaking essay was the first to use late-twentieth-century French theory to interpret African American literature. Gates drew on the work of several anthropologists and linguists who established that cultures, and languages in particular, structure our understanding of the world with binary terms taken to be opposites, such as up/down, good/evil, and raw/cooked. Roman Jakobson (1896–1982) was a Russian linguist and literary theorist; Morris Halle (1923–2008) was a Latvian-born American linguist; Claude Levi-Strauss (1908–2009) was a French anthropologist; Frederic Jameson (b. 1934) is an American literary critic.

1. Jakobson and Halle, *Fundamentals of Language* (The Hague: Mouton, 1971), pp. 4, 47–49.
2. [Claude Levi-Strauss], *Totemism* (New York: Penguin, 1969), p. 130.

mediated structure itself.[3] Perhaps it is not irresponsible or prema-
ture to call Levi-Strauss' contribution to human understanding a
classic one.

Frederic Jameson, in *The Prison-House of Language*, maintains
that

> the binary opposition is . . . at the outset a heuristic principle,
> that instrument of analysis on which the mythological herme-
> neutic is founded. We would ourselves be tempted to describe
> it as a technique for stimulating perception, when faced with a
> mass of apparently homogeneous data to which the mind and
> the eyes are numb: a way of forcing ourselves to perceive dif-
> ference and identity in a wholly new language the very sounds
> of which we cannot yet distinguish from each other. It is a
> decoding or deciphering device, or alternately a technique of
> language learning.

How does this "decoding device" work as a tool to practical criticism? When any two terms are set in opposition to each other the
reader is forced to explore qualitative similarities and differences,
to make some connection, and, therefore, to derive some meaning
from points of disjunction. If one opposes A to B, for instance, and
X to Y, the two cases become similar as long as each involves the
presence and absence of a given feature. In short, two terms are
brought together by some quality that they share and are then
opposed and made to signify the absence and presence of that quality. The relation between presence and absence, positive and negative signs, is the simplest form of the binary opposition. These
relations, Jameson concludes, "embody a tension 'in which one of

---

3. What has this rather "obvious" model of human thought to do with the study of mun-
dane literature generally and with the study of Afro-American literature specifically? It
has forced us to alter irrevocably certain long-held assumptions about the relation
between sign and referent, between signifier and signified. It has forced us to remember
that we must not always mean what we say; or to remember what queries we intended
to resolve when we first organized a discourse in a particular way. What's more, this
rather simple formulation has taught us to recognize texts where we find them and to
read these texts as they demand to be read. Yet, we keepers of the black critical activity
have yet to graft fifty years of systematic thinking about literature onto the consideration of our own. The study of Afro-American folklore, for instance, remains preoc-
cupied with unresolvable matters of genesis or with limitless catalogs and motif
indices. Afraid that Brer Rabbit is "merely" a trickster or that Anansi spiders merely
spin webs, we reduce these myths to their simplest thematic terms—the perennial
relation between the wily, persecuted black and the not-too-clever, persecuting white.
This reduction belies our own belief in the philosophical value of these mental constructs. We admit, albeit inadvertently, a nagging suspicion that these are the primitive
artifacts of childish minds, grappling with a complex Western world and its languages,
three thousand years and a world removed. These myths, as the slave narratives would,
did not so much "narrate" as they did convey a value system; they functioned, much
like a black sermon, as a single sign. The use of binary opposition, for instance, allows
us to perceive much deeper "meanings" than a simplistic racial symbolism allows.
Refusal to use sophisticated analysis on our own literature smacks of a symbolic inferiority complex as blatant as were treatments of skin lightener and hair straightener.

the two terms of the binary opposition is apprehended as positively having a certain feature while the other is apprehended as deprived of the feature in question.'"[4]

Frederick Douglass' *Narrative* attempts with painstaking verisimilitude to reproduce a system of signs that we have come to call plantation culture, from the initial paragraph of Chapter i:

> I was born in Tuckahoe, near Hillsborough, and about twelve miles from Easton, in Talbot County, Maryland. I have no accurate knowledge of my age, never having seen any authentic record containing it. By far the larger part of the slaves know as little of their ages as horses know of theirs, and it is the wish of most masters within my knowledge to keep their slaves thus ignorant. I do not remember to have ever met a slave who could tell of his birthday, they seldom come nearer to it than planting-time, harvest-time, cherry-time, spring-time, or fall-time. A want of information concerning my own was a source of unhappiness to me even during childhood. The white children could tell their ages. I could not tell why I ought to be deprived of the same privilege. I was not allowed to make any inquiries of my master concerning it. He deemed such inquiries on the part of a slave improper and impertinent, and evidence of a restless spirit. The nearest estimate I can give makes me now between twenty-seven and twenty-eight years of age. I come to this, from hearing my master say, some time during 1835, I was about seventeen years old.[5]

We see an ordering of the world based on a profoundly relational type of thinking, in which a strict barrier of difference or opposition forms the basis of a class rather than, as in other classification schemes, an ordering based on resemblances or the identity of two or more elements. In the text, we can say that these binary oppositions produce through separation the most inflexible of barriers: that of meaning. We, the readers, must exploit the oppositions and give them a place in a larger symbolic structure. Douglass' narrative strategy seems to be this: He brings together two terms in special relationships suggested by some quality that they share; then, by opposing two seemingly unrelated elements, such as the sheep, cattle, or horses on the plantation and the specimen of life known as slave, Douglass' language is made to signify the presence and

4. Frederic Jameson, *The Prison-House of Language: A Critical Account of Structuralism and Russian Formalism* (Princeton: Princeton Univ. Press, 1972), pp. 113; 35, citing [Nikolai] Troubetskoy's *Principes de phonologie*. See also Jonathan Culler, *Structuralist Poetics: Structuralism, Linguistics, and the Study of Literature* (Ithaca: Cornell Univ. Press, 1975), pp. 93, 225–27; Roland Barthes, *S/Z, An Essay*, trans. Richard Miller (New York: Hill and Wang, 1975), p. 24.
5. Frederick Douglass, *Narrative* (Boston: Anti-Slavery Office, 1845), p. 1. * * *

absence of some quality—in this case, humanity.[6] Douglass uses this device to explicate the slave's understanding of himself and of his relation to the world through the system of the perceptions that defined the world the planters made. Not only does his *Narrative* come to concern itself with two diametrically opposed notions of genesis, origins, and meaning itself, but its structure actually turns on an opposition between nature and culture as well. Finally and, for our purposes, crucially, Douglass' method of complex mediation— and the ironic reversals so peculiar to his text—suggests overwhelmingly the completely arbitrary relation between description and meaning, between signifier and signified, between sign and referent.

Douglass uses these oppositions to create a unity on a symbolic level, not only through physical opposition but also through an opposition of space and time. The *Narrative* begins "I was born in Tuckahoe, near Hillsborough, and about twelve miles from Easton, in Talbot County, Maryland." Douglass knows the physical circumstances of his birth: Tuckahoe, we know, is near Hillsborough and is twelve miles from Easton. Though his place of birth is fairly definite, his date of birth is not for him to know: "I have no accurate knowledge of my age," he admits, because "any authentic record containing it" would be in the possession of others. Indeed, this opposition, or counterpoint, between that which is *knowable* in the world of the slave and that which is *not*, abounds throughout this chapter. Already we know that the world of the master and the world of the slave are separated by an inflexible barrier of meaning. The knowledge the slave has of his circumstances he must deduce from the *earth*; a quantity such as time, our understanding of which is *cultural* and not *natural*, derives from a nonmaterial source, let us say the *heavens*: "The white children could tell their ages. I could not."

The deprivation of the means to tell the time is the very structural center of this initial paragraph: "A want of information concerning my own [birthday] was a source of unhappiness to me even during childhood." This state of disequilibrium motivates the slave's search for his humanity as well as Douglass' search for his text. This deprivation has created that gap in the slave's imagination between self and other, between black and white. What is more, it has

6. There is overwhelming textual evidence that Douglass was a consummate stylist who, contrary to popular myth, learned the craft of the essayist self-consciously. The importance of Caleb Bingham's *The Columbian Orator* (Boston: Manning and Loring, 1797) to Douglass' art is well established [see note 3 on p. 104]. John Blassingame is convinced of Douglass' use of Bingham's rhetorical advice in his writing, especially of antitheses. (Personal interview with John Blassingame, 7 May 1976.) For an estimation of the role of language in the political struggle of antebellum Blacks see Alexander Crummell, "The English Language in Liberia," in his *The Future of Africa* (New York: Scribners, 1862), pp. 9–57.

apparently created a relation of likeness between the slave and the animals. "By far," Douglass confesses, "the large part of slaves know as little of their ages as horses know of theirs." This deprivation is not accidental; it is systematic: "it is the wish of most masters within my knowledge to keep their slaves thus ignorant." Douglass, in his subtle juxtaposition here of "masters" and "knowledge" and of "slaves" and "ignorance," again introduces homologous terms. "I do not remember to have ever met a slave," Douglass emphasizes, "who could tell of his birthday." Slaves, he seems to conclude, are they who cannot plot their course by the linear progression of the calendar. Here, Douglass summarizes the symbolic code of this world, which makes the slave's closest blood relations the horses and which makes his very notion of time a cyclical one, diametrically opposed to the master's linear conception: "They [the slaves] seldom come nearer to [the notion of time] than planting-time, harvest-time, cherry-time, spring-time, or fall-time." The slave had arrived, but not *in time* to partake at the welcome table of human culture.

✻   ✻   ✻

Douglass' narrative demonstrates not only how the deprivation of the hallmarks of identity can affect the slave but also how the slave-owner's world negates and even perverts those very values on which it is built. Deprivation of a birth date, a name, a family structure, and legal rights makes of the deprived a brute, a subhuman, says Douglass, until he comes to a consciousness of these relations; yet, it is the human depriver who is the actual barbarian, structuring his existence on the consumption of human flesh. Just as the mulatto son is a mediation between two opposed terms, man and animal, so too has Douglass' text become the complex mediator between the world as the master would have it and the world as the slave knows it really is. Douglass has subverted the terms of the code he was meant to mediate: He has been a trickster. As with all mediations the trickster is a mediator and his mediation is a trick—only a trick; for there can be no mediation in this world. Douglass' narrative has aimed to destroy that symbolic code that created the false oppositions themselves. The oppositions, all along, were only arbitrary, not fixed.

Douglass first suggests that the symbolic code created in this text is arbitrary and not fixed, human-imposed not divinely ordained in an ironic aside on the myth of the curse of Ham,[7] which comes in the very center of the seventh paragraph of the narrative and which

---

7. Cf. Genesis 9.20–27. Although the myth has traditionally been called the curse of Ham, it is actually about a curse on Ham's son Canaan—by Ham's father, Noah—in response to some shameful act committed by Ham. In past centuries, some commentators interpreted black skin and slavery as results of the curse [Editors' note].

is meant to be an elaboration on the ramifications of "this class of slaves" who are the fruit of the unnatural liaison between animal and man. If the justification of this order is the curse on Ham and his tribe, if Ham's tribe signifies the black African, and if this prescription for enslavement is scriptural, then, Douglass argues, "it is certain that slavery at the south must soon become unscriptural; for thousands are ushered into the world, annually, who, like myself, owe their existence to white fathers, and those fathers," he repeats for the fourth time, are "most frequently their own masters."

* * *

Douglass has posited the completely arbitrary nature of the sign. The master's actions belie the metaphysical suppositions on which is based the order of his world: It is an order ostensibly imposed by the Father of Adam,[8] yet one in fact exposed by the sons of Ham. It is a world the oppositions of which have generated their own mediator, Douglass himself. This mulatto son, half-animal, half-man, writes a text (which is itself another mediation) in which he can expose the arbitrary nature of the signs found in this world, the very process necessary to the destruction of this world. "You have seen how a man was made a slave," Douglass writes at the structural center of his *Narrative*, "you shall see how a slave was made a man."[9] * * *

* * *

If we step outside the self-imposed confines of Chapter i to seek textual evidence, the case becomes even stronger. The opposition between culture and nature is clearly contained in a description of a slave meal, found in Chapter v.[1] "We were not regularly allowanced. Our food was coarse corn meal boiled. This was called *mush*. It was put into a large wooden tray or trough, and set down upon the ground. The children were then called, like so many pigs, and like so many pigs they would come and devour the mush; some with oyster-shells, others with pieces of shingle, some with naked hands, and none with spoons. He that ate fastest got most; he that was strongest secured the best place; and few left the trough satisfied." The slave, we read, did not eat food; he ate mush. He did not eat with a spoon; he ate with pieces of shingle, or on oyster shells, or with his naked hands. Again we see the obvious culture-nature opposition at play. When the slave, in another place, accepts the comparison with and identity of a "bad sheep," he again has inverted the terms,

8. I.e., by God [*Editors' note*].
9. Douglass, p. 77.
1. Douglass, p. 13–15.

supplied as always by the master, so that the unfavorable meaning that this has for the master is supplanted by the favorable meaning it has for the slave. There is in this world the planter has made, Douglass maintains, an ironic relation between appearance and reality. "Slaves sing most," he writes at the end of Chapter ii, "when they are most unhappy. . . . The singing of a man cast away upon a desolate island might be as appropriately considered as evidence of contentment and happiness, as the singing of a slave; the songs of the one and of the other are prompted by the same emotion."

Finally, Douglass concludes his second chapter with a discourse on the nature of interpretation, which we could perhaps call the first charting of the black hermeneutical circle and which we could take again as a declaration of the arbitrary relation between a sign and its referent, between the signifier and the signified. The slaves, he writes, "would compose and sing as they went along, consulting neither time nor tune. The thought that came up, came out—if not in the word, [then] in the sound;—and as frequently in the one as in the other."[2] Douglass describes here a certain convergence of perception peculiar only to members of a very specific culture: The thought could very well be embodied nonverbally, in the sound if not in the word. What is more, sound and sense could very well operate at odds to create through tension a dialectical relation. Douglass remarks: "They would sometimes sing the most pathetic sentiment in the most rapturous tone, and the most rapturous sentiment in the most pathetic tone. . . . They would thus sing as a chorus to words which to many would seem unmeaning jargon, but which, nevertheless, were full of meaning to themselves." Yet the decoding of these cryptic messages did not, as some of us have postulated, depend on some sort of mystical union with their texts. "I did not, when a slave," Douglass admits, "understand the deep meaning of those rude and apparently incoherent songs." "Meaning," on the contrary, came only with a certain aesthetic distance and an acceptance of the critical imperative. "I was myself within the circle," he concludes, "so that I neither saw nor heard as those without might see and hear." There exists always the danger, Douglass seems to say, that the meanings of nonlinguistic signs will seem "natural"; one must view them with a certain detachment to see that their meanings are in fact merely the "products" of a certain culture, the result of shared assumptions and conventions. Not only is meaning culture-bound and the referents of all signs an assigned relation, Douglass tells us, but *how* we read determines *what* we read, in the truest sense of the hermeneutical circle.

2. Douglass, p. 30.

WILLIAM L. ANDREWS

[Neither Individualism nor Authoritarianism]†

* * *

The *Narrative of the Life of Frederick Douglass* is one of the most remarkable success stories in the history of American autobiography. Without sounding self-congratulatory, the former slave made himself into an exemplar of Romantic individualism, to which transcendentalists like Theodore Parker and Margaret Fuller paid tribute in their reviews of his book.[1] In many respects Douglass's slave narrative represents the culmination of a major tradition in antebellum black autobiography that celebrated the lives of those who had fled the alien status of slave and had made a place for themselves in freedom as "a man and a brother," in the words of a famous antislavery motto. As he wrote his narrative, Douglass was determined to show not just that he had raised himself out of slavery but that he had rapidly been assimilated into the white world of the North, where he had attained a position of respect and influence in the antislavery movement. Among the Garrisonian abolitionists he had come into his own, had "found himself" in a crucial sense, for it was they who had shown him the way to the freedom that climaxes the *Narrative*, the liberation of his voice and with it the discovery of his vocation as an antislavery orator. Thus, when Douglass concluded his first autobiography in 1845, he pictured himself as a man secure in his life's mission. The pattern of his life story assumes the tripartite structure of the classic rites of passage that inform the process by which an individual negotiates crises in life in order to move from one status to another. Douglass's resistance to his status as a slave and his flight from it constitute a rite of separation; his experience as a lonely, displaced fugitive in the North corresponds to a rite of transition; as he achieves status and recognition in the North within the abolitionist movement, he undergoes a rite of incorporation.[2] Nothing at the end of the *Narrative* prepares us to see Douglass as

---

† From "Frederick Douglass," *My Bondage and My Freedom*, ed. William L. Andrews (Urbana: U of Illinois P, 1987), pp. xi–xxviii. Rpt. in *Critical Essays on Frederick Douglass*, ed. William L. Andrews (Boston: G. K. Hall & Co., 1991), pp. 136–47. Copyright 1987 by the Board of Trustees of the University of Illinois. Reprinted by permission of the University of Illinois. Bracketed page references are to this Norton Critical Edition.

1. See Parker's speech, "The American Scholar," in George Willis Cooke, ed., *The American Scholar*, vol. 8 of *Centenary Edition of Theodore Parker's Writings* (Boston: American Unitarian Association, 1907), p. 37. Margaret Fuller's review of Douglass's *Narrative* for the *New York Tribune* of June 10, 1845, is reprinted in Bell Gale Chevigny, *The Woman and the Myth: Margaret Fuller's Life and Writings* (Old Westbury, N.Y.: Feminist Press, 1976), pp. 340–42.

2. Arnold van Gennep, *The Rites of Passage*, trans. Monika B. Vizedom and Gabrielle L. Caffee (1909; Chicago: University of Chicago Press, 1960), pp. 11, 21.

a man who still had a great lesson in irony to learn, namely, as he observed in *My Bondage and My Freedom*, that for him "the settling of one difficulty only opened the way for another" [p. 224].

During the decade between his two autobiographies, Douglass was forced by a series of unexpected reversals in his life to take fresh stock intellectually, to rethink the significance of key concepts like bondage and freedom in light of his widening experience as a freeman. This process began in Great Britain during a twenty-one-month speaking tour on which Douglass had embarked after publication of the *Narrative* forced him to flee America for his safety. England's hearty welcome to the fugitive slave caused him in a letter to Garrison on New Year's Day, 1846, to question seriously all his "prejudices in favor of America." The "outcast" perspective that he had been forced to assume convinced him that throughout the United States, "all is cursed with the infernal spirit of slaveholding." Douglass's *Narrative* had been notably quiet on the topic of racism in the North, but his letter to Garrison exploded in a series of humiliating episodes in Massachusetts when he was refused admission to popular entertainments, public conveyances, a worship service, and an eating establishment, in each case because, in language Douglass attributed to his antagonists, "'*We don't allow niggers in here!*'" When he wrote *My Bondage and My Freedom*, Douglass made sure that this scathing denunciation of American bigotry was reprinted prominently and in full.

After his return from England in the spring of 1847, Douglass's decisions placed him increasingly at odds with Garrison and the ideology of the American Anti-Slavery Society. Against Garrison's counsel his black protégé undertook a new career as an independent antislavery journalist, launching the weekly *North Star* in Rochester, New York, on December 3, 1847.[3] Writing editorial defenses of his antislavery positions required Douglass to reexamine the principles of Garrisonianism, the effect of which was Douglass's growing realization that he could no longer subscribe fully to Garrison's intellectual leadership. By 1851 the relationship between the two men openly and acrimoniously ruptured when Douglass publicly declared the U.S. Constitution (which Garrison had termed a proslavery document) to be an instrument of emancipation and further committed his newspaper to political activism, which the Garrisonians had long disavowed. After Garrison successfully prohibited further funding of the *North Star* by the American Anti-Slavery Society, Douglass turned to Liberty party leader Gerrit Smith for financial aid. This decision to ally himself with a rival faction of abolitionists regarded by the Garrisonians as mischievous temporizers gained for

3. Benjamin Quarles, *Frederick Douglass* (Washington, D.C.: Associated Publishers, 1948), pp. 80–81.

Douglass the reputation among his former associates as "the most malignant" of "all the seceders and apostates from our ranks."[4]

One lesson Douglass learned from his falling-out with the Garrisonians was the necessity of solidarity and self-sufficiency among northern blacks as a bulwark against white paternalism. On the eve of the publication of *My Bondage and My Freedom*, he insisted that blacks realize that "OUR ELEVATION AS A RACE, IS ALMOST WHOLLY DEPENDENT UPON OUR OWN EXERTIONS." He justified this contention by noting that "we have called down upon our devoted head, the holy (?) horror of a certain class of Abolitionists, because we have dared to maintain our Individuality, and have opened our own eyes, and looked out of them, through another telescope." Douglass charged that, despite their reputation as the champions of the Negro, Garrison and his adherents were only theoretically, not practically, committed to "the Idea of our Equality with the whites." It was high time, therefore, for northern blacks to desert the false "self-appointed generals of the Anti-Slavery host" and become more communally self-reliant. It was equally incumbent on Afro-American writers to set aside their loyalties to everything but "the truth, and the whole truth." "The redemption of our whole race"—in the North as well as the South—"from every species of oppression" was at stake as never before.[5] Out of a deeper awareness of the guises of oppression in his past, and with a new standard of candor and sense of literary mission, Douglass wrote *My Bondage and My Freedom*.

From its opening pages, where James McCune Smith, known for his vehement criticism of Garrison, supplants Douglass's former mentor as prefacer of his memoir, one can see that *My Bondage and My Freedom* was not designed to serve as merely an updated, second installment of the *Narrative*. In its tone, structure, and dominant metaphors, the new book represents a thoughtful revised reading of the meaning of Douglass's life. A cursory comparison of the *Narrative* and *My Bondage and My Freedom* indicates that the latter is bigger, roomier, more detailed, and more expository, befitting the more reflective mood of its author in 1855. The few paragraphs allotted in the *Narrative* to the seven years he had spent in freedom are expanded to

4. Philip S. Foner, ed., *The Life and Writings of Frederick Douglass* (New York: International Publishers, 1950), vol. 2, p. 59. The first treatment of the Garrison-Douglass split is in Benjamin Quarles, "The Breach between Douglass and Garrison," *Journal of Negro History*, 23 (Apr. 1938), pp. 144–54. For an extensive discussion of Douglass's split with the Garrisonians, see Foner, *The Life and Writings of Frederick Douglass*, vol. 2, pp. 48–66; and Waldo E. Martin, *The Mind of Frederick Douglass* (Chapel Hill: University of North Carolina Press, 1984), pp. 25–48.
5. "Self-Elevation—Rev. S. R. Ward," *Frederick Douglass' Paper*, Apr. 13, 1855, as reprinted in Foner, *The Life and Writings of Frederick Douglass*, vol. 2, pp. 359–62.

seventy pages in the second autobiography so that Douglass could integrate his additional ten years as a freeman into the scheme of his life story. As he reflected on the significance of his rites of passage through Garrisonianism during his seventeen years in freedom, Douglass found himself rethinking his previous understanding of the pattern of his life in slavery. In 1855 he could no longer see his life reaching its climax in his incorporation into the Garrisonian sphere. What the *Narrative* treats as the denouement of Douglass's struggle for freedom is pictured in *My Bondage and My Freedom* as just another stage of ironic disillusionment in the former slave's quest for liberation. Why, Douglass seems to have asked himself as he wrote his second autobiography, had he not recognized much earlier the kind of bondage that his attachment to the Garrisonians had held in store for him? To answer this question Douglass probed the dynamics of love, authority, and power in almost all of the major relationships in his life, particularly those involving father figures.

The 1845 *Narrative* pictures Douglass's consuming goals in life as freedom and independence, the attainment of which is symbolized in the transformation of the former slave into a spokesman for abolitionism. In *My Bondage and My Freedom*, however, Douglass suggests that before the ideal of freedom had infused his consciousness, his heart had been profoundly touched by hunger for a home. The first two chapters of Douglass's 1855 autobiography nostalgically reminisce at length about "MY HOME—the only home I ever had" [p. 41], the "joyous circle" [p. 39] under the care of his grandmother Betsey Baily, with whom the slave boy lived until he was about seven years old. The *Narrative* says virtually nothing about the home that Betsey Baily provided young Frederick, but in 1855 it is described as a place of "the veriest freedom" [p. 40] and "sweet content" [p. 39] where the "authority of grandmamma" [p. 38] sealed the child in a protective ignorance that insulated him from all but a vague awareness of his actual unfree condition. It was only when he left home with his grandmother to walk the twelve miles from her Tuckahoe cabin to "Old Master's" plantation on the Wye River that Frederick received his "first introduction to the realities of slavery" [p. 45]. His initiation came in a moment of powerful disillusionment. His trusted grandmother, having hidden from him the reason why she had taken him away from home, left him without warning or explanation "almost heart-broken" among the strangers of "old master's domicile" [p. 44]. Douglass brings out the significance of this crucial early episode in his life in the simple statement, "I had never been deceived before" [p. 44]. He had believed implicitly in Betsey Baily, but she, the first authority figure in his life, had deceived him. In whom, then, could he place his trust, other than in himself? Under his grandmother's benign authority he had enjoyed an ideal blend of freedom from restraint and the security of a protective parent's nurture. Would it ever be possible to discover or recreate in a personal or communal relationship this kind of home, where individuality and authority could be reconciled?

In the 1845 version of his life Douglass portrays himself in slavery as an incipient rebel-individualist who learned early the necessity of defiance of authority. By 1855, however, he had come to recognize and admit that he had often been a seeker of authority, even "something of a hero worshiper, by nature" [p. 218], to use the autobiographer's own phrase, who had been all too ready to attach himself to paternal figures whom he identified unconsciously with all that home signified. The structure of Douglass's life in his second autobiography shows us an evolving dialectic between two sides of the man's personality: one side jealously guarding its private temple of the free self, the other zealously devoted to idealized authorities outside the self. The narrator of *My Bondage and My Freedom* identifies ultimately with neither of these alter egos, for each one's limitations necessitate its displacement by the other as Douglass moved through youth and young manhood in the South and the North. The goal of the writing of Douglass's second autobiography was freedom from the prisons of both individualism and authoritarianism in a truly communal Afro-American home.

In this introductory discussion of *My Bondage and My Freedom,* I can only outline the pattern of Douglass's psychological struggles after leaving his first home. Douglass's discussion of his childhood on Colonel Lloyd's plantation shows how early he became acquainted with whites as paternalistic authorities. Captain Aaron Anthony, young Frederick's "Old Master," whom he had learned to fear from his days with his grandmother, embodies the contradictions inherent in slavery as a paternalistic system. The 1845 *Narrative* depicts Anthony simply and briefly as "a cruel man," but ten years later Douglass gave this figure a more complex character. He could be gentle, affectionate, "almost fatherly" to the winsome child he called "his 'little Indian boy'" [p. 61]. Yet when provoked by an affront to his patriarchal pride and prerogative, as in Esther Baily's defiance of his commandment against her love for Ned Roberts, Anthony's pretense of familial regard for his "servants" exploded in naked passion and sadistic revenge. "A wretched man, at war with his own soul" [p. 62], Anthony, like his slave Esther, was a victim of the grotesque intimacies that arose from the perverse paternalism of the South's peculiar institution. Many masters like Aaron Anthony subscribed to a patriarchal interpretation of their relationship to their black "families," so that slaveowners might be justified in demanding obedience and loyalty in exchange for providing and caring for their slaves. However, by implicitly endorsing the mutual obligations of patron and servant, Anthony could not help but inspire in the minds of strong-willed slaves like Esther (and later her nephew Frederick) the idea that obligations gave rise to rights for *both* sides in the paternalistic arrangement.[6] Beneath the paternalistic pretensions of Thomas and Hugh Auld lay their assumed right to decide what their slave Frederick owed them and what he could rightfully expect of them in return. But because of the paternalistic relationship that these men and their kindly wives, Lucretia and Sophia, established with Frederick in his boyhood, the conviction that he always deserved not the "inch" that his masters would allot him but the "ell" he desired for himself fired within the slave the rebellious individualism that eventually freed him from bondage.

The reader of *My Bondage and My Freedom* cannot ignore, however, the genuine sense of loss that accompanied Douglass's repeated separation from or rejection of paternal (and sometimes maternal) authorities, from Betsey Baily to William Lloyd Garrison. By 1855 Douglass could see that the most threatening oppression in his life had been the most insidiously beguiling. In some ways it had been harder to break the emotional and intellectual bonds that had held him to messianic leaders like Garrison than it had been to resist the whip of "the snake" Edward Covey. Outright tyrants Douglass would fight implacably; when the issue was the elevation of another's individual authority via the expunction of his own, Douglass felt free to insist on his own will. On the other hand, when paternal authorities offered him the chance to transcend his isolate individuality in the name of a new identification with a higher principle or a larger community, Douglass often proved a willing true believer.

As a young slave whose reading had alienated him emotionally from the Baltimore home of Sophia and Hugh Auld, Frederick felt keenly his loneliness. His white master and later his white mistress treated him with suspicion, while the "stupid contentment" of his fellow slaves made them seem equally unreachable to the black boy who had become "too thoughtful to be happy" [p. 106]. Disillusioned by the earthly fathers and mothers who had deceived him, Frederick concluded that he was in "need of God, as a father and protector" [p. 109]. He soon attached himself to Charles Lawson, a black drayman who became his "spiritual father" [p. 111] and inspired in him a sense of his destiny and calling as a preacher and a freeman. As a result of the encouragement of "Father Lawson," the black teenager became confident that "my life was under the guidance of a

6. For a thorough discussion of paternalism and slavery, see Eugene D. Genovese, *Roll, Jordan, Roll: The World the Slaves Made* (New York: Random House, 1974), especially pp. 89–91, 146–47. The role of patriarchal honor in slave-master relationships is treated in Bertram Wyatt-Brown, *Southern Honor* (New York: Oxford University Press, 1982), pp. 362–65. See also Willie Lee Rose, "The Domestication of Domestic Slavery," *Slavery and Freedom*, ed. William W. Freehling (New York: Oxford University Press, 1982), pp. 18–36.

wisdom higher than my own" and that "in His own good time" his heavenly Father would "deliver [him] from bondage" [p. 111]. Lawson's ministrations, in other words, saved Frederick from an increasingly desperate sense of alienation and gave a larger purpose to his efforts at self-education. On the other hand, by convincing the youth that he should "trust in the Lord" for the future, Lawson inhibited the growth of Douglass's self-reliance, in which he would have to place profound trust later when he was hired out to Covey. The challenge of the slave-breaker to Douglass's sense of personhood forced the slave to set aside the faith of Lawson in "the authority of God" [p. 107] and see to it that his hands "were no longer tied by my religion" [p. 152]. Survival and progress as a self thus required that Douglass violently "backslide" from the religion of his black, as well as white, fathers. We are moved to see in this what might be termed a slave's "fortunate fall" into dignity, just as we are similarly invited to interpret Douglass's "apostasy" from Garrison's "holy cause" as his liberation from "something like a slavish adoration" [p. 242] of his Boston leaders. Yet it is important to remember that for Douglass the immediate result of such dissenting was usually alienation from the sense of community, larger purpose, or transcendent identity that had lured him into discipleship in the first place.

As we approach the end of *My Bondage and My Freedom*, Douglass's renunciations, one after another, of all the false authorities that in the past had betrayed his faith as well as his freedom become one of the major themes of his book. What is not so apparent, however, is the alternative he poses for psychologically and spiritually homeless Afro-Americans who could find no lasting fulfillment in antiauthoritarian individualism. This alternative emerges from several incidents in Douglass's past and again at the conclusion of his autobiography. Consider the aftermath of his battle with Covey. At first the narrator stresses the tonic effect his victory had on his personal sense of "self-respect" and "manly independence" [p. 155]. But what was perhaps of greater significance to the development of Douglass's ultimate mission as an orator and agitator for freedom were the Sabbath schools he undertook in 1835, the year after he left Covey's farm. After his disillusionment with the false godliness of his various Maryland masters, Douglass found a spiritual home in sub-rosa socioreligious communities that he created and led among his fellow slaves. What began as a gesture of largess from the comparatively well-educated teenager to his ignorant companions in bondage became the most mutually beneficial and egalitarian community that Douglass would ever experience in the South. "I never loved, esteemed, or confided in men, more than I did in these," Douglass says of his students in the Sabbath school that he conducted on William Freeland's plantation. "No band of brothers

could have been more loving. There were no mean advantages taken
of each other . . . and no elevating one at the expense of the other.
We never undertook to do any thing, of any importance, which was
likely to affect each other, without mutual consultation. We were
generally a unit, and moved together" [p. 168].

This fraternal instead of paternal relationship between leader and
followers stuck in Douglass's mind as an unprecedented model of
home. Paternalism tended to fragment the slaves' faith in their peers
in favor of the cultivation of their immediate superiors and inferiors. But the fraternalism of Douglass's Freeland band distributed
power laterally, not vertically, so that authority could not abuse community. The mutual self-reliance of these black men cemented
them into a unity of identity and purpose that liberated Douglass
from mere individualism. "I could have died with and for them"
[p. 171], he wrote of his closest friends in the school; with them,
therefore, he made his first break for freedom.

After his successful escape to the North, Douglass joined the Garrisonians, "young, ardent, and hopeful" [p. 221] of having finally
found the kind of community of freedom, brotherhood, and benevolent authority that he had long associated with home. Initially the
abolitionist fraternity seemed remarkably color-blind, causing their
new associate to "forget that my skin was dark and my hair crisped"
[p. 222]. Gradually, however, it became clear to the former slave that
racial prejudice often governed the ideas that his new "friends" had
about how to use him in their cause. Douglass probably was aware
that his relationship to Garrison had become "something like that
of a child to a parent," as the black man characterized it in a letter
to Senator Charles Sumner in 1852.[7] But not until the publication
of My Bondage and My Freedom did the full cost of Douglass's
attachment to his white abolitionist patrons become evident.

In his introduction to the book, James McCune Smith points out
that when Douglass launched his newspaper, the North Star, over
the opposition of Garrison, he could not have expected northern
blacks to rally automatically to him because "the wide gulf which
separated the free colored people from the Garrisonians, also separated them from their brother, Frederick Douglass." The actual distance that existed between Douglass the Garrisonian and the free
blacks of the North cannot be easily determined now. A number of
important black pundits (such as Smith) did intensely criticize the
American Anti-Slavery Society and those blacks (like Douglass) who
continued to adhere to it in the 1840s and 1850s. On the other hand,
after the full Douglass-Garrison split, most northern blacks defended

---

7. Douglass to Sumner, Sept. 2, 1852, in Foner, The Life and Writings of Frederick Douglass, vol. 2, p. 210.

Douglass against the harsh attacks on his integrity and leadership mounted by the many Garrison loyalists.[8] Regardless of the extent to which Douglass felt alienated from the free blacks of the North as a consequence of his involvement with the Garrisonians, the conclusion of *My Bondage and My Freedom* testifies to the author's determination to reidentify himself as a leader and spokesman of a nationwide Afro-American community. Separation from the Garrisonians had shown him that the best way of accomplishing the antislavery mission he had begun among them was to immerse himself in the cause of the quasi-free black people of the North. In short, the final image of Douglass in his second autobiography is that of a community-builder. Just as he had labored in his Sabbath school on Freeland's plantation to inspire within his companions a unifying spirit of hope, mutual trust, and aspiration toward freedom, so in the North, through his independent journalism and his new autobiography, would he promote similar ideals: "the moral, social, religious, and intellectual elevation of the free colored people" [p. 249].

"Progress is yet possible" [p. 249], Douglass exhorts the black readers of his second autobiography. It was no small part of his aim in 1855 to show black Americans how to progress toward the kind of "elevation" they all sought. The subtle argument of *My Bondage and My Freedom* is that the elevation of Frederick Douglass, whose "example of self-elevation" qualified him as James McCune Smith's "Representative American man" [p. 27], was not to be attributed merely to his individual exertions alone. By the mid-1850s Douglass could see how much his own life proved his maxim: "A man's character greatly takes its hue and shape from the form and color of things about him" [p. 61]. The mature Douglass recognized that his character, his needs, and the direction of his life had been profoundly shaped by the maternal, paternal, and fraternal relationships of his past. The repeated ironic reversals in his quest for freedom had taught him the primary necessity of distinguishing between true and false community as the basis on which real as opposed to delusory freedom depended. Thus, the pattern of his life in his second autobiography reflects his realization that any ascendant Afro-American needed a communal anchor before he or she could attain a truly liberating identity as both an individual and a part of a larger social whole. It is not clear that Douglass felt he had realized in his own self that balance of interdependent individuality and communality that had become his ideal at the end of *My Bondage and My Freedom*. But though the example of his own life illustrates how elusive

8. For a discussion of black criticism of the Garrisonians and of the black response to the rift between Douglass and Garrison, see Jane H. and William H. Pease, *They Who Would Be Free: Blacks' Search for Freedom, 1830–1861* (New York: Atheneum, 1974), pp. 68–93.

that ideal can be, Douglass's resolution to pursue it, fortified by his hard-won awareness that only through its attainment could he become truly free, brings his autobiography to both its conclusion and its climax. The ultimate assurance of "progress" in *My Bondage and My Freedom* leaves us with a sense of "new possibilities" for both the individual and society, a quality that Emerson felt would always be the lasting legacy of the biographies of "representative men."[9]

The highest achievement of a "representative man" in Emerson's view is to "preach the equality of souls" and "give a constitution to his people," thereby releasing them "from their barbarous homages," even to himself. * * *

As an exponent of "the equality of souls," Douglass joined with his Romantic literary contemporaries in emphasizing the idea that human beings, individually and collectively, share a potential for evolution toward a higher self-awareness, fulfillment, and ethical discernment. Some may be farther advanced on the path of self-realization than others, but this does not alter the fact that the human condition is perpetually liminal, that is, poised on a threshold, in transit from one level of knowledge to another. When Douglass concludes his autobiography by affirming that "progress is always possible" [p. 249], he underscores his faith in the transcendentalist creed of individual as well as social progress that writers like [Henry David] Thoreau and Fuller echo. His emphasis on black solidarity as an essential factor in the achievement of Afro-American progress is no more radical or less romantic a message to the oppressed than is Fuller's recommendation in favor of American women's banding together to be their own "best helpers."

The "constitution" that Douglass gave to "his people," that is, to black America, is not a finished political document but an open-ended personal history which, in its dual focus on life in slavery and in freedom, incorporates the crucial parameters of every antebellum Afro-American's experience and thus constitutes a truly representative and national work of black expression. Douglass's second autobiography also constitutes the full significance of the themes of slavery and freedom that writers like Fuller and Thoreau explore. *My Bondage and My Freedom* provides a grounding in specific historical and social reality for Fuller's and Thoreau's largely metaphorical applications of slavery and freedom to American society; moreover, Douglass's acknowledgment of the ironies of his own youthful idealism places in a cautionary perspective the transcendent optimism of a Thoreau or Fuller. Thoreau assures his reader that "there can be no very black

---

9. Ralph Waldo Emerson, "Uses of Great Men," *Representative Men* (Boston: Phillips, Sampson, 1850), p. 37.

melancholy to him who lives in the midst of Nature and has his senses still."[1] Douglass insists on the reality of black melancholy, especially among southern blacks, so as to impress upon his reader the real threat of slavery to subvert even the most aspiring mind, such as his own. But he also insists on the creative uses of black melancholy for slave singers and rebels like himself who needed more than a retreat to Nature to free themselves from slavery-imposed despair.

Douglass joins Thoreau and Fuller in emphasizing the many prejudices, particularly those involving race, that Americans in the North as well as the South had allowed to smother their natural love of freedom. The former slave dramatizes in his personal story the efficacy of both Thoreau's appeal to individual self-emancipation and Fuller's call for an alliance of the oppressed in their own behalf to combat slavery in its many guises. To an extent that neither Thoreau nor Fuller would risk, however, Douglass makes himself a negative as well as a positive example of the impact of bondage and freedom on an American consciousness. "Self-criticism," Douglass asserted a few years after the publication of *My Bondage and My Freedom*, is among "the highest attainments of human excellence"; an unsparing objectivity regarding the self provides "the germinating principle of all reform and all progress."[2] The self-criticism of Douglass's second autobiography, along with its warnings against hero-worship, help to release his readers from excessive "homage" to the myth of Frederick Douglass. This makes progress indeed possible, if nowhere else than on the intellectual front of the Afro-American struggle for independence. By contrast, Thoreau and Fuller, despite their use of the personal essay and autobiographical forms, seem to be either not interested in or inhibited about revealing themselves critically, particularly in circumstances of frustration or failure.[3] We do not learn much from *Walden* or [Fuller's] *Woman in the Nineteenth Century* about the process by which the narrators of these two classic books attained the enlightened and liberated perspective from which they speak so confidently.

My Bondage and My Freedom is that rare "I-narrative" of the American 1850s that not only preaches the message of the "representative" men and women of the American literary renaissance but also conducts its reader through the stages of the preacher's realization of his own identity, mission, and message. What we discover from Douglass's most compelling self-portrait in autobiography is not

---

1. Henry David Thoreau, *Walden*, ed. J. Lyndon Shanley (Princeton: Princeton University Press, 1971), p. 131.
2. Frederick Douglass, "Pictures and Progress," undated MS. in Frederick Douglass Papers, Library of Congress, reel 18, p. 151. Douglass wrote this lecture sometime in 1864 or 1865.
3. Lawrence Buell, *Literary Transcendentalism* (Ithaca: Cornell University Press, 1973) p. 269.

a self-made man but a man still in the making, characterized ultimately by what Melville termed "that lasting temper of all true,
candid men—a seeker, not a finder yet."[4]

NICK K. BROMELL

[Slavery, Work, and Song in Douglass's Autobiographies][†]

As its title suggests, Frederick Douglass's second version of his
autobiography is less a linear account of movement from slavery to
emancipation than a self-reflexive and self-circling meditation on a
condition in which freedom and bondage are simultaneously present.
As William Andrews has shown, whereas the *Narrative* is for the
most part the story of how a "thing" rediscovers himself as a "man,"
My Bondage and My Freedom is able to explore more fully what it
means to be a man, and specifically a black man in a racist society. [1]
To this account I would add that *My Bondage and My Freedom*
explores also the condition and work of being a writer, specifically an
African American writer. Whereas the *Narrative* concentrated on a
search for the origins of his decision to regain his humanity, in *My
Bondage and My Freedom* Douglass goes back to the experience of
slavery in order to find the origins of his identity as a writer.

To understand this search, we must understand first the position
Douglass finds himself in 1854, as he writes *My Bondage and My
Freedom*. He is a man who begins life performing the degraded and
exclusively manual labor entailed by slavery. Gradually, though, he
is able to achieve a measure of freedom by performing the relatively
free and skilled labor of working for hire as a ship caulker; he even
experiences a brief period when his master allows him to keep all
his surplus wages. After he escapes to the North, Douglass is able
to perform labor that is free in the literal sense of the word, but the
racism prevalent among working-class whites prevents him from performing the more skilled and relatively profitable labor of caulking.
He is forced instead to undertake the most menial kinds of manual
labor available—chopping wood, carrying freight, and so on. Then
he is discovered by the abolitionists. They allow him to perform the

---

4. Herman Melville, "Hawthorne and His Mosses," as reprinted in *Moby-Dick*, ed. Harrison Hayford and Hershel Parker (New York: W. W. Norton, 1967), p. 547.
† From *By the Sweat of the Brow: Literature and Labor in Antebellum America* (Chicago: U
Chicago P, 1993), pp. 194–202. Copyright © 1993 by the University of Chicago. Reprinted
with permission of the University of Chicago Press. Bracketed page references are to this
Norton Critical Edition.
1. William L. Andrews, *To Tell a Free Story: The First Century of Afro-American Autobiography, 1760–1865* (Urbana: University of Illinois Press, 1986), pp. 214–39.

relatively mental labor of lecturing, and then of writing his *Narrative*, but they attempt to restrict the scope of that work's mentality. Eventually, Douglass breaks ranks with the Garrisonians, establishes his own newspaper "to promote the moral . . . and intellectual elevation of the free colored people,"[2] and performs work that is at once more free and more mental than any he has done before.

In *My Bondage and My Freedom*, Douglass deliberately structures his history as a laborer in terms of an ascent (thwarted at times, to be sure) from manual to mental labor. * * * [However,] this movement is complicated and resisted not just by an occasional note of mockery, but by Douglass's increasing *acceptance* of his racial identity—an identity in which the connection between "self" and "body" is crucial.

Perhaps the most striking indication of this acceptance of his racial identity, and with it of the value of embodied labor, is to be found in the introduction which James M'Cune Smith wrote (and which Douglass must have approved) for *My Bondage and My Freedom*. Smith, a black physician, pointedly emphasizes that Douglass's ascent from manual to mental labor does not entail a rejection of the body and the skills it has learned.[3] Smith argues that for his work as an advocate of emancipation Douglass was well prepared by his experience, and specifically his work, as a slave. "And for this special mission, his plantation education was better than any he could have acquired in any lettered school. What he needed, was facts and experiences. . . . His physical being was well trained also, running wild until advanced into boyhood; hard work and light diet thereafter, and a skill in handicraft in youth." Douglass was a born worker and even in slavery found ample opportunity to exercise his energy and even some of his gifts: ". . . he worked, and he worked hard. At his daily labor he went with a will; with keen, well set eye, brawny chest, lithe figure, and fair sweep of arm, he would have been king

2. Frederick Douglass, *My Bondage, My Freedom* (Urbana: University of Illinois Press, 1987), p. 242 [p. 249]. All further page references will be made in the text.
3. Smith even provides a scientific theory to explain why Douglass's drama of self-elevation and self-culture does not entail abandonment of a past that has been located mainly in the body and its labors. "Naturalists tell us that a full grown man is a resultant or representative of all animated nature on this globe; beginning with the early embryo state, then representing the lowest forms of organic life, and passing through every subordinate grade or type, until he reaches the last and highest—manhood" (p. 17 [p. 27]). Thus, Douglass is great precisely in that he embodies the entire spectrum of what exists, from matter to spirit, from body to mind; his achievement (like that of all great men, according to Smith) is not that he transcends, but that he includes, or contains. This is another version of the [Henry David] Thoreauvian and [Walt] Whitmanesque wish that the sentient knowledge of the body and its labors might be accorded their full value and seen not just as a threshold to higher development, but as essential components of any complete man. "In like manner, and to the fullest extent, has Frederick Douglass passed through every gradation of rank comprised in our national make-up, and bears upon his person and upon his soul every thing that is American" (p. 17 [p. 27]).

among calkers, had that been his mission" (p. 12 [p. 22]). This is the man, then, who becomes for a while a Garrisonian. Like Douglass, Smith emphasizes the turn Douglass takes at this point from hard manual labor—"sawing wood, rolling casks, or doing what labor he might to support himself and young family" (p. 13 [p. 23])—to the mental labor of abolitionism. And, more explicitly than Douglass, he relates how the Garrisonians both promoted and sought to limit the exercise of his intellectual powers:

> In the society [of Garrisonians], . . . Mr. Douglass enjoyed the high advantage of their assistance and counsel in the labor of self-culture, to which he now addressed himself with wonted energy. Yet, these gentlemen, though proud of Frederick Douglass, failed to fathom and bring out to the light of day, the highest qualities of his mind; the force of their own education stood on their own way; they did not delve into the mind of a colored man for capacities which the pride of race led them to believe to be restricted to their own Saxon blood.

After his experiences in England, however, Douglass "awakened . . . to the consciousness of new powers that lay in him" and "rose to the dignity of a teacher and a thinker" (p. 15 [p. 24]).

From this point forward, the bulk of Smith's introduction consists of a description and analysis of Douglass's remarkable intellectual abilities and "mental processes" (p. 18 [p. 27]). He praises Douglass's singular clarity of "perception," his "unfailing memory," his "truthful common sense," his "wit," his "descriptive and declamatory powers," and his "logical force" (p. 20 [pp. 27–28]). But when he comes to "the most remarkable mental phenomenon in Mr. Douglass," his "style in writing and speaking," he confesses that he is at a loss to explain these, and that Douglass's writing style in particular is "an intellectual puzzle." "The strength, affluence and terseness may easily be accounted for, because the style of the man is the man; but how are we to account for that rare polish in his style of writing, which, most critically examined, seems the result of careful early culture among the best classics of our language" (p. 21 [p. 30]). Smith confesses that he was once tempted to attribute Douglass's literary genius to "the Caucasian side of his make-up," but that the "facts narrated in the first part" of *My Bondage and My Freedom* "throw a different light on this interesting question." In sum, Smith (like Douglass himself, as we shall see), locates Douglass's literary genius in his "negro blood," and more specifically in the figures of his grandmother ("a woman of power and spirit . . . marvelously straight in figure, elastic and muscular" and possessing great "skill in constructing nets, . . . perseverance in using them, . . . and widespread fame in the agricultural way") and his mother ("tall, and finely proportioned; of deep black, glossy complexion"). "These facts show," Smith concludes, "that for his energy, perseverance, eloquence, invective, sagacity, and wide sympathy, he is indebted to his negro blood. The very marvel of his style would seem to be a development of that other marvel,—how his mother learned to read" (pp. 21–22 [p. 32]).

*   *   *

* * * [Indeed,] Douglass * * * in *My Bondage and My Freedom* absolutely rejects *any* paternal contribution to his identity as a writer. Instead—and here the contrast with the *Narrative*, in which Douglass writes of his mother but says nothing about her relation to language, is instructive—Douglass explicitly locates the origin of his gifts as a writer in the "sable" body of his laboring mother:

> I learned, after my mother's death, that she could read, and that she was the *only* one of all the slaves and colored people in Tuckahoe who enjoyed that advantage. How she acquired this knowledge, I know not, for Tuckahoe is the last place in the world where she would be apt to find facilities for learning . . . I can, therefore, fondly and proudly ascribe to her an earnest love of knowledge. That a "field hand" should learn to read, in any slave state, is remarkable; but the achievement of my mother, considering the place, was very extraordinary; and, in view of that fact, I am quite willing, and even happy, to attribute any love of letters I possess, and for which I have got— despite of prejudice—only too much credit, *not* to my admitted Anglo-Saxon paternity, but to the native genius of my sable, unprotected, and uncultivated *mother*—a woman, who belonged to a race whose mental endowments, it is, at present, fashionable to hold in disparagement and contempt. (p. 42 [pp. 48–49])

This is the most crucial emendation of his 1845 *Narrative*. By referring to the "prejudices" of white racism and its "contempt" for the "mental endowments" of blacks, Douglass indicates that racism, not slavery, is the catalyst that has urged him to retrace the track of his past and to define his authorial identity in terms of race. At one level, Douglass is employing the already familiar vocabulary of the distinction between manual and mental labor and marveling that a mere "field hand" should have been able to acquire knowledge and perform the mental labor entailed by literacy. But Douglass superimposes on this scene a specifically racial dimension, and it is one that calls into question the dichotomy itself. Although the field hand *per se* could theoretically achieve an entirely new identity as a mental laborer, metamorphosing from corporeal to mental worker, this is not true of the *black* or "sable" field hand. This laborer will always remain black, will always labor in and through his or her black body. Douglass thus specifically and unequivocally locates the origin of his "love of letters" and his literary accomplishments in a figure that triply represents the embodied state: in a field hand who is a mother and who is also black; in his "sable . . . *mother*." By doing so, he expresses a willingness not only to think of himself as an African American writer, but also to acknowledge that this racial identity must have a bodily, a physical origin. For Douglass as an African American writer, "Genius" is not a spiritual chimaera flitting through and attempting to transcend the sinews of the body; it is "native" to and inseparable from that body. To abandon the body would be to renege on his African American identity.

* * * Douglass's affirmation of his racial identity, while crucial to his identity as a writer, also has its costs. To the degree that it requires him to value the body and bodily labor, it also threatens to return him to a condition of bondage and to the kind of identification with the body that [Harriet Beecher] Stowe, too, acknowledged and resented. The most concentrated and suggestive expression of Douglass's ambivalence toward the body and toward embodied expressivity is his meditation on the meaning and power of the slaves' songs. * * * Douglass is drawn to these songs in part because he remains loyal to the slave community and to its mode of expressiveness. More pointedly, he is drawn to them also because, as a mode of expressivity, slave songs are indissolubly associated with the labor of slavery and with the laboring body of the black slave. It is the deep affinity between the slave songs and slave labor that makes them such a powerful and multivalent icon to a freed slave who is discovering and defining his real work as an African American writer. The slave song gives voice to the doubleness of slave labor, to its expropriation of the slave's body and to its potentialities as a refuge from the degradations of slavery. Moreover, behind slave labor stands the slave's body, and as a form of expressivity the slave song never leaves that body behind. ("Stripped of all else," observed Alain Locke, "the Negro's own body became his prime and only artistic instrument, so that dance, pantomime and song became the only gateways for his creative expression.")[4]

* * *

Yet Douglass also registers a concern that the slave song is at the same time distinctly inappropriate as a model on which to pattern one's work as an African American writer. In the *Narrative* of 1845, Douglass had voiced three reservations about the songs sung by

4. Quoted in James E. Newton and Ronald L. Lewis, eds., *The Other Slaves: Mechanics, Artisans, and Craftsmen* (Boston: G. K. Hall, 1978), p. 205.

slaves. First, insofar as he located them only in the slaves' trips to the Great House Farm, he associated them with a slavish sycophancy, with the slaves' self-defeating desire "to please their overseers." Second, the songs worried him because they were so easily misunderstood and misused by white Americans in the North and in the South who found in them evidence of the slaves' "contentment and happiness." Third, he suggested that the spontaneous and improvisational nature of the songs, their conflation of "sound" and "word," helped render them not only "unmeaning jargon" to outsiders but "incoherent" and beyond the "comprehension" even of those who sang them, those within "the circle" of slavery.[5]

In *My Bondage and My Freedom*, written ten years later, Douglass still has these reservations about the songs, but in his account of them he makes crucial revisions indicative both of his new concern with his work as a writer and of his wavering loyalty toward an embodied identity. His first major change is to make clear that the songs were sung not only on trips to the Great House Farm but whenever and wherever the slaves worked. "Slaves are generally expected to sing as well as to work. A silent slave is not liked by masters or overseers. '*Make a noise*,' '*make a noise*,' and '*bear a hand*,' are the words usually addressed to the slaves when there is silence among them" (p. 64 [p. 71]). Douglass accents the songs' association with work again when he describes the outsiders' misunderstanding of the slave songs as, specifically, a misunderstanding of the slaves' attitude toward their work ("The remark is not infrequently made, that slaves are the most contented and happy *laborers* in the world" (p. 66 [p. 72]) [my emphasis]). These changes suggest, I would argue, that in *My Bondage and My Freedom* Douglass is returning to the slave songs with a new interest in their relation to slave work—an interest that grows out of his own concern to understand his work as a writer.

A second major revision Douglass makes is to explore further the nature and consequences of these songs' spontaneity. The *Narrative*'s implied linkage of improvisation with "incoherence" now becomes explicit: the "words of their own improvising [were] jargon to others but full of meaning to themselves" (p. 65 [p. 71]). In this version, moreover, he seems to stress that the songs not only resist full "comprehension" by those who sing them, but that they actually substitute for and thus impede the development of thought and self-consciousness among the slaves: "Once on the road [to the Great House Farm] with an ox team, and seated on the tongue of his cart, with no overseer to look after him, the slave was comparatively free;

5. Frederick Douglass, *Narrative of the Life of Frederick Douglass, An American Slave* (New York: Penguin Books, 1982), 57 [*Editors' note*].

and, if thoughtful, he had time to think" (p. 64 [p. 71]). But it is clear that most slaves were not eager to embrace this opportunity for thought. Instead, they sang.

Why did they sing? Why, when they had opportunity to "think," did the slaves become "*peculiarly* excited and noisy" (p. 65 [p. 71]) [my emphasis] and sing with unusual intensity of feeling? Douglass's implicit explanation is that they did so precisely because they could not and did not *want* to think. Their songs offered them an opportunity to express their rage and grief without actually having to think about it. As Douglass makes clear in the *Narrative*, to think about and be conscious of one's "condition"—to stare unblinkingly at what it is to be a slave—is to experience "torment." When Douglass himself becomes aware of his condition he often wishes he were not: "Anything, no matter what, to get rid of thinking! It was this everlasting thinking of my condition that tormented me. There was no getting rid of it." It should come as no surprise that the slaves preferred to sing their condition rather than to think about it.

Yet, crucially, this ability to "view" one's "wretched condition" as a slave is the consequence, for Douglass, of literacy. Thought is the gift, and curse, of reading and writing.

> As I read and contemplated the subject [of slavery], behold! that very discontentment which Master Hugh had predicted would follow my learning to read had already come, to torment and sting my soul to unutterable anguish. As I writhed under it, I would at times feel that learning to read has been a curse rather than a blessing. It had given me a view of my wretched condition, without the remedy. . . . In moments of agony, I envied my fellow-slaves for their stupidity. I have often wished myself a beast. ([*Narrative*,] p. 84)

Although he envies his fellow slaves their "stupidity," and wishes himself "a beast," Douglass nevertheless believes that the thought acquired by reading must be obtained and experienced. It is a necessary precondition of emancipation. This is why Douglass has misgivings about the slave songs' conflation of "word" and "sound" and this is why slaves outside the "circle" of slavery have a fuller understanding of the songs' meaning than those locked within it. Literacy, the acquisition of power over the "word," enables one to step outside the circle. Singing, by contrast, though it powerfully expresses feelings of anguish and sorrow, obstructs thought insofar as it allows one to vent one's feelings without understanding them.

To point out the ways in which *My Bondage and My Freedom* expresses an intensified ambivalence toward the slave song (and, thereby, to slave labor) is not to propose that *My Bondage and My Freedom* ceases to respect these. On the contrary, in the *My*

Bondage and My Freedom version of the slave-song passage, Douglass writes nothing that qualifies his feeling of obligation toward
the slave song. Presumably, as a writer he still feels that he received
from the songs his first "glimmering conception of the dehumaniz-
ing character of slavery." As a writer, he still locates in the songs
the emergence of a consciousness which, while much less developed
than that obtained from reading, nevertheless represents an
advance over a condition with no conceptions at all. And to the
degree that the slave song itself emerges from and expresses the
slave's labor (a connection Douglass emphasizes in *My Bondage and
My Freedom*), he must still trace his labor as a writer back not only
to the songs, but to the labor he performed as a slave.

*   *   *

ROBERT S. LEVINE

The Black Man and the Brotherhood[†]

Shortly before publishing *The Heroic Slave*, his novella about black
rebellion, in *Autographs for Freedom*, and two months before he
would serialize it over the four March 1853 issues of *Frederick
Douglass' Paper*, Douglass wrote Gerrit Smith about changing the
name of his paper to one of four possibilities: "'The Black man,' 'The
agitator,' 'The Jerry Level,' or 'The Brotherhood.'" Though he kept
the name unchanged, Douglass during the early to mid-1850s began
more emphatically to talk about himself as a black man. Thus *My
Bondage and My Freedom*, Douglass's second autobiography, does
not build toward a telos of Douglass joining a white-led antislavery
organization; instead, it offers a more open-ended conclusion in
which Douglass, in the spirit of the slave revolt depicted in the final
section of *The Heroic Slave*, links himself with the cause of black
freedom fighters. *Bondage and Freedom*'s prefatory material further
emphasizes black agency and community. In the 1845 *Narrative*, the
white abolitionists William Lloyd Garrison and Wendell Phillips
introduce Douglass as a former slave working in the spirit of the
Massachusetts Anti-Slavery Society. In *Bondage and Freedom*, Douglass's friend the black physician and social activist James McCune
Smith supplies the introduction, presenting Douglass as a representative American, but then placing him in a larger black diasporic

† From *The Lives of Frederick Douglass* (Cambridge, MA: Harvard UP, 2016), pp. 158–
70, 172–74. © 2016 by the President and Fellows of Harvard College. Reprinted and
adapted for this Norton Critical Edition by permission of Harvard University Press.
Bracketed page references are to this edition.

context by discussing him in relation to three black artists: the French writer Alexandre Dumas, the Anglo-American actor Ira Aldridge, and the American singer Eliza Greenfield, who was wildly popular in Europe. In his 1854 "The Claims of the Negro Ethno-logically Considered," Douglass pridefully states that it is a "physi-ological fact" that mixed-race blacks' "intellect is uniformly derived from the maternal side"; and in his introduction McCune Smith fol-lows Douglass in asserting that it was from his black grandmother and mother that Douglass got the intelligence and "strong self-hood" that "led him to measure strength with Mr. Covey, and to wrench himself from the embrace of the Garrisonians." As the comparison between Covey and the Garrisonians suggests, McCune Smith is unsparing toward the latter, claiming that they "did not delve into the mind of a colored man for capacities which the pride of race led them to believe to be restricted to their own Saxon blood."[1] Doug-lass makes similar claims about the Garrisonians in *Bondage and Freedom*. Douglass may have been of mixed blood, but in his sec-ond autobiography he presents himself much more self-consciously and aggressively as a black man who, like his black-skinned hero Washington, forges interracial friendships on his own terms and is prepared to fight for his compatriots.[2]

Approximately three times the length of the *Narrative, Bondage and Freedom* draws on the *Narrative*, and even quotes from it on occasion, while for the most part reconceiving key scenes, adding new scenes, and taking the life of Douglass in new directions. Like *The Heroic Slave, Bondage and Freedom* is marked by a complex and searching historicism. As Sundquist observes, Douglass in his sec-ond autobiography "now stands outside his former self as it appeared in the first narration so as to reflect on the process of construction." In his first autobiography, Douglass rarely pauses to consider the historiographical issues that he later addresses in the opening para-graphs of *The Heroic Slave* about archives, historical recovery, and black heroism. Those issues are central to *Bondage and Freedom*, in

1. Douglass to Gerrit Smith, letter of 14 January 1853, Gerrit Smith Papers, Syracuse University; Douglass, "The Claims of the Negro Ethnologically Considered: An Address Delivered in Hudson, Ohio, on 12 July 1854," *The Frederick Douglass Papers: Series One: Speeches, Debates, and Interviews,* ed. John W. Blassingame et al. (New Haven, CT: Yale University Press, 1981), vol. 2, 510; Douglass, *My Bondage and My Freedom*, xxxi, xxii [pp. 32, 24]. For a good discussion of Douglass's paratexts in his second autobiography, see John Sekora, "'Mr. Editor, If You Please': Frederick Doug-lass, *My Bondage and My Freedom*, and the End of the Abolitionist Imprint," *Callaloo* 17.2 (1994): 608–626. On theological debates about race, see Jared Hickman, "Doug-lass Unbound," *Nineteenth-Century Literature* 68.3 (2013): 323–62.

2. For a different, but complementary, perspective on Douglass and revolutionism, see Cody Marrs's fine discussion of Douglass's engagement with the European revolutions of the period, "Frederick Douglass in 1848," *American Literature* 85.3 (2013): 447–73. "Black-skinned hero Washington" refers to Madison Washington, leader of a rebellion aboard the ship *Creole* and hero of Douglass's novella *The Heroic Slave* (1852).

which Douglass regularly remarks on the role played by oral history and memory in his reconceived life history as a heroic slave and freeman.

Historiographical matters have an especially important place in the opening chapters of *Bondage and Freedom*'s long first part, "Life as a Slave," for the good reason that Douglass remains uncertain about his historical past (such as his birthdate and the identity of his father). He conveys some of that uncertainty in the *Narrative*, but in his second autobiography he is much more the historian. "Genealogical trees do not flourish among slaves," he writes early on, calling attention to the lack of archives for historical reconstruction. Thus he needs to rely on oral history and often vague memories to develop what becomes a racially self-conscious story about his indebtedness to his black matrilineal line. When he introduces his grandmother, for instance, he acknowledges the limits of his memory: "The first experience of life with me that I now remember—and I remember it but hazily—began in the family of my grandmother." Douglass's account of the pain that he felt at being separated from his grandmother when he was moved to the house of his master, and even his tales about her continued efforts to serve as his guardian and protector, derive from memories that he concedes never fully come into focus. The same is true for his account of his mother, whom, as he relates in the *Narrative*, he barely knew and thus found it difficult as a young child to mourn when he heard news of her death. But because he now wants to tell more about the woman to whom he feels indebted for his intelligence, he draws on oral history, from his grandmother and other sources, to remark on her literacy. Extolling "the native genius of my sable, unprotected, and uncultivated *mother*," and even comparing her to an Egyptian prince depicted in James Cowles Prichard's *Natural History of Man* (1843), he suggests the difficulty of learning about his mother when he describes her resting place (which is not mentioned in the *Narrative*): "Her grave is, as the grave of the dead at sea, unmarked, and without stone or stake."[3]

3. Douglass, *My Bondage and My Freedom*, 34, 35, 58, 60 [pp. 36, 36, 49, 50]. For a provocative discussion of Douglass's presentation of his mother in his second autobiography, see Michael A. Chaney, "Picturing the Mother, Claiming Egypt: *My Bondage and My Freedom* as Auto(bio)ethnography," *African American Review* 35.3 (2001): 391–408. Chaney calls attention to Douglass's at times contradictory deracialization of his mother. My own sense is that Douglass seeks to destabilize race by unsettling connections between color and intelligence, and by the end of his essay Chaney makes a similar point (405–6). On Douglass's presentation of his mother and grandmother in *Bondage and Freedom*, see also Cynthia Hamilton, "Frederick Douglass and the Gender Politics of Reform," *Liberating Sojourn: Frederick Douglass and Transatlantic Reform*, ed. Alan J. Rice and Martin Crawford (Athens: University of Georgia Press, 1999), 73–92; and Arthur Riss, "Sentimental Douglass," *The Cambridge Companion to Frederick Douglass*, ed. Maurice S. Lee (Cambridge: Cambridge University Press, 2009), 103–17. For an intriguing discussion of the importance of mothers to Barack

Working with "marks, traces, possibles, and probabilities,"[4] Douglass in his second autobiography presents himself as a historian of slavery on the Eastern Shore and of his younger self. Douglass states about his historical interest in slavery while still a slave at Colonel Lloyd's: "I could not have been more than seven or eight years old, when I began to make this subject my study." The boy historian was especially dependent on oral history in order to develop his knowledge of slavery beyond his immediate locale. For instance, when he describes the overseer Gore's brutal murder of Denby, which is also described in the *Narrative*, he makes clear that he was not actually there to view the horrible scene, and that his story has been constructed from accounts of black witnesses: "It is said that Gore gave Denby three calls, telling him that if he did not obey the last call [to get out of a creek], he would shoot him." Much of the other information that he recounts in the opening chapters of "Life as a Slave" have their sources in black oral history. He reports about Colonel Lloyd's favored black coachman, for instance: "It was whispered, and pretty generally admitted as a fact, that William Wilks was a son of Col. Lloyd, by a highly favored slave-woman." Of course there are similar whisperings about Douglass's connection to his white owner, Aaron Anthony, and thus to Thomas Auld's first wife, who is Anthony's daughter, but he remains forever uncertain about his patrilineal line and thus about key aspects of his personal history. Still, compared to the *Narrative*, it is with a larger historical vision and a fuller cast of characters that Douglass sets up his personal story, which doesn't move to center stage until chapter 9, "Personal Treatment of the Author." As in the *Narrative*, Douglass writes about his good fortune in being sent to Baltimore to live with Hugh and Sophia Auld, his efforts to teach himself to read and write while in Baltimore, his eventual return to the Eastern Shore to live with the "cruel" Thomas Auld and his new wife, and his increasing rebelliousness in response to Auld's cruelty.[5]

Douglass's depiction of his rebelliousness is considerably different from the moral-suasionist *Narrative*. Angered by Auld's miserly rationing of food, Douglass chooses to satisfy his hunger by stealing from him, which he justifies in this way: "Considering that my labor and person were the property of Master Thomas and that I was by him deprived of the necessaries of life—necessaries obtained by

Obama's and Douglass's autobiographies, see Robert B. Stepto, *A Home Elsewhere: Reading African American Classics in the Age of Obama* (Cambridge, MA: Harvard University Press, 2010), 7–26.

4. See Frederick Douglass, *The Heroic Slave: A Cultural and Critical Edition*, ed. Robert S. Levine, John Stauffer, and John R. McGivigan (New Haven: Yale University Press, 2015), p. 5.

5. Douglass, *My Bondage and My Freedom*, 91, 122, 115, 187 [pp. 67, 85, 81, 122].

my own labor—it was easy to deduce the right to supply myself with what was my own." In the guise of his teenaged self, Douglass then sets forth the position that he would regularly set forth *after* he had broken from Garrison and aligned himself with Gerrit Smith's Liberty Party: "I hold that the slave is fully justified in helping himself to the *gold and silver, and the best apparel of his master, or that of any other slaveholder; and that such taking is not stealing in any just sense of that word.*" The language resembles Madison Washington's when he explains to Listwell how he could justify stealing food while making his way north. (Listwell responds that Gerrit Smith would approve.) Though Douglass certainly didn't use this sort of language to Auld, it is precisely because Auld senses that Douglass has become rebellious that he sends him to "Covey, the Negro Breaker."[6]

It is at this point in his second autobiography that we see the important influence of *The Heroic Slave* on Douglass's reconception of himself as a Washington-like black rebel. Somewhat strangely, we could say about Douglass in *Bondage and Freedom* something like what the critic Ivy Wilson says about him in *The Heroic Slave*: It is as if the author is inserting himself into the protagonist, as if Douglass is attempting to make himself Douglass. To put this another way, in the 1845 *Narrative* Douglass chose to work with the script of the slave narrative that served the ends of Garrison and his antislavery society. In the 1855 *Bondage and Freedom*, he presents himself on his own terms, and one of the selves he chooses to present is that of a black freedom fighter who has joined hands with his black compatriots.

Arguably the most famous scene in the *Narrative* is Douglass's rebellion against the slave breaker Covey. In his first autobiography, Douglass emphasizes the significance of the rebellion at both its beginning—"You have seen how a man was made a slave; you shall see how a slave was made a man"—and conclusion—"It was a glorious resurrection, from the tomb of slavery, to the heaven of freedom." The framing and presentation of the rebellion make it a red-letter moment in the *Narrative*, the event that in many ways helped to create the man who would become the Garrisonian abolitionist of its final pages. But because Douglass now wants to present himself as a group leader, he chooses to downplay his heroic individualism in this second telling of his rebellion against Covey, showing how the other slaves on Covey's farm were critical to his success. Though Douglass retains some of the language from the Covey section in the *Narrative*, such as his apostrophe to the Chesapeake, he drops the language about heroic manhood and Christlike resurrection. In physically resisting Covey, Douglass does indeed

6. Ibid., 189, 190–91, 205 [pp. 123, 124, 132].

come to feel like "a freeman in *fact*, while I remained a slave in *form*," as he puts it in *Bondage and Freedom*.[7] But the more crucial development from the rebellion is his newfound sense of solidarity with his fellow slaves.

At Covey's, Douglass is regularly beaten; that remains a constant between the two autobiographies. But in *Bondage and Freedom*, Douglass presents himself as part of a larger community that includes Covey's cousin William Hughes, Caroline the black cook, a hired black man named Bill Smith (who is forced to breed slave children with Caroline), a slave named Eli, the slave Sandy Jenkins, and several others. As in the *Narrative*, after Douglass is viciously beaten by Covey, and Thomas Auld refuses to shelter him, Sandy offers him the root of an herb that, according to African traditions, should protect him (yet fails to). But in *Bondage and Freedom*, after Auld sends Douglass back to Covey, Sandy also invites him to dinner with his wife, a free black who is not mentioned in *Narrative*. Recalling that dinner years later, Douglass writes that "though I have feasted since, with honorables, lord mayors and alderman, over the sea, my supper on ash cake and cold water, with Sandy, was the meal, of all my life, most sweet to my taste, and now most vivid in my memory." The solidarity that he experiences at this healing dinner carries over into his account of the rebellion against Covey, which is successful (as Douglass presents it in *Bondage and Freedom*) precisely because of his solidarity with blacks. "We were all in open rebellion, that morning," Douglass writes. It is the slaves' refusal to assist the master that allows Douglass successfully to resist Covey; and it is Douglass's recognition of the important role of black community that keeps him from making the scene into a celebration of a single heroic slave. Douglass concludes the chapter with "Hereditary bondmen, know ye not / Who would be free, themselves must strike the blow"—the very words from Byron quoted by Henry Highand Garnet in his 1843 "Address to the Slaves of the United States," the speech at the African American Buffalo convention which had extolled Madison Washington, and which Douglass at that time had voted against from his moral-suasionist perspective; and of course very close to the words that the post-Garrisonian Douglass used as an epigraph to Part IV of *The Heroic Slave*.[8] As in the novella, Douglass's invocation of these lines at the end of the Covey section tells a larger autobiographical story about his changed

7. Douglass, *Narrative*, 65–66, 73; Douglass, *My Bondage and My Freedom*, 247 [p. 156].
8. Douglass, *My Bondage and My Freedom*, 227, 245, 249 [pp. 150, 154, 156]. On the importance of the Byron passage to *Bondage and Freedom*, see Phan, *Bonds of Citizenship*, 162–64; and on Douglass's more communal rendering of the rebellion against Covey, see Sekora, "'Mr. Editor, If You Please,'" 623–625.

perspective on black revolutionism in the years following the Buffalo convention.

That story of Douglass's evolving perspective on black revolutionism is given its fullest figuration in a subsequent chapter of *Bondage and Freedom* called "The Run-Away Plot," which focuses on Douglass's relationship with the slaves at William Freeland's plantation. In the *Narrative*, Douglass makes clear that he developed friendships at Freeland's and that the runaway plot was a group venture. But in *Bondage and Freedom*, those friendships are given much more emphasis; we even learn the names of most of his coconspirators. He also gives the runaway plot many more pages than he did in the *Narrative*. In fact, the chapter titled "The Run-Away Plot" is twenty-six pages in the 1855 printing of *Bondage and Freedom*, which makes it more than twice the length of "The Last Flogging," which describes the rebellion against Covey. As his use of the Byron quote suggests, in his retelling of the runaway plot in his second autobiography Douglass presents it as an insurrectionary plot in the tradition of the *Creole* and other black uprisings.[9]

In passages that are new to *Bondage and Freedom*, Douglass depicts the rebellious slaves at Freeland's as a black revolutionary "unit" that rejects the idea that "dark color [is] God's mark of displeasure." Meeting secretly at Douglass's Sabbath school, the slaves share "thoughts and sentiments . . . which might be called very incendiary, by oppressors and tyrants." Accordingly, Douglass describes the slaves as planning more than simply an escape. He writes: "These meetings must have resembled, on a small scale, the meetings of revolutionary conspirators, in their primary condition. We were plotting against our (so called) lawful rulers." In the *Narrative*, the runaway plot is conceived almost entirely in relation to the American revolutionary tradition; and indeed Douglass retains from his first autobiography the analogy he developed between the ideology of the rebellious black plotters and that of the Patrick Henry who declares, "GIVE ME LIBERTY OR GIVE ME DEATH." But when he writes in *Bondage and Freedom* that "incomparably more sublime, is the same sentiment, when *practically* asserted by men accustomed to the lash and chain," he decouples the sentiment from the specifics of the American Revolution, making it more in accord with the revolutionary spirit he depicts at the end of *The Heroic Slave*. And he adds something new from the 1845 rendering, asserting that he and his black compatriots "fully intended to *fight* as well as *run*, if necessity should occur for that extremity."[1]

---

9. See note 6 on pp. xi–xii [*Editors' note*].
1. Douglass, *My Bondage and My Freedom*, 269, 275, 269, 280, 284, 288 [pp. 168, 171, 168, 174, 176, 179].

Though the plot at Freeland's collapses when Freeland and his associates take Douglass and his fellow slaves into custody (Douglass cannot change that essential fact), the fighting spirit of the plot lives on in the blacks' consciousnesses and subsequent actions. The coconspirator slave Henry chooses to fight back, and his resistance distracts the whites long enough for Douglass to burn the passes he had written up for his fellow conspirators. Douglass remarks about his compatriots' refusal to divulge details of the plot or to implicate one another: "We were a band of brothers, and never dearer to each other than now." He even loves Sandy, to the point that he refuses to say absolutely that he had been their betrayer. As a result of their solidarity, the blacks are eventually returned to Freeland's farm, with the exception of Douglass, who is sent back to Hugh and Sophia Auld in Baltimore by his owner, Thomas Auld. There, Douglass becomes involved with the free blacks of the East Baltimore Improvement Society, who possibly help with his eventual escape. As he extolled the blacks on Freeland's farm, he now extolls the free blacks of Baltimore: "I owe much to the society of these young men."[2] Significantly, after making his escape from slavery (the details of which he continues to keep secret), Douglass records his indebtedness to a host of people who help to make him feel at home in New Bedford, including the unnamed blacks of New Bedford's African Methodist Episcopal Zion Church, who are described as so tightly committed to each other's welfare, and so resistant to the practice of slavery, that they are prepared to kill one of their members for threatening to betray a fugitive slave. Douglass doesn't dissent. Having reconceived of himself as a black revolutionary leader in the first part of *Bondage and Freedom*, he now turns in the second (and concluding) part to another large theme that he had addressed in *The Heroic Slave*: interracial friendship.

There is a wealth of new material about Douglass's life in the short concluding section, "Life as a Freeman." Nevertheless, the two most recent editors of *Bondage and Freedom* are in agreement about the limits of this second part. John Stauffer remarks that "representing himself as a free man seemed to induce in Douglass a crisis of language and aesthetics," while David W. Blight asserts that "in the second part, . . . Douglass's voice seems at times to fall flatter."[3] Perhaps the problem is that the final section, with its focus on Douglass's several years in New Bedford, his initial association with Garrison,

2. Ibid., 296, 319 [pp. 183, 197].
3. John Stauffer, "Foreword," Douglass, *My Bondage and My Freedom* (New York: Modern Library, 2003), xxv; David W. Blight, "Introduction," Douglass, *My Bondage and My Freedom* (New Haven: Yale University Press, 2014), xi.

his triumphal British tour, and his break with Garrison, doesn't seem quite as universal as the archetypal story of Douglass's rise from slavery to freedom. But this section, which is hardly flat, helps us to better understand why Douglass has written a second auto-biography just ten years after his first: he wants to address the political transformation that led to his break with Garrison. In 1845 and 1846, Douglass sought to assert his authority over the 1845 *Narrative* by publishing his own editions in Dublin, but even those revised autobiographies remained true to the Garrisonian storyline of the rise of an extraordinary slave to a position within the Massachusetts Anti-Slavery Society. In light of his public break from Garrison, Douglass sought to retell his life story, and as I have been arguing throughout this chapter, his evolving thinking about black revolutionism (with its focus on Madison Washington) had become crucial to his increasing differences with Garrison. To some extent Douglass writes that political and personal history into *The Heroic Slave*; and he foregrounds that history in the "Life as a Freeman" section of *Bondage and Freedom*. Though the account of Garrison in this section mainly addresses the 1845–1847 period, it is motivated by Douglass's reconception of himself as a black leader in the late 1840s and early 1850s, and in particular by his disputes with Garrison in the immediate wake of the publication of *The Heroic Slave*.

In 1853 and 1854, following the publication of a novella that implicitly and explicitly honored Gerrit Smith, Garrison went on the offensive, printing numerous articles in the *Liberator* on Douglass's bad politics, and even accusing him of having an affair with Julia Griffiths. Responding to the sharp criticism from Garrison, as well as from William C. Nell and other black Garrisonians, Douglass confessed in an article printed in the December 9, 1853, *Frederick Douglass' Paper*: "Their assaults are now unbearable." Particularly embarrassed by the charge of adultery, he had his wife, Anna, send Garrison a letter, probably authored by Douglass, declaring that theirs was a happy household: "SIR—It is not true, that the presence of a certain person in the office of Frederick Douglass causes unhappiness in his family. Please insert this in your next paper." Garrison printed the letter in the December 16, 1853, *Liberator*. In a subsequent raging attack precipitated by Douglass's various efforts to defend himself, Garrison pronounced on his former associate: "Mr. DOUGLASS now stands self-unmasked, his features flushed with passion, his air scornful and defiant, his language bitter as wormwood, his pen dripped in poison; as thoroughly changed in his spirit as was ever 'arch-angel ruined,' as artful and unscrupulous a schismatic as has yet appeared in the abolition ranks."[4] Douglass offered an extended response to Garrison in a March 1855 lecture in which he argued that while Garrison may have helped to revive antislavery activity in the United States, he "neither discovered its principles, originated its ideas, nor framed its arguments."[5] Several months after delivering this lecture, Douglass published *Bondage and Freedom*, whose opening paratexts trumpet the autobiography as a work that has been reconceived in light of his break with Garrison, his friendship with Gerrit Smith, and his alliance with the Liberty Party. In a striking full-page dedication to Smith, Douglass praises "HIS GENIUS AND BENEVOLENCE," and records his "GRATITUDE FOR HIS FRIENDSHIP," signing himself Smith's "FAITHFUL AND FULLY ATTACHED FRIEND." That dedication could be read as a slap in the face to Garrison. But the real slap comes in *Bondage and Freedom*'s "Life as a Freeman" section. In sharp contrast to the Listwell-Washington relationship in *The Heroic Slave*, Douglass presents his relationship with Garrison as a glaring instance of a bad interracial friendship.

Douglass begins his account of Garrison on an upbeat note, remarking on how he discovered the *Liberator* shortly after arriving in New Bedford: "I not only liked—I *loved* this paper, and its editor." But as the "loved" suggests, this is all in the past, and Douglass emphasizes the pastness of the past at the very moment that he introduces Garrison into his narrative: "Seventeen years ago, few men possessed a more heavenly countenance than William Lloyd Garrison, and few men evinced a more genuine or a more exalted piety." As in the *Narrative*, Douglass describes his first short speech before Garrison's society and his subsequent recruitment as a lecturer. Working with the conventions of the seduction novel, Douglass depicts himself as an innocent: "Young, ardent, and hopeful, I entered upon this new life in the full gush of unsuspecting enthusiasm." What he hadn't anticipated, he now says from his

---

4. Douglass, "The Liberator," *Frederick Douglass' Paper*, 9 December 1853, 2; *Liberator*, 16 December 1853, 196; William Lloyd Garrison, "The Mask Entirely Removed," *Liberator*, 16 December 1853, 196. Shocked by the venom of Garrison's attack, Harriet Beecher Stowe wrote him privately to ask: "Why is he [Douglass] any more to be called an apostate for having spoken ill-tempered things of former friends than they for having spoken severely and cruelly as they have of him? Where is this work of excommunication to end? Is there but one true anti-slavery church and all others infidels?" (Stowe to Garrison, letter of 19 December 1853, in *Life and Letters of Harriet Beecher Stowe*, ed. Annie Fields [Boston: Houghton, Mifflin, 1898], 214–15). Julia Griffiths returned to England early in 1855. For a helpful collection of letters and other primary documents about the conflict between Douglass and Garrison, see John Ernest, ed., *Douglass in His Own Time: A Biographical Chronicle of His Life, Drawn from Recollections, Interviews, and Memoirs by Family, Friends, and Associates* (Iowa City: University of Iowa Press, 2014), 63–101. See also William H. Pease and Jane H. Pease, "Boston Garrisonians and the Problem of Frederick Douglass," *Canadian Journal of History* 2.2 (1967): 29–48.

5. Douglass, "The Anti-Slavery Movement: An Address Delivered in Rochester, New York, on 19 March 1855," *FDP*, vol. 3, 19–20.

disillusioned perspective in 1855, is that he would be regarded as an inferior—a black subordinate—in a hierarchically based white antislavery organization who was expected to play the role of the escaped black slave. In an oft-quoted passage near the end of *Bondage and Freedom*, Douglass insists that Garrison mainly wanted him to speak about his history as a slave: "'Tell your story, Frederick,' would whisper my then revered friend, William Lloyd Garrison, as I stepped upon the platform." Douglass confides to his readers: "I could not always obey, for I was now reading and thinking."[6] In a subsequent chapter on his "Twenty-One Months in Great Britain," Douglass highlights his growing independence as an antislavery speaker and thinker, while making clear that he has been developing new interracial friendships, such as with the white British abolitionists who purchased him out of slavery.

Near the end of *Bondage and Freedom*, the reading and thinking Douglass returns to the story of his relationship with Garrison. Unlike the final pages of the *Narrative*, the concluding chapter is almost completely lacking in triumphalism; instead, it builds to a statement of mission. Douglass's main contention is that Garrison and his associates are bad friends because they are racists. Douglass moves the reader to this dispiriting insight by telling the story of the *North Star*. Instead of encouraging Douglass to establish a vital black newspaper, the Garrisonians angrily insist that he continue to lecture for their organization. Douglass attempts to gain the goodwill of his paternalistic "Boston friends" by moving to "Rochester, Western New York, among strangers, where the circulation of my paper could not interfere with the local circulation of the Liberator," but his relationship with Garrison continues to deteriorate, especially after he publicly announces his break from Garrisonian abolitionism in 1851. Douglass summarizes the next few years of his interactions with Garrison by stating that "the common punishment of apostates was mine." But he is no mere "apostate"; he is a black apostate. In the closing pages of *Bondage and Freedom*, Douglass discusses Garrison in the larger context of "American prejudice against color, and its varied illustrations in my own experience," commenting on Jim Crow cars and other manifestations of racism, and then on the Garrisonians. "When I first went among the abolitionists of New England, and began to travel," Douglass writes, "I found this prejudice very strong and very annoying. The abolitionists themselves were not entirely free from it."[7] In *The Heroic Slave*,

6. Douglass, *My Bondage and My Freedom*, 354–55, 359, 361 [pp. 218, 221, 222]. Douglass also chose not to obey the edict of Garrison's associate George Foster, who, for the sake of authenticity, tells him to retain "a *little* of the plantation manner of speech" in his lectures (362 [p. 223]).
7. Ibid., 394, 395, 396, 398 [pp. 243, 243, 244, 245].

the sympathizing character Listwell is hardly race-blind; he gazes obsessively at Washington's black body when he first eavesdrops on him. But when they announce themselves as friends, race seems secondary to their shared commitment to human freedom. In his wry comments on Garrison at the end of *Bondage and Freedom*, Douglass suggests that Garrison, for all the wrong reasons, never stopped seeing him as a black man.

And so it is as a prideful black leader that Douglass concludes his second autobiography. He states that precisely because he decided in 1847 to edit a black newspaper, "I have had my mind more directed to the condition and circumstances of the free colored people than when I was the agent of an abolition society." In ways that parallel the ending of *The Heroic Slave*, he situates himself in relation to blacks both within and beyond the United States by quoting the prophecy of Psalms 68.31: "Ethiopia shall yet reach forth her hand unto God." In the autobiography's final sentence prior to the appendix, Douglass states that he will be working "to advocate the great and primary work of the universal and unconditional emancipation of my entire race."[8] At various moments in his career Douglass affirms his connection to the human race, but here, at the end of his 1855 autobiography, the heroic slave and freeman conceives of himself in relation to black people. Taken together, *The Heroic Slave* and *Bondage and Freedom* can be read as a composite autobiography, as mediated by his thinking about Madison Washington, of Douglass's development of a racial consciousness that links him with a larger black diaspora. Crucial to the story that he tells in both works is an enhanced commitment to traditions of black revolutionism and an ongoing concern about the risks of interracial friendship.

JEANNINE DELOMBARD

From Talking Lawyerlike about Law[†]

* * *

* * * If the *Narrative of the Life of Frederick Douglass* is the consummate portrayal of the bondsman as victim of and witness to the crime of slavery, *My Bondage and My Freedom* offers the period's most thorough articulation of the dilemma of the free black abolitionist facing the bar of public opinion. In the *Narrative*, prefaces

---

8. Ibid., 405, 406 [pp. 249, 427].
† From *Slavery on Trial: Law, Abolitionism, and Print Culture* (Durham: U of North Carolina P, 2007), pp. 132–43, 149. Copyright © 2007 by the University of North Carolina Press. Used by permission of the publisher.

by well-known white advocates for the slave mimic the prosecutor's opening argument by introducing and framing the testimonial evidence that follows; appropriately, then, the prefatory materials with which Douglass begins his second narrative foreground the conundrum of black advocacy itself.

In a letter reproduced in the unsigned "Editor's Preface" to *My Bondage and My Freedom*, Douglass, responding to his editor's "urgent solicitation for such a work," reminds his reader, "I have often refused to narrate my personal experience in public antislavery meetings, and in sympathizing circles, when urged to do so by friends, with whose views and wishes, ordinarily, it were a pleasure to comply."[1] Instead, Douglass maintains, in "letters and speeches, I have generally aimed to discuss the question of Slavery in the light of fundamental principles, and upon facts, notorious and open to all; making, I trust, no more of the fact of my own enslavement, than circumstances seemed absolutely to require."[2] Picking up where the *Narrative* left off, Douglass's autobiography portrays its author as pleading the cause of his brethren in preference to narrating his "personal experience." Still, Douglass's claims seem more than a little disingenuous. After all, he had become an international celebrity through recitations of his "own enslavement" in print and on the lecture platform; he would retell the story of his "Bondage" in the current volume; and he would go on to recount that story yet again in a third autobiographical narrative, the *Life and Times of Frederick Douglass* (1881), publishing two further revised and expanded editions of that work before his death in 1895.

But in an era when, in Habermas's words, the "publicizing of private biographies" was beginning to supplant the ideal of reasoned debate in the public sphere, circumstances frequently seemed "absolutely to require" that Douglass root his philosophical antislavery argument in what critic Eric J. Sundquist has called the "wrenchingly personal" facts of his own enslavement.[3] Indeed, later in the same introductory letter, Douglass would draw on the very juridical language that Garrison had used to authorize the *Narrative* in order to elaborate his reasons for publishing this sequel. Emphasizing that *My Bondage and My Freedom* was intended "not to illustrate any

---

1. Frederick Douglass, *My Bondage and My Freedom*, in *Autobiographies*, by Frederick Douglass, ed. Henry Louis Gates, Jr. (New York: Library of America, 1994), 105 [p. 5].
2. Ibid.
3. Jurgen Habermas, *Structural Transformation of the Public Sphere: An Inquiry into a Category of Bourgeois Society*, trans. Thomas Burger and Frederick Lawrence (Cambridge, MA: MIT P, 1991), 171. Eric J. Sundquist, *To Wake the Nations: Race in the Making of American Literature* (Cambridge, MA: Harvard UP, 1993), 97. On the new importance of personality to Jacksonian rhetorical performance, see Terry Baxter, *Frederick Douglass's Curious Audiences: Ethos in the Age of the Consumable Subject* (New York: Routledge, 2004), 59–83.

heroic achievements of a man" but, rather, to shine "the light of truth upon a system, esteemed by some as a blessing, and by others as a curse and a crime," Douglass moved from a religious to a legal register to explain that "this system [slavery] is now at the bar of public opinion—not only of this country, but of the whole civilized world—for judgment."[4] Because "its friends have made for it the usual plea—'not guilty;' the case must, therefore, proceed. Any facts, either from slaves, slave-holders, or by-standers, calculated to enlighten the public mind, by revealing the true nature, character, and tendency of the slave system, are in order, and can scarcely be innocently withheld."[5] However eager he may have been to step down from the witness stand, Douglass implied, his autobiographical testimony had been effectively subpoenaed by the popular tribunal.

At the moment that he offered one of the era's most vivid evocations of the slavery debate as a trial before "the bar of public opinion," however, Douglass (always an astute observer of the racial politics of antebellum print culture) called attention to the unique rhetorical challenges such legal language posed for African Americans. Citing "special reasons why I should write my own biography, in preference to employing another to do it," Douglass explained, "Not only is slavery on trial, but unfortunately, the enslaved people are also on trial. It is alleged, that they are, naturally, inferior; that they are *so low* in the scale of humanity, and so utterly stupid, that they are unconscious of their wrongs, and do not apprehend their rights."[6] Linking the imputed criminality of slaves to their presumptive inferiority, Douglass acknowledged the importance of black literary production to demonstrating African Americans' ability to "apprehend their rights"—perceiving the fundamental principles of natural law that guaranteed those rights, as well as laying claim to the rights themselves.

* * *

As Douglass's shrewd use of the word "apprehend" implies, due to the nature of the inferiority ascribed to blacks, such vindication could not be accomplished merely by casting the former slave in the role of testifying eyewitness.[7] * * * For, as radical as the abolitionist call for black testimony may have seemed, that appeal was nevertheless rooted in Enlightenment racial thought, which conceded blacks to be skillful in description and other mimetic techniques

---

4. Douglass, *My Bondage*, 106 [p. 6].
5. Ibid.
6. Ibid.
7. On the Scottish Common Sense philosophy concept of "apprehension" elsewhere in *My Bondage*, see Maurice Lee, *Slavery, Philosophy, and American Literature, 1830–1860* (Cambridge: Cambridge UP, 2005).

associated with the production of narrative but deficient in a higher capacity for analysis and interpretation. Thomas Jefferson's classic formulation of this thesis in "Laws," Query XIV of his *Notes on the State of Virginia*, builds on the philosophy of David Hume and Immanuel Kant to justify Virginian legislators' refusal to "incorporate the blacks into the state" (and by extension the nation) largely on the basis of this deficiency.[8] * * *

"Comparing [blacks] by their faculties of memory, reason, and imagination," Jefferson finds "that in memory they are equal to the whites; in reason much inferior," and "in imagination they are dull, tasteless, and anomalous"; thus, like animals, "their existence appears to participate more of sensation than reflection."[9] Restricting his "judgment" to blacks of the diaspora, amongst whom "some have been liberally educated, and all have lived in countries where the arts and sciences are cultivated to a considerable degree, and have had before their eyes samples of the best works from abroad," Jefferson concludes, "Never yet, could I find that a black had uttered a thought above the level of plain narration."[1]

* * * Although Jefferson's language anticipates both the scientific racism and the romantic racialism that would increasingly characterize nineteenth-century racial thought, his conclusions were particularly devastating in the bourgeois Enlightenment world * * *, for in that milieu, civic inclusion was premised, at least theoretically, on the display of reason rather than social status.[2] To lack reason was to lack humanity; to be denied admission to the republic of letters authorized one's exclusion from the republic of laws."[3]

* * * It is precisely his white colleagues' inheritance of Jeffersonian racial thought, and most notably the opposition of blacks' "plain narration" to whites' "sober reasoning," that Douglass critiques in *My Bondage and My Freedom*'s best-known passage, from the chapter "Introduced to the Abolitionists":

8. Thomas Jefferson, *Notes on the State of Virginia*, ed. David Waldstreicher (New York: Bedford-St. Martin's, 2002), 169, 172, 175, 182. See also Emmanuel Chukwudi Eze, ed., *Race and the Enlightenment: A Reader* (Malden, MA: Blackwell, 1997), 29–33, 38–64.
9. Jefferson, *Notes*, 177.
1. Ibid.
2. See Habermas, *Structural Transformation*, 36. On Jefferson and nineteenth-century racial thought, see George M. Fredrickson, *The Black Image in the White Mind: The Debate on Afro-American Character and Destiny, 1817–1914* (Hanover, NH: Wesleyan UP, 1971); Alexander O. Boulton, "The American Paradox: Jeffersonian Equality and Racial Science," *American Quarterly* 47.3 (Sept. 1995): 467–92; Henry Louis Gates, *The Trials of Phillis Wheatley: America's First Black Poet and Her Encounters with the Founding Fathers* (New York: Perseus-Basic Civitas Books, 2003).
3. In Query XIV's triadic grouping of law, race, and education, the mutual interdependence of (white) citizenship and education makes blacks' imputed intellectual inferiority virtually synonymous with their civic exclusion. [See James Oakes, "Why Slaves Can't Read: The Political Significance of Jefferson's Racism," in James Gilrath, ed., *The South as an American Problem* (Athens: U of Georgia P, 1995), 191.—*Editors*]

During the first three or four months, my speeches were almost
exclusively made up of narrations of my own personal experience as a slave. "Let us have the facts," said the people. So also
said Friend George Foster, who always wished to pin me down
to my simple narrative. "Give us the facts," said Collins, "we will
take care of the philosophy." . . . "Tell your story, Frederick,"
would whisper my then revered friend, William Lloyd Garrison,
as I stepped upon the platform. I could not always obey, for I
was now reading and thinking. New views of the subject were
presented to my mind. It did not entirely satisfy me to *narrate*
wrongs; I felt like *denouncing* them. I could not always curb my
moral indignation for the perpetrators of slaveholding villainy,
long enough for a circumstantial statement of the facts which
I felt almost everybody must know. Besides, I was growing, and
needed room.[4]

Rejecting the Garrisonian demand that he limit his public speaking
to a "circumstantial statement of the facts," Douglass identifies a
dynamic that Holocaust scholar James E. Young sees as a defining
characteristic of testimonial literature.[5] Young describes testimony
as "'factually insistent' narrative" that "accomplishes not so much
the unmediated rendition of facts as it does a 'rhetoric of fact.'"[6] As
a result, Young explains, both testimonial texts and their authors are
assigned the impossible task of becoming "*traces*" or "material frag-
ments of experiences."[7] Hence, the need for formerly enslaved lecturers and writers to authorize their political interventions on the
basis of the physical victimization against which they testified.

* * *

The problem with this "rhetoric of fact" was not so much its claim
to unmediated representation as its tendency to separate, in the
words of Douglass's white colleague John Collins, "fact" from
"philosophy."[8] Mimicking the adversarial trial's apparent distinction between facts and analysis, narration and interpretation, the

4. Douglass, *My Bondage*, 367 [pp. 222–23].
5. On the appropriateness of Holocaust scholarship to the study of slavery and abolition,
see Paul Gilroy, *The Black Atlantic: Modernity and Double Consciousness* (Cambridge,
MA: Harvard UP, 1993), 215. The purpose here is better to understand, in theoretical
terms, the status of testimonial speech in the nexus of power relations from which it
arises. For a similar approach, see Marcus Wood, *Blind Memory: Visual Representations of Slavery in England and America, 1780–1865* (New York: Routledge, 2000),
20–53.
6. James E. Young, *Writing and Rewriting the Holocaust: Narrative and the Consequences
of Interpretation* (Bloomington: Indiana UP, 1988), 15, 9.
7. Ibid., 23.
8. On poststructuralism and the countermovement of Holocaust testimony to "documen-
tary realism," see Young, *Writing*, 17. On the critical pitfalls of reifying "experience,"
see Joan W. Scott, "The Evidence of Experience." *Critical Inquiry* 17.4 (Summer 1991):
773–97.

antislavery movement endowed its black witnesses with "testimonial authority"—recognition of the authenticity and facticity of their texts—at the expense of what we might call exegetical authority, recognition of their ability and right to construct meaning from these texts.[9] * * * Perhaps it is not surprising to find Boston lawyer George W. Searle—in phrasing much like that Douglass attributes to Collins—recalling of his late colleague Robert Morris, "He tried cases on facts, and left the refinements and technicalities of law to others who had mastered them."[1]

                              *   *   *

Critics have long recognized the importance of the *Columbian Orator*, and this moral suasionist "Dialogue" in particular,[2] to Douglass's preparation for—and publicizing of—his subsequent abolitionist career.[3] But what is seldom, if ever, acknowledged is the significant discrepancy between the rhetorical strategies adopted by the *Columbian Orator*'s idealized republican slave and those employed by Douglass as Garrisonian "eye-witness to the cruelty."[4] From this exchange, historian David Blight points out, young Frederick Bailey learned "that slavery was something subject to 'argument,' even between master and slave"—a discovery that offered a valuable example of "reason winning over power" to an adolescent "surrounded and imprisoned by the opposite message."[5]

9. Young, *Writing*, 38. See also ibid., 15–39.
1. *In Memoriam, Robert Morris, Sr. Born June 8, 1823. Died December 12, 1882.* (Boston: n.p., 1883?), 18. This comment may also refer to changes in legal education more generally, as Morris's generation of attorneys trained in law-office apprenticeships was replaced by the products of professional law schools. On legal training, see J. Clay Smith Jr., *Emancipation: The Making of the Black Lawyer, 1844–1944* (Philadelphia: U of Pennsylvania P, 1993), 33–92; Maxwell Bloomfield, *American Lawyers in a Changing Society, 1776–1876* (Cambridge, MA: Harvard UP, 1976), 302–09.
2. In *My Bondage and My Freedom*, Douglass refers to a popular anthology of rhetoric, *The Columbian Orator*, and discusses his response to one of the volume's selections, which he describes as "a short dialogue between a master and his slave" (104) [*Editors' note*].
3. See John W. Blassingame, Introduction, *The Frederick Douglass Papers*, series 1: *Speeches, Debates, and Interviews*, ed. John W. Blassingame et al. (New Haven, CT: Yale UP, 1979), xxii–xxiii; David W. Blight, "Editor's Introduction: The Peculiar Dialogue between Caleb Bingham and Frederick Douglass," in Bingham, *The Columbian Orator: Containing a Variety of Original and Selected Pieces Together with Rules, Which Are Calculated to Improve Youth and Others in the Ornamental and Useful Art of Eloquence*, ed. David W. Blight (New York: New York UP, 1998), xxii–xxiii; Shelley Fisher Fishkin and Carla L. Peterson, "'We Hold These Truths to Be Self- Evident': The Rhetoric of Frederick Douglass's Journalism," in *Frederick Douglass: New Literary and Historical Essays*, ed. Eric Sundquist (New York: Cambridge UP, 1990), 190–92; Robert S. Levine, *Martin Delany, Frederick Douglass, and the Politics of Representative Identity* (Chapel Hill: U of North Carolina P, 1997), 27; William S. McFeely, *Frederick Douglass* (New York: Touchstone-Simon and Schuster, 1991), 34–36; Waldo E. Martin, Jr., *The Mind of Frederick Douglass* (Chapel Hill: U of North Carolina P, 1985), 8–9; Sundquist, *To Wake*, 104–05; Gregory P. Lampe, *Frederick Douglass: Freedom's Voice, 1818–1845* (East Lansing: Michigan State UP, [1998]), 9–13, 101–02.
4. I am indebted to my former students Kristen Proehl and Briallen Hopper for first calling this discrepancy to my attention.
5. Blight, "Editor's Introduction," xxiv.

But, like Garrison, Douglass grew up in a print culture shaped by the lingering ideals of republicanism only to find himself contributing to a very different one, in which sensationalism and biographical storytelling increasingly trumped reason and argument. Strictly speaking, Aikin's eloquent slave devotes only two sentences to autobiographical narrative, sentences that are subordinated to a larger philosophical discussion about "power" versus "right."[6]

It is this kind of reasoned adversarial dialogue that Douglass in *My Bondage and My Freedom* claims Garrisonians reserved for themselves while restricting the former slave to a "circumstantial statement of the facts." But as the archival work of Newman, Rael, and Lapsansky shows us, Aikin's eighteenth-century fictive slave had his counterpart in the first generation of black pamphleteers whose turn to print culture as a court of public opinion would influence Garrisonian tactics. From the 1790s onward, these scholars note, autobiography provided the ballast for black political writing; for African American pamphleteers "the first-person perspective was an important method of clarifying, critiquing, and illuminating the issues at hand: racist laws, white stereotypes, black nationhood. Autobiographical frames of reference broadened outward into a world of analysis, formal social debate, and intellectual activity."[7] In contrast to the antebellum slave narrative, however, "the trick was to go beyond the personal to the transcendent."[8] Thus, it is only in the fourth and last article of David Walker's *Appeal* that the author assures his reader, "I do not speak from hear say—what I have written, is what I have seen and heard myself"; by contrast, Walker devotes Article I to demonstrating the need for black forensics: "Unless we try to refute Mr. Jefferson's arguments respecting us, we will only establish them."[9]

We can see these antecedents resurfacing in Douglass's revised self-fashioning in *My Bondage and My Freedom*. As James McCune Smith's introduction suggests, Douglass's second personal narrative represents his determined attempt, through a consolidation of the roles of antislavery witness and black advocate, to reconcile the proven extralegal tactics of Garrisonian abolitionism with the still-influential republican association of reason with citizenship,

---

6. Bingham, *Columbian Orator*, 210.
7. Richard Newman, Patrick Rael, and Phillip Lapsansky, "Introduction: The Theme of Our Contemplation," in *Pamphlets of Protest: An Anthology of Early African American Protest Literature, 1790–1860*, ed. Richard Newman, Patrick Rael, and Phillip Lapsansky (New York: Routledge, 2001), 22.
8. Ibid.
9. David Walker, *David Walker's Appeal, in Four Articles; Together with a Preamble, to the Coloured Citizens of the World, But in Particular, and Very Expressly, to Those of the United States of America*, ed. Sean Wilentz (New York: Hill and Wang, 1995), 76, 15.

especially where blacks were concerned.[1] Thus, even as McCune Smith's prefatory comments seem to affirm the volume's generic status as slave narrative by replicating traditional authenticating documents, his introduction radically revises that model, effectively following Aikin's "Dialogue" and black pamphleteers in subsuming the former slave's narrated "personal experience" to his impassioned but well-reasoned advocacy on behalf of his fellow African Americans.[2]

Signaling Douglass's independence from Garrisonian abolitionism in his opening paragraphs, the free African American doctor, activist, and author begins his introduction by reminding his readers that the "real object" of "the American anti-slavery movement" was "not only to disenthrall" but "also, to bestow upon the negro the exercise of all those rights, from the possession of which he has been so long debarred."[3] Presenting Douglass not merely "as a representative" to "the downtrodden" of "what they may themselves become," McCune Smith maintained that he was "a Representative American man—a type of his countrymen" and that *My Bondage and My Freedom* was, therefore, "an American book, for Americans, in the fullest sense of the idea."[4]

Because Douglass's eligibility as representative American was jeopardized by racism in the form of perennial murmurs that the famous orator's "descriptive and declamatory powers, admitted to be of the very highest order, take precedence of his logical force," McCune Smith carefully refuted such Jeffersonian slurs by insistently coupling the author's "uncommon memory" with his "keen and accurate insight into men and things," his "passion" with his "intellect," and (again) his "unfailing memory" with his "keen and telling wit."[5] In McCune Smith's account, Douglass's "plantation education," far from suppressing these "original gifts," actually "prepare[d] him for the high calling on which he has since entered—the advocacy of emancipation by the people who are not slaves" by providing the necessary "facts and experiences, welded to acutely wrought up sympathies" that could not be acquired elsewhere.[6] (The

---

1. For a critique of uplift ideology in McCune Smith's introduction and the work as a whole, see Levine, *Martin Delany*, 112–15.
2. On Douglass's use of a black-authored authenticating document, see Frances Foster, *Witnessing Slavery: The Development of Ante-bellum Slave Narratives* (Westport, CT: Greenwood, 1979), 148; and William L. Andrews, *To Tell a Free Story: The First Century of Afro-American Autobiography, 1760–1865* (Urbana: U of Illinois P, 1986), 217.
3. Douglass, *My Bondage*, 125 [p. 19].
4. Ibid., 125, 132, 137 [pp. 19, 27, 32–33]. On Douglass's representative Americanness, see Sundquist, *To Wake*, 86, 92, 101.
5. Douglass, *My Bondage*, 126, 133 [pp. 20–21, 27–28]. For a more direct critique of Jefferson's Query XIV, see James McCune Smith, "On the Fourteenth Query of Thomas Jefferson's *Notes on Virginia*," *Anglo-African Magazine* (Aug. 1859): 225–38. See also Gates, *Trials*, 64–65.
6. Douglass, *My Bondage*, 126 [p. 21].

awkwardness of his reference to "the advocacy of emancipation by the people who are not slaves" betrays the strain of articulating a black advocacy premised not on previous condition of servitude but on current assertions of civic agency.)

The Garrisonians' mistake, McCune Smith made clear, was to limit Douglass to such "facts and experiences" rather than encouraging that free play of "memory, logic, wit, sarcasm, invective, pathos, and bold imagery of rare structural beauty" that gave Douglass's post-*Narrative* oratory and writing its tremendous power.[7] Of "Wendell Phillips, Edmund Quincy, William Lloyd Garrison," and other white "men of earnest faith and refined culture," McCune Smith wrote, "these gentlemen, although proud of Frederick Douglass, failed to fathom, and bring out to the light of day, the highest qualities of his mind; the force of their own education stood in their own way: they did not delve into the mind of a colored man for capacities which the pride of race led them to believe to be restricted to their own Saxon blood."[8] In short, the movement's racism produced a crowd-pleasing but narrow representation of African American identity: "Bitter and vindictive sarcasm, irresistible mimicry, and a pathetic narrative of his own experiences of slavery, were the intellectual manifestations which they encouraged him to exhibit on the platform or in the lecture desk."[9]

More than simply exposing and condemning the prejudices of white abolitionists, however, McCune Smith's account turns such racial thought on its head. "Whilst the schools might have trained" Douglass "to the exhibition of the formulas of deductive logic," as they did his Yankee colleagues, "nature and circumstances," McCune Smith cannily asserts, "forced him into the exercise of the higher faculties required by induction":

> The first ninety pages of this "Life in Bondage," afford specimens of observing, comparing, and careful classifying, of such superior character, that it is difficult to believe them the results of a child's thinking; he questions the earth, and the children and the slaves around him again and again, and finally looks to "*God in the sky*" for the why and the wherefore of the unnatural thing, slavery. . . .
>
> To such a mind, the ordinary processes of logical deduction are like proving that two and two make four. Mastering the intermediate steps by an intuitive glance . . . it goes down to the deeper relation of things, and brings out what may seem, to some, mere statements, but which are new and brilliant generalizations, each resting on a broad and stable basis. Thus,

7. Ibid., 134 [p. 29].
8. Ibid., 129 [p. 24].
9. Ibid.

> Chief Justice Marshall gave his decisions, and then told Brother
> Story to look up the authorities—and they never differed from
> him.[1]

McCune Smith's identification of Douglass with American Colonization Society officer and slaveholder John Marshall is a comparison as apt as it is unexpected. After all, Jefferson's nemesis, Federalist
lawyer and Supreme Court Chief Justice Marshall, not only stood
as the personification of American constitutional law but was also
known for his comparative lack of formal legal training, his corresponding disinclination to "blackletter scholarship," and his uncommon mixture of "those qualities essential to legal greatness: a
capacious, retentive, and quick mind; sharp analytical skills; and a
logical prose style that bordered on eloquence"—the exact qualities
that McCune Smith has been careful to attribute to Douglass.[2] Like
Marshall, characterized by the "exercise of the higher faculties
required by induction," Douglass is, along with McCune Smith's
masculinist roll call of black abolitionists (Samuel Ringgold Ward,
Henry Highland Garnet, William Wells Brown, James W. C. Pennington, and Jermaine Wesley Loguen), uniquely qualified for the
"high calling" of advocating for the "full recognition of the colored
man to the right, and the entire admission of the same to the full
privileges, political, religious and social, of manhood."[3]

The comparison of Douglass to Marshall further implies that such
African Americans' firsthand experience of slavery or racism, far
from constraining them to the subordinate position of antislavery
witness, fits them to lead the movement. The image of Marshall telling "Brother Story to look up the authorities" thus offers an alternative model of abolitionist collaboration. In place of the unequal
relationship between the testifying slave witness and the white advocate who represents him, McCune Smith provides the example of
Marshall and Story as legal colleagues; characterized by mutual
respect, this fraternal model nevertheless grants authority and leadership to the "Brother" with the greater experience and skill.

McCune Smith's inversion of Jeffersonian claims to blacks' intellectual inferiority through his emphasis on Douglass's superior
capacity for induction retraces a similar movement in the

---

1. Ibid., 133, 134 [pp. 28, 29].
2. R. Kent Newmyer, "John Marshall," *in The Oxford Companion to the Supreme Court of
the United States,* ed. Kermit L. Hall (New York: Oxford UP, 1992), 523. For Marshall's
ambiguous position on slavery, see ibid., 526. On Marshall in a literary context, see
Robert A. Ferguson, *Law and Letters in American Culture* (Cambridge, MA: Harvard
UP, 1984), 23.
3. Douglass, *My Bondage,* 125 [p. 19].

Columbian Orator's "Dialogue between a Master and a Slave."[4] Opening with the master's accusatory address to his runaway slave—"Now, villain!"—the "Discourse" begins with the premise of black criminality that, in the master's deductive logic, is proven by the slave's illegal theft of himself.[5] But the slave wins both the argument and his freedom by demonstrating inductively from his own experience that it is the perpetrators of slavery, not slaves, who are the guilty criminals. Briefly recounting his own "treacherous kidnapp[ing]" in Africa as a preface to his philosophical query, "What step in all this progress of violence and injustice can give a right?" the slave clinches his argument with his pointed appropriation of the slaveholder's inaugural epithet: "Was it in the villain who stole me, in the slave-merchant who tempted him to do so, or in you who encouraged the slave merchant to bring his cargo of human cattle to cultivate your lands?"[6] Lest the connection between the villainy of the African slave trade and the crime of slaveholding remain unclear, the slave's next contribution to the dialogue dispatches the master's earlier appeal to providential design by responding, "You cannot but be sensible, that the robber who puts a pistol to your breast may make just the same plea. Providence gives him a power over your life and property; it gave my enemies a power over my liberty."[7]

Bingham's lesson was lost on neither the young Frederick Bailey nor the adult Frederick Douglass. Immediately following his discussion of the *Columbian Orator*, Douglass recalls in the *Narrative* that

4. *Notes*'s structure, Ferguson has shown, rests on the inductive logic of empiricism and the common law: "Only slavery resists rational management in Jefferson's hands, . . . precisely because it defies legal terminology and solution within the framework of an eighteenth-century lawyer. Slavery exists, but against natural law; it becomes, in consequence, a structural incongruity in *Notes*, spilling between and among sections." The anomalous, extralegal status of the slave disrupts not only *Notes*'s structural coherence but its logical progression as well. In contrast to the inductive legal logic that provides *Notes* with its structure, Jefferson's discussion of blacks and law moves in the opposite direction: observed evidence of blacks' inferiority is marshaled to support the premise of their necessary civic exclusion (*Law and Letters*, 38, 46, 51). See also Waldstreicher, "Introduction," 29–34. On the philosophical contexts for McCune Smith's emphasis on the superiority of induction, see Lee, *Slavery*, 108. David Waldstreicher, "Introduction: Nature, Race, and Revolution in Jefferson's America," in *Notes on the State of Virginia*, by Thomas Jefferson, ed. David Waldstreicher (New York: Bedford-St. Martin's, 2002), 29–34.

5. Bingham, *Columbian Orator*, 209. Conflating servitude and criminality, the word *villain* is especially charged here, given contemporary debates about the legal precedent for American slavery in the archaic English practice of villeinage. See William M. Wiecek, "The Origins of the Law of Slavery in British North America," *Cardozo Law Review* 17.6 (May 1996): 1715–18; A. Leon Higginbotham, Jr., *In the Matter of Color: Race and the American Legal Process: The Colonial Period* (New York: Oxford UP, 1978), 322–23, 338–44; Thomas D. Morris, *Southern Slavery and the Law, 1619–1860* (Chapel Hill: U of North Carolina P, 1996), 52–55.

6. Bingham, *Columbian Orator*, 210.

7. *Ibid.*

"the more I read, the more I was led to abhor and detest my enslavers," culminating in the realization that slaveholders are merely "a
band of successful robbers, who had left their homes, and gone to
Africa, and stolen us from our homes."[8] Through a combination of
reading and the "reflection" Jefferson found wanting in blacks,
the rhetoric of the abolitionist advocate becomes second nature to
the slave child.

Douglass drives this point home in the expanded treatment of
the *Columbian Orator* in *My Bondage and My Freedom*, where the
author explicitly identifies himself with Bingham's exemplary slave:
"It is scarcely necessary to say, that a dialogue, with such an origin,
and such an ending . . . powerfully affected me; and I could not help
feeling that the day might come, when the well-directed answers
made by the slave to the master, in this instance, would find their
counterpart in myself."[9] For Douglass, what was "finely illustrated
in the dialogue" was "the mighty power and heart-searching directness of truth, penetrating even the heart of a slaveholder, compelling him to yield up his earthly interests to the claims of eternal
justice."[1] Complicating the abolitionist adage that "argument pro-
vokes argument, reason is met by sophistry; but the narratives of
slaves go right to the hearts of men," Douglass here insists upon the
"mighty power" of a black-authored antislavery argument that irre-
sistibly employs forceful inductive reasoning grounded in personal
experience.[2]

As *My Bondage and My Freedom* illustrates, by 1855 Frederick
Douglass had become convinced of the need for black abolitionists
to leave the confines of the witness stand in order to advocate for
both immediate emancipation and the full citizenship of all African Americans.[3] Far from rejecting the adversarial trial model that

8. Frederick Douglass, *Narrative of the Life of Frederick Douglass, an American Slave,
Written by Himself: Authoritative Text, Contexts, and Criticism*, ed. William L. Andrews
(New York: W. W. Norton, 1997), 33. Compare Douglass, *My Bondage*, 227 [p. 106].
See also Fishkin and Peterson, "'We Hold,'" 195.
9. Douglass, *My Bondage*, 225–26 [p. 105].
1. Ibid., p. 226 [p. 105].
2. For an updated version of Bingham's "Dialogue," Douglass's own "Letter to His Old
Master," see Douglass, *My Bondage*, 412–18 [pp. 264–70]. On literary historical connections to Jefferson's *Notes*, see Dickson D. Bruce, Jr., *The Origins of African American Literature, 1680–1865* (Charlottesville: UP of Virginia, 2001), 69, 246. The most
suggestive synthesis of testimonial authority and civic assertion appears in a narrative
published six years after *My Bondage and My Freedom*, in the first year of the Civil
War. The title-page proclamation of J. H. Banks's *Narrative*, "I am a witness against
American slavery," prefaces an account that depicts Banks repeatedly engaging his
enslavers in extended debates over the justice of slavery and, at one point, contracting
with his fellow fugitives, who are "thus covenanted and leagued together as a band of
liberty-hunting pilgrims" J[ames] W. C. Pennington, *A Narrative of Events in the Life of
J. H. Banks, an Escaped Slave, from the Cotton State, Alabama, in America* (Liverpool,
1861), 21–24, 42–45, 60–62, 72.
3. On Douglass's nuanced understanding of citizenship in *My Bondage* as well as African
Americans' strategic embrace of normative citizenship, see Russ Castronovo, *Necro*

had provided the print debate over slavery with both its structure and its rhetorical power, Douglass's determined efforts to combine personal narrative and advocacy indicated his growing awareness of the extent to which, in the words of legal scholar Paul Gewirtz, "storytelling in law is narrative within a culture of argument," that "the trial process" is "a struggle over narratives."[4] For however much law may appear to assign discrete functions to the different personages in the criminal trial—that is, the witness's task is storytelling; the lawyer's, argumentation; the judge's, adjudication of law; and the jury's, adjudication of facts—the tendency of the adversarial process is inevitably to fragment, multiply, and disperse these activities.[5] Putting this insight into discursive practice, Douglass demonstrated how thoroughly he had learned to talk lawyerlike about law.

*   *   *

Douglass's growing commitment to talking lawyerlike about law represented not only a significant transformation in his post-*Narrative* self-fashioning, from witness to advocate, but also a determined effort to join his fellow black abolitionists in their efforts to expand and redefine African American participation in both the antislavery movement and the civic life of the nation.[6] Like his interpretation of the founding legal documents of the United States, his reading of Southern slave laws suggests that for Douglass, black advocacy meant not just breaking free of the discursive constraints associating blackness with plain narration and claiming the right to denounce as well as to narrate wrong—not just liberating himself from the racial hierarchy of the antebellum antislavery movement and asserting the necessary autonomy of black political speech. Far more powerfully, black advocacy meant rejecting the legal marginalization of African Americans and demanding full legal and political enfranchisement, beginning, but by no means ending, with emancipation and the right to due process.

Citizenship: Death, Eroticism, and the Public Sphere in the Nineteenth-Century United States (Durham, NC: Duke UP, 2001), 50–61, 206, 214.

4. Paul Gewirtz, "Narrative and Rhetoric in the Law," in *Law's Stories: Narrative and Rhetoric in the Law*, ed. Peter Brooks and Paul Gewirtz (New Haven, CT: Yale UP, 1996), 5,7.

5. See Carol J. Clover, "Law and the Order of Popular Culture," in *Law in the Domains of Culture*, ed. Austin Sarat and Thomas R. Kearns (Ann Arbor: U of Michigan P, 2000), 103–04, 118.

6. See Jane H. Pease and William H. Pease, *They Who Would Be Free: Blacks' Search for Freedom, 1830–1861* (New York: Atheneum, 1974); C. Peter Ripley, ed., *The Black Abolitionist Papers*, vol. 3 (Chapel Hill: U of North Carolina P, 1990), 20–57.

CODY MARRS

Frederick Douglass in 1848[†]

When revolutions rocked Europe in 1848, Frederick Douglass responded almost immediately by framing these movements across the Atlantic in global terms.[1] As the rebellions against monarchy spread from Paris to Prague, Douglass reprinted poems by Alphonse de Lamartine in his abolitionist newspaper, the *North Star*; wrote essays in which he tied class strife in the Old World to the contest over slavery in the New; and delivered lectures in which he heralded this upheaval as part of an international uprising against tyrants. "France," he declared, "is not alone"; it is "in direct communication with all the great cities" from London to Washington and Rome, "and the influence of her example is everywhere powerful." What the abdication of Louis Philippe, the dethroning of Metternich, and the Magyar uprising under Lajos Kossuth portended, according to Douglass's 1848 essay "The Revolution of 1848" (1999a, 106–7), was the eruption of a revolutionary zeitgeist throughout the Atlantic world, a "Spirit of Liberty" that, as he put it, united "the oppressed classes" and caused "thrones to crumble."

Yet for Douglass the revolts of 1848 manifested not simply as political events but as a chronopolitical phenomenon. In Europe's upheaval, he discerned nothing less than a universal freedom drive that was transhistorical as well as transnational. As he insisted in his speeches, essays, and editorials, the sudden and seemingly miraculous overthrowing of kings in France, Italy, and Hungary was more or less coextensive with the American Revolution of 1776, with the British abolition of slavery in 1833, and with past and future slave rebellions throughout the Western hemisphere. What Douglass took from these revolutions was accordingly not merely a newfound cosmopolitanism but a restructured understanding of transformation itself. In the wake of these insurrections, he became increasingly invested in an idea of historical connection based on deferral, and this sense of history shaped his thought for years to come, as he used the revolts of 1848 to discern patterns of protest

---

[†] From *American Literature* 85.3 (September 2013): 447–48, 451–56, 467. Copyright, 2013, Duke University Press. All rights reserved. Republished by permission of the copyright holder, Duke University Press. Bracketed page references are to this Norton Critical Edition.

1. The year 1848 saw antimonarchical revolutionary turmoil across Europe. In France, King Louis Philippe I (1773–1850) was forced to abdicate the throne; in Germany, Chancellor Klemens von Metternich (1773–1859) was forced to resign; and in Hungary, Lajos Kossuth (1802–1894) led a revolution against the Hapsburg Empire that resulted in the establishment of Hungary's first parliamentarian government [*Editors' note*].

and repression in the crisis over slavery in the 1850s, in the ensuing Civil War, and in the rise and fall of Radical Reconstruction.

His reflections on these rebellions shuttle between times and locations, weaving together disparate places, moments, and events in ways that elude linear and national chronologies. From his initial prophetic declarations about the coming "downfall of tyranny throughout the world" to his later uses of Europe's upheaval to reframe the American Founding, Douglass's writings about these rebellions advance a multi-linear sense of historical time (1999b, 97). His responses to 1848 therefore present an interesting theoretical challenge for prevailing models of postnationalist inquiry, which tend to construe literature's extraterritoriality in terms of space. Indeed, to the degree that postnationalist criticism's various strands—from hemispheric and translinguistic paradigms to studies of the Atlantic and the Pacific Rim—share a common conceptual foundation, it lies in the assumption that dislodging the nation as the chief organizing literary-critical category requires, first and foremost, reconceptualizing literature's geography. However, as Douglass's writings about 1848 make abundantly clear, the problem of extranationality is not only an issue of space. It is also, inescapably, an issue of temporal experience.

❊   ❊   ❊

❊ ❊ ❊ Time, he came to believe, tends not to progress in a straight line but to break off and return in unexpected ways. This sense of historical movement certainly owes much to Douglass's early experiences as a slave. His time on Colonel Lloyd's plantation, and in the shipyards of Baltimore; his early immersion in the slave songs and the other acoustics of bondage (like his Aunt Hester's scream); his famous brawl with Edward Covey; and his experiences as a fugitive—neither slave nor free, yet both—in the antebellum North all forged in him a profound, and deeply corporeal, understanding of the inescapable brokenness of the world. As he later wrote: "The thought of only being a creature of the *present* and the *past*, troubled me, and I longed to have a *future*—a future with hope in it. To be shut up entirely to the past and present, is abhorrent to the human mind; it is to the soul . . . what the prison is to the body" (1994a, 304–5 [p. 170]). His ensuing, lifelong struggle to integrate a future with his fractured past led him to develop something like a philosophy of history out of these experiences, a temporal viewpoint that fuses the sense of discontinuity ingrained in him on the plantation with a transnational vision of unity that sprang from his witnessing of 1848.[2]

2. Douglass's reading of gaps and fissures as constitutive rather than accidental to diachronic change differs from most Euro-American ideas of progress, which tend to

This worldview became pivotal for Douglass in the following years, as he revised his ideas about the nation's origins and revised his autobiography (first published in 1845). The much longer and significantly altered 1855 text, *My Bondage and My Freedom*, is formally split in two to mark the moment of emancipation. This event is nonetheless far more unstable than this structural divide would seem to indicate. Writing in the reactionary, post-1848 aftermath, Douglass draws a much thinner line between slavery and freedom, depicting his entry into the free state of New York—a scene that inaugurates part two ("My Life as a Freeman")—as anything but an unambiguous escape from bondage:

> Some apology can easily be made for the few slaves who have, after making good their escape, turned back to slavery, preferring the actual rule of their masters, to the life of loneliness, apprehension, hunger, and anxiety, which meets them on their first arrival in a free state. It is difficult for a freeman to enter into the feelings of such fugitives. He cannot see things in the same light with the slave, because he does not, and cannot, look from the same point from which the slave does. "Why do you tremble," he says to the slave—"you are in a free state;" but the difficulty is, in realizing that he is in a free state, the slave might reply. A freeman cannot understand why the slave-master's shadow is bigger, to the slave, than the might and majesty of a free state; but when he reflects that the slave knows more about the slavery of his master than he does of the might and majesty of the free state, he has the explanation. The slave has been all his life learning the power of his master—being trained to dread his approach—and only a few hours learning the power of the state. . . . A man, homeless, shelterless, breadless, friendless, and moneyless, is not in a condition to assume a very proud or joyous tone; and in just this condition was I, while wandering about the streets of New York and lodging, at least one night, among the barrels on one of its wharves. I was not only free from slavery, but I was free from home, as well. (351–52 [pp. 209–10])

---

prize linearity over recurrence. Another way to read these layered, chronopolitical responses to 1848 is, accordingly, through the politico-aesthetic figure of the "cut" or "break" in African American studies. James Snead (1990, 67) describes the "cut" as an underlying element of black aesthetics and argues that whereas European culture tends to code repetition as progress, the cultural traditions coming from Africa tend to present repetition as a variegated process in which "the thing (the ritual, the dance, the beat) is [always] 'there for you to pick it up when you come back to get it.'" Fred Moten (2003, 2–7), in a related vein, uses this phenomenon of the "break" to read Douglass's portrayal of plantation life, positing that Douglass's autobiographies expose the raw acoustics of slavery. In light of these insights, what makes Douglass's responses to 1848 significant, and all the more necessary to retrieve, is the way they broaden this vision of broken progression into a philosophy of history.

In this passage about the precariousness of negative liberty, the word "state" slips between its connotations, manifesting as a federal edifice, as a subnational geographical entity, and as a fluid condition unmoored from any security. The nation-state thereby emerges in Douglass's account as an almost unreal performative utterance, a locution that is "little more than a dream," and this ephemerality— dispelling any illusion of the nation's "majesty"—situates him somewhere between slavery and freedom, in an unfixed "state" bolstered neither by the ostensible rights of liberal freedom nor by the palpable "might" of the slave master. To reconstruct the stateless experience of fugitivity, Douglass draws from the patterns of progression-through-deferral that he wrested from the events of 1848 in order to refigure his own passage from slavery to freedom as a form of suspended uplift.

Revising his autobiography in the wake of "the American 1848," Douglass attempts to reach beyond the failed American nation. This transnational impulse extends throughout *My Bondage and My Freedom*, from his invocations of Milton and other British poets to his chapters about "undergo[ing] a transformation" during his trip to England (1994b, 372). As Douglass wrote to William Lloyd Garrison during his time abroad, escaping the "republican negro hate prevalent in our glorious land" made him realize that "I have no end to serve, no government to defend; and as to nation, I belong to none. . . . If ever I had any patriotism, . . . it was whipped out of me long since, by the lash of the American soul-drivers" (372). This stateless perspective fills out Douglass's amended description of the slave songs, which, in the 1855 text, places far more emphasis on these songs' innate communicability. The slaves, he recalls, "would make the dense old woods, for miles around, reverberate with their wild notes. These were not always merry because they were wild. On the contrary, they were mostly of a plaintive cast, and told a tale of grief and sorrow. In the most boisterous outbursts of rapturous sentiment, there was ever a tinge of deep melancholy." Yet this fusion of joy with sadness, he adds, is not locatable *solely* within the slave song, or even on American soil: "I have never heard any songs like those anywhere since I left slavery, except when in Ireland. There I heard the same *wailing notes*, and was much affected by them. It was during the famine of 1845–6" (184). There is something politically and aesthetically significant in these shared "notes," and it is a hidden history of the repressed, a latent commonality that exceeds the narrow universalism fostered by the state.

To draw out this inner universality, Douglass often turns to poetry. Almost all of his orations, essays, and autobiographies are replete with lines borrowed from Robert Burns, Lord Byron, Samuel

Taylor Coleridge, John Greenleaf Whittier, Thomas Moore, William Cowper, John Pierpont, Henry Wadsworth Longfellow, James Russell Lowell, Percy Bysshe Shelley, and Thomas Hood, among others. These poetic quotations are especially ubiquitous and structurally important in his post-1848 writings. Throughout many of these texts, poetry does not simply enter—it intervenes, descending below and rising up beyond the impassioned reason of Douglass's words in order to create a literary experience in which history is momentarily recircuited. In his "Revolution of 1848" speech, for instance, Douglass articulates the meaning of Europe's revolts not by quoting any politicians, or newspaper editors, or reformers, or even the revolutionaries themselves, but instead by invoking Shelley's posthumously published poem "Liberty":

> *From spirit to spirit—from nation to nation,*
> *From city to hamlet, thy dawning is cast;*
> *And tyrants and slaves are like shadows of night,*

> Standing in the far West, we may now hear the earnest debate of the Western world.—The means of intelligence is so perfect, as well as rapid, that we seem to be mingling with the thrilling scenes of the Eastern hemisphere. (Douglass 1999b, 105)

Analogizing human conflict to the earth's natural violence, Shelley's poem is about the rise of freedom from below. Liberty, Shelley (1994, 661) suggests in the surrounding stanzas, is the result of unfolding action: emerging from "underground" with the astounding capacity to "blind . . . volcanoes," it is a force at once ingrained and unfamiliar. At this moment of crisis, when France's new "Revolution has stirred the dormant energies of the oppressed classes all over [the globe]" (1999b, 106), Douglass draws from this vision of freedom in order to divulge the chronopolitical link between Europe's contemporary struggles, slavery's abolition, and the founding of the United States.

   This transnational vision, which Douglass came to by mixing the worldview of fugitivity with the cosmopolitanism made possible by 1848, also fills out many of his speeches about the Civil War. Throughout that conflict, he made a habit of drawing from Europe's poetry and history to explain the North's political situation. In one of these orations, which he delivered soon after the bombardment of Fort Sumter, Douglass connects the Union's struggle against the Confederacy to *The Giaour*, Byron's 1813 poem about love and revenge in the Orient. Reflecting on the common proposition that "revolutions never go backward," Douglass points out that this concept "is two-edged. It cuts both ways. . . . If revolutions never go backward, they are of course as likely to go forward in one section as the other—in the north, as in the South. The slaveholders have resolved to battle for slavery, and the people of the Free States will yet come forth to battle for freedom." After exposing these diverging velocities, Douglass enlists Byron's poem:

> Freedom's battle once begun,
> Bequeathed from bleeding sire to son,
> Tho' baffled oft is ever won.
> (quoted in Douglass 1985, 430)

These lines come from the opening sections of Byron's text, after the main character (a Western "giaour," or *infidel* in Turkish) has arrived at Thermopylae, the site of the famous Spartan resistance to Persian invaders in 480 BC. Meditating on the landscape's political history, the poem's narrator calls on today's generation to honor their ancestors by reclaiming their spirit of revolt:

> Snatch from the ashes of your sires
> The embers of their former fires;
> And he who in the strife expires
> Will add to theirs a name of fear
> That Tyranny shall quake to hear,
> And leave his sons a hope, a fame,
> They too will rather die than shame:
> For Freedom's battle once begun,
> Bequeath'd by bleeding Sire to Son,
> Though baffled oft is ever won.
> Bear witness, Greece, thy living page! (Byron 1883, 64)

Byron's narrator critiques Greece's contemporary citizens for having forgotten or erased this revolutionary heritage. As Douglass would later do repeatedly in his orations about the American Founding, Byron laments that the political bonds between past and present have been tragically severed, not by some external force but by an inner degradation that has emptied out people's historical consciousness:

> no foreign foe could quell
> Thy soul, till from itself it fell;
> Yes! Self-abasement paved the way
> To villain-bonds and despot sway.
> What can he tell who treads thy shore?
> No legend of thine old time,
> No theme on which the Muse might soar
> High as thine own in days of yore,
> When man was worthy of thy clime.
> The hearts within thy valleys bred,
> The fiery souls that might have led

Thy sons to deeds sublime,
Now crawl from cradle to the grave,
Slaves—nay, the bondsmen of a slave,
And callous, save to crime;
Stain'd with each evil that pollutes
Mankind. (Byron 1883, 64)

In reading these lines, Douglass likely saw a parallel between the United States of the 1850s and 1860s and Byron's Greece. In both countries a political heritage that originated in a "sublime" overthrow of tyranny has degenerated into a "callous" embrace of slavery. In Byron's poem this historical collapse is nonetheless incomplete, and this is the import of Douglass's three quoted lines: because freedom constructs its own self-generated history, it can resurge even when it appears to be either conquered or absent. Douglass, transporting these lines into a very different time and place, draws from their faith in liberty's veiled irrepressibility while injecting it with an altered meaning: this latent freedom drive recoded through Douglass manifests now not in Greek history but in the Union's struggle against the South. By transporting the split temporality of Byron's text into his own speech about the war, Douglass articulates a discontinuous narrative of freedom, and the latter is not merely the issue of some bloody apocalypse—providential or otherwise—but a sublime principle that extends multilinearly across time and space.

These poetic appropriations are a crucial part of the cosmopolitan vision that animates so much of Douglass's writing. * * * Both during and after the revolts of 1848, Douglass attempts to write beyond the nation, but he does so not simply by rejecting or denying its "flinty reality." Instead, he enlists extranational events and experiences (like the upheaval of 1848) in order to illuminate a common experience of deferred progress, an irrepressible recursivity that both proceeds through and transcends the state. Whether his subject is a founding document whose spirit has been misapprehended, or a civil war that resurrects prior struggles, or rebellions in Europe that recall the American Revolution (and vice versa), Douglass figures transnationalism as a form of experience that depends not only on an expanded sense of space but also on an awareness of history's cycles, gaps, and returns. To account for this worldview, or for extranational writing more generally, we must fashion a hermeneutic that is sensitive to the dialectical relation between national temporal consciousness and the transnational imaginary. And Douglass—in his imaginative movements across oceans and epochs, and in his critiques of the nation's mythologies—can help us get there.

References

Byron 1883. Lord Byron, *The Poetical Works of Lord Byron* (London: J. Murray).

Douglass 1985. Frederick Douglass, "Revolutions Never Go Backwards," in *The Frederick Douglass Papers*, series 1: *Speeches, Debates, and Interview*, vol. 3: *1855–65*, ed. John W. Blassingame (New Haven: Yale UP).

———— 1994a. Frederick Douglass, *My Bondage and My Freedom*, in *Autobiographics*, ed. Henry Louis Gates (New York: Library of America).

———— 1994b. Frederick Douglass, *The Life and Times of Frederick Douglass*, in *Autobiographies*, ed. Henry Louis Gates (New York: Library of America).

———— 1999a. Frederick Douglass, "The Revolution of 1848," in *Frederick Douglass: Selected Speeches and Writings*, ed. Philip S. Foner and Yuval Taylor (New York: Lawrence Hill Books).

———— 1999b. Frederick Douglass, "What of the Night?" in *Frederick Douglass: Selected Speeches and Writings*, ed. Philip S. Foner and Yuval Taylor (New York: Lawrence Hill Books).

Shelley 1994. Percy Bysshe Shelley, *The Complete Poems*, ed. Mary Shelley (New York: Modern Library).

CRISTIN ELLIS

From Amoral Abolitionism: Frederick Douglass and the Environmental Case against Slavery[†]

Early in his second and much-revised autobiography, *My Bondage and My Freedom* ([1855] 1994), Frederick Douglass reminds us that to be a slave is to be treated as a fungible commodity. Of his childhood on Colonel Lloyd's plantation (where he grew up a slave, and probable son, of the farm's overseer), Douglass recalls:

> [The Colonel's] slaves, alone, were an immense fortune. These small and great, could not have been fewer than one thousand in number, and though scarcely a month passed without the sale of one or more lots to the Georgia traders, there was no apparent diminution in the number of his human stock: the home plantation merely groaned at the removal of the young increase, or human crop, then proceeded as lively as ever. (163 [p. 55])

[†] From *American Literature* 86.2 (June 2014): 275–80, 283–85, 287–91. Copyright, 2014, Duke University Press. All rights reserved. Republished by permission of the copyright holder, Duke University Press. Bracketed page references are to this Norton Critical Edition.

Modern readers are likely to recognize this deadpan reference to slavery's "human crop" as a bit of free indirect discourse—a wry impersonation of Colonel Lloyd's casual disregard for the humanity of his "human stock." In reading this ironically, we follow generations of critics who identify Douglass's text with the genre of sentimental antislavery literature—a tradition which championed sympathy and decried the inhumanity of a system that splintered slave families and shattered the organic brotherhood of mankind.

One consideration this reading occludes, however, is the possibility that Douglass is not merely speaking rhetorically when he refers to Colonel Lloyd's slaves as a crop. In the decades before the Civil War, large swaths of the Old South—including Douglass's native Talbot County—were experiencing an environmental crisis of soil exhaustion that was in fact causing planters to become increasingly less economically dependent on the agricultural products of slave labor than on the value of those slaves themselves. As J. D. B. DeBow, the influential proslavery editor of a New Orleans–based business journal, summarized the alarming situation in 1852: "The best lands have become exhausted . . . [and] the only increase to be found in the elements or means to procure wealth, consists of the increase of slaves" (194). Soil exhaustion fueled Southern dependence on slave wealth in two ways: first, by decreasing the value of land it afflicted (raising the relative value of slave capital for those planters), and second, by driving up the market value of slaves (which more than doubled from 1840 to 1860) as planters migrated west to new cotton lands in search of virgin soil.[1] As a result, the "human crop" became big business: in 1850, the value of the "yearly increase" (or births) of the slave population constituted roughly 14 percent of the nation's gross fixed capital formation that year—worth some $52.9 million to the 1850 US economy,[2] or as much as $184 billion

1. The average market price for a slave jumped from $377 in 1840 to $778 in 1860 (see Carter 2006, tables Bb209–14). In today's terms, this represents an increase from roughly $10,700 to $22,200 per slave (estimates reflect the "real price" estimate of commodity value provided by Samuel Williamson and Louis Cain's "Measuring Worth" tool; see note 3 below).

2. "Gross fixed capital formation" measures the value of additions to an economy's fixed assets (such as outlays on machinery and infrastructure like roads, railways, and buildings) plus net changes in inventories (unsold stocks). In 1850, the value of the increase in the slave population was roughly $52.9 million, or 13.8 percent of that year's gross national capital formation, which is estimated at $383.5 million (all historical figures are given in 1860 dollars). It is important to bear in mind that this "yearly increase" would undoubtedly have constituted much more than 14 percent of the South's regional capital formation for 1850: although estimates of gross Southern capital formation are not available for this period, given that the value in the increase in slave "assets" was concentrated in the slaveholding South, and given how much of the nation's other fixed capital formation (such as manufacturing and railroad construction) was occurring at higher rates in the North, we may reasonably infer that slave "assets" would have represented a larger share of the region's economy (see Carter 2006, tables Ca232 and Ca237).

in today's dollars.³ Indeed, in the decade in which *My Bondage* was published, Southern wealth more than doubled, and fully half of that growth was accounted for by increases in the value and size of the slave population.⁴ From the perspective of wealth formation, then, the antebellum South was literally in the business of growing slaves—slaves had become a more valuable product to the South than the cash crops to which it still staked its regional pride. And the soaring value of those slave "stocks" tells a story about the slow implosion of soils in the region.

When read in light of this history of environmental crisis, Douglass's reference to Lloyd's "human crop" takes on a polemical salience distinct from the sentimental critique we are accustomed to attributing to him. For when Douglass informs us that Lloyd's plantation is selling off slaves for profit, or when, a few pages on, he confesses that "the most valuable part of [Lloyd's] property was his slaves" (170 [p. 60]), he is invoking what was, in 1855, a telltale sign of the South's agricultural collapse. Douglass's reference to Lloyd's "human crop" thus comes with a double barb: in addition to portraying the slaveholder's unfeeling inhumanity, it exposes his insolvency, invoking the pragmatic objection that slavery may be economically and environmentally hazardous.

What is potentially surprising about the macroeconomic rereading I am proposing is how independently it operates, as a critique of slavery, from the moral argumentation we have learned to expect from Douglass. Douglass is, of course, justly remembered as an apostle of conscience and a towering champion of human rights. Nonetheless, in this essay I shall seek to demonstrate that in *My Bondage*, he develops a pointedly amoral critique of slavery on the grounds of its practical unsustainability—an argument that imports a surprisingly utilitarian new refrain into his antislavery polemic.⁵ In what

3. Economists disagree about the best methods for making conversions from historical to present-day monetary values. In offering the estimate of $184 billion above, I am using the "economic power" conversion method endorsed by Samuel Williamson and Louis Cain in "Measuring Slavery in $2009" (2009). This method measures the relative value of the historical $52.9 million as a proportion of 1850 GDP, theoretically yielding a more accurate estimate of the value of slave "assets" to the Southern economy as a whole than does the rival "real price" method, which measures relative value of a commodity using the consumer price index (CPI). Using the latter method yields a more conservative estimated value of $1.5 billion in today's dollars. For a fuller justification of the accuracy of the "economic power" method for measuring the value of slaves, see Williamson and Cain. I arrived at both of the "economic power" and "real price" comparative figures using Williamson's and Cain's Measuring Worth tool available online at www.measuringworth.com/uscompare.

4. Between 1850 and 1860, Southern wealth grew from $2,844 billion to $6,322 billion. Of that 222 percent increase, 51 percent (or $1,773 billion) was represented by the increase in the total value of slave capital (see Wright 2006, tables 2.3 and 2.4).

5. In referring to Douglass's rhetoric as "amoral" throughout this essay, I do not mean to suggest that his appeal to economic sustainability is ultimately free of moral commitment. On the contrary, insofar as this new environmental antislavery proposes to

follows, I shall offer a reconsideration of the text's most significant landscapes in order to highlight this pragmatic turn in Douglass's late antislavery thought. In doing so, my most immediate aim is to revise our tendency to read Douglass perhaps too narrowly through the rubric of sentimental antislavery. Learning to recognize his strategic engagement with comparatively dispassionate economic and ecological antislavery logics can both broaden our understanding of his political thought and remind us of the important, yet widely forgotten role that environmental crisis played in shaping antislavery politics in America.

*   *   *

The Soil Crisis and Antislavery's Environmental Imaginaries

Although declining soil fertility had been a concern of Southern planters since the early days of the republic, by 1840 it was widely acknowledged that the region was facing a crisis of soil exhaustion. Up and down the southeastern seaboard, the evidence of environmental disaster became unmistakable in dwindling crop yields, metastasizing tracts of barren farmland, and homesteads left abandoned by planters gone west in search of virgin soils. Agriculturalists looked on in despair: "The lands in this Parish were once uncommonly fine and productive," laments one typical survey from South Carolina, "but by improvident culture they have greatly deteriorated" ("Agricultural Survey" 1840, 199). Census records paint a similarly stark picture, reporting in 1850 that over two-thirds of the South's total farm acreage lay fallow, either given up as exhausted or held back in reserve for when current fields failed (Majewski 2009, table 1). By comparison, nearly two-thirds of farmland in the Northeast was under active cultivation—a contrast underwriting the popular antebellum stereotype that the Mason-Dixon[6] formed (as New York Congressman John Taylor put it) "a dividing line between farms highly cultivated and plantations . . . overrun with weeds" (quoted in Ashworth 1995, 59).

This crisis was a source of acute embarrassment to a region that prided itself on its agricultural tradition. But far more pressing was the concern that soil exhaustion might permanently shift the

---

sustain the status quo of capitalist accumulation and liberal ideology more broadly, it implicitly condones a raft of moral commitments by which those systems operate, many of which we might well wish to interrogate. By calling Douglass's argument amoral, then, I instead mean to underscore that it specifically—indeed strategically—refrains from reexamining the culture's ideological commitments, that it works within the prevailing moral framework.

6. See note 1 on p. 128 [*Editors' note*].

balance of economic and political power in favor of the Northern states. By 1857, Northern farms were outproducing Southern farms by 30 percent, or about 60 million (1860) dollars, according to a study by North Carolinian abolitionist Hinton Rowan Helper (1857, 204). At the same time, soil exhaustion was widening the population gap between North and South by spurring emigration and mitigating against the emergence of cities and industry—two great population multipliers.[7] This growing gap fueled sectional alarm—epitomized in John Calhoun's[8] 1849 "Southern Address"— that Northern states would soon earn a majority of seats in federal government. Census records confirm that between 1830 and 1860, population in the South grew at half the rate it did in the North, and even excluding the growth in cities, population in the rural North outpaced the rural South by a third.[9] Declining soil fertility was thus not only a major economic concern to the South but a threat to its political influence within the republic, and as such it became an engine of growing sectional antagonism.

Agricultural historians now agree that Southern soil exhaustion was brought about by the region's prevailing crop system, which was then dominated by the monoculture of nutrient-intensive cash crops (typically cotton, tobacco, or rice) whose chemical demands on the soil were not offset by crop rotation or adequate fertilization. This crop system therefore produced annual deficits in soil nutrients that, when coupled with the fact that Southern soils have lower indigenous fertility than Northern soils to begin with, made the South particularly susceptible to soil exhaustion. At the time, however, the causes of the crisis were a matter of debate, producing a wide range of interpretations informed and inflamed by the most critical debate of the day: slavery. This Southern environmental crisis thus became a new site for the national referendum on slavery.

7. At the time, the most evident cause of the Old South's relatively stagnant population was massive emigration, as tens of thousands of farmers left the southeastern states every year in search of more profitable land. Modern historians now suggest growth was further stalled by the effect of soil exhaustion on patterns of land use in the region. In order to weather the continued failure of their soils, wealthy planters of the era began to "bank" acreage against the necessity of abandoning their present fields—a practice that intensified the consolidation of land ownership into ever-fewer and larger holdings. This distinctive pattern of land use increased the total acreage of plantations without increasing the workforce supported on them (because only a fraction of the acreage was farmed at one time), resulting in thinly dispersed populations that precluded the emergence of cities and industry. For a fuller account of the relation between soil exhaustion, land-use patterns, and demographic stagnation, see Majewski (2009), Rubin (1975), and Wright (2006).
8. See note 2 on p. 295 [*Editors' note*].
9. Between 1830 and 1860, the Southern population grew by 95 percent (86 percent in rural areas), compared to an increase of 175 percent (131 percent in rural areas) posted in Northern states (figures calculated from regional population statistics collected in Carter 2006, tables Aa, 36–92).

*   *   *

Thus the crisis of environmental decline in the Old South was interpreted according to at least three distinct antislavery logics. In this spectacle of failed crops and abandoned farms, sentimental abolitionists like Stowe and Dickens saw the rewards of moral degeneracy; Republicans saw the signs of perverted incentive; and some agriculturalists saw the effects of profligate farming practices institutionally perpetuated by slavery. As forms of environmental imaginary, however, only the latter interpretation could be described as properly *ecological*, since only it seems to recognize that restoring Southern soils would not simply be a matter of changing attitudes (of engendering sympathy or restoring the entrepreneurial spirit), but more particularly of accommodating cultural practices to the specific dynamics and limits of the landscape's material systems. The distinctions between these three discourses moreover gave rise to diverging expectations of slavery's endgame, which ranged from divinely appointed apocalypse to economic and ecological collapse from purely secular causes. Against this expanded field of antislavery's environmental imaginaries, we are now better equipped to discern the political logics of Douglass's carefully observed landscapes in *My Bondage and My Freedom*.

Landscapes of Protest in My Bondage and My Freedom

Douglass announces his newfound attention to slavery's environment in the very first lines of *My Bondage*. Revising the *Narrative*'s pointedly brief first sentence ("I was born in Tuckahoe, near Hillsborough, and about twelve miles from Easton, in Talbot county, Maryland") ([1845] 1994, 15), *My Bondage* opens with a leisurely panorama of Tuckahoe's landscape, lingering on "the worn-out, sandy, desert-like appearance of its soil, the general dilapidation of its farms and fences, [and] the indigent and spiritless character of its inhabitants" (139–40 [p. 35]). Since, as many critics have noted, the *Narrative*'s foreshortened introduction worked to underscore how little self-knowledge slavery afforded Douglass, *My Bondage*'s amplitude here represents a notable change in rhetorical tack. By way of justifying the sheer surfeit of detail, Douglass now explains that the nature of his birthplace is "a fact of some importance" if we wish to understand "anything" about him: "a man's character," he later adds, "greatly takes its hue and shape from the form and color of things about him" (171 [p. 61]). No longer merely an index of his genealogy's obscurity, then, Tuckahoe now illuminates it: in the absence of other parents, Douglass introduces himself as a son of this place.

For many readers, this dilation of vision marks the most striking difference between Douglass's two antebellum autobiographies:

where the *Narrative* is minimalist, *My Bondage* is expansive, fleshed out with richly textured observations of community, history, and landscape.[1] Drawn to the latter, ecocritics like Lawrence Buell, Lance Newman, and Ian Finseth have suggested that *My Bondage* qualifies as a rare instance of African American pastoralism.[2] * * *

Each of these ecocritical readings valuably contributes to our understanding of *My Bondage* by drawing our attention to the importance of landscape to this text. However, as I shall attempt to show, in leaning so heavily on the rubrics of pastoralism and communal holism—rubrics with deep ruts in the ecocritical field—they can be insensible to those features of Douglass's environmental imaginary that do not fit modern ecocritical convention so neatly. Where these readings construe the text's ruined landscapes as symptoms of an underlying crisis of human sympathy (evidenced in broken families, divided communities, and alienation from nature), I seek to show how Douglass frames ecological decline through the economic and ecological logics then circulating as alternative forms of antislavery environmental imaginary.

Returning to *My Bondage*'s opening panorama, for instance, we may be immediately struck by how pointedly Douglass's elaboration of Tuckahoe's "decay and ruin" invokes the tropes of Republican free-market ideology. The text's first sentence draws a syntactically straight line from Tuckahoe's "worn out" soil to "the indigent and spiritless character of its inhabitants." Douglass's antebellum audience would have had little trouble recognizing this community—with its "white population . . . indolent and drunken to a proverb, and . . . slaves, who seemed to ask, 'Oh! What's the use?' every time they lifted a hoe" ([1855] 1994, 140 [p. 36])—as archetypes of Republican political economy: here a contemptuous white worker, there a demoralized slave. The very perfection of their typecasting works to make Tuckahoe less a place than a parable of ecological exhaustion brought on by slavery's disincentivization of labor.

*   *   *

1. Among the early critics who stressed the importance of this newly wide-screen imaginary, William Andrews (1986, 217–39) notes how it refashions Douglass as the product of—rather than a heroic exception to—his Southern African American community, and Eric Sundquist (1993, 89–93) suggests how it similarly refigures violence as a systemic rather than simply occasional product of slaveholding society. To this earlier conversation, the recent ecocritical readings add the valuable insight that it is not just his social and institutional environments but also, significantly, the physical environment to which Douglass's attention so carefully turns in this text.
2. I say "rare" because, as Robert Butler (1995) and Michael Bennett (2001) have shown, slave narratives (including Douglass's *Narrative*) more typically obey an overtly antipastoral logic, locating redemption in urban centers and corruption in the rural landscapes of plantation slavery. The prevalence of antipastoralism among early African American texts thus makes it all the more significant, to ecocritical readers like Buell, that *My Bondage* expresses affection for the Southern countryside.

If Tuckahoe seems designed to instantiate a Republican argument against slavery, however, Douglass complicates this politics with his description of the next landscape of his early life—the Lloyds' Wye House plantation. Despite the fact that this was the backdrop to his first taste of life as a slave, Douglass recalls the plantation with a fondness that seems downright hazardous to his antislavery politics. "Here were . . . plenty of places of pleasant resort" ([1855] 1994, 161 [p. 53]), he reminisces; "It was just a place to my boyish taste" (166 [p. 57]). Lawrence Buell (quoted in Newman and Walls 2011, 67; Buell 1995, 44) accounts for this surprising warmth by suggesting that Douglass deliberately invokes the pastoral ideal in order to activate our "pastoral outrage" when he reveals how thoroughly slavery worked to pervert his natural "love of countryside." In doing so, Buell suggests, Douglass indicts slavery with alienating the slave from his "rightful estate" as an affectionate child of the land (1995, 44). Thus, though outwardly the antithesis of Tuckahoe's wasted dereliction, the Lloyds' plantation, on Buell's reading, proves another of slavery's corrupted pastorals.

Yet while Buell rightly calls our attention to the intensity of Douglass's affection for this landscape, the text strains against his pastoral interpretation in two ways. First, Douglass takes pains to emphasize the artificiality of the plantation's ostensibly pastoral features of rural independence and isolation from metropolitan corruption. As he describes it, the plantation's pastoral seclusion is a feat of protectionist engineering: the Lloyds have restricted all commerce with the outside world to the movements of a single boat and required their children to be educated at home in order to elaborately ensure that the estate remained shuttered to the least "ray of . . . public sentiment." Thus Douglass conjures a plantation whose pastoral isolation does not make it an uncorrupted and atemporal paradise so much as a fortress of contrived anachronism, a "full three hundred years behind the age" (160 [p. 52]). Comparing the influence of metropolitan opinion to the nourishing effect of sunlight, Douglass exposes pastoral traditionalism as a most unnatural technique for local domination. In doing so, he explodes the pietism of agrarian independence upon which the logic of American pastoralism depends.

But though I am suggesting that Douglass's account of the plantation is skeptical of pastoralism, it does not follow that he distrusts nature. On the contrary, his hostility to the plantation's pastoralism is fueled by a countervailing affinity for nature that he conceives in rambling over its grounds. Here he encounters a promiscuousness in nature that belies the plantation's pastoral pretense to "natural" seclusion. Thus, for instance, when the young Douglass hears a tree full of blackbirds "making all nature vocal with the . . . beauty of their wild, warbling notes," the source of his pleasure proves to be not the virtue of their music in itself, but the fact that their song "belonged to me, as well as to Col. Edward Lloyd" ([1855] 1994, 163 [p. 54]). This instant of self-recognition in the blackbird's uncapturable song begets a love affair with nature that culminates in Douglass's ecstatic discovery that "all nature was redolent" of freedom (179 [p. 106]): "It looked from every star, smiled in every calm, breathed in every wind, and moved in every storm" (179 [p. 106]). The "love of countryside" Buell attributes to pastoral convention thus takes the more particular form of appreciation for nature's nonexcludability, or what Stephen Best (2004) might call its fugitive property. Rather than vivifying his exclusion from the plantation's bounty, Douglass's admiration for nature highlights its errant accessibility.

Indeed, in *My Bondage*, nature not only cannot be possessed (like birdsong); it cannot even be definitively localized. At the plantation, nature is always a kind of news from elsewhere, visiting in migratory birds, flows of weather ("breath[ing] in every wind"), or the cosmic transit of starlight ("look[ing] from every star"). Nature thus conceived is not a territory—a pastoral margin, a green zone on the map—so much as a principle of transitivity: a global circulation of materials including light, air, and song, as well as newspapers, ideas, and fugitive slaves. In this sense, readings that posit Douglass's alienation from nature (including Buell's account of his pastoral exclusion, Finseth's [2009] narrative of his nostalgia for unpolluted community, and Newman's account of his quest for "restorative contact with [nature's] immanent divine" [2009, 144]) seem at odds with Douglass's own understanding of nature as deterritorializing material process. For Douglass, nature vouchsafes a liberty from which slavery could never alienate him—a freedom elemental to every restless atom on earth. It is therefore meaningless to speak of alienation from or reconciliation to nature since disarticulation from nature, thus conceived, would be impossible in the first place. Indeed, as Douglass reminds us, even in the plantation's airlessly artificial environment, "civilization is shut out, but nature cannot be" (160 [p. 52]). As such, nature's redemptive promise to the young Douglass consists of demonstrating the ubiquity of material circulation to a young slave taught to believe that nothing (or no one) could transcend the sovereign confines of the local.

A secondary effect of Douglass's processual conception of nature is to empty out the moralism of appeals to the natural. That is if, as I have represented it, Douglass's argument against the plantation can still be said to turn upon slavery's unnaturalness, he nonetheless conceives of the natural in terms distinct from the organic sympathy invoked by a Stowe or Dickens. For here slavery's unnaturalness inheres not first and foremost in its cruelty but rather in the plantation's extravagant efforts at self-sequestration. Thus, though as of yet it shows no signs of exhaustion, the plantation's deliberate archaism exemplifies the resistance to modernization that so many agriculturalists worried was driving Southern agriculture to environmental ruin. Like Tuckahoe's wasted soils, then, the plantation's baroque pastoralism invites our condemnation of slavery on the comparatively amoral grounds of its practical unsustainability.

Douglass's willingness to set aside moral appeal in *My Bondage*'s landscapes may, however, be most clearly displayed in the fact that the single landscape he endorses in this text is a paragon of cosmopolitan efficiency notably lacking in anything like a pastoral or communitarian ethos. In the contours of bustling New Bedford, MA, his first free home in the North, Douglass constructs a positive foil to slavery's landscapes of profligacy and ruin.[3] Taught to believe that "no people could become very wealthy without slavery," Douglass is struck, on his first walk through this world-class port, to find "the very laboring population of New Bedford . . . surrounded by more comfort and refinement . . . than a majority of the slaveholders on the Eastern Shore of Maryland" ([1855] 1994, 355 [p. 212]). He watches six men and "an old ox, worth eighty dollars" accomplish a task that "would have required fifteen thousand dollars worth of human bones and muscles to have performed in a Southern port" (356 [p. 213]). Recalling the "noisily fierce and clumsily absurd manner of labor-life" under slavery, he marvels at New Bedford's revelation of "industry without bustle, labor without noise, and heavy toil without the whip" (356 [p. 213]). His fervor for its parsimonious productivity carries well over into idealized distortion when he even claims the "carpenters struck where they aimed, and the caulkers wasted no blows in idle flourishes of the mallet" (356 [p. 214]). New Bedford's industrious landscape thus yields as concise an education in freedom's productivity as Tuckahoe's did in slavery's wasteful enervation.

But while this lesson is clearly consistent with Republican free-labor ideology, Douglass's audit of New Bedford's wealth ultimately looks beyond psychological motivation. Instead of talking up the

3. To my knowledge, ecocritical readings of this text's landscapes have overlooked its account of New Bedford more or less completely. It may be that, because it is an urban landscape, it has simply not registered as relevant to ecocritical interests. Yet when we follow Douglass in conceiving of nature not as a green space on the map but as a principle of material circulation, it is possible (as it is not for pastoral or even post-pastoral eco-criticism) to recognize his appreciation for the naturalness of this admittedly nonleafy environment.

productivity of New Bedford's incentivized laborers, Douglass highlights the town's "scrupulous regard to economy, both in regard to men and things" (356 [p. 213]). His survey leaves us with the clear impression that it is not, in the end, unleashed ambition so much as it is conscientious thrift that underwrites this town's success. Walking down one street, Douglass marvels as house after house reveals ingenious new labor-saving devices—"self-shutting gates, washing machines, pounding barrels, were all new things" to him (356 [p. 213]). And the same attention is paid to conserving nonhuman resources. In the drydocks, carpenters restore ships sold for junk down in Baltimore, making them "better and more valuable than they ever were before." In today's eco-speak, this is a "smart" economy—premised, as Douglass affirms, on "the superiority of mind over simple brute force" (355 [p. 213]). Recalling Grandmother Betsey's "wise prudence" as well as the continuously cultivated Northern farms to which Southern landscapes like Tuckahoe's were routinely contrasted, New Bedford demonstrates the profitability of prudential resource stewardship.[4]

As such, this landscape furnishes Douglass with a surprisingly pragmatic argument for abolition. New Bedford's chief virtue—its conscientious efficiency—is, after all, economic and ecological, but not particularly moral. Indeed, the most striking thing about Douglass's enthusiasm for New Bedford may be that it persists despite his recognition that New Bedford is deeply racially divided; indeed, shortly after his arrival, Douglass is forced out of his skilled job as a caulker by racist opposition. His idealized sense of New Bedford's exemplarity is thus manifestly not predicated on its moral superiority: New Bedford is not unified by interracial sympathy, shared belief, or anything else we might be tempted to call moral community. That is, New Bedford instantiates a functionally cooperative interdependence not premised on ethical regard, and thus in endorsing it, Douglass makes an economic and ecological case for abolition that sets aside, at least for now, the work of moral transformation. To skeptics unmoved by *My Bondage*'s witness to slavery's cruelty and divisiveness, these surveys of Southern and Northern landscapes would demonstrate that freedom is not solely a question of

---

4. To be sure, Douglass's portrait of victimless prosperity won entirely by gains in efficiency is thick with ideological overpainting. Anyone familiar with *Moby-Dick*'s contemporaneous account of New Bedford's oil economy ("all these brave houses and flowery gardens . . . were harpooned and dragged up hither from the bottom of the sea" (Melville [1851] 1992, 37) will rightfully suspect Douglass of soft-focusing the town's success. Even absent such comparison, we can sense distortion in his extravagant praise for the "well adjusted machine" of New Bedford's labor. Still, such signs of idealization only accent the fact that this landscape is designed to do specific political work for Douglass, exaggerating the disparity between freedom's efficiency and the ruinous wastefulness of life under slavery.

moral imperative but also of national economic and ecological survival.

✳   ✳   ✳

References

"Agricultural Survey" 1840. "Agricultural Survey of the Parish of St. Matthews," *Southern Cabinet of Agriculture, Horticulture, Rural, and Domestic Economy* 1.

Andrews 1986. William Andrews, *To Tell a Free Story: The First Century of Afro-American Autobiography, 1760–1865*. Urbana: U of Illinois P.

Ashworth 1995. John Ashworth, *Slavery, Capitalism, and Politics in the Antebellum Republic: Commerce and Compromise, 1820–1850* (Cambridge: Cambridge UP).

Bennett 2001. Michael Bennett, 'Anti-Pastoralism, Frederick Douglass, and the Nature of Slavery." In *Beyond Nature Writing: Expanding the Boundaries of Ecocriticism*, edited by Karla Armbruster and Kathleen Wallace, 195–210. Charlottesville: U of Virginia P.

Best 2004. Stephen Best, *The Fugitive's Properties: Law and the Poetics of Possession* (Chicago: U of Chicago P).

Buell 1995. Lawrence Buell, *The Environmental Imagination: Thoreau, Nature Writing, and the Formation of American Culture* (Cambridge, MA: Harvard UP).

Butler 1995. Robert Butler, "The City as Liberating Space in *Life and Times of Frederick Douglass*." In *The City in African American Literature*, edited by Yoshinobu Hakutani and Robert Butler, 21–36. Madison, NJ: Fairleigh Dickinson UP.

Carter 2006. *Historical Statistics of the United States, Colonial Times to 1970*. Millennial ed. Cambridge, UK: Cambridge UP.

DeBow 1852. J. D. B. DeBow, *The Industrial Resources of the Southern and Western States*. New Orleans: DeBow's Review. In Woodman (1996, 194–96).

Douglass [1845] 1994. Frederick Douglass, *Narrative*, in Henry Louis Gates, ed., *Autobiographies* (New York: Library of America).

———— [1855] 1994. Frederick Douglass, *My Bondage and My Freedom*, in Henry Louis Gates, ed., *Autobiographies* (New York: Library of America).

Finseth 2009. Ian Finseth, *Shades of Green: Visions of Nature in the Literature of American Slavery* (Athens: U of Georgia P).

Helper 1857. Hinton Rown Helper, *The Impending Crisis of the South: How to Meet It* (New York: Burdick Brothers), in Harold

D. Woodman, ed., *Slavery and the Southern Economy: Sources and Readings* (New York: Harcourt Brace, 1996).

Majewski 2009. John Majewski, *Modernizing a Slave Economy: The Economic Vision of the Confederate Nation* (Chapel Hill: U of North Carolina P).

Melville [1851] 1992. Herman Melville, *Moby-Dick: or, The Whale*. New York: Penguin.

Newman 2009. Lance Newman, "Free Soil and the Abolitionist Forests of Frederick Douglass's 'The Heroic Slave,'" *American Literature* 81.1: 127–52.

Newman and Walls 2011. Lance Newman and Laura Walls, "Cosmopolitics and the Radical Pastoral: A Conversation with Lawrence Buell, Hsuan Hsu, Anthony Lioi, and Paul Outka," *Journal of Ecocriticism* 3.2: 258–71.

Rubin 1975. Julius Rubin, "The Limits of Agricultural Progress in the Nineteenth-Century South." *Agricultural History* 49.2: 362–73.

Sundquist 1993. Eric Sundquist, *To Wake the Nations: Race in the Making of American Literature*. Cambridge, MA: Belknap P.

Williamson and Cain 2009. Samuel Williamson and Louis Cain, "Measuring Slavery in \$2009," www.measuringworth.com/slavery.php

Wright 2006. Gavin Wright, *Slavery and American Economic Development*. Baton Rouge: Louisiana State UP.

NEIL ROBERTS

From Comparative Freedom and Marronage in Frederick Douglass[†]

*   *   *

Douglass on Comparative Freedom

COMPARATIVE POLITICAL LANGUAGE

Douglass prominently introduces the adjectival political term *comparative* into *My Bondage and My Freedom*. He adds the words *comparative* and *comparatively* before nouns in sentences throughout *Bondage*, mirroring identical passages in *Narrative* as well as novel

---

[†] From *Freedom as Marronage* (Chicago: U of Chicago P, 2015), pp. 71–78, 86. Copyright © 2015 by University of Chicago. Reprinted by permission of University of Chicago Press. One of the author's notes has been omitted. Bracketed page references are to this Norton Critical Edition. "Marronage" conventionally refers to the condition of having fled from enslavement and becoming a "maroon" who avoids recapture without being legally recognized as "free." In the book from which this excerpt is drawn, Roberts argues that marronage is a condition of flight that can be understood as a site of (comparative) freedom.

scenario descriptions that the first autobiography does not mention. Douglass titles a subsection of the opening chapter "Comparative Happiness of the Slave-Boy and the Son of a Slaveholder," where he reflects upon the ways in which young slaves are relatively protected from the grueling labor that older slaves endure. In evaluating different slave overseers' stern measures, Douglass writes that the slaves on Colonel Lloyd's plantation who worked under Mr. Sevier's watchful gaze were not permitted to take any pleasure in the "comparatively moderate rule of Mr. Hopkins." Douglass's confrontation with Edward Covey resurrects him "from the dark and pestiferous tomb of slavery, to the heaven of comparative freedom." Austere slave life under Covey cannot measure up to the "comparative tenderness" of his life as a slave in Baltimore. Alienated slave property biologically has brothers and sisters, Douglass not exempted. Even so, he states that his two sisters and brothers "were, comparatively, strangers to me" because of forced early separation and the breakup of family units under slavery. The fugitive slave's existence in New York after his escape was "comparatively safe," given the possibility of capture and return back to the South. Additionally, on describing changing his last name, Douglass says the measure was a "comparatively unimportant matter" in relation to other issues facing fellow fugitives.[1]

Douglass's invocation of *comparative* and *comparatively* has precise significance with regard to freedom, since Douglass carefully uses poetic political language with specific intentionality. In "What to the Slave Is the Fourth of July?" delivered July 5th, 1852 at Corinthian Hall in Rochester, New York, Douglass inquires into whether the principles of political freedom embodied in the Declaration of Independence apply to American slaves, and if so why in practice are slaves prevented from experiencing what freedom offers individuals and social collectives.[2] Douglass places the address as the fifth appendix item in *Bondage*. That the speech occurs the day after the official American Independence celebrations grounds the context.

American slavery and the "slave's point of view" are the topic and subjective phenomenology of the orator.[3] Douglass speaks of "Fellow-Citizens" while simultaneously distancing himself from the ability to experience the fruits of full citizenship and freedom. The

1. Douglass, *My Bondage and My Freedom* (New York: Penguin Books, 2003), 29, 34–35, 90, 101, 181, 251, 252 [pp. 35, 83, 92, 132, 155, 210, 211].
2. For alternative appreciations of Douglass's famous abolitionist speech, consult Charles W. Mills, *Blackness Visible: Essays on Philosophy and Race* (Ithaca, NY: Cornell UP, 1998), 167–200; James Colaiaco, *Frederick Douglass and the Fourth of July* (New York: Palgrave MacMillan, 2006); Jason Frank, *Constituent Moments: Enacting the People in Postrevolutionary America* (Durham: Duke UP, 2010), 209–36. *Bondage* includes only an excerpt of the speech. The full text also is in print under the title "The Meaning of July Fourth for the Negro." [See "What to the Slave Is the Fourth of July?" (p. 320).—*Editors*]
3. Douglass, *Bondage*, 341 [p. 281].

pronouns *you, yours, I,* and *mine* are Douglass's linguistic mechanisms of differentiation. Douglass questions the hypocrisy of republican governance, not the idea of republicanism. Freedom is comparative, for the unfree slave looks at legally free white citizens and mourns a majority population incapable of acknowledging the fundamental crime against humanity structuring their society, governmental apparatuses, and livelihood. Freedom is irreducible to laws of states. Douglass exhorts:

> What have I, or those I represent, to do with your national independence? Are the great principles of political freedom and natural justice, embodied in that Declaration of Independence, extended to us? . . . This Fourth of July is *yours,* not *mine. You* may rejoice, *I* must mourn. To drag a man in fetters into the grand illuminated temple of liberty, and call him to join you in joyous anthems, were inhuman mockery and sacrilegious irony. . . . What to the American slave is your Fourth of July? I answer, a day that reveals to him, more than all other days in the year, the gross injustice and cruelty to which he is a constant victim. To him, your celebration is a sham; your boasted liberty, an unholy license; your national greatness, swelling vanity; your sounds of rejoicing are empty and heartless; your denunciations of tyrants, brass-fronted impudence; your shouts of liberty and equality, hollow mockery; your prayers and hymns, your sermons and thanksgivings, with all your religious parade and solemnity, are to him mere bombast, fraud, deception, impiety, and hypocrisy—a thin veil to cover up crimes which would disgrace a nation of savages.[4]

Victims of subjection have the capacity to alter their world. The unfree, Douglass suggests, are perceptive teachers of freedom's meaning.

Upon returning to the United States from Britain, Douglass declares his intention to "restore to 'liberty and the pursuit of happiness' the people with whom I had suffered, both as a slave and as a freeman." Along with inquiry into the Declaration of Independence, Douglass revisits principles of the American Constitution. His activism around slavery faces challenges from competing US constitutional interpreters, most of whom debate the doctrine of original intent and question whether the Constitution is to be understood as an anti- or pro-slavery text.[5] Recognizing the disjuncture between normative philosophical ideals and human social practices, Douglass formulates a relativistic notion of freedom that contains

4. Ibid., 340–41, 344 [pp. 281–82, 285].
5. Ibid., 289, 292–93 [pp. 241, 243–45]. Douglass expands on comparative constitutionalism in "The Constitution and Slavery" [1849], in Philip Foner and Yuval Taylor, eds., *Frederick Douglass: Selected Speeches and Writings* (Chicago: Lawrence Hill Books, 1999), 129–33.

fundamental baseline requirements while being attentive to the comparative experience of freedom in different settings.

The concept of comparative freedom is temporally stretched to account both for real-world debates on constitutionality during the period of slavery *and* for imagined, forward-looking arguments about post–chattel slavery topics from land economics to voting. Comparative freedom is akin to the classifications of certain contemporary scholars of poverty to the extent that international development specialists on the effects of poverty's unfreedom globally and domestically operationalize a comparative capability approach.[6] However, contrary to these poverty analysts' tendency to endorse a form of liberal political theory and to interpreters of Douglass who read him through the framework of liberalism, Douglass embraces a romantic vision that promotes a unique "true republicanism."[7] He does so to demonstrate how to escape a state of enslavement via flight. Douglass wants to point out the gradations of freedom and the ways in which attaining freedom is not simply a moral or physical quality, but is also psychological. Struggle has a role here, albeit not in terms of a struggle for recognition.[8] Comparative freedom necessitates a struggle against the Slave Power, the power of the master class. Struggle, the fact-form distinction, and assertion are the principles of method validating Douglass's rationale.

STRUGGLE

Douglass's oft-quoted words on struggle from the "West India Emancipation" speech echo the position he defends at length in *Bondage*:

6. Amartya Sen's *Development as Freedom* New York: Anchor Books, (1999) exemplifies this approach.
7. Douglass, *Bondage*, 279 [p. 233]. For interpretations of Douglass as a liberal thinker, see Sharon Krause, *Liberalism with Honor* (Cambridge: Harvard UP, 2002); Nick Bromell, "The Liberal Imagination of Frederick Douglass," *American Scholar* 77.2 (2008), 34–45; Peter C. Myers, *Frederick Douglass: Race and the Rebirth of American Liberalism* (Lawrence: UP of Kansas, 2008); Nick Buccola, *The Political Thought of Frederick Douglass* (New York: New York UP, 2012).
8. Scholars such as Paul Gilroy, Cynthia Willet, Margaret Kohn, and the early Angela Davis have compared intricately Douglass's thought to that of G. W. F. Hegel, particularly Hegel's theory of recognition put forth in the *Phenomenology of Spirit*. See Angela Y. Davis, *Lectures on Liberation* (Los Angeles: National Committee to Free Angela Davis, 1971); Paul Gilroy, *The Black Atlantic: Modernity and Double Consciousness* (Cambridge, MA: Harvard UP, 1993); Margaret Kohn, "Frederick Douglass's Master-Slave Dialectic," *Journal of Politics* 6.2 (2005): 497–514. I, however, do not read Douglass through the Hegelian master–slave dialectic for two reasons. First, unlike what we know about W. E. B. Du Bois's interaction with German thought, no evidence supports the contention that Douglass had interacted with German idealism by the time of *Bondage*. Douglass did not engage with German thought until *after Bondage*'s publication, mainly due to his association with the text's German translator, Ottelia Assing. Second, I wish to create a dialogue between scholars of freedom, slave narratives, and Romanticism in a way that the literature on struggles of recognition rarely addresses.

Let me give you a word on the philosophy of reform. The whole history of the progress of human liberty shows that all concessions yet made to her august claims, have been born of earnest struggle. The conflict has been exciting, agitating, all-absorbing, and for the time being, putting all other tumults to silence. It must do this or it does nothing. If there is no struggle, there is no progress. Those who profess to favor freedom and yet deprecate agitation, are men who want crops without plowing up the ground, they want rain without thunder and lightning. They want the ocean without the awful roar of its many waters. This struggle may be a moral one, or it may be a physical one, or it may be both moral and physical, but it must be a struggle. Power concedes nothing without demand. It never did and it never will.[9]

Bondage closes emphasizing the twin pillars of liberty and progress.[1] These pillars, designed to elevate an African-American political imaginary, resurface in speeches buttressing Douglass's trenchant belief in a progressive freedom emerging out of struggle. Without struggle, the slave cannot become free. Douglass articulates slavery to mean the granting of power to an agent to exercise the right of property over the body and soul of another agent. Although in bondage, the slave is agentic. Engaging in struggle serves as a major step endowing the shackled being with heightened slave agency. Douglass's classic fight with the slave-breaker Covey demonstrates this most clearly.

* * *

* * * He peered into the depths of the not-so-peculiar institution of slavery, shifting the view toward a comparative idea of freedom rooted in judging political freedom physically, psychologically, individualistically, and collectively. In reassessing the moment when he no longer feared death, Douglass determined why the struggle with Covey marked the turning point in his life. In the process, Douglass developed the concept of comparative freedom:

Well, my dear reader, this battle with Mr. Covey,—undignified as it was, and as I fear my narration of it is—was the turning point in my *"life as a slave."* It rekindled in my breast the smouldering embers of liberty; it brought up my Baltimore dreams, and revived a sense of my own manhood. I was a changed being after that fight. I was *nothing* before; I WAS A MAN NOW. It recalled to life my crushed self-respect and my self-confidence,

9. Douglass, *"West India Emancipation"* [1857], in Foner and Taylor, *Frederick Douglass: Selected Speeches and Writings*, 367.
1. Douglass, *Bondage*, 298 [p. 249].

and inspired me with a renewed determination to be A FREE-
MAN. A man, without force, is without the essential dignity of
humanity. Human nature is so constituted, that it cannot *honor*
a helpless man, although it can *pity* him; and even this it cannot do long, if the signs of power do not arise. He can only
understand the effect of this combat on my spirit, who has himself incurred something, hazarded something, in repelling the
unjust and cruel aggressions of a tyrant. Covey was a tyrant,
and a cowardly one, withal. After resisting him, I felt as I had
never felt before. It was a resurrection from the dark and pestiferous tomb of slavery, to the heaven of comparative freedom.
I was no longer a servile coward, trembling under the frown of
a brother worm of the dust, but, my long-cowed spirit was
roused to an attitude of manly independence. I had reached the
point, at which I was *not afraid to die*. This spirit made me a
freeman in *fact*, while I remained a slave in *form*. When a slave
cannot be flogged he is more than half free.[2]

FACT VERSUS FORM

Douglass radically amends the identical passage detailing the cre-
scendo of the fight with Covey from the first to the second autobiography. In the *Narrative*, Douglass speaks of the glorious
resurrection from the tomb of slavery to the heaven of "freedom,"
not "comparative freedom." Additionally, whereas the *Narrative*
describes a distinction between "slave in form" and "slave in fact,"[3]
Bondage includes a demarcation between "slave in form" and "freeman in fact." This latter distinction accentuates the novelty of comparative freedom as an ideal.[4]

2. Ibid., 180–81 [pp. 155–56].
3. Douglass, *Narrative*, 395 (Signet edition). There are other notable revisions in *Bondage*, such as Douglass's markedly different discussions of the slave woman, Caroline, in
the first two autobiographies (Andrews, *To Tell a Free Story*, 285–86). These accounts
take place when Douglass is describing Covey. In *Narrative*, Caroline does not appear
in the crux of the fight with Covey scene, and Douglass mentions her in a single, brief
section. Douglass refers to her simply as a "miserable woman" and a "wretched woman"
whose sole purpose was as a "breeder" (orig. emphasis, 387). By contrast, in *Bondage*,
Caroline becomes integral to the Douglass-Covey fight. Douglass describes Caroline
this time in "The Last Flogging" chapter as a "powerful woman" who "could have mastered me very easily, exhausted as I now was." Caroline was Covey's personal slave, and
when Covey demanded that she take hold of Douglass to strengthen his standing during the altercation, Caroline refused. Covey later "gave her several sharp blows" as a
result. "We were all in open rebellion, that morning" (2003, 179, 180) [pp. 154, 155].
Careful examination of Douglass's use of words across the autobiographies, even when
reading historical scenes in his oeuvre considered by readers the most familiar, is
essential to discerning the conceptual breakthrough on freedom in *Bondage*.
4. In the book from which this article has been excerpted, Roberts clarifies Douglass's
distinction between *fact* and *form* as follows: "The slave in form is the legal slave, the
slave of an institution, the commodity belonging to the master. Fact, on the other
hand, . . . denotes the psychological disposition of the [enslaved] agent" (76) [*Editor's
note*].

* * *

Four possible models illustrate Douglass's system regarding the dialectic of slavery and freedom, alignment and nonalignment. An agent can be (1) a slave in form and slave in fact, (2) a slave in form and free in fact, (3) free in form and a slave in fact, or (4) free in form and free in fact. Table 1 depicts these scenarios.

Table 1: Four models of an agent's fact-form alignment and nonalignment

	Slave in form	Free in form
Slave in fact	Model 1	Model 3
Free in fact	Model 2	Model 4

The least ideal condition is (1) and the most ideal state is (4). Against countless theories that classify slaves solely within model 1, Douglass suggests that slaves can be comparatively free while in bondage. Model 3 of his theory also offers a framework to answer questions posed by several theorists, including Rousseau in *Of the Social Contract* and Bob Marley in "Redemption Song"—the latter echoing Marcus Garvey—who ask how it is possible for one to be free legally and simultaneously unfree in psychological chains of dependence. For Douglass, it is not that the extreme models (1 and 4) are never fully realized. Models 1 and 4 describe conditions prior to and after the dialectical, intersubjective struggles experienced by enslaved agents. The capacity for activity is inherent in all slaves. Moments of struggle are catalytic in that they convert a slave's potential for agency into the actuality of the lived experience of freedom.

What Douglass ascertains is that his own process of flight from slavery to freedom begins as a result of the fight with Covey. Model 2 categorizes Douglass's observations at the fight's end. Douglass remains a slave in form despite winning the struggle against the agent, keeping him in an austere state of constraint. By victoriously preventing Covey from whipping him thereafter, Douglass psychologically experiences an embodied transformation. He has become a freeman in fact through experiencing what it means to be no longer completely under the mental will of the master. Douglass cannot be flogged any longer and is hence more than half free. Under the law, Douglass remains a slave. Nonetheless, he is comparatively free, having attained the status of a freeman in fact. That major psychological victory put him en route to model 4: the path toward jointly aligning freedom in form and freedom in fact. * * *

* * *

Comparative freedom rejects totalizing models claiming absolute slavery or absolute freedom. Slavery and freedom have extreme states. Struggle emerges within the critical gaps between these absolute conditions. Assertion continues the realignment process begun by struggle.

✳   ✳   ✳

Frederick Douglass challenges those, such as Hannah Arendt and Philip Pettit, whose respective republicanisms disavow the relationships among slavery, slave agency, and freedom. Furthermore, he goes beyond these thinkers by attempting to spell out the boundaries of slavery and freedom as well as the interstitial modes of flight connecting these opposing states. He demonstrates the value of the fugitive for thought and reasoning. Fugitivity is at once episodic and yet a permanent facet of everyday politics. Fugitives can evade and transform the world we live in. ✳ ✳ ✳

✳   ✳   ✳

JULIET HOOKER

From "A Black Sister to Massachusetts": Latin America and the Fugitive Democratic Ethos of Frederick Douglass[†]

The transnational dimensions of Frederick Douglass' political thought have been neglected in prevailing interpretations of him as a thinker thoroughly focused on the U.S., a perception further buttressed by his categorization as part of the assimilationist strand within African-American philosophy (Boxill 1992–1993) and as an exponent of American liberalism (Buccola 2012; Krause 2002; Myers 2008; Turner 2012). In contrast, this article seeks to enlarge the conceptual terrain of Douglass scholarship by locating a more geographically capacious Douglass whose engagement with Latin America reveals an important hemispheric dimension to his political thought. It joins recent analyses by historians and literary critics that highlight the centrality of Douglass' engagement with the rest of the Americas to his political ideas (Levine 2008; Nwankwo 2005; Polyné 2010), but shifts the locus of attention to suggest that we read Douglass more expansively as a theorist of democracy. Viewed through a hemispheric lens Douglass is revealed as a radically democratic thinker whose ideas can be utilized to sketch a fugitive democratic ethos that contains important resources for contemporary

† From *American Political Science Review* 109.4 (2015): 690–95, 701–02. © American Political Science Association 2015. Reprinted with permission of Cambridge University Press and the author. The author's first note has been moved. Bracketed page references are to this Norton Critical Edition.

democratic theory. Engaging with the hemispheric coordinates of Douglass' political reflections and investments and his support for a composite U.S. nationality via immigration during the 19th century can illuminate early 21st century debates about race, shifting demographics, and the character of U.S. democracy.

* * * The thread that unites Douglass' seemingly contradictory Caribbean interventions and his view of U.S. racial politics was his commitment to multiracial democracy. For Douglass, Latin America[1] and the Caribbean functioned as both models of racial egalitarianism and participants in the project of reshaping the U.S. polity.[2] Grappling with Douglass' writings on Latin America thus reveals a heretofore underappreciated element of his political thought: the articulation of a conception of democracy informed by black fugitivity that could enable the practice of egalitarian politics in multiracial polities. The question of the intellectual, moral, and civic capacities of nonwhites and the kinds of political relations that could be established between whites and nonwhites in the multiracial republics of the Americas were far from settled during the second half of the 19th century, as evidenced by the opposition of many white abolitionists in the U.S. to African-American social and political equality. It is in this context that Douglass articulates a distinctive conception of multiracial democracy, or the political coexistence on egalitarian terms of individuals of "all races and creeds" as fellow citizens. Unlike the myths of racial democracy formulated in Latin America during the 20th century, however, which conflate multiracial democracy and mestizaje, Douglass envisions a "composite nationality" anchored in the idea of a universal human right to migration and the Americas' political legacy of multiraciality. Reading Douglass as a democratic theorist thus reveals how his arguments about U.S. and Latin American racial politics intersect to formulate what I identify as a fugitive democratic ethos.

The distinctive features of this fugitive democratic ethos can be discerned by bringing together two strands of contemporary thinking on democracy and fugitivity—Sheldon Wolin's notion of "fugitive democracy" and black fugitive thought—thereby extending and amending each in important ways. Wolin (1994) understands

---

1. I use the term "Latin America" to encompass Haiti and the Caribbean coast of Central America—despite the fact that their complex geopolitical histories and linguistic differences do not align with dominant ideas of the region as Spanish-speaking with an Indo-Hispanic cultural heritage—because Douglass' conception of the Americas corresponds to this expansive use of the term. See Mignolo (2006) on its origins and implications.

2. Douglass and his African-American contemporaries undoubtedly overestimated Latin America's racial egalitarianism, as the region has been marked by racial hierarchy and antiblack and anti-indigenous racism since the colonial era (Andrews 2004; Wade 1997). For the present argument what matters is Douglass' belief that they represented a preferable alternative to U.S. racial politics, however.

democracy as "a project concerned with the political potentialities of ordinary citizens . . . becoming political beings through the self-discovery of common concerns and the modes of action for realizing them" (11). He suggests that rather than thinking about democracy as a form of government, it would be more useful to reconceive it as a political moment that is rare and episodic: "a mode of being which is . . . doomed to succeed only temporarily, but is a recurrent possibility" (23). Because the enlargement of the circle of those who can participate in politics generally requires the wholesale transformation of existing forms, democracy and revolution are related rather than opposed, and constitutionalism, rather than institutionalizing democracy, attenuates and limits it, because democratic founding moments are revolutionary moments "that activate the demos and destroy boundaries that bar access to political experience . . . revolutionary transgression is the means by which the demos makes itself political" (18). Democracy thus requires moments of "democratic renewal" when ordinary individuals can create "new cultural patterns of commonality" (24). Wolin's notion of democratic fugitivity thus envisions democracy as an uneven, multifaceted practice that is never fully achieved.

Douglass' understanding of citizenship/exclusion and approach to constitutional interpretation in his famous "What to the Slave is the Fourth of July" speech of 1852[3] proleptically articulates Wolin's qualms about the ossification of democracy, while introducing a novel question that Wolin did not consider: What if it is liminal or imperfect citizens[4] who have an enhanced access to the democratic? In the speech Douglass rhetorically performs the civic in-betweenness of slaves, fugitive ex-slaves, and free African-Americans by continually aligning and disaligning himself with the United States. He simultaneously addresses his white audience as "fellow citizens," yet reminds them that "This Fourth [of] July is *yours*, not *mine*. *You* may rejoice, *I* must mourn" (Douglass 1996, 116 [p. 327]). He interprets the U.S. founding as an anticolonial, revolutionary event in which the rule of law was flouted in the name of higher moral and political principles, suggesting that in the pre–Civil War era it was not-quite-citizen slaves and fugitive ex-slaves, as well as (black and white) abolitionists who were acting as exemplary citizens. The founding fathers, he argued: "preferred revolution to peaceful submission to bondage . . . They believed in order; but not in the order of tyranny. With them, nothing was '*settled*' that was not right . . . They seized upon eternal principles and set a glorious example in their

---

3. See pp. 320–30 above [*Editors' note*].
4. That is, persons who are not yet legal citizens but who act as (and could become) such, and those who are citizens according to the law but are not treated thus in practice.

defence [sic]" (113 [p. 325]). Douglass is a fugitive democratic thinker because he emphasizes the revolutionary and unsettled character of democratic politics, and asserts the right of ordinary citizens to inter- pret the law, such as when he exhorts his audience to read the consti- tution themselves in order to reach their own conclusions about whether it was an antislavery text (128). In his autobiographies Doug- lass also suggested that slavery led slaves to develop a different rela- tionship to the law; how else would it have been possible for them to engage in any kind of resistance, particularly escape? "Slaveholders made it almost impossible for the slave to commit any crime, known either to the laws of God or the laws of man. If he stole, he but took his own; if he killed his master, he only imitated the heroes of the revolution" (2003, 69). By connecting the law-breaking of fugitive slaves to the U.S. founding, Douglass suggests that these practices should be seen as constitutive to the praxis of citizenship. Douglass' analysis of the experiences of *actual* fugitives thus alters the tempo- rality of Wolin's concept, as it shows that beyond the evanescence of the political, individuals and groups with precarious claims to citi- zenship may nevertheless develop enhanced democratic subjectivi- ties. Today's fugitives, we might thus suggest, are the dreamers or Ferguson protesters[5] who enact exemplary democratic practices even as their status as citizens is precarious, and as their political activism renders them vulnerable to increased state reprisal.

In order to fully sketch this dimension of democratic fugitivity that goes beyond Wolin's concept it is thus also necessary to draw upon the tradition of black fugitive thought.[6] Fugitivity was a strategy that escaped slaves enacted both individually and collec- tively, and it is a recurring theme in black political thought (Davis 1971). We can provisionally identify a few key features of black fugitive thought: (1) taking seriously as political activities the sur- vival strategies of fugitives: secrecy, concealment, flight, outlawry, etc.; (2) a concern with the creation of autonomous, and at times clandestine, spaces where black political agency can be collec- tively enacted, which is often coupled with a rejection of the strat- egy of seeking inclusion into existing racial states due to pessimism about their ability to be reorganized on bases other than white

5. "Dreamers" refers to persons who qualify for the Deferred Action for Childhood Arrivals program (2012), which established a pathway toward citizenship for children brought to the United States without official documentation. "Ferguson protesters" refers to partici- pants in protests that began in August 2014 in Ferguson, Missouri, in response to the police shooting of an unarmed African American man, Michael Brown [*Editors' note*].

6. Other attempts to link black fugitivity and democratic theory include Du Bois' formula- tion of the term "abolition-democracy" in *Black Reconstruction*, Davis' (2005) use of Du Bois' concept to frame contemporary mass incarceration in light of the civic death of slavery, Balfour's (2011) excavation of the insights about U.S. democracy embedded in Du Bois' textual practices, and Gooding-Williams' (2009) suggestion that Douglass enacted a collective, non-rule-centered form of plantation politics.

supremacy; (3) embracing the intellectual orientations arising from fugitivity, such as "speaking out of turn" to reveal racial injustice, and imagining alternate racial orders, futures, and forms of subjectivity. Contemporary theorists have attempted to rethink freedom and justice from the perspective of the black fugitive (Best and Hartman Fall 2005; Hesse 2014), and Roberts (2015) in particular approaches Douglass as a theorist of fugitivity. He argues that Douglass provides an account of slave agency that allows us to move beyond the stalemate between static, polarized conceptions of negative and positive liberty that dominate debates about freedom in Western political thought: "Douglass develops a tradition of political theory centering attention on the psychological and physical acts of struggle and assertion that are integral to slave agency" (57). Douglass belongs to the tradition of black fugitive thought, not only because he was the most visible African-American fugitive of his time, but also because the experiences of liberation from enslavement and fugitivity shape his political thought in ineluctable ways. He recognized the fugitive's complicated relationship to the law, because in resisting enslavement and stealing themselves, slaves violated laws that did not recognize them as persons, only as chattel. Douglass also theorized the crucial psychological components of liberation—such as when he claimed that he became a free man in fact even though he remained a slave in form after his victory in the climatic battle with the slave-breaker Covey (74–8)—thereby revealing fugitivity as not simply a status, but a praxis and disposition.

While Douglass did not fully embrace all the implications of black fugitivity, his approach to democratic politics was shaped by important lessons derived from the actual experience of fugitivity that both extend Wolin's notion of democratic fugitivity and are in tension with it at times. Black fugitive thought, for example, has generally been concerned with the creation of autonomous spaces for black freedom (such as maroon communities) at the margins of or outside colonial states and their successors. Yet Douglass, for the most part, was committed to working toward the refoundation of the U.S. polity on more egalitarian terms; he envisioned its radical transformation based on an expansive notion of multiraciality that would decenter whiteness to an extent that arguably has not been achieved to this day. He may have stopped short of endorsing revolution in the U.S. context, but at key junctures Douglass' concern with black freedom led him to look for models of political agency and black self-government in other parts of the Americas, such as Haiti, which he recognized as a state founded by fugitive slaves (in others words, a maroon state). Douglass' political thought thus displays elements of both democratic fugitivity and black fugitivity. There are potential contradictions and tensions between democratic fugitivity and black fugitivity, however. For instance, democratic engagement requires exposure to the state, but it is precisely the rule of law that is revealed as insufficient and dangerous by the black fugitive; likewise a fugitive democratic orientation would seek to reshape the moral dispositions of the dominant racial order, but black fugitivity is oriented rather to sites of black freedom that refuse or challenge logics of coloniality and the nation-state. I thus trace the tensions between black fugitivity and democratic fugitivity in Douglass' political thought. Sediments of both are present throughout, but black fugitive commitments are most evident during those moments when Douglass despairs about the U.S., while fugitive democratic orientations are most apparent during Reconstruction, when he believed a revolutionary moment of democratic renewal was underway.

*   *   *

"A [Black] City Set on a Hill": Haiti, Nicaragua, and the Mosquito Kingdom

It is perhaps not surprising that Douglass' trenchant critique of U.S. democracy in 1852 in his fourth of July speech coincided with the emergence of an enlarged hemispheric sensibility that looked outward to the rest of the Americas for examples of black self-government. In 1852 *Frederick Douglass' Paper* was the discursive site of African-American reflections about Central America that directly contested U.S. racism in light of political models of multiracial democracy drawn from Nicaragua and the Mosquito Kingdom. Douglass' curatorial practices as a newspaper editor in the 1850s—which highlighted African-Americans' search for sites of black freedom outside the U.S.—can thus be read as a fugitive practice of concealing oneself in the service of sustaining an outlawed exercise of agency. By featuring other African-Americans writing openly about emigration, Douglass was able to champion multiracial democracy without alienating white abolitionists opposed to black equality. Yet African-American attempts to enact black fugitivity transnationally ran the risk of establishing proto-imperial relationships vis-à-vis local populations in Latin America, including black and indigenous peoples pursuing their own quests for political autonomy.

Douglass opposed African-American emigration, particularly white colonizationist schemes to remove African-Americans to Central America premised on the idea that black and white coexistence on equal terms was impossible in the U.S. (Fredrickson 1987, 149–50). Douglass refused to concede that democracy was only possible in the context of racial homogeneity; he also rejected the idea

of separate climatic zones suitable to being inhabited only by certain races (the temperate zone for whites, the tropics for blacks).
White colonizationists envisioned a kind of Jim Crow American continent that disavowed the possibility of political co-existence. Douglass' stance on African-American emigration was thus partly driven
by his commitment to multiracial democracy.

In contrast, advocates of voluntary black emigration, such as Douglass' onetime co-editor of *The North Star* and later rival Martin
Delany,[7] viewed it as a means of fulfilling black desires for freedom
and self-government. Douglass and Delany had a complicated intellectual relationship; they are generally viewed as representative of
two diametrically opposed poles within African-American political
thought: integrationism and Black Nationalism. Delany was the
most famous 19th century proponent of black emigration; unlike
Douglass he had given up hope for black equality in the U.S., and
highlighted African-Americans' connection to Africa, whereas Douglass emphasized their status as Americans. It is thus Delany rather
than Douglass that one would expect to have a hemispheric vision
connecting African-Americans to black populations in Latin America. As Levine (1997) and others have noted, however, this simplistic binary opposition overlooks the fact that there was also significant
overlap between Douglass and Delany's political ideas: "If Douglass
can be viewed as a U.S. nationalist whose racial thinking surfaced
at times of stress or dissonance, Delany can be viewed as a racial
thinker whose U.S. nationalism expressed itself at moments of hope-
fulness" (229). This contention is borne out by Douglass' endorse-
ment of black emigration for a brief period prior to the Civil War,
when the Dred Scott decision[8] and other developments made the
possibility of national inclusion in the U.S. appear distant.

In the 1850s his newspapers promoted emigration to Haiti and
Central America, and Douglass himself planned to visit Haiti in
order to report on conditions there for those interested in emigration. In "A Trip to Haiti" in *Douglass' Monthly* in May of 1861, he
explained that among his motives for going were "special ones growing out of things at present existing in this country. During the last
few years the minds of free colored people in all the States have been
deeply exercised in relation to what may be their future in the United
States. To many it has seemed that the portents of the moral sky
were all against us" (Douglass 1952b, 87–8). Haiti, a maroon state
built by rebellious slaves, beckoned disillusioned African-Americans:
"looking out into the world for a place of retreat, an asylum from

---

7. Martin Robison Delany (1812–1885) was an African American abolitionist, writer, and
   political activist. For a time, he coedited the *North Star* with Douglass [*Editors' note*].
8. See note 2 on p. 366 [*Editors' note*].

the apprehended storm" (88). In accordance with its prominence in U.S. debates about race and slavery during the 19th century, Haiti played an important role in Douglass' thinking about black freedom. The success of Haiti's experiment in black self-government had implications for the cause of black equality everywhere, including the U.S. Douglass explicitly extolled Haiti as an exemplary maroon community where black self-government was a reality:

> Born a slave as we were, in this boasted land of liberty . . . accustomed from childhood to hear the colored race disparaged and denounced, their mental and moral qualities held in contempt, treated as an inferior race, incapable of self-government, and of maintaining, when left to themselves, a state of civilization . . . we, naturally enough, desire to see, as we doubtless shall see, in the free, orderly and Independent Republic of Haiti, a refutation of the slanders and disparagements of our race. We want to experience the feeling of being under a Government which has been administered by a race denounced as mentally and morally incapable of self-government. (86)

Because of the central place it occupied in U.S. debates about race, civilization, and slavery, "both the press and the platform of the United States have long made Haiti the bugbear and scare-crow of the cause of freedom." One purpose of Douglass' trip was thus to reveal the truth about Haiti, "to do justice to Haiti, to paint her as she is," since "though a city set on a hill, she has been hid" (87). Here, Douglass' journalism was serving black fugitive goals, revealing Haiti as an alternative political ideal principally to U.S. blacks still living under slave law. Haiti was the living enactment of heroic black liberation in which blacks had been the principal actors; it was "the theatre of many stirring events and heroic achievements, the work of a people, bone of our bone, and flesh of our flesh" (85).

This was an era in which Douglass was especially attuned to black fugitivity. In his speech on the anniversary of West India emancipation in 1857, for example, he emphasized the importance of violent resistance by the enslaved (in contrast to his praise for the peaceful process by which it was achieved in the 1880 version of the speech). "The truth concerning the inauguration of freedom," he proclaimed in 1857, was that "a share of the credit of the result falls justly to the slaves themselves . . . They did not hug their chains;" what British abolitionists were trying to accomplish through persuasion, "the Slaves themselves were endeavoring to gain by outbreaks and violence" (Douglass 1857, 23). This is a moment when Douglass "extols the value of black revolutionary violence as modeled in the Southern Americas" (Levine 2008, 191), in part to exhort U.S.

blacks to display the same kind of civic virtue rather than "the stolid contentment, the listless indifference, the moral death which reigns over many of our people" (Douglass 1857, 19). There is an important tension in Douglass' theorization of slave agency between the degradation produced by slavery and the vital necessity of resistance, however, which is mapped onto the comparison between non-U.S. slaves and U.S. blacks in this speech. In the U.S., he argued: "Negroes will be hunted at the North, and held and flogged at the South so long as they . . . make no resistance, either moral or physical" (22). Yet Douglass did find examples of violent African-American resistance to slavery, such as his rather bloodthirsty suggestion that "every mother who, like Margaret Garner,[9] plunges a knife into the bosom of her infant to save it from the hell of . . . Slavery, should be held and honored as a benefactress" (22).[1] Yet his U.S. examples of slave resistance all involve individual heroism and inward-directed violence (infanticide and suicide), rather than collective uprisings against slavery.

In 1852, prior to Douglass' invocation of Caribbean models of political agency, Central America was prominently featured as a site of black freedom in *Frederick Douglass' Paper*. In April 1852 Delany published *The Condition, Elevation, Emigration, and Destiny of the Colored People of the United States*, in which he identified Central America (and Nicaragua specifically) as one of the most favorable destinations for black emigration (1968). It is not entirely clear whether Delany was already aware that he had been elected (in absentia) mayor of the port of San Juan del Norte when he wrote *Condition*, and Douglass never reviewed the book.[2] But Delany's

9. Margaret Garner was an African American woman who escaped from slavery in January 1856. When she and her family were pursued and captured under the terms of the Fugitive Slave Act of 1850, she chose to kill her daughter so she would not be re-enslaved. Garner and her daughter are the subject of Toni Morrison's novel *Beloved* (1987) [*Editors' note*].
1. Douglass' invocation of Garner also raises the question of whether his conception of freedom is masculinist (i.e., whether it reifies male experience as normative). Black feminists, for example, have argued that by repeatedly describing the harms of slavery and exclusion from citizenship as denials of black manhood, Douglass implicitly conceived freedom for black women in a limited form that corresponded to the attenuated civic status of white women (Davis 2010); they have also critiqued the representations of enslaved women in his autobiographies, arguing that he downplayed sexual violence against enslaved women and presented black women's pained bodies as spectacle (Franchot 1990). But Douglass' gender politics are complicated; he also supported women's suffrage and praised their political activism (in the speech cited above, for example, he recognized women's prominence in abolitionist movements), and some readers argue that in the later autobiographies he highlights the role of women, including his mother, grandmother, and the slave-woman Caroline. Situating Douglass within the tradition of black fugitive thought thus also requires considering the relevance of "gendered strategies of freedom" for an assessment of his gender politics, but fully developing this point is beyond the scope of this article.
2. San Juan's racial and geopolitical topography were complex. Because of its strategic importance as the Atlantic entrance to a possible interoceanic canal it was claimed by both the Mosquito Kingdom and Nicaragua, in a dispute that also involved Great

election was covered in *Frederick Douglass' Paper*, as was African-American emigration to San Juan, and Douglass also published a review of Ephraim G. Squier's *Nicaragua, Its People, Scenery, Monuments, and the Proposed Interoceanic Canal*. While Douglass did not write any of the articles lauding the Mosquito Kingdom and Nicaragua as examples of black self-government, as publisher of the paper he made the editorial decision to include them. Douglass' curatorial choices as a journalist in 1852 could thus be read as a fugitive practice, whereby the measure of concealment offered by publishing pro-emigrationist texts written by others allowed him to challenge prevailing racial hierarchies in the U.S.

In his two-part review of Squier's book, which appeared in *Frederick Douglass' Paper* in January of 1852, James McCune Smith[3] identified both the Mosquito Kingdom and Nicaragua as free states governed by blacks. Writing under the pseudonym "Communipaw," McCune Smith (1852a) explained to his African-American readers that "The British Government claims protection over the mouth of the San Juan, for its ally the colored King of the Musquitos. The American Government claims protection over the rest of the route, for their allies the colored republic of Nicaragua. For Nicaragua is a *colored republic!*" Mapping the one-drop rule[4] onto Squier's description of Nicaragua's racial composition, McCune Smith observed that taking the "North American view" of the question "Colored or Negroes" were the majority of the country's population. Reducing those originally counted as white (whose whiteness Squier himself had also questioned), and adding together those in the mixed-race and black categories, McCune Smith concluded that Nicaragua was mostly black, with a significant indigenous population, and few whites. Nicaragua's *criollo* elite, which tended to downplay the country's black and indigenous ancestry, would have no doubt vigorously disputed this characterization as a black republic, but it is consistent with African-American perceptions of Latin America as more racially egalitarian than the U.S.[5]

Britain and the U.S. During the colonial era black Creoles and indigenous Miskitus exercised significant autonomy on the Mosquito Coast, but were increasingly subject to Anglo hegemony after Britain officially reestablished its protectorate over the Mosquito Kingdom in 1843, and the discovery of gold in California in 1848 resulted in increased U.S. presence in the region.

3. See note 1 on p. 3 [*Editors' note*].

4. The "one-drop rule" refers to the principle of racial classification whereby a person with just one ancestor from sub-Saharan Africa—figuratively with just one drop of "blood" from that ancestor—was legally classified as "black" (or "Negro" or "colored") [*Editors' note*].

5. While it had outlawed slavery in 1821, Nicaragua was hardly exempt from racism. In their dispute with the Mosquito Kingdom over ownership of San Juan, for example, Nicaraguan officials deployed a racially coded discourse of civilization and savagery to delegitimize the political capacities of the region's black and indigenous inhabitants (Hooker 2010).

* * * McCune Smith (1852b) pointedly observed that Nicaragua's Foreign Relations minister at the time, Sebastian Salinas, was a mulatto: "Although Mr. Squiers carefully conceals it, the truth is that *Senior Salinas is a black man!* . . . Here in Nicaragua, the . . . freest . . . region on the face of God's earth, where black and white interchange all the civil and social relations on the same platform . . . we find a black diplomatist of the first water." Similarly, Douglass would later point to Latin America in a scathing rebuttal of Lincoln's flirtation with colonizationism in the midst of the Civil War in an editorial in *Douglass' Monthly* in September 1862: "Mr. Lincoln knows that in Mexico, Central America and South America, many distinct races live peaceably together in the enjoyment of equal rights" (Douglass 1952a, 268).

African-Americans seeking sites of black freedom in Central America confronted complicated racial politics upon their arrival, however, as illustrated by another article about San Juan del Norte that appeared in *Frederick Douglass' Paper* in May 1852 (a month after the publication of Delany's *Condition*). James Starkey, an African-American migrant, wrote a letter about attempts to export U.S.-style racial segregation to San Juan. Having departed the U.S. on a vessel captained by a Virginian who enforced segregation aboard the ship, Starkey (1852) expected to be able to meet whites "on equal ground" in San Juan, but was disappointed to find that in "a town containing five hundred inhabitants, of which one hundred are white Americans . . . the other four hundred, which are composed of Indians and colored persons from the American States, suffer themselves to be ruled at the will and pleasure of the few pale faces." Even more disturbing was the fact that it was sometimes transplanted African-Americans who sought to enforce racial segregation in deference to the sensibilities of their white customers. Starkey described an incident involving an African-American returning from California with white companions who was refused service by the "colored" landlord of a hotel, which resulted in a sound rebuke by the entire party and their moving to another "hotel kept by a *white* man . . . [where they] were entertained alike without distinction."[6] Starkey sought a space of black freedom in the Mosquito Kingdom, not just from slavery, but also from U.S.-style racial hierarchies:

> It is very strange that our people will suffer themselves to be carried away by this 'American character' even here, in a country like this, whose king is a colored man, and the police officers, colored men . . . And with this colored government, colored persons from the States, seek to enforce what they call

6. Mattox (2009) reads this incident as referring to locals, but throughout the letter the phrase "colored persons from the American States" refers to African-Americans.

the 'American character,' but more justly the slaveholding character, on their own color who come among them . . . Is it not
time that we had begun to appreciate freedom, and real liberty,
particularly, in a country like this?

Yet due to the presence of white Americans and transplanted
African-American subservience, slavery may not have existed, but
blacks were still not free.

Starkey's concern that white immigration to black/mixed-race
spaces in Central America could infuse them with "the slaveholding
character" that U.S. blacks sought to escape was not unfounded, as
the circumstances of Delany's election as mayor of San Juan reveal.
Delany's election, which was reported in *Frederick Douglass' Paper* in
May 1852, was orchestrated by a transnational, multiracial political
alliance between African-American migrants and San Juan's local
black/indigenous/mixed-race inhabitants, against an effort by white
U.S. citizens to exclude nonwhites from political participation. "In the
San Juan election purportedly won by Delany, white and black U.S.
Americans, Jamaicans, Miskito Indians, and Nicaraguans participated, pitting a white Cotton American ticket supported by southern
U.S. American residents against a 'native and colored' party" (Mattox
2009, 532–3). Delany's election was subsequently annulled, yet this
fugitive enactment of multiracial democracy epitomized the contradictions that plagued African-Americans' search for sites of black freedom in Central America. For Carolina (1852), a correspondent to
Frederick Douglass' Paper, the event represented an actualization of
fugitive democracy, when "the native and colored citizens of San Juan"
were impelled to organize politically to counter the exertions of "a portion of the inhabitants of this town . . . to deprive us of our rights as
citizens, to strip us of the rights of having a voice in choosing our own
rulers, to subject us if possible to a system of slavery, equaled only by
that of the Southern States of the United States of North America."
Read in light of black fugitivity, the precariousness of African-
American freedom (and citizenship!) in San Juan is clear, including
the threat of re-enslavement. Simultaneously, however, Delany's
selection as a candidate (when he did not reside in, and had never even
visited San Juan) points to the unequal power hierarchies within this
transnational alliance. Delany's black emigrationism thus involved a
trade-off in which spaces of black freedom for African-Americans
might be achieved at the expense of the Mosquito Kingdom's actual
(black and indigenous) citizens, who were already involved in a struggle to preserve their political autonomy from Nicaragua, the U.S., and
Britain. Douglass' hemispheric vision faced similar tensions.

In the 1850s Douglass (and Delany) found sites of black freedom,
models of a black "city on a hill," in Central America that

demonstrated that black self-government and multiracial democracy were possible. Douglass' black fugitive sensibilities during this period can be discerned in his decision to allow his newspapers to function as a discursive space where black collective political agency could be envisioned. The tensions inherent in African-American hemispheric visions would become even more apparent following emancipation, however, when Douglass (who rejected U.S. expansionism while slavery persisted) endorsed the incorporation of willing Caribbean nations as a means of remaking the U.S. in their more multiracial and (ostensibly) racially egalitarian image.

* * *

The fugitive democratic ethos that can be extracted from Douglass' political thought is particularly relevant today because it can serve as a resource in ongoing debates about racial justice, cultural diversity, and U.S. democracy. There is a striking parallel between 19th century fears of black supremacy elicited by attempts to enfranchise African-Americans and contemporary accusations of executive overreach and Caesarism against President Obama. Douglass' call for nonwhite incorporation in order to overcome white supremacy also stands in stark contrast to contemporary hostility toward Latino immigrants grounded in fears about the "browning" of the country and the displacement of its Anglo-Saxon political culture. His embrace of a composite U.S. nationality fueled by immigration in order to build an egalitarian multiracial polity where solidarities could be forged across racial and cultural boundaries serves as an important counterpoint to arguments that such developments threaten both whites' demographic majority and African-American interests. Highlighting the hemispheric valences within African-American political thought also upends the claim that only Latin America has produced positive conceptions of multiracial democracy. In light of recent attempts to read Douglass as an unabashed believer in the redemptive power of a deracialized American liberalism, it is also especially useful to highlight his at times quite radical black fugitive commitments to racial justice. When Douglass proclaimed of Haitian slaves, "when they struck for freedom they builded better than they knew,"[7] he should also be read as staking a claim for the revolutionary potential and relevance of black fugitivity as a resource for rethinking the spatial logic, temporal contours, and intellectual lineage of democratic theory.

---

7. Frederick Douglass, "Lecture on Haiti: The Haitian Pavilion Dedication Ceremonies Delivered at the World's Fair," Jackson Park, Chicago, January 2, 1893 [*Editors' note*].

References

Andrews, George Reid. 2004. *Afro-Latin America, 1800–2000*. New York: Oxford UP.

Balfour, Lawrie. 2011. *Democracy's Reconstruction: Thinking Politically with W.E.B. Du Bois*. New York: Oxford UP.

Best, Stephen, and Saidiya Hartman. Fall 2005. "Fugitive Justice." *Representations* 92.1: 1–5.

Boxill, Bernard. 1992–1993. "Two Traditions in African-American Political Philosophy." *The Philosophical Forum* 24.1–3: 119–35.

Buccola, Nicholas. 2012. *The Political Thought of Frederick Douglass: In Pursuit of American Liberty*. New York: New York UP.

Carolina. 1852. "San Juan de Nicaragua." *Frederick Douglass' Paper*, May 6.

Communipaw. 1852a. "Nicaragua." *Frederick Douglass' Paper*, January 8.

Communipaw. 1852b. "Nicaragua–No. II." *Frederick Douglass' Paper*, January 15.

Davis, Angela Y. 1971. *Lectures on Liberation*. Los Angeles: National United Committee to Free Angela Davis.

Davis, Angela Y. 2005. *Abolition Democracy: Beyond Empire, Prisons, and Torture/Interviews with Angela Y. Davis*. New York: Seven Stories P.

Davis, Angela Y. 2010. "Introduction." In *Narrative of the Life of Frederick Douglass, an American Slave, Written by Himself: A New Critical Edition*, 21–37. San Francisco: City Lights Publishers.

Delany, Martin R. 1968. *The Condition, Elevation, Emigration, and Destiny of the Colored People of the United States*. New York: Arno.

Douglass, Frederick. 1857. "West India Emancipation." In *Two Speeches by Frederick Douglass, one on West India Emancipation and the other on the Dred Scott Decision*. Rochester, NY: C. P. Dewey, 3–24.

Douglass, Frederick. 1893. *Lecture on Haiti*. Chicago: Violet Agents Supply Co.

Douglass, Frederick. 1952a. "The President and His Speeches." In *The Life and Writings of Frederick Douglass, Vol III: The Civil War, 1861–1865*, ed. Philip S. Foner. New York: International Publishers, 266–70.

Douglass, Frederick. 1952b. "A Trip to Haiti." In *The Life and Writings of Frederick Douglass, Vol. III: The Civil War, 1861–1865*, ed. Philip S. Foner. New York: International Publishers, 85–88.

Douglass, Frederick. 1996. "What to the Slave Is the Fourth of July?" In *The Oxford Frederick Douglass Reader*, ed. William L. Andrews. New York: Oxford UP, 108–30.

Douglass, Frederick. 2003. *The Life and Times of Frederick Douglass.* 1892 ed. Mineola, NY: Dover Publications.

Franchot, Jenny. 1990. "The Punishment of Esther: Frederick Douglass and the Construction of the Feminine." In *Frederick Douglass: New Literary and Historical Essays,* ed. Eric J. Sundquist. Cambridge, England: Cambridge UP, 141–65.

Fredrickson, George M. 1987. *The Black Image in the White Mind: The Debate on Afro-American Character and Destiny, 1817–1914.* Middletown, CT: Wesleyan UP.

Gooding-Williams, Robert. 2009. *In the Shadow of Du Bois: Afro-Modern Political Thought in America.* Cambridge, MA: Harvard UP.

Hesse, Barnor. 2014. "Escaping Liberty: Western Hegemony, Black Fugitivity." *Political Theory* 42.3: 288–313.

Hooker, Juliet. 2010. "Race and the Space of Citizenship: The Mosquito Coast and the Place of Blackness and Indigeneity in Nicaragua." In *Blacks & Blackness in Central America: Between Race and Place,* eds. Lowell Gudmundson and Justin Wolfe. Durham: Duke UP, 246–77.

Krause, Sharon R. 2002. *Liberalism with Honor.* Cambridge, MA: Harvard UP.

Levine, Robert S. 2008. *Dislocating Race and Nation: Episodes in Nineteenth-Century American Literary Nationalism.* Chapel Hill: U of North Carolina P.

Mattox, Jake. 2009. "The Mayor of San Juan del Norte? Nicaragua, Martin Delany, and the 'Cotton' Americans." *American Literature* 81.3: 527–54.

Mignolo, Walter. 2006. *The Idea of Latin America.* New York: Wiley-Blackwell.

Myers, Peter C. 2008. *Frederick Douglass: Race and the Rebirth of American Liberalism.* Lawrence: UP of Kansas.

Nwankwo, Ifeoma K. 2005. *Black Cosmopolitanism: Racial Consciousness and Transnational Identity in the Nineteenth-Century Americas.* Philadelphia: U of Pennsylvania P.

Polyné, Millery. 2010. *From Douglass to Duvalier: U.S. African Americans, Haiti and Pan Americanism, 1870–1964.* Gainesville: UP of Florida.

Roberts, Neil. 2015. *Freedom as Marronage.* Chicago: U of Chicago P.

Starkey, James R. 1852. "Letter." *Frederick Douglass' Paper,* May 27.

Turner, Jack. 2012. *Awakening to Race: Individualism and Social Consciousness in America.* Chicago: U of Chicago P.

Wade, Peter. 1997. *Race and Ethnicity in Latin America.* London: Pluto P.

Wolin, Sheldon S. 1994. "Fugitive Democracy." *Constellations* 1.1: 11–25.

Frederick Douglass: A Chronology

1818   Born near Tuckahoe Creek, in Talbot County, Mary-
        land. Named Frederick Augustus Washington Bailey.
        The son of an enslaved Black woman, Harriet Bailey,
        and a white man—perhaps his master, Aaron Anthony.

1819–23 Raised by his grandmother, Betsy Bailey, on Holme Hill
        Farm, some miles from the slave quarters and Anthony's
        residence (a house on the plantation of Colonel Lloyd,
        for whom Anthony works as the estate manager).

1824   Separated from his grandmother, begins living on the
        "Great House Farm," the Lloyd plantation. Anthony's
        daughter Lucretia, married to Thomas Auld, befriends
        him.

1826   Sent to Fell's Point, Baltimore, to live with the family
        of Hugh Auld, Thomas's brother.

1829–30 Works as an errand boy at Hugh Auld's shipyard, Auld
        and Harrison. Secretly begins teaching himself to read
        and write.

1833   Sent back to live with the family of Thomas Auld in
        St. Michaels, Maryland, after Thomas quarrels with
        Hugh.

1834   Deemed by Thomas Auld to be a resistant slave requir-
        ing discipline and sent to live with William Covey, a
        renowned "slave breaker." In August, successfully resists
        Covey's attempt to physically subdue him.

1835   Sent to work for William Freeland, a relatively humane
        master. While at Freeland's, covertly organizes a Sun-
        day school for his fellow enslaved people.

1836   Decides to attempt to escape enslavement, but his plans
        are discovered in April, he is sent to jail, and soon
        thereafter he is returned to live with Hugh Auld and
        family in Baltimore.

1838   Becomes engaged to Anna Murray, a free Black woman
        living in Baltimore, and with her assistance success-
        fully escapes to the north on September 3. After a brief
        stay in New York, where he and Murray marry, moves to

New Bedford, Massachusetts, and takes the last name Douglass.

1839   Subscribes to the abolitionist newspaper *The Liberator*, edited by William Lloyd Garrison. Addresses abolitionist meeting in New Bedford and thereby comes to the attention of the Massachusetts chapter of the American Anti-Slavery Society. Daughter Rosetta born June 24.

1840   Son Lewis Henry born October 9.

1841   Attends and is urged to speak at a meeting of the Massachusetts Anti-Slavery Society on Nantucket on August 10–11. His speech so impresses Garrison that he is soon thereafter hired to be an agent for the Society. Begins traveling and speaking at abolitionist meetings around New England. Moves to Lynn, Massachusetts, and buys a house.

1842   Son Frederick born March 3.

1843–44   Travels and gives antislavery speeches, gradually becoming famous in abolitionist circles.

1844   Shares the speakers' platform with well-known essayist Ralph Waldo Emerson in Concord, Massachusetts, on August 1. Son Charles Remond (named after Black abolitionist Charles Lenox Remond) born October 21.

1845   Begins work on his first autobiography, *Narrative of the Life of Frederick Douglass, An American Slave, Written by Himself*, which is published in mid-May and quickly becomes a best seller. Fearful that the book's popularity will enable his master to discover his whereabouts and recapture him, flees to Britain on August 16 and begins an eighteen-month speaking tour of Ireland, Scotland, and England.

1846–47   Tours Scotland, giving antislavery lectures to great acclaim. Joined by Garrison, meets with leaders of Chartist movement, which seeks economic and political reforms. Lets English friends buy him out of slavery; Hugh Auld (now Douglass's legal owner) receives $711.66 when Douglass's manumission documents are filed in Baltimore. On December 12, is formally emancipated.

1847   Leaves England and arrives in Boston on April 20. Informs Garrison and other abolitionist friends that in Britain he has raised money to start his own newspaper and that he plans to do so. Establishes *The North Star* in Rochester, New York, where he also begins an important friendship with wealthy abolitionist Gerrit Smith.

1848   Moves to Rochester and buys a house. Through news-
         paper editing, develops relationships with a wider circle
         of Black and white abolitionists, including James
         McCune Smith and Samuel Ringgold Ward, and
         becomes more informed about political and social
         issues of concern to free Blacks living in the north.
         Julia Griffiths, an abolitionist he met in England, moves
         to Rochester to help him manage the business affairs of
         The North Star.

1849   Daughter Annie born March 22.

1851   Publicly changes his mind on the constitutionality of
         slavery and now regards the Constitution as anti-
         slavery. Merges *The North Star* with the *Liberty Party
         Paper,* yielding a new, weekly publication, *Frederick
         Douglass' Paper.*

1853   Writes and publishes *The Heroic Slave,* a novella, in
         Autographs for Freedom, a collection of antislavery writ-
         ing edited by Julia Griffiths and sold to raise funds for
         Douglass's newspaper.

1855   Publishes second autobiography, *My Bondage and My
         Freedom,* in August. Like his earlier *Narrative,* it instantly
         becomes a best-seller.

1856   Meets and begins a close relationship with German
         journalist Ottilie Assing.

1858   Begins publishing *Douglass' Monthly.*

1859   Meets with abolitionist John Brown in Chambersburg,
         Pennsylvania, and refuses to join Brown's secret plot to
         attack the federal arsenal in Harper's Ferry, Virginia,
         and seize the armaments stored in it. After Brown's plan
         fails and Brown is captured, Douglass is implicated in
         the plot, flees to Canada, then returns to Britain.

1860   Ends publication of *Frederick Douglass' Paper.* Writes
         that Abraham Lincoln, the president-elect, is not a
         committed foe of slavery and expresses doubt that the
         South will secede from the Union. After daughter
         Annie dies, returns to Rochester.

1861   Civil War begins. Douglass argues that the purpose of
         the war should be ending slavery, not just preventing
         Southern secession.

1863   Attends meeting at Boston's Tremont Temple to cele-
         brate issuance of Emancipation Proclamation, Presi-
         dent Lincoln's order freeing the slaves in the South.
         Recruits soldiers for black regiment, the 54th Massachu-
         setts, which sons Lewis Henry and Charles Remond

demand to join. Meets with Lincoln in the White House to plead for equal treatment for Black soldiers. Ceases publication of *Douglass' Monthly*, ending his career as an editor.

1864   Returns to Maryland for first time in twenty-six years, reuniting with his sister Eliza. Endorses Lincoln.

1865   Attends Lincoln's inaugural, where he is personally greeted by the president.

1865–66   Demands Black male suffrage as indispensable to African American advancement.

1868   Campaigns for Union general Ulysses S. Grant's presidential campaign.

1870   Becomes publisher and editor of *New National Era*.

1871   Named assistant secretary of commission sent to investigate annexation of Dominican Republic.

1872   Rochester home destroyed by arson. Moves with family to Washington, D.C.

1874   Named president of Freedman's Savings Bank, which fails. Douglass closes *New National Era*.

1877   Appointed marshall of District of Columbia by President Rutherford B. Hayes.

1881   Recorder of deeds, Washington, D.C. Publishes *Life and Times of Frederick Douglass*, his third autobiography, which is a financial failure.

1882   Wife, Anna, dies.

1884   Marries his former secretary Helen Pitts.

1889   Appointed consul general to Haiti by President Benjamin Harrison.

1893   Is appointed by Haiti to be its commissioner at the World's Columbian Exposition in Chicago. Becomes a friend and an ally of Black antilynching activist Ida B. Wells.

1894   Delivers final great address, "Lessons of the Hour," an antilynching speech.

1895   Dies in Washington, D.C., soon after addressing a meeting of the National Council of Women. Buried in Rochester.

Selected Bibliography

• indicates works included or excerpted in this Norton Critical Edition.

Major Works by Frederick Douglass

Narrative of the Life of Frederick Douglass, An American Slave, Written by Himself. Boston: American Anti-Slavery Society, 1845.
My Bondage and My Freedom. New York: Miller, Orton & Mulligan, 1855.
Life and Times of Frederick Douglass, Written by Himself. Hartford, CT: Park Publishing, 1881.
Life and Times of Frederick Douglass, Written by Himself: His Early Life as a Slave, His escape from Bondage, and His Complete History to the Present Time. Boston: De Wolfe, Fiske, 1892.
Life and Writings of Frederick Douglass. Ed. Philip S. Foner. 5 vols. New York: International, 1950–75.
Frederick Douglass on Women's Rights. Ed. Philip S. Foner. Westport, CT: Greenwood, 1976.
The Frederick Douglass Papers. Ed. John W. Blassingame et al. 5 vols. New Haven: Yale UP, 1979–92.
Autobiographies. Ed. Henry Louis Gates, Jr. New York: Library of America, 1994.
Oxford Frederick Douglass Reader. Ed. William L. Andrews. New York: Oxford UP, 1996.

Some of Douglass's manuscripts are held at the Library of Congress as the Frederick Douglass Papers. Others are at the University of Rochester.

Biographies

Blight, David W. *Frederick Douglass' Civil War: Keeping Faith in Jubilee.* Baton Rouge: Louisiana State UP, 1989.
——— *Frederick Douglass: Prophet of Freedom.* New York: Simon and Schuster, 2018.
Foner, Philip S. *Frederick Douglass.* New York: Citadel P, 1950.
Holland, Frederic May. *Frederick Douglass: The Colored Orator.* New York: Funk & Wagnalls, 1891.
Huggins, Nathan Irvin. *Slave and Citizen: The Life of Frederick Douglass.* Boston: Little, Brown, 1980.
McFeely, William S. *Frederick Douglass.* New York: Norton, 1991.
Oakes, James. *The Radical and the Republican: Frederick Douglass, Abraham Lincoln, and the Triumph of Antislavery Politics.* New York: Norton, 2008.
Preston, Dickson J. *Young Frederick Douglass: The Maryland Years.* Baltimore: Johns Hopkins UP, 1980.
Quarles, Benjamin. *Frederick Douglass.* Washington, DC: Associated Publishers, 1948.

Stauffer, John. *Giants: The Parallel Lives of Frederick Douglass and Abraham Lincoln*. New York: Twelve, 2009.

Stauffer, John, Zoe Trodd, and Celeste-Marie Bernier, eds. *Picturing Frederick Douglass: An Illustrated Biography of the Nineteenth Century's Most Photographed American*. New York: Norton, 2015.

General Historical and Literary Studies

Andrews, William L., ed. *Critical Essays on Frederick Douglass*. Boston: G. K. Hall, 1991.

――――. *To Tell a Free Story: The First Century of Afro-American Autobiography, 1760–1865*. Urbana: U of Illinois P, 1986.

Baptist, Edward E. *The Half Has Never Been Told: Slavery and the Making of American Capitalism*. New York: Basic Books, 2014.

Blassingame, John W. *The Slave Community: Plantation Life in the Antebellum South*. New York: Oxford UP, 1979.

Butterfield, Stephen. *Black Autobiography in America*. Amherst: U of Massachusetts P, 1974.

Castronovo, Russ. *Necro Citizenship: Death, Eroticism, and the Public Sphere in the Nineteenth-Century United States*. Durham: Duke UP, 2001.

Davis, Charles T., and Henry Louis Gates, Jr., eds. *The Slave's Narrative*. New York: Oxford UP, 1985.

Delbanco, Andrew. *The Abolitionist Imagination*. Cambridge, MA: Harvard UP, 2012.

Fisher, Dexter, and Robert B. Stepto, eds. *Afro-American Literature: The Reconstruction of Instruction*. New York: Modern Language Association of America, 1979.

Foster, Frances Smith. *Witnessing Slavery: The Development of Ante-Bellum Slave Narratives*. Madison: U of Wisconsin P, 1979.

Frederickson, George M. *The Black Image in the White Mind*. New York: Harper & Row, 1971.

• Gates, Henry Louis, Jr. *Figures in Black*. New York: Oxford UP, 1987.

Johnson, Walter. *River of Dark Dreams: Slavery and Empire in the Cotton Kingdom*. Cambridge, MA: Harvard UP, 2013.

McDowell, Deborah E., and Arnold Rampersad, eds. *Slavery and the Literary Imagination*. Baltimore: Johns Hopkins UP, 1989.

McKivigan, John R., and Stanley Harrold, eds. *Antislavery Violence: Sectional, Racial, and Cultural Conflict in Antebellum America*. Knoxville: U of Tennessee P, 1999.

Meier, August. *Negro Thought in America, 1880–1915*. Ann Arbor: U of Michigan P, 1966.

Patterson, Orlando. *Slavery and Social Death: A Comparative Study*. Cambridge, MA: Harvard UP, 1982.

Ripley, C. Peter. "The Autobiographical Writings of Frederick Douglass." *Southern Studies* 24.1 (Spring 1985): 5–29.

――――, et al., eds. *The Black Abolitionist Papers*. 5 vols. Chapel Hill: U of North Carolina P, 1985–92.

Sekora, John, and Darwin T. Turner, eds. *The Art of Slave Narrative*. Macomb: Western Illinois UP, 1982.

Sinha, Manisha. *The Slave's Cause: A History of Abolition*. New Haven: Yale UP, 2016.

Smith, Valerie. *Self-Discovery and Authority in Afro-American Narrative*. Cambridge, MA: Harvard UP, 1987.

Stauffer, John. *The Black Hearts of Men: Radical Abolitionists and the Transformation of Race*. Cambridge, MA: Harvard UP, 2002.

Criticism and Political Theory

Acampora, Christa Davis. "Unlikely Illuminations: Nietzsche and Frederick Douglass on Power, Struggle, and the Aisthesis of Freedom." In *Critical Affinities: Nietzsche and African American Thought*. Ed. Robert Gooding-Williams. Albany: State U of New York P, 2006, 175–202.

Augst, Thomas. "Frederick Douglass, between Speech and Print." In *Professing Rhetoric: Selected Papers from the 2000 Rhetoric Society of America Conference*. Ed. Frederick Antczak, Cinda Coggins, and Geoffrey D. Klinger. Mahwah, NJ: Erlbaum, 2002, 53–61.

Archuleta, Micki. "Life, Liberty, and the Pursuit of Happiness: A Fugitive Slave on Individual Rights and Community Responsibilities." *Nineteenth Century Studies* 19 (2005): 35–45

Bennett, Nolan. "'To Narrate and Denounce': Frederick Douglass and the Politics of Personal Narrative." *Political Theory* 44.2 (2016): 240–64.

Bernier, Celeste-Marie. "From Fugitive Slave to Fugitive Abolitionist: The Oratory of Frederick Douglass and the Emerging Heroic Slave Tradition." *Atlantic Studies: Literary, Cultural, and Historical Perspectives* 3.2 (2006): 201–24.

Blight, David W. "The Private Worlds of Frederick Douglass." *Transition: An International Review* 61 (1993): 161–68.

Bromell, Nick. "A 'Voice from the Enslaved': The Origins of Frederick Douglass's Political Philosophy of Democracy." *American Literary History* 23.4 (2011): 697–723.

———. *By the Sweat of the Brow: Literature and Labor in Antebellum America*. Chicago: U of Chicago P, 1993.

———. *The Powers of Dignity: The Black Political Philosophy of Frederick Douglass*. Durham, NC: Duke UP, 2021.

Buccola, Nicholas. *The Political Thought of Frederick Douglass: In Pursuit of American Liberty*. New York: New York UP, 2012.

Cassuto, Leonard. "Frederick Douglass and the Work of Freedom: Hegel's Master-Slave Dialectic in the Fugitive Slave Narrative." *Prospects* 21 (1996): 229–59.

Castronovo, Russ. "'As to Nation, I Belong to None': Ambivalence, Disapora, and Frederick Douglass." *American Transcendental Quarterly* 9.3 (September 1995): 245–60.

Chaffin, Tom. *Giant's Causeway: Frederick Douglass's Irish Odyssey and the Making of an American Visionary*. Charlottesville: U of Virginia P, 2014.

Chaney, Michael A. "Heartfelt Thanks to Punch for the Picture: Frederick Douglass and the Transnational Jokework of Slave Caricature." *American Literature* 82.1 (2010): 57–90.

Colacio, James A. *Frederick Douglass and the Fourth of July*. New York: Palgrave MacMillan, 2006.

Crane, Gregg D. *Race, Citizenship, and Law in American Literature*. Cambridge, UK: Cambridge UP, 2002.

Culbertson, Graham. "Frederick Douglass's 'Our National Capital': Updating L'Enfant for an Era of Integration." *Journal of American Studies* 48.4 (2014): 911–35.

Diedrich, Maria. *Love across the Color Line: Ottilie Assing and Frederick Douglass*. New York: Hill & Wang, 1999.

DeLombard, Jeannine. "'Eye-Witness to the Cruelty': Southern Violence and Northern Testimony in Frederick Douglass's 1845 Narrative." *American Literature* 73.2 (June 2001): 245–75.

De Pietro, Thomas. "Vision and Revision in the Autobiographies of Frederick Douglass." *CLA Journal* 26.4 (June 1983): 384–96.

Duane, Anna Mae. "'Like a Motherless Child': Racial Education at the New York African Free School and in *My Bondage and My Freedom*." *American Literature* 82.3 (2010): 461–88.

Egan, Hugh. "'On Freedom': Emerson, Douglass, and the Self-Reliant Slave." *ESQ: A Journal of the American Renaissance* 60.2 (2014): 183–208.

• Ellis, Cristin. "Amoral Abolitionism: Frederick Douglass and the Environmental Case against Slavery." *American Literature* 86.2 (June 2014): 275–303.

Ernest, John. "Revolutionary Fictions and Activist Labor: Looking for Douglass and Melville Together." In *Frederick Douglass and Herman Melville: Essays in Relation.* Ed. Robert S. Levine and Samuel Otter. Chapel Hill: U of North Carolina P, 2008, 19–38.

Fagan, Benjamin. *"The North Star* and the Atlantic 1848." *African American Review* 47.1 (Spring 2014): 51–67.

Fanuzzi, Robert. "Frederick Douglass's 'Colored Newspaper': Identity Politics in Black and White." In *The Black Press: New Literary and Historical Essays.* Ed. Todd Vogel. New Brunswick, NJ: Rutgers UP, 2001, 55–70.

———. "The Trouble with Douglass's Body." *American Transcendental Quarterly* 13.1 (1999): 27–49.

Ferreira, Patricia J. "Frederick Douglass in Ireland: The Dublin Edition of His *Narrative.*" *New Hibernia Review* 5.1 (2001): 53–67.

Fought, Leigh. *Women in the World of Frederick Douglass.* New York: Oxford UP, 2017.

Frank, Jason. *Constituent Moments: Enacting the People in Postrevolutionary America.* Ithaca, NY: Cornell UP, 2010.

Frey, Raymond. "Douglass, Slavery, and Original Intent." *Proteus* 12.1 (Spring 1995): 15–17.

Fritz, Meaghan M., and Frank E. Fee. "To Give the Gift of Freedom: Gift Books and the War on Slavery." *American Periodicals* 23.1 (2013): 60–82.

Ganter, Granville. "'He Made Us Laugh Some': Frederick Douglass's Humor." *African American Review* 37.4 (Winter 2003): 535–52.

Giles, Paul. "Douglass's Black Atlantic: Britain, Europe, Egypt." In *The Cambridge Companion to Frederick Douglass.* Ed. Maurice S. Lee. Cambridge, UK: Cambridge UP, 2009, 132–45.

———. "Narrative Reversals and Power Exchanges: Frederick Douglass and British Culture." *American Literature* 73.4 (2001): 779–810.

Gilmore, Paul. "Aesthetic Power: Electric Words and the Example of Frederick Douglass." *American Transcendental Quarterly* 16.4 (December 2002): 291–311.

Gooding-Williams, Robert. *In the Shadow of Du Bois: Afro-Modern Political Thought in America.* Cambridge, MA: Harvard UP, 2009.

Gougeon, Len. "Militant Abolitionism: Douglass, Emerson, and the Rise of the Anti-Slave." *New England Quarterly* 85.4 (December 2012): 622–57.

Hamilton, Cynthia S. "Models of Agency: Frederick Douglass and 'The Heroic Slave.'" *Proceedings of the American Antiquarian Society* 114.1 (2004): 87–136.

Hickman, Jared. "Douglass Unbound." *Nineteenth-Century Literature* 68.3 (December 2013): 323–62.

Hutchins, Zachary McLeod. "Rejecting the Root: The Liberating, Anti-Christ Theology of Douglass's *Narrative.*" *Nineteenth-Century Literature* 68.3 (2013): 292–322.

Insko, Jeffrey. *History, Abolition, and the Ever-Present Now in Antebellum American Writing.* New York: Oxford UP, 2018.

Janmohamed, Abdul. "Between Speaking and Dying: Some Imperatives in the Emergence of the Subaltern in the Context of U.S. Slavery." In *Can the Subaltern Speak? Reflections on the History of an Idea.* Ed. Rosalind Morris. New York: Columbia UP, 2010, 139–55.

Jay, Gregory S. "American Literature and the New Historicism: The Example of Frederick Douglass." *Boundary 2* 17.1 (Spring 1990): 211–42.

Jenkins, Lee. "'The Black O'Connell': Frederick Douglass and Ireland." *Nineteenth Century Studies* 13 (1999): 22–46.

Jenkins, Melissa Shields. "'The Poets Are with Us': Frederick Douglass and John Milton." *Modern Language Studies* 38.2 (Winter 2009): 12–27.

Jones, Douglas A. "Douglass' Impersonal." *ESQ* 61.1 (2015): 1–35.

Lawson, Bill E., and Frank M. Kirkland, eds. *Frederick Douglass: A Critical Reader*. Malden, MA: Blackwell, 1999.

Lee, Maurice S., ed. *The Cambridge Companion to Frederick Douglass*. Cambridge, UK: Cambridge UP, 2009.

Levander, Caroline. "Witness and Participate: Frederick Douglass's Child." *Studies in American Fiction* 33.2 (Autumn 2005): 183–92.

Leverenz, David. "Frederick Douglass's Self-Refashioning." *Criticism: A Quarterly for Literature and the Arts* 29.3 (Summer 1987): 341–70.

Levine, Robert S. "Identity in the Autobiographies." In *The Cambridge Companion to Frederick Douglass*. Ed. Maurice S. Lee. Cambridge, UK: Cambridge UP, 2009, 31–45.

• ———. *The Lives of Frederick Douglass*. Cambridge, MA: Harvard UP, 2016.

———. *Martin Delany, Frederick Douglass, and the Politics of Representative Identity*. Chapel Hill: U of North Carolina P, 1997.

———. "Road to Africa: Frederick Douglass's Rome." In *Roman Holidays: American Writers and Artists in Nineteenth-Century Italy*. Eds. Robert K. Martin and Leland S. Person. Iowa City: U of Iowa P, 2002, 226–45.

———. "The Slave Narrative and the Revolutionary Tradition of American Autobiography." In *The Cambridge Companion to the African American Slave Narrative*. Ed. Audrey A. Fisch. Cambridge, UK: Cambridge UP, 2007, 99–114.

Levine, Robert S., and Samuel Otter. *Frederick Douglass and Herman Melville: Essays in Relation*. Chapel Hill: U of North Carolina P, 2008.

Lohmann, Christopher, ed. *Radical Passion: Ottilie Assing's Reports from America and Letters to Frederick Douglass*. New York: Peter Lang, 1999.

Mailloux, Steven. "Re-Marking Slave Bodies: Rhetoric as Production and Reception." *Philosophy and Rhetoric* 35.2 (2002): 96–119.

Martin, Waldo E. *The Mind of Frederick Douglass*. Chapel Hill: U of North Carolina P, 1984.

• Marrs, Cody. "Frederick Douglass in 1848." *American Literature* 85.3 (September 2013): 447–73.

———. *Nineteenth-Century American Literature and the Long Civil War*. Cambridge, UK: Cambridge UP, 2015.

McClish, Glen. "Frederick Douglass and the Consequences of Rhetoric: The Interpretive Framing and Publication History of the 2 January 1893 Haiti Speeches." *Rhetorica* 30.1 (2012): 37–73.

McDaniel, W. Caleb. *The Problem of Democracy in the Age of Slavery: Garrisonian Abolitionists and Transatlantic Reform*. Baton Rouge: Louisiana State UP, 2013.

McQuillan, Jennifer. "Parsing the Body: Frederick Douglass and the Recorporealization of Self." *Proteus* 28.1 (2012): 23–28.

M'Baye, Babacar. "Radical and Nationalist Resistance in David Walker's and Frederick Douglass's Antislavery Narratives." In *Literature of Protest*. Ed. Kimberly Drake. Ipswich, MA: Salem P, 2013, 113–43.

Mills, Charles. *The Racial Contract*. Ithaca, NY: Cornell UP, 1997.

Moses, Wilson J. "'The Ever-Present Now': Frederick Douglass's Pragmatic Constitutionalism." *Journal of African American History* 99.1–2 (2014): 71–88.

Myers, Peter C. *Frederick Douglass: Race and the Rebirth of American Liberalism*. Lawrence: UP of Kansas, 2008.

Nielsen, Cynthia R. "Resistance Is Not Futile: Frederick Douglass on Panoptic Plantations and the Un-Making of Docile Bodies and Enslaved Souls." *Philosophy and Literature* 35.2 (2011): 251–68.

Noble, Marianne. "Sympathetic Listening in Frederick Douglass's 'The Heroic Slave' and *My Bondage and My Freedom.*" *Studies in American Fiction* 34.1 (Spring 2006): 53–68.

Nwankwo, Ifeoma C. K. "Douglass's Black Atlantic: The Caribbean." In *The Cambridge Companion to Frederick Douglass.* Ed. Maurice S. Lee. Cambridge, UK: Cambridge UP, 2009, 146–59.

Phan, Hoang G. *Bonds of Citizenship: Law and the Labors of Emancipation.* New York: New York UP, 2013.

Pratt, Lloyd. "'I Am a Stranger with Thee': Frederick Douglass and Recognition after 1845." *American Literature* 85.2 (June 2013): 247–72.

———. "Progress, Labor, Revolution: The Modern Times of Antebellum African American Life Writing." *Novel: A Forum on Fiction* 34.1 (2000): 56–76.

Rice, Alan J., and Martin Crawford, eds. *Liberating Sojourn: Frederick Douglass and Transatlantic Reform.* Athens: U of Georgia P, 1999.

Riss, Arthur. *Race, Slavery, and Liberalism in Nineteenth-Century American Literature.* Cambridge, UK: Cambridge UP, 2006.

• Roberts, Neil. *Freedom as Marronage.* Chicago: U of Chicago P, 2015.

———, ed. *A Political Companion to Frederick Douglass.* Lexington: UP of Kentucky, 2018.

Ryan, Susan M. *The Grammar of Good Intentions: Race & the Antebellum Culture of Benevolence.* Ithaca, NY: Cornell UP, 2003.

Sale, Maggie Montesinos. *The Slumbering Volcano: American Slave Ship Revolts and the Production of Rebellious Masculinity.* Durham: Duke UP, 1997.

Sekora, John. "Black Message/White Envelope: Genre, Authenticity, and Authority in the Antebellum Slave Narrative." *Callaloo* 32 (1987): 482–515.

———. "'Mr. Editor, If You Please': Frederick Douglass, *My Bondage and My Freedom,* and the End of the Abolitionist Imprint." *Callaloo* 17.2 (Spring 1994): 608–26.

Shulman, George. *American Prophecy: Race and Redemption in American Political Culture.* Minneapolis: U of Minnesota P, 2009.

Stauffer, John. "Douglass's Self-Making and the Culture of Abolitionism." In *The Cambridge Companion to Frederick Douglass.* Ed. Maurice S. Lee. Cambridge, UK: Cambridge UP, 2009, 13–30.

———. "Frederick Douglass and the Aesthetics of Freedom." *Raritan* 25.1 (Summer 2005): 114–36.

Stephens, Gregory. "Arguing with a Monument: Frederick Douglass' Resolution of the 'White Man Problem' in His 'Oration in Memory of Lincoln.'" *Comparative American Studies* 13.3 (September 2015): 129–45.

Stepto, Robert B. *From Behind the Veil: A Study of Afro-American Narrative.* Urbana: U of Illinois P, 1979.

Sundquist, Eric J., ed. *Frederick Douglass: New Literary and Historical Essays.* Cambridge, UK: Cambridge UP, 1990.

———. *To Wake the Nations: Race in the Making of American Literature.* Cambridge, MA: Harvard UP, 1993.

Sundstrom, Ronald. "Frederick Douglass's Longing for the End of Race." *Philosophia Africana* 8.2 (August 2005): 143–70.

Sweeney, Fionnghuala. *Frederick Douglass and the Atlantic World.* Liverpool: Liverpool UP, 2007.

———. "'The Republic of Letters': Frederick Douglass, Ireland, and the Irish Narratives." *Éire-Ireland: A Journal of Irish Studies* 36.1–2 (Spring–Summer 2001): 47–65.

Tamarkin, Elisa. "Black Anglophilia; Or, the Sociability of Antislavery." *American Literary History* 14.3 (2002): 444–78.

Tang, Edward. "Rebirth of a Nation: Frederick Douglass as Postwar Founder in Life and Times." *Journal of American Studies* 39.1 (2005): 19–39.

Trodd, Zoe. "A Hole Story: The Space of Historical Memory in the Abolitionist Imagination." In *Agency in the Margins: Stories of Outsider Rhetoric.*

Ed. Anne Meade Stockdell Giesler. Madison, NJ: Fairleigh Dickinson UP, 2010, 68–90.

Turner, Jack. *Awakening to Race: Individualism and Social Consciousness in America*. Chicago: U of Chicago P, 2012.

Voss, Frederick S. *Majestic in His Wrath: A Pictorial Life of Frederick Douglass*. Washington, DC: Smithsonian Institution P, 1995.

Wallace, Maurice O. "Violence, Manhood, and War in Douglass." *The Cambridge Companion to Frederick Douglass*. Ed. Maurice S. Lee. Cambridge, UK: Cambridge UP, 2009, 73–88.

Walker, Peter F. *Moral Choices: Memory, Desire, and Imagination in Nineteenth-Century American Abolition*. Baton Rouge: Louisiana State UP, 1978.

Weinauer, Ellen. "Writing Revolt in the Wake of Nat Turner: Frederick Douglass and the Construction of Black Domesticity in 'The Heroic Slave.'" *Studies in American Fiction* 33.2 (2005): 193–202.

Wilson, Ivy G. "On Native Ground: Transnationalism, Frederick Douglass, and 'The Heroic Slave.'" *PMLA* 121.2 (2006): 453–68.

———. *Specters of Democracy: Blackness and the Aesthetics of Politics in the Antebellum U.S.* New York: Oxford UP, 2011.

Yancy, George. "African-American Philosophy: Through the Lens of Socio-Existential Struggle." *Philosophy & Social Criticism* 37.5 (2011): 551–74.

———. "Through the Crucible of Pain and Suffering: African-American Philosophy as a Gift and the Countering of the Western Philosophical Metanarrative." *Educational Philosophy and Theory* (2015): 1–17.

Yarborough, Richard, ed. "Frederick Douglass and Theology [Special Section]." *Nineteenth-Century Literature* 68.3 (December 2013): 287–362.

———. "Race, Violence, and Manhood: The Masculine Ideal in Frederick Douglass's 'The Heroic Slave.'" In *Haunted Bodies: Gender and Southern Texts*. Ed. Anne Goodwyn Jones and Susan Van D'Elden Donaldson. Charlottesville: UP of Virginia, 1997, 159–84.

Zwarg, Christina. "The Work of Trauma: Fuller, Douglass, and Emerson on the Border of Ridicule." *Studies in Romanticism* 41.1 (Spring 2002): 65–88.